W9-CGL-241

COLLECTING TOYS

A Collector's Identification & Value Guide

4th Edition

by Richard O'Brien

To
ED POOLE
everything a collector should be

Cover Design by Rebecca Lowers

BOOKS AMERICANA
INC.

ISBN 0-89689-048-1

Copyright ©1985 by Richard O'Brien, exclusive rights Books Americana Inc., P.O. Box 2326, Florence, Alabama 35630. All rights reserved. No part of the book may be used or reproduced in any manner whatsoever without permission, except in the case of brief quotations embodied in critical articles or reviews.

TABLE OF CONTENTS

ACKNOWLEDGEMENTS

More and more, this book seems to be becoming a collaborative effort, as I continually seek to improve and expand the information in each succeeding volume. If I have forgotten anyone here, my apologies. I'm extremely grateful for any help on this book, even to the tiniest correction.

Jim Harmon gets not only thanks but congratulations. Thanks for his continuing help with photos and prices on premiums, as well as for his excellent introduction to the subject. Congratulations for being signed by the Ralston Company to create new Tom Mix premiums; a dream come true for Jim, and a heartening encouragement to the rest of us dreamers.

Bill Kaufman, a friend for an embarrassing number of years, again came through whenever I whined for his photographic ministrations, as did the unfailing Ed Poole.

Ray Funk continued to bedazzle me with his generosity, C.B.C. Lee was as thorough and prompt as ever, as were Charles W. Best, Thomas W. Sefton, Jerry Wagner, Barbara and Jonathan Newman and their photographer-son, Jonathan A. Newman.

For new information on toy companies, thanks to Ed Laucus (Jones), Eddie Szpond (Auburn), Leslie Steinau Jr. and Leslie Steinau III (Molded Products), K. Warren Mitchell (Miller), Peter Ruben (Manoil), Walt Dineen (Barclay), Clayton W. Nimtz (Playwood Plastics), Dick MacNary (ID Models) Harold Frutchey (Beton).

Gramercy to Don Hultzman for the Herculean job on Battery toys and the big assistance on tin wind-ups. Equal heaps of gratitude to Joe Wallis for bringing his expertise to the subject of Britain's soldiers, and to Bruce and Blossom Abell for their authoritative contributions on the subject of Schoenhut.

For photos, and lending me toys to photograph, heartfelt thanks to Tony Salamone, Bill Adams, George Butler, Dick and Nancy Dice, Ron Chojnacki, Charles P. O'Brien, Bob Black Jr. and Don Mueller.

Gene Coffman was generous with price information (and a Metal Cast photo), as were Bill Adams and the redoubtable Hank Anton, who provided so many toy soldier prices averaged from his auctions, he swore he'd never do it again, and I don't blame him.

For additional information and corrections, thanks to ex-Barclay employee George Fall, to Lois Helen Brown for contributions on Built-Rite, to Al Dellinges for the Fould's premiums photo, to Bob Emmons and Larry Reno and Joe Miller for information on toy soldiers.

Without the auctioneers this book would be in great trouble as far as photographs go, so buckets of gratitude to Tara Ana Finley of Christie's East, Pamela Brown Sherer of PB Eighty-Four, Elizabeth Rice of Philips, Ted Hake, and David Mapes of Mapes Auctioneers & Appraisers.

Finally, thanks to my agent, Al Zuckerman, to Books Americana publisher Dan Alexander for his continuing courtesy, friendliness and helpfulness, to all those who contributed to the first three editions, to anyone I've missed, and to my daughter, Rebecca, for the exhausting task of averaging out these thousands of prices.

Additionally, as this book goes to press, thanks to Craig Ullery, Don Brett, Robert Ausley, Elizabeth Ausley, James T. Lane, Bob Kneale, Ron Cadieux, Bob Klinedinst and John Murray.

INTRODUCTION

This is the fourth edition of "Collecting Toys", and there have been some changes this time out. The first edition listed almost 4000 toys, the second added 1500, the third another 2000, and this, the fourth, lists yet another 700 or so toys, for a total of over 8000.

In addition, the size of the book has been enlarged to enable us to expand the listings and the number of photographs, the latter about double those of the third edition. Finally, the designation VALUE RARE has been replaced by No Price Found in the perhaps forlorn hope of persuading the hopeful that a toy whose value hasn't been established isn't necessarily worth the sun, moon and stars.

One of the pleasures for me in doing this book has been the opportunity it's afforded me to research the pre-WW II American toy soldier companies, about which little was known before "Collecting Toys" began. With my tug at the veils of Molded Products, Inc., I seem to have reached the end of the road with my research. All the major companies have been unearthed, and all the major information mined. What remains, and I hope to hear from any readers who can help with this, is catalog information on these companies, which would fill in some missing holes (such as dating and numbering), as well as any information at all on the numerous companies who were at the fringe during the Depression years, some of whom produced 3" lead figures, and some of whom manufactured what are now known loosely (and erroneously) as "small Barclays".

With the exception of Premiums, the prices in all categories this time have increased, some of them spectacularly. Almost 3500 prices have been revised since the last edition, with none of the remaining prices adjusted for inflation, as toys follow their own economic indicators. A number of the toys added in this edition are from the 1950s and 1960s, as these are becoming more and more collectible, as evidenced by sales and want lists.

It is my continuing hope that, although this book is primarily intended as a price guide, it be more than that; that it provide enjoyment and information for all those who are interested in toys. To that end, I would like to hear from anyone with well-researched background information, photos, and lists on companies not already comprehensively dealt with here. In addition, all corrections are gratefully received.

The prices shown alongside each toy were determined by my going through thousands of items on hundreds of sales lists, by poring through auction results, by strolling through flea markets and toy conventions, and by checking with knowledgable collectors and dealers and then, where possible, averaging out the prices. These figures, however, can serve only as a guide, as prices range widely on many items, and on scores of others only one example emerged as being bought, advertised or sold. Furthermore, in addition to the often great range of dealers' prices, auction prices can fluctuate widely, even in the course of the same auction, as interest can be feverish and monied, or totally spent-out, disinterested or uninformed. Thus there is a need for a book of this sort, and as the years and editions roll on, perhaps it can help serve as a stabilizing force, to the benefit of buyer and seller alike.

In my conversations with collectors and dealers about the idea of this book, the one point stressed over and over was condition, and the impact it has on the price of a toy. For this reason, since some readers will be turning to only one section of this book, and also since types of condition can vary with the different kind of toys, I have included several paragraphs on condition in each of the categories with which this book deals.

As much information as possible is given on the items listed. Where information is skimpy, it is because it was all I had. Sizes are noted wherever possible, and when just the number of inches is given, without specifying whether it is length or height, it is because that information did not appear in the list I received. Any words in quotes indicate the words are found on the toy. "Litho" is an abbreviation for a toy that is lithographed.

For those who wish to consider this field as an investment, and it can be a good one, it should be stressed that mint or near-mint condition provides considerably more financial safety than any of the other conditions, as this is the only condition sure to attract all collectors and dealers of any particular toy.

Richard O'Brien

VEHICLES
(See also Tin Wind-Up)

Average mint price of vehicles in the last edition was $139.63, this edition it is $159.36, an increase of 14%.

CAST IRON AUTOMOTIVE TOYS
by C. B. C. Lee

The manufacture of cast iron toys began shortly after the Civil War and had about reached its zenith by the beginning of the twentieth century. The first toy automobiles began to appear soon after their real life prototypes began chugging along the horse-carriage roads, by which time some of the great 19th century toy makers had already gone out of business. Among those that continued into the automotive era were Hubley, Dent, Wilkins, and Kenton. During the first three decades of this century, others came to the forefront, such as Arcade, Kilgore, A. C. Williams, and Champion. Others also made toy cars and trucks in smaller numbers or for a short period of time, such as Grey Iron, Freidag, and North and Judd. Many of these firms made no identifying marks on their toys, and it has only been in recent years that many very familiar toys have been correctly attributed, as catalogues, patents, and old advertisements have gradually come to light. Probably the greatest American toymaker of all was Ives, but this firm is thought to have made only one toy car, a clockwork-driven horseless carriage runabout with figure, measuring 6½" long and 6" to the top of the jockey-cap on the driver. This is a rare toy today, and one in excellent condition commands a considerable price (about $1600 as of this writing.) But other similar vehicles and varying smaller sizes by Hubley, Dent, Wilkens, etc. vary in value from around $20 to $300.

Value does not have much relationship to either age or size, however, having more to do with scarcity, complexity and nicety of design, detail, and "desirability". As with anything else in a free market, it is simply the rule of supply and demand.

Demand and "desirability" are affected by a number of factors. One of these is nostalgia, and the current market seems to have most of that hooked into the period from mid 1920s through the mid 1930s. In automotive toys, quality also peaked during this decade, but then, so did the squeeze of the Great Depression. The latter event shrunk Santa Claus's budget, depressed sales, and eventually resulted in a down-grading of quality. It also resulted in these most desirable of toys being the most scarce today.

As a general guide to factors affecting desirability, there are a few broad easy clues, however. Accuracy of scale and proportion, the use of many different cast parts, cast-in or decal logos and details, hand-painting (by the original maker, but NOT by some later child or collector!!), etc. all enhance the value. In most cases, a 4-inch roadster with a separate chassis, separate nickel-plated radiator and headlights, and a separate cast figure will be worth much more than a two-piece one with the halves riveted together. The Hubley Packard is a complex assembly of nearly 20 parts, with opening front doors, hinged hoods, plated radiator and motor, license plate, seats, and driver. It is a handsome toy, and was relatively expensive when originally marketed. A mint example today can sell for more than $5000. Nearly as complex, but much less scarce, the Kilgore Stutz roadster will sell for up to $700. Of similar value are the Arcade Buicks, Reo, Checker cab (with separate nickeled radiator) and several large buses. Because of scarcity, certain pieces of similar quality demand higher prices: White panel truck or moving van, $1000 plus; White A. C. F., and Mack buses, about $2000. The very rare Brinks Armoured truck by Arcade is worth even more. These high prices are due to extreme scarcity, many of these pieces being in fewer than ten known collections, and some having only 2 or 3 examples known in the country. For this reason, the market is very shallow, and only a few more coming on the market could drop the values dramatically. If someone found a case of twelve Brink's trucks in an old warehouse, he might sell the first one for $3000, but would have trouble getting $500 for the twelfth one. An example of this is the handsome Arcade Andy Gump 348 roadster. This was approaching $1000 in the inflating market a few years ago, but several have sold recently for under $250.

In small cars, around 4" long, the vast majority are currently worth between $10 and $40, but a few scarce ones, such as Arcade Nashes, Dent LaSalles, Kenton Pontiacs and other nickeled radiator members of this set, 4-casting nickeled-radiator cars by A. C. Williams and Champion, go for $100 or more.

Other special cases included some small trucks with logo publicity on them: Borden's Milk truck, a LIFE-SAVERS truck and size and shape of a roll of candy, etc. can sell for more than $300.

But these values are very volatile, both up and down, and may be badly obsolete even by the time this is printed. The lawyers long ago defined the "fair market value" as that price paid by a (knowledgeable) willing buyer to a (knowledgeable) willing seller.

A WORD OF CAUTION!!!

In recent years several American makers have begun to make cast-iron or brass copies of old toys, and more recently many more have been coming in from Taiwan and perhaps other sources. These are marketed as decorator pieces, and sell quite cheaply, for as little as $2.00. Many unscrupulous dealers are using these pieces to cheat unwary new collectors. They usually rust them hurriedly and sometimes make other modifications of tip-off parts (axles or screws) to fool the uninitiated. The Makers, "IRON ART", "UTEXIQUAL" and others here and abroad are running an honest enough business, but the dishonest dealers are using the products to turn a quick profit at the expense of naive buyers.

The fakes are usually easy to spot once one has gained a little experience. They are usually held together by a long screw, which is threaded all the way up to the hub, as are standard stove bolts in your local hardware store (only a few genuinely old toys are asembled with a screw rather than a long peaned rivet, and the few screws used often had only about ¼-inch threaded at the tip (the Hubley Packard is an important exception). Modern axles are usually a hollow rolled piece of sheet-metal, much like a long shear-pin, though a few are rods with threaded ends and sheet-metal acorn nuts. The castings themselves are the most dependable give-away, but require a little experience; a blind-man could tell in an instant. The old castings are thinner, lighter, and smoother; the modern ones being gritty, thick and coarse of detail.

CLINT SEELEY (8/28/27–3/6/84), a New England doctor, used the pen-name C.B.C. LEE when writing about toys, which he did prolifically. He contributed to books and magazines not only in this country but also in England, France, Italy, New Zealand, Australia and Japan and was in touch with collectors on five continents. His extensive research on the subject, and his generosity in sharing what he'd learned, will keep his name alive as long as interest remains in the hobby he so loved.

TOOTSIETOYS, DIE-CAST AND SLUSH
by C. B. C. LEE

Die-casting was an outgrowth of the invention of the Linotype machine, introduced at the Columbian Exposition at Chicago in 1893. A trade-journal publisher in that city named Samuel Dowst began to adapt the type-casting machine to making small promotional miniatures, collar buttons, and so on related to the Laundry Journal he also published. By the turn of the century, however, the die-casting business had become his principal business, and he was producing a myriad of small party favors, candy premiums, political items and penny jewelry. Amongst these were several charms and miniatures of automotive, trains, and aircraft. By 1911, he produced a small 477 mm. limousine with free-turning wheels. By 1914 a 77 mm. Ford touring car was marketed, and a matching pick-up truck was made two years later. All three of these stayed in the catalogue until the late 20s, and the truck as late as 1932. In 1922 a line of doll furniture was developed, and was trade-named Tootsietoy after the daughter of the company's president at that time, Tootsie Dowst. The name later was used to identify nearly all of the toys the company sold. However, it continued to make items for other buyers, and still makes the metal marker pieces used in the deluxe Monopoly game. Tootsietoys continue to be made today, the present name of the Company being the Strombecker Corporation.

As with other collectibles, the value of obsolete toys today is not greatly related to age. The oldest Tootsietoys were made in such large numbers and for so long a period that they are not hard to find today. Others, some of which were unpopular in their day, were not sold in great numbers and are rare today. The 1932 Funnies series of six pieces drawn from the contemporary comic strips is an example of this. These were made in a boxed set of 6, having cams on the axles, which imparted action to the figures as the toy was pushed along the floor, and having details and figures hand-painted in up to seven different colors. This boxed set sold for $1.00. The six pieces were also made in simplier non-action versions with simple paint and sold for 10¢ each. For reasons hard to understand today, these toys were not popular. Consequently they are very hard to find, and are more valuable. Some of the individual pieces must have been better liked by their owners and were played to death or lost, making them even scarcer. So, though all were made in about equal numbers, some are rarer than others. Uncle Walt Wallet in a roadster is the most valuable, often selling for more than $100. Uncle Willie and Mamie in a boat is at the other end, worth about half as much.

In regular production cars, LaSalles and a sort of pseudo-Lincoln have the greatest value, up to about $75, while other Fords, Yellow Cabs, and early Mack trucks are seldom above $25. Graham automobiles are presently worth about $35 except for the roadster and town car, worth about $45. A 1925 delivery truck, often called "Federal" by collectors, was made in stock versions having legends on the side panels saying: MILK, MARKET, LAUNDRY, GROCERY, BAKERY, and FLORIST. Their rarity is in about that order, MILK being worth about $20 up to FLORIST at about $100. This same line of small trucks were also made in small numbers with custom private liveries, and over a dozen such versions with store names on the sides are presently known to exist. There were probably more. These, too, vary in value according to scarcity, the commonest, HOSCHSCHILD KOHN & CO., presently being worth about $100. One which had the J. C. Penney logo on the side is worth twice that, and a few might find a buyer at even higher prices.

Other manufacturers also made die-cast toys, and a few of these are desirable enough to have some value. Barclay made a small series of separate body/chassis vehicles in the late 1930s, and a west coast firm, TIP-TOP Toys, which are of fair value. So are a few of the finer die-cast Manoils and ERIEs. Many others are in little demand, such as JANE FRANCIS, GOODIE, METAL MASTERS, IT'S A BEAUT, and certain Hubleys, Post-War items, including most of the Hubley, Tootsietoy, Midgetoy, Manoil, etc. output seldom sell for more than $2.00.

Slush casting was a process simple enough to be done in tiny factories, and even in home-industries during the depression. A few large manufacturers made toys in this way, most notably Barclay, Manoil, Savoye, Kansas Toy and Novelty, and others, but many were made by anonymous and small unidentifiable and local operations, using molds made and marketed by a few firms. Many slush-cast toys are of very little value today, but there are exceptions. Foremost among these were dealer promotional replicas of real cars, made by Banthrico and National Products. These can sell for up to $200. Other very accurate and detailed slush models, similar in size and scale to the contemporary Tootsietoys, can be worth up to $50, most notable among these being certain nicely cast models of the Reo Victoria, Packard, Chrysler Imperial, Cord coupe, late 20s, Buick and Model A Ford; these, and others made with an extra mold-part resulting in detailed radiator grilles, were made by the Lincoln White Metal Works. Other small accurate replicas, with the names cast on the door sides, were made by Tommy Toy.

As with other toys, condition is very important. The values quoted here are for those in like-new condition. Paint-wear can drop the value to half, and broken or missing parts can drop it to nearly nothing. Repairing can occasionally partially rescue an exceptionally rare piece, but more often depresses the value. Reproductions are beginning to appear on the market, and will also tend to depress the values of the real thing. As with anything else in a free market, cost is largely a matter of supply and demand, both of which can wax and wane cyclically. Let the buyer beware.

CONDITION OF A TOY
AND ITS RELATION TO PRICE

The price of a toy depends not only on its desirability, but on its condition. A toy in mint condition is generally worth twice what that same toy would bring in good condition, with "very good" falling about equally in between good and mint.

"Mint" means just that; the condition in which it was originally issued — perfect, regardless of age, not the slightest blemish. Needless to say this is a fairly rare state of affairs, but enough toys exist in mint condition to make it an employable term. Many people hoping to dispose of toys are tempted to call an item "mint" when it is really "near mint", "very good", or sometimes just "good". Inevitably this can result in unhappiness all around, and not infrequently, a cancelled sale.

"Good" signals a toy that has seen considerable wear, shows its age, but is basically sound. A collector will collect it, but will often not be wholly satisfied with it as an example of his collection, and thus prices are often drastically below that which the same item in mint can command.

Condition below good results in another drastic drop in price, and toys with missing parts, although otherwise in excellent condition, will usually fall into this lower-priced category. Rust, even small spots of it, can seriously lower the price of a toy. "Near-Mint", "Very Fine", "Fine" and similar terms often found in sellers' descriptions denote conditions between Mint and Very Good, and are priced accordingly.

The key to grading is to avoid wishful thinking. Grading can sometimes be a problem for the unitiated, but common sense will usually prevail, and when possible, a consultation with an expert in the field can often clear up lingering doubts. A toy in its original box is worth up to 10 to 20% more if the box is in mint condition, with the price dropping as its condition lessens.

VEHICLES

	G	VG	M
A. C. WILLIAMS Car Carrier with 3 Austins, 1920	225.00	337.50	450.00
A. C. WILLIAMS four-casting nickeled radiator car, approx. 4" long . . .	50.00	75.00	100.00
A. C. WILLIAMS Sedan, 6¾" long, circa 1931, cast iron, interchangeable body	75.00	112.50	150.00
A. C. WILLIAMS Stake Truck, 7" long, circa 1931, interchangeable body . .	85.00	127.50	170.00
A. C. WILLIAMS Studebaker, circa 1933-34, approx. 4" long, two tone sedan	35.00	52.50	70.00
A. C. WILLIAMS Touring Car, 9½" long, cast iron	250.00	375.00	500.00
ALL-NU "Field Kitchen", approx. 2½" long, "Made in USA" slush lead	NO PRICE FOUND		
ALL-NU Searchlight, approx. 2¾" long, "Made In USA", slush lead	NO PRICE FOUND		

	G	VG	M
ALL-NU Sound Detector, approx. 2¾" long, "Made In USA", slush lead	NO PRICE FOUND		
ALL-NU Tank "USA", 3" long, "Made In USA", slush lead	NO PRICE FOUND		
AMERICAN NATIONAL Army Truck, Mack "Giant", 26½" long . . .	200.00	300.00	400.00
AMERICAN NATIONAL "Juvenile Auto" dump truck pedal car, red and yellow tin, 57" long . . .	75.00	112.50	150.00
AMERICAN NATIONAL Packard Coupe, 30" long, 1920s, steerable front wheels	400.00	600.00	800.00
AMERICAN NATIONAL Packard car, 1920s coupe	100.00	150.00	200.00
AMERICAN NATIONAL Velie, child's pedal car, circa 1918	100.00	150.00	200.00
ANIMATE TOY "Baby Tractor", friction, "patented June 20, 1916"	16.00	24.00	32.00

ALL-NU Searchlight, "Field Kitchen", Sound Detector, Tank.
Photo by Bill Kaufman. Courtesy Evelyn Besser.

ANIMATE TOY "Baby Tractor", circa 1916.
Courtesy Good Old Days Store. Photo by Bill Kaufman.

ARCADE MANUFACTURING COMPANY
A Brief History
by C. B. C. Lee
(based on information from Dave Davison)

In 1869 a foundry in Freeport, Ill. was organized as a two-man partnership under the name of Novelty Iron and Brass Foundry, but was dissolved in 1885, when a new, larger factory was incorporated under the name of Arcade Manufacturing Co. It made industrial castings and household items, but no toys. After a disastrous fire in 1892 and management changes in 1893, toys began to appear in its catalogue, and by the early 1900s the line had become so extensive that a 50-page catalogue was issued showing a large line of notions and novelties, small stoves, banks and a few trains, including a unique pile-driver. But it was not until an enterprising young lawyer married the daughter of one of the officers and joined the firm in 1919 that the firm rapidly became one of the major makers of cast iron toys. Struck by the large number of Yellow Cabs in the streets of Chicago (my reference doesn't say he was hit or injured by them), the young man approached the Yellow Cab Company with a novel proposition: in return for the sole right to make toy replicas of the cab, the Yellow Cab Company would have the exclusive right to use the toy in its advertising. Success was instantaneous.

Arcade went on to duplicate this pattern with miniature Buicks, Chevrolets, Ford cars, McCormack-Deering and Harvester farm equipment, and several makes of trucks and buses. Arcade's slogan "They look real" was well justified by its products. In the booming 1920s the company's sales swelled so much that a new and larger plant was built in 1927. Two years later, the stock market crash heralded the great depression, and hard times hit the small car business just as it did the large ones. Cheap competition and dwindling demand for toys costing more than a dime had brought the company to the brink of bankruptcy by 1933. But, once again, the enterprising management gave the firm new life with an exclusive arrangement to provide souvenir replicas of the fairground buses made by G.M.C. for the Chicago Century of Progress. The depression caused a cheapening of quality, but World War II gave the firm business in military material. After the war, the company returned to making industrial and household hardware and a few toys, but cheaper toys of die-cast zamac, plastic, rubber and lithographed tin eclipsed the costlier cast iron toys. In 1946 the firm was sold to Rockwell Manufacturing Co. of Pittsburgh. Death and retirement soon finished the change of the old firm, and it followed its guiding directors into oblivion when Rockwell moved to Alabama.

Though the source is gone, the toys live on in collections across the land. Arcade is a prestigious name in cast iron automotive toys exceeded by none and approached by very few of its old competitors. No serious collection of cast iron toy cars, trucks, buses, or farm and construction equipment can pretend to be representative without its inclusion.

	G	VG	M		G	VG	M
ARCADE A.C.F. Bus ...	750.00	1125.00	1500.00	ARCADE Bus, 4" long, 1920s, 5 windows on each side	26.00	39.00	52.00
ARCADE Allis-Chalmers Tractor trailer, approx. 12" long, circa 1937	65.00	97.50	130.00	ARCADE Bus, 1930, 6¼" long, metal wheels	55.00	82.50	110.00
ARCADE "Allis Chalmers" tractor and wagon, white rubber tires, 9½" long .	16.00	24.00	32.00	ARCADE Bus, 8" long, seven side windows, circa 1930.	60.00	90.00	120.00
ARCADE "Allis Chalmers" tractor and wagon, 12¾" long	70.00	135.00	140.00	ARCADE Bus, circa 1940, 8¾" long	30.00	45.00	60.00
ARCADE Ambulance, "City Ambulance", 6" long, 1920	70.00	105.00	140.00	ARCADE Bus, 9" long, circa 1949	25.00	37.50	50.00
ARCADE Andy Gump car, No. 348 on license place	450.00	675.00	900.00	ARCADE Bus, 9½" long, early 1930s, dual rear wheels	33.00	49.50	66.00
ARCADE Anthony Company Dump Truck, reads "Anthony Company Inc., Streater, Illinois" in raised gold embossed letters on tailgate	250.00	375.00	500.00	ARCADE Bus, 12" long, early 1930s, dual rear wheels, driver	75.00	112.50	150.00
ARCADE Auto #1481, Plymouth, 3½" long ...	7.50	11.25	15.00	ARCADE Bus, with driver, cast iron, 13" long	220.00	330.00	440.00
ARCADE auto, looks like 1933 Plymouth, white rubber tires, approx. 4¾" long	16.00	24.00	32.00	ARCADE No. 316x bus, double-decker coach, 1932, rear stairway to top, 8¼" long	130.00	195.00	260.00
ARCADE auto, four-door hard top, 6" long	100.00	150.00	200.00	ARCADE No. 311 Bus, approx. 6" long, 1920s....	25.00	37.50	50.00
ARCADE Avery Tractor circa 1920s, 4¾" long ...	60.00	90.00	120.00	ARCADE No. 312 Bus ..	40.00	60.00	80.00
ARCADE Brinks Armored Truck	1250.00	1875.00	2500.00	ARCADE Bus, double-decker, rear stairway to top, circa 1938, 8" long.	80.00	120.00	160.00
ARCADE Bugatti Racer, 5½"	45.00	67.50	90.00	ARCADE Bus, double-decker, 10" long	40.00	60.00	80.00
ARCADE Buick Sedan, 8½" long, rubber tires, 1920.	550.00	725.00	1100.00	ARCADE "Caterpillar Tractor", No.268x, 1932, chain caterpillar treads, approx. 5½" long	35.00	52.50	70.00
ARCADE Buick, coupe, circa 1928, 8" long, spare tire on rear	700.00	1050.00	1400.00	ARCADE Caterpillar Tractor, 8" long, steel tracks, diesel	150.00	225.00	300.00
				ARCADE No. 269 very early Caterpillar tractor ...	200.00	300.00	400.00

ARCADE "Fageol Safety Coach" with metal wheels, approx. 12" long.
Photo by Bill Kaufman. Courtesy Good Old Days Store.

ARCADE Allis-Chalmers Tractor Trailer, circa 1936.
Courtesy Dick & Nancy Dice.

ARCADE "New York World's Fair" tourist train, 1939.
Photo by Bill Kaufman.

ARCADE Bus, Double-Decker, 10" long.
Courtesy Mapes Auctioneers & Appraisers.

ARCADE "Yellow Cab", 9" long, circa 1928, no driver.
Courtesy Mapes Auctioneers & Appraisers.

ARCADE Steamroller, "Austin Autocrat Worm Drive", 7" long.
Courtesy Mapes Auctioneers & Appraisers

ARCADE Fire Truck, hook and ladder, 18" long.
Courtesy Mapes Auctioneers & Appraisers.

	G	VG	M
ARCADE Century of Progress Bus, 1934, 10¼" long	45.00	67.50	90.00
ARCADE Century of Progress Greyhound bus, 10" long, circa 1933	44.00	66.00	88.00
ARCADE Century of Progress Greyhound bus, 12" long, circa 1940	60.00	90.00	120.00
ARCADE Century of Progress sightseeing bus, 14¼" long, 1933	70.00	105.00	140.00
ARCADE Chevrolet utility coupe, 1924, rubber tires, black with gold belt line, silver headlights, 6¾" long, with chauffeur	80.00	120.00	160.00

	G	VG	M
ARCADE corn cutter and binder	25.00	37.50	50.00
ARCADE corn planter	8.00	12.00	16.00
ARCADE No. 116 coupe with working rumble seat, 1920s, approx. 5" long	35.00	52.50	70.00
ARCADE disk harrow	7.00	10.50	14.00
ARCADE double-decker bus, open, 18 tin seats on roof, dual wheels on rear, "Made by ARCADE MFG. CO. FREEPORT, ILL." on each side, 13¾" long, circa 1930s	350.00	525.00	700.00

ARCADE Coupe, 7½" long.
Courtesy Mapes Auctioneers & Appraisers.

ARCADE Mack "Gasoline" truck, 13½" long.
Courtesy Mapes Auctioneers & Appraisers.

	G	VG	M
ARCADE Chevrolet Coupe 1928, 8" long, white rubber tires, spare tire on rear	120.00	180.00	240.00
ARCADE Corn Planter, rubber wheels	17.00	25.50	34.00
ARCADE Coupe, circa 1937, 3¾" long	37.50	56.25	75.00
ARCADE Coupe, 5" long, 1920s, two side windows	60.00	90.00	120.00
ARCADE Coupe, 5¼" long, circa 1920, metal wheels	34.00	51.00	68.00
ARCADE Coupe (Ford?), 6½" long, one side window, 1920s	50.00	75.00	100.00
ARCADE Coupe, 6¾" long, two side windows, early 1920s	60.00	90.00	120.00
ARCADE Coupe, 7½" long	100.00	150.00	200.00
ARCADE Coupe, 9" long, circa 1920s, spare tire on rear, two windows on side	300.00	450.00	600.00
ARCADE Coast to Coast bus, 10" long	35.00	52.50	70.00

	G	VG	M
ARCADE dump hay rake, 5"	22.00	33.00	44.00
ARCADE dump hay rake, 7"	40.00	60.00	80.00
ARCADE dump truck, 6" long, circa 1927	40.00	60.00	80.00
ARCADE dump truck, 7", 1920s or early 30s	50.00	75.00	100.00
ARCADE dump truck, open cab, 8" long, early 1920s	80.00	120.00	160.00
ARCADE dump truck with driver, 10½" long	190.00	285.00	380.00
ARCADE dump truck, Red Baby, 11" long, 1920s	150.00	225.00	300.00
ARCADE dump truck, Mack, 12" long	344.00	516.00	688.00

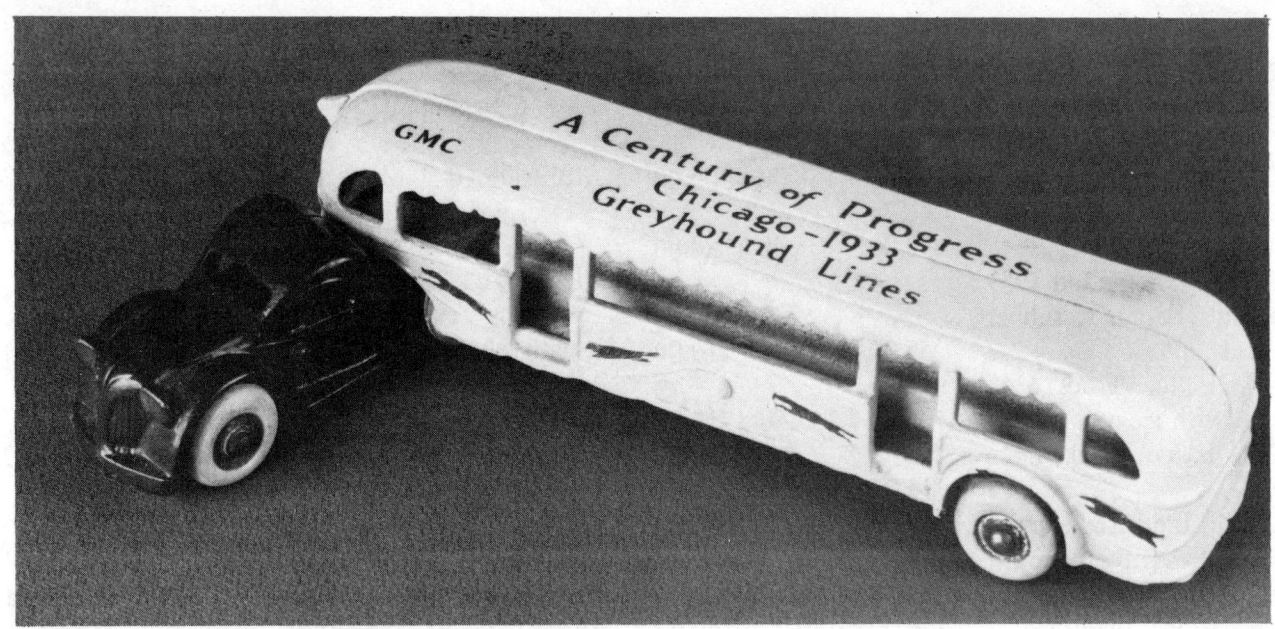

ARCADE "Century of Progress" Greyhound bus, 10" long, 1933.
Courtesy Mapes Auctioneers & Appraisers.

	G	VG	M		G	VG	M
ARCADE dump truck, Mack, 13"	250.00	375.00	500.00	ARCADE Fire Truck, 15"	120.00	180.00	240.00
ARCADE Fageol Coach (bus), circa 1932, 6" long	50.00	75.00	100.00	ARCADE Ford coupe with rumble seat No. 106...	22.00	33.00	44.00
ARCADE Fageol bus, 8" long, 7 windows on each side, 1920s	44.00	66.00	88.00	ARCADE Ford coupe with rumble seat No. 116 ...	40.00	60.00	80.00
ARCADE Fageol bus, 12½" long, dual wheels, circa 1930s	140.00	210.00	280.00	ARCADE Ford gondola, 13" long, circa 1927	150.00	225.00	300.00
ARCADE "Fageol Safety Coach", with metal wheels, approx. 12" long	90.00	135.00	180.00	ARCADE Ford stake truck, 7" long	40.00	60.00	80.00
ARCADE Fageol Safety Coach, 1920, 12½" long, rubber tires	100.00	150.00	200.00	ARCADE Ford touring Model T with driver ...	40.00	60.00	80.00
ARCADE Farm Mower ..	15.00	22.50	30.00	ARCADE Ford Tractor, 4"	40.00	60.00	80.00
ARCADE Farmal Tractor, Model B	160.00	240.00	320.00	ARCADE "Fordson" tractor, 1920s, 3½" long	26.00	39.00	52.00
ARCADE Fire Apparatus Truck, Mack, 21" long.	190.00	285.00	380.00	ARCADE Fordson Tractor, 4" long	30.00	45.00	60.00
ARCADE Fire Engine, 9" long, 1930s	40.00	60.00	80.00	ARCADE Fordson tractor with driver, cast iron 5¾"	58.00	87.00	116.00
ARCADE Fire Hook & Ladder Truck, 16" long, articulated	175.00	262.50	350.00	ARCADE Gasoline Truck, 5", spoked wheels	75.00	112.50	150.00
ARCADE Fire Hook and Ladder Truck, 18" long	150.00	225.00	300.00	ARCADE "Gasoline" truck, Mack, 5" long	44.00	66.00	88.00
ARCADE Fire Pumper, 13" long, six figures	150.00	225.00	300.00	ARCADE "Gasoline" Truck, Mack, 13" long	400.00	600.00	800.00
ARCADE Fire Truck, circa 1936, 13½" long, rubber tires, removable hose reel, bell, six firemen in blue coats, steam boiler	210.00	315.00	420.00	ARCADE "Gasoline" truck circa 1920s, 13" long, tin operating tank, rubber hose	475.00	712.50	950.00
				ARCADE "Gasoline" truck, Mack, 13½" long, circa 1925	100.00	150.00	200.00
				ARCADE Gasoline truck, Mack, "Independent Oil", 13½" long	900.00	1350.00	1800.00

	G	VG	M
ARCADE GMC Bus, 7½" coast to coast	75.00	112.50	150.00
ARCADE Greyhound bus, 1938, rubber wheels, 8½"	100.00	150.00	200.00
ARCADE Greyhound GMC Bus, 7½"	90.00	135.00	180.00
ARCADE Greyhound 1939 World's Fair bus, rubber wheels, 6½"	55.00	82.50	110.00
ARCADE "Ice" Truck, 6½" long, with ice and tongs	105.00	157.50	210.00
ARCADE Ice Truck, circa 1930s.............	115.00	172.50	230.00
ARCADE Industrial Derrick	350.00	525.00	700.00
ARCADE International Dump Truck, 1939, 11" long, rubber wheels....	120.00	180.00	240.00
ARCADE International Harvester Caterpillar tractor	80.00	120.00	160.00
ARCADE International Harvester Caterpillar tractor, large	200.00	300.00	400.00
ARCADE International Harvester dump truck, white rubber tires, circa 1929	100.00	150.00	200.00
ARCADE International pickup, circa 1939, rubber wheels, 9"	140.00	210.00	280.00
ARCADE International Truck 11" long, ...	80.00	120.00	160.00
ARCADE John Deere thresher, mid-1930s	75.00	112.50	150.00
ARCADE John Deere tractor	16.00	24.00	32.00
ARCADE Ladder Truck, 4" long	26.00	39.00	52.00
ARCADE Ladder Truck, 5¼"................	35.00	52.50	70.00
ARCADE limousine (or bus), circa 1920s, 12½" long.	100.00	150.00	200.00
ARCADE Mack "American Oil Co.", circa 1928, 10½" long................	300.00	450.00	600.00
ARCADE Mack bus	1500.00	2250.00	3000.00
ARCADE Mack Stake Truck, 7½"	150.00	225.00	300.00
ARCADE Mack Truck, 4¾"	30.00	45.00	60.00
ARCADE Mack Truck, circa 1928, 8½" long	100.00	150.00	200.00
ARCADE Mack Truck with dump body, driver, body cranks up and dumps, 1920s, 8½" long	100.00	150.00	200.00

	G	VG	M
ARCADE McCormick-Deering combine, 10", cast iron	110.00	165.00	220.00
ARCADE 10-20 McCormick-Deering Farm Tractor ..	100.00	150.00	200.00
Tractor	100.00	150.00	200.00
ARCADE "McCormick-Deering", manure spreader with shaft	60.00	90.00	120.00
ARCADE No. 450x McCormick-Deering thresher, 9½" long, 1932	100.00	150.00	200.00
ARCADE Model A convertible Coupe, 4"........	44.00	66.00	88.00
ARCADE Model A Coupe, 4¼", spare tire on back	60.00	90.00	120.00
ARCADE Model A coupe, rumble seat, 5" long....	110.00	165.00	220.00
ARCADE Model A Ford 6½" long, circa 1928-1931, with driver	150.00	225.00	300.00
ARCADE Model A Pickup, 8", metal wheels, circa 1928	60.00	90.00	120.00
ARCADE Model A truck, stake sides, circa 1928-1931	12.50	18.75	25.00
ARCADE Model A wrecker, circa 1929-31, 11" long .	150.00	225.00	300.00
ARCADE Model T Coupe, 4"	35.00	52.50	70.00
ARCADE Model T Ford coupe, driver, two side windows, 6½" long, circa 1922	150.00	225.00	300.00
ARCADE Model T Pickup, 8" long	125.00	187.50	250.00
ARCADE Model T Ford sedan with door in middle	40.00	60.00	80.00
ARCADE Model T Ford sedan, two-door, with driver, 6¼" long.......	75.00	112.50	150.00
ARCADE Model T Ford four-door car, 6".......	225.00	337.50	450.00
ARCADE Model T Ford touring car, 6¼" long, circa 1920, rubber tires, open-sided	135.00	202.50	270.00
ARCADE Model T, 6½" long, rubber tires	130.00	195.00	260.00
ARCADE Model T Touring Car, 1920, 6½" long, nickel plated wheels ...	75.00	112.50	150.00
ARCADE Motorcycle, Harley-Davidson, cop rider, 5½" long, 1930s .	55.00	82.50	110.00

	G	VG	M
ARCADE mower, rubber wheels	14.00	21.00	28.00
ARCADE Nash, approx. 4" long	44.00	66.00	88.00
ARCADE New York World's Fair bus, 10½" long	80.00	120.00	160.00
ARCADE "New York World's Fair" 11" long (with two trailers) cast iron tourist train, 1939-40, tin litho canopy, price with one trailer, add $25 for each additional trailer in mint	80.00	120.00	160.00
ARCADE No. 1 Farm Tractor	18.00	27.00	36.00
ARCADE Oliver Tractor, black rubber wheels ...	15.00	22.50	30.00
ARCADE Pickup Truck No. 1488, 3½" long	7.50	11.25	15.00
ARCADE Pickup Truck, Chev., 1920s, 8½" long	300.00	450.00	600.00
ARCADE Pile Driver, 10½"	80.00	120.00	160.00
ARCADE plow, one-gang, with black rubber tires..	3.00	4.50	6.00
ARCADE plow, two-gang	4.00	6.00	8.00
ARCADE Pontiac Sedan, 1935, 6⅛" long........	200.00	300.00	400.00
ARCADE Race Car with two figures	25.00	37.50	50.00
ARCADE Racer 3¾", circa 1932, rubber wheels ...	16.00	24.00	32.00
ARCADE Racer, solid wheels, 5½"..........	47.50	71.25	95.00
ARCADE Racer No. 1457, 5½" long, rubber wheels, circa 1935	30.00	45.00	60.00
ARCADE Rack Truck, Chevrolet, 1920s, 9" long	450.00	675.00	900.00
ARCADE Railroad spike driver, cast with small wheels, upright lever...	180.00	270.00	360.00
ARCADE Reo Coupe, rumble seat, 9"	300.00	450.00	600.00
ARCADE Reo coupe, smaller	100.00	150.00	200.00
ARCADE Road Grader, 4½".................	46.00	69.00	92.00
ARCADE Rumble coupe with driver, 6¾"	120.00	180.00	240.00
ARCADE "Safety Coach" tour bus, rubber tires, 12" long, with driver	70.00	105.00	140.00
ARCADE "Safety Coach" tour bus, steel wheels, driver, 12" long	100.00	150.00	200.00
ARCADE Sandloader, 8½" long, 1920s	220.00	330.00	440.00
ARCADE Sedan No. 2272	16.00	24.00	32.00
ARCADE Sedan circa 1937, cast iron, 8" long	60.00	90.00	120.00
ARCADE Sedan, 3¾" high, circa 1940	16.00	24.00	32.00
ARCADE Sedan, No. 1511, 5".................	35.00	52.50	70.00
ARCADE semi-truck, cast iron, 1920s, blue	22.00	33.00	44.00
ARCADE sickle bar mower	5.00	7.50	10.00
ARCADE "Silver Arrow" sedan, 7" long	66.00	99.00	132.00
ARCADE stake truck, cast iron, blue, 7" long	110.00	165.00	220.00
ARCADE stake truck, 1920s, 7½" long	150.00	225.00	300.00
ARCADE Steam Roller, 3½"	40.00	60.00	80.00
ARCADE Steam Roller, 4½"	44.00	66.00	88.00
ARACADE Steamroller, "Austin Autocrat Worm Drive", 7" long........	90.00	135.00	180.00
ARCADE Steam Roller, 7½" long	60.00	90.00	120.00
ARCADE Steam Shovel, 4½"	40.00	60.00	80.00
ARCADE tank No. 3960, 1930s, 3" long, spring-firing cannon	80.00	120.00	160.00
ARCADE taxi, four-door with driver, red, white and black, 7¾"	60.00	90.00	120.00
ARCADE threshing machine	37.50	56.25	75.00
ARCADE thresher machine, circa 1930	30.00	45.00	60.00
ARCADE tractor 273 ...	25.00	37.50	50.00
ARCADE Tractor 2880L, 2½"	7.50	11.25	15.00
ARCADE Tractor No. 2738, 3½"	20.00	30.00	40.00
ARCADE Tractor, Ford and Trailer	200.00	300.00	400.00
ARCADE Tractor Trailer No. 289, 3½"	18.00	27.00	36.00
ARCADE tractor with white rubber wheels	10.00	15.00	20.00
ARCADE transport service semi-truck	150.00	225.00	300.00

	G	VG	M
ARCADE truck, black rubber tires, 1930s	18.00	27.00	36.00
ARCADE red baby truck, with driver, open back, 11" long	90.00	135.00	180.00
ARCADE White bus	1000.00	1500.00	2000.00
ARCADE White dump truck, circa 1920s	300.00	450.00	600.00
ARCADE White moving van	900.00	1350.00	1800.00
ARCADE White panel truck	425.00	637.50	850.00
ARCADE Wrecker, circa 1930s, 4½"	20.00	30.00	40.00
ARCADE wrecker, circa 1930s, 6" long	45.00	67.50	90.00
ARCADE wrecker with driver and hard rubber wheels, 11" long	130.00	195.00	260.00
ARCADE wrecker with driver, 11½" long	70.00	105.00	140.00
ARCADE Wrecker, Mack, 13" long, 1920s	300.00	450.00	600.00
ARCADE Yellow Cab, 5" long	200.00	300.00	400.00
ARCADE "Yellow Cab", 8" long, 1920s	250.00	375.00	500.00

	G	VG	M
ARCADE "Yellow Cab", 9" long, circa 1928, no driver	90.00	135.00	180.00
ARCADE "Yellow Cab", No. 155, 1930s, actually orange and black, 8⅛" long, nickel-plated driver, white rubber tires, lead cowl lights	150.00	225.00	300.00
ARCADE Yellow Cab, 1934, "A Century of Progress", 6½"	200.00	300.00	400.00
ARCADE Yellow Cab with driver, 9" long, 1920 . . .	190.00	285.00	380.00
ARCADE Yellow Cab 15" long, circa 1924	150.00	225.00	300.00
ARCADE Yellow Cab 3, small	22.00	33.00	44.00
ARCADE Yellow Cab, Zephyr, late 1930s, 8¼" long	200.00	300.00	400.00
ARCADE Yellow coach bus	350.00	525.00	700.00
ARCADE Yellow coach bus, double-decker, 1925, 14" long	700.00	1050.00	1400.00

ARCADE Model T Touring 6¼" long
Courtesy Lloyd W. Ralston Auctions

ARCADE Rack Truck, Chevrolet, 1920s, 9" long
Courtesy Lloyd W. Ralston Auctions

ARCADE Yellow Cab, Zephyr, late 30's, 8¼" long.
Courtesy Lloyd W. Ralston Auctions

Top, L to R: Dump Truck, tin 5¾" long, Road Grader, 7½" long, cast iron, Truck, open back, cast iron, 4¼" long. Middle, L to R: Pickup Truck, 7¼" long, cast iron, 1920s, ARCADE "Allis Chalmers" tractor and wagon, 9½" long. Bottom, L to R: ARCADE "Allis Chalmers" tractor and wagon, 12¾" long, Coupe with rumble seat, tin, 5" long.
Courtesy Garth's Auctions Inc.

ARCADE Fageol Safety Coach, 1920, 12¼" long.
Courtesy Lloyd W. Ralston Auctions

Army Truck, pressed steel, cloth top, black wooden wheels, approx. 10" long	G	VG	M
	20.00	30.00	40.00

Army Truck, "USA", rubber, covered with impregnated canvas, white rubber tires, dual wheels, circa 1938	G	VG	M
	4.00	6.00	8.00

AUBURN RUBBER

This company also manufactured rubber tires for other companies, including Wyandotte.

	G	VG	M
AUBURN RUBBER ambulance, white or khaki, circa 1938	8.00	12.00	16.00
AUBURN Cadillac, 1936.	10.00	15.00	20.00
AUBURN Chevrolet, 1939	10.00	15.00	20.00
AUBURN Chrysler Airflow	9.00	13.50	18.00
AUBURN Cord automobile (first car produced by Auburn), circa 1936....	12.50	18.75	25.00
AUBURN David Bradley Manure Spreader	5.00	7.50	10.00
AUBURN Fire Engine, 8"	7.50	11.25	15.00
AUBURN Ford coupe, circa 1937	3.00	4.50	6.00
AUBURN Ford sedan, circa 1937	9.00	13.50	18.00
AUBURN Lincoln Convertible, 1942, 4¾" long....	7.50	11.25	15.00
AUBURN midget car, 10½" long	8.00	12.00	16.00
AUBURN milk truck, 4" long, circa 1940	3.00	4.50	6.00
AUBURN "Oldsmobile", coupe, 1936, "Aubrtoy", 3¾" long............	7.50	11.25	15.00
AUBURN Oldsmobile sedan, 4 door, 1940, 6" long ..	15.00	22.50	30.00
AUBURN Plymouth sedan, circa 1940	6.00	9.00	12.00
AUBURN Pumper, 9" long, late 1940s	5.50	8.25	11.00
AUBURN racing car, approx. 6½" long, circa 1939	6.00	9.00	12.00
AUBURN Racer, 10½" long	6.00	9.00	12.00
AUBURN Service Truck .	10.00	15.00	20.00
AUBURN Stake Truck, 4"	4.00	6.00	8.00
AUBURN tank, approx. 3" long	5.50	8.25	11.00
AUBURN tank, approx. 4½" long	13.00	19.50	26.00

	G	VG	M
AUBURN tractor with driver, circa 1938	6.00	9.00	12.00
AUBURN Tractor with field howitzer, set	10.00	15.00	20.00
AUBURN truck, open bed, 4" long, green, circa 1940..	15.00	22.50	30.00
AUBURN truck, open bed, 5¼" long, circa 1940, marked USA, khaki ...	15.00	22.50	30.00
AUBURN US Army Truck, approx. 4¾" long, Ford "U.S.A."	10.00	15.00	20.00
"Austin", cast iron, early 1930s	20.00	30.00	40.00
Austin Racer, 4" cast iron	7.00	10.50	14.00
"Austin" stakebody, 3¾" long, 1920s, cast iron ..	25.00	37.50	50.00
"Austin" wrecker, 4' long, 1920s, cast iron	30.00	45.00	60.00
Auto Express 546, 6" long with drivers and barrels	80.00	120.00	160.00
Auto Express 546, 7" long, cast iron	31.00	46.50	62.00
Auto, raked cab, cast iron, early 1930s, approx. 4" long	18.00	27.00	36.00
Auto Trailer, 12½" long, carries three cars, all two-door, circa 1932	150.00	225.00	300.00
Auto Trailer, 1920s, 22" long, with coupe, two-door sedan, and four-door sedan on trailer	80.00	120.00	160.00
Auto with house trailer, late 1930s, cast iron, 13½" .	150.00	225.00	300.00
Auto with trailer, circa 1938, 2½" long, both auto and trailer very streamlined .	30.00	45.00	60.00

AUBURN Racer, 10½" long.
Courtesy Mapes Auctioneers & Appraisers.

Arcade Buicks and Chevrolets: on top are Chevy 1924 coupe and 1928 sedan and coupe. The latter were later made with double-striping around the waistline, rarer and more valuable. Bottom row, the famous Arcade Buicks, Sedan and 4-passenger coupe.
Photo by C.B.C. Lee.

Arcade made other brands of cars and trucks; Top, 1922 Dodge coupe; 1931 Reo Royale coupe 9¼"; Mach high-lift coal truck, one of a very large range of various trucks; bottom: Yellow panel truck; White panel delivery; International-Harvester panel truck; each of these vans was issued in various private liveries, the best known being the I-H Hathaway Bakery, which was done in versions using either decal transfers or colored rubber stamping.
Photo by C.B.C. Lee.

Other toy makers also made some nice trucks and cars; Top: Champion panel truck; Dent Police Patrol (they also made a similar parcel delivery); and Freidag delivery truck; Bottom: Vindex Pontiac coupe, Hubley Chrysler Airflow, Dent sedan.
Photo by C.B.C. Lee.

Among the most valuable large iron toys are several non-Arcades; rear, Kenton touring car, Kilgore Model T Ford with moving figures; Dent Red Devil touring car (Kenton made a very similar Franklin); bottom, the famous Hubley Packard and Kilgore Stutz, both assembled from multiple castings and very choice items amongst advanced automotive toy collectors.
Photo by C.B.C. Lee.

Choicer small cast iron pieces include: Top row, A.C. Williams 1934 Ford (series included coupe and sedan); A.C.W. 1936 Ford (series included coupe, sedan, roadster and panel truck and in a simpler single-piece casting only three, omitting the roadster); A.C.W. generic take-apart (series included coupe, sedan and stake truck). Bottom row shows Arcade 1933 Nash (coupe and sedan); Arcade 1935 Ford (sedan and stake truck); Dent 1935 LaSalle (sedan, coupe, roadster, pick-up truck, wrecker and panel truck).
Photo by C.B.C. Lee.

Smaller realistic slush-mold cars. The center car in bottom row is marked Cord on door and "A TOMMY TOY" along the rocker panel on each side.
Photo by C.B.C. Lee.

Some desirable slush-cash include top row, Reo Victoria, Chrysler coupe, L29 Cord coupe. Bottom, a selection of late 20s models, some marked with car names "CHEVROLET", "CHRYSLER".
Photo by C.B.C. Lee.

These are a rare make of toy, evidently manufactured through most of the twenties and thirties in San Francisco by the TIP TOP TOY CO.
Photo by C.B.C. Lee.

These are by various English makers. There were many makers of die-cast, poured lead, slush, etc. in Europe, some of them highly desirable and costly.
Photo by C.B.C. Lee.

BARCLAY

BARCLAY: A number of unmarked vehicles were in the possession of the late Barclay-All Nu designer Frank Krupp. Most of these were too early to have been All-Nu and were checked with four early Barclay employees. The number of Xs in parenthesis after the toy's description indicate how many thought it had been Barclay. However, it is possible, since these are based on memories of several decades, that not all are Barclay. An X? indicates the employee believed it was Barclay but was not sure. Those not marked with Xs have been identified in other ways.

In 1984, 45 plaster castings retained by Barclay's chief of maintenance when he cleaned out the shut-down factory in 1971 were shown to the author in the course of his research. Included were soldiers, Disney figures, vehicles and an autogiro, many never produced. Some of the toys in this photo may now identify previously unmarked vehicles as being made by Barclay.

	G	VG	M		G	VG	M
BARCLAY (BV 1) Ambulance, No. 50, 3½" long, small cross	15.00	22.50	30.00	BARCLAY (BV 12) "Beer" truck, circa 1940, No. 376, approx. 3¾"	8.00	12.00	16.00
BARCLAY (BV 2) Ambulance, No. 50, 3½" long, large cross	15.00	22.50	30.00	BARCLAY (BV 13) Beer Truck No. 377, with barrels	7.50	11.25	15.00
BARCLAY (BV 3) Ambulance No. 50, 4¾" long	10.00	15.00	20.00	BARCLAY (BV 14) Bus, futuristic, "Made U.S.A."	5.00	7.50	10.00
BARCLAY (BV 4) Antiaircraft truck, no driver, 2¾" long, man firing AA gun, double barrel, circa 1940	18.00	27.00	36.00	BARCLAY (BV 15) Cannon Car, 3¼" long, gunner low	6.00	9.00	12.00
BARCLAY (BV 5) Antiaircraft gun vehicle, 2½" long, post WW II, black rubber tires	10.00	15.00	20.00	BARCLAY (BV 16) Cannon car, metal wheels, 3¼" long, (No. 53 Antiaircraft car in 1931 catalog)	6.00	9.00	12.00
BARCLAY (BV 6) Armored car, circa 1937, two protruding weapons	6.00	9.00	12.00	BARCLAY (BV 17) Cannon Car, 3¼" long, slight casting differences from headlight version	12.00	18.00	24.00
BARCLAY (BV 7) Armored car, streamlined, one protruding cannon, white rubber tires	10.00	15.00	20.00	BARCLAY (BV 18) Cannon Car, battery-powered headlight, 3½" long		No Price Found	
BARCLAY (BV 8) Army Car with two silver bullhorns, approx. 2½" long	10.00	15.00	20.00	BARCLAY (BV 19) Cannon Car, 4" long, moveable gun, gunner at side of gun	20.00	30.00	40.00
BARCLAY (BV 9) Army Tractor (Minneapolis-Moline "Jeep"), 2¾" long	9.00	13.50	18.00	BARCLAY (BV 20) Cannon Car, 4" long, moveable gun, gunner at rear	20.00	30.00	40.00
BARCLAY (BV 10) Austin Coupe, circa 1935, 2" long, XX	5.00	7.50	10.00	BARCLAY (BV 21) Cannon Truck, 4" long, with moveable cannon	12.50	18.75	25.00
BARCLAY (BV 11) Auto Carrier, circa 1941, 2-piece, "Barclay Made in U.S.A." on each piece	10.00	15.00	20.00	BARCLAY (BV 22) Cannon Truck, more streamlined version	9.00	13.50	18.00
				BARCLAY (BV 23) Chrysler Airflow, 4" long, circa 1936	4.00	6.00	8.00

Top, L to R: BARCLAY Ambulance No.50, small cross, BARCLAY Ambulance No.50, large cross. Bottom, BARCLAY Ambulance No.50, 4¾" long.
Photo by Ed Poole.

BARCLAY, top, L to R: BV 60; BV 63; BV 25; BV 28; BV 71; bottom, L to R: BV 37; BV 61; BV 55; BV 24.
Photo by Bill Kaufman. Courtesy George Buhler.

BARCLAY, L to R; BV 64; BV 72; BV 40.
Photo by Bill Kaufman. Courtesy Evelyn Besser.

BARCLAY, L to R: BV 54, BV 30, BV 81.
Photo by Bill Kaufman. Courtesy Evelyn Besser.

BARCLAY L to R, top: BV 11; BV 49; BV 14; BV 13. Bottom, L to R: BV 82; sedan for BV 61 set; BV 47.
Photo by Bill Kaufman. Courtesy George Buhler.

BARCLAY, L to R: BV 65; BV 52.
Photo by Bill Kaufman. Courtesy Evelyn Besser.

BARCLAY, L to R: BV 80; BV 10; BV 26; BV 59.
Photo by Bill Kaufman. Courtesy Evelyn Besser.

BARCLAY: Top, L to R: BV 15; BV 6; BV 4; BV 9.
   Middle, L to R: BV 56; BV 19; BV 20.
   Bottom, L to R: BV 16; BV 16; BV 18; BV 17.
Photo by Ed Poole

BARCLAY, top, L to R: BV57, BV 21 (cannon missing), BV 39.
   Middle, L to R; BV67, BV66, BV70.
   Bottom, L to R: BV 68, BV 5, BV 69, cannon 4" long, Post WWII.
Photo by Ed Poole

BARCLAY, top row, L to R: Howitzer, 4 wheels, loop hitch horozontal, Howitzer, 4 wheels, loop hitch vertical; BV 78 with wire hitch; BV 78 with peg hitch.
   Bottom row, L to R: BV 7; BV 76, wire hitch; BV 76, no hitch.
Photo by Ed Poole.

BARCLAY, L to R: BV 32; BV 33, BV 41.
Photo by Bill Kaufman. Courtesy Evelyn Besser.

	G	VG	M
BARCLAY (BV 24) "Coast to Coast" bus, "Barclay Toy", two-piece	No Price Found		
BARCLAY (BV 25) Coupe, 1930s, "Made in U.S.A."	7.50	11.25	15.00
BARCLAY (BV 26) Coupe, approx. 2½" long, slush lead, circa 1935, XXX..	7.00	10.50	14.00
BARCLAY (BV 27) Coupe, 1934, 4¼" long, XXX..	40.00	60.00	80.00
BARCLAY (BV 28) Coupe, 2-piece, 1930s, "Barclay Toy"	No Price Found		
BARCLAY (BV 31) Coupe, two-tone, approx. 3½" long, slush lead, X?X...	7.50	11.25	15.00
BARCLAY (BV 32) De Soto, 1938, 3⅛" long, XXX...	5.00	7.50	10.00
BARCLAY (BV 33) "Delivery" Truck, 2⅞" long, XXX	7.50	11.25	15.00
BARCLAY (BV 34) Double Decker Bux, 4"	7.00	10.50	14.00
BARCLAY (BV 35) Double Transport Set No. 440, four cars on upper and lower racks, 1960s, hinged for unloading	12.50	18.75	25.00
BARCLAY (BV 36) Esso Gas Truck, approx. 6" long	2.50	3.75	5.00
BARCLAY (BV 37) "Express" stake truck, 1930s	No Price Found		
BARCLAY (BV 38) Fire Engine No. 390?, moveable ladder, circa 1950s	4.00	6.00	8.00
BARCLAY (BV 39) Field Kitchen, 2" long.......	10.00	15.00	20.00
BARCLAY (BV 40) Fire Engine, approx. 2¾" long, 2 firemen, black metal wheels, 1930s, XX......	6.00	9.00	12.00
BARCLAY (BV 41) Fire Engine, 4" long, French-looking (Barclay often copied foreign toys), XXX	6.00	9.00	12.00
BARCLAY (BV 42) Ford, 1931, 2¼"	3.00	4.50	6.00
BARCLAY (BV 43) "Golden Arrow Racer", approx. 4½" long, slush lead, X?X	4.00	6.00	8.00
BARCLAY (BV 44) Mack Pick Up Truck, 3½"...	6.00	9.00	12.00

	G	VG	M
BARCLAY (BV 45) Milk Truck No. 377 with cans	5.00	7.50	10.00
BARCLAY (BV 46) Motorcycle with flat rider, full-dimensioned sidecar....	12.00	18.00	24.00
BARCLAY (BV 47) "Oil-Fuel" truck, circa 1940.	5.00	7.50	10.00
BARCLAY (BV 48) "Parcel Delivery", approx. 3½" long, slush lead, X?XXX	4.00	6.00	8.00
BARCLAY (BV 49) Police Car No. 317, slush mold, approx. 3¾" long, circa 1930s	13.00	19.50	26.00
BARCLAY (BV 50) Race Car, 3".............	3.50	5.25	7.00
BARCLAY (BV 51) Racer, 5½"	14.00	21.00	28.00
BARCLAY (BV 52) Racer, closed cockpit, approx. 7" long, circa 1939, slush lead, could be All-Nu, X?X .	5.00	7.50	10.00
BARCLAY (BV 53) Racer, early slush lead, 1920s-30s	7.50	11.25	15.00
BARCLAY (BV 54) Racer, two passengers, approx. 4¼" long, XXX.......	9.00	13.50	18.00
BARCLAY (BV 55) Racer with tail fin, "Made In U.S.A."	No Price Found		
BARCLAY (BV 56) Renault Tank, circa 1938......	14.00	21.00	28.00
BARCLAY (BV 57) Searchlight Truck, white rubber tires, circa 1940	7.00	10.50	14.00
BARCLAY (BV 57A) Searchlight Truck, second version	No Price Found		
BARCLAY (BV 58) Sedan, 4 door, approx. 5" long, maybe Chrysler, circa 1936	19.00	28.50	38.00
BARCLAY (BV 59) Sedan, two door, approx. 3⅛" long, rubber wheels, slush lead, circa 1935, XX........	10.00	15.00	20.00
BARCLAY (BV 60) Sedan, two-piece, 2-door, 1930s, "Barclay Toy"	5.00	7.50	10.00
BARCLAY (BV 61) Sedan and "Tourist Trailer", "Made U.S.A.", 1930s..	7.50	11.25	15.00
BARCLAY (BV 62) Silver Arrow Race Car, 5½"..	8.00	12.00	16.00

BARCLAY: Top, L to R: BV 53;   BV 71;   BV 49;   unlisted, BV 74.
Bottom, L to R: BV 46;   BV 4;   BV 6;   BV 68.
Photo by Bill Kaufman.

BARCLAY (BV83) Cannon Truck moveable cannon, 4" long . . . .
No Price Found

Photo by Ed Poole

BARCLAY, L to R: BV 31,   BV 48,   BV 43.
Photo by Bill Kaufman. Courtesy Evelyn Besser.

	G	VG	M
BARCLAY (BV 63) Station Wagon, 1930s, 2-piece, "Barclay Toy", approx. 3"	5.00	7.50	10.00
BARCLAY (BV 64) Steam-Roller, 3¼" long, traction type, slush lead with tin roof, X?X	12.50	18.75	25.00
BARCLAY (BV 65) Streamline Chromed Racer, approx. 6¾" long, circa 1939, open cockpit, could be All-Nu, X?XX	5.00	7.50	10.00
BARCLAY (BV 66) Tank "4562", one man in turret, 3¾" long	15.00	22.50	30.00
BARCLAY (BV 67) Tank "4562", two men in turret, 3¾" long	15.00	22.50	30.00
BARCLAY (BV 68) Tank T41, 4¼" long	5.00	7.50	10.00

	G	VG	M
BARCLAY (BV 69) Tank, 2½" long, man in turret	4.00	6.00	8.00
BARCLAY (BV 70) Tank 2¼" long (based on US M2 light tank)	7.00	10.50	14.00
BARCLAY (BV 71) Taxi, 3¼" long, circa 1940s, slush	5.00	7.50	10.00
BARCLAY (BV 72) Tractor, approx. 2½" long, caterpillar type, slush lead, XX	4.00	6.00	8.00
BARCLAY (BV 73) Tractor, circa 1940)	5.50	7.75	11.00
BARCLAY (BV 74) Trailer Truck, variously "Railway Express", or with Moving Company name, circa 1950s	3.00	4.50	6.00
BARCLAY (BV 75) Transport Set No. 330, 2 cars, 1960s	17.50	26.25	35.00
BARCLAY (BV 76) "US Army" bulldog truck, 2½" long, slush lead	8.00	12.00	16.00
BARCLAY (BV 77) "U.S. Army" truck, white rubber tires	10.00	15.00	20.00
BARCLAY (BV 78) Truck "U.S. Motor Unit", circa 1940, white rubber tires .	11.00	16.50	22.00
BARCLAY (BV 79) Wheel-A-Rific speedway track, two lead racers, black rubber wheels, 10' of plastic track, sold for $1.00 circa 1970	4.00	6.00	8.00
BARCLAY (BV 80) Wrecker, approx. 3¾" long, circa 1935, slush lead, XX	4.00	6.00	8.00
BARCLAY (BV 81) Wrecker, 4½" long, circa 1934, XXX	5.00	7.50	10.00
BARCLAY (BV 82) Wrecker, two-piece, 1930s, "Barclay Toy"	No Price Found		
BARCLAY (BV 83) Cannon Truck, moveable cannon, 4" long	No Price Found		

BV 57A
Photo by Ed Poole

BEAUT MFG. CO. of North Bergen, New Jersey: Beaut Mfg. Co. was founded in 1946 by Eugene Buhler and Irving Reader, former machinist and salesman, respectively, for Barclay Mfg. Co. The company put out five toys: a taxicab, a police car, a fire engine, a sedan and a child's wagon. The company was successful at first, employing ten people, and selling to Woolworth's and many overseas buyers. It ceased its toy-making activities (it continued until 1982 as a general machine shop) around 1950, because of competition from plastic toys.

BEAUT "Police" car (left) and "Taxi". Photo by Bill Kaufman. Courtesy George Buhler.

	G	VG	M		G	VG	M
BEAUT Fire Engine	2.00	3.00	4.00	BEST TOY No. 70 Pumper, 2¼"slush lead	3.00	4.50	6.00
BEAUT "Police" car, approx. 3¾"	2.00	3.00	4.00	BIG BANG carbide armored car, cast iron, 9½" long .	30.00	45.00	60.00
BEAUT Sedan, approx. 3¾"	2.00	3.00	4.00	BIG BANG motor tank, 9" long, circa 1933	9.00	13.50	18.00
BEAUT "Taxi", approx. 3¾"	2.00	3.00	4.00	BIG BOY Fire Hook and Ladder, 38" long	400.00	600.00	800.00
BEST TOY No. 35 Coupe, 2¼", slush lead, circa 1920s	3.00	4.50	6.00	Boattail Speedster, cast iron, 5" long, blue with nickel wheels, driver, circa 1920s	55.00	82.50	110.00
BEST TOY No. 49 "Nite Coach", 2½" slush lead .	3.00	4.50	6.00				
BEST TOY No. 55 Mack Truck and Trailer, slush lead, 4"	5.00	7.50	10.00				

BUDDY "L"

BUDDY "L": Buddy "L" toys were first manufactured by the Moline Pressed Steel Company, Moline, Illinois, in 1921, and were named after the son of the owner, Fred Lundahl. Lundahl had started the company about eight years earlier, manufacturing auto and truck parts (fenders, etc.). The toys were originally made as special items for his son, but as Buddy Lundahl's playmates began to clamor for similar toys of their own and their fathers began asking Lundahl senior to make duplicate toys for their sons, Lundahl went into the toy business. Buddy "L" toys were large, typically 21 to 24 or more inches long for trucks and fire engines. Construction was of very heavy steel, strong enough to support a man's weight. These were made until the early 1930s, when the line was modified and lighterweight materials were employed. Before this time, Fred Lundahl had died, having already lost control of the company. The company has changed names several times, being known as the Buddy "L" Corp., Buddy "L" Toy Co., etc., in recent years dropping the quotes around the L. Continuing to make toys till the present day, the company even put out a few wooden toys during World War II, when its main plant made nothing but war-related items. The early Buddy "L" trains are also popular, and tend to be worth even more than the vehicles. Buddy "L" material from the pre-1932 period is almost indestructible and as a consequence, 50% of the pieces found are either very rusty or have been repainted at some point. The basic metal seems to hold up forever, but repainting and rust drops the price well below "good".

Following is a list of pre-1932 Buddy "L" toys compiled by Thomas W. Sefton.

Large Trucks	G	VG	M		G	VG	M
BUDDY L 200 Express Truck 1921-31	100.00	150.00	200.00	BUDDY L 202 Coal Truck 1926-31	135.00	202.50	270.00
BUDDY L 201 Dump Truck (Ratchet) 1931-30	100.00	150.00	200.00	BUDDY L 202A Sand & Gravel Truck 1926-31 .	150.00	225.00	300.00
BUDDY L 201A Hydraulic Dump Truck 1926-31 . .	135.00	202.50	270.00	BUDDY L 203 Stake Truck 1921-24, 1926-28	150.00	225.00	300.00

BUDDY L Coca Cola Truck, wooden.
Courtesy Dick MacNary.

BUDDY L 201A Hydraulic Dump Truck.
Courtesy Mapes Auctioneers & Appraisers.

BUDDY L 205 Hook and Ladder.
Courtesy Mapes Auctioneers & Appraisers.

BUDDY L Steam Shovel
Courtesy Mapes Auctioneers & Appraisers.

No. 230 BUDDY "L" Sand Loader

No. 204-A BUDDY "L" Railway Express Truck

No. 205 BUDDY "L" Fire Truck

No. 207 BUDDY "L" Ice Truck

No. 203-B BUDDY "L" Baggage Truck.

No. 300 BUDDY "L" Sand Screener

No. 201-A BUDDY "L" Hydraulic Dump Truck

No. 205-B BUDDY "L" Hydraulic Aerial Truck   No. 205-AB BUDDY "L" Pumping Fire Engine

No. 209 BUDDY "L" Auto Wrecker

No. 220 BUDDY "L" Steam Shovel

No. 2005 Junior BUDDY "L" Steam Shovel

	G	VG	M
BUDDY L 203A Lumber Truck 1925-30	125.00	187.00	250.00
BUDDY L 203B Baggage Truck 1929-31	200.00	300.00	400.00
BUDDY L 204 Moving Van 1924-30	175.00	262.50	350.00
BUDDY L 204A Railway Express 1926-31	175.00	262.50	350.00
BUDDY L 206, 206B Street Sprinkler Truck 1924-31	150.00	225.00	300.00
BUDDY L 206A Oil Truck 1925-30	150.00	225.00	300.00
BUDDY L 207 Ice Truck 1926-31	175.00	262.50	350.00
BUDDY L 208 Coach 1928-31 (Lt. Green Motorbus)	175.00	262.50	350.00
BUDDY L 209 Auto Wrecker 1928-31 (Tow Truck)	150.00	225.00	300.00

Fire Trucks

	G	VG	M
BUDDY L 205 Hook & Ladder 1924-31	100.00	150.00	200.00
BUDDY L 205A Pumper 1925-30	100.00	150.00	200.00
BUDDY L 205AB (Working) Pumper 1930-31	200.00	300.00	400.00
BUDDY L 205 B Aerial Ladder 1926-30	125.00	187.50	250.00
BUDDY L 205C Insurance Patrol 1926-30	135.00	202.50	270.00
BUDDY L 205D Water Tower Truck (Working) 1930-31	300.00	450.00	600.00

Model T Series

	G	VG	M
BUDDY L 210 Flivver Truck 1925-30	150.00	225.00	300.00
BUDDY L 210A Flivver Roadster 1925-27	150.00	225.00	300.00
BUDDY L 210B Flivver Coupe 1925-30	150.00	225.00	300.00
BUDDY L 211 Ford Dump Cart 1926-30	175.00	262.50	350.00
BUDDY L 211A Ford Dump Truck 1926-30	200.00	300.00	400.00

	G	VG	M
BUDDY L 212 Ford Express Truck 1929-30	225.00	337.50	450.00
BUDDY L 212A One-Ton Ford Delivery Truck 1929-30	250.00	375.00	500.00

Construction Equipment

	G	VG	M
BUDDY L 220 Steam Shovel 1921-31	37.50	56.25	75.00
BUDDY L 220A Heavy Steam Shovel 1929-30 .	75.00	112.50	150.00
BUDDY L 220AB Heavy Shovel (on Treads) 1929-30	100.00	150.00	200.00
BUDDY L 230 Sand Loader 1925-31	100.00	150.00	200.00
BUDDY L 240 Small Derrick 1922-31	37.50	56.25	75.00
BUDDY L 241 Large Derrick 1922-31	75.00	112.50	150.00
BUDDY L 250 Overhead Crane 1924-27	200.00	300.00	400.00
BUDDY L 250A Traveling Crane 1928-30	200.00	300.00	400.00
BUDDY L 260 Pile Driver 1926-28	150.00	225.00	300.00
BUDDY L 270 Dredge (Clamshell) 1926-30	150.00	225.00	300.00
BUDDY L 270A Tractor Dredge (on Treads) 1929-30	175.00	262.50	350.00
BUDDY L 280 Concrete Mixer 1926-30	75.00	112.50	150.00
BUDDY L 280A Mixer (on Treads) 1929-31	100.00	150.00	200.00
BUDDY L 290 Road Roller 1929-31	300.00	450.00	600.00
BUDDY L 300 Sand Screener 1929-30	135.00	202.50	270.00
BUDDY L 350 Hoisting Tower 1929-31	250.00	375.00	500.00
BUDDY L 360 Aerial Tramway 1929-30	250.00	375.00	500.00
BUDDY L 400 Trencher 1928-31	200.00	300.00	400.00

End listing by Thomas W. Sefton

	G	VG	M		G	VG	M
BUDDY L "Army Truck, 21", circa 1940, cloth top	30.00	45.00	60.00	BUDDY L Timber Truck, wooden, 24" long, WW II	100.00	150.00	200.00
BUDDY L Circus Wagon with Animals, 23" long, wooden, rubber tires, No. 484	75.00	112.50	150.00	BUFFALO TOYS Silver Bullet Racer, 26" long	120.00	180.00	240.00
BUDDY L Coca Cola truck, wooden, 19" long, circa WWII, only three known	2100.00	3150.00	4200.00	Bus, 1930s, 15½" long, aluminum	60.00	90.00	120.00
BUDDY L Curtiss Candy Truck	87.50	131.25	175.00	Bus, late 1920s, 23½" long, six side windows	50.00	75.00	100.00
				Bus, cast iron, 4" long	12.50	18.75	25.00
BUDDY L Delivery Truck, 13", 1940s, "Store Door Delivery"	11.00	16.50	22.00	Bus, cast iron, 4½" long, five side windows, circa 1928	50.00	75.00	100.00
BUDDY L Dump Truck, 1940s, 22" long	10.00	15.00	20.00	Bus, cast iron, 4¾" long, circa 1920s	8.00	12.00	16.00
BUDDY L Dump Truck, 1930s, 23½" long, crank operated	45.00	67.50	90.00	Bus, cast iron, with driver, rubber tires, 13" long	175.00	262.50	350.00
BUDDY L Excavator Truck	42.50	63.75	85.00	Bus, double-decker, cast iron, four figures, 8" long	70.00	105.00	140.00
BUDDY L Ford Dump Truck, 1953, 24" long, hydraulic lift	30.00	45.00	60.00	Bus, cast iron, double-decker, 9½" long	140.00	210.00	280.00
BUDDY L Ford pickup, 1959	7.50	11.25	15.00	"C2 TO C Co." semi-trailer, cast iron steel wheels, small	8.00	12.00	16.00
BUDDY L Greyhound Lines Bus	60.00	90.00	120.00	"C. W. Brand Coffee" Dump Truck, approx. 11¼" long, 1930s	40.00	60.00	80.00
BUDDY L Jolly Joe's Popsicle Wagon, 17½" long, No. 472, wooden	75.00	125.00	200.00	Cabriolet with rumble seat, cast iron, circa 1920s	45.00	67.50	90.00
BUDDY L Moving Van, wooden, WWII, 26" long	100.00	150.00	200.00	"Cannonball Express" child's pedal car, red-painted, 37" long	150.00	225.00	300.00
BUDDY L Robotoy Dump Truck, with driver, operates on remote control	315.00	472.50	630.00	Car, cast iron, 1½" long, maybe Cracker Jack. Possibly smallest cast iron car	25.00	37.50	50.00
BUDDY L Sand & Gravel Truck, 13" long, circa 1950s	17.50	26.25	35.00	Car, cast iron, 4" long	100.00	150.00	200.00
BUDDY L Scarab	125.00	187.50	250.00	Car, cast iron, with people, 3" long	20.00	30.00	40.00
BUDDY L Station Wagon, 14½" long, 1950s	8.00	12.00	16.00	Caterpillar tractor, cast iron, red, with driver, chain treads	50.00	75.00	100.00
BUDDY L Station Wagon, 18½" long, wooden	37.50	56.25	75.00	CENTURY OF PROGRESS cast iron Greyhound bus, 11" detachable trailer	40.00	60.00	80.00
BUDDY L Sky View Cab, 18½" long, wooden, rubber tires, trunk and plastic roof open	100.00	150.00	200.00	CHAMPION Coupe, Reo type, 7½" long	180.00	270.00	360.00
BUDDY L Stock Car, 10½"	16.00	24.00	32.00	CHAMPION Gas and Motor Oil truck, 8" long, cast iron, circa 1930s	60.00	90.00	120.00
BUDDY L Telephone Maintenance truck, 26" long, 1940s	40.00	60.00	80.00	CHAMPION four-casting nickeled radiator car, approx. 4" long	40.00	60.00	80.00
BUDDY L "Texaco" tanker, large, promo sold at gas stations, 25" long	35.00	52.50	70.00	CHAMPION Mack Dump, 7" long, circa 1930s	50.00	75.00	100.00
				CHAMPION Mack Stake Truck, 7½" long	175.00	262.50	350.00

"Champion" Wrecker, 7½" long.
Courtesy Good Old Days Store   Photo by Bill Kaufman

"Champion", policeman on motorcycle
Courtesy Mapes Auctioneers & Appraisers

CHEIN Roadster, tin litho, circa 1925, 8½" long.
Courtesy Mapes Auctioneers & Appraisers

CLEVELAND TOY racer, aluminum, 13" long.
Courtesy Mapes Auctioneers & Appraisers

L to R: Sedan, two-door, "Made U.S.A.", convertible "Made U.S.A.", Trailer Truck cab, slush-cast.

	G	VG	M
CHAMPION Race car, 6" long, cast iron, detachable driver	22.50	33.75	45.00
CHAMPION Race car, 9" long, circa 1930s	38.00	57.00	76.00
"Champion" motorcycle and rider, 4½" long, cast iron	26.00	39.00	52.00
"Champion" motorcycle, cast iron, circa 1930, 7¼" long, rubber tires on wood hubs	34.00	51.00	68.00
Champion, policeman on motorcycle, 7" long, rubber tires	40.00	60.00	80.00
"Champion" Wrecker, 7½" long, cast iron	25.00	37.50	50.00
Checker Cab, circa 1920s, with driver, thin white rubber tires, with rear tire	300.00	450.00	600.00
CHEIN Army Truck, cannon on back, 8½" long, tin, early	12.50	18.75	25.00

	G	VG	M
CHEIN Army Truck, open bed, 8½" long, tin, early	12.50	18.75	25.00
CHEIN Hercules Motor Express, tin litho, 19½" long, Mack	60.00	90.00	120.00
CHEIN Roadster, tin litho, circa 1925, 8½" long	25.00	37.50	50.00
CHEIN "Royal Blue Line Coast to Coast Service"	300.00	450.00	600.00
CHEIN Touring car, tin litho, 7" long	37.50	56.25	75.00
"Chicago Century of Progress" bus, 2-piece, cast iron	17.50	26.25	35.00
Child's car, battery-operated, red-painted, 44" long	60.00	90.00	120.00
Child's car, battery-powered, 60" long	90.00	135.00	180.00
Chrysler Airflow, heavy sheet metal with wind-up motor. Tin grill, headlights and bumper, wooden wheels, 4" long	17.50	26.25	35.00

	G	VG	M
Chrysler Airflow, cast iron, 4½" long, 1930s	47.50	71.25	95.00
Chrysler Airflow, pressed steel, 6" long, circa 1937 .	20.00	30.00	40.00
Circus Band Wagon, plays record and moves, 17" long, comic musicians on top, circa 1922	350.00	525.00	700.00
"City Fire Dept. Truck", 1930, pressed steel, rubber tires, 26" long	220.00	330.00	440.00
CLARK friction auto, manufactured from 1899-1909	160.00	240.00	320.00
CLARK friction auto, circa 1901, wood body covered with steel	180.00	270.00	360.00
CLEVELAND TOY Racer, aluminum, steel wheels, circa 1935, 13" long	14.00	21.00	28.00

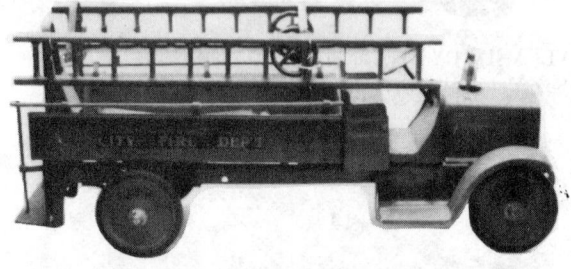

"City Fire Dept. Truck", 1930, 26" long.
Courtesy Lloyd W. Ralston Auctions

CONVERSE Auto with fringe top, 3-seat, 10½" long.
Courtesy Lloyd W. Ralston Auctions

Auto with house trailer, late 30s, cast iron 13½".
Courtesy Lloyd W. Ralston Auctions

	G	VG	M
CONVERSE Auto with fringe on top, 3-seat, 1905, painted, pressed steel, clockwork, rubber tires ...	320.00	480.00	640.00
CONVERSE Fire Engine ladder truck, bell, wooden headlight, 10", 1915	600.00	900.00	1200.00
CONVERSE Pick-Up Truck, very early, open cab	150.00	225.00	300.00
CONVERSE Touring Auto, 1910, pressed steel, canvas roof	400.00	600.00	800.00
Convertible, "Made USA", slush-cast, open, filled with people, 3" long, looks like MANOIL, but probably is BARCLAY	5.00	7.50	10.00
Convertible, futuristic, 1930s, with large streamlined fenders, black wooden wheels, heavy pressed steel, large size	3.00	4.50	6.00
COR-COR dump truck, dumps back or side to side, 23" long	60.00	90.00	120.00
COR-COR Graham Paige sedan, 20" long, electric ..	270.00	405.00	540.00
COR-COR Van, painted metal, circa 1928, 23" long	80.00	120.00	160.00
Cord, supercharged, 1930s, rubber, black rubber tires .	4.00	6.00	8.00
Coupe, cast iron, 6" long, 2-piece body	21.00	31.50	42.00
Coupe with rumble seat, tin, 1920s, 5" long	15.00	22.50	30.00
Coupe with rumble seat, possibly Plymouth, circa 1920s, cast iron, 6" long ..	125.00	187.50	250.00
Coupe, tin friction 17½" long	24.00	36.00	48.00
Coupe, two-door, modern, tin, battery-powered, electric side lamps, 9" long	20.00	30.00	40.00
Crash Car, 3-wheeled motorcycle, 5½" long	35.00	52.50	70.00
DAYTON Coal and Ice Truck, tin friction circa 1920	40.00	60.00	80.00
DAYTON Coupe, 12", 1928, pressed steel	40.00	60.00	80.00
DAYTON Coupe, 12½" long, circa 1920	26.00	39.00	52.00
DAYTON "Dayton Friction", pressed steel, rubber tires, 1920s, 14¼" long ..	100.00	150.00	200.00

	G	VG	M
DAYTON open touring car, dated 1909, friction motor, driver	110.00	165.00	220.00
DAYTON touring car, 13½" long, friction motor	220.00	330.00	440.00
DAYTON touring car, 13½" long, unpowered	90.00	135.00	180.00
Delivery Truck, 3½" long, cast iron	40.00	60.00	80.00
Delivery Truck, 10½" long, with driver, friction	40.00	60.00	80.00
Delivery Truck, "Packard", 28" long, steel	180.00	270.00	360.00
DENT "American Oil Co.", cast iron truck, approx. 10½" long	187.50	281.25	375.00
DENT bus, cast iron, sample, 6¼" long	50.00	75.00	100.00
DENT fire truck, cast iron, 7" long, sample	40.00	60.00	80.00

DENT Sedan, 7½" long, late 1920s.
Courtesy Lloyd W. Ralston Auctions

	G	VG	M
DENT fire ladder truck, 8½" long, with driver	25.00	37.50	50.00
DENT fire truck with ladder and men, cast iron, 18" long, sample	200.00	300.00	400.00
DENT hose reeler with men, cast iron, large	150.00	225.00	300.00
DENT La Salle, approx. 4" long	50.00	75.00	100.00
DENT Ladder truck, 10" long, two drivers	20.00	30.00	40.00
DENT Mack Dump Truck, 4½", circa 1925, iron wheels	30.00	45.00	60.00
DENT Model T two door sedan, iron wheels, circa 1925	60.00	90.00	120.00
DENT "Patrol", 6½" long, circa 1920s	50.00	75.00	100.00
DENT "Police Patrol", 8¾" long	375.00	562.50	750.00
DENT Steam Roller, cast iron, 6" long	40.00	60.00	80.00
DENT Sedan, 7½" long, spare tire, has stop and go light, full bumpers on front	450.00	675.00	900.00
DENT Yellow Cab, approx. 7¾" long	216.00	324.00	432.00
"Dept. of Street Cleaning" dump truck, 10½" long, circa 1935	10.00	15.00	20.00

DOEPKE "MODEL TOYS"
by Ray Funk
(See also Miscellaneous)

Doepke "Model Toys" advertised their toys as outlasting all others 3 to 1. The company's full title was the "Charles Wm. Doepke Mfg. Co., Inc." of Rossmoyne, Ohio. Each toy was an authorized replica of the actual thing and the decals and coloring were exactly as upon the real equipment or trucks, with the exception of the manufacturer having his own, in this case "Model Toys."

At the end of the Second World War, the Doepke Corp. hit the market with five models, first in a line of heavy duty metal operating replicas, employing metal tread or authentic miniature tires, either Goodyear or Firestone, with authentic tread and name and tire sizes, exactly as on the real tires. This, to the best of my knowledge, has never been done so perfectly, even in the model kits of today.

These toys all had rubber smoke stacks, and received the approval of Parents Magazine, P.T.A., Boy's Life Magazine, and all other experts and advocates of good toys at that period. The first five numbers were 2000, 2001, 2002, 2006, 2007. Why not 3, 4 and 5, I cannot say. Perhaps Doepke had toys planned for these numbers that fell through. Following is a listing of the Doepke vehicles.

RAY FUNK is a leading collector and authority on trains and other toys, as well as a collector and authority on comic books and Western literature.

No. 2000, Wooldridge H. D. earth hauler, bright yellow, four huge tires, 25" long, and weighing 10 lbs. The actual manufacturer's address is listed as Sunnyvale, Calif. I'm sure most of you have seen the John Wayne movie, "The Fighting Seabees", which used several of these, along with caterpillar bulldozers and road graders. These Wooldridge's caught my eye with their maneuvering ability, and could traverse the roughest terrain easily. Two long doors, the length of the bottom of the dirt-hauling area, could be released to deposit a load. Price was $14.75 new in 1945.

No. 2001, Barber-Greene high-capacity bucket loader, 13" high, 10 lbs., dark green, all steel and rolling on steel tread, was designed as a toy to load earth haulers. Handcrank operated, operated exactly as the real thing. Price $14.75.

No. 2002, Jaeger concrete mixer, bright yellow, 15" long, 8 lbs. on four wheels, steerable via draw bar (all model toys steered exactly like the real thing), though perhaps the best-detailed, was the poorest-selling toy, as although you could, it wasn't feasible to really mix concrete in them, due to small amount received versus cleaning time. This toy was priced at $10.75 to $13.75.

No. 2006, Adams diesel road grader, dark orange, 26" long, 14 lbs., all six wheels, three axles, and blade adjustable to all angles, exactly like the real thing, steerable via steering wheel, priced at $14.75.

No. 2007, Unit Mobile Crane, dark orange, 11½" long, 19½" boom, eight lbs. and eight ounces, adjustable side jacks, steered via a drawbar, with block and tackle, and removable operating clam shell as standard accessory. Priced at $14.75.

No number 2008, as the next year, No. 2009 was released and No. 2000 dropped. No. 2009 was a Euclid earth-hauler truck, with uncoupling four-wheel tractor to use to tow other toys. 27" long, 11 lbs., Euclid green, or light road-grader orange, the trailer dumped in the same way as the Wooldridge. Priced $14.75.

No. 2010, American-LaFrance pumper fire truck, 18" long, 7 lbs., bright red with chrome trim, ladder, bell, fire extinguisher, hoses and nozzle, a reservoir that held water for hand-operated pressure pump. A beautiful toy at $16.75.

No. 2011, Heiliner earth scraper, 29" long, 13 lbs., bright dark red, loaded and dumped and operated on four wheels as the Wooldridge did. Priced at $16.75.

No. 2012, Caterpillar D6 tractor and bulldozer, caterpillar yellow, 15" long, 7 lbs., with real bulldozer treads for sharp realistic turning (removable only by using punch and hammer to remove connecting pin from between two of the pads) and adjustable bulldozer blade, plus heavy draw bar. Truly a beautiful toy at $13.75. Diesel motor was cast metal.

No. 2013 eliminated and replaced No. 2001. No. 2013, Barber-Green mobile high-capacity bucket loader, 22" long, 12" high, 10 lbs., buckets on chains and rubber conveyor belt, adjustable and steered by steering wheel, priced at $19.75.

No. 2014, American La-France aerial ladder fire truck, 23" long, 42" extended ladder height, 11 lbs., bright red and chrome, bell, red light, adjustable side jacks, single unit truck steered by steering wheel, priced at $20.75.

This ends the listing of Doepke "Model Toys", doomed to extinction by its lower-priced, lighter-constructed imitators of lesser quality, some of which were started in the 1920s, and others that came into being in the 1950s, several of which are still around today, but none ever containing, before or after, the heavy-duty constructed realism and operating qualities as had the one and only "Model Toys".

Of the Doepke Model Toys that were mass produced, several had variations in their basic construction from time to time. Usually these changes were an elimination of the more intricate operating procedures, and had little or no effect on the toy's overall outward appearance.

In Antique Toy World, Philip Sayer wrote a two part article on the Doepke Co., and featured pictures of nearly all toys ever manufactured by the firm. The ones that were produced in such limited numbers (only one to a few), are mentioned and oft times described. Also listed are nearly all of the slight changes in the mass produced toys, though I could not (perhaps overlooked it) find mention of the change in the D-6 Caterpillar. The first models to hit the market have the front axles held tightly forward by springs, so when being pushed forward and they strike a solid object to climb over, there is some give to absorb the shock and protect the tract pads. Later models eliminated this and opted for simple axle wells as in the rear wheels. Had I not had both types, this slight change would have easily gone unnoticed.

It would seem that the Doepke Co. would accept orders to make model toys of the real thing for the actual producers, and the toys with the most allure, playability, and feasible mass production design, and greatest entertainment to be provided to the child that received one, would be mass produced. Of the others that would not withstand rough handling by young hands, or because of cost and time required to produce them, there were only one to a few produced as previously mentioned. This is no doubt the explanation for the number gaps between the marketed items.

Among the scarcer articles produced, were even a few automobiles, avidly sought after by collectors that have delved into this Company's past history to any depth. Of these, perhaps there were catalogs or brochures about them, though all I have ever seen are the ones dealing with the mass produced toys I have listed.

DOEPKE Catalog Illustrations of Nos. 2009 and 2011.
Photo by Bill Kaufman. Courtesy Ray Funk.

DOEPKE Catalog illustration of Model No. 2012.
Photo by Bill Kaufman. Courtesy Ray Funk.

DOPEKE Catalog illustration of Model No. 2010.
Photo by Bill Kaufman. Courtesy Ray Funk.

An ad for DOEPKE Model Toys
Photo by Bill Kaufman
Courtesy Ray Funk

	G	VG	M
DOEPKE No. 2000 Wooldridge H.D. Earth Hauler, 25" long	90.00	135.00	180.00
DOEPKE No. 2001 Barber-Greene high capacity bucket loader, 13" high.	84.00	126.00	168.00
DOEPKE No. 2002 Jaeger Concrete Mixer, 15" long	140.00	210.00	280.00
DOEPKE No. 2006 Adams Diesel Road Grader, 26" long	90.00	135.00	180.00
DOEPKE No. 2007 Unit Mobile Crane, 11½" long	78.00	117.00	156.00
DOEPKE No. 2009 Euclid Earth Hauler Truck, 27" long	150.00	225.00	300.00
DOEPKE No. 2010 American-LaFrance pumper fire truck, 18" long	70.00	105.00	140.00
DOEPKE No. 2011 Heiliner Earth Scraper, 29" long	60.00	90.00	120.00

	G	VG	M
DOEPKE No. 2012 Caterpillar D6 tractor and bulldozer, 15" long	150.00	225.00	300.00
DOEPKE No. 2013 Barber-Green mobile high-capacity bucket loader 22" long	62.50	93.75	125.00
DOEPKE No. 2014 American-LaFrance aerial ladder fire truck, 23" long	140.00	210.00	280.00
DOEPKE Fire Hook and Extension ladder truck, 29" long	No Price Found		
DOEPKE Jaguar, 17½" long	130.00	195.00	260.00
DOEPKE MG TD Roadster, heavy die-cast body, 14" long, steel frame, leaf springs in rear, A-frames on front, pneumatic rubber tires	125.00	187.50	250.00

	G	VG	M
Dual Road Race crossover track, 1/32 0-27, per track	2.50	3.75	5.00
"Dugan Brothers" ride-on van, metal	30.00	45.00	60.00
Dump Truck, 4½" long, cast iron, "2205"	17.50	26.25	35.00
Dump Truck, tin, 5¾" long, wooden wheels	3.00	4.50	6.00
Dump Truck, 6" long, pressed steel, circa 1939	24.00	36.00	48.00
Dump Truck, 7" long, cast iron, driver	25.00	37.50	50.00
Dump Truck (Beck), steers via horn on top of cab, late 1940s, large	25.00	37.50	50.00
DRUDGE "Hyster" lumber carrier	40.00	60.00	80.00
EAGLE bell toy, gong bell, East Hampton, Conn.	250.00	375.00	500.00
Electric car, cast iron, 3¾" long	60.00	90.00	120.00
"Electric Powered Rider Convertible", lithographed tin, circa 1950, 29" long, riding toy	15.00	22.50	30.00
ERIE streamlined auto with tail fin, tail fin has taillight mounted in it, approx. 4¼" long	5.00	7.50	10.00
ERIE super-charged streamline auto, looks like Cord, circa 1930s	4.00	6.00	8.00
Farm truck, "Speed", with driver, 7" cast iron	54.00	81.00	108.00
Fire Engine "9608" die cast, 6" long, Post-War	2.50	3.75	5.00
Fire Engine Pumper, friction, gear shift lever, with drivers	90.00	135.00	180.00
Fire Pumper, 5" long, cast iron, circa 1935	35.00	52.50	70.00
Fire Pumper, approx. 6½" long, cast iron	50.00	75.00	100.00
Fire Pumper, 8" long, cast iron	42.50	63.75	85.00
Fire Pumper, 11" long, cast iron	30.00	45.00	60.00
Fire Pumper, early wind-up, metal, 11"	90.00	135.00	180.00
Fire Truck, cast iron, 7" long	37.50	56.25	70.00
Fire Truck, friction, with driver, metal and wood, pat. Nov. 2, 1897	300.00	450.00	600.00

	G	VG	M
Fire Truck, pressed steel friction toy 10½" long, early, with driver	175.00	262.50	350.00
Ford coupe, 4" long, 1924	40.00	60.00	80.00
Ford coupe, blue, chrome wheels, 5" long	42.00	63.00	84.00
Ford coupe, cast iron, black, chrome wheels, circa 1920s, 5" long	35.00	52.50	70.00
Ford coupe, rubber, 1935.	2.50	3.75	5.00
Ford, FIRESTONE RUBBER, "Made at the Firestone Exhibit Great Lakes Exposition Cleveland 1935", 5" long	25.00	37.50	50.00
"Fordson" tractor with driver, cast iron, 5¾" long	70.00	105.00	140.0
Fordson tractor with hay rake, cast iron, 1930s	50.00	75.00	100.00
Friction car, cast iron and wood, with figures	50.00	75.00	100.00
Friction Car, 7¼", 1910 .	480.00	720.00	960.00
Friction toy with two riders, 1897	50.00	75.00	100.00
GMC "Greyhound Lines" cast iron bus, 7½" long, circa 1934	30.00	45.00	60.00
"Gasoline" truck, circa late 30s, red, approx. 2¾" long, slush	5.00	7.50	10.00
GIRARD Fire Chief Car, 15" long	60.00	90.00	120.00
GIRARD "Fire Chief Siren Coupe", 14½" long	50.00	75.00	100.00
GIRARD Fire truck, 12" long, 1920s,	40.00	60.00	80.00
GIRARD Roadster, 14½" long, electrified	40.00	60.00	80.00
GIRARD Tank Truck, 11½" long, wood wheels	14.00	21.00	28.00
GIRARD Touring Bus, painted tin, circa 1920, 12" long	40.00	60.00	80.00
GIRARD Truck with Trailer, 1930s, 17"	50.00	75.0	100.00

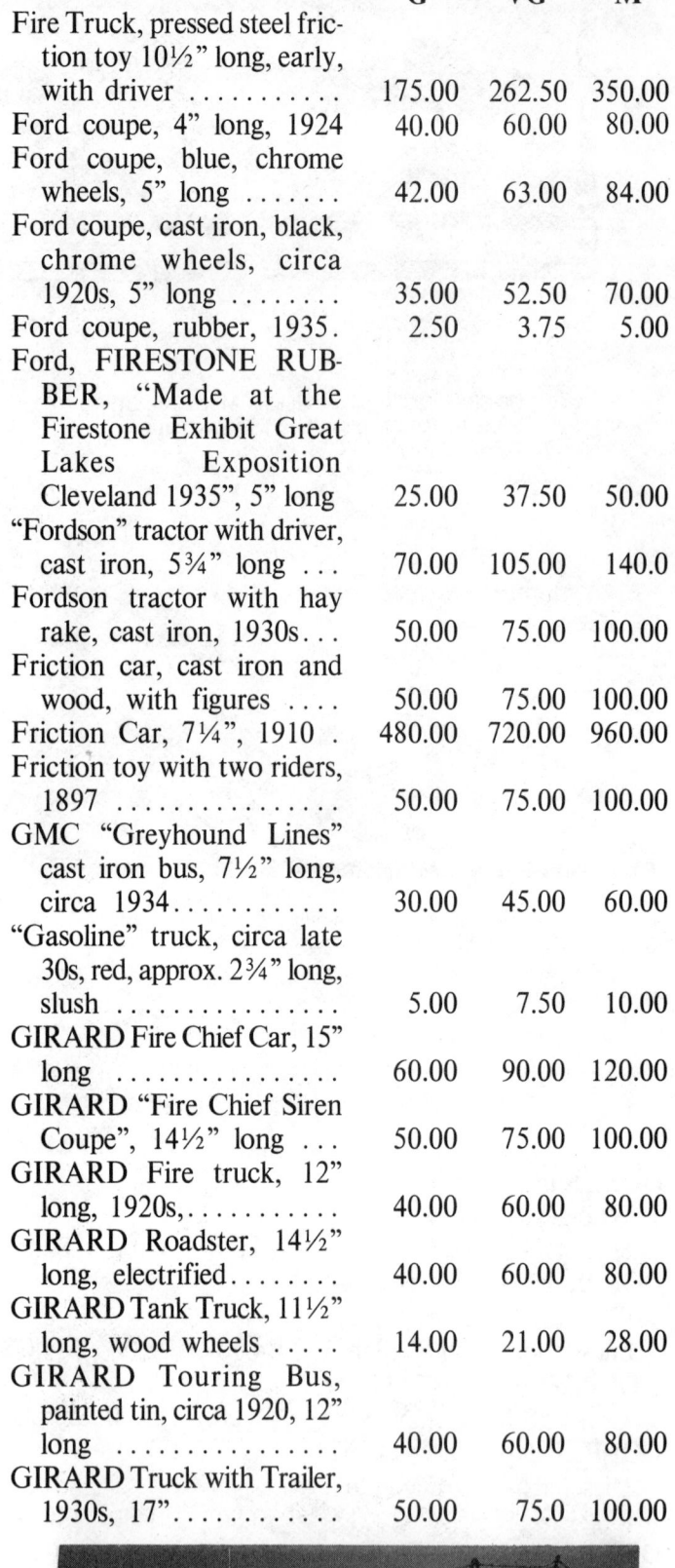

GIRARD Touring Bus
Courtesy Mapes Auctioneers & Appraisers

Fire Pumper, cast iron, 11" long
Photo by Bill Kaufman
Courtesy Good Old Days Store

Fire Pumper, cast iron, 5" long, circa 1935.
Courtesy Mapes Auctioneers & Appraisers

	G	VG	M
"Guided Missile Unit No. 10" truck, tin litho, circa 1960	5.00	7.50	10.00
Happy Sam driving wood truck, circa 1920s, 8" long	18.00	27.00	36.00
HILLCLIMBER "Ambulance", 10½" long, very early	400.00	600.00	800.00
HILLCLIMBER Armored Truck, 11" long, pressed steel friction	150.00	225.00	300.00
HILLCLIMBER Auto, woman driver, friction, very early, 6" long	250.00	375.00	500.00
HILLCLIMBER hook and ladder wagon, painted pressed steel friction, driver, 20" long	80.00	120.00	160.00
HILLCLIMBER Horseless Carriage, woman driver, cast iron and wood, very early, 7" long	200.00	300.00	400.00
HILLCLIMBER Racer with track, 7½" long	190.00	285.00	380.00
HOGE Fire chief car, 15" long	480.00	720.00	960.00
Hook and ladder, aluminum, with driver, 13" long	34.00	51.00	68.00
Hook and ladder truck, tin friction, 21" long	34.00	51.00	68.00
Hose Wagon, 1897, two riders, friction toy	54.00	81.00	108.00
"Huber" steam roller, cast iron, 7¼" long	90.00	135.00	180.00
Huber steam roller, cast iron, 7½" long	65.00	97.50	130.00
Huber steam roller, 8" long, cast iron, intricate, with chain	90.00	135.00	180.00
HUBER Steam Roller, cast iron, about 8" long	No Price Found		

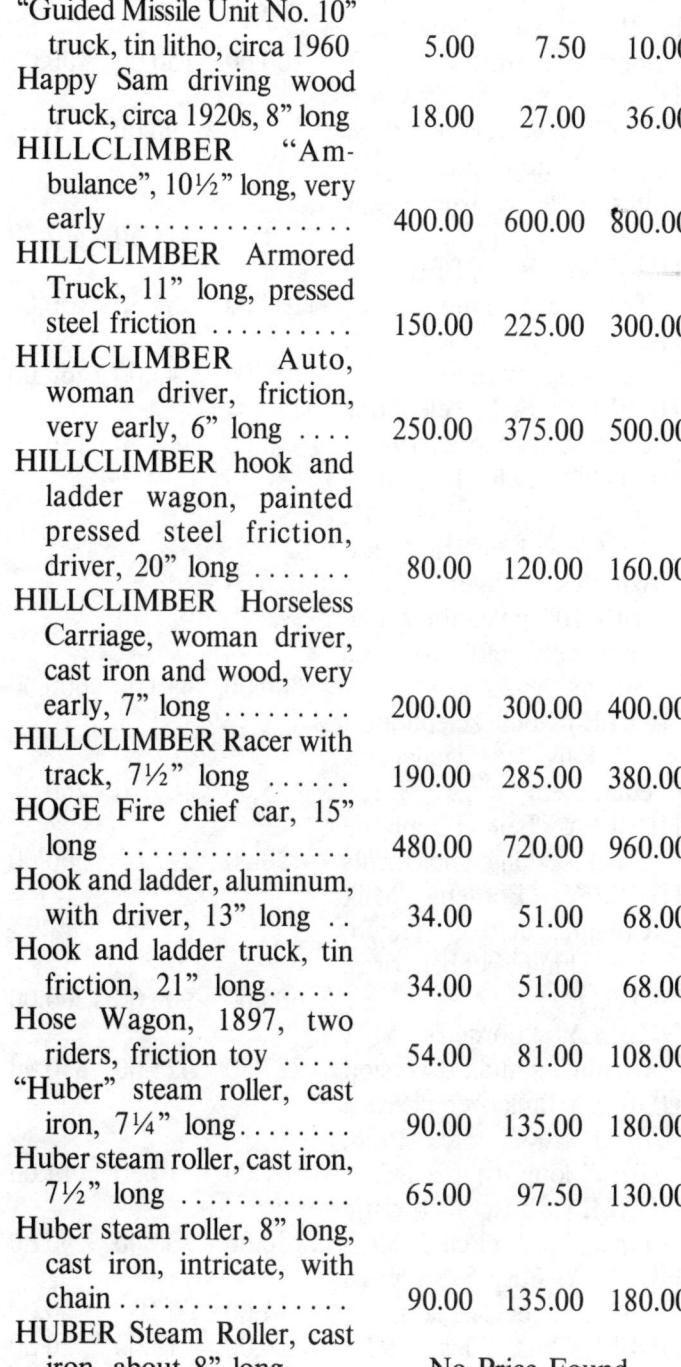

HILLCLIMBER Horseless Carriage, woman driver, 7" long.
Courtesy Mapes Auctioneers & Appraisers

Huber Steam Roller, 8" long.
Courtesy Mapes Auctioneers & Appraisers

HUBLEY: The Hubley manufacturing company was founded at least as early as 1894 by John Hubley, and made iron toys from the start at its plant in Lancaster, Pennsylvania. All toys at the beginning were cast iron, and some early toys included coal ranges, circus wagons and mechanical banks. Hubley's cast iron toys were popular almost from the start, and have long been collector's items, as they were well-made and attractive. By 1940, however, the cast iron toy, due to the increased cost of freight and foreign competition, was slowly becoming a thing of the past. At this time, when Hubley was the largest producer of cast iron toys and cap pistols in the world, it began to introduce die cast zinc alloy toys. During the Second World War, Hubley was 98% engaged in war production, turning out over five million M-74 bomb fuses, which the Hubley engineers played a large part in developing. Since the war, Hubley manufactures die cast toys and plastic toys exclusively. In 1952, Hubley manufactured 9,763,610 toys and 11,184,878 cap pistols, about ten times the amount of toys and pistols they produced in 1930, but with a line of toys 80% smaller than in 1930. It is the combination of the relative scarcity (and multiplicity) of the older toys, plus the preference by collectors for cast iron over die cast zinc alloy and plastic toys that makes the pre-World War II toys the most attractive to collectors. Hubley was acquired by Gabriel Industries in late 1965, and puts out holster sets, cap pistols, vehicles, hobby kits and a number of other toys.

HUBLEY Caterpillar 3¼" long.
Courtesy Mapes Auctioneers & Appraisers

HUBLEY Stake bed truck, 7" long.
Courtesy Mapes Auctioneers & Appraisers

	G	VG	M
HUBLEY Army Motor Truck No. 807 with driver, 15" long	200.00	300.00	400.00
HUBLEY Auto, 6½"	40.00	60.00	80.00
HUBLEY Auto carrier, 10" long, with three cars and one pickup truck, circa 1939	130.00	195.00	260.00

	G	VG	M
HUBLEY Auto Express, 9" long, cast iron	100.00	150.00	200.00
HUBLEY Avery tractor, 4¾" long, very early	60.00	90.00	120.00
HUBLEY auto circa 1950s, black plastic wheels, die cast	1.00	1.50	2.00
HUBLEY Bell Telephone Truck, 3¾" long	25.00	37.50	50.00
HUBLEY "Bell Telephone", 12" long, with tools	30.00	45.00	60.00
HUBLEY Bell Telephone truck, 12½" long, 1940s	75.00	112.50	150.00
HUBLEY Bell Telephone truck, 10" long, No. 41, 1936, with derrick and windlass, auger, trailer with 10" pole, three digging tools, and two loose ladders	300.00	450.00	600.00
HUBLEY "Bell Telephone", 13" long, just ladders as equipment	125.00	187.50	250.00
HUBLEY Bell Telephone Truck, 9" long, implements	150.00	225.00	300.00
HUBLEY "Borden's Milk Cream", deluxe version, 7½" long, rubber tires, clicker	600.00	900.00	1200.00
HUBLEY "Borden's Milk Cream", standard version	237.50	425.00	850.00
HUBLEY Bulldozer, die-cast, front scoop, circa 1950, 10¼" long, rubber treads	7.00	10.50	14.00
HUBLEY bus, (futuristic type), 3½", circa 1935	20.00	30.00	40.00
HUBLEY bus, 5½", circa 1938, rubber wheels	15.00	22.50	30.00
HUBLEY bus, 8" long, 1930s	10.00	15.00	20.00

	G	VG	M
HUBLEY Cadillac, 7" die cast	8.00	12.00	16.00
HUBLEY 2278 car and 2279 house trailer, circa 1939	70.00	105.00	140.00
HUBLEY Caterpillar Tractor, 3¼" long, driver in cab	17.50	26.25	35.00
HUBLEY Cement Mixer, 18" long	150.00	225.00	300.00
HUBLEY Chemical Truck with ladders, 13" long	50.00	100.00	150.00
HUBLEY Champion Stake Truck, 8½" long, 1930s, white rubber tires	70.00	105.00	140.00
HUBLEY Chrysler Airflow, 4½" long, take-apart body	56.00	84.00	112.00
HUBLEY Chrysler Airflow, 6¾" long, take-apart body	40.00	60.00	80.00
HUBLEY Chrysler Airflow, 8" long, electrified, white rubber tires on wood hubs	320.00	480.00	640.00
HUBLEY Chrysler Airflow racing car, circa 1938	26.00	39.00	52.00
HUBLEY Coal Truck, cast iron, with driver	1100.00	1650.00	2200.00
HUBLEY Coupe, 1933 Ford	46.00	69.00	92.00
HUBLEY Coupe roadster, rumble seat, 11" long, rubber tires	40.00	60.00	80.00
HUBLEY Crash Car, three-wheel motorcycle, chrome wheels	37.50	56.25	75.00
HUBLEY Crash Car, circa 1937, 4¾" long, white rubber tires	50.00	75.00	100.00
HUBLEY Digger, Mack General, 10" long	125.00	187.50	250.00
HUBLEY Dump Truck, 5½"	39.00	58.50	78.00
HUBLEY Dump Truck, circa 1938, 7½" long	30.00	45.00	60.00
HUBLEY Dump Truck, Mack, 1930s, 6 tires, 10¾" long	210.00	315.00	420.00
HUBLEY Fire Engine Pumper, circa 1920, 12½" long, cast iron, black rubber tires, driver, boiler-tender	75.00	112.50	150.00
HUBLEY Fire Engine pumper, early, No. 504	30.00	45.00	60.00
HUBLEY Fire Engine No. 526, 10½" long, circa 1936	34.00	51.00	68.00

	G	VG	M
HUBLEY Fire Engine, die cast, white rubber tires with wooden rims, circa 1941	6.00	9.00	12.00
HUBLEY Fire Ladder Truck, 8½", early	50.00	75.00	100.00
HUBLEY Fire Ladder Truck, 19½" long	260.00	390.00	520.00
HUBLEY Fire Truck with searchlight, white rubber tires with wooden rims	6.00	9.00	12.00
HUBLEY Fire Truck, 5"	29.00	43.50	58.00
HUBLEY "5 Ton Truck", 17" long, 8 wooden barrels, circa 1920	370.00	555.00	740.00
HUBLEY Ford coupe, 1936	15.00	22.50	30.00
HUBLEY Hook & Ladder Truck, 19½" long, cast iron	80.00	120.00	160.00
HUBLEY Huber road roller	205.00	307.50	410.00
HUBLEY Huber Road Roller, 14" long	300.00	450.00	600.00
HUBLEY Kiddietoy, "Patrol" stake truck, circa 1937	10.00	15.00	20.00
HUBLEY Ladder Truck circa late 1930s, 5"	24.00	36.00	48.00
HUBLEY Ladder Truck, 5"	41.00	61.50	82.00
HUBLEY Ladder Truck, terraplane front, 1930s, 6" long	30.00	45.00	60.00
HUBLEY Ladder Truck, 13½" circa 1940	90.00	135.00	180.00
HUBLEY Life Saver Truck, circa 1930, hole in rear is large enough to hold pack of Life Savers	50.00	75.00	100.00
HUBLEY Life Saver Truck, small hole in rear, can't hold Life Savers	150.00	225.00	300.00
HUBLEY Limousine, 7" long, six-door, 1920s	35.00	52.50	70.00
HUBLEY Log Truck with five chained logs, black rubber tires, die-cast, approx. 19" long	25.00	37.50	50.00
HUBLEY Mack Truck Steam Shovel-Digger, circa 1920, nickel wheels and scoop, 7" long	120.00	180.00	240.00
HUBLEY "Milk and Cream" truck, 1920, cast iron, 3½" long, white rubber tires	75.00	112.50	150.00

HUBLEY "Railway Express" truck, 5" long.
Courtesy Mapes Auctioneers & Appraisers

HUBLEY Motorcycle, Harley-Davidson with policeman, 1930s, 6½" long, swivel head, small wheels near feet.
Courtesy Mapes Auctioneers & Appraisers

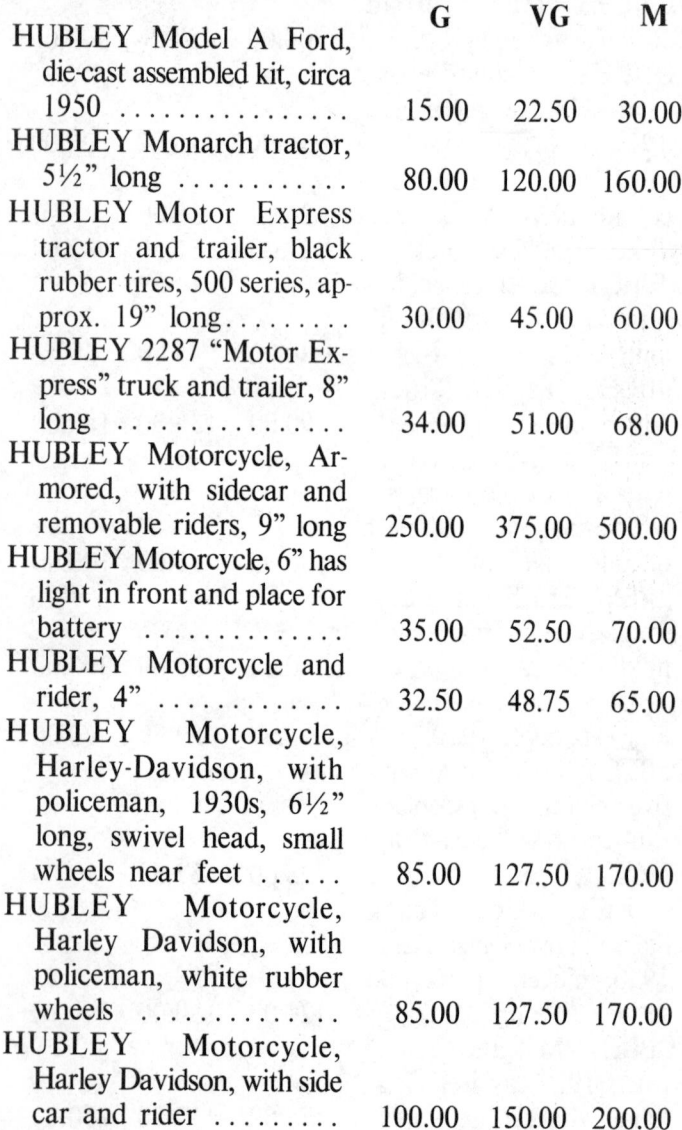

	G	VG	M
HUBLEY Model A Ford, die-cast assembled kit, circa 1950	15.00	22.50	30.00
HUBLEY Monarch tractor, 5½" long	80.00	120.00	160.00
HUBLEY Motor Express tractor and trailer, black rubber tires, 500 series, approx. 19" long	30.00	45.00	60.00
HUBLEY 2287 "Motor Express" truck and trailer, 8" long	34.00	51.00	68.00
HUBLEY Motorcycle, Armored, with sidecar and removable riders, 9" long	250.00	375.00	500.00
HUBLEY Motorcycle, 6" has light in front and place for battery	35.00	52.50	70.00
HUBLEY Motorcycle and rider, 4"	32.50	48.75	65.00
HUBLEY Motorcycle, Harley-Davidson, with policeman, 1930s, 6½" long, swivel head, small wheels near feet	85.00	127.50	170.00
HUBLEY Motorcycle, Harley Davidson, with policeman, white rubber wheels	85.00	127.50	170.00
HUBLEY Motorcycle, Harley Davidson, with side car and rider	100.00	150.00	200.00

	G	VG	M
HUBLEY Motorcycle No. 649 Hill Climber, 1936, 6¾" long	100.00	150.00	200.00
HUBLEY Motorcycle, Indian, 9½" long, policeman rider, nickel-plated cylinder	90.00	135.00	180.00
HUBLEY Motorcycle policeman with side-car, 4" long, 1920s	28.00	42.00	56.00
HUBLEY Motorcycle policeman with sidecar, 5" long	40.00	60.00	80.00
HUBLEY Motorcycle with detachable cop, 4¼" long, cast iron, "Made USA", circa mid 1930s	27.00	40.50	54.00
HUBLEY Motorcycle, policeman rider, 5", circa 1936	18.00	27.00	36.00
HUBLEY Motorcycle with policeman, 1920s, 5" long	34.00	51.00	68.00
HUBLEY Motorcycle with side car, 8½" long, No. 46-F, two demountable policemen, 1936	40.00	60.00	80.00
HUBLEY Motorcycle, two-cylinder Indian, with side car, no riders	50.00	75.00	100.00
HUBLEY Motorcycle "traffic car", four-cylinder Indian with stake sides on two-wheel cart	140.00	210.00	280.00
HUBLEY Motorcycle, Parcel Post delivery, with two-wheel cart	150.00	225.00	300.00

	G	VG	M
HUBLEY Motorcycle, four-cylinder P.D.Q. delivery	160.00	240.00	320.00
HUBLEY Motorcycle, three-wheel with stake sides, rider, chrome wheels ...	44.00	66.00	88.00
HUBLEY Motorcycle, "U.S. Mail", 9" long	170.00	255.00	340.00
HUBLEY Motorized Steam Pumper, 4" long, circa 1930s	12.50	18.75	25.00
HUBLEY Night Coach, 3½" white rubber tires	12.50	18.75	25.00
HUBLEY "Nucar Transport" with trailer 17" long, 4 cars	230.00	345.00	460.00
HUBLEY Packard, 15 parts, 1929, 11" long	2500.00	3750.00	5000.00
HUBLEY "Panama" digger, Mack, 13" long	550.00	825.00	1100.00
HUBLEY Parcel Post motorcycle and sidecar, Harley Davidson	1700.00	2550.00	3400.00
HUBLEY "Patrol", 15½" long, driver, policeman..	700.00	1050.00	1400.00
HUBLEY Pumper, circa late 1930s	50.00	75.00	100.00
HUBLEY Pumper, terra-plane front, 1930s, 6¼" long	25.00	37.50	50.00
HUBLEY Race Car, "1790", 5" long approx.	24.00	36.00	48.00
HUBLEY Race Car, driver, 7" long	22.50	33.75	45.00
HUBLEY Race Car, 2241, 7½" long, 1930s	22.50	33.75	45.00

	G	VG	M
HUBLEY Racer 629, 1936 6¾" long	12.00	18.00	24.00
HUBLEY Racer "#1", 8" long	40.00	60.00	80.00
HUBLEY Race Car, driver, rubber tires, 8" long ...	45.00	67.50	90.00
HUBLEY Race Car, die-cast, black rubber tires	3.50	5.25	7.00
HUBLEY Race Car, animated exhaust stacks, 8" long, driver	120.00	180.00	240.00
HUBLEY Race Car, animated exhaust stacks, rubber tires, driver, 8" long	25.00	37.50	50.00
HUBLEY Racer No. 5, painted and nickeled iron and aluminum, 9½" long, raise hood-see motor ...	250.00	375.00	500.00
HUBLEY Racing Motorcycle, 6½" long, rubber wheels	40.00	60.00	80.00
HUBLEY "Railway Express" Truck, 5" long, rubber tires	55.00	82.50	110.00
HUBLEY Road Roller, late 1920s, 8" long, driver ..	100.00	150.00	200.00
HUBLEY Sedan, 1920, cast iron, 7" long	37.50	56.25	75.00
HUBLEY Sedan, 1928, cast iron, 7" long	40.00	60.00	80.00
HUBLEY Sedan, circa 1938, 2-door, 3½", looks like Ford, rubber wheels ...	20.00	30.00	40.00
HUBLEY Service Car, 4¼" long	22.00	33.00	44.00
HUBLEY Service Car, 5" cast iron, including wheels, 1930s	75.00	112.50	150.00
HUBLEY 726 Shovel Truck, 10" long, circa 1930 ...	44.00	66.00	88.00
HUBLEY Stake Truck, circa late 1930s	5.00	7.50	10.00
HUBLEY No. 614 Stake Truck, circa 1930s	24.00	36.00	48.00
HUBLEY Stake Bed Truck, cast iron, 3½" long ...	15.00	22.50	30.00

HUBLEY Huber Road Roller
Courtesy Lloyd W. Ralston Auctions

HUBLEY Motorcycle, Harley-Davidson with policeman, 1930s.
Courtesy Lloyd W. Ralston Auctions

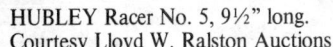

HUBLEY Racer No. 5, 9½" long.
Courtesy Lloyd W. Ralston Auctions

	G	VG	M
HUBLEY Stake bed truck, 7" long	20.00	30.00	40.00
HUBLEY Stake Truck with trailer - No. 927. Two pieces, 21" long	11.00	16.50	22.00
HUBLEY No. 452 stake-type truck, black rubber tires, circa post WW II	7.50	11.25	15.00
HUBLEY Station Wagon, circa 1940s-1950s	16.00	24.00	32.00
HUBLEY Steam Roller, 5"	75.00	112.50	150.00
HUBLEY Steam Shovel, "General", 9" long, rubber tires on hubs	85.00	127.50	170.00
HUBLEY Street Sweeper, 8" long, "The Elgin", cast iron	450.00	675.00	900.00
HUBLEY Studebaker Roadster, frame and body separate	56.00	84.00	122.00
HUBLEY Touring Auto, 1915, 9½" long, cast iron, chauffeur and rider	137.50	206.25	275.00
HUBLEY Tow Truck, 3¾" long, cast iron, circa 1930s	32.00	48.00	64.00
HUBLEY Tractor, Ford 6000	11.00	16.50	22.00
HUBLEY Tractor, steam boiler in front, 4¾" long, circa early 1920s	40.00	60.00	80.00
HUBLEY Tractor, 5", 1930s	60.00	90.00	120.00
HUBLEY Trailer Truck, circa 1936-38.........	10.00	15.00	20.00
HUBLEY Transitional Fire Patrol, 12" cast iron, driver, firemen, 1920 ..	325.00	487.50	650.00
"HUBLEY U.S.A." Airflow type, circa 1937, approx. 3½" long	4.00	6.00	8.00
HUBLEY Wrecker, chrome wheels, Service Car	24.00	36.00	48.00
HUBLEY Wrecker, 3½" .	16.00	24.00	32.00
HUBLEY Wrecker, 4½", rubber wheels, 1930 ...	30.00	45.00	60.00
HUBLEY Wrecker, 4¾" .	30.00	45.00	60.00
HUBLEY Wrecker, 6", circa 1940, white wheels on large hubs	50.00	75.00	100.00
HUBLEY Wrecking Truck, 1930, cast iron, rubber tires, 7½" long	14.00	21.00	28.00
HUBLEY Yellow Cab, 8"	225.00	337.50	450.00
"Ice" Stake Truck, circa 1940, streamlined fenders, pressed steel	15.00	22.50	30.00

	G	VG	M
Ice Cream Truck, cast iron, 8" long	120.00	180.00	240.00
International Diesel Crawler, PRODUCT MINIA-TURE, INC., 11", plastic with black rubber treads, 1950s	130.00	195.00	260.00
IVES horseless carriage runabout, 6½" long, 6" high to the top of jockey cap on driver	900.00	1350.00	1800.00
IVES steamer, cast iron, 19½" long, two drivers	200.00	300.00	400.00
Jaeger Cement Mixer, cast iron	70.00	105.00	140.00

Jaeger cement mixer.
Courtesy Mapes Auctioneers & Appraisers

	G	VG	M
Jeep, glass candy container, 4" long	2.00	3.00	4.00
"Jeepster", rubber tires, 14¼" long	2.00	3.00	4.00
John Deere tractor, rubber tires, cast iron, 7" long .	10.00	15.00	20.00
JONES Tank, throwing flame, flame touching hull	40.00	60.00	80.00
JONES Tank, throwing flame, flame not touching hull	65.00	97.50	130.00
JONES Tank, throwing flame, "No.25"	No Price Found		
JONES Tank, "22" on side .	50.00	75.00	100.00
KENTON Auto, 6" long, cast iron	60.00	90.00	120.00
KENTON Boat-tail cut-down speedster, 1910, 7" long	60.00	90.00	120.00
KENTON Buckeye Ditching Maching	205.00	302.50	410.00

KENTON Fire Pumper, 18" long, has gong.
Courtesy Mapes Auctioneers & Appraisers

	G	VG	M
KENTON Bus, Double-Decker, 6" long, 1920s..	200.00	300.00	400.00
KENTON Bus, Double Decker, 1920, 7¼" long	500.00	750.00	1000.00
KENTON Bus, 8" long, cast iron	170.00	255.00	340.00
KENTON Bus, 1920s, 10¾" long	180.00	270.00	360.00
KENTON Cement Mixer, rubber wheels, marked "Jaeger", 7" long, cast iron	50.00	75.00	100.00
KENTON Cattle Truck, 8" long, cast iron, circa 1938	50.00	75.00	100.00
KENTON Cement Mixer .	50.00	75.00	100.00
KENTON "Coal" dump truck, 8½" long	70.00	105.00	140.00
KENTON "Coast-to-Coast" bus	25.00	37.50	50.00
KENTON Emergency Truck, circa 1930s, black rubber tires, takes batteries for headlights and spotlight	40.00	60.00	80.00
KENTON Fire Apparatus Truck	150.00	225.00	300.00
KENTON Fire pump truck, early, with driver	190.00	285.00	380.00
KENTON Fire Pumper, 14½" long, 1920s	200.00	300.00	400.00

	G	VG	M
KENTON Fire Pumper, 18" long, circa 1920, has gone	150.00	225.00	300.00
KENTON Fire Truck, 15" long with pumper	180.00	270.00	360.00
KENTON Ice Truck, tongs and glass ice, 7½"	150.00	225.00	300.00
KENTON Jaeger cement mixer, 6½" long, iron wheels	115.00	172.50	230.00
KENTON Jaeger cement mixer, 8" long	130.00	195.00	260.00
KENTON Jaeger "Mixer", cast iron cement truck, 9" long	300.00	450.00	600.00
KENTON Ladder Truck, approx. 7½" long, cast iron	55.00	82.50	110.00
KENTON Ladder Truck, pressed steel ladders, 16" long	130.00	195.00	260.00
KENTON Ladder Truck, 17¼" long	150.00	225.00	300.00
KENTON Overland Circus cage truck with driver, 7½" long	110.00	165.00	220.00
KENTON Overland Circus with lion, 9" long	400.00	600.00	800.00
KENTON Patrol Wagon, marked "Patrol" on side, circa 1920s-1930s	200.00	300.00	400.00
KENTON Phaeton touring car, 12"	140.00	210.00	280.00

	G	VG	M
KENTON Pontiac, approx. 4" long	50.00	75.00	100.00
KENTON Road Grader, cast iron, 7½" long, rubber tires, nickel-plated moveable blade	75.00	112.50	150.00
KENTON Runabout Auto, 5" long, 1900	160.00	240.00	320.00
KENTON Runabout Auto, cast iron, 7" long, resembles a 1910 Franklin, has driver	260.00	390.00	520.00
KENTON Sedan, 7" long, late 1930s, rubber tires, take apart body	600.00	900.00	1200.00
KENTON Sprinkler Truck, early, 8"	150.00	225.00	300.00
KENTON Steam Roller, "Gallon Master", 6½" long	30.00	45.00	60.00
KENTON Steam Shovel, Marion, 7¼" long	270.00	405.00	540.00
KENTON Tank, cast iron, 2½" long	40.00	60.00	80.00
KENTON Touring Car, open, driver and passenger, 8½" long	180.00	270.00	360.00
KENTON Tow Auto, 1920s, 9½" long	700.00	1050.00	1400.00
KENTON Yellow Cab, 1950s, 6⅜" long	145.00	217.50	290.00
KEYSTONE Fire Truck, wood steering wheel, two ladders, 22" long	55.00	82.50	110.00
KEYSTONE Mail Truck, grating sides, 26½" long, circa 1932	310.00	465.00	620.00
KEYSTONE "Moving Van Long Distance Hauling"	200.00	300.00	400.00
KEYSTONE Packard Army Ambulance, 27" long	350.00	525.00	700.00
KEYSTONE Packard Army Truck, open cab, khaki paint, heavy canvas top marked "U.S. Army", 26" long, circa 1930	157.50	236.25	315.00
KEYSTONE Packard Dump Truck, front crank raises dump bed, 26" long, black with red trim	104.00	156.00	208.00
KEYSTONE Packard Fire Truck, circa 1925 with lights, rails and winch and fire hose	150.00	225.00	300.00

KEYSTONE "Moving Van Long Distance Hauling"
Courtesy Mapes Auctioneers & Appraisers

	G	VG	M
KEYSTONE Packard Mail Truck, 26½" long	88.00	132.00	176.00
KEYSTONE Packard Police Patrol, 29" long, 1930s	162.50	243.75	325.00
KEYSTONE Steam Roller, red and black, air pressure whistle, brass bell, 20" long	110.00	165.00	220.00
KEYSTONE Steam Shovel, 19"	12.00	18.00	24.00
KEYSTONE Steam Shovel, 20¾" long, black with red trim	100.00	150.00	200.00
KEYSTONE Truck Loader, steel, 17"	28.00	42.00	56.00
KEYSTONE U.S. Army Truck, with canvas cover	41.00	61.50	82.00
KEYSTONE Water Pump and Tower Truck, 21" long, ladders, brass railing, aluminum running board, brass bell, klaxon horn	44.00	66.00	88.00
KEYSTONE Water Tower Fire Truck with pump, circa late 1920s, 30" long	50.00	75.00	100.00
KEYSTONE "World's Greatest Circus" truck, 26" long, circa 1930s	500.00	750.00	1000.00
KEYSTONE Wrecker, 26" long	350.00	525.00	700.00
KILGORE Auto, "LF 1300A", driver	60.00	90.00	120.00
KILGORE Arctic Ice Cream Truck, 8" long	120.00	180.00	240.00
KILGORE Convertible with Rumble seat, 7", early 1930s, with driver	80.00	120.00	160.00
KILGORE Dump Truck, cast iron, circa 1934, 5¾" long	65.00	97.50	130.00

KENTON Bus, double-decker 1920s, 7¼" long.
Courtesy Lloyd W. Ralston Auctions.

KENTON Tow Auto, 1920s, 9½" long.
Courtesy Lloyd W. Ralston Auctions

KENTON "Jaeger" Cement Mixer Truck, 8" long.
Courtesy HAKE'S Americana & Collectibles

KENTON Sedan 7" long, late 30s.
Courtesy Lloyd W. Ralston Auctions.

KENTON, boat-tail, cut-down speedster,
1910, 7" long.
Courtesy Lloyd W. Ralston Auctions

KENTON Ladder Truck, pressed steel ladders, 16"
long.
Courtesy Lloyd W. Ralston Auctions

KINGSBURY Phaeton Auto, 1900, 9¼" long.
Courtesy Lloyd W. Ralston Auctions

KEYSTONE Packard Dump Truck 26" long.
Courtesy PB Eighty-Four New York

	G	VG	M
KILGORE Dump Truck, 7" long, 1930s	90.00	135.00	180.00
KILGORE Livestock Truck, 7" long, 1930s	100.00	150.00	200.00
KILGORE Packard Luxury Sedan, 8¼", take-apart body	350.00	525.00	700.00
KILGORE Pierce-Arrow roadster, 6⅛" take-apart body	110.00	165.00	220.00
KILGORE Roadster, 6" long, driver, rumble seat	100.00	150.00	200.00
KILGORE Sedan, 3¼" long	30.00	45.00	60.00
KILGORE Stutz Roadster, 13 parts	250.00	375.00	500.00
KILGORE "Toy Town Delivery" truck, 6⅛" long	100.00	150.00	200.00
KINSBURY Aerial Ladder Truck, pressed steel wind-up circa 1941, 24" long, ladder rises automatically to height of 38 inches			

	G	VG	M
when the truck runs into any obstruction, fireman on ladder climbs up and down by turning crank at base of ladder	83.00	124.50	166.00
KINGSBURY Airflow, circa 1934, pressed steel, rubber tires, 14" long	100.00	150.00	200.00
KINGSBURY Airflow, clockwork, 14" long	142.50	213.75	285.00
KINGSBURY auto, very early, 9¾" long, steel windup	300.00	450.00	600.00
KINGSBURY Brougham Sedan, 13" long, pressed steel windup	400.00	600.00	800.00
KINGSBURY Bus, 18" long, pressed steel	300.00	450.00	600.00
KINGSBURY Cannon Truck, very early, 11" long, clockwork	125.00	187.50	250.00

	G	VG	M
KINGSBURY Caterpillar, 8½" long, wind-up.....	100.00	150.00	200.00
KINGSBURY Cattle Truck, 19" long, 1930s........	15.00	22.50	30.00
KINGSBURY De Soto, 14½" long, pressed steel windup, circa 1938.....	37.50	56.25	75.00
KINGSBURY Dump Truck, tin, driver, 10" long....	150.00	225.00	300.00
KINGSBURY Dump Truck, early 30s, 16" long, clockwork............	250.00	375.00	500.00
KINGSBURY Fire Pumper, 11" long, very early, clockwork iron and steel	200.00	300.00	400.00
KINGSBURY Fire Pumper, 1920s, 23" long........	350.00	525.00	700.00
KINGSBURY Fire Truck, 18" long............	100.00	150.00	200.00
KINGSBURY Ford Sedan & House Trailer, 1937, 23" long, pressed steel..	110.00	165.00	220.00
KINGSBURY Golden Arrow Racer, 20" long, pressed steel windup....	140.00	210.00	280.00
KINGSBURY Ladder Truck, steel, driver, 22" long................	100.00	150.00	200.00
KINGSBURY ladder wagon fire truck, tin, rubber tires, 23½" long	12.50	18.75	25.00
KINGSBURY Phaeton Auto, 1900, rubber slip tires, 9½" long........	600.00	900.00	1200.00
KINGSBURY Rack Truck, 16" long, pressed steel windup	250.00	375.00	500.00
KINGSBURY Roadster, 13" long, electric headlights, spring motor, luggage rack	172.50	258.75	345.00
KINGSBURY Sedan, two-door, with trailer, 22½" long, 1930s, clockwork..	100.00	150.00	200.00
KINGSBURY Sunbeam Racer, sheetmetal, red with rubber tires on steel wheels, clockwork motor, 19" long............	240.00	360.00	480.00
KINGSBURY Tractor, mechanical, 8", with driver	80.00	120.00	160.00
KINGSBURY Tractor and cart, tin, with iron driver, white rubber wheels, circa 1930s...........	60.00	90.00	120.00
KINGSBURY Transit Truck, 1930s, 19" long.	20.00	30.00	40.00

	G	VG	M
KINGSBURY Truck with C Cap, 10" long, tin......	125.00	187.50	250.00
KINGSBURY Wind-Up Car, curved dash, driver, 9" long..............	150.00	225.00	300.00
KINGSBURY Wrecker, 13" long, pressed steel, windup	190.00	285.00	380.00
Ladder Truck, driver front and rear, cast iron, 5" long	18.00	27.00	36.00
Ladder Truck approx. 14" long, battery operated lights, wind-up........	65.00	97.50	130.00
LAKETOY "John Wanamaker" delivery van, 10½" long, wooden....	90.00	135.00	180.00
LANSING SLIK-TOY 7" aluminum passenger Sedan, circa 1940s.....	2.00	3.00	4.00
LINDSTROM Lumber Truck #160, steerable front wheels, tin, with driver, 10" long.............	55.00	82.50	110.00
LINDSTROM Steam Roller No. 181, mechanical, 12" long...............	20.00	30.00	40.00
Log Truck (Beck), steers via horn on top of cab, late 1940s, large..........	7.50	11.25	15.00
Mack Dump Truck, cast iron, 12" long............	60.00	90.00	120.00
Mack Dump Truck, cast iron, 1930s...............	37.50	56.25	75.00
"Mack" Ladder Truck, 18" long, cast iron........	130.00	195.00	260.00
Mack Stake Truck 4¼" long, cast iron............	63.00	94.50	126.00
Mack Stake Truck, 5" long, cast iron wheels, circa late 1920s...............	32.50	48.75	65.00
Mack Stake Truck, 5" long, white rubber wheels, circa 1930s...............	35.00	52.50	70.00
Mack Stake Truck, cast iron, 7" long.............	35.00	52.50	70.00

Mack Dump truck, cast iron, 1930s.
Courtesy Mapes Auctioneers & Appraisers

Mack Stake Truck, cast iron, 7" long.
Courtesy Mapes Auctioneers & Appraisers

MANOIL

MANOIL: List compiled by Terry Sells. Numbers and words italicized are MANOIL'S own description. 701-706 began production in 1934.

	G	VG	M
MANOIL *700 Sedan,* *futuristic*	17.50	26.25	35.00
MANOIL *701 Sedan,* *futuristic*	17.50	26.25	35.00
MANOIL *702 Coupe,* *futuristic*	20.00	30.00	40.00
MANOIL *703 Wrecker,* *futuristic*	25.00	37.50	50.00
MANOIL *704 Roadster,* *futuristic,* Pat. No. 95791	12.50	18.75	25.00
MANOIL *705 Sedan,* *futuristic,* Pat. No. 95792	15.00	22.50	30.00
MANOIL *706 Rocket,* *futuristic bus-like vehicle,* Pat. No. 95793	8.00	12.00	16.00
MANOIL *70 Soup Kit-* *chen,* large number	12.00	18.00	24.00
MANOIL *70A Soup Kit-* *chen,* small number	12.00	18.00	24.00
MANOIL *71 Shell Carrier* *With Soldier On Shell* *Box,* has loop	11.25	16.92	22.50
MANOIL *71A* Same as above, no loop	12.50	18.75	25.00
MANOIL *72 Water* *Wagon,* large number . . .	10.50	15.75	21.00
MANOIL *72A* Same as above, small number . . .	10.50	15.75	21.00

	G	VG	M
MANOIL *73 Tractor,* loop front	8.00	12.00	16.00
MANOIL *73A Tractor,* plain front	10.50	15.75	21.00
MANOIL *74 Armored Car* *with Anti-Tank Gun* . . .	16.00	24.00	32.00
MANOIL *75 Armored Car* *with Anti-Aircraft Gun.*	22.50	33.75	45.00
MANOIL *75A Armored* *Car with Siren, siren* cast separately	35.00	52.50	70.00
MANOIL *75A Armored* *Car With Siren, siren* cast with vehicle	6.00	9.00	12.00
MANOIL *95 Tank*	9.00	13.50	18.00
MANOIL *96 Large Shell* *on Truck*	9.00	13.50	18.00
MANOIL *97 Pontoon on* *Wheels*	16.00	24.00	32.00
MANOIL *98 Torpedo on* *Wheels*	13.00	19.50	26.00
MANOIL *103 Gasoline* *Truck*	13.00	19.50	26.00
MANOIL *104 Chemical* *Truck*	21.00	31.50	42.00
MANOIL 105 Five Barrel Gun on Wheels	12.00	18.00	24.00
MANOIL (MC5) Tank, composition	22.00	33.00	44.00

704 ROADSTER

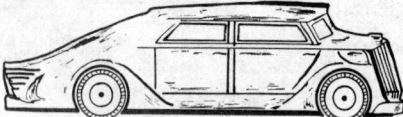

705 SEDAN

706 ROCKET

MANOIL Pre-World War II vehicles
Courtesy Peter and Marjorie Ruben

No. 713   BUS

No. 710 - OIL TANKER

No. 709 - FIRE ENGINE

No. 707 - SEDAN

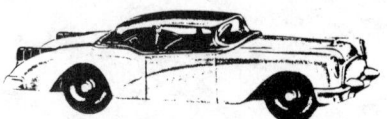

No. 716 - SEDAN

No. 717 - HARD TOP CONVERTIBLE

No. 718 - CONVERTIBLE

No. 719 - SPORT CAR

No. 715 - COMMERCIAL TRUCK has removable panels, as shown above

No. 714 - TOWING TRUCK

No. 720 - RANCH WAGON

MANOIL Postwar Vehicles
Courtesy Peter and Marjorie Ruben

No. 708 - ROADSTER

MANOIL Post-War Vehicles
Courtesy Peter and Marjorie Ruben

MANOIL 69 cannon, metal wheels, wood wheels, wood wheels variant.
MANOIL Vehicles, top row, L to R: 70, 71. Middle row, 71 with variant on wheel support, 72, 73 with front tow loop, 74. Bottom row: 75, 75A with siren cast separately, 75A siren cast integrally.
Photo by Ed Poole

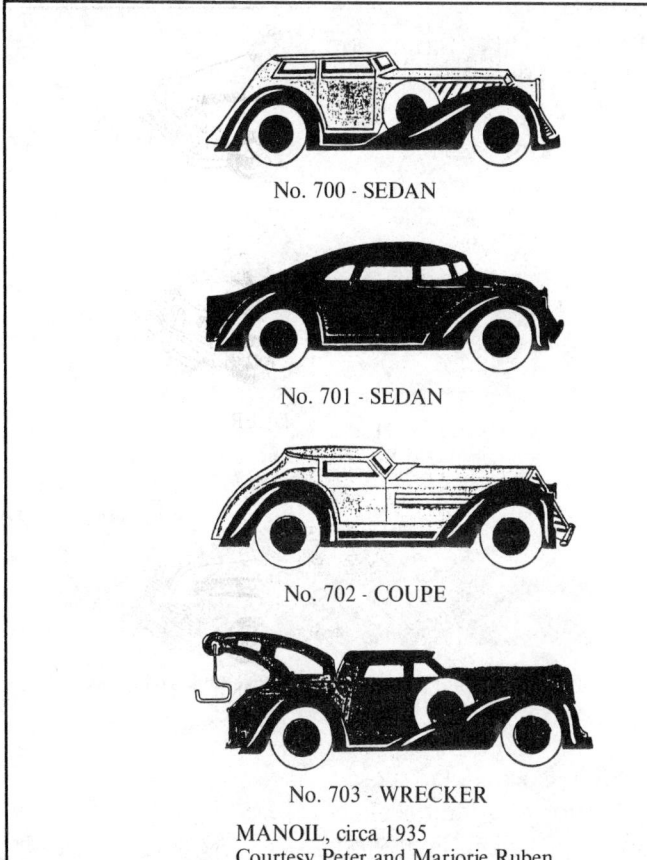

No. 700 - SEDAN

No. 701 - SEDAN

No. 702 - COUPE

No. 703 - WRECKER

MANOIL, circa 1935
Courtesy Peter and Marjorie Ruben

MANOIL, top L to R: 713, 716, P-7
 Bottom, L to R: 714, P-10, P-11, P-9
Courtesy Marjorie and Peter Ruben

| | 95 | 96 | 97 | 98 |

| | 103 | 104 | 105 | 200 |

MANOIL Vehicles and "Metal Action Cannon" No. 200.
Photo by Ed Poole

MANOIL Post War Vehicles

	G	VG	M
MANOIL 707 Sedan	7.00	10.50	14.00
MANOIL 708 Roadster, horizontal radiator.....	9.00	13.50	18.00
MANOIL 708A Roadster, vertical radiator.......	9.00	13.50	18.00
MANOIL 709 Fire Engine	9.00	13.50	18.00
MANOIL 710 Oil Tanker.	9.50	14.25	19.00
MANOIL 711 Aerial Ladder	No Price Found		
MANOIL 712 Pumper ...	No Price Found		
MANOIL 713 Bus	No Price Found		
MANOIL 714 Towing Truck	10.00	15.00	20.00
MANOIL 715 Commercial Truck	12.50	18.75	25.00
MANOIL 716 Sedan	10.00	15.00	20.00
MANOIL 717 Hard Top Convertible..........	10.00	15.00	20.00
MANOIL 718 Convertible	10.00	15.00	20.00
MANOIL 719 Sport Car .	10.00	15.00	20.00
MANOIL 720 Ranch Wagon	10.00	15.00	20.00

MANOIL Plastic Vehicles

	G	VG	M
MANOIL P-7 Roadster ..	.50	.75	1.00
MANOIL P-8 Sedan.....	.50	.75	1.00
MANOIL P-9 Pick-Up....	.50	.75	1.00
MANOIL P-10 Towing Truck	.50	.75	1.00
MANOIL P-11 Road Scraper	.50	.75	1.00
MANOIL P-12 Tractor...	.50	.75	1.00
MANOIL P-13 Dump Cart	.50	.75	1.00

MANOIL, Top L to R: 705, 708 early, 708 later
Bottom L to R: 707, 710, 709
Photo by Norbet Schachter
Courtesy Marjorie and Peter Ruben

MANOIL 712 Pumper (top); 711 Aerial Ladder (bottom).
Photo by Norbert Schachter.
Courtesy Marjorie and Peter Ruben

MARX Convertible Roadster, 1930s, 11" long.
Courtesy Lloyd W. Ralston Auctions

MARX Lonesome Pine trailer and convertible sedan, 19" long.
Courtesy Lloyd W. Ralston Auctions

	G	VG	M
MARX "City Sanitation Dept. Help Keep Your City Clean", circa 1940, 12¾" long............	25.00	37.50	50.00
MARX Coca Cola truck, 20" long, sprite decal, stamped steel, late 1940s to early 1950s........	50.00	75.00	100.00
MARX Convertible Roadster, 1930s, nickel plated tin, 11" long....	60.00	90.00	120.00
MARX Dump Truck, 17" long, No. 695B........	25.00	37.50	50.00
MARX Dump Truck, two-color, No.T751, circa 1930s................	45.00	67.50	90.00
MARX No. 1084 Dump Truck................	12.50	18.75	25.00
MARX "Electrically Lighted Truck and Trailer Set" No. T-5715, circa 1930s, 15" long...	20.00	30.00	40.00
MARX Falcoln with plastic bubble top, black rubber tires	20.00	30.00	40.00
MARX G-Man Pursuit car, No. 7000, 15" long, 1930s................	40.00	60.00	80.00
MARX Gang Buster Car No. 7200, approx. 14" long, 1930s...........	120.00	180.00	240.00
MARX Guided Missile Truck No. 4488.......	37.50	56.25	75.00
MARX "High-Boy Climbing Tractor" No. 950, 10½" long............	17.50	26.25	35.00
MARX "Heavy Gauge Tractor" No. 926......	7.50	11.25	15.00

	G	VG	M
MARX Air Force Truck, "Air Defense Group", ridem toy, 32" long, No. 3290	65.00	95.50	130.00
MARX Ambulance No. 8500, approx. 14" long, 1930s...............	27.00	40.50	54.00
MARX Ambulance No. 8600, approx. 14" long, 1930s...............	27.00	40.50	54.00
MARX "American Railroad Express Agency Inc.", early 1930s, open cab, 7"..	30.00	45.00	60.00
MARX American Truck Co. No. 65 moving truck, friction..............	30.00	45.00	60.00
MARX Auto Transport, 1950s with Tin Litho cars (2 of them), 34" long...	20.00	30.00	40.00
MARX "Auto Transwalk" No. T-50447B, 1930s truck with three cars.......	16.00	24.00	32.00
MARX "Chief-Fire dept. No. 1", "Friction Drive", circa 1948	3.00	4.50	6.00

MARX Coca-Cola Truck, 20" long.
Courtesy Richard MacNary

	G	VG	M
MARX Hi-way Express Truck	34.00	51.00	68.00
MARX Lazy-Dazy Dairy Farm Pick-Up Truck and Trailer, 22" long	30.00	45.00	60.00
MARX Lonesome Pine trailer and convertible sedan, 1930s, 19" long	55.00	82.50	110.00
MARX "Lumar Contractors" 962 dump truck	10.50	15.75	21.00
MARX M.D. War Dept. Ambulance, 1930s	90.00	135.00	180.00
MARX No. 1016 Machinery Moving Truck	10.00	15.00	20.00
MARX "Mammoth Truck Train" No. T-50-12345, circa 1930s, truck with five trailers	60.00	90.00	120.00
MARX Mystery Taxi, circa 1930s, press down to operate	30.00	45.00	60.00
MARX Navy Jeep No. 1078	33.00	49.50	66.00
MARX Panel Wagon	9.00	13.50	18.00
MARX "Power Grader" No. 1759, black or white wheels, 17½" long	7.50	11.25	15.00
MARX Pure Milk Dairy Truck with glass bottles, pressed steel, tin wheels, circa 1940	25.00	37.50	50.00
MARX REA Express Truck No. 1021	80.00	120.00	160.00
MARX Rex Mars Tank wind-up	60.00	90.00	120.00
MARX Road Grader, heavy-duty	10.00	15.00	20.00
MARX Rocker Dump No. 1752, 17½" long	11.00	16.50	22.00
MARX Side Dump Truck, four-color No. T-475, circa 1940	15.00	22.50	30.00

	G	VG	M
MARX Side Dump Truck and Trailer, No. T-4045, circa 1930s	15.00	22.50	30.00
MARX "Siren Fire Chief", circa 1930, "F.D. 1st Batt.", 15" long	75.00	112.50	150.00
MARX Siren Police Car No. 8300, 1930s, approx. 14" long	67.50	101.25	135.00
MARX Sports Coupe, 1930s, 15"	60.00	90.00	120.00
MARX Stake-type truck, 3-color, No. E-271, circa 1941	18.00	27.00	36.00
MARX No. 1008 Stake Truck	12.00	18.00	24.00
MARX "Tricky Taxi", friction, 4½" long	16.00	24.00	32.00
MARX "USA 41573147" Army Truck, circa 1952, 13¾" long	10.00	15.00	20.00
MARX "USA Army D-105", 7½" long, Mack Truck brown pressed steel, winds up	20.00	30.00	40.00
MARX Willys Jeep, steel, circa 1938, 12" long, hood opens, windshield folds down	20.00	30.00	40.00
MARX Willys Jeep and trailer, circa 1940s	21.00	31.50	42.00
MARX Wrecker Truck No. T-16, circa 1930s	12.50	18.75	25.00
McCormick-Deering Spreader, "Made in USA", steel, 10½" long, black rubber, 1950s	25.00	37.50	50.00
METAL CAST Tank, slush lead, circa 1946	40.00	60.00	80.00

Metal Cast Tank
Photo by Ed Poole

METAL MASTERS	G	VG	M
METAL MASTERS Ambulance wind-up, circa 1940	15.00	22.50	30.00
METAL MASTERS Bus, 7" long, 1930s	10.00	15.00	20.00
METAL MASTERS Bus, black rubber tires	6.00	9.00	12.00
METAL MASTERS Bus, black plastic wheels, circa WW II, approx. 7" long	7.50	11.25	15.00
METAL MASTERS pickup truck with black plastic wheels, approx. 7" long .	6.50	9.75	13.00
METAL MASTERS station wagon, like model 100, but not wind-up	12.50	18.75	25.00
METAL MASTERS station wagon, model 100, wind-up, circa 1940	20.00	30.00	40.00
METAL MASTERS Tow Truck No. 600, circa 1940, "Towing ABC Service"	12.50	18.75	25.00
METAL MASTERS Tow Truck with spring wind-up motor, like No. 600 otherwise	22.50	33.75	45.00
METALCRAFT "Bunte Candies" 12" truck	60.00	90.00	120.00
METALCRAFT Coca Cola Truck, 11" long, pressed steel, rubber tires, circa late 20s-early 30s, 10 bottles in rack, "Every Bottle Sterilized"	155.00	232.50	310.00
METALCRAFT Coca Cola Truck, 10 bottles, 10½" long, 1930s	40.00	60.00	80.00
METALCRAFT Coca Cola Truck, 12" long, 10 bottles, late 1930s, long nose, stamped metal . . .	No Price Found		
METALCRAFT Coca Cola Truck, circa 1928, with bottles in racks	170.00	255.00	340.00
METALCRAFT Delivery Truck Van, 11" long, steel	75.00	112.50	150.00
METALCRAFT "Goodrich Silvertone Tires" wrecker	34.00	51.00	68.00
METALCRAFT "Heinz" truck, circa 1932 "Baked Beans, Bottled Vinegar", "Rice Flakes", 12" long .	90.00	135.00	180.00

METALCRAFT Coca-Cola truck, late 1930s, 12" long.
Courtesy Richard L. MacNary

METALCRAFT	G	VG	M
METALCRAFT "Meadow Gold Butter" truck 13" long, battery lights	80.00	120.00	160.00
METALCRAFT "White King Delivery" truck, 12" long	125.00	187.50	250.00
Model A Ford, coupe with spare tire on back, cast iron	30.00	45.00	60.00
Model A Tow Truck, cast iron, no maker imprinted, 7" long	45.00	67.50	90.00
Model T Ford, cast iron, 5" long	75.00	112.50	150.00
Model T, cast iron 6" long	114.00	171.00	228.00
Model T Ford, cast iron, 8½" long	14.00	21.00	28.00
Model T Ford coupe, gray, with animated figures, cast iron, 1920s	160.00	240.00	320.00
Model T Ford, tin	50.00	75.00	100.00
Model T Ford "C" Cab Truck, cast iron, circa early 1920s, 8½" long .	44.00	66.00	88.00
Model T Speedster, 10" long	50.00	75.00	100.00
Motorcycle "Cop", 3¾" long, cast iron	16.00	24.00	32.00
Motorcycle, cast iron, white rubber tires, 3" long	10.00	15.00	20.00
Motorcycle, Harley-Davidson, rider, 6" long .	22.00	33.00	44.00
Motorcycle, Harley-Davidson, cast iron, 9" long	56.00	84.00	112.00
Motorcycle with sidecar, policeman rider, 4" long, cast iron	35.00	52.50	70.00
NONPAREIL Ambulance	14.00	21.00	28.00
NONPAREIL Dry Goods .	14.00	21.00	28.00
NONPAREIL Police Patrol	14.00	21.00	28.00
NONPAREIL Toyville Express	14.00	21.00	28.00

NORTH & JUDD. Research by collector C.B.C. Lee suggests that this company, located at the time in New Britain, Connecticut, made cast iron toys for only one year, probably 1930, for S. H. Kress. Their original designs appear to have been marked with the company's name, but their copies for the most part are unmarked. The company is still in business, making quality hardware.

	G	VG	M
Austin Convertible, open top, marked "North & Judd"		No Price Found	
Austin Sedan, two-door, marked "North & Judd".		No Price Found	
Bus, looks like Dent, 4.667" long		No Price Found	
Ford Model A Coupe, looks like Arcade, length of left cab 1.528", has driver in window, trunk at rear		No Price Found	
Ford Model T stake truck, like Arcade's, but marked			
"Anchor Truck Co." (an anchor is North & Judd's trademark)		No Price Found	
Motorcycle cop, like Hubley's "Cop", separate nickeled driver is held by mushrooms at front of handlebars and on driver's feet		No Price Found	
Semi-Trailer Stake Truck, marked "North & Judd".		No Price Found	
Tractor, looks like Arcade, but has nickeled driver, 2.988" long		No Price Found	

	G	VG	M
NYLINT Austin & Western Telescopic Crane, 21"	37.50	56.25	75.00
NYLINT "Elgin Street Sweeper"	25.00	37.50	50.00
NYLINT Road Grader, 18" long	25.00	37.50	50.00
OHIO Armored Car, circa WW I, friction, 7¼" long	110.00	165.00	220.00
OHIO Coupe, 2-door, 17" long, pressed steel	77.50	116.25	155.00
OHIO Delivery Truck, 1920s, painted pressed steel, friction, 12" long	130.00	195.00	260.00
OHIO Fire Ladder Truck, 13½" long, 1920s	175.00	262.50	350.00
OHIO Fire Patrol, 9¾" long, pressed steel, cast iron, wood, very early	170.00	255.00	340.00
OHIO Fire Truck, 10½" long, pressed steel, cast iron, wood, very early	250.00	375.00	500.00
OHIO Fire Truck, 19½", friction	150.00	225.00	300.00
OHIO Pickup Truck, 13" long, 1920s, friction	60.00	90.00	120.00
OHIO Roadster, 7½" long, cast iron and wood, friction, very early	175.00	262.50	350.00
OHIO Roadster, 13" long, 1920s	90.00	135.00	180.00
OHIO Roadster, 18" long, 1920s, friction, pressed steel	140.00	210.00	280.00

OHIO Fire Truck, 19½" long, 1910. Courtesy Lloyd W. Ralston Auctions.

OHIO Armored Car, C. WW I, 7¼" long. Courtesy Lloyd W. Ralston Auctions

OHIO Delivery Truck, 1920s, 12" long. Courtesy Lloyd W. Ralston Auctions

OHIO Roadster, 18" long, 1920s. Courtesy Lloyd W. Ralston Auctions

	G	VG	M
OHIO Touring Auto, friction	22.50	33.75	45.00
OHLSSON & RICE, midget race car, aluminum body, rubber tires, circa 1940s	25.00	37.50	50.00
Oil and Gas Truck, cast iron, 8" long	80.00	120.00	160.00
Oil Truck circa 1936, pressed steel 10¾" long	30.00	45.00	60.00
Packard Van Truck, 27" long, screen side, pressed steel	100.00	150.00	200.00
"Patrol" Motorcycle and rider, circa 1940, 6¼" long, cast iron	20.00	30.00	40.00
"Patrol" stake truck, Wyandotte? pressed steel, 4⅞" long	2.75	4.13	5.50
Pedal Car, "American National Company Toledo Ohio, USA", sheet metal and wooden, dashboard with dials, rubber tread on wheels, 46" long	80.00	120.00	160.00
Pedal Car, circa 1905, chain drive, wooden spoke wheels	150.00	225.00	300.00
Pedal Car, Cadillac, circa 1915 TOLEDO METAL WHEEL CO. lithographed dashboard	120.00	180.00	240.00
Pedal Car, Fire Truck, Mack	200.00	300.00	400.00
Pedal Car, "Ford, 1896", Tubular frame with wire wheels, sheet metal seat with wooden back rest and steering lever, plate under seat has diagram of motor, 39" long	20.00	30.00	40.00
Pedal Car, "Ford" emblem on radiator, painted steel	150.00	225.00	300.00
Pedal Car, green and yellow-painted, metal	24.00	36.00	48.00
Pedal Car, Hudson, wood and steel, folding windshield, tilt-up steering wheel	100.00	150.00	200.00
Pedal Car, Lincoln, 1931	400.00	600.00	800.00
Pedal Car, Nash Sideway, 34" long, 1920s	500.00	750.00	1000.00
Pedal Car, Open Coupe, 1920s or early 1930s, GLENDRON, 36" long	80.00	120.00	160.00

Pedal Car, "Ford"
Courtesy Mapes Auctioneers & Appraisers

	G	VG	M
Pedal Car, Packard Dual Cowl Phaeton, 6' long, AMERICAN NATIONAL	2200.00	3300.00	4400.00
Pedal Car, Packard Roadster, 1920s, AMERICAN NATIONAL, 45" long	600.00	900.00	1200.00
Pedal Car, "Packard", early, wire wheels	75.00	112.50	150.00
Pedal Car, "Pioneer" race car, metal and wood	350.00	525.00	700.00
Pedal Car, Winner, circa 1906	280.00	420.00	560.00
Pickup Truck, cast iron, 3½" long, 1920s, white rubber tires on wooden wheels	20.00	30.00	40.00
Pickup Truck, cast iron, 4" long	40.00	60.00	80.00
Pickup Truck, 7¼" long, cast iron, 1920s	25.00	37.50	50.00
Pickup Truck, tin friction toy, 19" long, 1920s	120.00	180.00	240.00
Pickup Truck, tin or pressed steel, circa 1937-38 6", wood wheels	8.00	12.00	16.00
Plastic automobile, very early, futuristic	2.00	3.00	4.00
PLAYBOY Dump Truck 22" long, tan	55.00	82.50	110.00
PLAYBOY "Intercity Bus", 23½" long, cream color	135.00	202.50	270.00
Race Car, cast iron, 9"	60.00	90.00	120.00
Racer "Parker Special", simple body of heavy steel with steel wheels, 11" long	15.00	22.50	30.00

	G	VG	M
Race Car, friction, with driver, circa 1925	50.00	75.00	100.00
Race Car, 8" long, circa 1918	34.00	51.00	68.00
Race Car with driver, cast iron, 9½" long, "5"	140.00	210.00	280.00
Racer, 7½" pressed steel with driver, white rubber tires, rubberband and gear powered	9.00	13.50	18.00
Racing Car, cast iron, 6½" long, with figure	30.00	45.00	60.00
Racing Car, cast iron, with driver, full figure, spiked wheels, early 1920s	30.00	45.00	60.00
Racing Car, cast iron, 7¼"	20.00	30.00	40.00
Racing Set, 1930s, 3 tin racing cars, small tin garage	9.00	13.50	18.00
"Radio Police" slush mold police car coupe, white rubber tires, circa 1940..	5.00	7.50	10.00
"Railway Express" truck, cast iron, early 1930s, 5" long	40.00	60.00	80.00
RALSTOY "Antiaircraft Unit", 5½" long........	10.00	15.00	20.00
RALSTOY Mayflower Moving Van..........	9.00	13.50	18.00
RALSTOY Tank, 3" long, "U.S. Army"..........	7.50	11.25	15.00
RALSTOY Transporter with tank, cannon No.34, plane, 9" overall length..	15.00	22.50	30.00
RENWAL die-cast pickup truck, black rubber tires, approx. 7" long	7.50	11.25	15.00
REPUBLIC Taxi Cab with driver, sheetmetal, friction motor, circa 1926.......	55.00	82.50	110.00
Road Grader, 7½" long, cast iron, rubber wheels..	30.00	45.00	60.00
Road Race Cars, ¹/₃₂, 1962-1965............	3.50	5.25	7.00
Roadster, cast iron, early, driver, 7" long........	60.00	90.00	120.00
Roadster, pressed steel, circa 1936, rumble seat.......	25.00	37.50	50.00
Roadster Tow Truck, cast iron, 5" long..........	20.00	30.00	40.00
"Rocket Launcher" truck, "U.S.A.F.", friction, pressed steel and plastic, circa 1960	5.00	7.50	10.00
Sedan, two-door, "Made U.S.A.", slush cast,			

RALSTOY (None imprinted with company name)
Top: Transporter with tank, Cannon No. 34, Plane, 9" overall.
Middle: "Antiaircraft Unit", 5½" long, Cannon No. 23, 2¾" long.
Bottom: Tank 3" long, "U.S. Army", Cannon 3¾" long.
Photo by Ed Poole

	G	VG	M
possibly Manoil, late 1930s	4.00	6.00	8.00
Sedan, cast iron, four door, driver, 8" long	125.00	187.50	250.00
Sedan motor car, cast iron.	50.00	75.00	100.00
Sedan, die cast, black rubber tires, approx. 7" long, circa 1930s	7.50	11.25	15.00
Sedan, tin friction, four door, 9½"	13.00	19.50	26.00
Sedan, tin friction, 17¾" long, 1920s	50.00	75.00	100.00

"SMITTY TOYS"
by Ray Funk

A line of large cast metal and aluminum toy trucks hit the market in 1945, the Smith-Miller "Smitty Toys", "Famous Trucks in Miniature", produced in Santa Monica, California. These trucks were doomed from the beginning, as they were entering a highly competitive market, one that had toy producers of trucks dating back to the 30s and earlier, such as Buddy "L", Structo, Marx, Hubley, and in 46 Ny-lint, Tonka, in early 50s, and in the mid-1950s, Eldon plastics. However, despite the heavy competition, they fought to stay on the market for a full ten years, into 1955, outclassing virtually all toy trucks before and after, by far, although the last year they changed their profile from Mack Trucks to Auto-Car diesels, with opening doors and steering wheels that actually steered like the real thing. Their first trucks had two different classes, expensive replicas, and, still not cheap, though not actually true replicas, of a smaller type of truck of no name that looked to be a half-breed Ford. I will list the cheaper line first.

No. 401 Tow Truck, 15" long, No. 402 Dump Truck 11½" long, No. 403 Scoop Dump, 14" long (same dump with scoop), all complete cast, cast wheels and rubber tires.

The larger scale models were cast and aluminum, such as No. 404 Lumber Truck (six wheels), 19" long, $10.75; No. 404T Lumber Trailer, 17" long, $6.95; No. 405 Silver Streak, 28" long (14 wheels) six wheel tractor and eight wheel bogey'd heavy duty grain trailer, $15.95; No. 406 Bekins Van, 29" long, six wheel tractor and four-wheel trailer (single axle); No. 407 Searchlight Truck, long (six wheel) based frame 18½" long with platform that has diesel motor (to hold batteries) and huge searchlight, at $16.95; No. 408 Blue Diamond ten wheel huge dump truck, last double set of duals bogey'd, 18½" long, $17.95; No. 409 Pacific Intermountain Express (P.I.E.) six wheel tractor semi with eight wheel bogey'd aluminum trailer, 29" long, $19.75; No. 410 Aerial Ladder semi, six wheel tractor, and four wheel single axle trailer, 36" long, ladder extends to 48" high, $27.95. By 1950 some mid-West stores had the aerial ladder priced at $37.50, and various of the other higher-priced.

Later, various modifications were produced, one a straight Box bed truck, using the searchlight truck with metal box and rear double doors. Then yet another variation was the box truck employing the eight wheel bogey set-up, and the log trailer base with a same box to make a ten wheel straight truck and eight wheel trailer, as there were many on the California highways. Then the long base tractor (ten-wheeler) with bogey on rear eight wheels, hooked to Silver Streak and P.I.E. trailers, and yet other variations such as the P.I.E. eight wheel trailer minus top and raising rear door, as high-side grain hauler, and finally a long refrigerator trailer with small side door, all using ten-wheel tractors.

At the same time the company was putting the smaller wheels on the P.I.E. and Silver Streak trailers, and using the small six-wheeled cast "Half-Breeds" tractors, priced at lower competitive prices.

Their first Mack trucks were of the older 1940s types with running boards, old-type fenders and raised separate headlights, and all had fuel tanks, the later Mack trucks being 1954 Macks with air horn on top.

The final year saw a complete change, Smith dropping out and Ironson coming in, changing the name to M.I.C. toys, Miller-Ironson Corporation, and to the best of my knowledge they produced only four different, all cast trucks, and though no truck company name, definitely Auto-Car diesels. One was a heavy-duty tow truck as tows large semis, a flat bed with removable side racks, and turn-down hydraulically lowering tailgate (up and down), door handles that worked to open doors, seat, steering wheel and front wheel which were steered like on the "model toy" fire trucks and others of the "model toy" line, the last, fire truck #410 with Mack Tractor, I cannot say, as I only have the cab and no catalog or advertisement of this toy.

Honorable mention must be made, before closing, that one company in Minnesota, owned by Teamsters President Beck's son (in the late 1940s) put out a huge cast metal truck, mostly loggers and dumpers, which steered via a horn on top of the cab, and two, Wyandotte put out in 1950, a very realistic cab over semi six wheel tractor of cast and eight wheel bogey'd long aluminum trailer, with beautifully realistic cast center replica wheels and rubber tires. The fifth wheel on the tractor was operational to couple and uncouple from the trailer, and though of no name, the cast tractor was finely detailed, fuel tanks and all. The Wyandotte sold at $10 while the aforementioned, name unknown, and very short-lived trucks, sold at $20 each, a much too high price for the 1940s. All are now gone, but live on in the minds of those who played with them. There were a few minor variations of the Smith-Miller which I did not mention, and no doubt possibly some on all items that I do not know about, nor have catalogs depicting. Any added information would be appreciated.

Evidence via photographs, etc., has unearthed the fact that there are more in this toy truck line than I had listed.

An early Smitty truck is an all pot metal truck, mostly painted as an armored bank truck with square box and locking doors.

I received a picture of a tanker, using the small bastard six wheel tractor, and trailer having the dual-tandem setup. As by the pictures there did not seem to be any spare room in the wheel wells, I must assume that this was only produced with the small wheels and tractor. It is bright yellow, and has "SHELL" on the trailer.

Still yet another produced in the early years, a cattle hauling truck. This one was large as the largest S.M. and had the large early Mack with long frame. I have found this truck, minus wheels, so I can only assume that it was produced as many others with similar tractor frames as an 18 and also 14 wheeler. The enclosed trailer features double doors on the rear with latch, slotted vented sides and truck was same yellow as tanker, other than frame and fenders (all actually one piece on the early 'Macks') were gloss black, making an eye catching toy, colorwise. Eventually I hope to restore this item and have it pictured for your enjoyment.

How many different trucks, or variations Smitty produced, I have no idea, as I begin to suspect that like Doepke, at times they too made up a one, or few of a kind.

(NOTE: New versions of SMITTY vehicles, using original and new parts, are currently being produced — See Leading Collectors and Dealers)

SMITTY Coca Cola Truck
Courtesy R. L. MacNary

SMITTY Aerial Ladder Fire Truck, early, open cab. (Truck in photo restored.)
Photo courtesy Ed Stivers

SMITTY "Bank of America" Armored Truck
Courtesy Good Old Days Store

SMITTY Catalog illustrations of Models 402, 401.
Photo by Bill Kaufman.   Courtesy Ray Funk.

SMITTY Catalog illustration of models 408, 404 and 404T.
Photo by Bill Kaufman.   Courtesy Ray Funk.

SMITTY Catalog illustration of Models 406 and 405.
Photo by Bill Kaufman.   Courtesy Ray Funk.

	G	VG	M
SMITTY (Smith-Miller) No. 401 Tow Truck, 15" long	50.00	75.00	100.00
SMITTY No. 402 Dump Truck, 11½" long	30.00	45.00	60.00
SMITTY No. 403 Scoop Dump, 14" long	30.00	45.00	60.00
SMITTY No. 404 Lumber Truck, 19" long.......	205.00	307.50	410.00
SMITTY No. 404T Lumber Trailer, 17" long	22.50	33.75	45.00
SMITTY No. 405 Silver Streak 6-wheel tractor, 28" long	35.00	52.00	70.00
SMITTY No. 406 Bekins Van, 29" long, six-wheel tractor and four-wheel trailer...............	110.00	165.00	220.00
SMITTY No. 407 Search-light Truck, 18½"long, "Hollywood Filmad" ...	55.00	82.50	110.00
SMITTY No. 408 Blue Diamond 10-wheel dump truck, 18½" long	170.00	255.00	340.00
SMITTY No. 409 Pacific Intermountain Express (P.I.E.) six-wheel tractor semi with eight wheel aluminum trailer, 29" long...............	70.00	105.00	140.00
SMITTY No. 410 Aerial Ladder semi, six-wheel tractor, and four-wheel trailer, 36" long, "SMFD"	225.00	337.50	450.00
SMITTY Aerial Ladder fire truck, early, open cab ...	No Price Found		
SMITTY Box Truck with Box trailer, front truck ten-wheeler	75.00	112.50	150.00
SMITTY Box Truck with Box trailer, front truck is six-wheeler	75.00	112.50	150.00
SMITTY Bank of America Armored Truck, No. 602B, 14½" long	75.00	112.50	150.00
SMITTY Coca Cola truck, 13" long, aluminum, late 1940s to early 1950s ...	No Price Found		
SMITTY (MIC) Dump truck, 17" long, "GT-601"	225.00	337.50	450.00
SMITH (MIC) Heavy Duty Tow Truck, 17" long ..	150.00	225.00	300.00

	G	VG	M
SMITTY House Trailer, 24" long, removable roof, furnished interior ..	80.00	120.00	160.00
SMITTY Mobil Oil Truck, 22½" long...........	130.00	195.00	260.00

SMITTY Catalog illustrations of models 407, 403, 409.
Photo by Bill Kaufman.   Courtesy Ray Funk.

SMITTY Catalog illustration of Model 410.
Photo by Bill Kaufman.   Courtesy Ray Funk.

	G	VG	M
Steam Pumper, "Boston", with lamp, cast iron wheels, 15½" long	1400.00	2100.00	2800.00
Stake Truck, cast iron, white rubber tires......	8.00	12.00	16.00
Steam Pumper fire truck, cast iron, 5"..........	4.00	6.00	8.00
Steam Pumper truck, cast iron, hard rubber wheels, driver, 12" long	60.00	90.00	120.00
Steam Pumper, tin and wooden chain and fric-tion drive with driver, "National", 10"	75.00	112.50	150.00
Steam Pumper, tin and wooden friction drive, 11" long..............	20.00	30.00	40.00
Steam Roller, steam-engine powered	80.00	120.00	160.00

STRUCTO Tank, 11" long, No. 48
Courtesy Mapes Auctioneers & Appraisers

	G	VG	M
Steam Roller, cast iron, 4¾" long, circa early 1930s	46.00	69.00	92.00
Steam Shovel, "Sand Digger", 28" long	25.00	37.50	50.00
STEELCRAFT Army Truck, MACK, circa 1930, 22" long	30.00	45.00	60.00
STEELCRAFT Coca Cola Truck, 12 bottles on side	105.00	152.50	210.00
STEELCRAFT Fire Truck, 25" long	300.00	450.00	600.00
STEELCRAFT "Heinz, Rice Flakes, Baked Beans, Bottle Vinegar" truck	42.50	63.75	85.00
STEELCRAFT Model T Roadster pedal car, 50" long, Lic. #65-287	300.00	450.00	600.00
STEELCRAFT Railway Express Truck, 26" long	300.00	450.00	600.00
STEELCRAFT Shell Motor Oil truck with oil barrels	72.50	108.75	145.00
STEELCRAFT Tank truck, sheet metal, 25½" long	25.00	37.50	50.00

	G	VG	M
STEELCRAFT "U.S. Mail", 27¼" long, circa 1928	190.00	285.00	380.00
STRUCTO Army Truck with canvas top, 21" long	30.00	45.00	60.00
STRUCTO Army Van, 17½" long, pressed steel and canvas	85.00	127.50	170.00
STRUCTO Bearcat Racer, 12¼" long, clockwork .	175.00	262.50	350.00
STRUCTO Camper with cloth top, 12"	5.00	7.50	10.00
STRUCTO Coupe, convertible, circa 1920s	67.50	106.25	135.00
STRUCTO Caterpillar Tractor with Trailer, heavy spring clockwork motor, steel treads	60.00	90.00	120.00
STRUCTO Caterpillar Whippet Tank, 12" long, heavy spring clockwork motor enameled green, red and black, may read "Patented 1920", on sale in 1929, No. 48	54.00	81.00	108.00
STRUCTO Delivery Truck, tin electric lights	60.00	90.00	120.00

	G	VG	M
STRUCTO Dump Truck, open cab, circa 1930, 18" long	185.00	287.50	370.00
STRUCTO Dump Truck, "Structo Excavating Co. No. 605 Phone 351" black rubber tires	15.00	22.50	30.00
STRUCTO Dump Wagon, cast iron, rubber tires	10.00	15.00	20.00
STRUCTO Fire Dept. Emergency Patrol Truck, red bubble light, 12" long, 1950s	20.00	30.00	40.00
STRUCTO Garbage Truck, 21" long	26.00	39.00	52.00
STRUCTO Gasoline Truck No. 912, 1950s, 13" long	18.00	27.00	36.00
STRUCTO Guided Missile Launcher No. 906 with plastic launcher, missiles of wood and vinyl, 13" long	18.00	27.00	36.00
STRUCTO Guided Missile Launching Truck, truck metal, missiles, etc., plastic, rubber tires	15.00	22.50	30.00
STRUCTO Hydraulic Dumper, 14" long	9.00	13.50	18.00
STRUCTO Moving Van, 16" long, open cab, circa 1929	63.00	94.50	126.00
STRUCTO Package Delivery Storage Truck	11.00	16.50	22.00
STRUCTO Pick Up Truck, 13"	6.00	9.00	12.00
STRUCTO Police Patrol Truck, 17" long	50.00	75.00	100.00
STRUCTO Renault Tank, clockwork, green with red turret	125.00	187.50	250.00
STRUCTO Roadster, 16" long, 1920s, clockwork	250.00	375.00	500.00
STRUCTO Sand Loader, 12" high, circa 1928	10.00	15.00	20.00
STRUCTO Searchlight Truck, truck metal, light and generator plastic, uses batteries, has rubber tires	18.00	27.00	36.00
STRUCTO Steam Shovel, 14" x 11"	40.00	60.00	80.00
STRUCTO Steam Shovel, 16"	29.00	43.50	58.00
STRUCTO Steam Shovel, 21" x 18"	35.00	52.50	70.00

	G	VG	M
STRUCTO "Structo Telephone Co.", 12" long, circa 1948	20.00	30.00	40.00
STRUCTO Tank, 11" long, #48	60.00	90.00	120.00
STRUCTO Tank, olive drab with orange turret, ten metal wheels, 12" long	60.00	90.00	120.00
STRUCTO Tractor 8½" long with cast iron driver, early, caterpillar type	70.00	105.00	140.00
STRUCTO Truck Assortment No. 317: Dump truck, blue, Stake truck, Lumber truck. Each 9" long, 3½" wide, 3½" tall. Heavy gauge metal, rubber wheels, original box folds to form garage. 1920s...Price per set	25.00	37.50	50.00
STRUCTO U.S. Mail Delivery Truck, tin	100.00	150.00	200.00
Studebaker Phaeton, 1920s, cast iron	75.00	112.50	150.00
STRUCTO Wrecker, "Toyland Garage"	15.00	22.50	30.00
STURDITOY Ambulance, 26" long, open cab, circa 1929	60.00	90.00	120.00
STURDITOY American Railway Express Truck, circa 1920s	50.00	75.00	100.00
STURDITOY Dump Truck, 1920s, 25" long	100.00	150.00	200.00
STURDITOY Dump Truck, 1920s, 26½" long	350.00	525.00	700.00
STURDITOY Pumper, 26" long, circa 1930	133.00	195.00	266.00
SUN RUBBER Airflow Stake Truck, large	12.00	18.00	24.00
SUN RUBBER Ambulance, brown	14.00	21.00	28.00
SUN RUBBER, auto, license No. S500R, 1930s	6.00	9.00	12.00
SUN RUBBER, Bus, white rubber tires 4½" long	7.00	10.50	14.00
SUN RUBBER, Chrysler Airflow auto, white rubber tires	17.50	26.25	35.00

SUN RUBBER Scout Car, Tank. Photo by Ed Poole.

	G	VG	M
SUN RUBBER Coupe No. 35	12.00	18.00	24.00
SUN RUBBER Racer, 5" long, silver	4.00	6.00	8.00
SUN RUBBER, Scout Car 7" long, four men firing machine guns, circa 1946	8.00	12.00	16.00
SUN RUBBER Tank, 6" long	6.00	9.00	12.00
SUN RUBBER Trailer Truck, white rubber tires	7.50	11.25	15.00

	G	VG	M
SUN RUBBER Truck, futuristic, 5" long	3.50	5.25	7.00
SUN RUBBER U.S. Army Truck, 4½"	3.50	5.25	7.00
Tank, step-top, slush lead, 2" long	3.00	4.50	6.00
Tin Auto with tin wheels, circa 1930s, looks like Chrysler Airflow (similar to Volkswagen)	3.00	4.50	6.00
TIP-TOP Coupe, pre WW II, made in California	8.00	12.00	16.00
TIP-TOP Wrecker, metal wheels, pre WW II	8.00	12.00	16.00
TOLEDO METAL WHEEL CO. Fire Pumper Pedal Car, red-painted, 59" long	220.00	330.00	440.00

TOMMY TOY: The following vehicles have been identified by Charles E. Weldon Jr., son of one of the owners of Tommy Toy. He is sure these are Tommy Toy, but admits there is always a chance he could be mistaken on some. Certainly the Cannon Truck, aside from the hubs, looks just like Barclay's, which was produced in the same years. Some others resemble Metal Cast, Savoye, and other company's vehicles. However, since slush molds did tend to change hands, production of a vehicle by one company would not preclude later manufacture of the same toy by another company. American Alloy is known to have produced copies of Tommy Toy's soldiers using new molds. The only vehicle known to bear the Tommy Toy trademark is the 810 Cord.

	G	VG	M
TOMMY TOY Aerial Ladder Truck (like SAVOYE), late 20s type	12.50	18.75	25.00
TOMMY TOY Airflow type auto (like KANSAS-TOY), circa 1935	2.50	3.75	5.00
TOMMY TOY, "Ambulance", late 20s-early 30s type	15.00	22.50	30.00
TOMMY TOY "Beer Truck" with wooden barrels, late 1930s	7.50	11.25	15.00
TOMMY TOY Cannon Truck, mid-30s (like BARCLAY; BARCLAY's had wooden hubs)	4.00	6.00	8.00
TOMMY TOY Convertible, no driver, mid-late 30s	5.00	7.50	10.00
TOMMY TOY Convertible with driver, mid-late 30s	7.50	11.25	15.00
TOMMY TOY Cord, 810	15.00	22.50	30.00
TOMMY TOY "Delivery Deluxe" delivery truck (like SAVOYE), late 30s	10.00	15.00	20.00
TOMMY TOY Double-Decker Bus, closed top, early 30s	7.50	11.25	15.00
TOMMY TOY Double-Decker Bus, open top, extended hood (like SAVOYE), late 1920s	15.00	22.50	30.00
TOMMY TOY Double-Decker Bus, open top, no hood (like BARCLAY), late 1930s	10.00	15.00	20.00
TOMMY TOY Dump Truck, late 1930s (resembles KANSAS TOY, BEST TOY, MANHATTAN TOYS)	7.50	11.25	15.00
TOMMY TOY "General Trucking", late 30s	5.00	7.50	10.00
TOMMY TOY Ladder Truck, mid 30s	12.50	18.75	25.00
TOMMY TOY "Milk" truck, late 1930s	5.00	7.50	10.00
TOMMY TOY "Milk Truck", grilled window, circa late 1930s	5.00	7.50	10.00

TOMMY TOY: Top row: "Motorcoach"; Bottom row, L to R: "Police Patrol", solid windows, "Police Patrol", open windows, "Ambulance".
Photo by Bill Kaufman
Courtesy Charles E. Weldon Jr.

TOMMY TOY: Top row, L to R: "Oil" tanker, Cannon Truck, convertible with driver, "Packard".
Bottom row, L to R: "Beer Truck", "Milk Truck", smooth windows, Convertible, no driver.
Photo by Bill Kaufman
Courtesy Charles E. Weldon Jr.

TOMMY TOY: Top row, L to R: Racing Car, large; Racing Car, small.
Bottom row, L to R: Airflow type coupe, Sedan towing "Tourist" trailer, tractor.
Photo by Bill Kaufman
Courtesy Charles E. Weldon Jr.

TOMMY TOY: Top row, L to R: Pumper, Aerial Ladder Truck, Ladder Truck.
Bottom, L to R: Pumper, large; Pumper, small.
Photo by Bill Kaufman
Courtesy Charles E. Weldon Jr.

TOMMY TOY: Top, L to R: "Milk Truck", smooth window, "Milk Truck", grilled window, "General Trucking", "Milk" truck.
Bottom, L to R: Double-decker bus, closed top; Double-decker bus, open top, extended hood; Double-decker bus, open top, no hood.
Photo by Bill Kaufman
Courtesy Charles E. Weldon Jr.

TOMMY TOY: Top row, L to R: Towing Car, Coupe, Wrecker, Dump Truck.
Bottom row, L to R: "Delivery Deluxe", Sedan, four-door; Sedan for towing "Tourist" trailer.
Photo by Bill Kaufman
Courtesy Charles E. Weldon Jr.

	G	VG	M
TOMMY TOY "Milk Truck", smooth window, circa late 30s.........	5.00	7.50	10.00
TOMMY TOY "Motorcoach", mid-30s (like SAVOYE)............	17.50	26.25	35.00

	G	VG	M
TOMMY TOY "Oil" tanker, "Cap 80000" (like METAL CAST, which has different capacity number), 1930s, attaches to TOMMY TOY Towing Car Coupe........	6.25	9.38	12.50

	G	VG	M
TOMMY TOY "Packard", coupe, mid-30s.........	15.00	22.50	30.00
TOMMY TOY "Police Patrol", open windows, late 20s-early 30s type...	50.00	75.00	100.00
TOMMY TOY "Police Patrol", solid windows, late 20s-early 30s type...	10.00	15.00	20.00
TOMMY TOY Pumper, mid 1930s............	12.50	18.75	25.00
TOMMY TOY Pumper, large, red hubs, late 30s.	10.00	15.00	20.00
TOMMY TOY Pumper, small, late 30s.........	5.00	7.50	10.00
TOMMY TOY Racing Car, large, circa mid-30s.....	5.00	7.50	10.00
TOMMY TOY Racing Car, small, circa mid-30s.....	2.50	3.75	5.00
TOMMY TOY Sedan, four-door, circa 1935........	15.00	22.50	30.00
TOMMY TOY Sedan towing "Tourist" trailer, circa 1936-37..............	17.50	26.25	35.00
TOMMY TOY Towing Car Coupe (like SAVOYE), early 30s type..........	6.25	9.37	12.50
TOMMY TOY Tractor....	2.50	3.75	5.00

	G	VG	M
TOMMY TOY Wrecker, late 1930s............	2.50	3.75	5.00
TONKA Carnation Milk Truck, earliest TONKA, 1950, painted and decal, pressed steel, 12" long...	31.00	46.50	62.00
TONKA Dump Truck, 11½", early	24.00	36.00	48.00
TONKA Ford Tractor Trailer, "Jolly Green Giant", early, 24" long..	40.00	60.00	80.00
TONKA Mobile Clam, 1950s, 27" long	15.00	22.50	30.00
TONKA Mobile Dragline, 1950s, 27" long........	12.00	18.00	24.00
TONKA Transport, 22", early	50.00	75.00	100.00

TONKA Carnation Milk Truck, earliest TONKA.
Courtesy Lloyd W. Ralston Auctions

TOOTSIE TOY
(Compiled by C.B.C. LEE)

	G	VG	M
TOOTSIETOY 4528 Limousine circa 1910, in 1911-1928 catalogs......	10.00	15.00	20.00
TOOTSIETOY 4570 Ford, Model T, open tourer, 1914, in catalog 1915-1926............	15.00	22.50	30.00
TOOTSIETOY 4610 Ford Model T pick-up truck, 1914, in catalog 1919-1932............	15.00	22.50	30.00
TOOTSIETOY 4629 (Yellow Cab) sedan, 1921, in catalog 1923-1933............	5.50	8.25	11.00
TOOTSIETOY 4630 (Federal) "Grocery" delivery van, 1921, in catalog 1924-1933......	30.00	45.00	60.00

	G	VG	M
TOOTSIETOY 4631 (Federal) "Bakery" delivery van, 1921, in catalog 1924-1933..............	50.00	75.00	100.00
TOOTSIETOY 4632 (Federal) "Market" delivery van, 1921, in catalog 1924-1933..............	25.00	37.50	50.00
TOOTSIETOY 4633 (Federal) "Laundry" delivery van, 1921, in catalog 1924-1933..............	25.00	37.50	50.00
TOOTSIETOY 4634 (Federal) "Milk" delivery van, 1921, in catalog 1924-1933..............	20.00	30.00	40.00
TOOTSIETOY 4635 (Federal) "Florist" delivery van, 1921, in catalog 1924-1933..............	70.00	105.00	140.00

TOOTSIETOY vans in the 4630s made in special custom liveries for private department stores, including "Boggs & Buhl", "Watt & Shand", "Pomeroy's", "Hochschild Kohn & Co.", "Bamberger's", "Alling Rubber Co.-Toys", "Jordan Marsh Co.", etc. Prices range on these from $125 to $350 in mint condition.

	G	VG	M		G	VG	M
TOOTSIETOY 4636 coupe, 1921, in catalogue 1924-1933	9.50	14.25	19.00	TOOTSIETOY 4655 Ford, Model A coupe, 1928, in catalog 1928-1933	9.50	14.25	19.00
TOOTSIETOY 4638 Mack stake truck, 1922, in catalog 1925-1933	12.50	18.75	25.00	TOOTSIETOY 4656 (Buick) coupe in tinplate garage, 1930, in catalog 1931-1932	32.50	48.75	65.00
TOOTSIETOY 4639 Mack coal truck, 1922, in catalog 1925-1933	12.50	18.75	25.00	TOOTSIETOY 4657 (Buick) sedan in tinplate garage, 1930, in catalog 1931-1932	32.50	48.75	65.00
TOOTSIETOY 4640 Mack tank truck, 1922, in catalog 1925-1933	12.50	18.75	25.00	TOOTSIETOY 4658 Mack insurance patrol in garage, in catalog 1931-1932	32.50	48.75	65.00
TOOTSIETOY 4641 closed tourer, 1924, in catalog 1925-1933	17.50	26.25	35.00	TOOTSIETOY 4666 Bluebird I Daytona record car, 1927, in catalog 1932-1941	11.50	17.25	23.00
TOOTSIETOY 4642 cannon, in catalogue 1931-1941	5.50	8.25	11.00	TOOTSIETOY 4670 Mack tractor and two semi-trailers, 1927, "A&P", "American Express", in catalog 1929-1932	50.00	75.00	100.00
TOOTSIETOY 4643 Mack AA Gun truck, 1922, in catalog 1931-1941	12.50	18.75	25.00				
TOOTSIETOY 4644 Mack searchlight truck, 1922, in catalog 1931-1941	12.50	18.75	25.00	TOOTSIETOY 4680 "Overland Bus Lines", in catalog 1929-1933	25.00	37.50	50.00
TOOTSIETOY 4645 Mack "US Mail - Airmail Service", 1922, in catalog 1931-1933	17.50	26.25	35.00	TOOTSIETOY 23 racer with driver, in catalog 1927-1933	11.00	16.50	22.00
TOOTSIETOY 4646 Caterpillar tractor, in catalog 1931-1939	15.00	22.50	30.00	TOOTSIETOY 190 Mack auto transport (3 Buicks), 1922, in catalog 1931-1933	50.00	75.00	100.00
TOOTSIETOY 4647 (Renault) tank, 1915, in catalog 1931-1941	17.50	26.25	35.00	TOOTSIETOY 190 Mack auto transport (4 Buicks) 1922, in catalog 1933-1936	75.00	112.50	150.00
TOOTSIETOY 4648 steamroller, in catalog 1931-1934	35.00	52.50	70.00				
TOOTSIETOY 4651 (Fageol) safety coach circa 1927, in catalog 1927-1933	9.50	14.25	19.00	TOOTSIETOY 5101 Funnies Set, "Andy Gump" roadster, in catalog 1932-1933, standard version	75.00	112.50	150.00
TOOTSIETOY 4652 fire engine - hook and ladder, in catalog 1927-1933	20.00	30.00	40.00	TOOTSIETOY 5102 Funnies Set, "Uncle Walt" roadster, in catalog 1932-1933, standard version	100.00	150.00	200.00
TOOTSIETOY 4653 fire engine-water tower, in catalog 1927-1933	17.50	26.25	35.00				
TOOTSIETOY 4654 farm tractor, in catalog 1927-1932	17.50	26.25	35.00	TOOTSIETOY 5103 Funnies Set, "Smitty" motorcycle with sidecar, in catalog 1932-1933, standard version	67.50	101.25	135.00

TOOTSIETOY 0802
Photo by Bill Kaufman
Courtesy Good Old Days Store

TOOTSIETOY 0805
Photo by Bill Kaufman
Courtesy Good Old Days Store

TOOTSIETOY Jeep CJ3, 3", 1950
Photo by Ed Poole

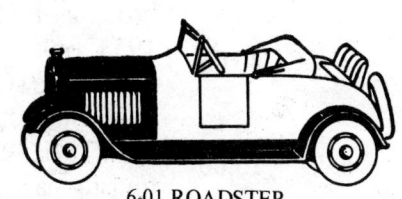

6-01 ROADSTER

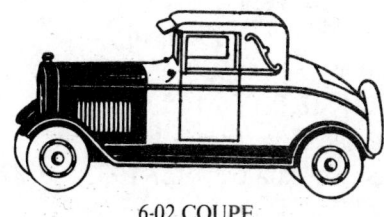

6-02 COUPE

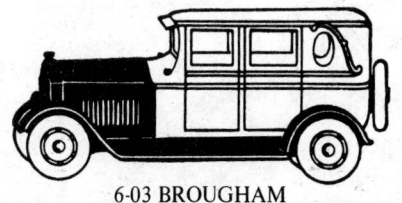

6-03 BROUGHAM

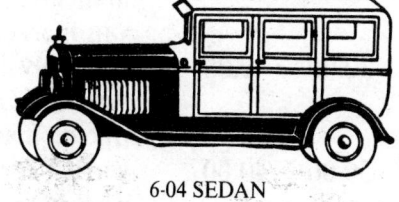

6-04 SEDAN

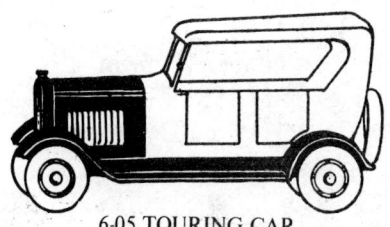

6-05 TOURING CAR

6-06 DELIVERY TRUCK

No. 4652 HOOK AND LADDER

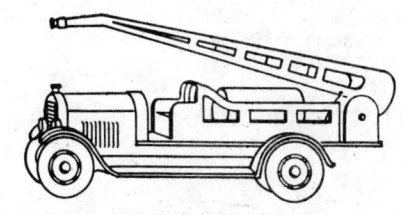

No. 4653 WATER TOWER

	G	VG	M
TOOTSIETOY 5104 Funnies Set, "Moon Mullins" police wagon, in catalog 1932-1933, standard v . . .	85.00	127.50	170.00
TOOTSIETOY 5105 Funnies Set, "Kayo" ice wagon, in catalog 1932-1933, standard v	92.50	138.75	185.00
TOOTSIETOY 5106 Funnies Set, "Uncle Willie" rowboat, in catalog 1932-1933, standard v	62.50	93.75	125.00
TOOTSIETOY 6001 Buick Roadster, 1926, in catalog 1927-1933	17.50	26.25	35.00

	G	VG	M
TOOTSIETOY 6002 Buick coupe, 1926, in catalog 1927-1933	17.50	26.25	35.00
TOOTSIETOY 6003 Buick Brougham, 1926, in catalog 1927-1933	17.50	26.25	35.00
TOOTSIETOY 6004 Buick sedan, 1926, in catalog 1927-1933	17.50	26.25	35.00
TOOTSIETOY 6005 Buick closed touring car, 1926, in catalog 1927-1933	30.00	45.00	60.00

	G	VG	M
TOOTSIETOY 6006 Buick screenside panel delivery, 1926, in catalog 1927-1933	17.50	26.25	35.00
TOOTSIETOY 6101 Cadillac roadster, 1926, in catalog 1927-1933	22.50	33.75	45.00
TOOTSIETOY 6102 Cadillac coupe, 1926, in catalog 1927-1933	22.50	33.75	45.00
TOOTSIETOY 6103 Cadillac brougham, 1926, in catalog 1927-1933	22.50	33.75	45.00
TOOTSIETOY 6104 Cadillac sedan, 1926, in catalog 1927-1933	22.50	33.75	45.00
TOOTSIETOY 6105 Cadillac closed touring car, 1926, in catalog 1927-1933	37.50	56.25	75.00
TOOTSIETOY 6106 Cadillac panel delivery van, 1926, in catalog 1927-1933	22.50	33.75	45.00
TOOTSIETOY 6201 Chevrolet roadster, 1926, in catalog 1927-1933	20.00	30.00	40.00
TOOTSIETOY 6202 Chevrolet coupe, 1926, in catalog 1927-1933	20.00	30.00	40.00
TOOTSIETOY 6203 brougham, 1926, in catalog 1927-1933	20.00	30.00	40.00
TOOTSIETOY 6204 Chevrolet sedan, 1926, in catalog 1927-1933	20.00	30.00	40.00
TOOTSIETOY 6205 Chevrolet closed touring car, 1926, in catalog 1927-1933	35.00	52.50	70.00
TOOTSIETOY 6206 Chevrolet panel delivery van, 1926, in catalog 1927-1933	20.00	30.00	40.00
TOOTSIETOY 6301 Oldsmobile roadster, 1926, in catalog 1927-1933	20.00	30.00	40.00
TOOTSIETOY 6302 Oldsmobile coupe, 1926, in catalog 1927-1933	20.00	30.00	40.00
TOOTSIETOY 6303 Oldsmobile brougham, 1926, in catalog 1927- 1933	20.00	30.00	40.00
TOOTSIETOY 6304 Oldsmobile sedan, 1926, in catalog 1927-1933	20.00	30.00	40.00

	G	VG	M
TOOTSIETOY 6305 Oldsmobile closed touring car, 1926, in catalog 1927-1933	35.00	52.00	70.00
TOOTSIETOY 6306 Oldsmobile panel delivery van, 1926, in catalog 1927-1933	20.00	30.00	40.00
TOOTSIETOY 6-01 roadster, 1926, in catalog 1933 only	35.00	52.50	70.00
TOOTSIETOY 6-02 coupe, 1926, in catalog 1933 only	35.00	52.50	70.00
TOOTSIETOY 6-03 brougham, 1926, in catalog 1933 only	35.00	52.50	70.00
TOOTSIETOY 6-04 sedan, 1926, in catalog 1933 only	35.00	52.50	70.00
TOOTSIETOY 6-05 closed touring car, 1926, in catalog 1933 only	52.50	78.75	105.00
TOOTSIETOY 6-06 panel delivery van, 1926, in catalog 1933 only	35.00	52.50	70.00
TOOTSIETOY, un-numbered, Ford Model A van marked "U.S. Mail", sold only in sets	22.50	33.75	45.00
TOOTSIETOY 4654 farm tractor made in special version for Army Field battery set No. 5071, with cannons	32.50	48.75	65.00
TOOTSIETOY Box trailer and road-scraper raker, sold only in boxed set Farm Tractor No. 7003	67.50	101.25	135.00
TOOTSIETOY 6665 Ford Model A sedan, 1928, in catalog 1929-1933	20.00	30.00	40.00
TOOTSIETOY 101 Buick coupe (see no. 4656), 1930, in catalog 1932-1934	7.50	11.25	15.00
TOOTSIETOY 102 Buick roadster, 1930, in catalog 1932-1934	5.00	7.50	10.00
TOOTSIETOY 103 Buick sedan (see no. 4657) 1930, in catalog 1932-1934	5.00	7.50	10.00
TOOTSIETOY 104 Mack insurance patrol (see 4658), in catalog 1932-1934	10.00	15.00	20.00

TOOTSIETOY 105 Mack	G	VG	M	TOOTSIETOY 109 Ford?	G	VG	M
tank truck, in catalog				stake pick-up truck, in			
1932-1934	10.00	15.00	20.00	catalog 1932-1934	12.50	18.75	25.00
TOOTSIETOY 198 Cater-				TOOTSIETOY 110			
pillar tractor, in catalog				Bluebird I Daytona			
1932-1934	10.00	15.00	20.00	record car, 1927, in			
				catalog 1932-1934	10.00	15.00	20.00

In the 1933 catalog, rubber tires were introduced, and many earlier models became available with optional rubber tires. Their catalog number was then preceded by the digit "0", so that the "Yellow Cab" with rubber tires, for example, was designated as 04629. New models with rubber tires only were also shown with a prefix of "0", so that the 1932 Macks, Grahams, etc., are thus listed below. However, all "0" prefixes were dropped in the 1937 and later catalogs. Also in the 1933 catalog, use of the new alloy (Zamac) was announced. Earlier models had been of lead and lead alloys. Some lead contamination in later castings resulted in the deterioration of the zamac. Lead-free zamac endures well.

	G	VG	M		G	VG	M
TOOTSIETOY 0191 Mack				TOOTSIETOY 0805 Mack			
dumper train, 3 carts,				"Tootsietoy Dairy" semi-			
1932 in catalog				trailer truck, 1932, in			
1933-1941	45.00	67.50	90.00	catalog 1933-1939	30.00	45.00	60.00
TOOTSIETOY 0192 Mack				TOOTSIETOY 0806			
"Tootsietoy Dairy" train				Graham wrecker, 1932,			
semi-trailer plus two full				in catalog 1933-1939	17.50	26.25	35.00
trailers, 1932, in catalog				TOOTSIETOY 0807			
1933-1941	55.00	82.50	110.00	delivery motorcycle			
TOOTSIETOY 0198 Mack				(adapted from 5103), in			
car transport (three				catalog 1933-34	32.50	48.75	65.00
Fords), 1932, in catalog				TOOTSIETOY 0808			
1935-1941	47.50	71.25	95.00	Graham "Tootsietoy			
TOOTSIETOY 0801 Mack				Dairy" van, 1932, in			
"Express" stake semi-				catalog 1933-1938	35.00	52.50	70.00
trailer, 1932, in catalog				TOOTSIETOY Graham			
1933-1941	22.50	33.75	45.00	"Commercial Tire &			
TOOTSIETOY 0802 Mack				Supply Co." delivery van			
"Domaco" tank semi-				was sold only in sets.			
trailer, 1932, in catalog				05300 set is shown in			
1933-1939	30.00	45.00	60.00	1935 catalog	45.00	67.50	90.00
TOOTSIETOY 0803 Mack				TOOTSIETOY 0809			
"Long Distance Hauling",				Graham ambulance,			
cargo van, semi-trailer,				1932, in catalog			
1932, in catalog				1935-1941	35.00	52.50	70.00
1933-1936, tin top	35.00	52.50	70.00	TOOTSIETOY 0810 Mack			
TOOTSIETOY 0804 "City				"Railway Express Co."			
Fuel Co.", ten-wheel				van (with Wrigley's ad),			
truck, 1932, in catalog				1932, in catalog			
1933-1935	35.00	52.50	70.00	1935-1939	35.00	52.50	70.00
TOOTSIETOY 0804 "City							
Fuel", four wheels only,							
in catalog 1936-1938	37.50	56.25	75.00				

The larger 1932 Macks were first issued in two-piece castings and dual wheels. In 1936 they were issued as one-piece castings with single rear wheels, worth about $10 less in mint. The tractor for the dumper train was never cast in the later one-piece (set 0191), and the car transport (0198) was never issued in the earlier two-piece casting. TOOT-SIETOY Graham Series: There were several minor changes in chassis castings. Initially, there were none without spare tire on either the sides or the rear. The "convertible" coupes and sedans listed below are castings identical to the non-convertible coupe and sedan, but painted two-toned with tan top. The same applies to the later 1934 Fords and 1935 LaSalles.

	G	VG	M

TOOTSIETOY 0511
Graham roadster, five-wheel, 1932, in catalog 1933-1935 . . . . — 37.50 56.25 75.00

TOOTSIETOY 0512
Graham coupe, five-wheel, 1932, in catalog 1933-1935 . . . . — 27.50 41.25 55.00

TOOTSIETOY 0513
Graham sedan, five-wheel, 1932, in catalog 1933-1935 . . . . — 27.50 41.25 55.00

TOOTSIETOY 0514
Graham convertible coupe, five-wheel, 1932, in catalog 1933-1935 . . . . — 30.00 45.00 60.00

TOOTSIETOY 0515
Graham convertible sedan, five-wheel, 1932, in catalog 1933-1935 . . . . — 30.00 45.00 60.00

TOOTSIETOY 0516
Graham town car, five-wheel, 1932, in catalog 1933-1935 . . . . — 37.50 56.25 75.00

TOOTSIETOY 0611
Graham roadster, six-wheel, 1932, in catalog 1933-1935 . . . . — 40.00 60.00 80.00

TOOTSIETOY 0612
Graham coupe, six-wheel, 1932, in catalog 1933-1935 . . . . — 30.00 45.00 60.00

TOOTSIETOY 0613
Graham sedan, six-wheel, 1932, in catalog 1933-1935 . . . . — 30.00 45.00 60.00

TOOTSIETOY 0614
Graham convertible coupe, six-wheel, 1932, in catalog 1933-1935 . . . . . . — 32.50 48.75 65.00

TOOTSIETOY 0615
Graham convertible sedan, six-wheel, 1932, in catalog 1933-1935 . . . . . . — 32.50 48.75 65.00

TOOTSIETOY 0616
Graham town car, six-wheel, 1932 in catalog 1933-1935 . . . . — 37.50 56.25 75.00

TOOTSIETOY (number not known) Graham roadster, four-wheel, 1932 . . . . — 45.00 67.50 90.00

TOOTSIETOY (number not known) Graham coupe, four-wheel, 1932, in catalog 1935?-1939 (Build-A-Car) . . . . — 27.50 41.25 55.00

TOOTSIETOY (number not known) Graham sedan, four-wheel, 1932, in catalog 1935?-1939 (Build-A-Car) . . . . — 25.00 37.50 50.00

TOOTSIETOY 0712
LaSalle coupe, 1935, in catalog 1936-1938 . . . . . . — 55.00 82.50 110.00

TOOTSIETOY 0713
LaSalle sedan, 1935, in catalog 1936-1938 . . . . . . — 55.00 82.50 110.00

TOOTSIETOY 0714
LaSalle convertible coupe, 1935, in catalog 1936 only . . . . — 57.50 86.25 115.00

TOOTSIETOY 0715
LaSalle convertible sedan, 1935, in catalog 1936 only . . . . — 57.50 86.25 115.00

TOOTSIETOY 0716 (Briggs Lincoln) prototype "Doodlebug", 1933, in catalog 1936-1937 . . . . . . — 30.00 45.00 60.00

TOOTSIETOY 6015 Lincoln (only the grille is accurate, the rest of the body being the same as the Briggs prototype, which was never publicly sold) Zephyr, 1936, in catalog 1937-1939 . . . . . . — 75.00 112.50 150.00

TOOTSIETOY 6016 Lincoln wrecker, 1936, in catalog 1937-1938 . . . . . . — 100.00 150.00 200.00

TOOTSIETOY Ford Series: The coupe and sedan in single color and convertible versions and the wrecker were issued in 1935 as 1934 Fords, having a separate grill-piece like the Grahams, the rubber tires mounted on metal hubs. The following year they were recast in one piece as 1935 Fords with slight changes also to the hood louvres and fender skirts and fitted with solid rubber wheels. The roadster, pick-up truck, etc., were not in the 1934 series.

C.B.C. LEE

	G	VG	M		G	VG	M
TOOTSIETOY 0111 Ford V-8 sedan, 1934, in catalog 1935 only	22.50	33.75	45.00	1935-1936	10.00	15.00	20.00
TOOTSIETOY 0111 Ford V-8 sedan, 1935, in catalog 1936-1939	12.50	18.75	25.00	TOOTSIETOY 0118 DeSota Airflow sedan, 1935, in catalog 1935-1939	17.50	26.25	35.00
TOOTSIETOY 0112 Ford V-8 coupe, 1934, in catalog 1935 only	22.50	33.75	45.00	TOOTSIETOY 0120 Oil Tank Truck, in catalog 1936-1939	12.50	18.75	25.00
TOOTSIETOY 0112 Ford V-8 coupe, 1935, in catalog 1936-1939	12.50	18.75	25.00	TOOTSIETOY 0121 Ford pick-up truck, 1935, in catalog 1936-1939	12.50	18.75	25.00
TOOTSIETOY 0113 Ford V-8 wrecker, 1934, in catalog 1935 only	27.50	41.25	55.00	TOOTSIETOY 0123 Ford "Special Delivery van, 1936, in catalog 1937-1939	15.00	22.50	30.00
TOOTSIETOY 0113 Ford V-8 wrecker, 1935, in catalog 1936-1941	15.00	22.50	30.00				

This "camelback" van was also issued in several custom liveries by use of a tin-plate insert on the side panels. Price on these in mint condition is $5 and up. - C.B.C. LEE

	G	VG	M		G	VG	M
TOOTSIETOY 0114 Ford V-8 convertible coupe, 1934, in catalog 1935 only	25.00	37.50	50.00	TOOTSIETOY 1006 "Standard" oil truck, in catalog from 1939 to at least 1941	15.00	22.50	30.00
TOOTSIETOY 0115 Ford V-8 convertible sedan, 1934, in catalog 1935 only	25.00	37.50	50.00	TOOTSIETOY 1007 "Sinclair" oil truck, in catalog from 1939 to at least 1941	15.00	22.50	30.00
TOOTSIETOY 180 set, Lincoln Zephyr and Roamer house-trailer issued in 1938 with clockwork motor, in 1939 without motor, 1936, in catalog 1938-1939	150.00	225.00	300.00	TOOTSIETOY 1008 "Texaco" oil truck, in catalog from 1939 to at least 1941	15.00	22.50	30.00
TOOTSIETOY 187 Mack car transport (up-tilted), 1932, in catalog 1941	87.50	131.25	175.00	TOOTSIETOY 1009 "Shell" oil truck, in catalog from 1939 to at least 1941	15.00	22.50	30.00
TOOTSIETOY 4634 Army supply truck (adapted from 1042), in catalog 1939-1941	27.50	41.25	55.00	TOOTSIETOY 1010 "Wrigley" box van, in catalog from 1940 to at least 1941	25.00	37.50	50.00
TOOTSIETOY 4635 Armored Car, in catalog from 1938 to at least 1941	22.50	33.75	45.00	TOOTSIETOY 1011 Farm tractor, in catalog 1941	25.00	37.50	50.00
TOOTSIETOY 0116 Ford V-8 roadster, 1935, in catalog 1936-1939	15.00	22.50	30.00	TOOTSIETOY 1016 (Auburn) roadster "torpedo", 1934, in catalog 1936 to at least 1941	6.50	9.75	13.00
TOOTSIETOY 0117 Zephyr railcar, in catalog				TOOTSIETOY 1017 torpedo coupe, in catalog from 1936 to at least 1941	5.00	7.50	10.00

	G	VG	M
TOOTSIETOY 1018 torpedo sedan, in catalog from 1936 to at least 1941	5.50	8.25	11.00
TOOTSIETOY 1019 pick-up truck, in catalog from 1936 to at least 1941	5.50	8.25	11.00
TOOTSIETOY Greyhound bus (see 1045), in catalog 1941	15.00	22.50	30.00
TOOTSIETOY (no number known) Transamerica bus, in set only, in 1941 catalog	60.00	90.00	120.00
TOOTSIETOY 1027 wrecker, in catalog 1938-1941	5.00	7.50	10.00
TOOTSIETOY 1040 hook & ladder, in catalog 1937-1941	22.50	33.75	45.00
TOOTSIETOY 1041 hose car, in catalog 1937-1941	20.00	30.00	40.00
TOOTSIETOY 1042 Insurance patrol with open rear, in catalog 1937-1938	20.00	30.00	40.00
TOOTSIETOY 1042 Insurance patrol with single rear ladder and rear fireman in catalog 1939-1941	22.50	33.75	45.00
TOOTSIETOY 1043 Ford and small house trailer, 11935, in catalog 1937-1941	25.00	37.50	50.00
TOOTSIETOY 1044 Roamer house-trailer (see 180 set), in catalog 1937 only	42.50	63.75	85.00
TOOTSIETOY 1045 Greyhound deluxe bus, 1935, in catalog 1937 to at least 1941	15.00	22.50	30.00
TOOTSIETOY 1046 station wagon, circa 1939, in catalog 1940 to at least 1941	17.50	26.25	35.00
TOOTSIETOY 230 (LaSalle) sedan, circa 1939, in catalog 1940 to at least 1941	7.50	11.25	15.00
TOOTSIETOY 231 coupe, circa 1939, in catalog 1940 to at least 1941 . . .	7.50	11.25	15.00
TOOTSIETOY 232 open touring car, circa 1939, in catalog from 1940 to at least 1941	7.50	11.25	15.00
TOOTSIETOY 233 boat-tail roadster, circa 1939, in catalog from 1940 to at least 1941	7.50	11.25	15.00
TOOTSIETOY 234 box van, in catalog from 1940 to at least 1941 . . .	7.50	11.25	15.00
TOOTSIETOY 235 oil tank truck, in catalog from 1940 to at least 1941	7.50	11.25	15.00
TOOTSIETOY 236 fire engine, hook & ladder, in catalog from 1940 to at least 1941	7.50	11.25	15.00
TOOTSIETOY 237 fire engine, insurance patrol, in catalog from 1940 to at least 1941	7.50	11.25	15.00
TOOTSIETOY 238 fire engine, hose wagon, in catalog from 1940 to at least 1941	7.50	11.25	15.00
TOOTSIETOY 239 station wagon, circa 1939, in catalog from 1940 to at least 1941	7.50	11.25	15.00

TOOTSIETOY 260 Paramount Air-N-Lite taxi "Yellow", 261 Paramount Air-N-Lite taxi "Checker", 262 fire engine and 263 hook & ladder were a "Giant Series", shown in 1941 catalog but never released.

End of List by C.B.C. LEE

POST-WAR TOOTSIETOYS

	G	VG	M
American La France Pumper, 3", 1954......	4.00	6.00	8.00
Austin-Healy 100-6 4-passenger roadster, 1956, 6"..............	9.00	13.50	18.00
Austin-Healy 100-6, 1955, 9"...................	No Price Found		
Buick Century Estate Wagon, 1954, 6".......	7.00	10.50	14.00
Buick LeSabre Experimental Roadster, 1951, 6"......	5.00	7.50	10.00
Buick Roadmaster 4-door sedan, 1949, 6"........	No Price Found		
Buick special experimental coupe, 1954, 6"........	15.00	22.50	30.00
Buick Special Fastback, 1947, 4"..............	20.00	30.00	40.00
Buick Super Estate station wagon, 1948, 6".......	6.00	9.00	12.00
Buick Y Experimental Roadster, 4", 1938 (postwar release)........	15.00	22.50	30.00
Cadillac 60 special 4-door sedan, 1948, 6".......	10.50	15.75	21.00
Cadillac 62 4-door sedan, 6", 1954..............	10.00	15.00	20.00
Caterpillar Bulldozer, 1956, 6"...................	5.00	7.50	10.00
Same as above, with blade.	6.00	9.00	12.00
Caterpillar Scraper 1956, 6"	5.00	7.50	10.00
Chevrolet Bel Air four door sedan, 3", 1955.....	3.00	4.50	6.00
Chevrolet Cameo Pickup, 4", 1956..............	5.50	8.25	11.00
Chevrolet Deluxe Panel Truck, 1950, 4".......	6.50	9.75	13.00
Same as above, as Army Ambulance...........	10.00	15.00	20.00
Chevrolet Deluxe Panel Truck, 1950, 3", civilian.	4.00	6.00	8.00
Chevrolet El Camino camper truck with boat atop, 1960, 6"........	No Price Found		
Chevrolet El Camino pickup truck, 1960, 6"........	4.50	6.75	9.00
Chevrolet Fleetline 2-door sedan, 1950 fastback, 3".	5.00	7.50	10.00
Chevrolet Semi with Gooseneck Trailer, 6", 1959	No Price Found		
Chrysler New Yorker 4-door sedan, 1953, 6"..	5.00	7.50	10.00
Chrysler 300 2-door hard-top, 1955, 6".........	7.50	11.25	15.00

	G	VG	M
Chrysler Thunderbolt experimental roadster, 1942, (postwar) 6"..........	13.00	19.50	26.00
Chrysler Windsor convertible, 1941 (released postwar), 4"..........	2.00	3.00	4.00
Chrysler Windsor convertible, 1950, 6".........	5.00	7.50	10.00
Chrysler Windsor convertible, 1960, 4".........	5.00	7.50	10.00
Corvette Roadster, 1954-55, 4"...................	4.50	6.75	9.00
Dodge D100 Panel Truck, 6", 1956..............	6.00	9.00	12.00
Dodge Pickup Truck, 1950, 4"...................	7.50	11.25	15.00
Ferrari Racer, 6", 1956....	3.25	4.88	6.50
Ford B Hot Rod, 1931 (made 1960), 3"........	3.50	5.25	7.00
Ford C600 Oil Tanker, 1956, 3"..............	3.50	5.25	7.00
Ford C600 Truck, 1962, 6"	3.25	4.88	6.50
Ford Country Sedan Station Wagon, 6", 1959.......	7.00	10.50	14.00
Ford Country Sedan Station Wagon, 1960, 3".......	4.00	6.00	8.00
Ford Country Sedan Station Wagon, 1962, 6".......	7.00	10.50	14.00
Ford Custom Convertible, 3", 1949.............	4.00	6.00	8.00
Ford Custom 4-door sedan, 1949, 3".............	6.00	9.00	12.00
Ford Customline V-8 2-door sedan, 3", 1955........	1.75	2.62	3.50
Ford Econoline Pickup, 1962, 6"..............	7.00	10.50	14.00
Ford F1 Pickup, 1949, 3"..	3.50	5.25	7.00
Ford F6 Oil Tanker, 1949, 6"...................	1.00	1.50	2.00
Ford F6 Oil Tanker, 4", 1949	4.50	6.75	9.00
Ford F6 Stake Truck, 4", 1949 (no stakes, looks like long pickup).......	5.50	8.25	11.00
Ford F100 Styleside Pickup, 3", with rear window, 1957	4.50	6.75	9.00
Same as above, without rear window	No Price Found		
Ford F-600 Stake Truck with tin cover, 1955, 6".	10.00	15.00	20.00
Ford Fairlane 500 convertible, 1957, 3"..........	4.00	6.00	8.00

	G	VG	M		G	VG	M
Ford Falcon, two-door sedan, 1960, 3"	3.00	4.50	6.00	Jeep CJ5, 1960, 6"	4.50	6.75	9.00
Ford Farm Tractor, 1956, 6"	No Price Found			Same as above, Army version	5.00	7.50	10.00
Ford LTD 2-door hardtop, 4", 1960 (last metal Tootsietoy)	No Price Found			Same as above, snowplow version	No Price Found		
				Jeepster, 1947, 3"	5.00	7.50	10.00
Ford Mainline four-door sedan, 1952, 3"	5.00	7.50	10.00	Kaiser Sedan, 6", 1947....	13.50	20.25	27.00
				Lancia Racer, 1956, 6" ...	4.00	6.00	8.00
Ford Ranch Wagon, 1954, 4"	6.00	9.00	12.00	Lincoln Capri 2-door hardtop, 1952, 6"	5.50	8.25	11.00
Ford Ranch Wagon, 1954, 3"	3.50	5.25	7.00	Mack B Line, 1955, 6", Cement Mixer...........	6.50	9.75	13.00
Ford Special Deluxe convertible, 1940 (sold 1960), 6"	5.00	7.50	10.00	Same as above, Hook and Ladder	17.50	26.25	35.00
Ford V-8 Hot Rod, 1940 (made 1960), 6"	4.50	6.75	9.00	Same as above, Moving....	5.00	7.50	10.00
				Same as above, Log.......	No Price Found		
GMC 3571 Greyhound Bus, 1948, 6"	6.00	9.00	12.00	Same as above, Oil	10.00	15.00	20.00
				Same as above, Open Stake	6.50	9.75	13.00
GMC Greyhound Scenicruiser Bus, 1957, 6"	4.50	6.75	9.00	Same as above, Pipe......	No Price Found		
Hook and Ladder Truck, No. 1040 (postwar release), 4"	9.00	13.50	18.00	Mack L-Line Dump, 1947, 6"	3.50	5.25	7.00
Hose Car No. 1041 (postwar), 4"	15.00	22.50	30.00	Mack L-Line Fire Pumper, 6", 1947..............	10.00	15.00	20.00
International K1 panel, truck, 1941, 4" (postwar release)	4.00	6.00	8.00	Mack L-Line with fire trailer (ladder), 1947, 6".	5.00	7.50	10.00
International K11 Oil Tanker, 1946, 6"	7.00	10.50	14.00	Mack L-Line Truck, 6", 1947, Log	No Price Found		
International Metro Van, 1960, 6"	No Price Found			Same as above, Moving Van..................	4.00	6.00	8.00
International RC 180, 1955, 6", gooseneck Army version with launcher......	5.00	7.50	10.00	Same as above, Pipe......	No Price Found		
				Same as above, Stake, closed side............	5.00	7.50	10.00
Same as above, gooseneck..	4.50	6.75	9.00	Same as above, stake trailer	10.00	15.00	20.00
Same as above, grain trailer	5.00	7.50	10.00	Same as above, "Tootsietoys Coast to Coast" trailer truck.................	5.00	7.50	10.00
Same as above, oil........	4.00	6.00	8.00				
Same as above, moving van	6.50	9.75	13.00	Same as above, Tow......	7.50	11.25	15.00
Same as above, boat transport	No Price Found			Mercedes 190SL Coupe, 1956, 6"	15.00	22.50	30.00
Same as above, car transport	4.00	6.00	8.00	Mercedes 300 SL Gullwing Coupe, 1955, 9"........	No Price Found		
Jaguar type D 1957, 3"....	4.00	6.00	8.00	Mercury custom sedan, four-door, 1952, 4".........	4.00	6.00	8.00
Jaguar XK120 roadster, 3", 1954	5.50	8.25	11.00	Mercury Fire Chief car, 1949, 4".............	4.00	6.00	8.00
Jaguar XK 140 coupe, 1956, 6"	7.00	10.50	14.00	Mercury Sedan, four-door, 1949, 4".............	8.00	12.00	16.00
				Metro Van, HO series.....	11.00	16.50	22.00
Jeep, CJ3, Army version, 4", 1950.............	4.00	6.00	8.00	MG TF roadster, 6", 1954.	6.00	9.00	12.00
				Same as above, 3".......	5.00	7.50	10.00
Same as above, civilian version	5.00	7.50	10.00	Nash Metropolitan Convertible, 3", 1954.........	5.00	7.50	10.00
Same as above, 3", Army..	3.00	4.50	6.00	Offenhauser Hill Climber Racer, 1947, 3"	3.50	5.25	7.00
Same as above, 3", Civilian.	3.00	4.50	6.00				

	G	VG	M
Oldsmobile 88 convertible, 4", 1949	17.50	26.25	35.00
Oldsmobile Dynamic 88 convertible, 6", 1959	4.50	6.75	9.00
Oldsmobile 98 Holiday 2-door hardtop, 1955, army version, 4"	5.00	7.50	10.00
Same as above, civilian version	4.00	6.00	8.00
Packard Patrician 4-door sedan, 1956, 6"	7.50	11.25	15.00
Plymouth Belvedere 2-door hardtop, 1957, 3"	3.50	5.25	7.00
Plymouth Special Deluxe 4-door Sedan 3", 1950	4.00	6.00	8.00
Pontiac Chieftain Deluxe Coupe Sedan, 4", 1950	No Price Found		
Pontiac Chieftain Fire Chief Coupe Sedan, 4"	12.00	18.00	24.00
Pontiac Safari Station Wagon, 2-door, 1955, 9"	4.00	6.00	8.00
Pontiac Star Chief 4-door sedan, 1959, 4"	4.50	6.75	9.00
Porsche Spyder Roadster, 1956, 6"	7.00	10.50	14.00
Rambler Super Cross-Country 6-cylinder station wagon, 4", 1960	4.50	6.75	9.00
School Bus, HO series	5.00	7.50	10.00
Studebaker Champion Coupe, 1947	9.00	13.50	18.00
Studebaker Lark custom convertible, 3", 1960	5.00	7.50	10.00
Thunderbird Coupe, 4", 1955	3.25	4.38	6.50
Thunderbird Coupe, 3", 1955	3.25	4.38	6.50
Triumph TR3 Roadster, 3", 1956	3.50	5.25	7.00
Twin Coach Bus, 1950, 3"	No Price Found		
Volskwagen 113 Beetle, 1960, 6"	3.50	5.25	7.00
Same as above, 3"	2.00	3.00	4.00
White Army Half Track, 1941 (postwar), 4"	6.00	9.00	12.00

END POSTWAR TOOTSIETOY LISTING

L to R: TOOTSIETOY Herbie & Smitty motorcycle and sidecar. TOOTSIETOY Andy Gump in Roadster. Courtesy PB Eighty-Four, New York

Tow Truck, cast iron, 6" long.
Courtesy Mapes Auctioneers & Appraisers

L to R: TOOTSIETOY Moon Mullins Police Patrol Car. TOOTSIETOY Uncle Willie and Mamie in Boat. TOOTSIETOY Kayo Ice Truck.
Courtesy PB Eighty-Four, New York

	G	VG	M
Touring car, tin, friction, 6"	10.00	15.00	20.00
Touring car, tin and wooden friction drive, with cast iron driver and two cast iron women, 10½" long.	100.00	150.00	200.00
Tow truck, cast iron, 6" long	30.00	45.00	60.00
Tow truck, cast iron, 7½", rubber wheels	75.00	112.50	150.00
Tractor, cast iron, 3"	40.00	60.00	80.00
Tractor, cast iron with wooden wheels, 4"	9.00	13.50	18.00
Tractor, cast iron with driver, 4½" long	32.00	48.00	64.00
Tractor with front loader and driver, cast iron, rubber wheels, 9½" long	200.00	300.00	400.00
Trailer truck, wooden, plastic wheels, "Coast to Coast Fast Freight", approx. 8¼" long	3.00	4.50	6.00
Trailer Truck Cab, slush cast, possibly METAL CAST, late 1930s	1.00	1.50	2.00
Trailer Truck "C to C C Co.", circa 1929, approx. 6¾" long	20.00	30.00	40.00
TRAVELEER Land Coach Traveler, Trailer Co. L.A., 1927	80.00	120.00	160.00

66

	G	VG	M
Truck, cast iron, flat back, 1920s, approx. 4¼" long, looks like Model A Ford semi-tractor	17.00	25.50	34.00
Truck, open back, 4¼" long, cast iron, wheels marked "Hamilton Corhart"	15.00	22.50	30.00
Truck cab with interchangeable flat bed and tank, sheet metal with wooden wheels, 10¾"	7.00	10.50	14.00
TURNER Bulldog mac closed cab dump truck, red and green steel, 23" long	70.00	105.00	140.00
TURNER Dump, friction, 15½" long, circa early 1930s	90.00	135.00	180.00
TURNER Fire Engine Pumper, 15" long	22.00	33.00	44.00
TURNER Hook and ladder, 15" long, circa 1930s	40.00	60.00	80.00
TURNER Lincoln Sedan, 26" long	600.00	900.00	1200.00
TURNER Packard Roadster, 16½" long, 1920s	200.00	300.00	400.00
TURNER Speedster, 1920s, 17" long, circa late 1920s, early 1930s	110.00	165.00	220.00
Two-door sedan, slung-back cab, 1930s, slush-mold die cast, white rubber tires	5.00	7.50	10.00
"U.S.A." US Army Truck, 1935 Ford, rubber, approx. 4¾" long	10.00	15.00	20.00
"U.S. Army Shooting Tank", 6" wood, pre WW II, 6" long, metal action	4.00	6.00	8.00
U.S. Army truck, boat, and cement carrier, three pieces	3.00	4.50	6.00
U.S.A.W. No. 60118 half-track, black wooden wheels, die-cast, approx. 4¾"	3.50	5.25	7.00
Van "Bamberger's", early with driver, "Market, Halsey & Washington Sts." (may have been TOOTSIETOY)	900.00	1350.00	1800.00
Van, "Strawbridge & Clothier", early "Eighth & Market Sts." &may have been TOOTSIETOY)	600.00	900.00	1200.00

	G	VG	M
VINDEX hay loader	42.50	63.75	85.00
VINDEX "P&H" power shovel, cast iron, 12" (17" extended), wheels in caterpillar base, handle revolves rig	400.00	600.00	800.00
VINDEX Racer, cast iron, "2", 11½" long, circa 1920s	100.00	150.00	200.00
WEEDEN Auto, live steam, 8¾", early	250.00	375.00	500.00
WEEDEN steam road roller, 1920s, 7" long, brass, tin, cast iron, steam toy fired by alcohol	80.00	120.00	160.00
WILKENS fire engine, circa 1900, with driver, steam boiler	50.00	75.00	100.00
WILKENS, Olds, 1904, curved dash, wind-up, 10"	600.00	900.00	1200.00
WILLIAMS Car Carrier, with three Austins	120.00	180.00	240.00
WILLIAMS Coupe, rumble seat, side mounts, 1930, cast iron, rubber tires, 6¾" long	50.00	75.00	100.00
WILLIAMS "Gasoline" truck, circa 1920, 5½" long, cast iron	26.00	39.00	52.00
WILLIAMS Lincoln Touring Car, 7" long	70.00	105.00	140.00
WILLIAMS Model T Coupe, 6" long	66.00	99.00	132.00
WILLIAMS Racer, boat-tailed, 6½" long	90.00	135.00	180.00
WILLIAMS Sedan, circa 1930, cast iron, 6½" long, streamlined rear fender	115.00	172.50	230.00
WILLIAMS Steamroller, 5½", 1930s	34.00	51.00	68.00
Willys Knight, cast iron, 8" long, 1920s, with driver	50.00	75.00	100.00
WOLVERINE "Mystery Car", press down to make car move, circa 1938	50.00	75.00	100.00
WOLVERINE Speeding Bus "5 Via Main St." tin litho, driver and occupants, 14" long, "19302", press down on rear to move	24.00	36.00	48.00
Wrecker, cast iron, circa 1933, approx. 4¾" long	19.00	28.50	38.00

WYANDOTTE, officially known as the All Metal Products Company, was located, before World War II, in Wyandotte, Michigan. It appears to have begun its toy manufacturing in the 1920s with pistols and pop guns, moving into vehicle production in 1935. During the War it made clips for the M-1 rifle, and after the War moved to Piqua, Ohio, going out of business in 1956.

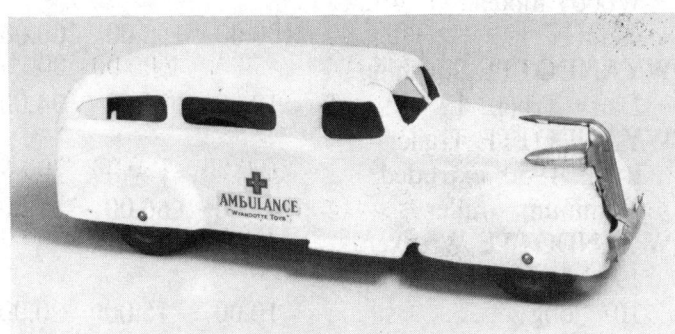

WYANDOTTE "Ambulance"
Courtesy Mapes Auctioneers & Appraisers

WYANDOTTE Stake Truck, 10" long, battery-operated headlights.
Courtesy Mapes Auctineers & Appraisers

WYANDOTTE Circus Truck, 10¾"

	G	VG	M
WYANDOTTE Ambulance, 11¼" long, swinging rear door	41.00	61.50	82.00
WYANDOTTE Army Truck, 10" long, steel with wood wheels	12.50	18.75	25.00
WYANDOTTE boattail racer, 8½" long, steel, red with white rubber tires, electric headlamps	20.00	30.00	40.00
WYANDOTTE Circus Truck, 10¾" long	55.00	77.50	110.00

	G	VG	M
WYANDOTTE Circus Truck No. 503, 11" long	65.00	97.50	130.00
WYANDOTTE Coffin Nose Cord, 13" long, pressed steel, rubber tires	140.00	210.00	280.00
WYANDOTTE Coupe, 2-door, about 1930, 6"	12.00	18.00	24.00
WYANDOTTE Coupe, 6", circa 1940	5.00	7.50	10.00
WYANDOTTE Coupe, circa 1935, red with white rubber tires, electric headlights, 8½" long	25.00	37.50	50.00
WYANDOTTE Dump Truck, 6", 1930s	10.00	15.00	20.00
WYANDOTTE Dump Truck, pressed steel, approx. 6½" long, circa 1940	12.00	18.00	24.00
WYANDOTTE Dump Truck, steel, 7" long, circa 1937	13.00	19.50	26.00
WYANDOTTE Dump Truck, 12"	12.00	18.00	24.00
WYANDOTTE Dump Truck, circa mid-1930s, 15" long, white rubber tires	65.00	97.00	130.00
WYANDOTTE Dump Truck, 1930s, 12½" long	16.00	24.00	32.00
WYANDOTTE "Express" trailer truck, tin wheels	15.00	22.50	30.00
WYANDOTTE Fire Truck, 12", with ladder, ringing bell	12.00	18.00	24.00
WYANDOTTE Ice Truck, marked "ICE" on sides, circa 1940	25.00	37.50	50.00
WYANDOTTE LaSalle car with trailer, 25½" long, 1930s	44.00	66.00	88.00
WYANDOTTE Pickup Truck, 6" long, circa late 1930s	12.00	18.00	24.00
WYANDOTTE Race Car, 8½" long, pressed steel, rubber tires, circa 1937	25.00	37.50	50.00
WYANDOTTE School Bus, 1930s, 24" long	40.00	60.00	80.00
WYANDOTTE Sedan, 6", circa 1940	10.00	15.00	20.00

	G	VG	M
WYANDOTTE Sedan & House Trailer, 25½" long, pressed steel, circa 1939	90.00	135.00	180.00
trailer alone	20.00	30.00	40.00
WYANDOTTE Sedan, streamlined (looks like LaSalle), 15"	150.00	225.00	300.00
WYANDOTTE Semi-trailer Stake Truck "Valley Farms Livestock Produce" 2-piece, 8½" long, 1940s	20.00	30.00	40.00
WYANDOTTE Stake Truck, 5½" long, rubber wheels	11.00	16.50	22.00
WYANDOTTE Stake Truck about 1930, 6¾".	9.50	14.25	19.00
WYANDOTTE Stake Truck 1930s, 7½", white rubber wheels	10.00	15.00	20.00
WYANDOTTE Stake Truck, 10" long, battery-operated headlights	17.00	25.50	34.00
WYANDOTTE Stake Truck, 12" long, circa 1930s	26.00	39.00	52.00

	G	VG	M
WYANDOTTE Stake Truck, 20"	20.00	30.00	40.00
WYANDOTTE Station Wagon, Cadillac, 1941, Woody model, 21" long, metal	100.00	150.00	200.00
WYANDOTTE Sunshine Dairy Truck, 12"	17.00	25.50	34.00
WYANDOTTE Trailer truck, 1950, extruded aluminum trailer	44.00	66.00	88.00
WYANDOTTE Wrecker, 1930s, wooden wheels, 10" long	10.00	15.00	20.00
WYANDOTTE "Wyandottey", pressed steel two-door sedan, sweeping long fenders, circa WW II black plastic wheels	5.00	7.50	10.00
Yellow Cab, 1930s, 7½" long, white rubber tires, rear suitcast rack	290.00	345.00	580.00
Yellow Cab, cast iron, with driver, 7¾" long	110.00	165.00	220.00
Yellow Cab, 9" long, cast iron	100.00	150.00	200.00

ANIMAL-DRAWN

The average mint price in this section in the last edition was $338.07, with the average mint price in this edition $354.19, an increase of 5%.

In this category, the toys generally commanding the highest prices are horse-drawn cast iron pieces. One reason for the eye-opening prices is that horse-drawn cast iron toys have considerable value apart from their lure as toys. There is an air of genuine Americana about them, and they are likely to attract the interest of many who otherwise pay no attention to toys (decorators figure largely in this area).

Since prices are often so high, reproductions, whether honest or dishonest, can be a problem. Things to look for when a reproduction is suspected include a rougher surface than an old toy would have (recastings are invariably rougher), uneven fit of pieces, a blurring of details, and "aging" that doesn't have the patina of age. Since at least one company, John Wright (formerly Grey Iron), is still manufacturing turn-of-the-century horse-drawn vehicles, some of them from the original molds, it is wise to become familiar with the field before investing heavily.

CONDITION OF A TOY AND ITS RELATION TO PRICE

The price of a toy depends not only on its desirability, but on its condition. A toy in mint condition is generally worth twice what that same toy would bring in good condition, with "very good" falling about equally in between good and mint.

"Mint" means just that; the condition in which it was originally issued — perfect, regardless of age, not the slightest blemish. Needless to say this is a fairly rare state of affairs, but enough toys exist in mint condition to make it an employable term. Many people hoping to dispose of toys are tempted to call an item "mint" when it is really "near mint", "very good", or sometimes just "good". Inevitably this can result in unhappiness all around, and not infrequently, a cancelled sale.

"Good" signals a toy that has seen considerable wear, shows its age, but is basically sound. A collector will collect it, but will often not be wholly satisfied with it as an example of his collection, and thus prices are often drastically below that which the same item in mint can command.

Condition below good results in another drastic drop in price, and toys with missing parts, although otherwise in excellent condition, will usually fall into this lower-priced category. Rust, even small spots of it, can seriously lower the price of a toy. "Near-Mint", "Very Fine", "Fine" and similar terms often found in sellers' descriptions denote conditions between Mint and Very Good, and are priced accordingly.

The key to grading is to avoid wishful thinking. Grading can sometimes be a problem for the uninitiated, but common sense will usually prevail, and when possible, a consultation with an expert in the field can often clear up lingering doubts. A toy in its original box is worth up to 10 to 20% more if the box is in mint condition, with the price dropping as its condition lessens.

ANIMAL-DRAWN

	G	VG	M		G	VG	M
"ALDERNEY DAIRY" Milk Truck two-horse wood and lithographed paper	140.00	210.00	280.00	**ALTHOFF BERGMAN** Milk Cart, "Pure Milk", 14" long, c. 1880	430.00	645.00	860.00
ALL-NU Trotter, lead alloy, 1941, approx. 4" long	20.00	30.00	40..00	**ARCADE** (All ARCADE toys are cast iron) ARCADE Bakery wagon, 13"	200.00	300.00	400.00
				ARCADE "Big Six Circus & Wild West" wagon, 14½" long (see Movies - "Tom Mix Big Six Circus", appears to be the same except for name)	150.00	225.00	300.00
				ARCADE Cart, wicker, horse, driver, cast iron	66.00	99.00	132.00
				ARCADE Coal car with horse	35.00	52.50	70.00
				ARCADE Contractors Dump Wagon, 14" long, horse team, driver	66.00	99.00	132.00

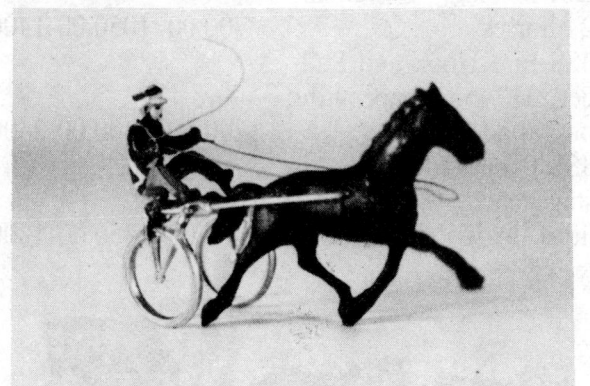

ALL-NU Trotter.
Photo by Bill Kaufman
Courtesy Evelyn Besser

ARCADE "Contractors Dump Wagon"
Courtesy Mapes Auctioneers & Appraisers

	G	VG	M
ARCADE "Contractors Dump Wagon", 13¼" two-horse driver, 1930s..	70.0	105.00	140.00
ARCADE Farm Wagon, two-horse, driver......	192.50	288.75	385.00
ARCADE McCormick Deering Farm Wagon, two-horse.............	90.00	135.00	180.00
ARCADE McCormick Deering manure spreader, with team of horses.....	50.00	75.00	100.00
ARCADE McCormick Spreader with team of horses...............	190.00	285.00	380.00

ARCADE McCormick Deering Spreader.

	G	VG	M
ARCADE Sulky plow, one horse, 10½"...........	70.00	105.00	140.00
Bakery Wagon, one horse, 13" long, cast iron.....	33.00	49.50	66.00
BARCLAY "Animal Cage" circus wagon, circa 1930s, lead and tin, approx. 9⅞" long, slush lead	20.00	30.00	40.00
BARCLAY Coach and Four, approx. 10¼" long, slush lead, circa 1930s...	40.00	60.00	80.00
BARCLAY Covered Wagon with oxen, under 6½" long, 1930s, "1849".....	30.00	45.00	60.00

BARCLAY Covered Wagon
Photo by Don Pielin

BARCLAY Coach and Four, approx. 10¼" long.
Photo by Bill Kaufman   Courtesy Evelyn Besser

	G	VG	M
"BARNUM AND BAILEY" circus cage, elephant drawn, 1930, painted, stained and litho wood, 35" long.......	330.00	495.00	660.00

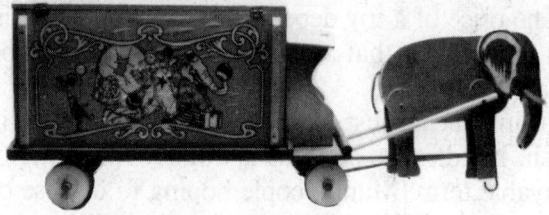

"Barnum and Bailey" Circus Cage, 35" long.
Courtesy Lloyd W. Ralston Auctions

	G	VG	M
BLISS Cinderella Coach, 1890, paper litho on wood, 26" long, 2 horses, 4 coachmen, lift off roof, blocks inside tell Cinderella story........	1700.00	2550.00	3400.00

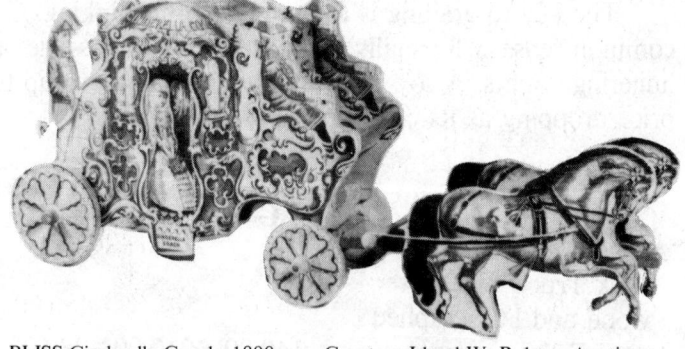

BLISS Cinderella Coach, 1890.   Courtesy Lloyd W. Ralston Auctions

	G	VG	M
BLISS Fire Hook and Ladder, 29" long, 2 firemen, 2 horses..............	700.00	1050.00	1400.00
BLISS Fire Hook and Ladder, 31" long, paper litho on wood..............	1200.00	1800.00	2400.00
BLISS Pansy 4 horse stagecoach, 1890, paper litho on wood, 31" long.	900.00	1350.00	1800.00

BLISS Pansy 4-horse stagecoach, 1890.Courtesy Lloyd W. Ralston Auctions

"Borden's Farm Products",	G	VG	M
wood, horse-drawn wagon pull-toy with articulated legs	40.00	60.00	80.00
Bread Wagon "Bread and Cakes" with driver, tin horse, 12½"	350.00	525.00	700.00
Brewery Wagon, cast iron and pressed steel, two horse with driver, 20½"	250.00	375.00	500.00
Buckboard, cast iron, 14" long, one horse and driver	100.00	150.00	200.00
Buggy, pressed steel, cast iron wheels and horse	20.00	30.00	40.00
Buggy with driver, cast iron, 6½" long	33.00	49.50	66.00
CARPENTER Cart, animated, pat. 1883, cast iron	120.00	180.00	240.00
CARPENTER Cart, two-wheel, one horse, no driver, pat. 1882	150.00	225.00	300.00
CARPENTER Dump Cart, 2-horse	150.00	225.00	300.00
CARPENTER Fire Patrol, cast iron, 2-horse, driver and 3 figures, 1885, 16½" long	312.50	468.75	625.00
CARPENTER Fire Wagon, one horse, one fireman	108.00	162.00	216.00
CARPENTER Hook and Ladder, cast iron, 2-horse, with driver and rear man, ladders, circa 1883-1890, 26½" long	200.00	300.00	400.00
CARPENTER Horse and carriage, 1880 painted cast iron, 14" long	130.00	195.00	260.00
CARPENTER Jog, cart, 2-horse, animated, cast iron	200.00	300.00	400.00

CARPENTER Horse and carriage, 1880, 14" long.
Courtesy Lloyd W. Ralston Auctions

CARPENTER Ox Cart, 2	G	VG	M
oxen, cast iron, circa 1880-1903, 11" long	100.00	150.00	200.00
CARPENTER Pumper, 2-horse, 18" long, No. 33	140.00	210.00	280.00
CARPENTER Tally Ho, 27½" long, 4-horse, cast iron, seven festive riders in coach	1700.00	2550.00	3400.00
CARPENTER Wagon, 2-wheel, prancing horse and driver, 11" long	80.00	120.00	160.00
Carriage, cast iron, one-horse, 7½" long	60.00	90.00	120.00
Carriage, one horse, cloth and wicker, 56" long	20.00	30.00	40.00
Carriage, metal and wood, one horse, malleable iron horse with articulated legs and tail, carriage made of wood	220.00	330.00	440.00
Cart, bull-pulled, cast iron two-wheeled cart	30.00	45.00	60.00
Cart, cast iron lion, two wheels, 8" long	30.00	45.00	60.00
Cart, one horse, cast iron, 9" long	25.00	37.50	50.00
Cart one horse, 8" long, early tin	40.00	60.00	80.00

CARPENTER "Tally-Ho", 27½" long.
Courtesy PB Eighty-Four, New York

Cart one Horse, tin 15" long.
Courtesy Lloyd W. Ralston Auctions

Cart, one horse, painted tin, 1890, 15" long	110.00	165.00	220.00
Cart with driver and buffalo, 7½" long, cast iron	350.00	525.00	700.00

72

	G	VG	M
Cart with cast iron woman and prancing horse, 10¼" long	70.00	105.00	140.00
Cart with elephant, cast iron, 7" long	25.00	37.50	50.00
Cart, stake sides, 1-horse, 7" long, early cast iron	20.00	30.00	40.00
Chariot drawn by tin horse, highly decorated, 13½" long	40.00	60.00	80.00
CHEIN "Dispatch" Wagon, 1-horse, 11½" long	32.50	48.75	65.00
Chief's Wagon, cast iron "Chief", one horse, circa 1915-1920, 12" long	50.00	75.00	100.00
"Chief" fire chief wagon, cast iron, one-horse, 15½" long	86.00	129.00	172.00
Circus Wagon, iron and tin, two horses, lion cage, 9" long	100.00	150.00	200.00
Circus Wagon, cast iron and wood, containing carved wood bear, 13" long	110.00	165.00	220.00
Coal Wagon, cast iron, small	50.00	75.00	100.00
"Coal" Wagon, cast iron, with driver and coal shovel, 9¼" long	66.00	99.00	132.00
Conestoga Wagon, cast iron, with cloth cover and two horses, 12½"	7.50	11.25	15.00
Conestoga Wagon, lithographed walking horses, iron wheels, 18" long	34.00	51.00	68.00
Confectionary Wagon, early 1-horse	400.00	600.00	800.00]
"Contractor's Dump Wagon", cast iron, three horse, driver, 13" long	46.00	69.00	92.00
Courtland Circus Parade, tin	12.50	18.76	25.00
Covered Wagon, 13" long, cast iron, cloth top, one horse, driver	170.00	255.00	340.00
Covered Wagon, tin, driver and horse, Indian head lithographed on side	12.00	18.00	24.00
DENT buckboard, rider, one horse, very early, primitive-looking	33.00	49.50	66.00
DENT Cart, horse and driver, 10" long	60.00	90.00	120.00

DENT Hook and Ladder, 1915, 14" long. Courtesy Lloyd W. Ralston Auctions

DENT Pumper, 1915, 14½" long.   Courtesy Lloyd W. Ralston Auctions

	G	VG	M
DENT Cart, lady driver, horse, 11" long	70.00	105.00	140.00
DENT Cart, mule, driver	50.00	75.00	100.00
DENT Contractors Dump Wagon, two horse, 15" long	30.00	45.00	60.00
DENT Coupe, one horse, driver, 9¾"	46.00	69.00	92.00
DENT Dump Cart, black man, mule	50.00	75.00	100.00
DENT Fire Engine Pumper, silver with white horses, two horse, 21" long	100.00	150.00	200.00
DENT Fire Engine steam pumper, three horses, 21" long	70.00	105.00	140.00
DENT Fire Hook & Ladder, 27" long	150.00	225.00	300.00
DENT Fire Patrol, 15½" long, 3-horse, firemen figures	200.00	300.00	400.00
DENT Fire Patrol, "Patrol", circa 1905, 3-horse, 22" long, cast iron, driver, 6 riders	250.00	375.00	500.00
DENT Fire Pumper, circa 1908, 15½" long, 3-horse, driver, paint and nickel plate	87.50	131.25	175.00
DENT Fire Snorkle Wagon, 3-horse, driver	160.00	240.00	320.00
DENT Hansom Cab, 14" long, cast iron, circa 1905, lady passenger, driver	185.00	277.50	370.00
DENT No. 57 Hansom cab, two-wheeled, one horse	64.00	96.00	128.00
DENT Hook and ladder, three-horse, extra large	180.00	270.00	360.00

DENT Hook and ladder, painted cast iron, 1915, 14" long, mechanized horses	**G**	**VG**	**M**
DENT Hook and ladder, painted cast iron, 1915, 14" long, mechanized horses	160.00	240.00	320.00
DENT Hook and ladder, cast iron, with figures, ladders	175.00	262.50	350.00
DENT Hose-reel, three horse, 24", 10" horse, figures	200.00	300.00	400.00
DENT Hose-reel, large, three-horse, figures and hose	200.00	300.00	400.00
DENT horse and cart, cart is tin	20.00	30.00	40.00
DENT horse and cart, low sides, all cast iron	20.00	30.00	40.00
DENT "Ice" wagon, two horse, 12"	30.00	45.00	60.00
DENT "Ice" wagon, one horse, 14" long	80.00	120.00	160.00
DENT "Ice" Wagon, cast iron, black horse pulling yellow and orange ice wagon, with driver, circa 1910, 15½" long	90.00	135.00	180.00
DENT Ladder Wagon, 1890, 43½" long, 4-horse, may be longest cast iron toy made	420.00	630.00	840.00
DENT Ox Wagon, 2 oxen, driver, 16" long, cast iron	70.00	105.00	140.00
DENT ox cart, stake sides, one ox	10.00	15.00	20.00
DENT police patrol, three horses, driver and four patrolmen, 21" long	155.00	232.50	310.00
DENT pony cart with driver, stake sides, horse	30.00	45.00	60.00
DENT pony cart No. 20 has driver, team of horses, stake sides on cart	70.00	105.00	140.00
DENT Pumper, painted cast iron, 1915, 14½" long, moving horses	100.00	150.00	200.00
DENT Road Cart, 1-horse, driver in top hat, 2 seats, 16" long	200.00	300.00	400.00
DENT small truck wagon, stake sides	75.00	112.50	150.00

DENT one horse truck wagon, stake sides, with dirver, 16" long	**G**	**VG**	**M**
DENT one horse truck wagon, stake sides, with dirver, 16" long	60.00	90.00	120.00
DENT sulky with jockey	30.00	45.00	60.00
DENT surrey, horse has wheel attached to one leg	44.00	66.00	88.00
Dog cart (baby carriage), black cloth top, 5½" long, tin	10.00	15.00	20.00
Dog Cart, tin, 10" long, circa 1875	125.00	187.50	250.00

Dog Cart, tin, 10" long, circa 1875
Courtesy Mapes Auctioneers & Appraisers

Donkey and cart, cast iron, with driver	66.00	99.00	132.00
Donkey and cart, tin, 8" long, iron star wheels	16.00	24.00	32.00
Donkey and cart, tin, 8½" long	9.00	13.50	18.00
Dray, cast iron, one horse, black horse pulling yellow dray	90.00	135.00	180.00
Dray Wagon, cast iron, driver and two horses, 18" long	50.00	75.00	100.00
"Dry Goods" cloth and wood two-horse drawn wagon pull-toy, circa 1860, 26" long	80.00	120.00	160.00
Dump Cart, "Hard and Soft Coal — Coke and Kindlings", tin, 19" long	260.00	390.00	520.00
"Dump Cart", horse pulling cart pull toy, 7¾" long	32.00	48.00	64.00
Dump Truck, cast iron and tin, one horse	33.00	49.50	66.00

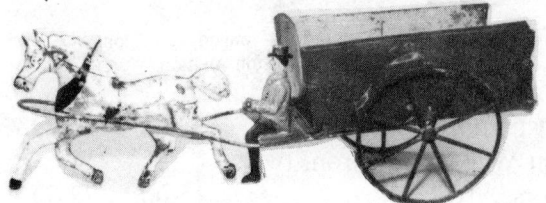

Dump Cart, "Hard and Soft Coal- Coke and Kindlings"
Courtesy Lloyd W. Ralston Auctions

	G	VG	M
FALLOWS Cart, tin, 12" long	70.00	105.00	140.00
FALLOWS Cart and horse, painted tin, 1870, 8½" long	30.00	45.00	60.00
FALLOWS Covered wagon painted tin, litho paper scenes on sides, 12" long.	260.00	390.00	520.00
FALLOWS "Dump Cart", 1-horse, 16" long, tin, circa 1890	180.00	270.00	360.00
FALLOWS "Fine Groceries" delivery wagon, 11½" long	600.00	900.00	1200.00
FALLOWS Fire Pumper, 18" long, two horse, very early	2900.00	4350.00	5800.00
FALLOWS Fire Pumper, 24" long, tin, very early.	2500.00	3750.00	5000.00
FALLOWS Horse and carriage, 1890, American painted and stenciled tin, 12½" long	100.00	150.00	200.00
FALLOWS "Pure Milk" wagon, 1895, painted and stenciled tin, 12½" long.	350.00	525.00	700.00
FALLOWS Streetcar, 10" long, two-horse	160.00	240.00	320.00

FALLOWS Horse and Carriage, 1890, 12½" long
Courtesy Lloyd W Ralston Auctions

FALLOWS "Pure Milk" wagon, 12½" long.
Courtesy Lloyd W. Ralston Auctions

	G	VG	M
Farm Wagon and donkey, cast iron, 10½" long	33.00	49.50	66.00
Farm Wagon, cast iron, two horse, 10"	15.00	22.50	30.00
Farm Wagon, cast iron, 14" long, two unusual horses, with driver	40.00	60.00	80.00

FALLOWS Covered Wagon, 12" long
Courtesy Lloyd W. Ralston Auctions

	G	VG	M
Farm Wagon, cast iron, large heavy horses, body wood, 25½" long	83.00	124.50	166.00
Farm Wagon, tin, with horse, 10½" long	10.00	15.00	20.00
"Fine Groceries", tin wagon, two horses, 14" long	60.00	90.00	120.00
Fire Hose Reel, cast iron, horse-drawn, 6"	35.00	52.50	70.00
"Fire Patrol" cast iron three horse wagon contains two firemen and driver 17" long	160.00	240.00	320.00
"Fire Patrol" three-horse, 18¾" long, driver, riders.	150.00	225.00	300.00
"Fire Patrol" cast iron, two horse, three firemen and driver, circa 1910, 19" long	375.00	562.00	750.00
Fire Pumper cast iron, three horse, 11¼"	120.00	180.00	240.00
Fire Pumper, cast iron, two horse with driver, 13" long	128.00	192.00	256.00
Fire Pumper, cast iron, three horse, 14½" long	33.00	49.50	66.00
Fire Pumper, cast iron, two horse, driver, 19¾" long.	230.00	345.00	460.00
Fire Pumper, circa 1910, cast iron, three horse, 17½" long	200.00	300.00	400.00
Fire Pumper, cast iron, three horse with driver, fireman, circa 1910, 18¼" long	150.00	225.00	300.00

Fire Pumper, cast iron, two horse, driver 10¾" long.
Photo courtesy Garth's Auctions Inc.

	G	VG	M
GEORGE BROWN Cab, driver, one-horse, 8½" long	560.00	840.00	1120.00
GEORGE BROWN Cart and Horse, 1880, painted and stenciled tin, 7½" long	90.00	135.00	180.00
GEORGE BROWN Doctor's Buggy, 14" long, tin and cast iron	650.00	975.00	1300.00
GEORGE BROWN Dump Cart, painted tin, 1885, 8¼" long	50.00	75.00	100.00
GEORGE BROWN Dump Cart, 1880, 13" long, tin, back gate lifts out for dumping	60.00	90.00	120.00
GEORGE BROWN "Eagle Chariot", painted tin, 1870, 11" long	210.00	315.00	420.00
GEORGE BROWN Gig, tin, 9" long	150.00	225.00	300.00
GEORGE BROWN Gig, tin, 10" long, 1-horse	100.00	150.00	200.00
GEORGE BROWN Goat Cart, 7" long	90.00	135.00	180.00
GEORGE BROWN Horse Cart, 1870, tin, 11½" long	105.00	157.50	210.00
GEORGE BROWN Ox cart, 1880, painted tin, 9" long	280.00	420.00	560.00
GEORGE BROWN Peddle Wagon, tin, circa 1880, 20" long, two wheeled horses, driver, awning	110.00	165.00	220.00
GEORGE BROWN Rockaway, passenger cart, 2-horse, 13" long	1100.00	1650.00	2200.00
GEORGE BROWN Sulk, 8¾" long	250.00	375.00	500.00

	G	VG	M
GEORGE BROWN Yankee Notins Peddler Wagon, 16½" long	1200.00	1800.00	2400.00

GEORGE BROWN Cart and Horse, 1880, 7½" long.
Courtesy Lloyd W. Ralston Auctions

GEORGE BROWN Dump Cart, 1885, 8¼" long.
Courtesy Lloyd W. Ralston Auctions

GEORGE BROWN Ox Cart, 9" long.
Courtesy Lloyd W. Ralston Auctions

GEORGE BROWN Eagle Chariot.
Courtesy Lloyd W. Ralston Auctions

	G	VG	M
GIBBS cart and horse, paper litho on wood, 13" long	70.00	105.00	140.00
GIBBS Chariot, horse 7½"	75.00	112.50	150.00
GIBBS "Delivery 14", one-horse, articulated	50.00	75.00	100.00

	G	VG	M
GIBBS "Groceries The Great Atlantic and Pacific Tea Co." mule-drawn cart, 12"..........	225.00	337.50	450.00
GIBBS Gypsy Wagon, two-horse	100.00	150.00	200.00
GIBBS Hay cart, paper litho and painted wood, iron wheels, 1910, 19" long.................	70.00	105.00	140.00
GIBBS pony cart, Shetland pony, paper litho on wood, cart tin, 7" long..	20.00	30.00	40.00
GIBBS "Pony Circus" wagon, two-horse, 13¾" long, paper litho on tin and wood, cast iron wheels................	90.00	135.00	180.00
GIBBS TEA CO. Mule cart	310.00	465.00	620.00
GIBBS "Yankee" cart and horse, wood and tin 18¾"................	37.50	56.25	75.00

GIBBS Hay Cart, 1910, 19" long.
Courtesy Lloyd W. Ralston Auctions

	G	VG	M
Gig, cast iron, one horse, figure	45.00	67.50	90.00
GIRARD Wagon, 2 tin horses, stake sides......	30.00	45.00	60.00
Goat Cart, 7½" long, iron goat and wheels, tin cart.	30.00	45.00	60.00
Goat Cart, 10½" long, tin, early	40.00	60.00	80.00
"Golden Pasture Farm Products, Milk & Cream" 1915, horse-drawn milk wagon, steering mechanism for child to ride, painted and stenciled wood, 30" long........	175.00	262.50	350.00

"Golden Pasture Farm Products, Milk and Cream".
Courtesy Lloyd W. Ralston Auctions

	G	VG	M
Gong Bell Pull Toy, two cast iron horses........	34.00	51.00	68.00
Grass Cutter, two horse, driver, two-wheeled cart, cast iron.............	500.00	750.00	1000.00
Hansom Cab, cast iron, no horse or figures.......	700.00	1050.00	1400.00
Hansom Cab, 8" long.....	40.00	60.00	80.00
Hansom Cab with driver, cast iron, 9½" long.....	35.00	52.50	70.00
Hansom Cab, cast iron, with driver, 9¾".......	24.00	36.00	48.00
Hansom Cab with driver, cast iron 9¾"..........	50.00	100.00	150.00
Hansom Cab, one horse, driver, 10" long, cast iron	70.00	105.00	140.00
HARRIS Cart, mule, driver, 10" long.............	165.00	247.50	330.00
HARRIS, Gloomy Gus standing in tin cart pulled by iron horse, 7½" long.	46.00	69.00	92.00
HARRIS Goat Cart, shell-type, 5" long, cast iron..	30.00	45.00	60.00
HARRIS Goat Cart, two goats, cast iron........	200.00	300.00	400.00
HARRIS Transfer Wagon, 1903, 18½" long, 3-horse	125.00	187.50	250.00
HARRIS Wagon, mule, 12" long.................	30.00	45.00	60.00
"Hood's Milk", RICH TOYS, wood and tin, horse-drawn wagon pull-toy..................	46.00	69.00	92.00
Hook and Ladder, cast iron, tin and wood, two-horse with driver and three ladders, 16½" long........	26.00	39.00	52.00
Hook and Ladder, cast iron and tin, three horse, two firemen, ladders, 21" long	33.00	49.50	66.00
Hook and Ladder, cast iron, two-horse, 22¾" long...	50.00	75.00	100.00
Hook and Ladder, cast iron, three-horse, with driver, 25" long..............	130.00	195.00	260.00
Hook and Ladder truck, cast iron, three-horse, 25½" long............	60.00	90.00	120.00
Hook and Ladder truck, cast iron, three-horse, two drivers, four ladders, circa 1910-1914, 31¼" long...	266.00	399.00	532.00
Hook and Ladder, pressed steel and iron, figures, ladders, unusual hanging horses	94.00	141.00	188.00

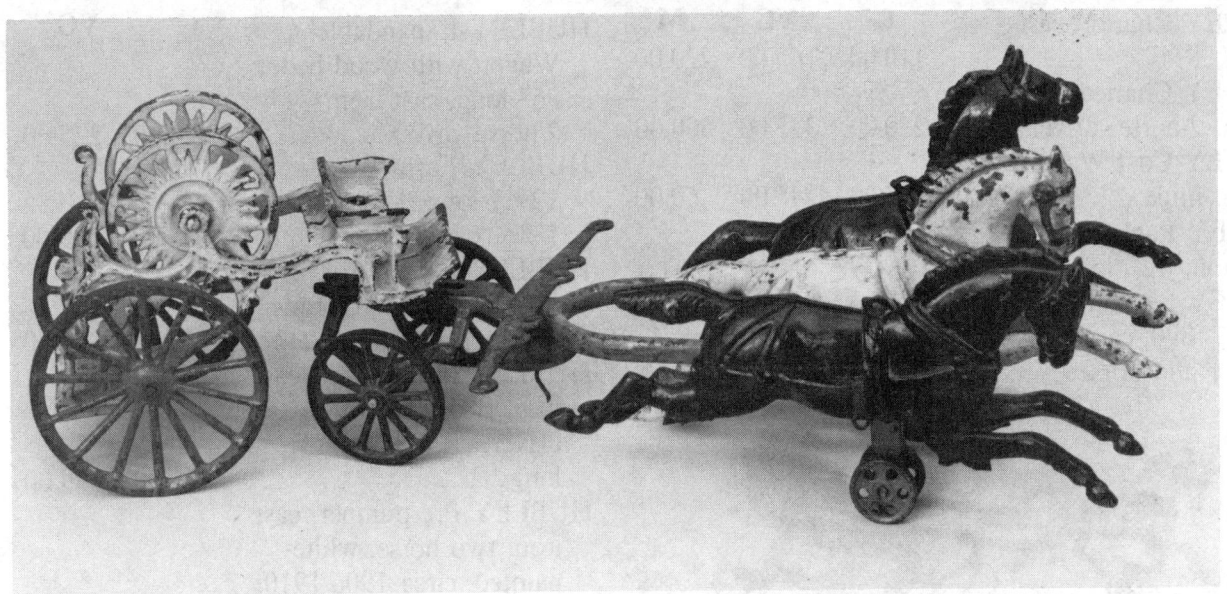

Hose Reel, cast iron, 3-horse, 19" long.
Courtesy Mapes Auctioneers & Appraisers.

	G	VG	M
Hook and Ladder, three horses, 27½" long, driver	140.00	210.00	280.00
Hook and Ladder, wood ladder with figurines, three-horse, 29½" long..	200.00	300.00	400.00
Horse and Cart, lithograph paper on wooden horse, tin cart	14.00	21.00	28.00
Horse pulling two wheel cart, tin	250.00	375.00	500.00
Horse with open carriage and driver in top hat, tin 5½" long	64.00	96.00	128.00
Hose Reel, cast iron, one horse with driver, 11" long	80.00	120.00	160.00
Hose Reel, cast iron, one horse with driver, 12" long	90.00	135.00	180.00
Hose Reel Wagon, cast iron with driver and cord fire hose, one horse, 12½" long	110.00	165.00	220.00
Hose Reel, early, two-horse with driver, cast iron, 14¼"	60.00	90.00	120.00
Hose Reel, early, two-horse, cast iron, 14½" long, with figure	80.00	120.00	160.00
Hose Reel, cast iron, 19" long, 3-horse, circa 1910.	200.00	300.00	400.00
Hose Reel, Wagon, cast iron, driver, two horses, man standing on rear bumper, 21" long	24.00	36.00	48.00

	G	VG	M
Hose Reel, cast iron, circa 1910-1914, three horse with driver and fireman, 21" long	200.00	300.00	400.00
Hose Wagon, cast iron, two firemen, three horses and bell, 21½" long	130.00	195.00	260.00
Hose Reel, early, cast iron, unusual horse	175.00	262.50	350.00
HUBLEY Brake, 2-seat, 16½" long, driver, 3 women passengers	2200.00	3300.00	4400.00
HUBLEY Brake, four-seated, 4-horse, 8 articulated passengers, 28" long, sold in good-very good condition for $5750			
HUBLEY Brake, 3-seated, 18" log, 2 plumed horses, cast iron	2200.00	3300.00	4400.00
HUBLEY Brougham, 16" long, cast iron & chrome, horse and driver	230.00	345.00	460.00
HUBLEY Brougham, top-hatted driver, 1-horse, 17" long	240.00	360.00	480.00
HUBLEY Cane Wagon, 15" long	42.00	63.00	84.00
HUBLEY Cart, 5½" long, driver	50.00	75.00	100.00
HUBLEY Cart, 8" long, horse and driver	18.00	27.00	36.00
HUBLEY Cart, wood, iron wheels, iron horse, 10½" long, 1910	15.00	22.50	30.00

HUBLEY Chariot, cast	G	VG	M
iron, 8¾"	110.00	165.00	220.00
HUBLEY Chariot, 9½" long, 2-horse, driver.....	250.00	375.00	500.00
HUBLEY Coal Wagon, 9" long, mule	30.00	45.00	60.00
HUBLEY Eagle Milk Wagon, 12" long.......	125.00	187.50	250.00
HUBLEY Essex Trap, 13" long, 1890, cast iron, driver and horse........	160.00	240.00	320.00

HUBLEY Sleigh, one-horse, 15" long.
Courtesy Lloyd W. Ralston Auctions

HUBLEY Sleigh, two-horse, 15" long.
Courtesy Lloyd W. Ralston Auctions

HUBLEY Sleigh, one-horse, 14½" long.
Courtesy Lloyd W. Ralston Auctions

HUBLEY Landau Carriage, 1905, 16½" long.
Courtesy Lloyd W. Ralston Auctions

HUBLEY "Ice" Wagon, 9½" long, 1920s.
Courtesy Lloyd W. Ralston Auctions

HUBLEY Expandable	G	VG	M
Wagon with wood bed, 26" long, cast iron, 2-horse driver.........	150.00	225.00	300.00
HUBLEY Farm Wagon, 12½" long, 1-horse, circa 1915, cast iron.........	33.00	49.00	66.00
HUBLEY Fire Patrol, 21", driver, 4 firemen, prancing horse team........	230.00	345.00	460.00
HUBLEY fire pumper, cast iron, two horses with driver, circa 1910, 14" long.................	66.00	99.00	132.00
HUBLEY fire pumper, cast iron, two horse, white-painted, circa 1906-1910, 19" long..............	200.00	300.00	400.00
HUBLEY fire pumper, two horse, cast iron, with driver and two firemen, 20" long..............	60.00	90.00	120.00
HUBLEY fire pumper, three-horse with driver, circa 1906-1910, 20½" long..................	130.00	195.00	260.00
HUBLEY fire pumper, two horses, cast iron with American Eagle, circa 1905-1910, 21" long....	110.00	165.00	220.00
HUBLEY Gig, lady driver, 15" long, horsedrawn...	300.00	450.00	600.00
HUBLEY Hansom Cab, driver cast in window, horse.................	250.00	375.00	500.00
HUBLEY Hook and ladder, three-horse, two firemen, two wooden ladders, circa 1906-1910, 27¾" long...	120.00	180.00	240.00
HUBLEY Hook and Ladder, 2-horse, 28" long, cast iron.............	150.00	225.00	300.00
HUBLEY hook and ladder wagon, three-horse, 33" long with eagle and shield on side..............	160.00	240.00	320.00
HUBLEY Hose reel, cast iron, three-horse with driver, circa 1906, 19" long.................	170.00	255.00	340.00
HUBLEY "Ice Wagon", 1920s, 9½" long.......	30.00	45.00	60.00
HUBLEY "Ice"Wagon, 14" long, 1910, cast iron, driver, horse, paint and nickel plate...........	225.00	337.50	450.00

HUBLEY "Ice" Wagon, 15" long, 2-horse, cast iron..	G	VG	M
	100.00	150.00	200.00
HUBLEY "Ice" Wagon, 15½" long, 2-horse, cast iron, black horses pulling green wagon, with driver, circa 1906	350.00	525.00	700.00
HUBLEY Landau Carriage, 1905, painted cast iron, 16½" long	375.00	562.50	750.00
HUBLEY Log Wagon, 15" long, two oxen, driver, circa 1905	110.00	165.00	220.00

HUBLEY "Royal Circus Calliope"

HUBLEY "Royal Circus Giraffe Cage"

HUBLEY "Royal Circus Clown on Trapeze Van"

HUBLEY "Royal Circus Lion Cage"

	G	VG	M
HUBLEY Log Wagon, 19" long, horse	80.00	120.00	160.00
HUBLEY lady in sleigh, circa 1900, 15" long	240.00	360.00	480.00
HUBLEY Monkey Trapeze circus mirror van, 12½" long	300.00	450.00	600.00
HUBLEY Royal Circus, animals, driver, 2 horses, 15" long	450.00	675.00	900.00
HUBLEY Royal Circus, 16" long	300.00	450.00	600.00
HUBLEY Royal Circus Bandwagon, 22" long, 4-horse, 7 riders, cast iron	650.00	975.00	1300.00
HUBLEY Royal Circus Bandwagon, circa 1920, 22½" long, cast iron, 2 horses, 7 riders	1000.00	1500.00	2000.00
HUBLEY "Royal Circus" Band Wagon, 30" long, 8 musicians and driver, 1920s	800.00	1200.00	1600.00
HUBLEY "Royal Circus" Calliope	500.00	750.00	1000.00
HUBLEY "Royal Circus" Clown on Trapeze van, 16½" long, 1920, oval-mirrored sides	1000.00	1500.00	2000.00
HUBLEY "Royal Circus" Farmer Van, 1920, 16" long, head revolves and disappears in top of wagon as toy pulled	No Price Found		
HUBLEY "Royal Circus" Giraffe Cage with large and small giraffes, driver, 1920, 27" long	1500.00	2250.00	3000.00
HUBLEY Royal Circus Lion Cage, 9" long	100.00	150.00	200.00
HUBLEY Royal Circus Polar Bear Cage, 1920s, 11¾" long	215.00	322.50	430.00
HUBLEY Royal Circus Rhino Wagon	750.00	1125.00	1500.00
HUBLEY Royal Circus Tiger Wagon, 1920s, 11½" long	500.00	750.00	1000.00
HUBLEY "Royal Circus" Tiger Wagon Cage, 1920, 16" long, driver, 2 tigers	275.00	412.50	550.00
HUBLEY Santa Claus Sleigh, 16" long, 1910, 2 reindeer, cast iron	330.00	495.00	660.00

	G	VG	M
HUBLEY Santa Claus, Sleigh, 17" long, early...	300.00	450.00	600.00
HUBLEY Shell Cart and horse, 7", 1905.........	50.00	75.00	100.00
HUBLEY Sleigh, one horse, painted cast iron, 1910, 14½" long............	130.00	195.00	260.00
HUBLEY Sleigh, one-horse, woman with moveable arms, 14¾", early......	175.00	262.50	350.00
HUBLEY Sleigh, one horse, 1900, painted cast iron, nickel plated 15" long...	130.00	195.00	260.00
HUBLEY Sleigh, 2 horse, 1910, painted and nickel plated cast iron, 15" long	180.00	270.00	360.00
HUBLEY Spring Wagon, horse, driver, cast iron...	110.00	165.00	220.00
HUBLEY Sulky, 8½" long.	30.00	45.00	60.00
HUBLEY Surrey, clockwork, 1894, 9" long, cast iron, brass works, five colors, first of Hubley's toys.........	225.00	337.50	450.00
HUBLEY Surrey, 18" long, 2-horse, driver	80.00	120.00	160.00
HUBLEY Trotter, 1900, 8¾" long, cast iron, horse and driver........	110.00	165.00	220.00)
HUBLEY Trotter Gig, lady driver, 11" long........	60.00	90.00	120.00
HUBLEY Wagon, 12" long, horse, cast iron........	40.00	60.00	80.00
Ice Cart, tin, horse-drawn..	66.00	99.00	132.00
"Ice" wagon, one horse, 12", cast iron..........	34.00	51.00	68.00
Ice Wagon, cast iron, two-horse, 12" long........	50.00	75.00	100.00
IDEAL Fire Pumper, 2-horse, 20½" long, cast iron, 2 riders..........	166.00	249.00	332.00
"Ideal Fire Department", 30" long, 3-horse, cast iron.................	200.00	300.00	400.00
IVES Coal Wagon, late 1890s, 13¼" long, driver, mule	110.00	165.00	220.00
IVES Doctor's cart, two wheels, 10¼".........	250.00	375.00	500.00
IVES dog pulling stake cart	100.00	150.00	200.00
IVES Donkey Cart, one of 4 walking animal toys by IVES, circa 1890, 15" long, cast iron........	550.00	825.00	1100.00

	G	VG	M
IVES "Fast Mail" wagon, 17" long, cast iron, walking horses............	400.00	600.00	800.00
IVES "Fire Patrol", 19" long, circa 1890, 1 horse, 5 riders, driver	340.00	510.00	680.00
IVES Fire Patrol, 20½" long, 2-horse, driver, 6 firemen, cast iron, circa 1880-1910.............	200.00	300.00	400.00
IVES Gig, 1890s, driver with top hat, 5½" long..	25.00	37.50	50.00
IVES Hansom Cab with walking horse..........	2200.00	3300.00	4400.00
IVES Hook and Ladder, circa 1890, 29" long, 2 horse, 2 riders, cast iron.	160.00	240.00	320.00
IVES Hose Cart, 1883, 17½" long, 2 horse.....	200.00	300.00	400.00
IVES Hose reel, cast iron, one horse, driver, "Phoenix", circa 1880-1910, 15" long....	150.00	225.00	300.00
IVES Ice Wagon with mules, 1896..........	210.00	315.00	420.00
IVES Phoenix Pumper, circa 1890, 19" long, cast iron, rarest of IVES pumpers	300.00	450.00	600.00
IVES Police Patrol Wagon, 1890s, 20½" long, 6 patrolmen, driver.......	300.00	450.00	600.00
IVES Steam pumper, two-horse, 20½"..........	300.00	450.00	600.00
IVES Walking Horse, pull toy, late 19th century, horse which walks by means of wheel mechanism under it, pulling a two-wheeled cart..	300.00	450.00	600.00
IVES & BLAKESLEE Fire Pumper, 1893, 25" long, cast iron, largest cast iron pumper made by IVES..	750.00	1125.00	1500.00

KENTON: Kenton Lock Manufacturing Co. was incorporated in May, 1890, in Kenton, Ohio. In November of 1894, it became the Kenton Hardware Manufacturing Company, and around this period, began producing toys. It ceased production of horse-drawn toys in the early 1920s (except for a 1930s beer wagon), but in 1939 introduced a completely new line of horse-drawn pieces, running through 1954.

KENTON Plantation Cart, 1910.
Courtesy Mapes Auctioneers & Appraisers

	G	VG	M
KENTON Bakery wagon, marked "Bakery", 1941	225.00	337.50	450.00
KENTON Band Wagon, musicians, driver, rider on horse	75.00	112.50	150.00
KENTON Boar Cart, 8" long, circa 1910, cast iron, Egyptian driver	260.00	390.00	520.00
KENTON Cabriolet, painted cast iron, 2nd series made into 1950s, 15" long	105.00	157.50	210.00
KENTON Cement Mixer, driver, horse, 14" long	245.00	367.50	490.00
KENTON Chariot, 6" long, cast iron	22.50	33.75	45.00
KENTON Chariot, 7½" long with comic driver, 1910, cast iron	120.00	180.00	240.00
KENTON Chariot, 3-horse, cast iron	300.00	450.00	600.00
KENTON "Chief" wagon, one-horse, driver, 12¼" long	375.00	562.50	750.00

	G	VG	M
KENTON Circus Cage Wagon, two horses, two riders, driver, animal in cage	75.00	112.50	150.00
KENTON "Coal" cart, donkey pulling, black driver	140.00	210.00	280.00
KENTON Contractor's Wagon, with black driver, 15½"	200.00	300.00	400.00
KENTON covered wagon, cast iron, two-horse	20.00	30.00	40.00
KENTON Delivery Wagon No. 5 with driver and 2 horses	75.00	112.50	150.00
KENTON Delivery Cart, donkey, cast iron	66.00	99.00	132.00
KENTON Dog Cart, 7" long, greyhound pulling dog riding	100.00	150.00	200.00
KENTON dray, 13¼" long	37.50	56.25	75.00

	G	VG	M
KENTON dray, cast iron, two horse, black and white horses pulling green dray, with driver, 13½" long................	50.00	75.00	100.00
KENTON dray No. 5, painted cast iron, 1930, 14½" long............	55.00	82.50	110.00
KENTON dray wagon with horse and driver, cast iron, 14¾"............	100.00	150.00	200.00
KENTON dray, cast iron, two-horse, two dark horses pulling a green cart, with driver, 14¾" long.................	74.00	111.00	148.00
KENTON Dump Cart, mule................	60.00	90.00	120.00
KENTON Dump Wagon, 10¼" long, early 1900s..	40.00	60.00	80.00
KENTON dump wagon, two-horses, lever releases bottom wagon..........	50.00	75.00	100.00
KENTON Express Wagon, horse, driver, cast iron...	80.00	120.00	160.00
KENTON Express Wagon, 11" long..............	25.00	37.50	50.00

	G	VG	M
KENTON fire ladder wagon, front driver only, 12" long..............	25.00	37.50	50.00
KENTON fire ladder wagon, horse-drawn, 17" long, drivers front and rear..................	22.50	33.75	45.00
KENTON Fire Pumper, 20" long, 2 horse, driver.	100.00	150.00	200.00
KENTON fire pumper, cast iron, 26½" long, horses 11" long..............	220.00	330.00	440.00
KENTON Fire Wagon, 23" long, 2-horse, driver, equipment, bell, wagon nickel-plated..........	150.00	225.00	300.00
KENTON goat cart, 7", figure with large ears....	75.00	112.50	150.00
KENTON gravel wagon, 13" with two horses....	60.00	90.00	120.00
KENTON Hansom Cab, 10" long, one horse, top-hatted driver..........	90.00	135.00	180.00
KENTON Hansom Cab, 12" long..............	140.00	210.00	280.00
KENTON Hansom cab, 15½" long, figures, horse	107.50	160.25	215.00

KENTON Hook & Ladder, 1915, 26" long.
Courtesy Lloyd W. Ralston Auctions

KENTON Hose Reel, 1920, 13½" long.
Courtesy Lloyd W. Ralston Auctions

KENTON Dray No.5, 14½" long.
Courtesy Lloyd W. Ralston Auctions

KENTON Cabriolet, 2nd series made into the 1950s, 15" long.
Courtesy Lloyd R. Ralston Auctions

	G	VG	M
KENTON Farm Wagon, 14" long, driver, 1 horse.	150.00	225.00	300.00
KENTON Farm Wagon, two-horse cast iron, 14½" with figure.......	30.00	45.00	60.00
KENTON Farm Wagon, 15" long, driver, 1 horse, early	90.00	135.00	180.00
KENTON Farm Wagon, two-horse, 15" with driver	135.00	202.50	270.00

	G	VG	M
KENTON Hook and Ladder Wagon, 20" long, 2-horse, driver........	100.00	150.00	200.00
KENTON Hook and Ladder Wagon, 20" long, nickel-plated, 2-horse, driver	80.00	120.00	160.00
KENTON Hook and Ladder, 16" long, 3-horse, cast iron..............	70.00	105.00	140.00

KENTON hook and ladder, wagon, three horses, 17" long	G	VG	M
	130.00	195.00	260.00
KENTON hook and ladder, cast iron, three-horse, circa 1910, 19" long	50.00	75.00	100.00
KENTON Hook and ladder, 1915, painted cast iron, ladders, 26" long	150.00	225.00	300.00
KENTON hose reel, 1920, painted cast iron, 13½" long	220.00	330.00	440.00
KENTON Hose Reel, cast iron, 14½" long, circa 1905, two-horse	300.00	450.00	600.00
KENTON "Ice" wagon, 15" long, 2-horse, driver, 1920s, cast iron	104.00	156.00	208.00
KENTON landau, cast iron, white horse pulling green carriage with driver, circa 1910, 15" long	250.00	375.00	500.00
KENTON log wagon, one horse with driver, 14½" long	60.00	90.00	120.00

KENTON Bakery Wagon

KENTON Log Wagon, 15" long, black man, 2 oxen, early 1900s, cast iron	200.00	300.00	400.00
KENTON "Milk" wagon, with horse and driver	75.00	112.50	150.00
KENTON, "Overland Circus" calliope wagon	120.00	180.00	240.00
KENTON "Overland Circus" two-horse, cast iron with driver, cage containing bear, circa 1940s-1950s, 13¾" long	30.00	45.00	60.00
KENTON "Overland Circus" cast iron, two-horse with driver, cage containing cloth bear, 14" long	235.00	352.50	470.00
KENTON Overland Circus Wagon, 6 musicians and driver, 15" long	180.00	270.00	360.00

KENTON "Overland Circus" cast iron, two-horse with driver, cage containing cast iron bear, 14" long, 1940s	G	VG	M
	235.00	352.00	470.00
KENTON Ox Cart, 5" long, cast iron	30.00	45.00	60.00
KENTON Ox Cart, 7"	30.00	45.00	60.00
KENTON Ox Cart, 12½" long	50.00	75.00	100.00
KENTON Ox Wagon, two oxen 18" long	180.00	270.00	360.00
KENTON "Patrol" No. 526, 2-horse, driver, riders 17" long	150.00	225.00	300.00
KENTON Plantation Cart, 1910, 10" long, black driver, mule	67.50	101.25	135.00
KENTON "Polar Ice" wagon, 2-donkey	250.00	375.00	500.00
KENTON Police Patrol with mule team, 16"	180.00	270.00	360.00
KENTON Pumper, 3 horses, 18"	175.00	262.50	350.00
KENTON Rabbit, 5" long, pulling cart with two wheels and seat, cast iron	37.50	56.25	75.00
KENTON Rhino Cart, 8" long	70.00	105.00	140.00
KENTON Sand and Gravel dump wagon, 15" long, driver, 2 horses	40.00	60.00	80.00
KENTON Stake Wagon, two horse	120.00	180.00	240.00
KENTON two horse stake wagon, 15" long, driver with reins	100.00	150.00	200.00
KENTON Sulky, driver cast to sulky, 6" long	30.00	45.00	60.00
KENTON Sulky, two-wheel race cart with jockey and horse, 6"	40.00	60.00	80.00
KENTON sulky and driver, cast iron, 7" long	70.00	105.00	140.00
KENTON surrey, two-horse cast iron with driver and passenger, 12½"	20.00	30.00	40.00
KENTON surrey, with fringe top, driver and passenger, two-horse (circa 1943?) 13" long	50.00	75.00	100.00
KENTON surrey, one horse, approx 1940, 16" long	83.00	124.50	166.00
KENTON team of horses with log and black driver	240.00	360.00	480.00

84

KENTON	G	VG	M
KENTON 3.2 Beer Delivery Wagon, 14½" long, 1930s, cast iron, 2-horse, driver, 10 wooden kegs..	110.00	165.00	220.00
KENTON Victoria cab and horse, cast iron, with driver and woman, 15½" long..................	60.00	90.00	120.00
KENTON No. 3, one-horse wagon, with driver, 15" long.................	60.00	90.00	120.00
KENTON No. 5 wagon, one horse, 15" long.....	45.00	67.50	90.00
KENTON wagon with driver, two-horse, 10¼" long..................	28.00	42.00	56.00
KINGSBURY Dray, 2-horse, cast iron, 20¼".	150.00	225.00	300.00
KINGSBURY Ladder Truck, 13", 1900, cast iron, tin and wood......	106.00	159.00	212.00
KINGSBURY Hook & Ladder, 25½" long, 3-horse, 2 riders, rubber covers on wheels, cast iron and pressed steel...	200.00	300.00	400.00
KINGSBURY Hook and Ladder, 2-horse, driver, 3 ladders, 27" long.......	300.00	450.00	600.00
"The Klondike Ice Co., New York" tin ice wagon, two-horse, 17½" long..................	120.00	180.00	240.00
Ladder Wagon, cast iron, two ladders and three galloping horses, 13½" long..................	10.00	15.00	20.00
Ladder Wagon, cast iron, with two horses, three sections of ladder, bell, 25½" long............	110.00	165.00	220.00
Ladder Wagon, cast iron with two drivers, four sections of ladder and three horses, Dart type, 30½" long..................	100.00	150.00	200.00
LANCASTER hook and ladder, two-horse cast iron, 25" long..........	60.00	90.00	120.00
LANCASTER hook and ladder, cast iron, 28" long, two horses, two drivers...............	50.00	75.00	100.00
LANCASTER hook and ladder, 28" long, iron, three horses, two drivers.	57.00	85.50	114.00

LANCASTER HUBLEY	G	VG	M
No. 58 Surrey, no driver.	30.00	45.00	60.00
LANCASTER HUBLEY No. 174, surrey with one seat, driver, horse.......	60.00	90.00	120.00
Landau, four-horse, 24" with driver...........	150.00	225.00	300.00
LEHMANN "Africa" tin friction toy, ostrich pulling cart...............	130.00	195.00	260.00
LEHMANN "Duo" Rooster pulling egg cart with a rabbit perched on top, tin friction	200.00	300.00	400.00
Log Wagon, cast iron with driver and two oxen, 15¼" long...........	170.00	255.00	340.00
Mail Cart, tin, horse-drawn.	35.00	52.50	70.00
MARX Covered Wagon, tin litho, 9" long, friction...	11.00	16.50	22.00
MASON & PARKER, buckboard, one-horse, 1910, pressed painted steel, 31" long.........	150.00	225.00	300.00
MASON & PARKER Cart and Horse, 1910, painted pressed steel, 13" long mechanical action from axle..................	110.00	165.00	220.00

MASON & PARKER Buckboard, one-horse, 31" long.
Courtesy Lloyd W. Ralston Auctions

MASON & PARKER Cart and horse, 13" long.
Courtesy Lloyd W. Ralston Auctions

	G	VG	M
McCormick Deering farm wagon, two-horse, 12½" long, cast iron.........	22.50	33.75	45.00
MERRIAM, cab and horse, 1880, painted and stenciled tin, 8½" long.......	400.00	600.00	800.00

MERRIAM Wagon and horse, American painted & stenciled tin, 1890, 19½" long	G	VG	M
	1600.00	2400.00	3200.00

MERRIAM Cab & Horse, 1880, 8½" long.
Courtesy Lloyd W. Ralston Auctions

MERRIAM Wagon and Horse, 1890, 19¼" long.
Courtesy Lloyd W. Ralston Auctions

	G	VG	M
Mess Cart, WW I-type, tin, two horse drawn, painted	26.00	39.00	52.00
Milk wagon, goat-drawn, possibly George Brown, painted tin, 6" long	60.00	90.00	120.00
"Milk" wagon with driver, 12½" long	12.00	18.00	24.00
"Milk" wagon, driver and one horse, 12¾" long	34.00	51.00	68.00
Mower, two horses and driver, cast iron, 10" long	66.00	99.00	132.00
"National Express" wagon, tin litho, horse 15" long	90.00	120.00	180.00
Omnibus, "People's" tin, with two horses, driver, circa 1880s-1890s	2600.00	3900.00	5200.00
Ox Cart, cast iron, 5" long, with ox	28.00	42.00	56.00
Ox Cart, cast iron, 11½" long	110.00	165.00	220.00
"Pansy" Stage Coach, REED, 28" long, 4 horse, driver, lithographed alphabet blocks	534.00	801.00	1068.00
Phaeton, one-horse with driver, 16" long	200.00	300.00	400.00
Plow, one horse, cast iron, 10¾"	60.00	90.00	120.00
Police Patrol Wagon, cast iron, 11½" long, figures and driver, one horse	40.00	60.00	80.00

	G	VG	M
"Police Patrol", cast iron, one-horse, 12"	60.00	90.00	120.00
"Police Patrol" wagon, cast iron, with driver and five policemen and two horses, 15"	150.00	225.00	300.00
PRATT & LETCHWORTH Artillery, 34" long, circa 1890, cast iron, hand-painted, 4-horse caisson, cannon, 4 riders, one sold in excellent condition for $9500.00			
"PRATT & LETCHWORTH" Cart, 10" long	17.50	26.25	35.00
PRATT & LETCHWORTH Dray, one horse, cast iron and wood, 1890, 12" long	200.00	300.00	400.00

PRATT & LETCHWORTH Dray, one-horse, 12" long.
Courtesy Lloyd W. Ralston Auctions

	G	VG	M
PRATT & LETCHWORTH Gig, cast iron and pressed steel, 10½" long, seven colors, one horse, one rider	140.00	210.00	280.00
PRATT & LETCHWORTH Hansom Cab, circa 1892, cast iron, 13" long	250.00	375.00	500.00
PRATT & LETCHWORTH Hay Cart, 10½" long	200.00	300.00	400.00
PRATT & LETCHWORTH hose reel, one horse, 14¼"	425.00	637.50	850.00
PRATT & LETCHWORTH Sulky, 8½" long	66.00	99.00	132.00
PRATT & LETCHWORTH-WELKER & CROSBY Dray, 14½" long, one-horse, driver	300.00	450.00	600.00
Pull Toy, tin, horse and cart, iron wheels, 11" long	100.00	150.00	200.00
Pull Toy, horse and covered delivery wagon, tin 5¼" long	25.00	37.50	50.00

	G	VG	M
Pull Toy, horse and wagon, two wheels, tin 9¼" long	40.00	60.00	80.00
Pull Toy, horse pulling water wagon, tin, iron wheels, 6¾" long.......	162.50	243.75	325.00
Pull Toy, horse-drawn carriage, tin, 12" long......	60.00	90.00	120.00
Pull Toy, horse pulling water wagon, tin, iron wheels, 7¼" long.......	40.00	60.00	80.00
Pumper, 15½" long, driver part of casting, 2-horse, early	75.00	112.50	150.00
Pumper, cast iron, with driver and two horses...	100.00	150.00	200.00
Pumper, cast iron, three horses with figure, 13" long.................	30.00	45.00	60.00
REED "Band Chariot" 28½" long, 14 bandsmen	400.00	600.00	800.00
Royal Circus Wagon, two horses with driver and animal in cage........	174.00	261.00	348.00
"Sand and Gravel", wagon with driver, cast iron, 9½" long............	16.00	24.00	32.00
Sand and Gravel Wagon, cast iron, 10" long, two horses	15.00	22.50	30.00
Sand and Gravel Wagon, single horse with driver, cast iron, 10½" long....	90.00	135.00	180.00
"Sand and Gravel" wagon, cast iron, driver, two-horse, 14¾" long......	40.00	60.00	80.00
"Sand and Gravel" wagon, with driver and two horses, cast iron, 15" ...	30.00	45.00	60.00
Santa and Sleigh, cast iron, 16x7"	250.00	375.00	500.00
Santa Claus in wooden sleigh pulled by reindeer, 25" long, Santa composition, reindeer plush with cast pewter antlers, early .	350.00	525.00	700.00

Santa Claus in wooden sleigh pulled by reindeer, 25" long.
Photo Courtesy Garth's Auctions Inc.

	G	VG	M
Santa Claus, reindeer pulling sled, two reindeer pulling white sled containing black-painted Santa Claus	46.00	69.00	92.00
Sheep, cast iron, pulling two-wheeled tin wagon, 8" long..............	25.00	37.50	50.00
"Sheffield Farms Company", wood horse-drawn milk wagon, horse has articulated legs, 21" long..	160.00	240.00	320.00
Spring Wagon, cast iron with driver, horse, 11"..	10.00	15.00	20.00
Spring Wagon, cast iron, driver, one horse, 14½" long..................	12.00	18.00	24.00
Spring Wagon, driver and two horses, cast iron, 14½" long............	17.00	24.50	34.00
Spring Wagon, driver and two horses, miniature pick, shovel, sledgehammer, 14¼" long, cast iron	75.00	112.50	150.00
Spring Wagon, cast iron, two horses, 15"........	10.00	15.00	20.00
Stagecoach with cowboy driver and two horses, 11" long, cast iron......	30.00	45.00	60.00
Stagecoach, 6-horse, 27" long, cast iron.........	25.00	37.50	50.00
Stake Bed Wagon, cast iron, one horse, 14¾".......	70.00	105.00	140.00
"Stanley" surrey with driver, lady passenger, two-horse, 14¾" long............	20.00	30.00	40.00
Steam Pumper with stationary driver, two horses, cast iron, 9¼" long..................	15.00	22.50	30.00
Steam Pumper, cast iron, stationary driver, three horses, 10½" long......	15.00	22.50	30.00
Steam Pumper, cast iron, 15" long with stationary driver and two horses...	120.00	180.00	240.00
Steam Pumper, cast iron, two horses, stationary driver, 15¼" long......	100.00	150.00	200.00
Steam Pumper, cast iron, driver, three horses, bell, 17½" long............	70.00	105.00	140.00
Steam Pumper, two-horse, cast iron with driver, 18" long.................	116.00	174.00	232.00

	G	VG	M
Steam Pumper, cast iron, driver and two horses, 20½" long	180.00	270.00	360.00
Steam Pumper, cast iron, three horses and bell, 21¼" high	150.00	225.00	300.00
Steamer with driver, two horses, 17"	183.00	274.50	366.00
STEVENS Black Man in cart whipping mule, painted cast iron, mechanical, 1890, 9"	200.00	300.00	400.00

STEVENS Black Man in cart whipping mule, 9" long.
Courtesy Lloyd W. Ralston Auctions

	G	VG	M
Sulky, cast iron, horse and rider, cart mounted with four bells, 6½"	60.00	90.00	120.00
Sulky, cast iron, with driver, 7¼" long	12.50	18.75	25.00
Sulky, cast iron, with driver, circa 1890s, 8½" long . . .	60.00	90.00	120.00
Sulky, cast iron, with rider, 8¾"	20.00	30.00	40.00
Sulky Rig, horse and driver pull toy, comic style, 10" long, 8" high, 1¼" thick	14.00	21.00	28.00
Surrey, cast iron, two-horse, 13" long	10.00	15.00	20.00
"Teddy Bear" enclosed cart, painted litho tin, 1915, 9" long	210.00	315.00	420.00

"Teddy Bear" Enclosed Cart, 9" long.
Courtesy Lloyd W. Ralston Auctions

	G	VG	M
Transfer Wagon, cast iron, two-horse, driver	95.00	142.50	190.00
"Transfer Wagon", three horses and driver, cast iron, wagon bolted to team, 19" long	120.00	180.00	240.00

	G	VG	M
"Transfer" Wagon, cast iron, driver and two horses, 19½" long	17.00	25.50	34.00
"Trotter, jockey and horse" cast iron, 6" long	10.00	15.00	20.00
"United States Transfer Co. No. 7", wood wagon with cast iron wheels, 2 stuffed horses, 31" long	120.00	180.00	240.00
U.S. Mail wagon, tin, two-horse, 17" long	110.00	165.00	220.00
Wagon, two-wheeled, with driver, cast iron, 7¼" . .	10.00	15.00	20.00
Wagon, cast iron, mule, driver, two-wheeled wagon, 9½" long	50.00	75.00	100.00
Wagon, two-seater, cast iron, one horse	80.00	120.00	160.00
Walking horse and sulky cart, horse of wood, moving legs and cart of tin, wheels cast iron, 7" long .	65.00	97.50	130.00
Water Tower with three horses, cast iron and pressed steel, 43" long, horse 11" long	200.00	300.00	400.00
WILKINS Artillery, 10" long, circa 1895, 2-horse, rider on caisson, seat top lifts off, cannon	180.00	270.00	360.00
WILKINS Buckboard, cast iron	33.00	49.50	66.00
WILKINS Caisson, horse-drawn, 18" long	320.00	480.00	640.00
WILKINS Cane Wagon, mule, driver, 11" long . . .	50.00	75.00	100.00
WILKINS Carriage, driver in derby, 1-horse, passenger	416.00	624.00	832.00
WILKINS Cart, animated, 6"	120.00	180.00	240.00
WILKINS Cart and Horse, 10" long	225.00	337.50	450.00
WILKINS Cart and horse, 12" long, driver	175.00	262.50	350.00
WILKINS Chariot, 7" long, four-horse	90.00	135.00	180.00
WILKINS "City Truck", cast iron, two-horse with driver	300.00	450.00	600.00
WILKINS Delivery Wagon, 21" long, driver, prancing horse team	100.00	150.00	200.00
WILKINS Dog Cart, 7½" long, 1890, cast iron	30.00	45.00	60.00

WILKINS Streetcar, "Broadway Car Line 75", horse-drawn.
Courtesy Mapes Auctioneers & Appraisers

	G	VG	M
WILKINS Dog Cart, 10½" long, circa 1890, cast iron, large St. Bernard-type dog, rider in cap...	200.00	300.00	400.00
WILKINS Donkey cart, 13¼" long............	175.00	262.50	350.00
WILKINS Dray, 15" long, cast iron.............	120.00	180.00	240.00
WILKINS, Dray, 16" long, 2-horse, cast iron.......	160.00	240.00	320.00
WILKINS Dray, 17½" long, two mules, driver..	300.00	450.00	600.00
WILKINS Dray, cast iron and tin barrel, drawn by two horses, driver in derby hat, circa 1910, 20½"	150.00	225.00	300.00
WILKINS Fire Chief buggy, one horse with rider	45.00	67.50	90.00
WILKINS Fire Chief Engine pumper, two horses, 19" long.......	60.00	90.00	120.00
WILKINS Fire Hose Reel, 10½" long............	190.00	275.00	380.00
WILKINS Fire Ladder Truck, cast iron, 20" long, 3-horse, circa 1910, two firemen	200.00	300.00	400.00

	G	VG	M
WILKINS Fire Patrol wagon, four firemen in wagon, 12" long........	30.00	45.00	60.00
WILKINS Fire Patrol, 2-horse, 2 men, cast iron.	70.00	105.00	140.00
WILKINS Fire Pumper, 20" long, 2-horse, driver.	300.00	450.00	600.00
WILKINS Gentleman's Cart, 1900, 10" long, gentleman driver, white horse................	80.00	120.00	160.00
WILKINS Gig, fancy, and driver, 10" long........	40.00	60.00	80.00
WILKINS "Groceries" wagon, one-horse, 13½" long, circa 1900........	100.00	150.00	200.00
WILKINS Hansom Cab, cast iron.............	50.00	75.00	100.00
WILKINS Hook and Ladder, 24" long..........	80.00	120.00	160.00
WILKINS Hook and Ladder, 27" long, prancing team, cast iron........	225.00	337.50	450.00
WILKINS hook and ladder, two-horse, horses sit on pegs, has ladders, figures.	240.00	360.00	480.00

WILKINS Hose Reel, 18"	G	VG	M
long, circa 1890, 1-horse, cast iron	400.00	600.00	800.00
WILKINS Ice Wagon, horse, tin and cast iron, 10" long	34.00	51.00	68.00
WILKINS Ox Cart, cast iron	17.50	26.25	35.00
WILKINS Phaeton, woman driver, 16" long, late 1800s	180.00	270.00	360.00
WILKINS Plantation Cart, 1910, cast iron and pressed steel, tilt dump, 11" long	36.00	54.00	72.00
WILKINS Plow, one horse, driver, 10½" long	800.00	1200.00	1600.00
WILKINS Pony Cart, 7½" long, one horse, driver	200.00	300.00	400.00
WILKINS Spring Wagon, driver, horses	80.00	120.00	160.00
WILKINS steam engine, two-horse, with driver, 17" long	140.00	210.00	280.00

WILKINS Fire Ladder Truck, cast iron, 3-horse, 20" long, circa 1910. Courtesy Mapes Auctioneers & Appraisers

WILKINS Streetcar,	G	VG	M
"Broadway Car Line 75", horse-drawn	350.00	525.00	700.00
WILKINS Wagon, driver, mule, 9" long	30.00	45.00	60.00
WILLIAMS Sulky, 8" long, circa 1920, cast iron	15.00	22.50	30.00

MECHANICAL BANKS

The average mint price in this category in the last edition was $1226.55 and in this edition is is $1460.80, an increase of 19%.

After trains, mechanical Banks are perhaps the most avidly pursued of all the toys cataloged in this book, and the most collectible remain these which were produced in cast iron from around 1870 to 1908, over three hundred different types being produced during that period. One factor that adds to their interest is that many were manufactured with an eye to adult trade as well as to that of children (the "Tammany" bank, for instance). As a result, prices are high, and have been so long before any of the other toys in this book were thought of as collector's items. With prices of this sort, the problem of counterfeiting arises, and care is urged in the purchase of any high-priced bank. Briefly, counterfeits tend to be rougher, to fit together less smoothly, and to have the the patina or "look" of age.

CONDITION OF A TOY BANK AND ITS RELATION TO PRICE

The price of a toy bank depends not only on its desirability, but on its condition as well. A bank in mint condition (and since these toys have been carefully collected virtually since their inception, this is not an exceptional condition) is generally worth twice what that same bank would bring in good condition, with "very good" falling about equally in between good and mint.

"Mint" means just that; the condition in which a toy was originally issued — perfect, regardless of age, not the slightest blemish. Many people hoping to dispose of toys are tempted to term an item "mint" when it is really "near mint", "very good", or sometimes even just "good". Inevitably this can result in unhappiness all around, and not infrequently, a cancelled sale.

"Very Good" indicates a toy which has obviously seen use, with signs of wear and aging, but in general having a freshness to its appearance that makes it attractive and collectible to all but the most discriminating.

"Good" signals a toy which has seen considerable wear, shows its age, but is basically sound. A collector will collect it, but will often not be wholly satisfied with it as an example of his collection, and thus prices are often drastically below that which the same item in mint can command.

Condition below good results in another drastic drop in price, and banks with missing parts, although otherwise in excellent condition, will usually fall into this lower-priced category (the failure of the actual mechanism, however, has little effect on price). Rust, even small spots of it, can seriously lower the price of a toy. "Near Mint", "Fine", "Very Fine" and similar terms often found in sellers' descriptions denote conditions between Mint and Very Good, and are priced accordingly.

The key to grading is to avoid wishful thinking. Grading can sometimes be a problem for the uninitiated, but common sense will usually prevail, and when possible, a consultation with an expert in the field can often clear up lingering doubts.

	G	VG	M
ACROBAT BANK, 5" high	950.00	1425.00	1900.00
ALLIGATOR IN TROUGH patented 1867	5000.00	7500.00	10000.00
ALWAYS DID DESPISE A MULE, black jockey on mule, 1879, 10" long....	295.00	442.50	590.00
ALWAYS DID DESPISE A MULE, Black on bench being kicked by mule, 1897.................	225.00	337.50	450.00
AMERICAN BANK sewing machine..............	1200.00	1800.00	2400.00
ARTILLERY BANK, Union officer with mortar firing at fort, 1877......	205.00	307.50	410.00

Astronaut's Bank — gold moon with rocket on stand, has rings showing orbit of space capsule, ring has astronaut's

	G	VG	M
names: "Shepard, Grissom, Glenn, Carpenter, Schirva, Cooper", little plane up side of rocket shoots money into moon, 11" high, pot metal.........	9.25	13.88	18.50
BAD ACCIDENT, Mule and black on two-wheeled car, 1887..............	230.00	345.00	640.00
BEAR HUGGING TREE.	125.00	187.50	250.00
BILL E. GRIN...........	370.00	555.00	740.00
BIRD ON ROOF	200.00	300.00	400.00

BOOK OF KNOWLEDGE REPRODUCTION OF ORIGINAL BANKS, circa 1950; Artillery Bank; Bulldog Bank; Creedmore; Eagle and Eaglets; Jonah & Whale; Magician; Man

	G	VG	M
and Pig; Man Milking Cow; Teddy and the Bear; Trick dog, Trick Pony, Tree Trunk and Buffalo. (Note — original markings sometimes filed away from bottom and sold as originals) Price per each..	20.00	30.00	40.00
BOY ON TRAPEZE......	250.00	375.00	500.00
BOY ROBBING NEST....	600.00	900.00	1200.00
BOY SCOUT............	600.00	900.00	1200.00
BOY SCOUT CAMP, Scout cooking, scout with flag, etc., 1910............	400.00	600.00	800.00
BOYS STEALING WATERMELONS	2000.00	3000.00	4000.00
BREAD WINNER.......	1200.00	1800.00	2400.00
BUFFALO, BUCKING...	750.00	1125.00	1500.00

	G	VG	M
BUILDING SAVINGS patented August 13, 1878, dog springing forward grabs coin from man's hands..........	1200.00	1800.00	2400.00
BULL & BEAR, brass model	800.00	1200.00	1600.00
BULL DOG, dog swallows coin.................	210.00	315.00	420.00
CALAMITY patented August 29, 1905, J&E Stevens Co., three football players	2000.00	3000.00	4000.00
CAT AND MOUSE BANK	575.00	862.50	1150.00
CHARLIE MCCARTHY, sitting with legs crossed on top of trunk, drop coin in back and mouth moves, pot metal, copytright 1938, 5¾" high........	50.00	75.00	100.00

ALWAYS DID DESPISE A MULE
Courtesy PB Eighty-Four, New York

BUILDING SAVINGS
Courtesy PB Eighty-Four, New York

AMERICAN BANK.
Courtesy Lloyd W. Ralston Auctions

CAT AND MOUSE
Courtesy PB Eighty-Four, New York

CALAMITY
Courtesy PB Eighty-Four, New York

BAD ACCIDENT
Courtesy PB Eighty-Four, NY

DOG ON TURNTABLE
Courtesy PB Eighty-Four, NY

**MAMA KATZENJAMMER
AND THE KIDS**
Courtesy PB Eighty-Four NY

PUNCH AND JUDY
Courtesy PB Eighty-Four, NY

ACROBAT
Courtesy PB Eighty-Four, NY

**BOYS STEALING
WATERMELONS**
Courtesy PB Eighty-Four, NY

ORGAN BANK, monkey only
Courtesy Lloyd W. Ralston
Auctions

INITIATING BANK
Courtesy Lloyd W. Ralston
Auctions

ORGAN BANK
Courtesy PB Eighty-Four, NY

**ORGAN GRINDER AND
BEAR**
Courtesy PB Eighty-Four, NY

SPEAKING DOG
Courtesy PB Eighty-Four, NY

DENTIST
Courtesy PB Eighty-Four, NY

STUMP SPEAKER
Courtesy PB Eighty-Four, NY

TEDDY AND THE BEAR
Courtesy PB Eighty-Four, New York

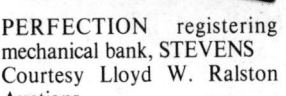

PERFECTION registering mechanical bank, STEVENS
Courtesy Lloyd W. Ralston Auctions

SANTA CLAUS AT THE CHIMNEY
Courtesy PB Eighty-Four, NY

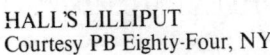

HALL'S LILLIPUT
Courtesy PB Eighty-Four, NY

TANK AND CANNON
Courtesy PB Eighty-Four, NY

	G	VG	M
CHEIN Monkey, seated, tips hat when coin dropped in, tin litho, 5" high.	25.00	37.50	50.00
CHIEF BIG MOON, Indian in teepee, etc. 1899	450.00	675.00	900.00
CHIMPANZEE	1000.00	1500.00	2000.00
CHINESE RECLINING, 1882	1750.00	2625.00	3500.00
CIRCUS TICKET TAKER	160.00	240.00	320.00
CLOWN ON GLOBE, 1873	450.00	675.00	900.00
COLUMBUS	175.00	262.50	350.00
CONFECTIONARY	600.00	900.00	1200.00
COW KICKING cow kicks over boy	600.00	900.00	1200.00
CREEDMORE BANK, man firing into tree, 1877, 10" long	140.00	210.00	280.00

	G	VG	M
CROWING ROOSTER	70.00	105.00	140.00
DANCING BEAR, several figures, building	200.00	300.00	400.00
DAPPER DAN	160.00	240.00	320.00
DARKTOWN BATTERY, black pitcher and catcher, 1888	515.00	782.50	1030.00
DARKY AND CABIN, 1885			
DENTIST BANK, white dentist working on black patient, 1880	1400.00	2000.00	2800.00
DINAH, bust of black woman, 6½"	110.00	165.00	220.00
DOG CHARGES BOY, bronze finish	300.00	450.00	600.00
DOG ON TURNTABLE, JUDD MFG. CO.	210.00	315.00	420.00
DOG STANDING	130.00	195.00	260.00
EAGLE AND EAGLETS, 1883	210.00	315.00	420.00
ELEPHANT, late cast iron, HUBLEY	30.00	45.00	60.00
ELEPHANT, semi-mechanical, cast iron, trunk flips up to catch coin, 5" high	90.00	135.00	180.00
ELEPHANT AND CLOWNS	450.00	675.00	900.00
ELEPHANT AND HOWDAH, 1920	150.00	225.00	300.00
FERRIS WHEEL, HUBLEY/BAUER	800.00	1200.00	1600.00
FORTUNE TELLER patented February 19, 1901, safe, complete with roll of fortunes	300.00	450.00	600.00
THE FORTY-NINER, donkey moves ears and tail	100.00	150.00	200.00
FRENCH'S AUTOMOTIVE, cast iron	500.00	750.00	1000.00
FROG AND SNAKE IN POND lithographed tin mechanical bank in the form of a snake striking at a frog which opens its mouth to receive the coin	2500.00	3750.00	5000.00
FROG, GOAT AND OLD MAN	275.00	412.50	550.00
FROG ON LATTICE, STEVENS, 1870s	140.00	210.00	280.00
FROG ON ROCK, KILGORE MFG. CO.	125.00	187.50	250.00

	G	VG	M
FROG ON STUMP, 1872.	90.00	135.00	180.00
GEM, Dog and building...	137.50	206.25	275.00
GIANT, giant holding a club	9000.00	13500.00	18000.00
GIRL SKIPPING ROPE, with key	4750.00	7125.00	9500.00
GLOBE SAVINGS FUND BANK	200.00	300.00	400.00
GUESSING BANK	400.00	600.00	800.00
HALL'S EXCELSIOR BANK, monkey cashier..	75.00	112.50	150.00
HALL'S LILLIPUT, 1875..	105.00	157.50	210.00
HOME building with two pillars, teller at window..	70.00	105.00	140.00
HORSE RACE	500.00	750.00	1000.00
HUMPTY DUMPTY	135.00	202.50	270.00
INDEPENDENCE HALL	165.00	247.50	330.00
INDIAN SHOOTING BEAR, 1888	315.00	472.50	630.00
INITIATING BANK FIRST DEGREE	1900.00	2850.00	3800.00
JOCKO	300.00	450.00	600.00
JOLLY NIGGER, bust....	56.00	84.00	112.00
JOLLY NIGGER, high hat, 8" high	97.50	146.25	195.00
JOLLY NIGGER, moves ears	50.00	75.00	100.00
JONAH AND THE WHALE, cast iron (Jonah in boat)	500.00	750.00	1000.00
JOHAN AND WHALE (Jonah emerges), offered at $25,000 in1982, no condition stated.			
JUMBO ON PLATFORM.	200.00	300.00	400.00
KATZENJAMMER KIDS.	375.00	562.50	750.00
"Keep 'Em flying" dime register, tin	15.00	22.50	30.00
LEAP FROG BANK, two boys, tree, 1891	640.00	960.00	1280.00
KICK INN Lithographed paper and wood mechanical bank, PRESTO, a mule standing in front of a small building	250.00	375.00	500.00
LIBERTY BELL	130.00	195.00	260.00
LIGHTHOUSE BANK, 1891	250.00	375.00	500.00
LION AND MONKEYS..	200.00	300.00	400.00
LION HUNTER	1350.00	2025.00	2700.00
LITTLE JOE	120.00	180.00	240.00
LOCOMOTIVE	400.00	600.00	800.00
MAGIC	425.00	637.50	850.00
MAGICIAN BANK, 1882.	800.00	1200.00	1600.00

	G	VG	M
MAMA KATZENJAM-MER AND THE KIDS 5¾"	1500.00	2250.00	3000.00
MAMMY FEEDING CHILD	900.00	1350.00	1800.00
MASON AND HOD CAR-RIER, 1887	750.00	1125.00	1500.00
MERRY GO ROUND, semi-mechanical	80.00	120.00	160.00
MEYERS No. 84, Jumbo Elephant	80.00	120.00	160.00
MILKING COW	115.00	232.50	330.00
MONEY BOX BANK, hand-carved on wood base, 10¼"	800.00	1200.00	1600.00
MONEY MOVES THE WORLD, ATLAS BANK	175.00	262.50	350.00
MONKEY AND COCONUT	150.00	225.00	300.00
MONKEY AND LION BANK, 1783	100.00	150.00	200.00
THE MORTAR, square fort	500.00	750.00	1000.00
MOSQUE	300.00	450.00	600.00
MULE BUCKING Black man riding a mule	500.00	750.00	1000.00
MULE ENTERING BARN	250.00	375.00	500.00
NATIONAL BANK	300.00	450.00	600.00
NAUGHTY GIRL BANK, modern	22.50	33.75	45.00
NEW CREEDMORE Meyer no. 54	160.00	240.00	320.00
NEW BANK, cast iron, cir-ca 1875, brass policeman in building, 4½" long....	160.00	240.00	320.00
NORTH POLE J&E Stevens Co., eskimos and dog sled	1400.00	2100.00	2800.00
NOVELTY BANK, house-like bank, 1873	180.00	270.00	360.00
ORGAN BANK, monkey and revolving cat and dog, 7¼" high	250.00	375.00	500.00
ORGAN BANK monkey only	125.00	187.50	250.00
ORGAN BOY AND GIRL patented June 13, 1882, monkey flanked by boy and girl holding tambourine	450.00	675.00	700.00
ORGAN GRINDER AND BEAR	600.00	900.00	1200.00
ORGAN GRINDER AND MONKEY, 1929	90.00	135.00	180.00
OWL, slot in back, cast iron	175.00	262.00	350.00
OWL, slot in head	150.00	225.00	300.00
OWL, turns head, cast iron.	130.00	195.00	260.00

HUMPTY DUMPTY
Photo Courtesy PB Eighty-Four, New York

WILLIAM TELL
Courtesy PB Eighty-Four, New York

CLOWN ON GLOBE
Courtesy PB Eighty-Four, NY

CHEIN Monkey
Courtesy Garth's Auctions Inc.

OWL, turns head.
Courtesy PB Eighty-Four, NY

FORTUNE TELLER
Courtesy PB Eighty-Four, NY

CHIEF BIG MOON
Courtesy PB Eighty-Four, New York

JONAH AND THE WHALE
Courtesy Garth's Auctions Inc.

EAGLE AND EAGLETS
Courtesy PB Eighty-Four, New York

	G	VG	M		G	VG	M
PADDY AND HIS PIG...	515.00	772.50	1030.00	PEGLEG BEGGAR......	325.00	487.50	650.00
PANORAMA, building....	300.00	450.00	600.00	PELICAN, cast iron, "boy			
PATRONIZE THE BLIND				thumbs nose".........	200.00	300.00	400.00
MAN AND HIS DOG				PETER PAN LEAGUE...	175.00	262.50	350.00
patented February 19,				PICTURE GALLERY....	1300.00	1950.00	2600.00
1878, J&E Stevens Co...	1600.00	2400.00	3200.00	PIG, BISMARCK........	300.00	450.00	600.00

TRICK PONY
Courtesy PB Eighty-Four, New York

NEW CREEDMORE
Courtesy PB Eighty-Four, New York

MASON AND HOD-CARRIER
Courtesy PB Eighty-Four, New York

TRICK DOG
Courtesy PB Eighty-Four, New York

LION HUNTER
Courtesy PB Eighty-Four, New York

DARKTOWN BATTERY
Courtesy PB Eighty-Four, New York

PRESTO-MOUSE ON ROOF
Courtesy PB Eighty-Four, New York

FROG AND SNAKE IN POND
Courtesy PB Eighty-Four, New York

HORSE RACE
Courtesy PB Eighty-Four, New York

	G	VG	M		G	VG	M
PIG IN HIGH CHAIR....	232.50	348.75	465.00	PUMP, BUCKET........	200.00	300.00	400.00
PREACHER IN PULPIT..	2000.00	3000.00	4000.00	PUNCH & JUDY,			
PRESTO, shape of building.	87.00	130.00	174.00	Shepherd Hardware, Buffalo, N.Y., circa 1890...	375.00	562.50	750.00
PRESTO-MOUSE ON ROOF lithographed paper on wood..............	10000.00	15000.00	20000.00	RABBIT, tall............	110.00	165.00	220.00
PROFESSOR PUG FROG'S GREAT BICYCLE FEAT...........	900.00	1350.00	1800.00	RABBIT, small, circular base..................	90.00	135.00	180.00
				RABBIT IN CABBAGE PATCH..............	190.00	285.00	380.00

GIRL SKIPPING ROPE
Courtesy PB Eighty-Four, New York

PADDY AND HIS PIG
Courtesy Garth's Auctions Inc.

FROG ON ROCK
Courtesy PB Eighty-Four, New York

TABBY
Courtesy PB Eighty-Four, New York

FROG ON LATTICE
Courtesy PB Eighty-Four, New York

	G	VG	M
RED RIDING HOOD....	7000.00	10500.00	14000.00
RISQUE PIG bank, twist tail..................	100.00	150.00	200.00
ROLLER SKATING.....	6000.00	9000.00	12000.00
ROOSTER	175.00	262.50	350.00
Perfection REGISTERING BANK	2000.00	3000.00	4000.00
ST. BERNARD, semi-mechanical	35.00	52.50	70.00
SANTA CLAUS AT CHIMNEY	400.00	600.00	800.00
SHOOT THE CHUTE....	1500.00	2250.00	3000.00
SNAPPING BULLDOG, Pat. 1878.............	525.00	762.50	1050.00
SPEAKING DOG BANK, J.E. Stevens, pat. 1885...	420.00	630.00	840.00
SQUIRREL AND TREE STUMP	200.00	300.00	400.00

	G	VG	M
STRATO BANK, pot metal, rocket and planet, 8" long, 1950s...........	3.75	5.25	7.50
STUMP SPEAKER, cast iron	450.00	675.00	900.00
TABBY................	60.00	90.00	120.00
TAMMANY BANK, 1875, 5¾" high..........	100.00	150.00	200.00
TANK AND CANNON, 1916	367.50	551.25	735.00
TEDDY AND THE BEAR, man firing at bear in tree, 1907	334.00	501.00	668.00
TELEPHONE	60.00	90.00	110.00
3-STAR ELEPHANT, brass	120.00	180.00	240.00
TRICK DOG, clown with hoop, dog and barrel, 1888 version, has six-part base	234.00	351.00	468.00

	G	VG	M
TRICK DOG............	125.00	187.50	250.00
TRICK DOG, 1888, cast iron, HUBLEY.........	80.00	120.00	160.00
TRICK DOG, clown with hoop, dark dog and dark barrel, 1929...........	133.00	199.50	266.00
TRICK PONY...........	214.00	321.00	428.00
TRICKY PIG..........	112.50	169.25	225.00
TRUST BANK.........	150.00	225.00	300.00
TWO FROGS..........	190.00	285.00	380.00
UNCLE REMUS.........	650.00	975.00	1300.00
UNCLE SAM, cast iron...	200.00	300.00	400.00
UNCLE SAM, has umbrella in left hand, 1886.......	272.50	408.75	545.00

	G	VG	M
UNCLE TOM, with lapels and one star..........	60.00	90.00	120.00
UNCLE TOM, with lapels, one star, brass base.....	400.00	600.00	800.00
U.S. AND SPAIN, cast iron	1400.00	2100.00	2800.00
WATCHDOG SAFE......	105.00	157.50	210.00
WEEDEN'S, tin..........	175.00	262.50	350.00
WILLIAM TELL, 1896...	220.00	330.00	440.00
WIRELESS BANK, 1913..	65.00	97.50	130.00
WOODPECKER.........	350.00	525.00	700.00
WORLD'S FAIR.........	473.00	709.50	946.00
ZOO	375.00	562.50	750.00

PAPER TOYS
(See also Premiums, Comic Character)

The average price for a mint paper toy in the last edition was $20.18, and in this edition it is $25.25, an increase of 25%.

AMERICAN PAPER TOYS
By Barbara and Jonathan Newman

The subject of paper toys has been only superficially treated even in books limited to just that medium. Even though, some brief introduction should be attempted. They have been called cut-outs, punch outs and press outs. By whatever name, forts, planes, trains, ships and much much more have been produced in paper. What adult does not have some memories (usually fond, often frustrating) of crisp booklets, shiny boxes, or just complicated sheets of paper and cardboard toys?

Throughout the period from the end of the last century to the period after World War II, paper was, if not king, certainly close to the throne. It was in many ways, the plastic of its day. Every subject matter found in toys can be found in its own version in paper or cardboard.

Certainly for a start, no collector of military toys or toy soldiers can be unfamiliar with the whole world of paper soldiers, even through they were never quite as popular in this country as in Europe where paper soldiers were born almost 200 years ago. American companies by the turn of the century were turning out paper troops by the thousands. The most popular was easily the McLoughlin Bros. Company which started out with paper toys in 1856 in N.Y.C. and moved to Springfield, Massachusetts in 1920. Their range included beautifully lithographed covered boxed sets of cardboard figures on wooden stands, or, for the young boy with less resources, over a hundred different sheets of American and foreign armies to be cut out and mounted on stands by the purchaser.

During this same general time period, centered around the 10 years from 1895 to 1905, almost every major newspaper in the country (at least those Big City ones with large Sunday editions) had Sunday "Art Supplements" which varied their "give away" fare from Armies or Navies of the world to historical panoramas illustrating our history, from political figures and personalities of the day to cut-out dolls of celebrities with vast wardrobes of clothes. Even the "Globe Quadruple Perfecting Press" itself was offered as a cut out to construct a complete diorama as the Boston Sunday Globe's offering of August 6th, 1896.

Paper houses and villages, a great favorite with little girls of the day, were sold by a wide variety of companies. The earlier ones included the ubiquitous McLoughlin Bros. and Milton Bradley (yes, they're still around) and more recent ones were the World War II era giants in the field, Built-Rite and Megow.

In fact, while there was no shortage in the 20's and 30's, it's WW II that was really the Golden Age of paper toys in this country. The reason is obvious and the lack of any alternative material to paper even caused the King of toy companies, Lionel, to produce as its only offering in the war, a complete train set in die-cut cardboard. Who would have thought such a poor substitute in 1943 would be a sought after and valuable rarity today? If you have one in mint condition you've got a real gem in both the world of toy trains and paper toys.

During these war years every conceivable type of toy, usually given a wartime, patriotic theme, was available. Punchout cardboard sets of "Rap-A-Jap", "Sink The Axis", "Camouflage Defense Force", books of punch out Naval Craft by Rigby, etc. were the birthday, Christmas or other presents of the forties. A whole range of Built-Rite forts, trenches, troops and doll houses are among our own fond memories.

The list and illustrations could go on and on and someday soon perhaps a reasonably definitive book will be written. For the meantime, just settle for a brief taste in words and pictures to either jog your own memory or kindle an interest in a lifetime passion for paper toys.

BARBARA and JONATHAN NEWMAN own and operate The Paper Soldier in Clifton Park, NY which specializes in antique and new paper toys from around the world. As collectors and dealers they are recognized leading experts on all toys made of paper and cardboard.

CONDITION OF A PAPER TOY AND ITS RELATION TO PRICE

The price of a paper toys depends not only on its desirability, but on its condition. A paper toy in mint condition is generally worth twice what that item would bring in good condition, with "very good" falling about equally in between good and mint.

"Mint" means just that; the condition in which it was originally issued — perfect, regardless of age, any white sections being near white to white, no printing or cutting defects, still retains original printing lustre, no damage, no matter how slight, to any part.

"Very Good" indicates a paper toy that has obviously seen some wear, and perhaps use, but in general having a crispness to its appearance that makes it attractive and collectible to all but the most discriminating.

"Good" signals a paper toy that has seen considerable wear, shows its age, but is basically sound. A collector will collect it, but will often not be wholly satisfied with it as an example of his collection, and thus prices are often drastically below that which the same toy in mint can command.

Condition below good results in another drastic drop in price, and paper toys with parts cut out or missing, although otherwise in excellent condition, will usually fall into this lower-priced category, as will anything brittle, no matter how "mint" it may appear otherwise.

"Near-Mint", "Fine", "Very Fine" and similar terms often found in sellers' descriptions denote conditions between Mint and Very Good, and are priced accordingly.

The key to grading is to avoid wishful thinking. Grading can sometimes be a problem to the uninitiated, but common sense will usually prevail, and when possible, a consultation with an expert in the field can often clear up lingering doubts.

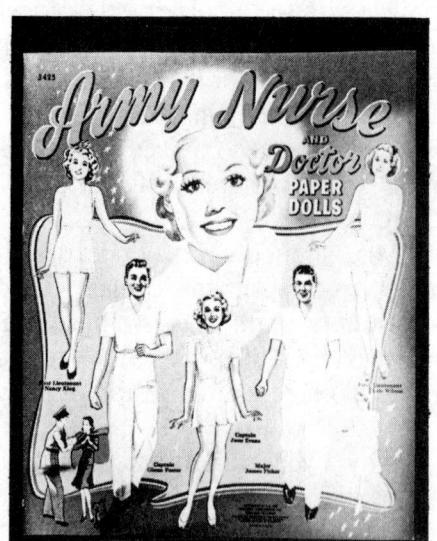

ARMY NURSE AND DOCTOR PAPER DOLLS
Photo by Jonathan A. Newman
Courtesy Barbara and Jonathan Newman

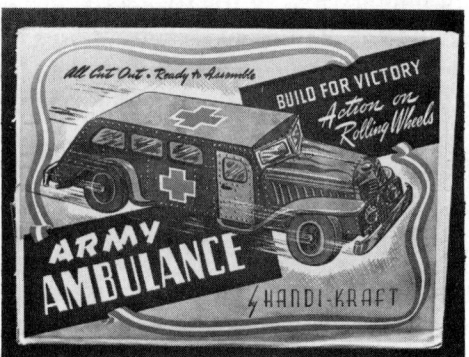

ARMY AMBULANCE. BUILD FOR VICTORY ACTION ON ROLLING WHEELS.
Photo by Jonathan A. Newman
Courtesy Barbara and Jonathan Newman

ALL-NU Cardboard soldiers, No.111, 109, 106, 108
Photo by Jonathan A. Newman
Courtesy Barbara and Jonathan Newman

(Note: Where not specifically noted, paper toys listed are paper dolls)

	G	VG	M
AIR-HOSTESS, 1947 SAALFIELD 2546.....	10.00	15.00	20.00
ALICE FAYE, 1941, MERRILL 4800...........	65.00	97.50	130.00
ALL-NU decal sheet of soldiers, meant to be attached to heavy cardboard backing, circa 1942, by Frank Krupp........	8.00	9.00	10.00
ALL-NU soldiers, 5" high on heavy cardboard, circa 1942-3			
100 Officer marching with sabre................	1.50	2.25	3.00
101 Marching, slope arms, WW I helmet.........	1.50	2.25	3.00
102 Bugler, campaign cap..	1.50	2.25	3.00
103 Signalman, WW I helmet................	1.50	2.25	3.00

	G	VG	M
104 Officer kneeling with binoculars.............	1.50	2.25	3.00
105 Kneeling, firing rifle with WW I helmet......	1.50	2.25	3.00
106 Throwing grenade, WW I helmet..............	1.50	2.25	3.00
107 Fixed bayonet, WW I helmet...............	1.50	2.25	3.00
108 Charging with gas mask, WW I helmet..........	1.50	2.25	3.00
109 Charging with rifle, port arms, WW I helmet.....	1.50	2.25	3.00
110 Seated machine gunner, WW I helmet..........	1.50	2.25	3.00
111 Flag-bearer, WW I helmet...............	1.50	2.25	3.00
112 General McArthur....	2.50	3.75	5.00
113 Nurse.............	1.50	2.25	3.00

	G	VG	M
114 2 Men carrying wounded soldier on stretcher, WW II helmets.........	1.50	2.25	3.00
115 2 Men firing rifles from prone position, WW II helmets...............	1.50	2.25	3.00
116 Soldier on wireless radio radio.................	1.50	2.25	3.00
117 3 Soldiers w/rifles leaving boat, WW II helmets.	1.50	2.25	3.00
118 2 paratroopers, one w/tommy gun, WW II helmets...............	1.50	2.25	3.00
119 Ski trooper...........	1.75	2.63	3.50
120 Soldier advancing w/fle, WW II helmet......	1.50	2.25	3.00
150 3 Men in jeep, WW I helmets..............	1.50	2.25	3.00
151 5-man team with cannon, WW I helmets.....	1.50	2.25	3.00
152 2 men manning wheeled AA gun, WW I helmets.	1.50	2.25	3.00
153 Tank with 3 men.....	1.50	2.25	3.00
154 Ambulance..........	1.00	1.50	2.00
155 Truck w/soldiers in rear, WW II helmets.........	1.50	2.25	3.00
ALL-NU Boxed Set of 24 of the above soldiers.......	No Price Found		
AMERICAN BEAUTIES, PAPER DOLLS, circa 1942, REUBEN LILJA & CO. No. 917..........	5.00	7.50	10.00
AMERICAN BEAUTY PAPER DOLLS with dresses worn by White House first Ladies 1789-1951, MERRILL No. 154815, 1951......	7.50	11.25	15.00
AMERICAN DEFENSE BATTLES PUNCH-OUT BOOK by George Trimmer, MERRILL No. 3430, 1940...........	20.00	30.00	40.00
AMERICAN FAMILY PAPER-DOLL BOOK "Costumes for all the family from 1610 to now", GRINNELL No.C1002............	15.00	22.50	30.00
AMOS & ANDY — Cutout cardboard of just Andy, 8½" high, stand-up..	2.50	3.75	5.00
ANIMAL PAPER DOLLS TO DRESS, 1950, SAALFIELD 2598, Bear, Monkey, Pig, Kitten....	6.00	9.00	12.00

	G	VG	M
ANIMALS TO PAINT, 1910, SAALFIELD.....	3.00	4.50	6.00
ANN BLYTHE, 1952 MERRILL No. 2550-25.	14.00	21.00	28.00
ARMY AIRFORCES AIRCRAFT IDENTIFICATION SILHOUETTE MODEL — Feb. 1943, ¹/₇₂ scale of Japanese fighter Najajima T-97, A.N.F. 7x11" envelope........	5.00	7.50	10.00
ARMY AMBULANCE, circa 1942, HANDI-KRAFT	12.50	18.75	25.00
ARMY CUT OUTS, 1937, SALLFIELD No. 245...	25.00	37.50	50.00
ARMY NURSE AND DOCTOR PAPER DOLLS, 1942, MERRILL 3425	11.00	16.50	22.00
AROUND THE WORLD WITH BOB AND BARBARA, 1946, CHILDRENS PRESS No. 3000.............	5.00	7.50	10.00
ASSEMBLE 9 MODEL WARPLANES, 4 Model Tanks, 1941, Fawcett Publications, LOWE....	20.00	30.00	40.00
AVA GARDNER, 1949, 1952 WHITMAN No. 119215	20.00	30.00	40.00
BABY BROTHER by Queen Holden, 1929, WHITMAN 920.......	20.00	30.00	40.00
BABY FIRST STEP, 1965, (Mattel) WHITMAN No. 1997	2.50	3.75	5.00
BABYLAND 1955, MERRILL No. 3642........	10.00	15.00	20.00
BABY PAT 1963 WHITMAN No. 2072........	2.00	3.00	4.00
BABY SITTER PAPER DOLLS, LOWE No. 945.	10.00	15.00	20.00
BARBARA BRITTON Paper Dolls with Magic Stay-On Costumes, 1954, SAALFIELD 5190, Boxed Set................	20.00	30.00	40.00
BARBIE AND KEN 1962 WHITMAN No. 4797, 7x12" boxed set........	3.50	5.25	7.00
BARBIE AND SKIPPER 1964 WHITMAN No. 1957, Yachting outfits...	2.50	3.75	5.00

 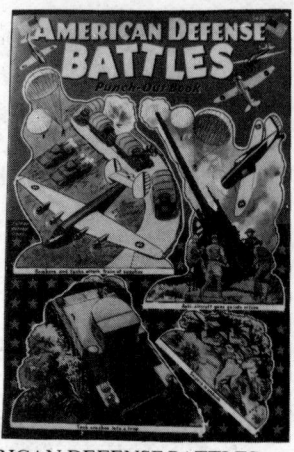

Left, ALICE FAYE. Right, AMERICAN DEFENSE BATTLES
PUNCH-OUT BOOK.
Photo by Jonathan A. Newman
Courtesy Barbara and Jonathan Newman

	G	VG	M
BARBIE BOUTIQUE 1973 WHITMAN No. 1954...	1.50	2.25	3.00
BEAUTIFUL PAPER DOLLS by Betty Campbell, 1941, SAALFIELD No. 242, has some of same paper dolls as LITTLE MISS AMERICAN PAPER DOLLS	10.00	15.00	20.00
BELLE OF THE BALL PAPER DOLLS, 1948, SAALFIELD 2702	7.00	10.50	14.00
BETSY McCALL, 1971, WHITMAN No. 4744...	2.50	3.75	5.00
BETSY McCALL AROUND THE WORLD PAPER DOLLS, circa 1962	5.00	7.50	10.00
BETSY McCALL DRESS'N PLAY PAPER DOLLS, 1963, STANDARD/ TOYCRAFT/McCALL No. 802 12x18" boxed set	7.50	11.25	15.00
BETSY ROSS AND HER FRIENDS — 1963, PLATT AND MUNK No. 224B, 7x11" boxed set	5.00	7.50	10.00
BETTY AND JOAN, 1941, 1945, WHITMAN No. 1015, Joan also appears in Mary and Joan, Lois & Joan	6.00	9.00	12.00

BETTY BONNETT —
HER FAMILY AND
FRIENDS by Sheila
Young, GEORGE W.
JACOBS & CO., Phila.

	G	VG	M
1915. Each series with 6 sheets and folder. First series	85.00	125.50	170.00
Second series	80.00	120.00	160.00
Third series	80.00	120.00	160.00
BETTY GRABLE, 1951, MERRILL No. 1558....	30.00	45.00	60.00
BETTY SUE — A CUT OUT DOLL — circa 1940 No. 1010	9.00	13.50	18.00
THE BEVERLY HILLBILLIES — Jed, Jethro, Granny and Elly May WHITMAN No. 1955, 1964	3.50	5.25	7.00
BIG-GIRL PAPER DOLLS, 1940, McLOUGHLIN BROS. No. 707, actually MILTON BRADLEY...	7.50	11.25	15.00
BIG INVASION PUNCH-OUT BOOK, 1964, WHITMAN No. 1936, Punchout of beach landing	4.00	6.00	8.00
BILD-A-SET CONSTRUCTOR KIT No. 85, boxed, Erector-type set of cardboard	6.00	9.00	12.00
BINSON-FREEMAN PRE FLIGHT TRAINER, cockpit and how to fly course	75.00	112.50	150.00
BIRTHDAY PARTY STAND-UP CUT-OUT DOLLS, 1944, NATIONAL SYNDICATE DISPLAYS, INC., 20 boys and girls	17.50	26.25	35.00
BLUE BONNET PAPER DOLLS by Florence Salter, MERRILL No. 3444, 1942	9.00	13.50	18.00
BLUE FEATHER AND SILVER CLOUD, 1940s, ABBOTT No. 1356, Indian dolls	9.00	13.50	18.00
BOARDING SCHOOL DOLLS AND CLOTHES, 1942, MERRILL No. 3492....	11.00	16.50	22.00
BOB HOPE AND DOROTHY LAMOUR, 1942, WHITMAN No. 976	42.50	63.75	85.00

BOB HOPE & DOROTHY
LAMOUR CUT-OUT BOOK

Top Right: BETTY BONNET -
HER FAMILY AND FRIENDS
- Second Series
Photo by Jonathan A. Newman
Courtesy Barbara and Jonathan
Newman

BIRTHDAY PARTY STAND-
UP CUT-OUT DOLLS
Photo by Jonathan A. Newman
Courtesy Barbara and Jonathan
Newman

BILD-A-SET CONSTRUCTOR KIT
Photo by Jonathan A. Newman
Courtesy Barbara and Jonathan Newman

Left, BETTY GRABLE Paper Dolls. Right, BOOTS AND HER
BUDDIES PAPER DOLLS.
Photo by Jonathan A. Newman
Courtesy Barbara and Jonathan Newman

	G	VG	M
BOBBY SOCKS CUT OUT DOLLS designed by Doris Lane Butler, 1945, WHITMAN No. 988	10.00	15.00	20.00
BOMBERS by Schomburg, WHITMAN No. 961, 1943, B-17, B-25, B-24, Douglas A-20A, Short "Stirling"	25.00	37.50	50.00
BOOK OF AIRPLANES, A, WHITMAN No. 923, 1930	9.00	13.50	18.00
BOOK OF PAPER DOLL CUT-OUTS, THE, 1927, SAALFIELD No. 2051	20.00	30.00	40.00
THE BRADY BUNCH, 1973, WHITMAN No. 1976	1.50	2.25	3.00
BRENDA LEE Teenage Celebrity, 1961, LOWE No. 2785	6.00	9.00	12.00
BRENDA LEE, 1964, No. 4360 DE JOURNETTE, 6½x10" boxed set, includes toy phonograph and records	10.00	15.00	20.00
BRIDAL PARTY, 1950, WHITMAN No. 1187, five dolls	5.00	7.00	10.00
BRIDE AND GROOM,, 1949, MERRILL No. 3443	10.00	15.00	20.00
BRIDE AND GROOM, 1949, MERRILL No. 1555	10.00	15.00	20.00
BRIDE AND GROOM MILITARY WEDDING PARTY, 1941, MERRILL No. 3411, 16 dolls	20.00	30.00	40.00
BRIDE DOLL CUT-OUT BOOK, 1940s, SAMUEL LOWE No. 1043	9.00	13.50	18.00
BROTHER AND SISTER STATUETTE DOLLS, 1950, WHITMAN 1182-15, two heavy cardboard 7½" dolls	6.00	9.00	12.00
BUFFY paper Dolls ("Family Affair") 1968, WHITMAN No. 1955	5.00	7.50	10.00
BUFFY AND JODY, 1970 ("Family Affair"), WHITMAN 4764, Two magic dolls with Stay-On wardrobes	4.00	6.00	8.00

BUILT-RITE

BUILT-RITE began in 1922 as a manufacturer of cardboard boxes. Somewhere along the line, at least as early as 1934, it began to produce cardboard construction toys, and appears to have manufactured them into the 1950s, with its greatest period of success probably enjoyed during and just prior to WW II. The company remains in business as Warren Paper Products Co., making card games, games and puzzles. Numbers and words in bold print here are Built-Rite's own descriptions.

BUILT-RITE No. 20 Army Battery Set
Photo by Ed Poole

BUILT-RITE Airport No. 26.
Photo by Jonathan A. Newman
Courtesy Barbara and Jonathan Newman

BUILT-RITE Fort No. 25, with Barclay soldiers
Photo by Ed Poole

BUILT-RITE Army Trench, Set No.14.
Photo by Jonathan A. Newman
Courtesy Barbara and Jonathan Newman

	G	VG	M
No.1 Toy Soldiers, WW I helmets, per each.......	1.50	2.25	3.00
No.2 Toy Trench.........	10.00	15.00	20.00
No.7 Private Garage, brick.	7.50	11.25	15.00
No.7 Army Plane Hanger	12.50	18.75	25.00
No.8 House, brick........	20.00	30.00	40.00
No.9 House, stucco and brick.................	20.00	30.00	40.00
No.10 House, two story, brick and shingle.......	25.00	37.50	50.00
No.14 "Front Line" Trench and soldier set, with trench, 6 WW II soldiers.	4.00	6.00	8.00
No.15 Commercial Garage.	17.50	26.25	35.00
No.16 Ford, no ramp......	17.50	26.25	35.00
No.17 Service Station.....	25.00	37.50	50.00
No.18 Airport..........	20.00	30.00	40.00
No.19 Railroad Station....	15.00	22.50	30.00
No.20 Railroad Tunnel....	8.00	12.00	16.00
No.20 Army Battery Set...	37.50	56.25	75.00
No.22 Army Outpost......	12.50	18.75	25.00

	G	VG	M
No.25 Ford, one ramp.....	50.00	75.00	100.00
No.25A-26-piece Fort and Soldier set same fort as 25, WWII soldier, 2 sand-bag foxholes and fibreboard pistol........	60.00	90.00	120.00
No.26 Airport...........	25.00	37.50	50.00
No.28 Garage and Super Service Station.........	20.00	30.00	40.00
No.33 Lokdwood Dolls, late 1940s, paper dolls........	5.00	7.50	10.00
No.33 House, Tudor type..	25.00	37.50	50.00
No.34 House, two story....	25.00	37.50	50.00
No.36 House............	25.00	37.50	50.00
No. 36F 3-Room Furnished Doll House............	25.00	37.50	50.00
No.45 Living Room Furniture	12.50	18.75	25.00
No.46 Dining Room Furniture	12.50	18.75	25.00
No.47 Bedroom Furniture..	12.50	18.75	25.00

	G	VG	M
No.48 Bathroom Furniture.	12.50	18.75	25.00
No.49 Kitchen Furniture...	12.50	18.75	25.00
No.50 Army Raiders' Victory Unit, 28 pieces, truck, tank, AA gun, jeep, semitrack truck, 20 soldiers, WW II........	17.50	26.25	35.00
No.55 5 Miniature cardboard houses..........	20.00	30.00	40.00
No.56 5 Miniature buildings, church, school, RR station, firehouse, drugstore.	21.00	31.50	42.00
No.57M 8 Piece Farm Set.	10.00	15.00	20.00
No.60 Navy Battle Fleet and Coast Artillery Gun.....	12.50	18.75	25.00
No.66 3-Piece Kitchen Set..	No Price Found		
No.75 Living Room Furniture.............	12.50	18.75	25.00
No.76 Dining Room Furniture.............	12.50	18.75	25.00
No.77 Bed Room Furniture.	12.50	18.75	25.00
No.77 American Ranger Fighters, 8 vehicles, WWII soldiers........	19.00	28.50	38.00
No.78 Kitchen Furniture...	12.50	18.75	25.00
No.100A Fortress, circa 1938, two ramps........	60.00	90.00	120.00
No.105 Farm Set with 20 plastic animals........	15.00	22.50	30.00
No.111 Railroad Accessory Set.................	12.00	18.00	24.00
No.112 American Fighters - Includes 110A fortress with soldiers, cannons, etc, 55 pieces, no flag on tower...............	75.00	112.50	150.00
No.115 Doll House, Garage Set (with car).........	25.00	37.50	50.00
No.119 Farm Set.........	21.00	31.50	42.00
No.120 Five Room Suburban Doll House.......	**25.00**	**37.50**	**50.00**
No.128 Miniature Village and Scenery Set.......	25.00	37.50	50.00
No.156 Miniature Houses and Buildings..........	25.00	37.50	50.00
No.201 26 Piece Guardsman Set, 2 trenches, artillery base, cannon, pistol, WWII soldiers........	25.00	37.50	50.00
No.202 Train Scenery (28 pieces, Terminal, Scenery, etc).................	No Price Found		
No.204F Furnished Country Estate.............	25.00	37.50	50.00
No.210 Railroad Station and Accessories..........	10.00	15.00	20.00

	G	VG	M
No.212 Station and Railroad Accessories...........	20.00	30.00	40.00
No.300 Stock and Grain Elevator..............	5.00	7.50	10.00
No.415 House, circa 1943, 13x20" boxed set with 19" house and garage, 27 pieces of furniture, sedan, baby buggy, shrubbery, etc.............	30.00	45.00	60.00
No.460 Pocket Size Series of Minatures Paperdoll Set..................	6.00	9.00	12.00
No.566 Village...........	20.00	30.00	40.00
No.1001 Modern Stock Farm................	12.50	18.75	25.00
No.1422 Fort and Soldiers (94 pieces, 2-ramp fort)..	No Price Found		
No.2050 Country Estate, house, bushes, dog, cat, baby buggy...........	13.00	19.50	26.00
Bathroom Furniture Set, 7¼ x 8¼" boxed set.....	12.50	18.75	25.00

End BUILT—RITE Listing

	G	VG	M
CAMOUFLAGE DEFENSE FORCE — Airplane, soldiers, anti-aircraft guns all hidden within farm buildings. Heavy cardboard. JAY LINE MANUFACTURING CO., 431, boxed. Circa 1943............	17.50	26.25	35.00
CAREER GIRLS WITH CLOTH-LIKE CLOTHES, 1944, WHITMAN NO.937 by Doris Lane Butler............	7.50	11.25	15.00
CHARMIN' CHATTY, 1964, WHITMAN No.1959..............	2.50	3.75	5.00
CHARMING PAPER DOLLS, circa 1960, SAALFIELD No.1357..	2.00	3.00	4.00
CHEERLEADER — TEEN AGE DOLL, 1950? STEPHENS PUBLISHING CO. NO.182, Mary and Elaine and four pages of clothes...............	2.25	3.38	4.50
CHILDREN FROM OTHER LANDS, 1961, WHITMAN No.2089, 8 cut-out dolls and native costumes............	4.00	6.00	8.00

CLAUDETTE COLBERT PAPER DOLLS
Photo by Jonathan A. Newman
Courtesy Barbara and Jonathan Newman

COLLEGE STYLE PAPER DOLLS
Photo by Jonathan A. Newman
Courtesy Barbara and Jonathan Newman

CUT-OUT DOLLS PUPPIES AND
KITTENS
Photo by Jonathan A. Newman
Courtesy Barbara and Jonathan Newman

	G	VG	M
CHILDREN IN THE SHOE, 1949, MERRILL NO.1562	6.00	9.00	12.00
CINDERELLA STEPS OUT, LOWE No.1242	6.00	9.00	12.00
CIRCUS DAY—1946 by Art Tanchon, STEPHENS PRINTING NO.135, Animals, clown, circus cages and wagons	3.00	4.50	6.00
CIRCUS PAPER DOLLS, 1952, NO.2610, SAALFIELD	4.00	6.00	8.00
CLAIRE MCCARDELL— designer of the American look, 1956, WHITMAN No.2067	9.00	13.50	18.00
CLAUDETTE COLBERT, 1943, SAALFIELD No.2451	25.00	37.50	50.00
CLOTH-LIKE CLOTHES FOR 3 CUTE GIRLS, 1949, WHITMAN No.1178:15, Flocked clothes	7.50	11.25	15.00
CLOTHES MAKE A LADY, 1941, LOWE No.1029	8.00	12.00	16.00
COKE CROWD, THE, 1946, MERRILL No.3445, 8 teens, costumes	11.00	16.50	22.00
COLLEGE STYLE PAPER DOLLS 1941, MERRILL 3400	11.00	16.50	22.00
COLORGRAPHIC STATUE-ETTES, 1943, 3-Dimensional stand-up paper dolls of Marine, Soldier, Sailor Nurse, WAAC, WAVE, boxed	7.50	11.25	15.00

	G	VG	M
COMET MODEL AIRPLANE CO. Die Cut Glider, 5½x8" sheet containing die cut U.S. Army fighter printed in 1942 by the Comet Model Airplane Co.	3.00	4.50	6.00
COMMANDO MACHINE GUN 1940s. Thin cardboard cut-out makes model over 25" long	10.00	15.00	20.00
CONNIE FRANCIS, 1963, WHITMAN No.1956	5.00	7.50	10.00
CORONATION CUT-OUT MODEL BOOK	22.50	33.75	45.00
CORONATION GLITTER MODEL BOOK	10.00	15.00	20.00
CORONATION PAPER DOLLS AND COLORING BOOK, 1953, SAALFIELD No.4450, 10½x15" book. Queen Elizabeth, Prince Philip, young Prince Charles and Princess Ann	12.50	18.75	25.00
COWBOY AND COWGIRL Cut-outs, 1950, MERRILL No.3449	6.00	9.00	12.00

CIRCUS DAY Cut-Out Book.
Photo by Jonathan A. Newman. Courtesy Barbara and Jonathan Newman

	G	VG	M
COWBOY CUTOUTS Circa 1930s, PLATT AND MUNK.............	6.00	9.00	12.00
COWBOYS AND INDIANS CUTOUTS, 1937 SAALFIELD..........	7.00	10.50	14.00
COWGIRL JILL AND COWBOY JOE, MERRILL No.3459........	6.00	9.00	12.00
THE CRADLE CROWD, 1948, Four doll babies with cloth-like clothes, WHITMAN No. 1173..	3.50	4.75	7.00
CUT AND STICK-OUR ARMY AND NAVY IN ACTION, MERRILL No.4835, 1942.........	20.00	30.00	40.00
CUT-ME OUT PAPER DOLLS, 1940s, ABBOTT No.1358..............	5.00	7.50	10.00
CUT-OUT DOLLS, PUPPIES AND KITTEN,S WHITMAN No.931, 1939................	20.00	30.00	40.00
CUT-OUT DOLLS WITH PAINTS AND CLOTHES TO COLOR, by Avis Mac, WHITMAN No.983, circa 1930s 11x18" book with four 17" children and 16 pages of clothing and sheet of paints........	20.00	30.00	40.00
CYD CHARISSE 1956, WHITMAN No.2084...	15.00	22.50	30.00
DANCING DOLLS with famous costumes, MERRILL No. 3448, 1954, ballet dancers.........	7.50	11.25	15.00
DAVY CROCKETT PUNCH OUT BOOK, 1955, No.1943........	11.25	16.88	22.50

	G	VG	M
DEANNA DURBIN, 1940, MERRILL No.3480....	25.00	37.50	50.00
DEBS AND SUB DEBS Paper Doll Book, 1941, No.2361 SAALFIELD, 20 Punchouts.........	20.00	30.00	40.00
DECALCO-LITHO CO. Paper Dolls Sheets. Circa 1920s, 8x10½" sheets, 1.Woman and girl and 9 outfits. 2.Woman and girl and 10 outfits. 3.Two women and 7 outfits. Price per sheet.........	4.00	6.00	8.00
DENNISON'S CREPE PAPER DOLL OUTFIT No.36................	20.00	30.00	40.00
DENNISON'S DOLLS AND DRESSES No.37, circa 1930............	20.00	30.00	40.00
DIANE AND DAPHNE THE ROUND ABOUT DOLLS BOOK, 1937, No.545 McLOUGHLIN BROS. Large cut-outs by Campbell.............	17.50	26.25	35.00
DIANA LYNN PAPER DOLLS, 1953, SAALFIELD 157910...	9.00	13.50	18.00
DICK THE SAILOR, circa 1942, SAMUEL LOWE No.L1074.............	7.50	11.25	15.00
DISNEYLAND PARK PUNCH OUT, 1960, No.175..............	2.50	3.75	5.00
DODIE FROM MY THREE SONS TV Series, 1971, ARTCRAFT No.5115, Dodie and dolly............	3.50	5.25	7.00
DOLLS FROM STORYLAND by Vivian Robbins, 1948, MERRILL 1554...........	7.50	11.25	15.00
DOLLS THAT WALK — "They Walk—They Dance — They Play", designed by Emily Sprague Wurl, WHITMAN No.977, 1939, two identical girls and two identical boys.........	17.50	26.25	35.00

DOUBLE WEDDING 15
PAPER DOLLS

DENISON'S CREPE PAPER
DOLL OUTFIT No.36

Courtesy Barbara and Jonathan
Newman   Photo by Jonathan A. Newman

	G	VG	M
DONNA REED PAPER DOLLS, 1960, SAALFIELD/ART-CRAFT No.5197, 9x12" boxed set............	12.50	18.75	25.00
DORIS DAY, 1952, WHITMAN No.210325......	15.00	22.50	30.00
DOROTHY PROVINE, 1962, WHITMAN No.1964.............	12.50	18.75	25.00
DOUBLE DATE CUT-OUT DOLLS by Eileen Fon Vaughan, 1949, WHITMAN No. 962...	5.50	8.25	11.00
DOUBLE WEDDING, 1939, MERRILL 3472..	21.00	31.50	42.00
DOWN ON THE FARM, 1940s, LOWE 1056.....	9.00	13.50	18.00
DR. KILDARE AND NURSE SUSAN, early 1960s, LOWE No.2740..	6.00	9.00	12.00
DRESS-UP DOLL BOOK, THE, 1953 TREASURE BOOKS No.T-167......	5.00	7.50	10.00
DRESS UP FOR THE NEW YORK WORLD'S FAIR by Judy and Barry Martin, SPERTUS No.700, 1963..........	3.50	5.25	7.00
DRESS-UP PAPER DOLL CUT-OUTS 1947, REUBEN LILJA & CO.	5.50	8.25	11.00
DRUM MAJOR AND MAJORETTE PAPER DOLLS, 1941, MER-RILL No.3415.........	14.00	21.00	28.00
8 AGES OF JUDY, THE by Fern Bisil Peat, 1941, LOWE L 1025, Judy as baby and ages 1-7......	20.00	30.00	40.00

	G	VG	M
ELIZABETH TAYLOR, 1950, WHITMAN No.973-10.............	15.00	22.50	30.00
ESKIMO CUT OUTS by Milo Winter, 1939, WHITMAN 1054......	5.00	7.50	10.00
ESTHER WILLIAMS, 1950, MERRILL 1563, 3 dolls	25.00	37.50	50.00
EVE ARDEN PAPER DOLLS, 1953, SAALFIELD 158510...	12.50	18.75	25.00
EVELYN RUDY — Little Star of Screen and Television, 1958, SAALFIELD No.1745..............	10.00	15.00	20.00
FABULOUS HIGH FASHION MODELS, 1958, BONNIE BROOKS/CHILD CRAFT No.2776.......	4.50	6.75	9.00
FAIRY FOLK CUT-OUT PAPER DOLLS by Margaret Carlson, STILL & EDWARDS CO., INC., 1920s..........	11.00	16.00	22.00
FAMILY PRINCESS PAPER DOLLS, 1958, MERRILL No.1548....	9.00	13.50	18.00
FAMILY AFFAIR, 1968, WHITMAN No.4767...	3.50	5.25	7.00
FAMILY OF PAPER DOLLS, 1947, SAALFIELD 2564.....	10.00	15.00	20.00
FAMILY OF PAPER DOLLS BY QUEEN HOLDEN, WHITMAN No.991, Mother, Father, Nurse, 6 kids..........	22.50	33.75	45.00
FARM CUT-OUTS by Milo Winter, 1938, WHITMAN No.1054, 6½x10½", six pages of heavy paper cut-outs....	5.00	7.50	10.00
THE FASHION BOOK OF THE ROUND ABOUT DOLLS, 1936, McLOUGHLIN BROS. Over an inch thick, eight stand-up dolls, plus scissors and pack of paper dolls clothes in package. By Betty Campbell......	20.00	30.00	40.00
FASHION CUT-OUTS with Sturdibilt Dolls, 1940s, LOWE No.1243........	6.00	9.00	12.00

FAIRY FOLK CUT-OUT PAPER DOLLS,
Little Bo-Peep.
Photo by Jonathan A. Newman
Courtesy Barbara and Jonathan Newman

GRACE KELLY 2 CUT-OUT DOLLS
AND CLOTHES
Photo by Jonathan A. Newman
Courtesy Barbara and Jonathan Newman

GLENN MILLER MARION HUTTON
TURNABOUT DOLL BOOK
Photo by Jonathan A. Newman
Courtesy Barbara and Jonathan Newman

	G	VG	M
FIFTEEN ABC BLOCKS TO PLAY AND LEARN, 1933, WHITMAN No.976, book containing 15 die-cut blocks to put together. Illustrations of nursery rhymes, alphabet letters, animals and numbers on each block	10.00	15.00	20.00
FIRE FIGHTERS IN ACTION, SAALFIELD, 1938	11.00	16.50	22.00
FIRE HOUSE P-18 by MEGOW, 1945, Brick firehouse. Boxed set	7.50	11.25	15.00
FIVE LITTLE PEPPERS, LITTLE WOMEN AND ANNIE LAURIE, 1941, LOWE L1030, 3-book set	25.00	37.50	50.00
THE FLYING NUN, 1968, 1969, ARTCRAFT No.4417	6.00	9.00	12.00
FOUR SISTERS PAPER DOLLS, 1943, SAALFIELD No.269	7.50	11.25	15.00
FOURTEEN DOGS TO CUT OUT AND STAND UP, Copyright 1930, WHITMAN, No.935, 12 pages of dogs, cardboard punchouts	10.00	15.00	20.00
FRENCH INFANTRY — Milton Bradley? circa 1915, approx. 6" high.			

	G	VG	M
Single figure, each cardboard	1.50	2.25	3.00
FRONTIER FORT, 1952, MERRILL No257225	4.50	6.75	9.00
FUN FARM, Reed and Associates	2.50	3.75	5.00
GENE AUTRY RANCH CUT-OUT BOOK, 1940, MERRILL Publishers	12.50	18.75	25.00
GENE AUTRY MELODY RANCH CUT-OUT DOLLS, 1950, WHITMAN No.990-10	17.50	26.25	35.00
GENE AUTRY RANCH cut-out book, 1953	15.00	22.50	30.00
GIGI PERREAU PAPER DOLLS, 1951, SAALFIELD 1542	7.00	10.50	14.00
GIGI PERREAU, 1951, SAALFIELD No2605	7.50	11.25	15.00
GIRL FRIEND-BOY FRIEND PAPER DOLLS, 1955, SAALFIELD No.1605	6.00	9.00	12.00
GIRL FRIENDS paper dolls, 1944, WHITMAN No.974	8.00	12.00	16.00
GIRL PILOTS OF THE FERRY COMMAND, 1943, MERRILL 4852	20.00	30.00	40.00
GIRLS IN UNIFORM PAPER DOLLS BOOK, circa 1942 No.L1048	12.50	18.75	25.00
GLAMOUR PARADE CUT-OUT DOLLS, STEPHENS PUBLISHING CO.,			

	G	VG	M
No.184, 1950s? Four models and four pages of clothes	3.50	5.25	7.00
GLENN MILLER MARION HUTTON TURNABOUT DOLL BOOK, 1942, LOWE No.21041	37.50	56.25	75.00
GLORIA JEAN PAPER DOLL CUT-OUTS, 1940, SAALFIELD No.1661..	27.50	41.25	55.00
GONE WITH THE WIND, 1940, MERRILL No.3404, 18 dolls.......	95.00	142.50	190.00
GONE WITH THE WIND, 1940, MERRILL 3405, 5 dolls	92.50	138.75	185.00
GOOD NEIGHBOR PAPER DOLLS, 1944, SAALFIELD No.2487..	7.00	10.50	14.00
GRACE KELLY 2 CUT-OUT DOLLS AND CLOTHES No.2049 WHITMAN, 1955......	15.00	22.50	30.00
GRACE KELLY, 1956, WHITMAN No.2069...	12.50	18.75	25.00
GULLIVER'S TRAVELS No.1261 cut-outs, 1939, SAALFIELD	24.00	36.00	48.00
HAIR-DO DOLLS BY QUEEN HOLDEN, 1948, WHITMAN 991..	15.00	22.50	30.00
HARRY THE SOLDIER, 1941, SAMUEL LOWE No.L1074	7.50	11.25	15.00
HAYLEY MILLS, "THE MOONSPINNERS", 1964, WHITMAN No.1960	9.00	13.50	18.00
HEAVY CRUISER "This Is The Navy", circa 1943 SKYLINE MFG. CO...	5.00	7.50	10.00
HEE HAW, 1971, ART-CRAFT No.5139.......	4.00	6.00	8.00
HEIDI AND PETER, circa 1970, SAALFIELD No.1355	2.00	3.00	4.00
HERE COMES THE BRIDE, 1952, WHITMAN No.118915......	7.00	10.50	14.00
HERE'S THE BRIDE, 1953, WHITMAN No2109..........	6.00	9.00	12.00
HIGH SCHOOL GIRLS, 1948, MERRILL No1551	11.00	16.50	22.00

	G	VG	M
HISTORICAL DOLLS TO CUT OUT AND DRESS, 1962, PLATT & MUNK No.226B, 7x11" boxed set. Mother, father, and two children of heavy cardboard, plus outfits	4.00	6.00	8.00
HOLIDAY PAPER DOLLS, 1950s, SAALFIELD No.1742..	2.50	3.75	5.00
HOLLYWOOD FASHION DOLLS 1939, SAALFIELD No.397, 12 male and female dolls, clothes...............	17.50	26.25	35.00
HOLLYWOOD FASHIONS, 1949, SAALFIELD No.1535..	6.00	9.00	12.00
HOUR OF CHARM PAPER DOLLS, 1943, women musicians, SAALFIELD No.2481..	25.00	37.50	50.00

HOUSE FOR SALE.
Photo by Jonathan A. Newman
Courtesy Barbara and Jonathan Newman

JAUNTY JUNIORS.
Photo by Jonathan A. Newman
Courtesy Barbara and Jonathan Newman

LITTLE MARY MIXUP AND HER FRIEND PEGGY.
Photo by Jonathan Newman
Courtesy Barbara and Jonathan Newman

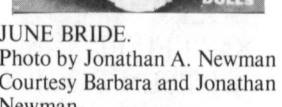

JUNE BRIDE.
Photo by Jonathan A. Newman
Courtesy Barbara and Jonathan Newman

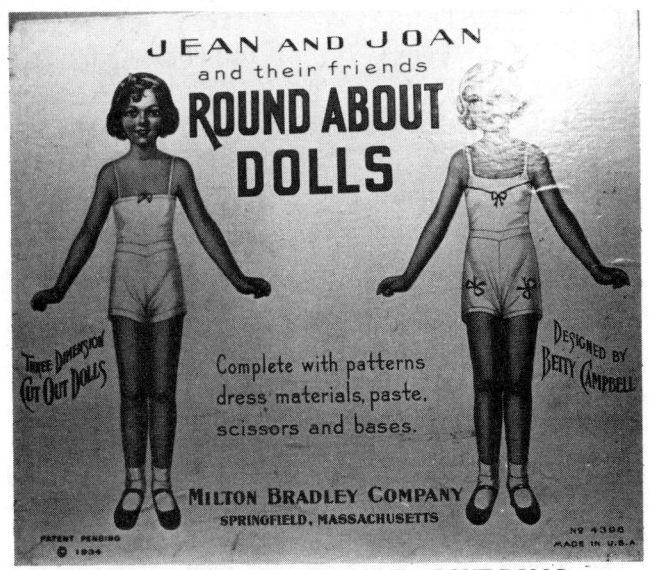

JEAN AND JOAN AND THEIR ROUND ABOUT DOLLS
Photo by Jonathan A. Newman
Courtesy Barbara and Jonathan Newman

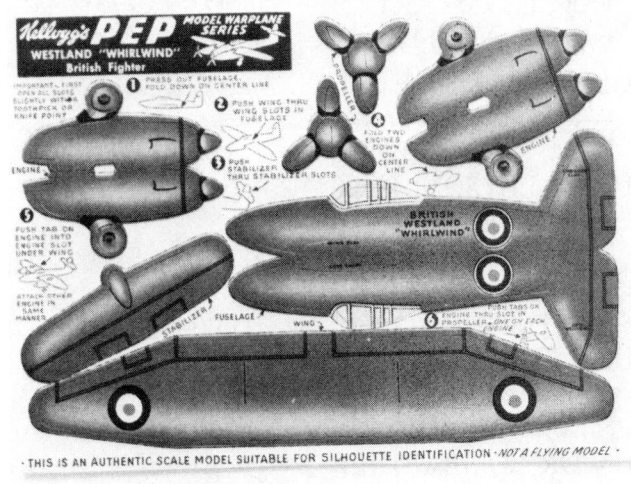

KELLOGG'S PEP Warplane, cardboard, circa 1944.
Courtesy HAKE'S Americana & Collectibles

	G	VG	M
HOUSE FOR SALE, 1962, LOWE No.9042	12.50	18.75	25.00
HOUSE THAT JACK BUILT, circa 1895, BLISS, R.I., paper litho, house and story's characters with stands	200.00	300.00	400.00
HOODY DOODY Puppet Show Punch-out Book Copyright 1952, WHITMAN No.211129, Punchout cardboard puppets may be controlled by strings. Includes Howdy, Bluster, Inspector, Dilly Dally, Clarabell and Flubadub	17.50	26.25	35.00
HOODY DOODY STICKER FUN, copyright 1951, WHITMAN No.219525	7.50	11.25	15.00
HOWDY DOODY STICKER FUN, copyright 1953, WHITMAN No.215825	7.50	11.25	15.00
HOWDY DOODY STICKER FUN CIRCUS, Copyright 1955, WHITMAN No.2165	7.50	11.25	15.00
I LOVE LUCY-LUCILLE BALL AND DESI ARNAZ, 1953, WHITMAN No.2101	10.00	15.00	20.00
JACK AND JILL, 1962, MERRILL No.1561, 6 dolls and clothes from storyland	4.00	6.00	8.00

	G	VG	M
JANE RUSSELL, 1955, SAALFIELD No.2611	12.50	18.75	25.00
JANET LEIGH Cutouts and Coloring Books, 1953, MERRILL No.2554	12.50	18.75	25.00
JANET LEIGH; 1958, ABBOTT No.1805	6.00	9.00	12.00
JAUNTY JUNIORS, 1946, No.903	7.50	11.25	15.00
JEAN AND JOAN AND THEIR FRIENDS, ROUND ABOUT DOLLS designed by Betty Campbell, 1934, boxed set, MILTON BRADLEY No.4396	25.00	37.50	50.00
JEANETTE MACDONALD, 1941, MERRILL 3640	57.50	86.25	115.00
JIMMY & JANE VISIT GENE AUTRY AT MELODY RANCH, 1951, WHITMAN No.118415	15.00	22.50	30.00
JOAN'S WEDDING by Florence Sarah Winship, clothes designed by Ruth M. Ruhman, 1942, WHITMAN No.990	10.00	15.00	20.00
JUDY AND JACK/PEG & BILL CUT-OUT DOLLS by Pelagie Doane, 1940, LOWE No.L1024	12.50	18.75	25.00
"JULIA"—DIAHANN CARROLL, Julia, Corey, Marie and Earl J. Wag-			

	G	VG	M
gedorn, 1968, ART-CRAFT No.5140......	5.00	7.50	10.00
JULIA with Julia, Earl J. Waggedord and Corey, 1969, SAALFIELD.....	5.00	7.50	10.00
JUNE ALLYSON, 1950, 1952, WHITMAN No.119015............	11.00	16.50	22.00
JUNE ALLYSON, 1953, WHITMAN 1173:15....	11.00	16.50	22.00
JUNE BRIDE by Art Tanchon, 1946, STEPHENS No.136..............	5.00	7.50	10.00
JUNIOR BOMBARDIER, 1953, EINSON & FREEMAN CO. No.202	12.50	18.75	25.00
JUNIOR PROM by Newman, 1942, LOWE 1042................	7.50	11.25	15.00
KAREN GOES TO COLLEGE! 1955, MERRILL No.1564.............	4.50	6.75	9.00

KIDDIELAND VILLAGE.
Photo by Jonathan A. Newman
Courtesy Barbara and Jonathan Newman

LITTLE FOLKS' FRIENDS
Photo by Jonathan A. Newman
Courtesy Barbara and Jonathan Newman

LITTLE FRIENDS FROM HISTORY
Photo by Jonathan Newman
Courtesy Barbara and Jonathan Newman

LOTS OF LITTLE PAPER DOLLS
Photo by Jonathan A. Newman
Courtesy Barbara and Jonathan Newman

	G	VG	M
KIDDIELAND VILLAGE, circa 1935, WHITMAN No.2004, 11½x15" boxed set, nine buildings and 65 cut-out figures........	22.50	33.75	45.00
KITTY GOES TO KINDERGARTEN, 1956, MERRILL No.1548....	4.50	6.75	9.00

	G	VG	M
LENNON SISTERS, 1957, WHITMAN No.1979...	10.00	15.00	20.00
LENNON SISTERS, 1961, WHITMAN, No.1983...	9.00	13.50	18.00
LETTIE LANE PAPER FAMILY — Third Series, 1909, GEORGE W. JACOBS & CO. Original house folder and six sheets.............	75.00	112.50	150.00
LIBERTY BELLES PAPER DOLL BOOK, 1943, No.3477, MERRILL............	10.00	15.00	20.00
LITTLE BALLERINA, 1953, MERRILL No.154215............	5.00	7.50	10.00
LITTLE BALLET DANCERS, 1950s? SAALFIELD No.1743..	2.50	3.75	5.00
LITTLE BROTHERS AND SISTERS, 1953, WHITMAN No.971:10, Tim, Kay, Ann and Pete.....	5.00	7.50	10.00
LITTLE FOLKS FRIENDS, 1915, SAALFIELD No.156...	3.50	5.25	7.00
LITTLE FRIENDS FROM HISTORY by Muriel Wilhoite, RAND McNALLY No.186, 1936	17.50	26.25	35.00
LITTLE FRIENDS PAPER DOLLS 1950s, SAALFIELD No.1746..	4.50	6.75	9.00
LITTLE MISS AMERICA Paper Doll Book, 1941, SAALFIELD No.2358, 15 punchouts by Campbell.............	12.00	18.00	24.00
LITTLE NURSE CUT-OUT BOOK, early 1940s, REUBEN H. LILJA AND CO., INC. No.909.	4.00	6.00	8.00
LITTLE RED SCHOOL HOUSE KINDERGARTEN, THE, by Margo Voight, McLOUGHLIN BROS., 1940, 2 teachers, 23 children.............	15.00	22.50	30.00
LITTLE WOMEN, circa 1970, ARTCRAFT No.5127.............	2.50	3.75	5.00
LOIS AND JOAN CUT-OUT DOLLS, 1941, 1945, WHITMAN			

	G	VG	M
No.1015 (Joan also appears in Betty & Joan and Lois & Joan)..........	6.00	9.00	12.00
THE LONE RANGER RIDES AGAIN punch-out set, DE-JOURNETTE MFG. CO., makes fences, figures of LR and Tonto, horses, campfire	7.50	11.25	15.00
LOOK-ALIKE CUT-OUT DOLLS, 1952, WHITMAN No.97210, two mother and daughter pairs of dolls..............	5.00	7.50	10.00
LOOK WHO I AM! 1952, HART PUBLISHING CO. by Doris Stelberg, 18" doll with 15 costumes Spiral bound..........	5.00	7.50	10.00
LORI MARTIN IN NATIONAL VELVET 1962, WHITMAN No.4612, 6x11½" boxed set, paper dolls	7.50	11.25	15.00
LOST HORIZON, 1973, ARTCRAFT No.5112..	5.00	7.50	10.00
LOTS OF LITTLE PAPER DOLLS by Angela Tuite Price, 1949, SAALFIELD No.1537	7.00	10.50	14.00
LUCILLE BALL DESI ARNAZ CUT-OUT DOLLS WITH LITTLE RICKY, 1953, WHITMAN 2116:25	15.00	22.50	30.00

LUCILLE BALL DESI ARNAZ CUT-OUT DOLLS WITH LITTLE RICKY
Photo by Jonathan A. Newman
Courtesy Barbara and Jonathan Newman

THE LETTIE LANE PAPER FAMILY
Photo by Jonathan A. Newman
Courtesy Barbara and Jonathan Newman

	G	VG	M
LUCILLE BALL PAPER DOLLS, 1944, SAALFIELD 2475	22.00	33.00	44.00

	G	VG	M
MADAME HATTIE FASHIONS, 1940s, REUBEN LILJA 908...	11.00	16.50	22.00
MAGIC MARY, 1955, MILTON BRADLEY No.4010-1, 10½x10½" boxed set, complete with magnetic doll and strips to put on clothes..........	6.00	9.00	12.00
MAKE YOUR OWN BATTLE SET MECHANIZED FORCE, 1942, ELECTRIC CORPORATION OF AMERICA...	17.50	26.25	35.00
MARGE AND GOWER CHAMPION, 1959, WHITMAN	12.50	18.75	25.00
MARTHA HYER PAPER DOLLS, 1958, SAALFIELD 4423.....	12.50	18.75	25.00
MARY AND JOAN, 1941, 1945, WHITMAN No.1015 (Joan also appears in Lois & Joan and Betty & Joan)..........	6.00	9.00	12.00
MARY BELLE CUT OUT DOLL by Fern Bisel Peat, SAALFIELD No.2100, four separate sheets, 17" doll with three sheets of clothes, 1934..........	22.50	33.75	45.00
MARY JANE — A CUT OUT DOLL, by Florence Winship, 1939, 1941, WHITMAN No.1010 with suitcase for accessories.............	7.50	11.25	15.00
MARY LEE — A CUT OUT DOLL WHITMAN No.1010, circa 1939.....	7.50	11.25	15.00
MARY MARTIN, 1942, SAALFIELD 2427.....	24.00	36.00	48.00
MARY OF THE WACS — A Young American, by Hilda Miloche and Wilma Kane, WHITMAN No.1012, 1943.........	10.00	15.00	20.00
MARY POPPINS, 1973, WHITMAN No.1977...	5.00	7.50	10.00
MARYBELLE MERCER'S FRONT AND BACK DOLLS WITH WRAPAROUND DRESSES by Queen Holden No.978...	20.00	30.00	40.00

McLOUGHLIN BROS. OF BROOKLYN, NEW YORK

McLoughlin Brothers was the largest American producer of paper soldiers, and one of the earliest in the paper-doll field. The firm, which traced its founding to 1828, began producing paper dolls at least as early as 1857. Among the other paper toys it sold were dollhouse furniture, toy theatres with actors and scenery, and blocks. The company was sold in 1920.

	G	VG	M
McLOUGHLIN BROS., circa 1884, Mounted U.S. Calvary, Hussar type, charging, several different poses. Price per figure...	1.00	1.50	2.00
McLOUGHLIN BROS. Infantry soldiers, printed 1857, price per each $5, complete set $150-175...			
McLOUGHLIN BROS., Infantry circa 1875, price per each...	1.50	2.25	3.00
McLOUGHLIN BROS. Zouaves, 1884, price per each...	1.00	1.50	2.00
McLOUGHLIN BROS. Brass Band, 1890, price per each...	1.00	1.50	2.00
McLOUGHLIN BROS. Grenadiers, 1890, price per each...	1.00	1.50	2.00
McLOUGHLIN BROS. Zouaves 0203, 1905, price per each...	.50	.75	1.00
McLOUGHLIN BROS. French soldiers 4026, 1917, per sheet...	6.00	9.00	12.00
McLOUGHLIN BROS. Paper Dolls 1860-1890, price per cut set, $25-50; uncut $50-150 depending on title, date, etc.			
McLOUGHLIN BROS. 100 Soldiers on Parade circa 1898...	125.00	187.50	250.00
McLOUGHLIN BROS. 100 Soldiers on Parade, second set, circa 1898...	125.00	187.50	250.00
McLOUGHLIN BROS. 260 series, circa 1889-1895: c. U.S. Regulars, spiked helmet, each	.75	1.13	1.50
d. U.S. Infantry...	.75	1.13	1.50
e. Mounted U.S. Cavalry, hussar type, charging...	.75	1.13	1.50
f. West Point Cadets...	.75	1.13	1.50
g. U.S. Regulars...	.87	1.31	1.75
h. U.S. Infantry...	.75	1.13	1.50
i. Bandsmen, various instruments, each...	.75	1.13	1.50
j. Navy—USS Boston...	.75	1.13	1.50
k. Grenadier Guards, each	.75	1.13	1.50
l. Anapolis Cadets, each..	.75	1.13	1.50
McLOUGHLIN BROS. Printed 1898, sailor 5¼" high, landing party for USS Texas...	1.50	2.25	3.00
McLOUGHLIN BROS. U.S. Infantry from Spanish-American War circa 1898. Approx. 6" high on wooden blocks. Price per figure...	1.50	2.25	3.00
McLOUGHLIN BROS. Circa 1898, small glossy series, 4½" high, West Point Cadets. Price per figure...	1.50	2.25	3.00
McLOUGHLIN BROS. Circa 1898, glossy series, g. U.S. Regulars, full dress, 5" high...	1.50	2.25	3.00
McLOUGHLIN BROS. circa 1898, British Infantry red coats, spiked helmets, 6" high on small wooden blocks. Price per figure..	1.50	2.25	3.00
McLOUGHLIN BROS. circa 1898, U.S. Zouaves, Civil War era, blue coats, red baggy trousers, 6" high on small wooden blocks...	1.50	2.25	3.00
McLOUGHLIN BROS. "02" series, circa 1905-1910 a. British Highlanders b. U.S. Zouaves c. U.S. Continentals d. U.S. Navy e. U.S. Infantry in Campaign Uniforms (Spanish American War) h. American Indians, kneeling and standing. Price per figure...	.75	1.13	1.50
McLOUGHLIN BROS. Same as above. g. West			

	G	VG	M
Point Cadets (round base), circa 1915............	.50	.75	1.00
McLOUGHLIN BROS. No. 0103 Dutch Paper Doll, boy of the Village of Vollendam. Circa 1910, 10½x10½" sheet.......	6.00	9.00	12.00
McLOUGHLIN BROS. No.0201, circa 1905-1910, British Highlanders. Single figure	.88	1.31	1.75
McLOUGHLIN BROS. Series 0202, circa 1910, American Indian, kneeling and standing types. Price per figure........	.88	1.31	1.75

McLOUGHLIN BROS. 100 SOLDIERS ON PARADE, Boxed Set
Photo by Jonathan A. Newman
Courtesy Barbara and Jonathan Newman

McLOUGHLIN BROS. THE NEW PRETTY VILLAGE
Photo by Jonathan A. Newman
Courtesy Barbara and Jonathan Newman

McLOUGHLIN BROS.	G	VG	M
Series 0205, circa 1915, round base, U.S. Navy. Price per figure........	.50	.75	1.00

McLOUGHLIN BROS.	G	VG	M
Series 0205, circa 1915, West Point Cadets, single figure	.75	1.13	1.50
McLOUGHLIN BROS. Circa 1915. Boy Scouts holding rifles across chests	.88	1.31	1.75
McLOUGHLIN BROS. Series No.4026 10½x10½" Paper soldiers on sheet, seven soldiers plus officer (5½" high) in field uniform. Circa 1916. 1. Belgium. 2. France. 3. Italy. 4. Britain. Price per sheet	5.00	7.50	10.00
McLOUGHLIN BROS. NEW FOLDING DOLL HOUSE, 1897, boxed set, cardboard with lithographed paper......	100.00	150.00	200.00
McLOUGHLIN BROS. NEW PRETTY VILLAGE—Church set, 1897	30.00	45.00	60.00
McLOUGHLIN BROS. NEW PRETTY VILLAGE No.5, Little Folks Hotel from the Boat Set............	6.00	9.00	12.00

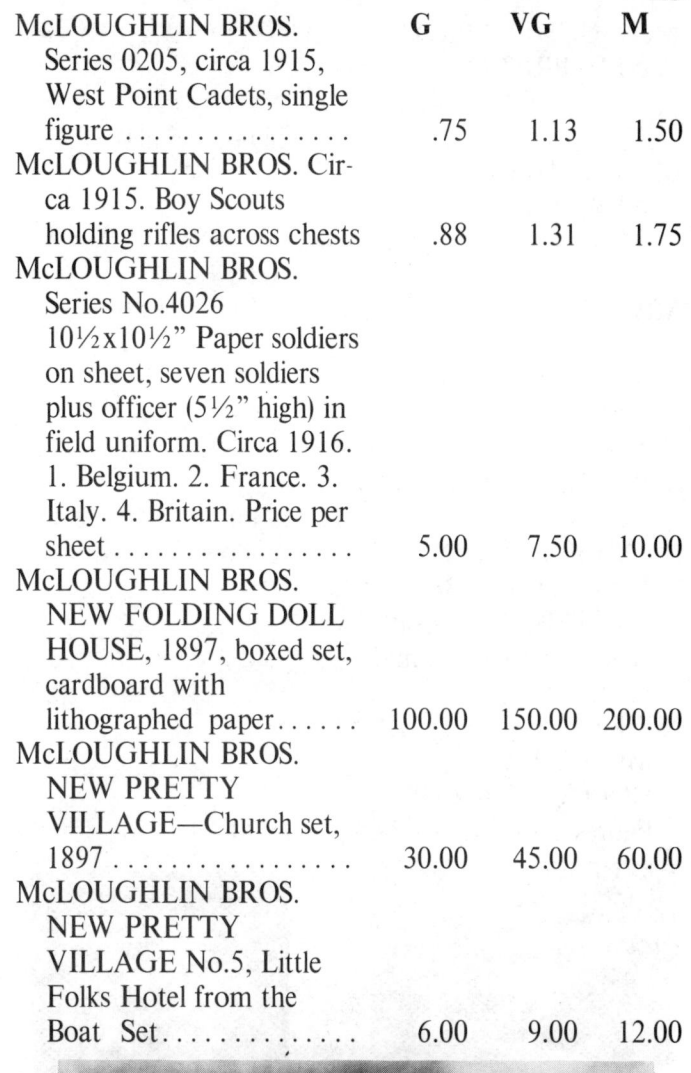

McLOUGHLIN BROS. Building from New Pretty Village
Photo by Jonathan A. Newman
Courtesy Barbara and Jonathan Newman

McLOUGHLIN BROS.			
NEW PRETTY VILLAGE No.3, Log Cabin from School set...	5.00	7.50	10.00

McLOUGHLIN BROS. NEW PRETTY VILLAGE School Set, 1897	G	VG	M
	35.00	52.50	70.00
McLOUGHLIN BROS. NEW PRETTY VILLAGE, individual bldgs	6.00	9.00	12.00
ME AND MIMI, 1957, A Bonnie Story Book Doll, 6x8" in the style of the Little Golden Books. A doll and her Dolly Story Book, plus dolls and their dresses	7.00	10.50	14.00
MEXICAN CUT OUTS by Milo Winter, 1938, WHITMAN 1054, six pages of people, animals, houses, etc.............	5.00	7.50	10.00
MICKEY AND MINNIE MOUSE PAPER DOLLS, 1930s 2 10" figures with clothes.....	75.00	112.50	150.00

MODEL TANKS CONSTRUCTION KIT
Photo by Jonathan A. Newman
Courtesy Barbara and Jonathan Newman

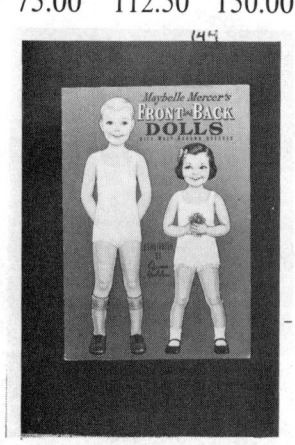

Make Your Own Battle Set
Mechanized Force
Photo by Jonathan A. Newman
Courtesy Barbara and Jonathan
Newman

MAYBELLE MERCER'S FRONT AND BACK DOLLS
Photo by Jonathan A. Newman
Courtesy Barbara and Jonathan Newman

MODEL WAR PLANES CONSTRUCTION KIT
Photo by Jonathan A. Newman
Courtesy Barbara and Jonathan Newman

MODEL AIRPLANES, SAMUEL LOWE No.1069, 1941, WW II airplanes, international...	32.50	48.75	65.00
MODEL BATTLESHIP by Reed, circa 1945, 7x10"..	4.00	6.00	8.00
MODEL FLAT-TOP by Reed, circa 1945........	4.00	6.00	8.00
MODEL TANKS, SAMUEL LOWE No.1065, 1941.........	20.00	30.00	40.00
MODEL TANKS CONSTRUCTION SET, boxed seet, 1942, LOWE No.1267	17.50	26.25	35.00

MODEL WAR PLANES CONSTRUCTION SET, boxed set, 1942, LOWE No.1266	G	VG	M
	17.50	26.25	35.00
MODERN MISS IN PAPER DOLLS, 1942, by Van Swearingen, SAALFIELD 2397.....	9.00	13.50	18.00
MOLLY BEE, 1962, WHITMAN No.2091.........	6.00	9.00	12.00
MOMMY AND ME, 1954, WHITMAN NO.977:10.	5.00	7.50	10.00
MOTHER AND DAUGHTER by Patrie Winston, GRINNEL LITHOGRAPHIC No.C-1005, 15" mother, 11" daughter, 2 scotties, 1940	12.00	18.00	24.00

	G	VG	M
MOUSEKETEER CUT OUTS, 1957, WHITMAN No.1974.........	6.00	9.00	12.00
MOVIE STARLETS, 1946, WHITMAN No.960, GAIL RUSSELL, DIANA LYNN, OLGA SAN JUAN, MARJORIE REYNOLDS, JOAN CAULFIELD..........	35.00	52.50	70.00
MOVIE STARLETS PAPER DOLLS, circa 1949, STEPHENS PUBLISHING CO., No. 178. Four dolls—Miss Premiere, Miss Stardust, Miss Hollywood, Miss Preview and four pages of costumes...........	2.50	3.75	5.00
MRS. BEASLEY Paper Doll Book, 1970 ("Family Affair" TV show) WHITMAN No.1973.........	2.50	3.75	5.00
MY FAIR LADY, 1965, OTTENHEIMER PUBLISHERS No.2960-2, by Evon Hartmann.............	7.50	11.25	15.00
MY PAPER DOLL'S SEWING KIT, 1940, by Margot Voight, GRINNELL C-1018.........	11.00	16.50	22.00
MY TWIN BABIES WITH OLDER BROTHER AND SISTER, 1940, WHITMAN 970.......	11.00	16.50	22.00
MY VERY FIRST PAPER DOLL BOOK, 1957, A Bonnie Book No.4732 SAMUEL LOWE......	2.50	3.75	5.00
NANCY AND HER DOLLS WITH SEVEN BUSY DAYS OF FUN, 1944, SAALFIELD No.2478..............	8.00	12.00	16.00
NANNY AND THE PROFESSOR, 1971, ARTCRAFT No.5114.......	3.50	5.25	7.00
NATIONAL VELVET, 1961, WHITMAN No.1958..............	9.00	13.50	18.00
NAVY SCOUTS PAPER DOLL BOOK, 1942, MERRILL No.3428....	20.00	30.00	40.00

	G	VG	M
NEW SHIRLEY TEMPLE IN PAPER DOLLS, THE, 1942, SAALFIELD No.2425	40.00	60.00	80.00
NEW YORK WORLD'S FAIR MAKE A MODEL, 1963, by Ottenheimer. SPERTUS No.600-50. Includes Unisphere, Swiss Ride, N.Y. Port Authority, Heliport, etc...........	7.50	11.25	15.00
NIGHT BEFORE CHRISTMAS WITH CUTOUTS Whitman No.948	7.50	11.25	15.00
19 FARMYARD ANIMALS TO CUT OUT AND STAND UP—Copyright 1930, WHITMAN No.935, 12 pages	10.00	15.00	20.00
NU-MATIC 7" paper pop gun	30.00	45.00	60.00
OKLAHOMA WITH SHIRLEY JONES AND GORDON MACRAE, 1956, WHITMAN No.1954	13.00	19.50	26.00
ON GUARD, 1942, LOWE No.L535	13.00	19.50	26.00

OUR HAPPY FAMILY CUT-OUT SHEETS
Photo by Jonathan A. Newman
Courtesy Barbara and Jonathan Newman

ON GUARD A PUNCH OUT BOOK
Photo by Jonathan A. Newman
Courtesy Barbara and Jonathan Newman

	G	VG	M
ONE HUNDRED SOLDIERS PUNCHOUT BOOK, 1943, WHITMAN 999.......	17.50	26.25	35.00
OUR HAPPY FAMILY CUT-OUT SHEETS, 1928, SAM'L GABRIEL SONS CO. No.D141....	27.50	41.25	55.00

OUR SOLDIERS CUT OUT
ARMY UNIFORMS
Photo by Jonathan A. Newman
Courtesy Barbara and Jonathan
Newman

OVER 80 TURN-ABOUT
STAND-UP SOLDIERS
Photo by Jonathan A. Newman
Courtesy Barbara and Jonathan
Newman

MODEL AIRPLANES.
Photo by Jonathan A.
Newman. Courtesy Barbara
and Jonathan Newman

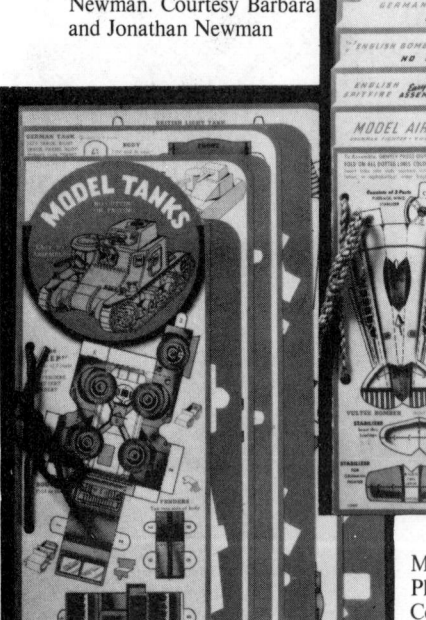

MODEL TANKS.
Photo by Jonathan A. Newman
Courtesy Barbara and Jonathan
Newman

NEW SHIRLEY TEMPLE IN
PAPER DOLLS.
Photo by Jonathan A. Newman
Courtesy Barbara and Jonathan
Newman

	G	VG	M
OUR NURSE NANCY— A Young American, by Hilda Miloche and Wilma Kane, 1943, cutouts, WHITMAN No.1012...	7.50	11.25	15.00
OUR SAILOR BOB, 10" doll with uniforms, WHITMAN, circa 1943.	7.50	11.25	15.00
OUR SOLDIER JIM, 1943, WHITMAN No.3980, designed by Hilda Miloche and Wilma Kane, 10½" standup doll with uniforms	7.50	11.25	15.00
OUR SOLDIERS CUT OUT ARMY UNIFORMS by Nat Falk, DELL, 1941, 4 cutout dolls and several uniforms	15.00	22.50	30.00
OUR WAVE JOAN— A Young American, by Hilda Miloche and Wilma Kane, 1943, WHITMAN No.1012	10.00	15.00	20.00
OUTDOOR PAPER DOLLS, 1941, SAALFIELD No.1958, fourteen dolls and four pages of clothes	4.25	6.38	8.50
OVER 80 TURN-ABOUT, STAND-UP SAILORS, 1943, LOWE No.141	11.25	16.38	22.50
OVER 80 TURN-ABOUT, STAND-UP SOLDIERS, 1943, LOWE No.140	12.50	18.75	25.00
PAPER DOLL FAMILY AND THEIR HOUSE by Florence and Margaret Hoopes, 1934, SAALFIELD No.4125 . .	22.00	33.00	44.00
PAPER DOLL FAMILY AND THEIR TRAILER, MERRILL No.3436, 1938	20.00	30.00	40.00
PAPER DOLL "JOAN" AND PAPER DOLL "BOBBY" by Queen Holden, 1928, WHIT-MAN 907	15.50	22.75	31.00
PAPER DOLL OUTFIT, AMERICAN TOY WORKS No.102, boxed set	20.00	30.00	40.00

	G	VG	M
OUR NEW HOME, 1930, story by Susan S. Popper, pictures by Helen E. Ohrenschall, SAM'L GABRIEL SONS, hardcover book, 6 pages of rooms 6 gummed pages of people, furniture, etc.	35.00	52.50	70.00

PAPER DOLL FAMILY AND
THEIR TRAILER
Photo by Jonathan A. Newman
Courtesy Barbara and Jonathan
Newman

PAPER DOLL OUTFIT
DRESSES AND HATS

Photo by Jonathan A. Newman
Courtesy Barbara and Jonathan
Newman

PAPER DOLLS TO CUT OUT
AND PAINT
Photo by Jonathan A. Newman
Courtesy Barbara and Jonathan
Newman

PAPER DOLLS JULIA MARIE
Photo by Jonathan A. Newman
Courtesy Barbara and Jonathan
Newman

PLAYHOUSE PAPER DOLLS.
Photo by Jonathan A. Newman
Courtesy Barbara and Jonathan
Newman

PAPER DOLLS OF ALL NA-
TIONS NEW YORK WORLD'S
FAIR, 1939.
Photo by Jonathan A. Newman
Courtesy Barbara and Jonathan
Newman

	G	VG	M
PAPER DOLL PLAYMATES, 1940, SAALFIELD No.154, nurse, 19 children, costumes, toys	15.00	22.50	30.00
PAPER DOLLS FROM MOTHER GOOSE, 1957, SAALFIELD No.2758 Mary, Bo-Peep, Boy Blue, Bobbie Shaftoe, Miss Muffett, Jack Horner	2.50	3.75	5.00
PAPER DOLLS JULIA AND MARIA by Angela Tuite Price, 1958, SAALFIELD No.1530	6.00	9.00	12.00
PAPER DOLLS OF ALL NATIONS-NEW YORK WORLD'S FAIR, 1939, SAALFIELD, No.227	18.00	27.00	36.00
PAPER DOLLS OF EVE ARDEN, 1956, SAALFIELD 1706	11.00	16.50	22.00
PAPER DOLLS PETER AND PEGGY, 1935, WHITMAN No.965, 64 pages by Dixon. Very large punchouts on front and back	12.50	18.75	25.00
PAPER DOLLS TO CUT OUT AND PAINT, 1920s, SAALFIELD No.1180	23.00	34.50	46.00
PAPER DOLLS—UNITED WE STAND by Margot Voight, SAALFIELD No. 113, 6 children with uniforms	11.00	16.50	22.00

	G	VG	M
THE PATRIDGE FAMILY, 1971, ARTCRAFT No.5137	3.50	5.25	7.00
PARTRIDGE FAMILY, 1972, ARTCRAFT No.5143	3.50	5.25	7.00
PAT BOONE, 1959, WHITMAN No.1968	7.50	11.25	15.00
PAT CROWLEY, 1955, WHITMAN No.2050	11.00	16.50	22.00
PATIENCE AND PRUDENCE, 1958, LOWE No.2736 (Popular singers of the 1950s)	5.00	7.50	10.00

	G	VG	M
PATSY, 1946, CHILDRENS PRESS No.30002, Patsy, dog, doghouse, etc.	10.00	15.00	20.00
PATSY A WOODEN DOLL WITH DRESSES (actually a 10" standup cardboard doll with wood backing) circa 1938, WHITMAN 3037	9.00	13.50	18.00
PATSY ANN AND HER TRUNK FULL OF CLOTHES BY QUEEN HOLDEN, 1939, WHITMAN No.992	19.00	27.50	38.00
PATTI PAGE 1958 book of paper dolls	10.00	15.00	20.00
PATTY'S PARTY PAPER DOLLS, circa 1950, STEPHENS PUBLISHING CO. No.175	2.50	3.75	5.00
PERT AND PRETTY, 1948, MERRILL No.1552	8.00	12.00	16.00
PETER AND PEGGY, 1950, WHITMAN No.99210	3.50	5.25	7.00
PETER AND PEGGY, JERRY AND JOAN PAPER DOLLS by Rachel Taft Dixon, 1935, WHITMAN No.985	15.00	22.50	30.00
PHOTO FASHIONS, 1953, WHITMAN No.973	3.50	5.25	7.00
PIG TAILS, 1949, MERRILL No.344410	6.00	9.00	12.00
PILOT AND STEWARDESS PAPER DOLL BOOK No.3423, 1941, MERRILL	10.00	15.00	20.00
THE PINK WEDDING, 1952, MERRILL No.1559	7.50	11.25	15.00
PIPER LAURIE, 1953, MERRILL No.2551	13.50	19.75	27.00
PLAYHOUSE DOLLS, 1949, STEPHENS PUBLISHING CO. No.165, Four dolls and four pages of clothes	2.50	3.75	5.00
PLAYHOUSE PAPER DOLLS designed by Doris and Marion Henderson, LOWE No.1028, 1941	10.00	15.00	20.00

PILOT AND STEWARDESS AIRLINER PAPER DOLLS
Photo by Jonathan A. Newman
Courtesy Barbara and Jonathan Newman

PLAYHOUSE PAPER DOLLS
by Doris and Marion Henderson
Photo by Jonathan A. Newman
Courtesy Barbara and Jonathan Newman

	G	VG	M
PLAYHOUSE PAPER DOLLS, 1947, SAALFIELD No.381	4.00	6.00	8.00
PLAYMATES, 1952, WHITMAN No.99510	3.50	5.25	7.00
PLAYTHINGS TO CUT OUT AND STAND UP, circa 1935, WHITMAN No.934. Contains ventroliquist's dummy, floating ships, general's hat, lantern, animals, other moving toys	5.00	7.50	10.00
PLAY TIME, 1952, WHITMAN 210525	5.00	7.50	10.00
PLAYTIME PALS, 1946, LOWE No.1045	4.50	6.75	9.00
POLLY PATCHWORK AND HER FRIENDS by Pelagie Doane, 1941, LOWE No.1024	7.00	10.50	14.00
POLYANNA CUT-OUT DOLLS, 1941, WHITMAN 995	9.00	13.50	18.00
POPULAR PAPER DOLLS, 1942, SAALFIELD No.1973	7.50	11.25	15.00
PORTRAIT GIRLS WITH CLOTH-LIKE CLOTHES, 1947, designed by Hilda Miloche and Wilma Kane, WHITMAN No.1170	7.50	11.25	15.00
POWER MODELS CUT OUT DOLLS BOOK, 1942, WHITMAN, No.981, Six dolls	10.00	15.00	20.00
PRESSED BOARD DOLLS AND THEIR DRESSES, box set, LOWE No.1942.	12.50	18.75	25.00

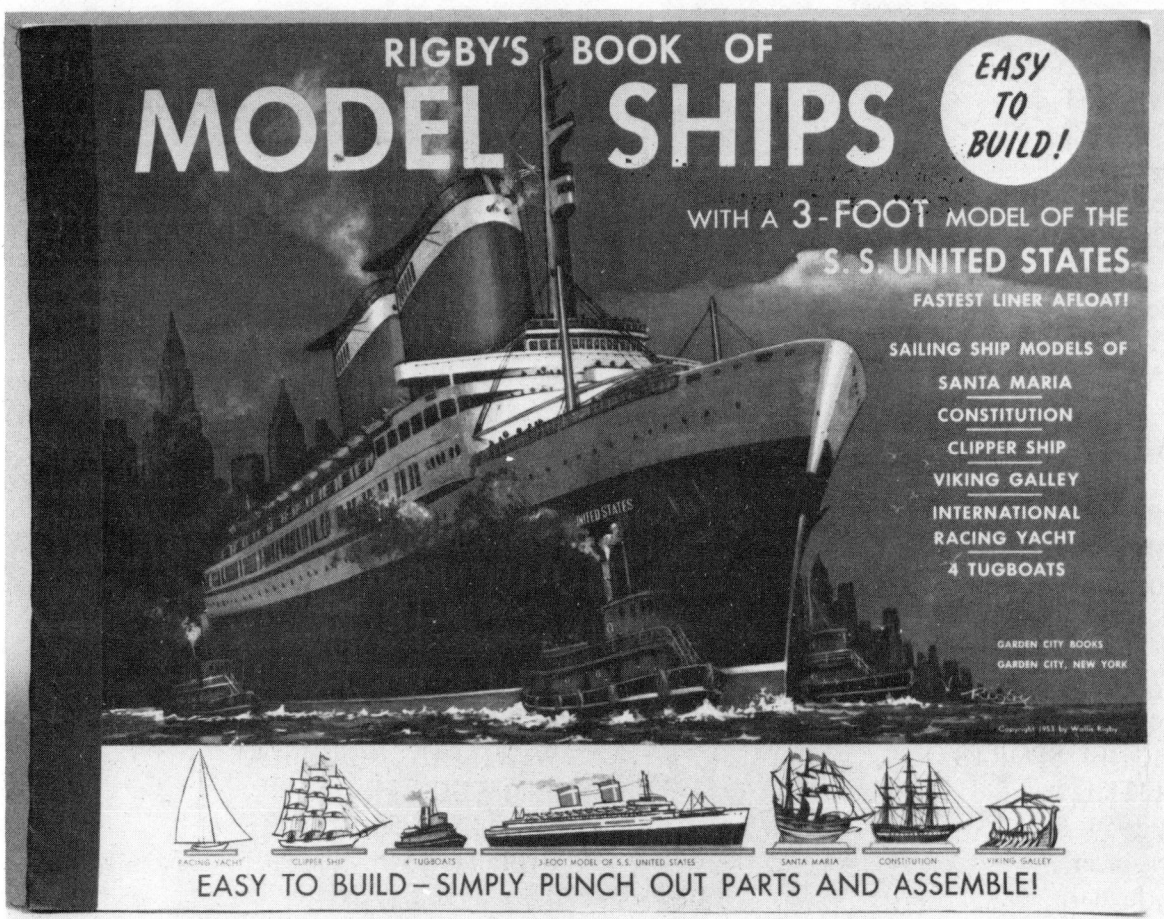

RIGBY'S Book of Model Ships. Courtesy Mapes Auctioneers & Appraisers.

	G	VG	M
PRE-TEEN PAPER DOLLS circa 1960s, SAALFIELD No.1366..	2.00	3.00	4.00
PRINCE AND PRINCESS PAPER DOLLS, 1949, SAALFIELD No.2706..	6.00	9.00	12.00
PROM TIME, 1962, WHITMAN No.2084, 2 dolls and party clothes...	2.00	3.00	4.00
QUEEN HOLDEN! QUEEN HOLDEN! BETTY AND BOB, 1952, 12½" high children, WHITMAN 99110.....	6.00	9.00	12.00
QUEEN HOLDEN! QUEEN HOLDEN! HAIR-DO DOLLS, 1948, 3 dolls, clothes and 31 different hair-dos, WHITMAN No.991..........	15.00	22.50	30.00
QUIZ KIDS PAPER DOLLS, 1942, SAALFIELD 2430.....	25.00	37.50	50.00
RAGGEDY ANN AND ANDY, 1953, by Ethel Hays, SAALFIELD 2719	16.00	24.00	32.00

	G	VG	M
RAGGEDY ANN AND ANDY PAPER DOLLS, 1944, SAALFIELD No.2719-15............	14.00	21.00	28.00
RAGGEDY ANN AND ANDY PAPER DOLLS, 1944, SAALFIELD No.2741 by Ethel Hays..	9.00	13.50	18.00
RAGGEDY ANN AND ANDY, 1968, WHITMAN No.4740.........	3.00	4.50	6.00
"RAP-A-JAP", circa 1943, WOODBURN MFG. No.C1...............	10.00	15.00	20.00
READY CUT VILLAGE, 1930s, no mfg. listed....	15.00	22.50	30.00
RICKY NELSON paper dolls, 1959...........	6.00	9.00	12.00
RIDERS OF THE WEST PAPER DOLLS, 1950, SAALFIELD No.2716-15	6.00	9.00	12.00
RIGBY'S BOOK OF MODEL SHIPS, 1953...	5.00	7.50	10.00
RIGBY'S EASY TO BUILD MODELS OF FIGHTING PLANES...	15.00	22.50	30.00

	G	VG	M
RIGBY'S EASIER TO BUILD MODELS OF NAVAL CRAFT, 24 models of warships, 27 pages, 11½x14", designed by Wallace Rigby, 1944, includes Battleship North Carolina, aircraft carrier, cruiser, destroyer, etc....	15.00	22.50	30.00
RIGBY FLYING MODELS OF JET AND ROCKET PLANES, ten planes, 1949, GARDEN CITY BOOKS.............	10.00	15.00	20.00
RIGBY'S MODEL BOOK OF FLYING CLIPPERS, 11x14" book designed by Wallace Rigby, two scale models of Douglas DC-Jet Clipper and Douglas DC-7C, 1957.........	10.00	15.00	20.00
RIGBY'S MODEL SPORTS CARS OF THE WORLD, 1954, includes 18" "sports-racer", Chevette, Jaguar, Mercedes-Benz, etc......	10.00	15.00	20.00
ROBIN HOOD AND MAID MARIAN, 1950s, SAALFIELD, No.1761, paper dolls...........	3.50	5.25	7.00
ROCK HUDSON paper dolls, 1957, WHITMAN No.2087.............	6.00	9.00	12.00
ROSEMARY CLOONEY, SAMUEL LOWE No.1256.............	10.00	15.00	20.00
ROSEMARY CLOONEY, 1958, SAMUEL LOWE No.2487.............	11.00	16.50	22.00
ROWAN & MARTIN'S LAUGH-IN PUNCH OUT PAPER DOLL BOOK, 1969 SAALFIELD No.1325, Rowan, Martin, Jo Ann Worley, Arte Johnson, Judy Carne and Goldie Hawn...............	6.00	9.00	12.00
ROY ROGERS AND DALE EVANS, 1950, WHITMAN No.1186...	15.00	22.50	30.00
ROY ROGERS AND DALE EVANS, 1954, WHITMAN No.1950...	17.50	26.25	35.00

	G	VG	M
ROY ROGERS CUT OUT DOLLS, 1948, WHITMAN No.995.........	16.00	24.00	32.00
ROY ROGERS STICKER FUN BOOK, 1953, No.2161.............	5.00	7.50	10.00
ROYALTY CUT-OUT BOOKS: A PROCESSION OF THE KNIGHTS OF THE GARTER.............	20.00	30.00	40.00
ROYALTY CUT-OUT BOOKS: TROOPING THE COLOUR........	20.00	30.00	40.00
RUTH NEWTON'S CUT OUT DOLLS AND ANIMALS "with over 80 pieces to cut out and play with", 1934, 11x17".....	12.50	18.75	25.00
SALLY ANN A CUT OUT DOLL, circa 1940, WHITMAN No.1010...	6.00	9.00	12.00
SALLY'S SILVER SKATES, 1956, MERRILL No.1549.........	5.00	7.50	10.00
SALLY THE STANDING DOLL, 1940s, LOWE No.1042.............	6.00	9.00	12.00
SANDRA AND SUE STATUETTE DOLLS AND THEIR CLOTHES, by Lee Lunzer, 1948, WHITMAN No.1180...	6.00	9.00	12.00
SANDRA DEE, 1959, Boxed, two dolls and 34 costume pieces, SAALFIELD No.5511..	10.00	15.00	20.00
SANDY AND SUE, 1963, WHITMAN No.1956...	1.75	2.63	3.50
SCHOOL GIRL PAPER DOLLS, 1942, SAALFIELD No.2400..	11.00	16.50	22.00
SCISSORS BIRD PAPER DOLLS, 1946, STEPHENS No.137....	2.00	3.00	4.00
SERVICE KIT OF AMERICA'S ARMED FORCES - ON LAND - ON SEA - IN THE AIR, 1942, LOWE No.265....	12.50	18.75	25.00
6 GOOD LITTLE DOLLS, no date, STEPHENS PUBLISHING CO. No.183.............	2.50	3.75	5.00

SERVICE KIT OF AMERICA'S ARMED FORCES ON LAND
ON SEA AND IN THE AIR
Photo by Jonathan A. Newman
Courtesy Barbara and Jonathan Newman

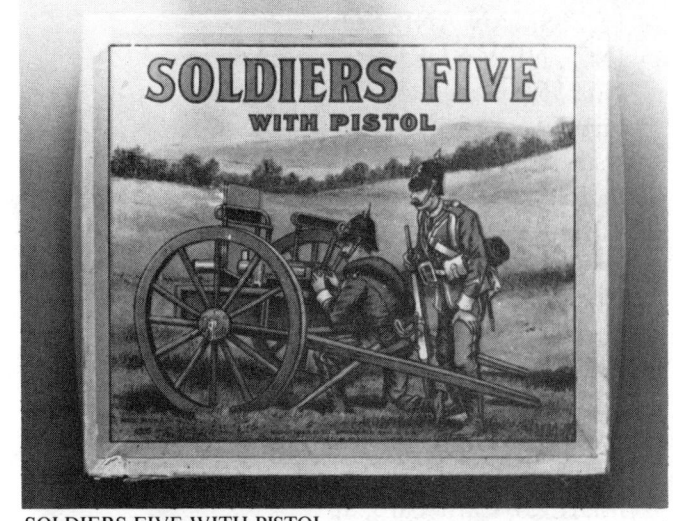

SOLDIERS FIVE WITH PISTOL
Photo by Jonathan A. Newman
Courtesy Barbara and Jonathan Newman

SHARPSHOOTERS, box and contents.
Photo by Jonathan A. Newman.
Courtesy Barbara and Jonathan Newman

SOLDIERS by Concord.
Photo by Jonathan A. Newman
Courtesy Barbara and Jonathan
Newman

STREAMLINE FLYER,
Photo by Jonathan A. Newman
Courtesy Barbara and Jonathan Newman

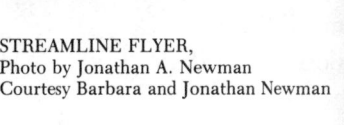

	G	VG	M
6 MOVIE STARLETS, 1942, ANNE NAGEL, PEGGY MORAN, JANE FRAZEE, ANNE GWYNNE, HELEN PARRISH, ANN GILLIS	25.00	37.50	50.00
SHARP SHOOTERS, circa 1915, MILTON BRADLEY No.4103, boxed set with two sets of five cardboard soldiers and one officer on stands	30.00	45.00	60.00
SKATING PARTY PAPER DOLL BOOK, 1941, No.2328, SAALFIELD, 17 Punchouts	6.00	9.00	12.00
SKATING STARS, 1954, WHITMAN No.2105	3.50	5.25	7.00
SMART PAPER DOLLS, 1940, SAALFIELD No.1935	11.00	16.50	22.00
SMASH THE AXIS, 1943, ELECTRIC CORP. OF AMERICA	10.00	15.00	20.00
SNOW WHITE AND THE SEVEN DWARFS PAPER DOLLS, 1938, 12x17", WHITMAN No.970	37.00	55.50	74.00
SNOW WHITE AND THE SEVEN DWARFS, circa 1970, WHITMAN No.1998	2.00	3.00	4.00
SOLDIERS, circa 1940, CONCORD TOY CO. boxed set contains 9 press-out soldiers, 3½" each, wooden cannon and ammunition	7.50	11.25	15.00

	G	VG	M
SOLDIER SET by J. PRESSMAN AND CO. INC., NEW YORK, No.1551, circa 1940, contains five cardboard soldiers, 4½" high, and marbles	5.00	7.50	10.00
SOLDIERS, cardboard, approx. 6" high on wooden blocks, Navy, both officer and sailors circa 1920. Price per single figure	1.00	1.50	2.00
SOLDIERS, Cardboard, approx. 6" high on wooden blocks. Sailor, U.S.	1.00	1.50	2.00
SOLDIERS, Cardboard, approx. 6" high on wooden blocks. U.S. Infantry in campaign hats, mounted. Price per single figure	.88	1.31	1.75
SOLDIERS, Cardboard, approx. 6" high on wooden blocks. U.S. Infantry circa 1910, khaki uniforms with red trim. Officers, enlisted men. Price per single figure	1.00	1.50	2.00
SOLDIERS, Cardboard, approx. 6" high on wooden blocks. West Point Cadets	1.00	1.50	2.00
SOLDIERS FIVE, circa 1920, boxed set, MILTON BRADLEY No.4395, five cardboard soldiers, pistol	25.00	37.50	50.00
SOLDIERS ON PARADE, early, Milton Bradley No.4518, set of 10	12.50	18.75	25.00
SPACEPORT, U.S.A., 1953, WHITMAN	5.00	7.50	10.00
SPORTS TIME, 1952, WHITMAN No.210525.	5.00	7.50	10.00
SQUARE DANCE PAPER DOLLS, 1950, SAALFIELD No.2717	6.00	9.00	12.00
SQUARE DANCE PAPER DOLLS by J. Voelz, LOWE 968-10	3.00	4.50	6.00
STAGE DOOR CANTEEN, 1943, SAALFIELD 2468	20.00	30.00	40.00
STAND-UP DOLLS, HONEY AND BUNNY, MERRILL No.3403, 1936	20.00	30.00	40.00

STATUETTE DOLLS AND THEIR CLOTHES
Photo by Jonathan A. Newman
Courtesy Barbara and Jonathan Newman

SALLY THE STANDING DOLL

	G	VG	M
STATUETTE DOLLS, 1943, WHITMAN No.992, Two women	9.00	13.50	18.00
STATUETTE DOLLS AND THEIR CLOTHES, 1942, WHITMAN, No.998	8.00	12.00	16.00
STATUETTE DOLLS AND THEIR CLOTHES, 1946, WHITMAN No.986, Two girls and a boy	7.50	11.25	15.00
STENCILS LARGE AND SMALL by Roy Best, circa 1935, No.954 (Whitman?) folder of 30 animals to punch out and use as stencils. Comes with tiny box of crayons.	7.50	11.25	15.00
STOCK FARM SET, circa 1944, CONCERN No.123, boxed, 100 die-cut pieces, including house, barn, silo, chicken house, tractor, etc.	7.50	11.25	15.00
THE STORY OF CINDERELLA, A Fold-A-Way Toy book designed by Will Pente. Circa 1925, REILLY & BRITTON CO.	3.50	5.25	7.00
STREAMLINE FLYER, 10¾"x13½" boxed set, CONCORD TOY CO., No.122, circa 1940. Contains engine, station, crossing gates, crossing signal, baggage truck, baggage and people	9.00	13.50	18.00
STYLE SHOP PAPER DOLLS, 1943, SAALFIELD No.1516	6.00	9.00	12.00

	G	VG	M
SUB-DEB PAPER DOLLS by Irving Nurick, 1941, MERRILL No.3408, 12 teenage boys and girls dolls, clothes..........	10.00	15.00	20.00
SUE AND TOM CUT-OUT DOLLS BOOK, THE, 1946, LOWE No.149....	6.00	9.00	12.00
SUNBONNET SUE, 1951, WHITMAN No.2062-29.	4.00	6.00	8.00
SUNSHINE CUT-OUTS, Sports Series, Spring, by M&F Hoopes, 1926, 4-part foldout, STOLL & EDWARDS CO........	15.00	22.50	30.00

SUNSHINE CUT-OUTS SPORTS SERIES - SPRING
Photo by Jonathan A Newman
Courtesy Barbara and Jonathan Newman

	G	VG	M
SUSAN DEY AS LAURIE ("Partridge Family TV show), 1972, ART-CRAFT, Fashions by Kate Greenaway.......	3.50	5.25	7.00
SWEETHEART PAPER DOLLS, 1943, SAALFIELD No.2458..	11.00	16.50	22.00
SWEETIE PIE TWINS, 1949, STEPHENS PUBLISHING CO. No. 166, Jane and Jean.....	2.50	3.75	5.00
SWING-A-PLANE by J.L. Schilling Co., Model of a Flying Tiger, 1944, flies on string.............	3.00	4.50	6.00
TAMMY, 1963, A LITTLE GOLDEN STORY BOOK with paper dolls to cut out and dress. Illustrated by Ada Salvi...	2.00	3.00	4.00
TARZAN OF THE APES, 1933 figure set........	20.00	30.00	40.00
TEEN GAL CUT OUT DOLLS, 1943, by HIlda			

STAND-UP DOLLS HONEY AND BUNNY
Photo by Jonathan A. Newman
Courtesy Barbara and Jonathan Newman

	G	VG	M
Miloche and Wilma Kane, WHITMAN No.980....	10.00	15.00	20.00
TEEN TOWN, 1949, MERRILL No.3443........	8.50	12.75	17.00
THAT GIRL — MARLO THOMAS, 1967, SAALFIELD No.1351..	3.50	5.25	7.00
THAT GIRL — MARLO THOMAS, 1967, SAALFIELD No.1379..	3.50	5.25	7.00
THEY STAND UP, by Avis Mac, 1939, WHITMAN No.932, 13x18" with five children..............	17.50	26.25	35.00
30 TOY SOLDIERS, circa 1943, WHITMAN No.2950..............	12.50	18.75	25.00
THIS IS BUNNY ONE OF THE FIVE CUT-OUT DOLLY SISTERS, 1939.	11.00	16.50	22.00
THIS IS DOTTY ONE OF THE FIVE CUT-OUT DOLLY SISTERS, WHITMAN, 1939......	11.00	16.50	22.00
THIS IS MARGIE ONE OF THE FIVE CUT-OUT DOLLY SISTERS, WHITMAN, 1939......	11.00	16.50	22.00
THIS IS PATSY, ONE OF THE FIVE CUT-OUT DOLLY SISTERS, WHITMAN, 1939......	11.00	16.50	22.00
THIS IS PEGGY ONE OF THE FIVE CUT-OUT DOLLY SISTERS, WHITMAN No.1002, 1939..............	11.00	16.50	22.00
THIS IS THE NAVY No.500A, SKYLINE MFG., Destroyer and PT Boat, circa 1942........	4.00	6.00	8.00

THIS IS BUNNY - ONE OF THE FIVE CUT-OUT DOLLY SISTERS
THIS IS PATSY - ONE OF THE FIVE CUT-OUT DOLLY SISTERS
Photo by Jonathan A. Newman
Courtesy Barbara and Jonathan Newman

THIS IS THE NAVY No.501 circa 1942, SKYLINE MFG., Heavy Cruiser	G	VG	M
THIS IS THE NAVY No.501 circa 1942, SKYLINE MFG., Heavy Cruiser	5.00	7.50	10.00
THREE BEARS CUT OUT BOOK, Copyright 1939, WHITMAN No.1020, Goldilocks and 3 Bears..	11.25	16.88	22.50
THREE FLYING MODELS of Famous Allied Fighting Planes by Judd Reed, 9x12", contains Hell Cat, Spitfire and Stormovik planes. Included is "American Ace Spotter", with turning dial of 48 3-view silhouettes of 16 planes in little windows, 1944	10.00	15.00	20.00
THREE LITTLE GIRLS WHO GREW AND GREW AND THIS IS HOW THEY GREW, 1945, WHITMAN No.99410	7.00	10.50	14.00
THREE LITTLE GIRLS WHO GREW AND GREW AND GREW AND THIS IS HOW THEY GREW, with cloth-like clothes, flocked, 1945, WHITMAN No.1176	7.00	10.50	14.00
THREE LITTLE PIGS CUT OUT BOOK, Copyright 1939, WHITMAN No.1020, Pigs and Big Bad Wolf.........	11.25	16.88	22.50
THREE SWEET BABY DOLLS TO CUT OUT AND DRESS, 1954, WHITMAN No.975....	2.50	3.75	5.00
THRILLTOWN RAILROAD, 1943, REED, Pullman Passenger Set.........	21.00	31.50	42.00
TINY CHATTY TWINS PAPER DOLLS, 1963, WHITMAN NO.1985...	2.00	3.00	4.00
TOBY TYLER CIRCUS PLAYBOOK PUNCH OUT, 1959, No.1936....	5.00	7.50	10.00

TOM CORBETT SPACE CADET Punch Out Book, 1952, SAALFIELD

	G	VG	M
No.4304, 14" long, 10½" wide	6.50	9.75	13.00
TOM THE AVIATOR, circa 1942, SAMUEL LOWE No.L1074......	7.50	11.25	15.00
TONI HAIR-DO CUT-OUT DOLLS, LOWE No.1284, 1950	10.00	15.00	20.00
TOP NOTCH PAPER DOLLS, 1948, SAALFIELD No.1504..	6.50	9.75	11.00
TOY MODELS: WARPLANE AND TANK PUNCHOUT, 1941, FAWCETT PUBLICATIONS, LOWE	20.00	30.00	40.00
TOY TOWN, 1916, series of 50 different buildings by AMERICAN COLOR-TYPE CO. boxed set....	25.00	27.50	50.00

TONI HAIR-DO CUT-OUT DOLLS
Photo by Jonathan A. Newman
Courtesy Barbara and Jonathan Newman

TRANSFER PICTURES, Copyright 1939, WHITMAN No.1085, 100 decalcomanias.........	7.50	11.25	15.00
TREASURE HOUR PUPPET BOOK No. 4, 1968, MURRAY SALES AND SERVICE, The Rustlers of Rocky Ranch, a play of cowboys and Indians in five scenes. Cut-out section makes model theatre .	6.00	9.00	12.00
TRICIA, 1969, ARTCRAFT No.4248......	4.00	6.00	8.00

TRICIA PAPER DOLLS, 1970, SAALFIELD No.1248, White House

	G	VG	M
tour game, White House stand-up doll of Tricia Nixon and costumes....	7.50	11.25	15.00
TRUDY PHILLIPS AND HER CROWD, 1954, WHITMAN No.2104...	7.50	11.25	15.00
TUESDAY WELD Paper Dolls, 1960, SAALFIELD No.5112 boxed two dolls and 58 costume pieces...	7.50	11.25	15.00
TURNABOUTS DOLL BOOK, THE 1940s, LOWE NO.1048, dolls printed front view on each side..............	12.50	18.75	25.00
TV STAR TIME PAPER DOLLS, circa 1950s, AB-BOTT No.1367........	2.50	3.75	5.00
TV TAP STARS PAPER DOLLS, LOWE 99010..	3.50	5.25	7.00
22 ANIMALS TO CUT OUT AND STAND UP, copyright 1930, WHIT-MAN No.935, rabbits, bears, owls, squirrels, etc.	10.00	15.00	20.00
TWIGGY Paper Doll, 1967, WHITMAN No.1999, withh "plastilon" Twiggy dress for small girls......	5.00	7.50	10.00
TYRONE POWER & LIDA DARNELL, 1941, MERRILL No.3438....	42.50	67.75	85.00
UMBRELLA GIRLS, 1956, MERRILL No.2562, wrap-around dresses.....	6.00	9.00	12.00
UNCLE SAM'S LITTLE HELPERS PAPER DOLLS by Ann Kovach, 1943, SAALFIELD 2450	10.00	15.00	20.00
UNITED STATES SOLDIERS, 1942, SAMUEL LOWE No.L1063............	12.50	18.75	25.00
U.S. COMMANDOS BOOK, 1943, LOWE No.1089..............	15.00	22.50	30.00
U.S. INFANTRY — Spanish American War, approx. 6" high soldier on small wooden block.....	1.00	1.50	2.00
VICTORY GIRLS - ARLENE THE AIRLINE HOSTESS, circa 1940s, LOWE.........	10.00	15.00	20.00

VICTORY PUNCH-OUTS TANKS SOLDIERS SAILORS PLANES
Photo by Jonathan A. Newman
Courtesy Barbara and Jonathan Newman

	G	VG	M
VICTORY PUNCH-OUT TANKS, SOLDIERS, SAILORS, PLANES, circa 1943, LOWE No.848.	7.50	11.25	15.00
VICTORY VOLUNTEERS, 1942, dolls with uniforms by Merlin, MERRILL No.3424	20.00	30.00	40.00
VIRGINIA MAYO, 1957, SAALFIELD, No.4422..	13.00	19.50	26.00
WACS AND WAVES, 1943, WHITMAN No.985	17.50	26.25	35.00
WALKING PAPER DOLL FAMILY No.1074, SAALFIELD 1934.....	20.00	30.00	40.00
WALT DISNEY'S BABES IN TOYLAND 1961, GOLDEN Punch-Out Book No.10363........	6.00	9.00	12.00
WALT DISNEY'S JANE AND MICHAEL FROM MARY POPPINS, 1963, WATKINS / STRATH-MORE 1892-6........	3.50	5.25	7.00
WALT DISNEY'S LET'S BUILD DISNEYLAND, 1957, WHITMAN No.1986, forms sets for Adventureland, Frontierland, Tomorrowland and Fantasyland........	5.00	7.50	10.00
WALT DISNEY'S MARY POPPINS, 1964, WHITMAN No.1982........	3.50	5.25	7.00

	G	VG	M
WALT DISNEY MATCH AND PATCH STICKER FUN, 1953, WHITMAN, Mickey Mouse, Donald Duck, Pluto, Goofy, etc.	5.00	7.50	10.00
WALT DISNEY PRESENTS HAYLEY MILLS in THAT DARN CAR, 1965, WHITMAN No.1955	4.50	6.75	9.00
WALT DISNEY STICKER FUN BOOK, 1951, WHITMAN	5.00	7.50	10.00
WALT DISNEY STICKER FUN WITH PETER PAN, 1952, WHITMAN	5.00	7.50	10.00
WAR BETWEEN THE STATES, 1959, GOLDEN PRESS No.GF152	5.00	7.50	10.00
WAR PLANE CUT OUTS, 1943, 10"x14", heavy stock, 8 different scale models	10.00	15.00	20.00
WEDDING PAPER DOLLS, 1970, WHITMAN No.1970	2.00	3.00	4.00
WE'RE A FAMILY CUT-OUT DOLLS, 1954, WHITMAN No.1181	4.25	6.38	9.50
WHITE HOUSE PARTY DRESSES, 1961, MERRILL No.1550	5.00	7.50	10.00
WHITMAN No.1146, little 3½"x7½" paper doll books, copyright 1939. A. Nancy and Tommy. B. Ann and Arthur. C. Kitty and Billy. D. Muriel and David. E. Cynthia and Bobby. F. Judy and Dick.	6.00	9.00	12.00
WHITMAN PAPER DOLL BOOK, 1933, No.3059, four dolls, ten sheets of clothes in folder	12.50	18.75	25.00
WINNIE'S NEW WARDROBE by Geraldine Cline, 1939, McLOUGHLIN BROS. No.555	9.00	13.50	18.00
YOUNG PATRIOT INVASION SET, circa 1944, COLORGRAPHIC No.500, contains destroyer, amphibian tractor, tank, jeep, anti-tank gun, bomber and dive bomber, 10½x13" boxed set	17.50	26.25	35.00
YOUNG PATRIOT — LEARN TO KNOW YOUR ARMY, 1943, COLORGRAPHIC No.350, tank, howitzer, jeep, antitank gun, bomber, fighter and soldiers. Guns shoot, bombs drop, etc.	17.50	26.25	35.00
YOUNG PATRIOT — LEARN TO KNOW YOUR NAVY, 1943, COLORGRAPHIC construction set No.360, 10x14" boxed set includes battleship, destroyer, aircraft carrier, mosquito boat, submarine, planes, depth charges, etc., with moveable parts	17.50	26.25	35.00
ZIEGFELD GIRL paper dolls, No."1", 1941, MERRILL No.3466	60.00	90.00	120.00
ZOO CUT OUTS by Milo Winter, 1938, WHITMAN No.1054, six pages of heavy cut-out animals.	5.00	7.50	10.00

TIN WIND-UP
(See also Movie, Comic Character)

The average mint price for tin wind-ups in the last edition was $145.65, and in this volume averages $163.55, an increase of 12%. Unlike most toys in this book, tin wind-ups do not "feel" particularly good in the hand, and depend more on the lure of motion and colorful lithography. Esthetically the most appealing, perhaps, are those of Lehmann, a German company which also patented a number of its toys in the United States, and which holds a strong attraction for a large number of collectors.

CONDITION OF A TOY AND ITS RELATION TO PRICE

The price of a tin wind-up toy depends not only on its desirability, but on its condition. A wind-up in mint condition is generally worth twice what that same toy would bring in good condition, with "very good" falling about equally in between good and mint.

"Mint" means just that; the condition in which it was originally issued — perfect, regardless of age, not the slightest blemish. Needless to say this is a fairly rare state of affairs, but enough toys exist in mint condition to make it an employable term. Many people hoping to dispose of toys are tempted to call an item "mint" when it is really "near mint", "very good", or sometimes just "good". Inevitably this can result in unhappiness all around, and not infrequently, a cancelled sale.

"Good" signals a toy that has seen considerable wear, shows its age, but is basically sound. A collector will collect it, but will often not be wholly satisfied with it as an example of his collection, and thus prices are often drastically below that which the same item in mint can command.

Condition below good results in another drastic drop in price, and toys with missing parts, although otherwise in excellent condition, will usually fall into this lower-priced category. Rust, even small spots of it, can seriously lower the price of a toy. "Near-Mint", "Very Fine", "Fine" and similar terms often found in sellers' descriptions denote conditions between Mint and Very Good, and are priced accordingly.

The key to grading is to avoid wishful thinking. Grading can sometimes be a problem for the uninitiated, but common sense will usually prevail, and when possible, a consultation with an expert in the field can often clear up lingering doubts. A toy in its original box is worth up to 10 to 20% more if the box is in mint condition, with the price dropping as its condition lessens.

	G	VG	M
"Acrobatic Marvel" monkey on pole, with rocking base, circa 1937........	60.00	90.00	120.00
Aircraft Carrier, circa post WW II, tin litho, approx. 15" long.............	22.50	33.75	45.00
"Aircraft Carrier X53", with five jet planes, tin litho, circa 1950s...........	10.00	15.00	20.00
ANIMATED TOY "U.S. Baby Tank", pat. 6/20/16, 2½" long.............	7.50	11.25	15.00
AUTOMATIC TOY CO. Cross-Over Trolley Set...	45.00	67.50	90.00
AUTOMOTIVE TOY "Magic Crossroads" track, 2 windup cars, circa 1950	30.00	45.00	60.00
Baby L racing boat, 1930, 11" long..............	90.00	135.00	180.00
AUTOMATIC TOY CO. "Rocket Space Ship			

Baby L. Racing Boat, 11" long.
Courtesy Lloyd W. Ralston Auctions

	G	VG	M
No.305, 8½" long, sparks, 1940s	35.00	52.50	70.00
Band, two monkeys and a clown, cloth suits, 4½" high.................	20.00	30.00	40.00
Banjo Player, early, musical	55.00	82.50	110.00
Barber — animal, perhaps cat, with animal customer in chair, circa 1940s.....	15.00	22.50	30.00
"Barnum & Bailey", c. 1935, elephant pulling a four-wheeled cart loaded with a collapsible cage containing a camel, a monkey, a lion and a giraffe, each mounted on four wheels.	100.00	150.00	200.00
Battleship, "U.S.S. Washington"..........	12.50	18.75	25.00
Biplane, very early, Wright Bros.-like paper propellor blades, 6" long........	300.00	450.00	600.00
Billiards Player, painted, c.1910...............	300.00	450.00	600.00
Bird in Cage, 3½" high....	60.00	90.00	120.00
Bird with flapping wings, 6½" long.............	57.50	86.25	115.00
Black boy eating watermelon, with dog			

Buffalo Toy Aero-Speeders

Carousel with four double horse and riders that alternate with four women in cars, velvet top with ball fringe, flag finial, 17" high	G	VG	M
	950.00	1275.00	1900.00
Carousel with four men in canoes, propellors with paper vanes, 11" high...	800.00	1200.00	1600.00
CARTER "Pan-Gee The Funny Dancer", 1921...	200.00	300.00	400.00
Cat pushing cage with two mice, 8¼" long........	200.00	300.00	400.00
Caterpillar Tractor, "1916", rubber treads, tin wind-up	60.00	90.00	120.00

Caterpillar Tractor, "1916"
Photo by Bill Kaufman
Courtesy Good Old Days Store

	G	VG	M
CHEIN Alligator with native on its back.......	65.00	97.50	130.00
CHEIN Barnacle Bill, looks like Popeye, 1930s......	42.50	63.75	85.00
CHEIN "Barnacle Bill in a Barrel", 1930s, 7" high...	110.00	165.00	220.00
CHEIN bear with hat, pants, shirt, bow-tie, circa 1938	10.00	15.00	20.00
CHEIN "Ski-Boy", 8" long, 1930s	50.00	75.00	100.00
CHEIN Cabin Cruiser, 1940s, 9" long........	10.00	15.00	20.00
CHEIN chick, brightly colored clothes and polka dot bowtie, 4" high........	10.00	15.00	20.00
CHEIN Chicken pulling wheelbarrow, 6x3½", 1930s	10.00	15.00	20.00
CHEIN Clown with umbrella	15.00	22.50	30.00
CHEIN "Dan-Dee Dump Truck"	100.00	150.00	200.00
CHEIN "Drummer Boy" 9" high, with shako, circa 1930s	30.00	45.00	60.00
CHEIN duck, 4" high, waddles, 1930............	14.00	21.00	28.00

	G	VG	M
biting his backside, 6½" high................	110.00	165.00	220.00
Boy on St. Bernard on rocker, 6¾" long.......	110.00	165.00	220.00
Boy on Tricycle, 8" high...	30.00	45.00	60.00
Buffalo Bill, hand-painted, hand-soldered	100.00	150.00	200.00
Buffalo Toys, "Aero Speeders", 1920s, carousel with 3 planes, screw-rod spring drive, 10" tall.....	100.00	150.00	200.00
Bumper Car, 6½" long....	10.00	15.00	20.00
"The Cackling Hen of Paradise", 8" long, turn side handle and hen cackles; Patented.......	14.00	21.00	28.00
"Cakewalk Dancers", short black man dancing with tall, heavy black woman.	300.00	450.00	600.00
Camel, 5¼" high.........	28.00	42.00	56.00
"Candy" cart driven by monkey in cap, also marked "candy", circa 1950s..	15.00	22.50	30.00
Car with electric headlights, hard rubber wheels, 9" long.................	22.00	33.00	44.00
Carousel with four biplanes and pilots, paper vanes, flag finial, 17" high.....	900.00	1200.00	1800.00

Chein "Roller Coaster" 1930s

Chein "Roller Coaster" 1950's

Chein "Ferris Wheel" 1930's.

	G	VG	M
CHEIN Ferris Wheel, 16½" high, 6 compartments, ringing bell, 1930's......	50.00	75.00	100.00
CHEIN "Mark 1" cabin cruiser, 8½" long, 1957..	10.00	15.00	20.00
CHEIN "Mechanical Aquaplane" No.39, boat-like pontoons, 1932, 8½" long, 7½" wingspan.....	55.00	82.50	110.00
CHEIN Pelican..........	6.00	9.00	12.00
CHEIN Penguin in tuxedo type jacket, circa 1940...	12.50	18.75	25.00
CHEIN "Playland Merry-Go-Round", 1930's, 9½" high.................	65.00	97.50	130.00
CHEIN "Playland Whip" No.340, 4 bump cars, driver's head wobbles....	66.00	99.00	132.00
CHEIN Rabbit in shirt and pants, circa 1938.......	10.00	15.00	20.00
CHEIN "Ride A Rocket" carnival ride, circa 1950s, 19".................	60.00	90.00	120.00
CHEIN "Roller Coaster", includes 2 cars, circa 1938.	55.00	82.50	110.00
CHEIN "Roller Coaster"', 1950s, includes 2 cars...	50.00	75.00	100.00

	G	VG	M
CHEIN duck, long-beaked, in orange sailor suit, not Donald Duck, but similar. Waddles, 6" high.......	10.00	15.00	20.00
CHEIN Ferris Wheel, "The Giant Ride", 16" high....	45.00	67.50	90.00

CHEIN "Barnacle Bill in a Barrell".
Courtesy PB Eighty-Four, New York

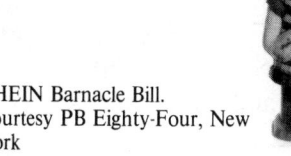

CHEIN Barnacle Bill.
Courtesy PB Eighty-Four, New York

	G	VG	M
CHEIN Turtle with Native on back	50.00	75.00	100.00
Chicken pulling chick in cart, 7½" long	25.00	37.50	50.00
Chicken, 8", cackles	12.50	18.75	25.00
Circus-Type Trainer, baton in hand, revolves, with rooster on each side, 3½" long, musical	22.00	33.00	44.00
Clown Dancer, 8" high	12.00	18.00	24.00
Clown in Donkey Cart, 7½" long	32.00	48.00	64.00
Clown in Hoop, 6½" high	60.00	90.00	120.00
Clown Musicians, four, on a pedestal, musical, 8" high	200.00	300.00	400.00
Clown pulled by goat	16.00	24.00	32.00
COURTLAND Black Diamond Coal Co., dump	3.00	4.50	6.00
COURTLAND Earthmoving truck "We Move The Earth" on trailer, Walt Reach Toy	18.00	27.00	36.00
COURTLAND Fire Patrol, 9" long	15.00	22.50	30.00
COURTLAND Ice Cream Car, "Ice Cream 5¢", man driving, bell on cart, c.1940	12.50	18.75	25.00
COURTLAND Logging Truck, "Walt Reach Toy", 13"	22.50	33.75	45.00
COURTLAND Pickup truck, 7"	12.00	18.00	24.00
Dachshund, 7" long	75.00	112.50	150.00
Dancing dogs, two, and boy with whip	100.00	150.00	200.00
Dancing horse, two small bells on top of bridle, 7½" high	60.00	90.00	120.00
Dodgem-type car, man and woman riders, circa 1938	30.00	45.00	60.00
Dog, monkey on back, 9" high	8.00	12.00	16.00
Duck, walks, quacks	9.00	13.50	18.00
Duckling	2.50	3.75	5.00
Elephant, 6" long	43.00	64.50	86.00
Ferris Wheel carrying eight gondolas, the gondolas containing a total of 16 small bisque dolls, 33½" high	666.00	999.00	1332.00
Ferris Wheel, carved with figures and music box, 17"	230.00	345.00	460.00
Fish, speckled trout, 5½" long, litho	8.00	12.00	16.00

	G	VG	M
Freight cart pulled by man in cap, with luggage on cart, circa 1940	5.00	7.50	10.00
GIRARD bus with driver, 12½" long	25.00	37.50	50.00
GIRARD "Flasho The Mechanical Grinder", 1920s	70.00	105.00	140.00
GIRARD "Goble, The Gobbling Goose"	20.00	30.00	40.00
GIRARD Man pushing wheelbarrow, 5½"	5.00	7.50	10.00
GIRARD Monoplane, high wing, one engine, 1921-22, 13" long	70.00	105.00	140.00
GIRARD Railroad Handcar	43.00	64.50	86.00

GIRARD Railroad Handcar
Courtesy Mapes Auctioneers & Appraisers

GIRARD Monoplane, high wing, one-engine, 1920.
Courtesy Lloyd W. Ralston Auctions

	G	VG	M
Hansom Cab, horse moves backward and forward, as wheels rotate, driver atop cab, 5¾" long	80.00	120.00	160.00
Hopping Rabbit, 4½" long, mid 1930s	15.00	22.50	30.00
HY LINE car, ultra-streamlined two-door coupe type, circa 1938	45.00	67.50	90.00
HY-LO, BUFFALO TOYS Ferris Wheel, 14½" high	60.00	90.00	120.00
Indian, like cigar store Indian, circa 1937	15.00	22.50	30.00

IVES Destroyer, "3009". Courtesy PB Eighty-Four, New York

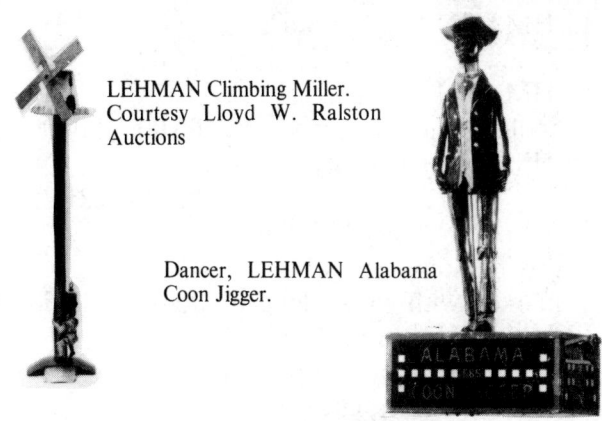

LEHMAN Climbing Miller. Courtesy Lloyd W. Ralston Auctions

Dancer, LEHMAN Alabama Coon Jigger.

IVES Tugboat "King" Courtesy PB 84 New York

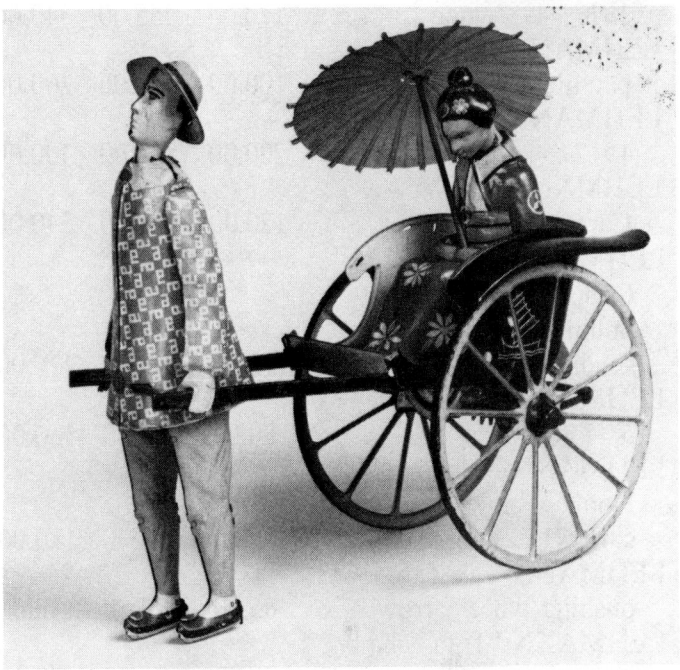

LEHMANN Masuyama
Courtesy Mapes Auctioneers & Appraisers

	G	VG	M
IVES "Destroyer" "3009", 1923, painted, 9" long...	200.00	300.00	400.00
IVES Submarine, 10½" long	150.00	225.00	300.00
IVES Tugboat "King".....	75.00	112.50	150.00
KATZ TOYS NY "The Question Mark" airplane, 18" wingspan, high-wing, two-motor............	140.00	210.00	280.00
KINGSBURY Biplane, circa 1925, single engine, rubber wheels, 16" long.....	120.00	180.00	240.00
KINGSBURY Convertible with rumble seat, electric headlamps, hard rubber wheels, 12½" long......	30.00	45.00	60.00
KINGSBURY fireman's ladder truck, hard rubber wheels, driver, 23½" long	30.00	45.00	60.00
KINGSBURY Monoplane, high wing, single engine, wind-up wheels and spins prop via rubber band, 1930s, 11" long........	100.00	150.00	200.00
KINGSBURY Roadster, electric headlamps, 12½" long.................	100.00	150.00	200.00
KINGSBURY Station Wagon, 1920s..........	90.00	135.00	180.00
LEHMANN "Ajax" Warrior with two clubs......	250.00	375.00	500.00
LEHMANN "Alabama Coon Jigger", "Lehmann, Oh-My", 10" high......	210.00	315.00	420.00
LEHMANN "Am Pol", Amundsen driving, figure behind with umbrella, map of North Pole......	350.00	525.00	700.00
LEHMANN "Anxious Bride", chauffeur on tricycle, woman in car......	400.00	600.00	800.00
LEHMANN "Bucking Bronco, Wild West", 6½" long	150.00	225.00	300.00
LEHMANN "Climbing Miller", cardboard blades.	140.00	210.00	280.00
LEHMANN "Daredevil" Zebra Cart...........	135.00	202.50	270.00
LEHMANN "Dude"......	550.00	825.00	1100.00
LEHMANN "Express", porter pulling cart, circa 1927, 6" long.........	94.00	141.00	188.00
LEHMANN, "Li La", early car with two excited women passengers, driver in top hat and dog with turning head, 5½" long..	300.00	450.00	600.00

LEHMANN Bird "Lu-Lu", 2"	G 5.00	VG 7.50	M 10.00
LEHMANN "Masuyama", coolie pulling rickshaw...	100.00	190.00	200.00
LEHMANN "Naughty Boy"	187.50	281.25	375.00
LEHMANN "Na-Ob", man driving horse cart, wheels marked with elf, 6" long.	75.00	112.50	150.00
LEHMANN "Nunu" No.733, rickshaw with puller and rider, circa 1913, 4½" long	170.00	255.00	340.00
LEHMANN "OHO" patented 1903	100.00	150.00	200.00
LEHMANN "Paddy Pig" c. 1912	200.00	300.00	400.00
LEHMANN "Power Carriage"	120.00	180.00	240.00
LEHMANN "Quack-Quack", mother duck pulling cart with three small ducks	112.50	168.75	225.00
LEHMANN "Rad-Cycle", 5" long, circa 1927	80.00	120.00	160.00
LEHMANN Stubborn Donkey, clown in donkey cart, 7½" long	90.00	135.00	180.00
LEHMANN Tap Tap, man pushing wheelbarrow	65.00	97.50	130.00
LEHMANN "Tom" climbing monkey, 8" long	60.00	90.00	120.00
LEHMANN "Tut-Tut", man in car with horn, 6¾" long	300.00	450.00	600.00
LEHMANN Walking Couple	450.00	675.00	900.00
LEHMANN Walking Sailor, 7½" high	100.00	150.00	200.00
LEHMANN "Zig Zag" patented 1903, 5" long	400.00	600.00	800.00
LINDSTROM Bird	30.00	45.00	60.00
LINDSTROM "Betty", 1930's, 8" tall, shako walker	65.00	97.50	130.00
LINDSTROM Bumper Car	35.00	52.50	70.00
LINDSTROM "Dancing Lassie", 8" tall, shako, 1930s	65.00	97.50	130.00

Lindstrom Toys 1930's, Sweeping Mammy, Betty, Mammy (Shakos)

	G	VG	M
LINDSTROM "Lindstrom's Ferry Boat", approx. 8¼", litho	30.00	45.00	60.00
LINDSTROM "Lindstrom Flyer", 14" long	40.00	60.00	80.00
LINDSTROM, "Mammy", 1930's 8" tall, shako walker	65.00	97.50	130.00
LINDSTROM "Miss America" speedboat	30.00	45.00	60.00
LINDSTROM "Parcel Post No.2" truck	125.00	187.50	250.00
LINDSTROM Speedboat, circa 1950, 18½" long	45.00	67.50	90.00
LINDSTROM Sweeping Girl	20.00	30.00	40.00
LINDSTROM "Sweeping Mammy", No.1750, 1930s, 8" tall, shako walker while sweeping	75.00	112.50	150.00
LUPOR METAL PRODUCTS N.Y. Racer No.8, 1930s	8.00	12.00	16.00
Man and Woman Dancing, both white, 8" high	250.00	375.00	500.00
Man pushing Wheelbarrow, black man, 6"	75.00	112.50	150.00
Marine, hand on belt, smiling, circa 1940	15.00	22.50	30.00

LOUIS MARX: By the 1950s, LOUIS MARX was the largest manufacturer of toys in the world; six large factories in the U.S., and ownership of interest in factories in seven other countries. Marx, born in Brooklyn in 1896, was working for "Toy King" Ferdinand Strauss when he was in his teens, and by the age of twenty his energy and enterprise had made him a director of that company. A falling out with Strauss persuaded him to go into business for himself, and in 1921 he and his brother began making their own toys, including some adaptations of items by the now-defunct Strauss. Marx's watchword seems to have been quality at the lowest possible price, and he was such a favorite with toy buyers that he had virtually no need for salesmen or advertising. Although Marx made virtually every type of toy with the exception of dolls, his tin wind-up toys are probably the most favored by toy collectors. Marx eventually sold his company to the Quaker Oats Company, who in 1976 sold it to Europe's largest toy manufacturer, Dunbee-Combex-Marx. The company went into bankruptcy in 1980. Louis Marx died in 1982 at the age of 85.

	G	VG	M
MARX Acrobatic Marvel, early	75.00	112.50	150.00
MARX Acrobatic Marvel, late	20.00	30.00	40.00
MARX Air Mail Biplane, 1930, 4-engine	115.00	172.50	230.00
MARX Air Mail Monoplane, 1930, 2-engine	70.00	105.00	140.00
MARX Airplane, U.S. Army No.6, 2-engine, no guns, 18" wingspan	45.00	67.50	90.00
MARX Airplane No.90, light fuselage	10.00	15.00	20.00
MARX Airplane No.90, medium fuselage	15.00	22.50	30.00
MARX "Ambulance" with siren	90.00	135.00	180.00
MARX Ambulance, "M.D. War Dept.", 1930s	90.00	135.00	180.00
MARX "Army Dive Bomber" No.482	62.50	93.75	125.00
MARX Army Staff Car, 1930s, litho steel	125.00	187.50	250.00
MARX "Army Staff Car", W-601158, with flasher and siren, 11" long, 1940s	70.00	105.00	140.00
MARX "Beat!! The Komikal Kop", 1930s	92.50	138.75	185.00
MARX Armored Trucking Co.	80.00	120.00	160.00
MARX Balky Mule, pre-war	30.00	45.00	60.00
MARX "Big Parade", moving vehicles, soldiers, etc., 1929	65.00	97.50	130.00
MARX Big Three Aerial Acrobats, 1920	90.00	135.00	180.00
MARX Big Lizzie car, early 1930s, 7¼" long	70.00	105.00	140.00
MARX Bomber, two engine, 18" wingspan	30.00	45.00	60.00
MARX Boy on Trapeze	17.00	25.50	34.00

MARX Big 3 Aerial Acrobats. Courtesy Lloyd W. Ralston Auctions

MARX Walking Clancy. Courtesy PB Eighty-Four, New York

MARX Air Mail Biplane, 4-engine, 1930. Courtesy Lloyd W. Ralston Auctions

	G	VG	M
MARX Brutus Dippy Dumper, celluloid figure, circa 1930, eccentric car	120.00	180.00	240.00
MARX Bulldozer Climbing Tractor, caterpillar type, circa 1950s, 10½" long	38.50	58.25	77.00
MARX Bumper Auto, streamlined, circa 1939, large bumpers front and rear	42.00	63.00	84.00
MARX "Busy Bridge", vehicles on bridge, 1935	75.00	112.50	150.00
MARX, "Busy Miners", 1930s, 16½" long, includes 2¼" tin litho miner's car	45.00	67.50	90.00

MARX "Busy Bridge"
Courtesy PB Eighty-Four New York

MARX Balky Mule
Courtesy Mapes Auctioneers & Appraisers

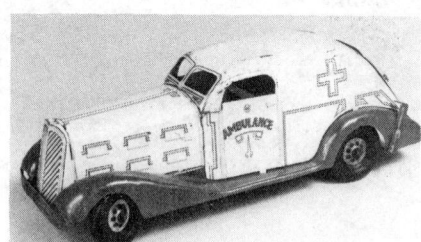

MARK "Ambulance" with siren
Courtesy Mapes Auctioneers & Appraisers

MARX "Royal Van Co."
Courtesy Mapes Auctioneers & Appraisers

	G	VG	M
MARX "The Butter and Egg Man" walker	75.00	112.50	150.00
MARX Cadillac Roadster, 13" long, trunk with tools on luggage carrier, 1930.	110.00	165.00	220.00
MARX Cat with ball in front, two wheels in back, circa 1938	20.00	30.00	40.00
MARX Caterpillar Climbing Tractor, circa 1950s, 10" long	15.00	22.50	30.00
MARX "Charleston Trio", one adult, two child dancers, 1921	182.50	273.75	365.00
MARX Chicken Snatcher, black holding chicken, dog biting at the seat of his pants, circa 1927	150.00	225.00	300.00
MARX Climbing Tractor, post-war, 8½" long	24.00	36.00	48.00
MARX Climbing Tractor, late 20's, farm boy at wheel, detachable	20.00	30.00	40.00
MARX "Climbing, Fighting Tank"	15.00	22.50	30.00
MARX "Coast Defense", circular, with three can-			

	G	VG	M
non, revolving airplane, 1929	100.00	150.00	200.00
MARX "Cowboy Rider", circa 1941, cowboy with lariat on dapple or black horse.	60.00	90.00	120.00
MARX Crazy Dora nodder head	9.00	13.50	18.00
MARX "Dapper Dan Coon Jigger", 1910	140.00	210.00	280.00
MARX Dare Devil Flyer, 1929	85.00	127.50	170.00
MARX "Dippy Dumper", early	60.00	90.00	120.00
MARX Donkey pulling cart, with rider	32.00	48.00	64.00
MARX Doughboy Tank, two side turrets, revolving top turret, 9¼" long, 1930, soldier with gun pops out	60.00	90.00	120.00
MARX Fireman on ladder, 24" high	71.50	107.25	143.00
MARX '1st Batt. F.D. Chief's Car", 16", siren, battery headlilghts	40.00	60.00	80.00
MARX "Flipo the Jumping Dog, See Me Jump", on			

	G	VG	M
hind legs, circa 1940, 3½x4"	30.00	45.00	60.00
MARX "Flying Fortress 2095" sparkling aeroplane, 1940's 4 engines	50.00	75.00	100.00
MARX "Funny Flivver" circa 1925.	150.00	225.00	300.00
MARX G-Man Pursuit Car, 1930s	20.00	30.00	40.00
MARX, "George the Drummer Boy", 1930s, 9" tall with moving eyes	50.00	75.00	100.00
MARX, "George the Drummer Boy", 1930s, 9" tall with stationary eyes	45.00	67.50	90.00
MARX "Giant King Racer", circa 1930s, "711"	20.00	30.00	40.00
MARX Giant Reversing Tractor Truck with tools, "Hauling", 14" long, circa 1950s	29.00	43.50	58.00
MARX Golden Pecking Goose, 9½" long, dated July 8, 1924, hops along, pecking at ground	70.00	105.00	140.00
MARX "Hee-Haw" balky mule, 1929, 10¾" long, six-color litho, goes backward, forward and rears, farmer and his dog on seat and 5 milk cans in cart	50.00	75.00	100.00
MARX Highboy Climbing Tractor, circa 1950s, 10½" long	16.00	24.00	32.00
MARX Highboy Tractor, sparkles, circa 1950s, 10" long	30.00	45.00	60.00
MARX "Honeymoon Express", old-fashioned train on circular track, 1927 . .	75.00	112.50	150.00
MARX "Honeymoon Express", circa 1940, circling train and plane, 9⅜" dia.	65.00	97.50	130.00
MARX "Honeymoon Express", streamlined train on circular track, 1947, 9⅜" dia.	50.00	75.00	100.00
MARX Jalopy Pickup Truck, 7"	17.00	25.50	34.00
MARX "Joy-Rider", 1929, 8" long, College Boy			

	G	VG	M
driver with bag, wording on car "goes backward, forward, circles and rears" head moves	104.00	156.00	208.00
MARX Jumpin' Jeep, circa WW II, 6"	40.00	60.00	80.00
MARX "King Racer", 1920s	130.00	195.00	260.00
MARX "Limping Lizzie" Car	40.00	60.00	80.00
MARX "Looping Plane", No.182	25.00	37.50	50.00
MARX "Looping Plane", No.382	25.00	37.50	50.00
MARX Lucky Stunt Flyer .	140.00	210.00	280.00
MARX "Main Street", moving vehicles, traffic cop, etc., 1929	60.00	90.00	120.00
MARX Mammy's Boy, eyes move, litho	80.00	120.00	160.00
MARX "Mechanical Speedway Racer"	10.00	15.00	20.00
MARX "Mechanical Tractor", 6" long, circa 1930s .	30.00	45.00	60.00
MARX Mechanical Tractor with Earth Grader, 21½" long, circa 1950s	18.00	27.00	36.00
MARX Merrymakers, four mice, three in band, one a dancer, 1929, with marquee	350.00	525.00	700.00
MARX Same as above without marquee	300.00	450.00	600.00
MARX "Midget Climbing Fighting Tank", approx. 5½" long, circa 1935, Pat. No. 1,334,539	25.00	37.50	50.00
MARX Midget Climbing Tractor, 5½" long, circa 1950	30.00	45.00	60.00
MARX "Midget Special", race car-driver in old headgear and goggles, 5" long, No.2 racer, 1930s . .	20.00	30.00	40.00
MARX "Midget Special" race-car driver in old headgear and goggles, 5" long No.7 racer, 1930s . .	20.00	30.00	40.00
MARX Minstrel figure, 11" high	60.00	90.00	120.00
MARX Motorcycle Policeman with side-car, "Police Squad", "3" license plate reads "102D", approx. 8" long, 5¾" high, circa 1940	75.00	112.50	150.00

	G	VG	M
MARX "Motorcycle Trooper", 1935.........	50.00	75.00	100.00
MARX Mystery Tunnel...	22.50	33.75	45.00
MARX "Mystic Motorcycle", circa 1930s........	40.00	60.00	80.00
MARX "New York", circular, with train, 1929...	90.00	135.00	180.00
MARX Nodding Goose...	20.00	30.00	40.00
MARX "Old Jalopy"......	50.00	75.00	100.00
MARX "P.D." Motorcyclist, "Pat. 2001625", approx. 4" long.......	20.00	30.00	40.00
MARX "P.D." Police motorcycle w/side car, wood wheels, on-off lever, 1930s, 3½" long........	30.00	45.00	60.00
MARX Peter Rabbit, eccentric car..............	25.00	37.50	50.00
MARX "Pinched" roadster, motorcycle cop in circular track, circa 1927.......	80.00	120.00	160.00
MARX "Police Patrol", motorcycle with sidecar, 1935	40.00	60.00	80.00
MARX Racer No. 5......	18.00	27.00	36.00
MARX Racing car, 12" litho, circa 1940, two-man team............	25.00	37.50	50.00
MARX Racing car, "27", litho, plastic driver circa 1950	10.00	15.00	20.00
MARX Range Rider......	55.00	82.50	110.00
MARX "Red Cap" Porter.	65.00	102.50	130.00

MARX "Reversible Coupe, The Marvel Car"
Courtesy Mapes Auctioneers & Appraisers

MARX Renfrew Tank....	65.00	102.50	130.00
MARX "Reversible Coupe" "The Marvel Car", circa 1938	55.00	82.50	110.00
MARX Reversing Road Roller	25.00	37.50	50.00
MARX "Ride 'Em Cowboy"	45.00	67.50	90.00
MARX "Ring-A-Ling Circus", early ringmaster and circus animals........	110.00	165.00	220.00
MARX "Roadside Rest Service Station", four pumps, car, garage, 1930	75.00	112.50	150.00

Marx "Speed Boy Delivery"

	G	VG	M
MARX "Rocket Fighter" circa 1950s, complete with tail fin and sparking mechanism	125.00	187.50	250.00
MARX Rocket Racer, 1930s	40.00	60.00	80.00
MARX "Rodeo Joe", 1933.	100.00	150.00	200.00
MARX "Roll Over Plane", circa 1920s............	60.00	90.00	120.00
MARX Rookie Pilot, 7" long, No.77, circa 1940..	20.00	30.00	40.00
MARX Rooster pulling Wagon, 1930s.........	25.00	37.50	50.00
MARX Royal Bus Line, 10" long..............	30.00	45.00	60.00
MARX "Royal Coupe"....	110.00	165.00	220.00
MARX "Royal Van Co." "We Haul Anywhere", 9" long.................	40.00	60.00	80.00
MARX "Sand and Gravel Truck — Builders Supply Co.", 1920............	25.00	37.50	50.00
MARX Scenic Express Train Set, circa 1950s...	15.00	22.50	30.00
MARX "Service Station Pumps" (3?), 1920......	25.00	37.50	50.00
MARX Sheriff Sam Whoopee Car..........	25.00	37.50	50.00
MARX "Sky Hawk" airport tower, two planes, tower 7½" high.............	50.00	75.00	100.00
MARX Skybird Flyer, 1930s	75.00	112.50	150.00
MARX Soldier, prone, firing rifle, WW I helmet..	15.00	22.50	30.00
MARX Space Tank.......	45.00	67.50	90.00
MARX "Sparkling Climbing Tank", 1939...........	37.50	56.25	75.00
MARX Sparkling Climbing Tractor, 8½" long, circa			

	G	VG	M
MARX "Spic Coon Drummer", 1924, 8½" high...	330.00	495.00	660.00
MARX "Streamline Speedway", two racing cars...	36.00	54.00	72.00
MARX, "Subway Express", with plastic tunnel, 1950s, 9⅜" diameter.....	40.00	60.00	80.00
MARX "Sunnyside Service Station", four pumps, car and garage, 1939.......	110.00	165.00	220.00
MARX "Tidy Tim" Streetcleaner, pushing wagon, 1933..........	117.50	176.25	235.00
MARX "Toyland Farm Products", 1930s, milk wagon, 10½" long......	52.50	78.75	105.00
MARX "Toytown Dairy", horsedrawn cart, 10½" long, 1930s...........	55.00	82.50	110.00
MARX Tractor, early 1940s	10.00	15.00	20.00
MARX Tractor and Trailer set, 1930s, similar to climbing tractor set, but with rounded and radiator front and copper finish metal. Tin plow attaches to front, silver metal trailer attaches to rear; has tin, copper finish and "balloon" tires........	35.00	52.50	70.00
MARX Tractor & trailer, 16½" long, circa 1950s..	25.00	37.50	50.00
MARX "Tricky Motorcycle", 1930s, 4¼" long, non-fail action........	40.00	60.00	80.00

Marx Tank

	G	VG	M
MARX Trolley, headlight, bell, 9" long..........	48.00	72.00	96.00
MARX Turn Over Tank No.3	15.00	22.50	30.00
MARX "U.S. Army" bomber, post-War, 1940s, two-engine	21.00	31.50	42.00
MARX "Uncle Wiggily, He Goes A Ridin'", 1935...	See Comic Character		
MARX Walking Clancy...	220.00	330.00	440.00
MARX Walking Drummer Boy, "Let The Drummer			

Marx "Subway Express", Chein "Boy Skier"	G	VG	M
1950s	20.00	30.00	60.00
MARX "Sparkling Climbing Tractor and Trailer", 16" long, circa 1950s.......	30.00	45.00	60.00
MARX Sparkling Heavy Duty Bulldog Tractor with Road Scraper, circa 1950s, 11" long........	25.00	37.50	50.00
MARX Sparkling Soldier Motorcycle, circa 1940..	34.00	51.00	68.00
MARX Sparkling Super Power Tank, circa 1950s, 9½" long.............	30.00	45.00	60.00
MARX Sparkling Tank, 4" long................	15.00	22.50	30.00
MARX "Sparkling Tractor", tractor with plow blade, 1939	40.00	60.00	80.00
MARX Sparkling Tractor and Trailer Set, "Marbrook Farms", circa 1950s, 21" long........	45.00	67.50	90.00
MARX Sparkling Warship, 14" long.............	30.00	45.00	60.00
MARX "Speed Boy Delivery", (Motorcycle delivery), 1930s, 9¾" long, battery operated lights	100.00	150.00	200.00
MARX Speedway coupe, battery to be inserted for headlights	35.00	52.50	70.00
MARX "Spic and Span, the Hams What Am", drummer and dancer, 1924...	325.00	487.50	650.00

MARX Charleston Trio

MARX Main Street

MARX Chicken Snatcher

MARX Hee-Haw

MARX Honeymoon Express

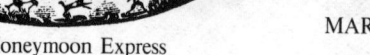

MARX Pinched

	G	VG	M
Boy Play While You Swing And Sway", circa 1939	125.00	187.80	250.00
MARX Wee Scottie, 5" long	20.00	30.00	40.00
MARX Whoopee Car, laughing cows on wheels, driver looks like cowboy, 1929	48.00	72.00	96.00
MARX Whoopee Car, "Yale-Princeton" pennants on wheels	77.00	115.50	154.00
MARX Xylophonist, 5"	15.00	22.50	30.00
MARX Zeppelin, 27" long, 1930s	60.00	90.00	120.00
MARX Zippo Monkey	14.00	21.00	28.00
Merry-Go-Round, 11" high	30.00	45.00	60.00
Monkey on Tricycle	26.00	39.00	52.00
Motorcycle with Rider	70.00	105.00	140.00
"Movie Man" TOURING Car, rare	1100.00	1650.00	2200.00
Newsboy, "Extra", with cap and bell, circa 1940s	20.00	30.00	40.00
OHIO ART Boat, 14" long	10.00	15.00	20.00
OHIO ART Hot Job Floatplane	45.00	67.50	90.00
ORI-O Tailspin 4"puppy	3.50	5.25	7.00
ORKIN Coast Guard Cutter, 25" long	200.00	300.00	400.00
"Parcel Post U.S. Mail" truck, 8½" long, early	120.00	180.00	240.00
Patrol Car No.7, no mfg. listed, circa 1948	11.00	16.50	22.00
Pecking Bird, 5" long	25.00	37.50	50.00
Pecking Chicken, 5½" high	25.00	37.50	50.00
Pool Players, two men playing pool, 14½" long	75.00	112.50	150.00
"PT 10", tin litho PT boat, circa 1941	20.00	30.00	40.00

	G	VG	M
Pump Cart with figure, 4¾" long	50.00	75.00	100.00
Roadster, orange and green	20.00	30.00	40.00
"Robot Bus" 14" long	25.00	37.50	50.00
Santa Claus in red cloth suit and holding Christmas tree, 5½" high	70.00	105.00	140.00
Santa Claus with green sleigh, Christmas tree, presents and white celluloid reindeer, bell, sleigh on three wheels, 8½" long	30.00	45.00	60.00
"Skidoodle", NIFTY, circa 1920, family in odd-looking car	300.00	450.00	600.00
Speedboat, "G.E. 200", tin litho, circa 1930	15.00	22.50	30.00
Spinning Globe, tin litho, two tin planes circling it, circa 1930	66.00	99.99	132.00
"Spirit of America" airplane PNX211, NY to Paris litho on wings	20.00	30.00	40.00
Stagecoach, 8¾" long, with horses	50.00	75.00	100.00
Steam Roller, circa 1925	45.00	67.50	90.00
Steam Shovel, large size, rubber wheels, early	10.00	15.00	20.00
STRAUSS "Alabama Coon Jigger", 1910, 9¾"	120.00	180.00	240.00
STRAUSS "Alabama Coon Jigger - Tombo" 1918, 10½" high, 3"x5" base	90.00	135.00	180.00
STRAUSS "Big Trixo", climbing monkey, 10" long	27.50	41.25	55.00

"Skidoodle", NIFTY
Photo Courtesy PB
Eighty-Four

STRAUSS Hooligans Hack
Courtesy Mapes Auctioneers & Appraisers

STRAUSS "Alabama Coon Jigger"
Courtesy Mapes Auctioneers & Appraisers

	G	VG	M
STRAUSS Black Porter pulling wheelbarrow 6¼"	75.00	112.50	150.00
STRAUSS "Bus Deluxe", 1920s, 12" long	200.00	300.00	400.00
STRAUSS Check-A-Cab	200.00	300.00	400.00
STRAUSS Circus Wagon, containing lion and tamer, 8½" long, no engine compartment	200.00	300.00	400.00
STRAUSS Circus Wagon, 10" long, has engine compartment	200.00	300.00	400.00
STRAUSS "Dizzie Lizzie"	42.00	63.00	84.00
STRAUSS "Ham and Sam The Minstrel Team", piano player and banjoist, 1921, 6½" long	170.00	255.00	340.00
STRAUSS "Haul Away Truck" No.22, dump body	40.00	60.00	80.00
STRAUSS Hooligans Hack	60.00	90.00	120.00
STRAUSS Interstate Double Decker Bus, 1920	200.00	300.00	400.00
STRAUSS "Jackee The Horn Pipe Dancer", 8½" long	125.00	187.50	250.00

	G	VG	M
STRAUSS "Jazzbo Jim The Dancer on the Roof", 1910, 10" high	85.00	127.50	170.00
STRAUSS "Jenny the Balky Mule", 10" long, six-color litho, goes backward, forward and rears, farmer holding extended tin grain pail from his seat in front of mule's face to keep him moving vegetables in cart	75.00	112.50	150.00
STRAUSS Joco the Golfer	75.00	112.50	150.00
STRAUSS Knock-Out Prize Fighters, ca 1910, 7" high	100.00	150.00	200.00
STRAUSS "Leaping Lena"	115.00	172.50	230.00
STRAUSS "Long Haulage Truck"	210.00	315.00	420.00
STRAUSS "Mailplane"	48.00	72.00	96.00
STRAUSS Monkey driving 3-wheel cart pulled by bulldog, 1930s, 4½" high	18.00	27.00	36.00
STRAUSS "Play Golf"	150.00	225.00	300.00
STRAUSS "Red-Cap Porter", porter pushing a large trunk	170.00	255.00	340.00
STRAUSS "Red Star Van"	40.00	60.00	80.00
STRAUSS Rollo Chair, black man pushing boardwalk chair, "Stock, DRGM, December 6, 1921"	170.00	255.00	340.00
STRAUSS Santa Claus in Sleigh, 1921, 6" high, 2 reindeer	210.00	315.00	420.00
STRAUSS "Speedwagon"	40.00	60.00	80.00
STRAUSS "Tip Tip" man with wheelbarrow	80.00	120.00	160.00
STRAUSS "Trikauto"	40.00	60.00	80.00
STRAUSS "Yell-o Taxi"	200.00	300.00	400.00

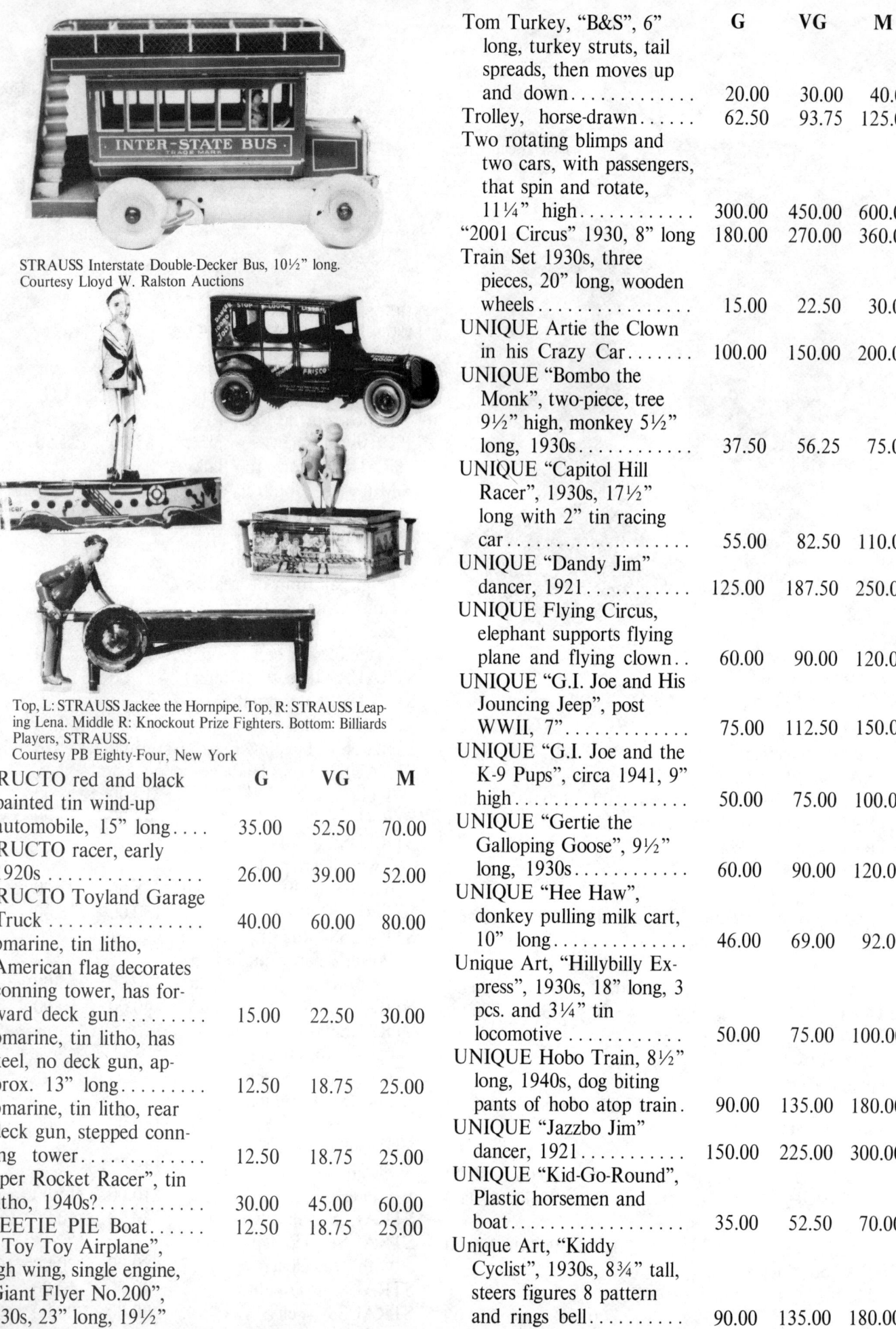

STRAUSS Interstate Double-Decker Bus, 10½" long.
Courtesy Lloyd W. Ralston Auctions

Top, L: STRAUSS Jackee the Hornpipe. Top, R: STRAUSS Leaping Lena. Middle R: Knockout Prize Fighters. Bottom: Billiards Players, STRAUSS.
Courtesy PB Eighty-Four, New York

	G	VG	M
STRUCTO red and black painted tin wind-up automobile, 15" long....	35.00	52.50	70.00
STRUCTO racer, early 1920s	26.00	39.00	52.00
STRUCTO Toyland Garage Truck	40.00	60.00	80.00
Submarine, tin litho, American flag decorates conning tower, has forward deck gun	15.00	22.50	30.00
Submarine, tin litho, has keel, no deck gun, approx. 13" long	12.50	18.75	25.00
Submarine, tin litho, rear deck gun, stepped conning tower	12.50	18.75	25.00
"Super Rocket Racer", tin litho, 1940s?	30.00	45.00	60.00
SWEETIE PIE Boat	12.50	18.75	25.00
"Tip Toy Toy Airplane", high wing, single engine, "Giant Flyer No.200", 1930s, 23" long, 19½" wingspan	75.00	102.50	150.00

	G	VG	M
Tom Turkey, "B&S", 6" long, turkey struts, tail spreads, then moves up and down	20.00	30.00	40.00
Trolley, horse-drawn	62.50	93.75	125.00
Two rotating blimps and two cars, with passengers, that spin and rotate, 11¼" high	300.00	450.00	600.00
"2001 Circus" 1930, 8" long	180.00	270.00	360.00
Train Set 1930s, three pieces, 20" long, wooden wheels	15.00	22.50	30.00
UNIQUE Artie the Clown in his Crazy Car	100.00	150.00	200.00
UNIQUE "Bombo the Monk", two-piece, tree 9½" high, monkey 5½" long, 1930s	37.50	56.25	75.00
UNIQUE "Capitol Hill Racer", 1930s, 17½" long with 2" tin racing car	55.00	82.50	110.00
UNIQUE "Dandy Jim" dancer, 1921	125.00	187.50	250.00
UNIQUE Flying Circus, elephant supports flying plane and flying clown..	60.00	90.00	120.00
UNIQUE "G.I. Joe and His Jouncing Jeep", post WWII, 7"	75.00	112.50	150.00
UNIQUE "G.I. Joe and the K-9 Pups", circa 1941, 9" high	50.00	75.00	100.00
UNIQUE "Gertie the Galloping Goose", 9½" long, 1930s	60.00	90.00	120.00
UNIQUE "Hee Haw", donkey pulling milk cart, 10" long	46.00	69.00	92.00
Unique Art, "Hillbilly Express", 1930s, 18" long, 3 pcs. and 3¼" tin locomotive	50.00	75.00	100.00
UNIQUE Hobo Train, 8½" long, 1940s, dog biting pants of hobo atop train.	90.00	135.00	180.00
UNIQUE "Jazzbo Jim" dancer, 1921	150.00	225.00	300.00
UNIQUE "Kid-Go-Round", Plastic horsemen and boat	35.00	52.50	70.00
Unique Art, "Kiddy Cyclist", 1930s, 8¾" tall, steers figures 8 pattern and rings bell	90.00	135.00	180.00

UNIQUE Rodeo Joe Whoopie Car
Courtesy Mapes Auctioneers & Appraisers

L to R: UNIQUE Sky Rangers, MARX Skybird Flyer.
Courtesy Phillips, New York

Top: "2001" Circus. Bottom: UNIQUE
Krazy Kar, 1940.
Courtesy Lloyd W. Ralston Auctions

	G	VG	M
UNIQUE Krazy Kar, litho.	110.00	165.00	220.00
UNIQUE "Lincoln Tunnel", moving vehicles, cop, 1935, 24" long	65.00	97.50	130.00
UNIQUE Musical Sail-Way Carousel with 3 kids in spinning plastic boats, 9" tall	30.00	45.00	60.00

	G	VG	M
UNIQUE Pecking Goose, Witch and Cat	127.50	191.25	255.00
UNIQUE Rodeo Joe Crazy Car	75.00	112.50	150.00
UNIQUE "Rollover Motorcycle Cop, 1935	60.00	90.00	120.00
UNIQUE "Sky Rangers" plane and zeppelin revolving from tower, 1933	100.00	150.00	200.00

Walking Man, carrying red top hat over his head, head revolves to reveal three different faces. Photo courtesy PB Eighty-Four

S.S. Wolverine Oceanliner

	G	VG	M
Walking Man, carrying red top hat over his head, head revolves to reveal 3 different faces..........	150.00	225.00	300.00
WALT REACH TOY CO. Rocking R Ranch......	9.00	13.50	18.00
WILKINS Roadster, early with driver, 9" long.....	135.00	202.50	270.00
WILKINS Auto, early, woman driver, 9" long..	130.00	195.00	260.00
WOLVERINE Acrobat....	50.00	75.00	100.00
WOLVERINE "Drummer Boy", 14" high.........	40.00	60.00	80.00
WOLVERINE "Drum Major", No.27, patent 1892546, 1930s, 13¼" tall on circular base (4¼" dia.)................	75.00	112.50	150.00
WOLVERINE, "Drum Major", No.27, patent 1892546, 1930s, 13⅝" tall on rectangular base (4½"x6½")...........	75.00	112.50	150.00
WOLVERINE Jet Roller, Coaster and small car, 21" long (extended)........	45.00	67.50	90.00
WOLVERINE, "Merry-Go-Round", 1930s, 11" diameter, 12" high, includes four tin-litho flags.	100.00	150.00	200.00
WOLVERINE "Loop-A-Loop", 1930s, 19" long, includes small car.......	50.00	75.00	100.00
WOLVERINE Roller Coaster, "Loop-A-Loop".	40.00	60.00	80.00
WOLVERINE "S.S. Wolverine", 14½" long..	15.00	22.50	30.00

	G	VG	M
WOLVERINE "Sandy Andy Circus", dancing toy..	34.00	51.00	68.00
WOLVERINE "Sunny Andy" Tank, 14" long.....	30.00	45.00	60.00
WOLVERINE "Zilotone" with six interchangeable records, 1930s........	200.00	300.00	400.00
"The Wonder Cyclist", boy on tricycle, circa 1930, 8¾" high.............	90.00	135.00	180.00
WOODHAVEN Tractor, 1916................	25.00	37.50	50.00
World on base, wind-up plane circles it.........	36.00	54.00	72.00
WYANDOTTE Duck pulling tin Easter cart, 15" long, litho, wooden wheels..............	10.00	15.00	20.00
WYANDOTTE "Hoky-Poky" handcar with 2 clowns................	22.50	33.75	45.00
WYANDOTTE "Red Ranger Ride 'Em Cowboy", circa 1930s...	50.00	75.00	100.00
WYANDOTTE "Ride 'Em Cowboy".............	45.00	67.50	90.00

Unique Art-"Kiddy Cyclist", Marx "Lone Ranger", Marx "Toytown Dairy"

"Battery-Operated" Flutter Birds, Answer Game Robot, Climbing Linesman
Courtesy Don Hultzman.   Photo by Ron Chojnacki.

Unique "G.I. Joe & K-9 Pups", Marx "Golden Pecking Goose",
Marx "Busy Miners", Marx "Figaro Cat", Unique Art "Gertie-the
Galloping Goose"

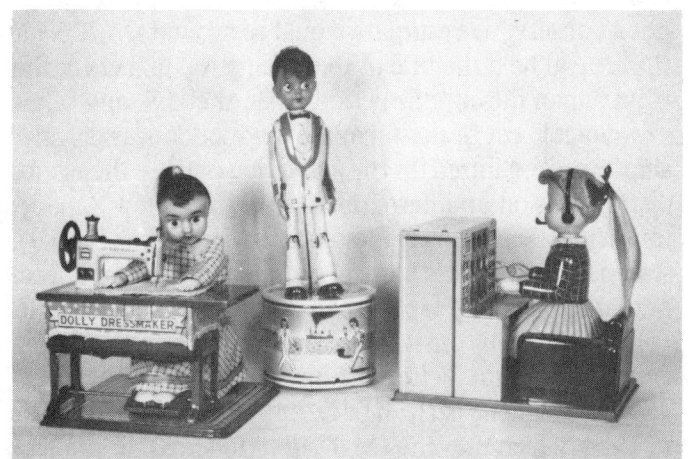

"Battery-Operated" Dolly Dressmaker, Twist Dancer, Switchboard Operator
Courtesy Don Hultzman.   Photo by Ron Chojnacki.

BATTERY-OPERATED TOYS
by Don Hultzman

Mint prices in this category averaged $93.10 in the last edition, and $100.26 in this, an increase of 8%.

During the years preceding World War II, the Japanese toy industry was content with making cheap imitations of American and European toys, mostly out of recycled tin cans. Immediately after the war and through the 1960's, the Japanese came into their own with a new and different dimension in the toy world — the battery-operated toy.

Previously, early U.S. and European toy makers used batteries in their toys to add realism to their boats, cars, trains and airplanes by adding flashlight bulbs where headlights, spotlights, tail-lights and navigation lights were required. Later, batteries were used to power horns, buzzers and electromagnets as well as lights, but these early mechanical toys still depended on a spring or small flywheel to function as a mechanical toy should. There was just so much these early toys could do until the Japanese toy revolution opened up a whole new area with their clever automatons.

Starting in 1946, the Japanese toy makers began to replace the wind-up clockwork mechanisms and friction-drive mechanical toys with mini-electric motors powered by one or more batteries. These small electric motors could run much longer than the spring powered or friction drive mechanisms and with this advantage, the Japanese toy makers designed and manufactured the most ingenious and complicated automatons imaginable. There were able to simulate just about every conceivable type of human-animal motions and behavioral actions. This ingenuity carried over into a multitude of different types of novelty toys. Just how many different types of automata and vehicles were manufactured is unknown, but a conservative estimate would be around the 700 mark. Multiply this figure by the thousands and it was no wonder that Japan held the title of the leading toy maker for the next 20 years. About 95% of the battery-operated toys came from Japan during this period while the U.S. and other countries manufactured the remaining 5% of these toys.

Since most of the Japanese production was destined for the U.S. and European market, international distributorships were organized for the marketing of these thousands of toys. Cragstan, Linemar and Rosko were some of the largest distributors on an international scale, but a few American toy makers hopped on the band wagon in marketing these toys under their brand names, such as Marx, Ideal, Hubley and Daisy (the BB gun people). Therefore many of the trademarks stamped on Japanese battery-operated toys are not necessarily that of the original manufacturer, but of the distributor or marketer. Many Japanese toy shops and factories manufactured, assembled and sold their products through a central factory which in turn was under contract to an international marketer. As a result it is very difficult to pinpoint a specific designer or manufacturer of any battery-operated toy.

Some of the early Japanese toy makers such as the Masutoku Toy Factory (later Masudaya Toy Co.), founded in 1924 (which uses the "M-T" or "Modern Toy" trademark) and the Nomura Toys, Ltd., founded in 1923 (which uses the "T-N" trademark), are probably a couple of the original designers and manufacturers of many of the hundreds of different automations exported from Japan. "Alps", the trademark of the Alps Shoji, Ltd., (Alps Toy Midzuno Co.), founded in 1948 and "SAN", the mark of the Marusan Co., founded in 1946, can also be accountable for the creation of many original battery toys. In fact, Marusan Co., and Bandai, founded in 1950, as well as the Taijo Kogyo Co., founded in 1959, can be credited with some of the most spectacular scale model, battery-operated cars ever made in the batt-op category. "ATC", (Asahi Toy Co., founded in 1950), "T.P.S." (Toplay Ltd., founded in 1956), and "Haji", (founded in (1951), of the Mansei Toy Co., have their trademark on many more toys. The alphabet soup continues with many other toy companies using only a single letter or letters like "K", "S", "J", "KO", "Y", and "S&E", etc. Why only letters is a mystery, unless they represent many subsidiaries of the parent company. Besides being clever, the Japanese have left toy collectors very confused, but this is a small disadvantage compared to the fun of collecting battery-operated toys.

After peaking in the late 60's, the Japanese tin toy production began to decline due to increased labor costs, increased safety restrictions, inflation and competition from the cheaper die-cast and plastic toy makers. Many of the original toy companies either folded or diversified into the electronic field, using the IC-microchip the same way they used the mini-electric motor to develop new electronic products. It seems that presently, Japan has relinquished its toy monopoly to China, Hong Kong, Korea and Taiwan, in favor of its automotive and electronic industry. The battery operated toys now coming from these countries consist mostly of plastic, are higher priced, lack quality and are presently not very collectable. There is no comparison to the beauty of these toys with those from Japan. Tin and plastic just have never been compatible in a quality toy and this tends to "turn off" most serious toy collectors.

It is generally agreed upon by battery-operated toy collectors that the period of the 40's-60's should be considered as the "Golden Age of the Battery Operated Toy". During this 20 year period, most of the quality toy companies were founded and the most desirable and beautiful toys were produced. They were high in quality, most complex, and the detail and lithography most fascinating. These are the ones most sought after and in demand today. Prices of these toys are generally increasing as they become more scarce, and more and more toy collectors are beginning to focus on their desirability and are willing to pay as much for them as they have for many of the early classical tin wind-ups. Top prices go for the most complex toys, comic character, space, robots, scale-model cars, Blacks, and the older and earlier figurals.

The "Ball Playing Bear" is a good example of one of the first batt-op toys of the late 40's. As in most early toys, it uses one D-cell; is made of tin and celluloid, and has six actions going on and is very difficult to find complete with accessories.

Although tens of thousands of battery-operated toys were in circulation during this period, it is a rarity and a thrill to find one in mint condition, with original box, as the mortality rate of these toys was extremely high. Corrosion from leaking batteries left in them by their absent-minded owners took a high toll as well as deterioration of rubber parts due to age. (Rubber hoses of the water-drinkers and the rubber bellows of the bubble blowers were classic victims of aging and hardening of the rubber.) Rust was inevitable with the wet-toys that depended on water or bubble solutions to perform. Lubricants dried out or stiffened, rendering the toy inoperable, wires frequently worked loose or broke and electrical contacts corroded. Accidents, abuse, tampering and interfering with the toy while it was going through its cycle added enormously to the mortality rate. Reversing battery polarity by not following instructions burned out and ruined many a fine toy. Like a precision watch, the more complex the toy, the more delicate the mechanism and the more susceptible it becomes to damage due to negligence and abuse, such as physically interfering with the actions of the toy, and stopping it before it completes its cycle will damage the many levers and gears inside the toy, making it useless. Many toys require accessory parts to perform correctly and these were often lost, such as bowls for the bubble-blowers, trays, balls, umbrellas, discs, flags, clothes, etc. Top prices usually go for the complete toys with no parts missing.

The original box for battery-operated toys is extremely important, probably more so than other mechanical toys, because the intructions were often printed on the box lid. Also a picture or illustration of the toy showing any accessory parts the toy might need as well as the correct battery insertion was noted, if not on the actual toy's battery compartment. Finally, the name of the toy, if not lithographed on the toy itself, was printed on the box and very often, the name of the toy was nowhere near the actual appearance of the toy. Many times the name of the toy was given for its function rather than what it was supposed to be and since many toys did not have their identity stamped on them, the box lid was the only means of identifying the toy. The toy listing that follows are names of toys actually identified from their original boxes or the toy itself. Therefore the original box usually adds 10% to the value of the toy.

The value of a battery-operated toy depends not only on its scarcity, desirability and condition, but also on the number of actions taking place during its performance cycle. These toys are classified as MAJOR or MINOR toys. Major action toys will have **three** or **more** actions taking place while performing, and will command top price, whereas minor action toys have only one or two actions and will have a correspondingly lower price. The actions of a major or minor toy include all the individual movements taking place during one cycle and include any lights, sound, or smoke effects. Also the major battery toys must have **all** actions functioning and in proper sequence. There should be no missing parts and the toy itself should be constructed mostly of tin, about 85-90%, and the rest plastic or vinyl such as heads, limbs, accessories, etc. Usually the more plastic, the lower the value of the toy, regardless of condition.

The following list of battery-operated toys are, for the most part, major action toys, and include, if known, the manufacturer or distributor derived from the box or lithographed on the toy itself. A "?" indicates that the name of this toy has not been verified by the author. Also the circa or year, if known, will follow, along with the most obvious or helpful dimensions and any special notes if necessary. The prices are the average market prices based on supply and demand, and not on "auction" or "will pay anything for this toy" price. Geographic area is another factor in their pricing and these were based on the going prices in the midwestern states.

A "RARE" toy is one that is difficult to find on the open market because: 1. It had a limited production, or; 2. It is of such a fragile nature that it is difficult to find complete or in operating condition, or; 3. They are so popular and highly collectible that they exist only in private collections.

DON HULTZMAN confesses he has always been a collector of toys, but didn't really get serious about the hobby until ten or so years ago, not only collecting but also repairing them. Born and raised in Cleveland, Ohio, he received a masters degree in Guidance and Administration at Kent State, and is currently employed by the Parma City School System as a school counselor. He does free-lance writing as a science consultant to the encyclopedia department of World Publishing Co. and lives in Brunswick Hills, Ohio. Many of his tin wind-up toys can be seen in the 1983 MGM movie "A Christmas Story".

CONDITION OF A TOY AND ITS RELATION TO PRICE

The value of a battery operated toy depends not only on its desirability, rarity and complexity, but very much on its condition. A toy in "mint" condition is generally worth twice as much as a toy in "good" condition. A toy in "very good" condition will be equally priced between "good" and "mint".

"Mint" means just that — the condition in which the toy was originally issued — **perfect** — regardless of age. It will also be in perfect mechanical condition, complete with all accessory parts when applicable, and will look "brand new". The cloth or fur (plush) covering on some battery toys may reveal some discoloration (yellowing) due to age, but this should not affect its value as a "mint" toy as long as it is clean. All toys in this category must be in perfect working condition. The original box in mint condition will significantly enhance the value of any "mint" toy.

"'Very good" indicates the condition of a battery toy that has seen some use and is starting to show its age. It will still be in perfect working order and have all its accessory parts where applicable. It will have some age-soiling, but will have no rust or corrosion. Overall, it will have an appearance of "freshness" and still be highly desirable to the fussy collector.

"Good" applies to a battery toy that has seen considerable use, wear and tear, some age soiling, but still in perfect working condition with no missing parts or accessories. The "wet" toys may show some slight surface rust that can be easily removed. A toy in "good" condition is still a welcome addition to any toy collection, but will be targeted for upgrading by a piece in better condition.

Any battery toy below the condition of "good" will reflect a drastic reduction in value. Toys in good shape, but missing accessory parts, will not lose as much value as those that are severely rusted, corroded, painted over, have parts broken off and are totally inoperable. These "poor" toys are usually collected for their "scrap value" by the toy repairer and seldom are they worth more than $10.00.

The key to grading is to use common sense and avoid wishful thinking. Since grading the condition of a toy may be difficult at times, consulting with an expert in the field, if possible, could clear up any lingering doubts. (See back section of this guide for references of toy collectors.)

GUIDELINES FOR THE CARE AND REPAIR OF YOUR BATTERY OPERATED TOY
by Don Hultzman

Your prized battery toy needs T.L.C. and when it stops working, you now have a frustrating disaster on your hands. To avoid this, the following suggestions should be of some help:

Battery toys, like other mechanical toys, should be operated periodically to keep them loosened up. A lightweight spray lubrication now and then will help considerably if the mechanism is accessible. Do not over-lubricate as the excess may stain any cloth or fur covering on some battery toys.

A good quality car wax or polish will keep the lithographed and bare metal parts looking like new — especially on the "wet" toys. Always test an obscure lithographed area to make sure the polish doesn't soften or dissolve the paint. Care should be exercised when polishing metal parts adjoining any cloth or plush covering, as the substance may stain the coverings. Light surface rust usually disappears with a careful polishing. Nothing can be done for deep rust or corrosion without ruining the value of the toy. Repainting will only further reduce the value and is not recommended.

Should your battery toy fail to operate, the following steps might be helpful:
1. Make sure it is not gunked-up and that no moving parts are binding.
2. Make sure the battery contacts are not dirty or corroded — if so then clean them with crocus cloth. ALWAYS USE FRESH BATTERIES!
3. Lightly tap the toy with your finger or **lightly** nudge one of the moving parts while the switch is "on".

If none of the above steps work, then your toy needs "major surgery". This means the toy must be completely torn down, repaired and reassembled. Most battery toys are repairable as long as they have not been destructively tampered with and no parts are missing or corroded beyond repair. This job is best left to an expert in toy repair and should never be attempted by one who doesn't know what he is doing. Expert repairs will not affect the value of a battery toy so long as the repair is **undetectable** and the toys looks and functions **exactly** as it did before the repair. Such repairs are acceptable in toy collecting circles. Expert repairs are also expensive but well worth the investment if it means the difference between a "mint" (and prized toy) and one below the grade of "good", since an inoperable toy is practically worthless, regardless of condition.

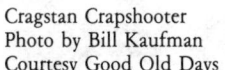

Cragstan Crapshooter
Photo by Bill Kaufman
Courtesy Good Old Days

Charlie Weaver
Photo by Bill Kaufman
Courtesy Good Old Days

Bartender
Photo by Bill Kaufman
Courtesy Good Old Days

Piggy Cook
Photo by Bill Kaufman
Courtesy Good Old Days

Gino-Neopolitan Balloon
Blower
Photo by Bill Kaufman
Courtesy Good Old Days

"A-B-C Fairy Train", 1950s, M-T Co., 14½" long, one pc., four actions	40.00	60.00	80.00
"Amtrak Locomotive" 1960s, ST Co., 16" long, minor toy	15.00	22.50	30.00
"Andy Gard - Brink's Armored Car - Bank", 1950s, General Molds & Plastics Corp. 6¾" long, minor toy	12.50	18.75	25.00
"Andy Gard Combat Knight No.143", 1960s, General Molds & Plastics Corp., 10¼" high, three actions, includes lance, stanchion, 3 plastic rings and helmet plume	20.00	30.00	40.00
"Animated Santa on Rotating Globe," 1950s, HTC Co., 15" high, five actions	100.00	150.00	200.00
"Animated Squirrel", 1950s, S&E Co., 8½" tall, eight actions, Rare	75.00	112.50	150.00
"Answer Game Machine" robot, 1960s, Ichida Co., 14½" tall, educational toy, eight actions	250.00	375.00	500.00
"Apollo Lunar Module", 1970s, DSK Co., 6" high, four actions, mostly plastic	40.00	60.00	80.00
"Apollo-X Moon Challenger", rocket, 1960s, T-N Co., 16" long, six actions	30.00	45.00	60.00

"Army Radio Jeep-J1490", 1950s, Linemar Co., 7¼" long, four actions	20.00	30.00	40.00
"Astro Dog", 1960s, Y-M Co., 11" tall, three actions	25.00	37.50	50.00
"Atomic Fighter" robot, 1950s, S-H Co., 11" tall, five actions	75.00	112.50	150.00
"Atom Rocket 7", vehicle with fins, 1950s, M-T Co., 9½" long, four actions	50.00	75.00	100.00
"Attacking Martian" Robot, 1950s, S-H Co., 11½" tall, 7 actions - two cycles	100.00	150.00	200.00
"Ball Blowing Clown", 1950s, T-N Co., 11" tall, three actions with ball	50.00	75.00	100.00
"Ball Playing Bear", 1940s, no marking, 10½" tall, six actions, includes five celluloid balls and one umbrella - Rare	100.00	150.00	200.00
"Balloon Blowing Monkey", 1950s, Alps Co., 11⅛" tall, five actions with balloon	40.00	60.00	80.00
"Balloon Blowing Teddy Bear", 1950s, Alps Co., 11⅛" tall, five actions with balloon	40.00	60.00	80.00
"Balloon Vendor", 1960s, Y Co., 12" tall, four actions, includes four plastic balloons and tin tray	30.00	45.00	60.00
"Barber Bear", 1950s, S&E Co., (Linemar) 9½" tall, five actions	100.00	150.00	200.00

150

"Mod Monster, Blushing Frankenstein", Hootin' Hollow Haunted House, Frankenstein Monster

Tricky Dog-House, Sky Taxi (Panam), Slurpy Puppy

B-Z Porter, Cragstan "Tugboat", Goodtime Charlie, Picnic Bunny

Treasure Chest Bank, Santa Bank, Hole-In-One Bank, Poverty Pup Bank.

Maxwell Coffee Loving Bear, Bird Watching Bear, Peanut Vendor

Ko-Kart, Dino the Dinosaur & Fred Flintstone, Pinnochio playing "London Bridge".

Bulldozer, Shaking Old-Timer Car, Tractor

Drinking Captain, Hi Jinks of the Circus, Cragstan "Playboy"

Courtesy Don Hultzman.   Photos by Ron Chojnacki.

	G	VG	M
"Barking Boxer Dog", 1950s, Marx, 7" long, minor toy	10.00	15.00	20.00
"Barking Spaniel Dog", 1950s, Marx, 7" long, minor toy	10.00	15.00	20.00
"Barney Bear Drummer", 1950s, Alps Co., 11" tall, five actions, resembles "Steiff" bear	70.00	105.00	140.00
"Barnyard Rooster", 1950s, Marx, 10" high, five actions	40.00	60.00	80.00
"Bartender", 1960s, T-N Co., 11½" tall, six actions	15.00	22.50	30.00
"Batmobile", 1972 National Periodical Publications, 12" long, three actions	30.00	45.00	60.00
"Battery Locomotive No. 123", 1950s, T-N Co., 10" long, three actions	10.00	15.00	20.00
"Bear Target Game", 1950s, M-T Co., 9½" high, five actions	40.00	60.00	80.00
"Bear - the Cashier", 1950s, M-T Co., 7½" high, five actions	100.00	150.00	200.00
"Bengali - The Exciting New Growling, Prowling Tiger", 1961, Marx Co., - Linemar Div., 18½" long from nose to end of tail, 2 cycles, three actions	50.00	75.00	100.00
"Betty Bruin - Cashier", 1950s, Linemar, 9" tall, six actions	125.00	187.50	250.00
"Beauty Parlor Bear", 1950s, S&E Co., 9½" high, seven actions	125.00	187.50	250.00
"Big Hunter-Automatic Gun", 1950s, Tada Co., 21" long - extended, three actions	25.00	37.50	50.00
"Big King Circus Truck", 1950s, M-T Co., 13" long, three actions	20.00	30.00	40.00
"Big Shot Cadillac", 1950s, T-N Co., 10" long, four actions - Rare	45.00	67.50	90.00
"Big Wheel Coca Cola Truck", 1970s, Taiyo Co., three actions	25.00	37.50	50.00
"Biller Train No.573", 1950s, T-N Co., 13" long, includes rubber cable track and two hopper cars, a minor toy - Rare	40.00	60.00	80.00

	G	VG	M
"Bimbo-the Clown", 1950s, Alps Co., 9¼" tall, three actions (includes detachable hat)	75.00	112.50	150.00
"Bird Watching Bear" (?), 1950s, M-T Co., 10" tall, three actions - Rare	75.00	112.50	150.00
"Blinky-the-Clown", 1950s, no marking, 10½" tall, five actions, includes multicolor paper hat	100.00	150.00	200.00
"Blow-Up-Ball Locomotive", 1950s, M-T Co., 9½" long, minor toy, includes celluloid ball	30.00	45.00	60.00
"Blushing Willie", 1960s, Y Co., 10" tall, four actions	15.00	22.50	30.00
"Bobby Drinking Bear", 1950s, Y Co., 10" tall, six actions	60.00	90.00	120.00
"Boeing 727 Jet Liner", 1960s, Y Co., 17½" long, 16¼" wingspan, three actions	25.00	37.50	50.00
"Boeing 727 Jet Plane", 1960s, M-T Co., 12½" long, 10⅜" wingspan, three actions	25.00	37.50	50.00
"Bongo, Drumming Monkey", 1960s, Alps Co., 9½" high, three actions, includes plastic hat	42.50	63.75	85.00
"Breakfast Chef", 1960s, K Co., 8¼" tall, minor toy (includes plastic egg and coffee maker	20.00	30.00	40.00
Broadway Trolley", 1950s, M-T Co., 10½" long, four actions - two cycles	30.00	45.00	60.00
"Bubble Blowing Bear", 1950s, M-T Co., 9½" high 4"x5" base, four actions	90.00	135.00	180.00
"Bubble Blowing Lion", 1950s, M-T Co., 7½" high, 3½"x7" base, four actions	30.00	45.00	60.00
"Bubble Blowing Monkey", 1950s, Alps Co., 10" tall, four actions, includes plastic bowl for bubble solution	45.00	67.50	90.00
"Bubble Blowing Washing Bear", 1950s, Y Co., 8" high, three actions, (includes plastic washtub)	60.00	90.00	120.00

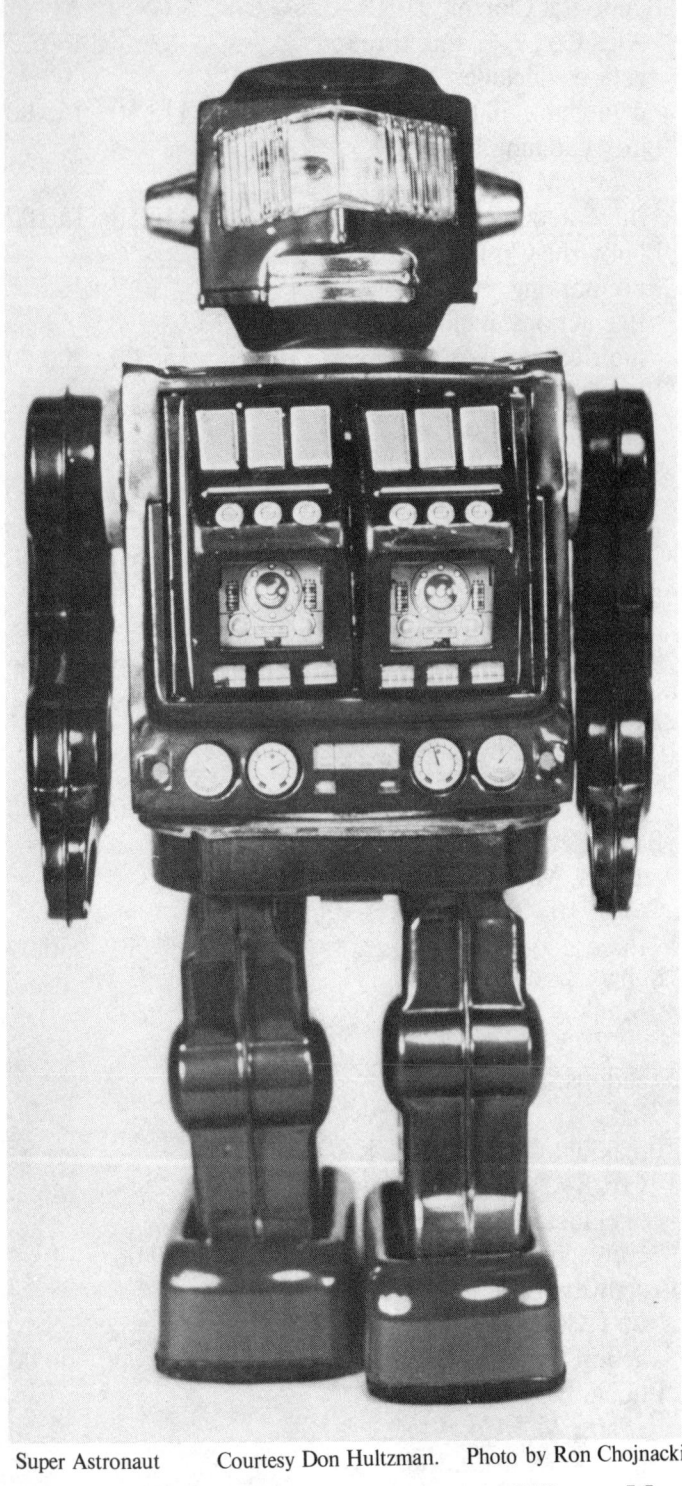

Super Astronaut   Courtesy Don Hultzman.   Photo by Ron Chojnacki.

	G	VG	M
"Busy Shoe Shining Bear", 1950s, Alps Co., 10" high, five actions	40.00	60.00	80.00
"Butt Stompin' Ashtray", 1977, Poynter Prod., 7¼" high, four actions, (includes tin manhole cover, ashtray insert and 4½" high plastic shoe)	20.00	30.00	40.00
"Buttons-Puppy With A Brain", 1960s, Marx, 12" high, 8 actions	125.00	187.50	250.00
"B-Z Porter" Baggage truck, 1950s, M-T Co., 7½" long, 6½" high, minor toy, includes three pcs. of luggage (tin)	60.00	90.00	120.00
"Cable Train", 1940s, T-N Co., 12" long, four pc. set, minor toy	35.00	52.50	70.00
"Cadillac" car, 1949, Ashai Toy Co., 10" long, three actions	50.00	75.00	100.00
"Calypso Joe", 1950s, Linemar, 11" tall, four actions	100.00	150.00	200.00
"Candy Vending Machine Bank", 1950s, Wonderful Toy Co., 9" high, five actions	100.00	150.00	200.00
"Capitol Airlines Viscount 321", 1950s, Linemar, 11" long, 14" wingspan, four actions	40.00	60.00	80.00
"Champion Weight Lifter", 1960s, Y-M Co., 10" tall, five actions	30.00	45.00	60.00
"Chaparral 2F", car, 1960s, Alps Co., 11" long, five actions	40.00	60.00	80.00
"Charlie-The Drumming Clown", 1950s, Alps Co., six actions (includes detachable drum and cymbals)	40.00	60.00	80.00
"Charlie Weaver, 1962, T-N Co., 12" tall, six actions . .	20.00	30.00	40.00
"Chef Cook", 1960s, Y Co., 11½" tall with hat on, five actions (includes tin litho egg and hat)	30.00	45.00	60.00
"Chief Robotman", 1950s, K.O. Co., 12" tall, four actions	250.00	375.00	500.00
"Chimp With Xylophone", 1970s, Y Co., 12" long,			

	G	VG	M
"Bulldozer", 1950s, T-N Co., 7½" long, five actions . . .	30.00	45.00	60.00
"Bulldozer", 1950s, M-T Co., 11" long, six actions .	25.00	37.50	50.00
"Bunny-The Magician", 1950s, Alps Co., 14½" tall, five actions, (includes card-ribbon apparatus for card trick)	75.00	112.50	150.00
"Busy Housekeeper, The", 1950s, Alps Co., 8½" tall, four actions	75.00	112.50	150.00

Flower Watering Pup, Rock 'N Roll Monkey, Barney Bear Drummer

Silver Mountain Express, Spirit of 1776

Happy Singing Bird in Cage, Cragstan-One Arm Bandit, Comic Hungry Bug, Mag-oo

Chimpy, Drumming Monkey, Happy Santa One-Man Band, Fred Flintstone's Bedrock Band, Dalmation One-Man Band

Courtesy Don Hultzman.

Puzzled Puppy, Shutter Bug, Popcorn Vendor

Military Police Car, Desert Patrol Jeep

Teddy-the Rhythmical Drummer, Major Tooty, McGregor, Cycling Daddy

Pepi-Tumbling Monkey, Yo Yo Monkey, Jo Jo-the Flipping Monkey
Photos by Ron Chojnacki.

	G	VG	M
8" high, minor toy (includes 4 records and hammer)	25.00	37.50	50.00
"Circus Elephant-With Blowing Ball and Parasol", 1950s, T-N Co., 9¾" high, three actions (includes celluloid ball and tin litho umbrella), Rare .	100.00	150.00	200.00
Chimpy the Drumming Monkey, 1950s, Alps Co., 9" high, six actions, includes detachable drum & cymbals	50.00	75.00	100.00
"Circus Fire Engine", 1960s, M-T Co., 11" long, four actions	40.00	60.00	80.00
"Circus Lion", 1950s, Rock Valley Toy Co., (Via), 11" high, four actions, includes whip and flannel carpet with levers, (2 cycles)	100.00	150.00	200.00
"Climbing Linesman", 1950s, T.P.S. Co., 24" high when assembled, three actions, (incudes 3 tin pole sections), Rare . . .	100.00	150.00	200.00
"Clown-The Magician No.40244", 1950s, Alps Co., 12" tall, six actions, includes card-ribbon apparatus for card trick	75.00	112.50	150.00
"Cock-A-Doodle-Doo Rooster", 1950s, Mikuni Co., 8" high, four actions	40.00	60.00	80.00
"Cola Drinking Bear" (?), 1950s, Alps Co., 10" high, five actions	50.00	75.00	100.00
"Colonel Hap Hazard" Robot, 1968, Marx Co., 11¼" tall, four actions . .	175.00	262.50	350.00
"Comic Hungry Bug" VW auto, 1970s, Tora (S-T) Co., 7¾" long, five actions	15.00	22.50	30.00
"Continental Blue Locomotive", 1960s, M-T Co., 12½" long, 4 actions	15.00	22.50	30.00
"Cragstan Astronaut", 1950s, Daiya Co., 14" tall, four actions	300.00	450.00	600.00
"Cragstan Biplane", 1950s, T-N Co., 9½" long, 11½" wingspan, four actions . . .	50.00	75.00	100.00

	G	VG	M
"Cragstan Crapshooter", 1950s, Y Co., 9½" tall, four actions, includes pair of small dice	30.00	45.00	60.00
"Cragstan Crapshooting Monkey", 1950s, Alps Co., 9" tall, three actions, includes pair of small dice	40.00	60.00	80.00
"Cragstan Dishwasher-Automatic", 1960s, Alps Co., 9" high, (includes 24 pc. dish set, 2 dish baskets and metal tray), minor toy	25.00	37.50	50.00
"Cragstan Great Astronaut", 1960s, Alps Co., 14" tall, five actions	250.00	375.00	500.00
"Cragstan's Mr. Robot", 1960s, Y Co., 10½" tall, four actions	150.00	225.00	300.00
"Cragstan One-Arm Bandit", 1960s, Y Co., 6¼" high, three actions, includes 3"x3¼" sign	25.00	37.50	50.00
"Cragstan Peanut Vendor", 1950s, T-N Co., 8" tall, five actions (includes felt hat)	100.00	150.00	200.00
"Cragstan Playboy", 1960s, Cragstan Co., 13" high, five actions	40.00	60.00	80.00
"Cragstan Roulette Player", 1950s, Y Co., 9½" tall, five actions, includes small ball and detachable table	40.00	60.00	80.00
"Cragstan Talking Robot", 1960s, Y Co., 10½" tall, three actions	100.00	150.00	200.00
"Cragstan Telly Bear", 1950s, S&E Co., 8" high, six actions	90.00	135.00	180.00
"Cragstan Tootin'-Chuggin' Locomotive", 1950s, Cragstan Co., 24" long, three actions (longest single piece battery toy made)	15.00	22.50	30.00
"Cragstan Tugboat", 1950s, San Co., 12¾" long, three actions	30.00	45.00	60.00
"Cragstan Vertol 1107 Helicopter", 1950s, T-N Co., 13½" long, four actions, includes rotors	40.00	60.00	80.00
"Cragstan Western Locomotive", 1950s,			

Cragstan Co., 12" long, four actions........... 30.00 45.00 60.00

"Cragstan's Two Gun Sheriff", 1950s, Y Co., 9½" tall, five actions (includes tin hat)......... 75.00 112.50 150.00

"Crane Tractor", 1950s, SKK Co., 7½" long, 11½" high extended.... 45.00 67.50 90.00

"Cry-Baby-In-Buggy" (?), 1950s, T-N Co., 11¾" long, 7" high, minor toy, includes plastic baby bottle to activate switch.... 40.00 60.00 80.00

"Cycling Daddy", 1960s, Bandai Co., 10" high, four actions........... 50.00 75.00 100.00

"Daisy-The Jolly Drumming Duck", 1950s, Alps Co., 9" high, seven actions, (includes detachable drum and cymbals, Rare...... 100.00 150.00 200.00

"Dalmatian One-Man Band No.90262", 1950s, Alps Co., 9" high, six actions, includes cymbals and stand................ 60.00 90.00 120.00

"Dancing Merry Chimp", 1960s, Kuramochi Co., (C-K), 11" tall, five actions.............. 30.00 45.00 60.00

"Dandy-The Happy Drumming Pup", 1950s, Alps Co., 8½" high, six actions, (includes detachable drum and cymbals)...... 40.00 60.00 80.00

"Dapper Jigger Dancer", 1950s, Haji Co., 12" tall, minor toy............ 50.00 75.00 100.00

"Dennis the Menace"- (Playing London Bridge), 1950s, Rosko, 9" high, three actions, includes xylophone............ 75.00 112.50 150.00

"Dentist Bear", 1950s, S&E Co., 9½" tall, 6¾" x 4¼" base, seven actions, includes detachable head. 125.00 187.50 250.00

"Desert Patrol Jeep", 1960s, M-T Co., 11" long, four actions, includes turret gunner.............. 40.00 60.00 80.00

"Destroyer 206" boat, 1950s, Y Co., 14" long, six actions, includes detachable

Barking Spaniel Dog, Sleeping Baby Bear, Barking Boxer Dog, Papa Bear-Smoking

Cragstan "Tootin-Chuggin Locomotive", Greyhound Bus Scenicruiser.

Ball Blowing Clown, Sammy Wong-the Tea Totaler, Nutty Nibs

Frankie-the Rollerstaking Monkey, Buttons-Puppy with a Brain, Jocko-the Drinking Monkey, Blushing Willie
Courtesy Don Hultzman.   Photos by Ron Chojnacki.

156

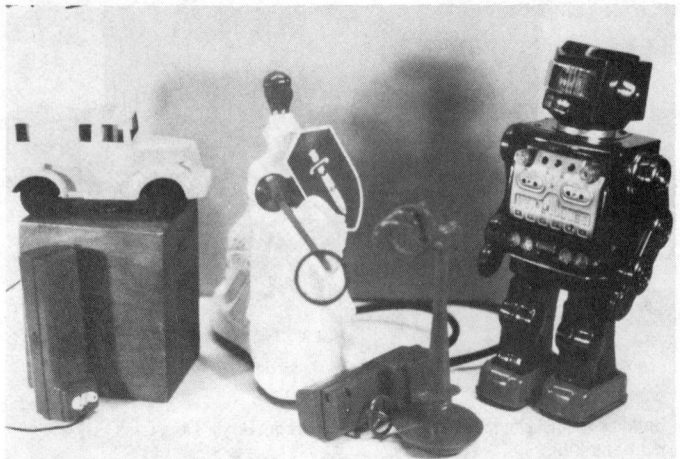

Andy Gard Brinks Armored Car Bank, Andy Gard Combat Knight, Swivel-O-Matic Robot

Surrey Jeep, Continental Blue Locomotive

Roaring Gorilla, Mighty Kong, Dancing Merry Chimp

Butt Stompin' Ashtray, Army Radio Jeep, Blow-Up Ball Locomotive   Courtesy Don Hultzman.   Photos by Ron Chojnacki.

Railroad Handcar, Winner-25-Rocket, Biller Train No.573

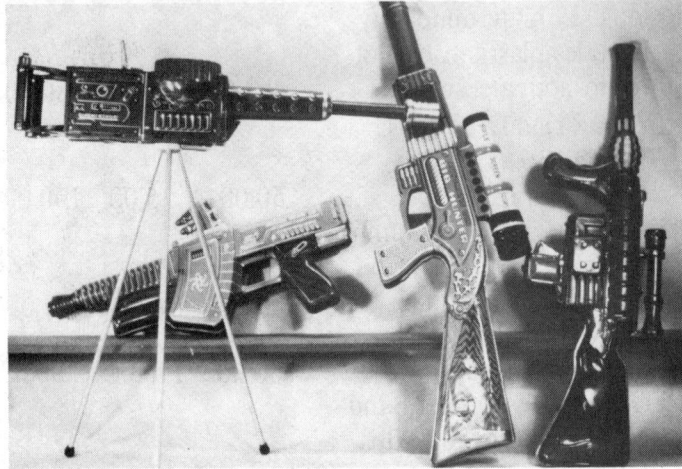

Ray Gun, Universal Machine Gun, Big Hunter Automatic Gun, Flashy-Ray Gun

Balloon Vendor, Miss Friday, Sam the Shaving Man, Gino the Neapolitan Balloon Blower

Balloon Blowing Bear, Balloon Blowing Monkey, Bubble Blowing Monkey

Tank (M-4), Tank X-3), Tank (M-103)

James Bond's Aston-Martin

Dennis The Menace-Xylophone Player, Chimp-Xylophone Player

Bongo Monkey, Chef Cook, Cola Drinking Bear

Courtesy Don Hultzman.   Photos by Ron Chojnacki.

Happy Fiddler Clown, Roarin' Jungle Lion, Mama Dog Feeding,
Hungry Baby Dog

Patrol Helicopter, Cragstan Biplane, T360-Monoplane

Western Badman-Red Gulch Bar, Drinker's Saving Bank

Happy the Clown Puppet Shown Drummer Mickey Mouse, Clown-
the Magician

Smoking Grandpa in Rocking Chair, Rocking Chair Bear, Mama
Bear & Hungry Baby Bear, Pop Drinking Bear

	G	VG	M
antenna and five depth charges	40.00	60.00	80.00
"Dino Robot", 1960s, S-H Co., 11" tall, five actions .	150.00	225.00	300.00
"Dino the Dinosaur and Fred Flintstone", 1961 Marx, 22" long, eight actions	100.00	150.00	200.00
"Disney Acrobat", (Pluto or Mickey), 1950s, Linemar Co., 9¼" tall, minor toy .	100.00	150.00	200.00
"Disneyland Fire Engine", 1950s, Linemar Co., 18" long, five actions	100.00	150.00	200.00
"Dolly Dressmaker", 1950s, T-N Co., 7" high, ten actions, includes cloth sample ("Dolly Seamstress" on box) Rare............	100.00	150.00	200.00
"Donald Duck Trolley", 1960s, M-T Co., 11" high, three actions...........	70.00	105.00	140.00
"Dozo-The Steaming Clown", 1960s, T-N Co., Rosko Toys, 10" tall, five actions	75.00	112.50	150.00
"Drill", 1950s, Linemar Co., 6" long, includes attachments, minor toy....	10.00	15.00	20.00
"Drinker's Savings Bank", 1960s, Illfelder Co., 9" high, minor toy........	25.00	37.50	50.00
"Drinking Captain", 1960s, S&E Co., 12" tall, six actions	40.00	60.00	80.00
"Drum Monkey", 1970s, Yada Co., 8" high, three actions	15.00	22.50	30.00
"Drumming Clown Charlie, The", 1950s, Alps Co., 9½" tall, six actions, includes drums and cymbals	45.00	67.50	90.00
"Drumming Mickey Mouse", 1950s, Linemar, 10" tall, four actions....	250.00	375.00	500.00
"Drumming Polar Bear", 1960s, Alps Co., 12" tall, three actions...........	20.00	30.00	40.00
"Dump Truck No.7343", 1960s, T-N Co., 10¼" long, seven actions......	30.00	45.00	60.00
"El Toro-Cragstan Bullfighter", 1950s, T-N Co., 9½" long, four actions, includes detachable tin matador...........	50.00	75.00	100.00

	G	VG	M
"Electric Remote Control Robot", 1950s, M-T Co, 7½" tall, four actions...	350.00	525.00	700.00
"Electric Robot", 1950s, Marx, 14½" tall, five actions	100.00	150.00	200.00
"Fairlane 500" car, 1958, Y Co., 11" long, five actions	100.00	150.00	200.00
"F.D. Fire Engine", 1960s, Y-M Co., 10" long, 12" high when ladder is extended, four actions.....	20.00	30.00	40.00
"Feeding Bird Watcher", 1950s, Linemar, 9" high five action, (includes detachable tin branch and bird), Rare...........	100.00	150.00	200.00
"Fighting Bull", 1970s, Rock Valley Tech Co., 12" long, nose to tail tip, four actions, two cycles......	25.00	37.50	50.00
"Fire Boat", 1950s, M-T Co., 15" long, five actions	30.00	45.00	60.00
"Fire Chief No.8 Car, 1960s, Y Co., 11¼" long, three actions	10.00	15.00	20.00
"Fire Chief Mystery Action Car", 1960s, T-N Co., 9¾" long, four actions...	40.00	60.00	80.00
"Fire Engine", 1950s, Y Co., 12" long, ladder extends 16", six actions........	30.00	45.00	60.00
"Fishing Bears-Bank", 1950s, Wonderful Toy Co., 9½" tall, six actions.........	150.00	225.00	300.00
"Fishing Kitty", 1950s, Linemar, 9" high, seven actions, includes tray and plastic fish	75.00	112.50	150.00
"Fishing Polar Bear or Forest Bear", 1950s, Alps Co., six actions.........	45.00	67.50	90.00
"Flashy-Ray Space Gun", 1950s, T-N Co., 18½" long, a minor toy.......	20.00	30.00	40.00
"Flower-Watering Pup", 1950s, Cragstan Co., 8" high, five actions.......	75.00	112.50	150.00
"Flutter Birds", 1950s, Alps Co., 26½" high when assembled, six actions, includes detachable pulley assembly	65.00	97.50	130.00
"Flying Dutchman-PH-KLM Airliner", 1950s, T-N Co., 11" long, 14" wingspan, five actions...........	40.00	60.00	80.00

Santa Claus Sitting on Roof, Santa Copter, Royal Bunny in Buggy

Cragstan "Crapshooter", Tumbles-the Bear, Overland Stage Coach

Warpath Indian, Nutty Mad Indian, Indian Joe

Furry Morris, Piggy Cook, Cragstan "Crapshooting Monkey"

Tank (M-81), Tank (M-35), Tank (M-56), Tank (M-197)

Pinky The Clown, Circus Elephant, Tom & Jerry Handcar (Tom)

Cragstan's Two Gun Sheriff, Bimbo the Clown, Mother Bear -
Sitting and Knitting in Her Old Rocking Chair.

Courtesy Don Hultzman

Bear-the Cashier, Old Fashion Telephone Bear, Washing Bear, Ice
Cream Eating Bear

Photos by Ron Chojnacki

	G	VG	M
"Ford" car, 1958, Y Co., 11" long, five actions....	20.00	30.00	40.00
"Fork Lift Truck", 1960s, M-T Co. 11" long, five actions..............	20.00	30.00	40.00
"Frankenstein Monster", 1960s, T-N Co., 14" tall, six actions............	65.00	97.50	130.00
"Frankie-The Rollerskating Monkey", 1950s, Alps Co., 12" tall..........	35.00	52.50	70.00
"Fred Flintstone Bedrock Band", 1962, Alps Co., 9½" high, four actions..	100.00	150.00	200.00
"Funland Cup Ride", 1960s, Sonsco Co., 7" tall, 6"x6" base, three actions, includes 6" umbrella......	30.00	45.00	60.00
"Galloping Cowboy Savings Bank", 1950s, Y Co., (Cragstan), 8" high, 6½" long, minor toy........	50.00	75.00	100.00
"Gama Mercedes Benz 220 SE Sedan", 1960s, Mignon Co., 9" long, three actions..........	20.00	30.00	40.00
"Gino-Neapolitan Balloon Blower", 1960s, Tomiyama Co., (Rosko), 10" tall, five actions, includes bubble solution plastic tray...........	40.00	60.00	80.00
"Go-Kart", 1950s, Rosko Co., 10" long, three actions, includes detachable head................	35.00	52.50	70.00
"Good Time Charlie", 1960s, M-T Co., 12" tall, seven actions..........	30.00	45.00	60.00
"Grand-Pa Car", 1950s, Y Co., 9" long, four actions	30.00	45.00	60.00
"Greyhound Bus-Scenicruiser", 1950s, I.Y. Metal Toy Co., 16" long, three actions..........	25.00	37.50	50.00
"Happy Clown Theater", (with Pinocchio-like puppet), 1950s, Y Co., 10" tall, three actions......	75.00	112.50	150.00
"Happy Fiddler Clown, The", 1950s, Alps Co., 9½" high, four actions, includes tin lith violin, Rare...............	125.00	187.50	250.00
"Happy Santa", 1960s, Z Co., 11" tall, three actions	75.00	112.50	150.00
"Happy Santa" (Walking), 1950s, Alps Co., 11" tall, five actions..........	75.00	112.50	150.00
"Happy Santa-One Man Band", 1950s, Alps Co., 9" high, six actions, includes cymbals and stand.	60.00	90.00	120.00
"Happy Singing Bird", 1950s, M-T Co., 9" high, bird 3" long, 5⅝" dia. base, three actions.....	30.00	45.00	60.00
"Happy the Clown" (with Pinocchio-like puppet), 1950s, Y Co., 10" tall, three actions..........	75.00	112.50	150.00
"Happy Tractor", 1960s, Daiya Co., 8" long, four actions................	15.00	22.50	30.00
"Hi Bouncer Moon Scout" robot, 1968, Marx Co., 11¼" tall, five actions, includes five plastic balls...	250.00	375.00	500.00
"High Jinks of the Circus", 1950s, T-N Co., 14" high, extends to 29", six actions	75.00	112.50	150.00
"Hole-In-One Bank", 1960s, no marking, 8½" long x 3½" wide, minor toy, includes marked test coin and golfer.............	20.00	30.00	40.00
"Holiday Sink-Stove Combination", 1950s, T-N Co., 9" high, minor toy, includes 3 pc. pan set....	25.00	37.50	50.00
"Hoopy-the Fishing Duck", 1950s, Alps Co., 10" high, seven actions (includes magnetic fish and detachable "pond")......	100.00	150.00	200.00
"Hootin' Hollow Haunted House", 1960s, Marx, 11" high, eight actions, Rare.	200.00	300.00	400.00
"Hooty the Happy Owl", 1960s, Alps Co., 9" tall, six actions..........	45.00	67.50	90.00
"Hot Rod" car, 1950s, T-N Co., 10" long, minor toy.	15.00	22.50	30.00
"Ice Cream Loving Bear" (?), 1950s, M-T Co., 9½" high, three actions, Rare.	50.00	75.00	100.00
"Indian Joe", 1960s, Alps Co., 12" tall, four actions	30.00	45.00	60.00
"Interceptor", target game, 1950s, S&E Co., 13" high, 16" wingspan, four actions..............	60.00	90.00	120.00

	G	VG	M
"Leo-The Growling Pet Lion With Magic Face-Change", 1970s, Toyiyama Co., 9" long, 2 cycles, three actions.....	30.00	45.00	60.00
"Love - Beetle - Volks", 1960s, K.O. Co., 10" long, three actions......	10.00	15.00	20.00
"Jaguar" car, 1960s, T-T Co., 10½" long, minor toy..................	15.00	22.50	30.00
"James Bond-007 Car-M101", 1960s, Daiya Co., 11" long, seven actions, includes ejectable driver..	60.00	90.00	120.00
"Jeep-USA", 1950s, TKK Co., 12½" long, a minor toy..................	30.00	45.00	60.00
"Jeep No.10560", 1950s, Cragstan, 5½" long, a minor action toy........	10.00	15.00	20.00
'Jig-Saw-Matic", 1950s, Z Co., 7¼" high, 4½"x8½", a minor action toy.................	20.00	30.00	40.00
"Jo-Jo-the Flipping Monkey", 1970s, TN Co., (Illfelder), 10" high, minor toy.................	25.00	37.50	50.00
"Jocko-the Drinking Monkey", 1950s, Linemar, 11" tall, four actions, includes top hat...	30.00	45.00	60.00
"Jolly Bambino", 1950s, no trademark, 9" high, five actions, includes candy pieces, Rare..........	75.00	112.50	150.00
"Jolly Drummer Chimpy", 1950s, Alps Co., 9" high, 6 actions, includes cymbals and stand..........	40.00	60.00	80.00
"Jolly Santa on Snow", 1950s, Alps Co., 12½" tall, four actions, two cycles.............	60.00	90.00	120.00
"Josie-The Walking Cow", 1950s, Daiya Co., 14" long, 8½" high, seven actions, two cycles.......	40.00	60.00	80.00
"Jumbo-The Bubble Blowing Elephant", 1950s, Y Co., 7¼" high, three actions, includes plastic bowl for bubble solution........	30.00	45.00	60.00
"Jungle Jumbo", 1950s, B.C. Co., 9" high, five actions.	60.00	90.00	120.00

	G	VG	M
"Jungle Trio", 1950s, Linemar, 8" high, eight actions, includes tin litho whistle	125.00	187.50	250.00
"Kitchen-ette Stove and Sink", 1940s, no marking 6½" long x 6¾" high, a minor toy, includes kitchen utensils and side tray, and stoppers.......	20.00	30.00	40.00
"Knight in Armour", 1950s, M-T Co., 12" high, five actions, includes crossbow and arrows............	50.00	75.00	100.00
"Knitting Grandma", 1950s, T-N Co., 8½" tall, three actions	50.00	75.00	100.00
"Kooky-Spooky Whistling Tree", 1950s, Marx Co., 14¼" tall, six actions, (two color schemes) Rare.	400.00	600.00	800.00
"Lighted Freight Train", 1950s, Y Co., four actions, 25½" long, five pcs, 8 section track.........	30.00	45.00	60.00
"Lincoln" car, 1958, Y Co., 11¼" long, five actions..	100.00	150.00	200.00
"Linda Lee Laundromat", washing machine, 1940s, T-N Co., 6½" high, a minor toy.............	10.00	15.00	20.00
"Locomotive-Continental Blue", 1970s, M-T Co., 13" long, four actions...	10.00	15.00	20.00
"Lotus 49-Ford F-1" car, 1960s, Junior Co., - J-Toy, 15¾" long, six actions	30.00	45.00	60.00
"Mag-oo, Mr. Magoo Car", 1961, Hubley Co., 9" long, five actions, includes cloth roof top..........	70.00	105.00	140.00
"Major Tooty", 1960s, Alps Co., (R.F.), 14" tall, three actions, includes drum and hat..............	50.00	75.00	100.00
"Mama Bear and Hungry Baby Bear" ?, 1950s, Y Co., 9½" high, six actions	60.00	90.00	120.00
"Mama Dog and Hungry Baby Dog" (?) 1950s, Y Co., 9½" high, six actions	70.00	105.00	140.00
"Mambo-The Jolly Drumming Elephant", 1950s, Alps Co., 9½" high, six actions, includes cymbals and stand.............	50.00	75.00	100.00

162

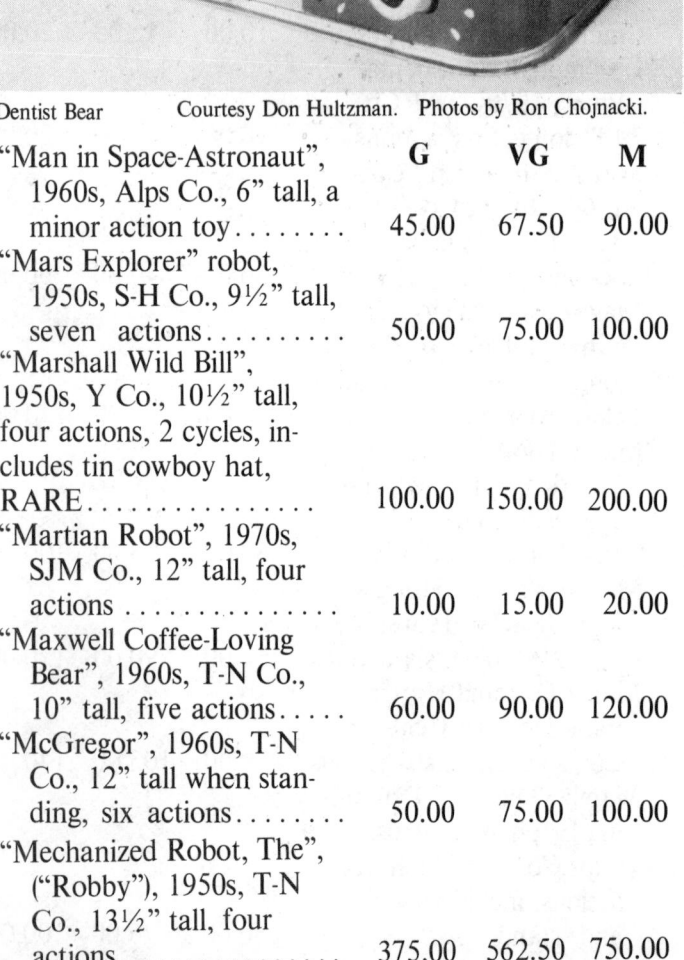

Dentist Bear   Courtesy Don Hultzman.   Photos by Ron Chojnacki.

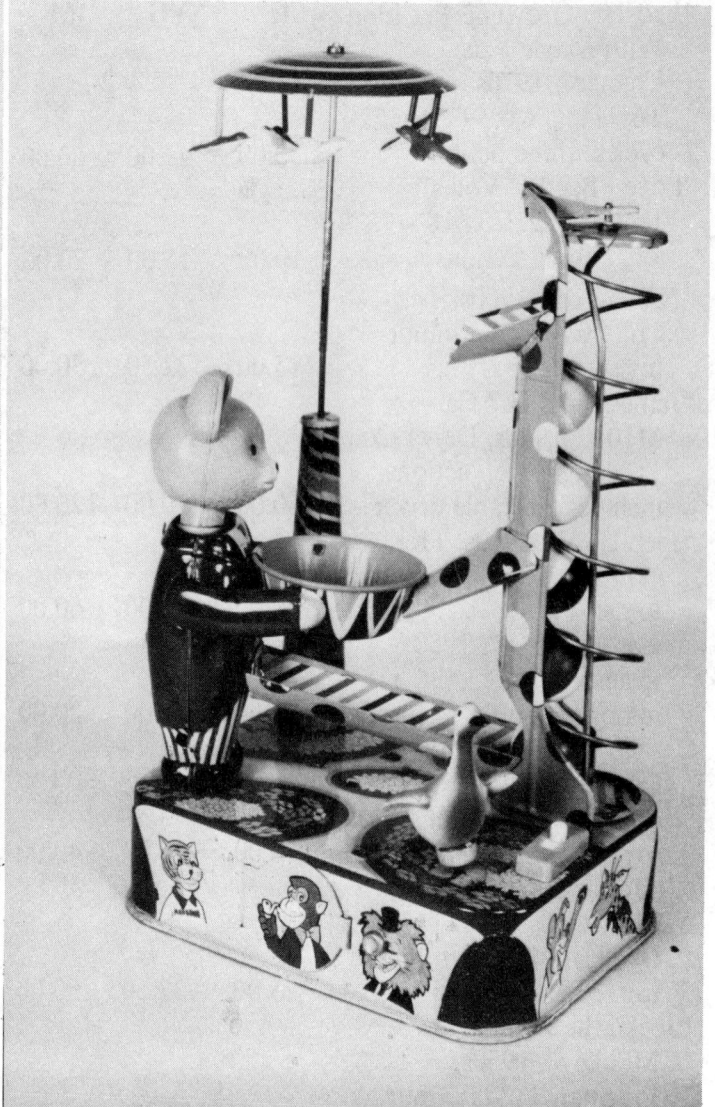

Ball Playing Bear

	G	VG	M
"Man in Space-Astronaut", 1960s, Alps Co., 6" tall, a minor action toy	45.00	67.50	90.00
"Mars Explorer" robot, 1950s, S-H Co., 9½" tall, seven actions	50.00	75.00	100.00
"Marshall Wild Bill", 1950s, Y Co., 10½" tall, four actions, 2 cycles, includes tin cowboy hat, RARE	100.00	150.00	200.00
"Martian Robot", 1970s, SJM Co., 12" tall, four actions	10.00	15.00	20.00
"Maxwell Coffee-Loving Bear", 1960s, T-N Co., 10" tall, five actions	60.00	90.00	120.00
"McGregor", 1960s, T-N Co., 12" tall when standing, six actions	50.00	75.00	100.00
"Mechanized Robot, The", ("Robby"), 1950s, T-N Co., 13½" tall, four actions	375.00	562.50	750.00

	G	VG	M
"Mercedes 220S No.5720 Hydro Car", 1950s, Schuco Co., 10" long, minor action	100.00	150.00	200.00
"Mercedes 230 SL Car", 1950s, Alps Co., 10½" long, minor action	75.00	112.50	150.00
"Mercedes 230 SL No.5500 Real Car", 1950s, Schuco Co., 10¾" long, minor action	100.00	150.00	200.00
"Mercedes No.5307 Sport Car", 1950s, Schuco Co., 10¾" long, minor action.	100.00	150.00	200.00
"Mercedes No.5503 Phanomenal Car", 1950/60s, Schuco Co., 8¾" long, minor action	75.00	112.50	150.00
"Mercedes Radio-Controlled Car", 1960s, M-T Co., 15½" long, minor action, includes radio transmitter	100.00	150.00	200.00

Circus Lion

Happy Santa-Walking, Santa on Hand Car

Cragstan "Schoolbus", Cragstan "Western Locomotive", New Bell Ringer Choo-Choo

Mr. Fox the Magician-blowing magic bubbles, Professor Owl, Mr. Fox the Magician with the Magical Disappearing Rabbit.

Peter-the Drumming Rabbit, Picnic Bear, Bunny-the Magician

Funland Cup Ride, Big Shot Cadillac

Bubble Lion, Wild West Rodeo, Cragstan "Bullfighter"

Courtesy Don Hultzman.

Trumpet Playing Monkey, Monkey On A Picnic, Busy Housekeeper
Photos by Ron Chojnacki.

	G	VG	M
"Mercedes Razzia Car No.5509", 1950/60s, Schuco Co., 8¾" long, three actions	75.00	112.50	150.00
"Mercury Explorer", 1960s, T.P.S. Co., 8" long, five actions	60.00	90.00	120.00
"Mickey Mouse and Donald Duck Fire Engine", 1960s, M-T Co., 16" long, three actions	55.00	87.50	110.00
"Mickey Mouse Sand Buggy", 1960s, M-T Co., 11" long, four actions	60.00	90.00	120.00
"Mickey Mouse Trolley", 1960s, M-T Co., 11" high, three actions	70.00	105.00	140.00
"Mickey the Magician", 1960s, Linemar, 7½" tall, four actions, includes celluloid rabbit	150.00	225.00	300.00
"Mighty Kong", 1950s, Marx, 11" tall, five actions	100.00	150.00	200.00
"Miltary Police Car", 1950s, Linemar, 8½" long, six actions	45.00	67.50	90.00
"Milk Drinking Kitty" (?), 1950s, T-N Co., 10" tall, 4"x4" base, six actions	30.00	45.00	60.00
"Mischievous Monkey", 1950s, M-T Co., 18" tall, six actions, includes tree and monkey	75.00	112.50	150.00
"Miss Friday-The Typist", 1950s, T-N Co., 8" tall, six actions, removable head	60.00	90.00	120.00
"Mix-ette Mixer", 1940s, KDP Co., 9" high when assembled, a minor toy, includes mixer stand and bowl	15.00	22.50	30.00
"Mr. Atomic" robot, 1950s, Cragstan, 11" tall, three actions, rare	500.00	750.00	1,000.00
"Mr. Chief" Robot, 1950s, K-O Co., 12" tall, four actions	250.00	375.00	500.00
"Mr. Fox, the Magician-Blowing Magical Bubbles", 1950s, Y Co., 9" tall, four actions, includes plastic bowl for bubble solution	75.00	112.50	150.00

	G	VG	M
"Mr. Fox, the Magician-With the Magical Disappearing Rabbit", 1960s, Y Co., 9" tall, five actions, includes plastic rabbit	100.00	150.00	200.00
"Mr. McPooch (smoking)", 1950s, SAN Co., 8" high, four actions	45.00	67.50	90.00
"Mr. Mercury" robot, 1960s, Marx Co., (Linemar), 13" tall, seven actions	250.00	375.00	500.00
"Mod Monster-Blushing Frankenstein", 1960s, T-N Co., 13¼" tall, five actions	75.00	112.50	150.00
"Monkey On A Picnic", 1950s, Alps Co., 9½" high, seven actions	75.00	112.50	150.00
"Moon Traveler-Apollo Z", 1960s, T-N Co., 12" long, 15" extended, five actions	50.00	75.00	100.00
"Mother Bear-Sitting and Knitting In Her Old Rocking Chair", 1950s, M-T Co., 9½" high, four actions	75.00	112.50	150.00
"Musical BankOrgan Grinder & Monkey", 1950s, HTC Co., 8" tall, four actions, includes test coin and detachable celluloid monkey	125.00	157.50	250.00
"Musical Bulldog Playing Piano", 1950s, SAN Co., 8½" tall, 6"x9" base, four actions- Rare	100.00	150.00	200.00
"Musical Jolly Chimp", 1960s, C-K Co., 10½" high, five actions, two cycles	15.00	22.50	30.00
"Mystery Fire Chief Car No.81", 1950s, Sanshin Co., 9¼" long, three actions	30.00	45.00	60.00
"Mystery Police Car", 1960s, T-N Co., 9¾" long, 6" wide, 4" high, three actions	45.00	67.50	90.00
"Neptune Tugboat", 1950s, M-T Co., 15" long, 7" high, four actions	30.00	45.00	60.00
"New Astronaut" robot, 1970s, S-H Co., 9½" tall, six actions	20.00	30.00	40.00
"New Bell Ringer Choo Choo", locomotive, 1960s,			

	G	VG	M
M-T Co., 10" long, three actions	15.00	22.50	30.00
"News Service Car", 1960s, TPS Co., 10" long, four actions	30.00	45.00	60.00
"Non-Stop Robot", 1960s, M-T Co., 15" tall, three actions	450.00	675.00	900.00
"Nutty Mad Indian", 1960s, Marx, 12" tall, four actions	30.00	45.00	60.00
"Nutty Nibs", 1950s, Linemar, 11½" tall, a minor action toy, includes litho bowl of nuts and steel ball, Rare	225.00	337.50	450.00
"007 Secret Agent's Car", (Impala), 1960s, Spesco Co., (Joy Toy), 15" long, five actions	50.00	75.00	100.00
"Old Fashioned Car", 1950s, S-H Co., 10" long, four actions	25.00	37.50	50.00
"Old Timer Automoball", 1950s, M-T Co., 10" long, three actions, includes celluloid ball	25.00	37.50	50.00
"Old-Fashioned-Telephone Bear" (?), 1950s, M-T Co., 9½" high, four actions			
"Old Ford Touring Car", 1950s, Z Co., 10" long, four actions	20.00	30.00	40.00
"Overland Choo Choo Express" locomotive, 1950s, M-T Co., 14" long, a minor action toy	10.00	15.00	20.00
"Overland Stage Coach", 1960s, Ichida Co., 18" long, four actions	40.00	60.00	80.00
"Pacific Piping Express Locomotive", 1960s, Kanto Toy Co., 14" long, four actions	15.00	22.50	30.00
"Panda Bear", 1970s, M-T Co. (Masudaya Co.), 10" long, four actions, mostly plastic	15.00	22.50	30.00
"PaPa Bear Smoking", 1950s, SAN Co., 8" tall four actions	40.00	60.00	80.00
"Patrol Auto-Tricycle", 1960s, T-N Co., 19" long, 7½" high, four actions	50.00	75.00	100.00
"Patrol Helicopter No.7",			

	G	VG	M
1960s, Bandai Co., 11" long, four actions	20.00	30.00	40.00
"P.D. No.5- Police Patrol Car", (Buick), 1960s, Asakusa Toy Co., 11½" long, three actions	15.00	22.50	30.00
"Pepi-Tumbling Monkey", 1960s, Yanoman Toy Co., 9½" high, minor toy	22.50	33.75	45.00
"Pete-the Space Man", 1960s, Bandai Co., 5" tall, minor action (Walking Mate Series)	20.00	30.00	40.00
"Peter-The Drumming Rabbit", 1950s, Alps Co., (VIA-Cragstan), 13" tall, five actions	50.00	75.00	100.00
"Picnic Bear", 1950s, Alps Co., 109" high, four actions	50.00	75.00	100.00
"Picnic Bunny", 1950s, Alps Co., 10" tall, four actions	40.00	60.00	80.00
"Picnic Poodle", 1950s, STS Co., 7" long-7" high, four actions, two cycles	20.00	30.00	40.00
"Piggy Barbecue", 1950s, Y Co., 9½" tall, five actions, includes chef's hat and tin litho fried egg	40.00	60.00	80.00
"Piggy Cook", 1950s, Y Co., 9½" tall, 4"x6" base, five actions, includes chef's hat and tin litho fried egg	40.00	60.00	80.00
"Pinky The Clown", 1950s, Rock Valley Toy Co., (Via) 10¼" tall, five actions, (includes tin litho propeller-ball on nose) Rare	100.00	150.00	200.00
"Pinocchio-Playing London Bridge", 1962, T-N Co., (Rosko), 10" tall, three actions, includes xylophone	75.00	112.50	150.00
"Piston Action Bulldozer", 1960s, Linemar Co., 7½" long two cycles	20.00	30.00	40.00
"Planet Rover", wheeled tank, 1960s, J Co., 9" long, 6½" high, six actions	45.00	67.50	90.00
"Polar Bear", 1970s, Alps Co., 8" long, three actions	15.00	22.50	30.00
"Policeman", 1950s, A-I Co., 14" tall, 6" x 6" base, four actions	40.00	60.00	80.00

166

Musical Bulldog

Animated Squirrel, Cock-A-Doodle-Doo Rooster, Josie-the-Cow, Sparky-the-Seal

Old Fashioned Telephone Bear, Cragstan Telly Bear, V.I.P. the Busy Boss, Telephone Bear

Courtesy Don Hultzman.

Tom & Jerry Choo-Choo, Old Timer Automoball

Broadway Trolley, Battery Locomotive No.123, A-B-C Fairy Train, Smoking Pop Locomotive-the General

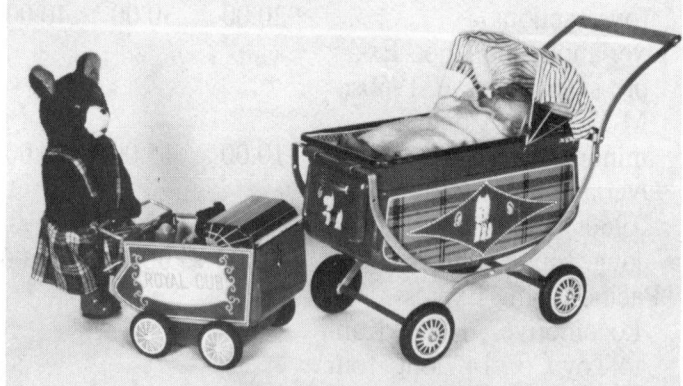

Royal Cub in Buggy, Cry-Baby-In-Buggy

Silver Streak Locomotive, Silver Bell Choo-Choo, Western Locomotive
Photos by Ron Chojnacki.

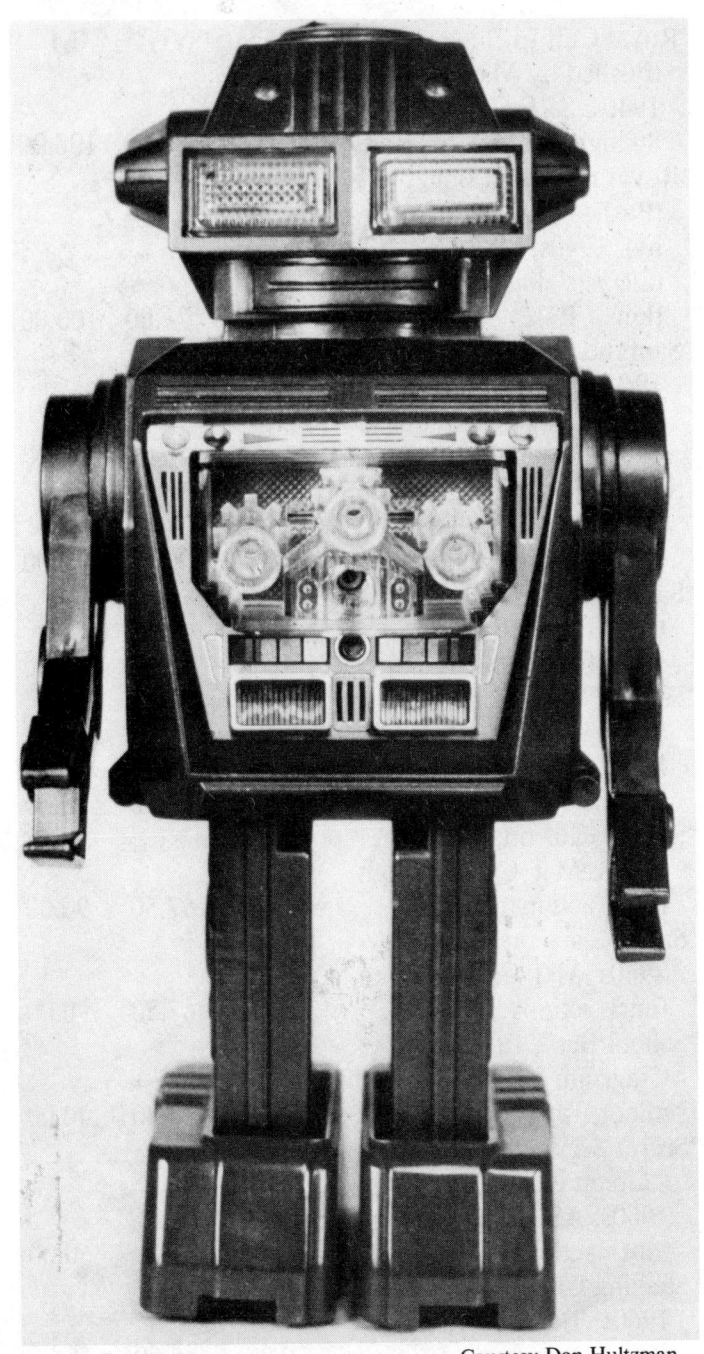

Smoking Robot   Courtesy Don Hultzman.

New Astronaut

Photos by Ron Chojnacki.

	G	VG	M
"Popcorn Vendor" No.s-4035, 1960s, S&E Co., 8" high, 7" long, six actions, includes litho umbrella	105.00	157.50	210.00
"Pop Drinking Bear", (?), 1950s, M-T Co., 10" tall, 4"x4" base, five actions	40.00	60.00	80.00
"Porsche-With Visible Engine", 1964, Bandai Co., 10" long, three actions	30.00	45.00	60.00
"Poverty Pup", bank, 1966, Poynter Products Co., 6" long, 4¼" high, three actions	20.00	30.00	40.00

	G	VG	M
"Pretty Peggy Parrot", 1950s, T-N Co., 12" long, four actions	100.00	150.00	200.00
"Princess-the French Poodle", 1950s, no markings, 9" long, 8" high, five actions	15.00	22.50	30.00
"Professor Owl", 1950s, E-T Co., 8" high, five actions, includes two discs	90.00	135.00	180.00
"Puffy Morris", 1960s, Y Co., 10" tall, five actions, uses real cigarette	45.00	67.50	90.00
"Puzzled Puppy", 1950s, M-T Co, 7½" long, 5" high, five actions	45.00	67.50	90.00

"R.R. Line Locomotive", 1950s, Marx, 6½" long, four actions	G	VG	M
	15.00	22.50	30.00
"R-35 Robot", 1950s, M-T Co., 7½" tall, five actions	165.00	247.50	350.00
"Radar Robot", 1950s, T-N Co., 8½" tall, three actions	325.00	487.50	650.00
"Railroad Hand Car", 1950s, KDP Co., 8" long, a minor toy, includes rubber track	40.00	60.00	80.00
"Railway Yard-Shuttle Train", 1950s, ATC Co., 8" long, track 28" long, three actions, includes locomotive boxcar and track	45.00	67.50	90.00
"Ray Gun", machine gun, 1950s, T-N Co., 17½" long, three actions, includes tripod	20.00	30.00	40.00
"Ricki-The Begging Poodle", 1950s, Rock Valley Toys (VIA), 9" long, 8" high, 5 actions	15.00	22.50	30.00
"Robert Robot", 1950s, Ideal Toy Co., 14" tall, three actions	100.00	150.00	200.00
"Road Grader", 1960s, T-N Co., 12" long, three actions	15.00	22.50	30.00
"Roaring Gorilla", (white gorilla), 1950s, T-N Co., 9¼" tall, five actions	80.00	120.00	160.00
"Roarin' Jungle Lion", (?), 1950s, Marx Co., 16" long, nose to tail tip, four actions, 2 cycles	50.00	75.00	100.00
"Robot", 1960s, Y Co, 10½" tall, three actions	250.00	375.00	500.00
"Robot 2500", 1970s, Durham Industries, 10½" tall, four actions	15.00	22.50	30.00
"Rocking Santa", 1950s, Alps Co., 10" high, four actions, RARE	125.00	187.50	250.00
"Rock 'n' Roll Monkey, 1950s, Rosko Co., 13" tall, five actions, includes plastic hat	75.00	112.50	150.00
"Rocking Chair Bear", (?), 1950s, M-T Co., 10" high, five actions	40.00	60.00	80.00

"Royal Cub In Buggy" (Pushed by Mama Bear), 1940s, S&E Co., 8" long, 8" high, six actions, Rare	G	VG	M
	50.00	75.00	100.00
"Royal Bunny In Buggy", (Pushed by Mama Bunny), 1940s, S&E Co., 10" tall, 7½" long, four actions, Rare	50.00	75.00	100.00
"Sam-the Shaving Man", 1960s, Plaything Toy Co., 11½" tall, seven actions, includes metal mirror	50.00	75.00	100.00
"Sammy Wong-The Tea Totaler", 1950s, T-N Co., 10" tall, four actions	60.00	90.00	120.00
"Santa Bank" 1960, HTC Co., (Trim a tree), 11" high, four actions	100.00	150.00	200.00
"Santa Claus" No.M-750 (Sitting on House), 1960s, H.T.C. Co., 8" high, four actions	60.00	90.00	120.00
"Santa Claus on Handcar", 1960s, M-T Co., 10" high, three actions	45.00	67.50	90.00
"Santa Claus on Scooter", 1960s, M-T Co., 10" high, four actions	45.00	67.50	90.00
"School Bus", 1950s, Cragstan, 20½" long, a minor toy	20.00	30.00	40.00
"Secret Service Action Car" ("Green Hornet" motif), 1960s, ASC Co., 11" long, four actions	30.00	45.00	60.00
"Shaking Classic Car", 1960s, T-N Co., 7" long, four actions	30.00	45.00	60.00
"Shaking Old-Timer Car No.2511-1", 1960s, T-N Co., 9" long, four actions, includes plastic driver	30.00	45.00	60.00
"Shark-U-Control Racing Car", 1961, Remco Ind., Inc., 19" long, all plastic, minor toy	20.00	30.00	40.00
"Shoe-Shaking Dog", 1950s, M-T Co., 8" long, 6" tall, five actions	20.00	30.00	40.00
"Shoe Shine Bear", 1950s, T-N Co., 9" tall, five actions	75.00	112.50	150.00
"Shoe Shine Joe", 1950s, Alps Co., 11" high, six actions	60.00	90.00	120.00

Kooky-Spooky Whistling Tree, Feeding Bird Watcher

Milk Drinking Kitty, Fishing Kitty, Shoe Shine Bear, Busy Shoe
Shining Bear, Knitting Grandma

Blacksmith Bear

Musical Jolly Chimp, Grand-Pa Car, Circus Fire Engine

	G	VG	M
"Shoe Shine Monkey", 1950s, T-N Co., 9" high, five actions	45.00	67.50	90.00
"Shooting Bear", 1950s, SAN Co., 9½" tall, five actions	70.00	105.00	140.00
"Shooting Gorilla", 1950s, M-T Co., 12" high, four actions, includes gun and			

Mix-ette Mixer, Wash-O-Matic Washing Machine, Jig-Saw-Matic
Jigsaw, Kitchen-ette Stove & Sink

	G	VG	M
darts	50.00	75.00	100.00
"Shutterbug" photographer, 1950s, T-N Co., 9" tall, five actions	80.00	120.00	160.00
"Shuttling Train and Freight Yard", 1950s, Alps Co., 11" long, track 51" long, four actions, includes			

Teddy-Go-Cart, Mambo-the Jolly Drumming Elephant.

F.D. Fire Engine, Fire Engine, Fire Chief Mystery Action Car, Police Motorcycle Cop

Champion Weight Lifter

Cragstan Automatic Dishwasher, Bengali Tiger, Holiday Sink/Stove Combination

Fighting Bull, Breakfast Chef, Near Sighted Pup

Ricki-the Begging Poodle, Picnic Poodle, Princess-the French Poodle

Courtesy Don Hultzman.

Dump Truck No.7343, Bulldozer, Crane Tractor Photo by Ron Chojnacki.

	G	VG	M
locomotive, baggage car, two platforms, litho luggage	50.00	75.00	100.00
"Silver Bell Choo Choo", 1950s, Kanto Co., 12" long, three actions	10.00	15.00	20.00
"Silver Mountain Express Locomotive", 1960s, M-T Co., four actions, 15¾" long	10.00	15.00	20.00
"Silver Mountain Locomotive," 1950s, M-T Co., 16" long, three actions	10.00	15.00	20.00
"Silver Streak Locomotive No.6682", 1950s, M-T Co., 16" long, four actions	20.00	30.00	40.00
"Singing Bird In Cage", 1950s, T-N Co., 9" high, 4"x6" rectangular base, four actions	25.00	37.50	50.00
"Sky Patrol Flying Saucer", 1950s, K-O Co., 7½" diameter, seven actions, includes detachable antenna	50.00	75.00	100.00
"Sky Taxi-Panam-Boeing Vertol 107", 1970s, Haji Co., 12¾" long, three actions, includes 2 detachable rotors	20.00	30.00	40.00
"Sleeping Baby Bear", 1950s, Linemar, 9" long, six actions, includes detachable Alarm Clock	60.00	90.00	120.00
"Slurpy Pup", 1960s, T-N Co., 6½" long, 4" high, four actions	10.00	15.00	20.00
"Smoking Bunny", 1950s, SAN Co., 10½" tall, four actions	45.00	67.50	90.00
"Smoking Elephant", 1950s, SAN Co., 8" tall, four actions	45.00	67.50	90.00
"Smoking Grandpa" (in Rocking Chair), 1950s, SAN Co., 8" tall, four actions, (Type I - eyes open)	55.00	82.50	110.00
"Smoking Grandpa" (in Rocking Chair), 1950s, SAN Co., 8" tall, four actions, (Type II - eyes closed)	70.00	105.00	140.00
"Smoking Pop Locomotive-the General", 1950s, San			

	G	VG	M
Co., 10¼" long, four actions	30.00	45.00	60.00
"Smoking Popeye", 1950s, Linemar, 9" tall, five actions, Rare	200.00	300.00	400.00
"Smoking Robot", 1960s, no trademark, 10" tall, four actions (all plastic)	30.00	45.00	60.00
"Smoking Spaceman", 1950s, Linemar Co., 12" tall, six actions	300.00	450.00	600.00
"Space Capsule", 1960s, M-T Co., 10" long, four actions, includes styrofoam saucer and astronaut	40.00	60.00	80.00
"Space Fighter" robot, 1970s, S-H Co., 9" tall, six actions	10.00	15.00	20.00
"Spaceman" robot, 1950s, T-N Co., 9¼" tall, four actions	175.00	262.50	500.00
"Spaceman" robot, 1950s, Linemar, 7½" tall, three actions	35.00	52.50	70.00
"Space Patrol" vehicle, 1950s, K Co., 9" long, six actions	50.00	75.00	100.00
"Space Robot (X-70)", 1960s, T-N Co., 12" tall, five actions	250.00	375.00	500.00
"Space Robot Trooper", 1950s, K-O Co., 7½" tall, three actions	175.00	262.50	350.00
"Space Rocket-Solar X", 1960s, T-N Co., 15½" tall, five actions	45.00	67.50	90.00
"Space Scooter", 1960s, M-T Co., 10½" high, 8" long, three actions	45.00	67.50	90.00
"Space Ship", 1970s, M-T Co., 9" long, three actions	10.00	15.00	20.00
"Space Ship X-5", 1970s, M-T Co., 8" diameter, four actions	10.00	15.00	20.00
"Space Tank", 1960s, K-O Co., 6" long, four actions	75.00	112.50	150.00
"Sparky-the Seal", 1950s, M-T Co., 6" high, 7" long, four actions, two cycles, includes celluloid ball	50.00	75.00	100.00
"Spirit of 1776", locomotive No.4406, 1976, M-T Co., 15¾" long, five actions . .	15.00	22.50	30.00
"Steam Roller" (Road Roller), 1950s, T-N Co., (Rosko), 12" long with			

	G	VG	M
trailer, four actions......	40.00	60.00	80.00
"Strutting My Fair Dancer", (Dancing Sailor Girl), 1950s, Haji Co., 12" tall, (two pieces), a minor toy.	40.00	60.00	80.00
"Super Astronaut", Robot, 1960s, S-H Co., 11½" tall, five actions, two cycles	100.00	150.00	200.00
"Super Astronaut" robot, 1960s, SJM Co., 12" tall, four actions..........	10.00	15.00	20.00
"Super Space Capsule", 1960s, S-H Co., 9" high, four actions..........	40.00	60.00	80.00
"Surrey Jeep", 1960s, T-N Co., 11" long, three actions	42.50	63.75	85.00
"Switchboard Operator" (?), 1950s, Linemar, 7½" high, four actions, Rare..	105.00	157.50	210.00
"Swivel-O-Matic Astronaut" robot, 1960s, S-H Co., 11½" tall, five actions, 2 cycles	100.00	150.00	200.00
"T 360 Monoplane", 1950s, S&E Co., 12" long, 14½" wingspan, four actions...	60.00	90.00	120.00
"Talking Police Car - Mystery Action", 1960s, Y Co., 14" long, three actions	30.00	45.00	60.00
"Tank M-4 Combat Tank", 1960s, Taiyo Co., 11½" long, 13" with gun barrel extended, five actions....	30.00	45.00	60.00
"Tank M-35", 1950s, HTC Co., 8" long, three actions	25.00	37.50	50.00
"Tank-M-41", 1970s, J Co., 8¼" long, four actions...	10.00	15.00	20.00
"Tank M-48-T", 1960s, T-N Co., 8¼" long, four actions	20.00	30.00	40.00
"Tank M-56", 1940s, M-T Co., 7½" long, wheel drive, seven actions.....	30.00	45.00	60.00
"Tank M-81", 1960s, M-T Co., 8½" long, seven actions	15.00	22.50	30.00
"Tank M-103", 1950s, M-T Co., 7" long, three actions	25.00	37.50	50.00
"Tank M-107-U.S. Army", 1950s, Y Co., 6" long, four actions, includes four missiles	25.00	37.50	50.00

	G	VG	M
"Tank M-X", 1950s, T-N Co., 8½" long, five actions	25.00	37.50	50.00
"Tank X-3" (explorer Defense), 1950s, Cragstan Co., 7¾" long, five actions, includes six cartridge shells...........	50.00	75.00	100.00
"Tank-Daisy-Matic No.80", 1965, Daisy Mfg. Co., 8½" long, five actions, includes darts...........	50.00	75.00	100.00
"Tarzan", 1960s, SAN Co., 13" tall, three actions....	75.00	112.50	150.00
"Teddy the Artist", 1950s, Y Co., 8½" high, 5¼" x 7" base, 3 actions, includes removable tray and 10 patterns...............	130.00	195.00	260.00
"Teddy-the Rhythmical Drummer", 1960s, Alps Co., 11" tall, three actions	20.00	30.00	40.00
"Telephone Bear", 1950s, Linemar, 7½" high, five actions	90.00	135.00	180.00
"Telephone Bear - Ringing and Talking In His Old Rocking Chair", 1950s, M-T Co., 10" high, four actions	80.00	120.00	160.00
"Television Spaceman", 1960s, Alps Co., 14" tall, five actions...........	40.00	60.00	80.00
"Television Truck" 1950s, Linemar Co., 14" long, three actions...........	40.00	60.00	80.00
"Thunderbird" car, 1961, Y Co., 11" long, five actions	90.00	135.00	180.00
"Tin Man" Robot, 1960s, Remco Industries, Inc., 21" tall, all plastic, four actions	20.00	30.00	40.00
"Tiny Jeep", 1950s, WACO Co., 4¼" long, minor action	7.50	11.25	15.00
"Tiny Tank", 1950s, WACO Co., 4¼" long, minor action	7.50	11.25	15.00
"Tom and Jerry Choo Choo", 1960s, M-T Co., 10¼" long, five actions..	50.00	75.00	100.00
"Tom and Jerry Handcar- Jerry", 1960s, M-T Co., 7¾" high, 7¾" long, three actions..........	50.00	75.00	100.00

Tin-Man, Animated Santa

Charlie-the Drumming Clown, Daisy the Jolly Drumming Duck, Teddy-the Artist, Dandy-the Happy Drumming Pup

	G	VG	M
"Tom and Jerry Handcar-Tom", 1960s, M-T Co., 9¾" high, 7¾" long, three actions..........	50.00	75.00	100.00
"Tom-Tom Indian", 1961, Y Co., 10½" tall, four actions..............	40.00	60.00	80.00

	G	VG	M
"Torpedo Boat-PT 107", 1950s, Linemar 11½" long, three actions......	35.00	52.50	70.00
"Tractor", 1950s, Showa Co., 7½" long, four actions, includes litho tin figure (driver)..........	30.00	45.00	60.00
"Tractor", 1960s, Y Co., 6" long, three actions......	15.00	22.50	30.00
"Treasure Chest" bank, 1960s, Illfelder Co., 11" tall, five actions, two cycles, risque toy-pg rated	37.50	56.25	75.00
"Tricky Dog House", No.673, 1960s, Y Co., 6¾" high, 7¼" long, 6¾" wide, four actions..	25.00	37.50	50.00
"Tubby the Turtle", 1950s, Y Co., 7" long, three actions	15.00	22.50	30.00
"Trumpet Playing Monkey", 1950s, Alps Co., 9" high, four actions, includes tin horn	60.00	90.00	120.00
"Tugboat", 1950s, Marx, 6½" long, a minor toy...	20.00	30.00	40.00
"Tumbles, the Bear", 1960s, Y-M Co. (Yanoman), 8½" tall, minor toy, includes porter's hat......	40.00	60.00	80.00
"UFO-X05", 1970s, M-T Co., 7½" diameter, three actions	10.00	15.00	20.00
"Union Mountain Cable Lines", Monorail set, 1950s, T-N Co., car 8" long, 16 pc. oval track, 22" x 32", minor toy....	25.00	37.50	50.00
"United Mainliner Stratocruiser", 1950s, Linemar, 19½" long, 13" wingspan, four actions...	40.00	60.00	80.00
"United States Ocean Liner", 1950s, Linemar Co., 14" long, three actions	40.00	60.00	80.00
"Universal Machine Gun", 1950s, T-N Co., 14¾" long, three actions......	20.00	30.00	40.00
"V.I.P.-the Busy Boss", 1950s, S&E Co., 8" high, six actions............	90.00	135.00	180.00
"Visible Ford Mustang", 1960s, Bandai Co., 10" long, four actions........	25.00	37.50	50.00

	G	VG	M
"Volkswagen-Elektrik", 1950s, Mignon Co., 8½" long, three actions......	12.50	18.75	25.00
"Volkswagen No.7653", 1960s, Bendai Co., 10" long, three actions......	10.00	15.00	20.00
"Volkswagen With Visible Engine", 1960s, K.O. Co., 7" long, three actions....	10.00	15.00	20.00
"Volkswagen With Visible Engine No.4049", 1960s, Bandai Co., 8" long, three actions	15.00	22.50	30.00
"Wagon Master", 1960s, M-T Co., 18" long, four actions	25.00	37.50	50.00
"Walking Bear With Xylophone", 1950s, Linemar Co., 10" high, seven actions.........	100.00	150.00	200.00
"Warpath Indian", 1950s, Alps Co., 12" tall, three actions	30.00	45.00	60.00
"Wash-O-Matic" washing machine, 1940s, T-N Co., 5¾" high, 4¼" diameter, a minor toy, includes lid .	10.00	15.00	20.00
"Western Badman", (Red Gulch Bar), 1960s, M-T Co., 9¾" high, eight actions, includes 3 plastic bottles and 2 plastic glasses RARE..........	150.00	225.00	300.00
"Western Express"-Locomotive, 1960s, Kanto Toy Co., 14" long, four actions	15.00	22.50	30.00

	G	VG	M
"Western Locomotive", 1950s, M-T Co., 10½" long, four actions......	45.00	67.50	90.00
"Western Special Locomotive", 1950s, M-T Co., 12" long, five actions	20.00	30.00	40.00
"Wheel-A-Gear"-Robot, 1960s, Taiyo Co., 14" tall, five actions............	75.00	112.50	150.00
"Wild West Rodeo", 1950s, Linemar, 6½" long, 8" high, five actions, includes plastic bowl for bubble solution..............	45.00	67.50	90.00
"Windy the Elephant", 1950s, T-N Co., 9¾" high, three actions, includes celluloid ball and tin litho umbrella, RARE	100.00	150.00	200.00
"Winner-23", Rocket, 1950s, KDP Co., (Exelo), 5½" long, minor action, includes rubber track......	75.00	112.50	150.00
"Yeti-the Abominable Snowman", 1960s, Marx, 12" tall, four actions....	150.00	225.00	300.00
"Yo-Yo Monkey", 1960s, Y-M Co., 12" tall-spring extension to 32", minor....	20.00	30.00	40.00
"Zoom Motorboat", 1950s, K Co., 12" long, three actions	15.00	22.50	30.00

SOLDIERS
(See also Paper)

The average mint price of American dimestore soldiers in the last edition was $13.50, and in this edition is $31.58, an increase of 132%.

To help correct some errors in the otherwise excellent new book "The American Dimestore Soldier Book", there is **no** indication that Barclay made any of the pieces generally referred to by collectors as "Small Barclays" (see Unknowns section). The only toys known to have been produced by All-Nu are those listed in the various sections of this book. Tommy Toy was out of business before World War II, so could not have produced any post-War soldiers. The plastic soldiers that are copies of Barclay pieces were not made by Barclay, which produced no plastic toys. These were made by an as yet unknown company in the 1950s.

Several new soldiers and variations have been found since the last edition, made by Barclay, Manoil, Grey and All-Nu. In addition, several "new" companies have been discovered.

Some lead soldiers suffer from "lead rot". This can often be cured by soaking them overnight in oil (baby oil will do), cleaning them off, and then soaking them overnight in vinegar. Cleaned off again, most seem to remain free of the condition.

CONDITION OF A TOY SOLDIER AND ITS RELATION TO PRICE

The price of a toy soldier depends not only on its desirability, but on its condition.

"Mint" means just that; the condition in which it was originally issued — perfect, regardless of age, not the slightest blemish. Needless to say this is a fairly rare state of affairs, but enough soldiers exist in mint condition to make it an employable term. Many people, hoping to dispose of toys, are tempted to term them "mint" when they are really "near mint", "very good" or sometimes even just "good". Inevitably this can result in unhappiness all around, and not infrequently, in a cancelled sale.

"Very Good" indicates a soldier which has obviously seen use; with signs of wear and aging, but with most of its paint remaining and in general having a freshness to its appearance that makes it seem attractive and collectible to all but the most discriminating.

"Good" signals a soldier that has seen considerable wear, but has at least one half to one third of its original paint, and is basically sound. A collector will collect it, but will often not be wholly satisfied with it as an example of his collection, and thus prices are well below that which the same item in mint can command.

Condition below good results in another drastic drop in price, generally to $3 or or less, and figures with missing parts, although otherwise in excellent condition, will usually fall into this lower-priced category. At present, a BARCLAY soldier minus its tin helmet (signalled by a large round hole in the top of its head) is worth about half of what it would otherwise bring. Rust, even small spots of it on the cast iron soldiers, can seriously lower their price, as can repainting of any of the soldiers. "Near-Mint", "Fine", "Very Fine" and similar terms often found in sellers' descriptions, denote conditions between Mint and Very Good, and are priced accordingly.

The key to grading is to avoid wishful thinking. Grading can sometimes be a problem for the uninitiated, but common sense will usually prevail, and when possible a consultation with an expert in the field can often clear up lingering doubts. A toy in its original box is worth up to 10 to 20% more if the box is in mint condition, with the price dropping as condition lessens.

BARCLAY
(See Vehicles, Animal-Drawn, Aircraft and Miscellaneous)

Barclay Mfg. Co. was the largest manufacturer of toy soldiers in the U.S. prior to World War II, selling millions of figures annually. The company, named after Barclay Street in West Hoboken, New Jersey (now 10th Street in Union City) began in 1924 or late 1923, owned by an elderly Frenchman, Leon Donze, and by Michael Levy (c. 1895-10/9/64), who became affiliated by buying a partnership. Levy eventually took over the company (around 1932) and it was he who turned it into a major one. From about five employees in 1924, the company expanded to a pre-War peak of 400 workers, and moved several times as it was forced to expand. Barclay's soldiers came in four styles prior to World War II. The first, which were probably produced almost from Barclay's beginning, were small, with the mounted figures having moving arms. The second, approximately 3¼" high, with a separate tin helmet, seem to have begun production in 1934, and were designed and sculpted by Barclay employee Frank Krupp. This figure (the tin helmet was subcontracted) was rather stiff and is known by collectors as "short stride" because its marching figures' feet were close together. The third style, again by Krupp, also had a separate tin helmet, was more realistic, and is known as "long stride". These were on sale as early as 1937. In February, 1938, a clip was designed to hold on the tin helmets, as the formerly glued-on helmets frequently came off, and drew complaints from the chain stores such as Woolworth's, which sold Barclay toys.

The fourth style, introduced about 1939-1940, when Barclay moved from slush casting to die casting its soldiers, was by free-lance artist Olive Kooken (1904-1964), and is known as "cast helmet", as the soldiers featured helmets that were an integral part of the figure. Barclay's soldiers were made of antimonial lead, consisting of about 13% antimony and the rest lead. When slush-molding was done, only one mold was made of each single figure. The lead would be poured into the mold, rocked, and immediately poured out, thus providing a hollow figure. Later, the die-cast molds produced a number of the same figures at the same time. During the Second World War BARCLAY laid off all but four of its employees, and did sub-contract work. It was never as successful after the war, and finally closed down in 1971, by this time employing only 50-75 people. Although BARCLAY assigned numbers to its figures from the beginning for its own records, many of the soldiers themselves bore no numbers. Figures listed with a question mark after the number are based on the memory of longtime BARCLAY employee George Fall, whose memory, judged against known BARCLAY numbers, is quite accurate, but not infallible. All short stride BARCLAYS have separate helmets.

Pre-1934
(All bold words and numbers are BARCLAY'S OWN DESCRIPTION)

	G	VG	M
(Ba) 87? **Mounted Officer, moving arm holding sword, on rearing horse**	40.00	60.00	80.00
(Baa) 87? Same as above on cantering horse	40.00	60.00	80.00
(Bb) 87? **Mounted Officer, moving arm holding bugle, on rearing horse**	40.00	60.00	80.00
(Bba) 87? Same as above, on cantering horse	40.00	60.00	80.00
(Bc) 87? **Mounted Officer, moving arm holding pistol on cantering horse**	40.00	60.00	80.00
(bd) 88? **Mounted Cowboy with lasso**	No Price Found		
(be) 89? **Mounted Indian, moving arm holding rifle**	12.00	18.00	24.00
(Bf) 90? **Mounted Cowboy with pistol**	No Price Found		
(BfA) 90? **Mounted Cowboy with moving arm, holding rifle**	20.00	30.00	40.00
(Bfa) Indian chief on foot, 54 mm high, blue and red-striped headdress, looks like Ideal I-14	No Price Found		
(Bfb) Indian brave on foot, 54 mm high, carrying rifle across stomach	No Price Found		
(Bg) Cavalryman mounted, 2¾" high, no moving parts, modeled on French soldier, circa late 1920s-early 30s	10.00	15.00	20.00
(Bh) Mounted soldier with steel helmet, circa early 30s, no moving parts, approx. 2¼" high	7.50	11.25	15.00
(Bi) Baseball fielder, approx. 1⅞" high, circa 1920s	25.00	37.50	50.00
(Bj) Baseball pitcher, circa 1920s	25.00	37.50	50.00

Ba   Baa   Bb   Bba

Bc   Be   Bg   Bh

Photo by Ed Poole
Courtesy Tony Salamone

B1   B2   B2A

B3   B3A   B4

Photo by Ed Poole

	G	VG	M
(Bk) Baseball batter, circa 1920s	25.00	37.50	50.00
(Bl) Mounted Indian on rearing horse	17.00	25.50	34.00

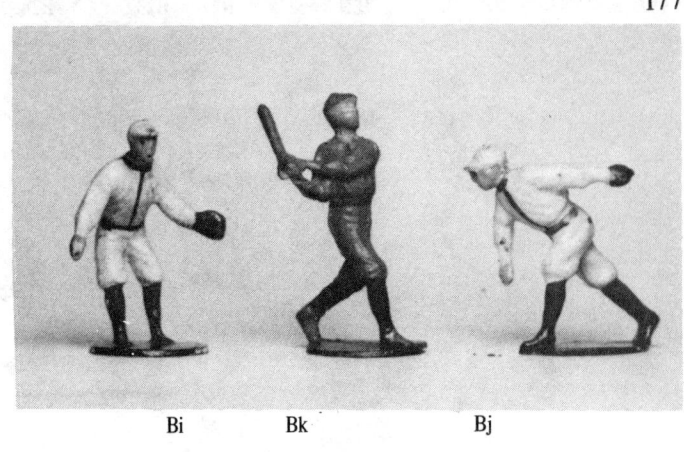

Bi   Bk   Bj

1934 and After	G	VG	M
(BA) Paint Your Own Army Set No. 2003, circa 1935-1936, boxed.......	125.00	187.50	250.00
(BAa) Paint Your Own Army Set No.2003, larger size than above, same toys, with compartment for one more. In set bought in September, 1980, compartment contained two two-dimensional lead elephants. Barclay employees queried don't remember these........	No Price Found		
(Bl) 98 Mounted Indian....	9.00	13.50	18.00
(B1a) Mounted Indian, two feathers..............	22.50	37.50	45.00
(B2) 99 Mounted Cowboy..	6.00	9.00	12.00
(B2A) 99 Mounted Cowboy, variation in gunbelt, saddle, etc...............	6.00	9.00	12.00
(B2B) Mounted Cowboy with lasso, horse's tail down................	12.50	18.75	25.00
(B2C) Mounted Cowboy with lasso, horse's tail up.	No Price Found		
(B3) 187? Mounted in grey, cap, intermediate size....	13.50	20.75	27.00
(B3A) Mounted in khaki or grey cap, larger black, grey or brown horse.....	8.00	12.00	16.00

B5   B6   B7   B9   B10   B11   B12

B13   B14   B15   B16   B17   B18   B19

Photo by Bill Kaufman

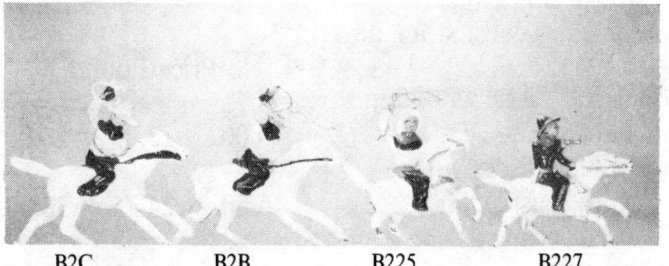

B2C   B2B   B225   B227
Photo by Don Pielin

Bl   BfA

B1a

	G	VG	M
(B4) 187? Mounted in colored jacket and cap, may be Chinese or Japanese..	21.00	31.50	42.00
(B5) 701 Flagbearer, tin helmet, short stride.....	10.00	15.00	20.00

B20   B21   B22 B23   B24   B25 B25a B26   B27   B28

B29   B30   B31   B32   B33   B34   B35 B36   B37

B25a Courtesy Bill Adams

Photo by Bill Kaufman

	G	VG	M
(B6) 701 Flagbearer, tin helmet, long stride......	8.00	12.00	16.00
(B7) 701 Flagbearer, cast helmet..............	6.00	9.00	12.00
(B8) 705 Flagbearer, Cuban flag variation painted for 10 Woolworth's in Cuba, not known if tin helmet, cast helmet or pot helmet	No Price Found		
(B9) 702 Machine-Gunner, kneeling, short stride....	5.00	7.50	10.00
(B10) 702 Machine-Gunner, kneeling, long stride.....	4.50	6.75	9.00
(B11) 702 Machine-Gunner, kneeling, cast helmet....	4.50	6.75	9.00
(B12) 703 Kneeling, firing, short stride............	6.50	9.75	13.00
(B12A) 703 kneeling, firing, short stride, in front of fingers, fat portion of gun and thin portion of barrel about equal length......	9.00	13.50	18.00
(B13) 703 Kneeling, firing, long stride, tin helmet...	6.00	9.00	12.00
(B14) 704 Marching, shoulder arms, short stride	6.50	9.75	13.00
(B15) 704 Marching, shoulder arms, long stride, tin helmet..............	4.00	6.00	8.00
(B16) 705 Port Arms, short stride................	5.00	7.50	10.00
(B17) 705 Port Arms, cast helmet..............	6.50	9.75	13.00
(B18) 706 Rifle across waist, short stride...........	8.00	12.00	16.00
(B18a) Same as above, with shorter rifle, sling around hand	No Price Found		
(B19) 706 Tall, tin helmet, solid puttees, only 4 known..............	200.00	300.00	400.00

	G	VG	M
(B20) 706 Advancing with leveled rifle, tin helmet, long stride............	12.50	18.75	25.00
(B21) 706 Advancing with leveled rifle, cast helmet..	7.00	10.50	14.00
(B22) 707 At Attention, cast helmet..............	7.50	11.25	15.00
(B23) 708 Officer with sword, short stride......	12.50	18.75	25.00
(B24) 708 Same as above, in blue................	10.00	15.00	20.00
(B25) 708 Officer with sword, tin helmet, long stride................	5.00	7.50	10.00
(B25a) 708 Officer with sword, tin helmet, long stride, no chest strap, also in blue...............	No Price Found		
(B26) 708 Same as B25 in blue................	10.00	15.00	20.00
(B27) 708 Officer with sword, cast helmet......	16.50	24.75	33.00
(B28) 708 Same as above, in blue................	14.00	21.00	28.00
(B29) 709 Bugler, short stride................	13.00	19.50	26.00
(B30) 709 Bugler, long stride, tin helmet............	5.50	8.25	11.00
(B31) 710 Drummer, short stride................	8.00	12.00	16.00
(B32) 710 Drummer, long stride, tin helmet.......	9.00	13.50	18.00
(B33) 711 Drum major, short stride............	7.50	11.25	15.00
(B34) 711 Drum major, long stride, tin helmet.......	5.50	8.25	11.00
(B35) 743 Cadet officer, short stride............	6.00	9.00	12.00

B38 B39 B40 B42 B41 B43 B44

B45 B46 B47 B48 B49 B51 B52

Photo by Bill Kaufman

B12   B12a

Photo by K. Warren Mitchell

B53 B60 B54 B55 B56 B57 B58 B59

B61   B62   B63
B64 B65 B66 B67 B68 B69

B70 B71 B72 B73 B74 B75 B76

Photo by Bill Kaufman

	G	VG	M
(B36) 742? Cadet with rifle, short stride............	7.50	11.25	15.00
(B37) 742? Same as above, but painted as wooden soldier, only two known.	No Price Found		
(B38) Cadet with rifle, long stride................	6.00	9.00	12.00
(B39) Ethiopian with rifle, circa 1935-36..........	100.00	150.00	200.00
(B40) Ethiopian Officer, circa 1935-36............	90.00	135.00	180.00
(B41) Italian Officer, circa 1935-36..............	80.00	120.00	160.00
(B42) Italian Infantryman, circa 1935-36, rifle tip off in photo..............	55.00	82.50	110.00
(B43) Japanese, charging with rifle, circa 1937....	37.50	56.25	75.00
(B44) Japanese Officer, circa 1937 (this is the original Ethiopian officer, painted as a Japanese)..........	100.00	150.00	200.00
(B45) Chinese Officer in steel helmet, circa 1937......	150.00	225.00	300.00
(B46) Chinese rifleman, circa 1937.................	40.00	60.00	80.00
(B47) 717 Indian, rifle across waist...............	4.00	6.00	8.00
(B48) 716 Indian with knife.	5.00	7.50	10.00
(B49) 719 Sailor, marching, short stride, white......	9.00	13.50	18.00
(B50) 719 Same as above, in blue.................	6.50	9.75	13.00
(B51) 719 Sailor in bell-bottoms, blue or white...	6.50	9.75	13.00
(B52) 719 Sailor in puttees, blue or white........	5.00	7.50	10.00
(B53) 720? Sailor Flagbearer, long stride.............	8.00	12.00	16.00
(B54) 721 Naval Officer, short stride, tin top to cap	30.00	45.00	60.00
(B55) 721 Naval Officer, short stride............	10.00	15.00	20.00
(B55a) 721 Naval Officer, same as above, in blue...	No Price Found		
(B56) 721 Naval Officer, long stride..............	7.50	11.25	15.00
(B57) 722 Marine, short stride, tin top to cap.....	30.00	45.00	60.00
(B58) 722 Marine, short stride................	5.50	8.25	11.00
(B59) 722 Marine, long stride.................	6.25	9.38	12.50
(B60) 723? Sailor Signalman	7.50	11.25	15.00
(B61) 728 Prone machine-gunner, tin helmet......	7.50	11.25	15.00

	G	VG	M
(B62) 728 Prone machine-gunner, cast helmet.....	7.50	11.25	15.00
(B63) 728 Prone machine-gunner, cast helmet, slightly smaller version...	9.00	13.50	18.00
(B64) 729? Crawling with rifle, tin helmet..........	8.00	12.00	16.00
(B65) 730 Signalman, tin helmet................	8.00	12.00	16.00
(B66) 731 Kneeling with pigeons, tin helmet......	6.50	9.75	13.00
(B67) 732 Kneeling with phone, tin helmet.......	5.50	8.25	11.00
(B68) 733 Kneeling with shell, tin helmet........	6.00	9.00	12.00
(B69) 734 Walking with boxes, tin helmet.......	6.00	9.00	12.00
(B70) 735 Looking through rangefinder, tin helmet...	7.50	11.25	15.00
(B71) 736 sentry in overcoat, tin helmet.............	5.50	8.25	11.00
(B72) 737 Tommy-gunner, tin helmet.............	6.50	9.75	13.00
(B73) 737 Tommy-gunner, cast helmet............	8.00	12.00	16.00
(B74) 738 Grenade-thrower, rifle butt on ground, tin helmet................	4.50	6.75	9.00
(B75) 738 Grenade-thrower, tall, tin helmet, solid puttees	No Price Found		
(B76) 738 Grenade-thrower, rifle off ground, tin helmet................	10.00	15.00	20.00
(B77) 738 Grenade-thrower, rifle off ground, cast helmet................	6.00	9.00	12.00
(B78) 739 Fifer, tin helmet..	7.50	11.25	15.00
(B79) 740 French horn, tin helmet................	6.50	9.75	13.00
(B79a) Seated machine-gunner, cast helmet, bandage-type puttees....	7.50	11.25	15.00
(B80) 741 Pilot............	4.50	6.75	9.00
(B81) Doctor with bag, white or brown..............	6.00	9.00	12.00
(B82) Kneeling Nurse......	5.00	7.50	10.00
(B83) 744 Nurse, hand on hip..................	4.50	6.75	9.00
(B84) Prone, firing rifle, tin helmet................	8.50	12.75	17.00
(B85) Wounded, sitting, arm in sling..............	7.00	10.50	14.00

B77 B78 B79 B79a B80 B81 B81 B82 B83

B84 B85 B86 B87 B88

B89 B90 B91 B92 B93

B94 B95 B96 B97 B98 B99 B100

B101 B102 B102a B103 B104 B105 B106

B107 B107a B108 B109 B110 B111 B112

B107a Courtesy Jeff Maund

B113 B114 B115 B116 B117 B118

B119 B120 B121 B122 B124

Above photos by Bill Kaufman

B18a B120a B120 B177 B179 B180
B181 B190 B191 B192 B193
Photo by Don Pielin

B123 B125 B126 B127
B128 B129 B130
Photo by Bill Kaufman

B139
Photo by Ed Poole

B131 B132 B133 B134 B135 B140 B141
B142 B143 B144 B145 B146
Photo by Bill Kaufman

	G	VG	M
(B86) 747 Standing, firing rifle, short stride	5.00	7.50	10.00
(B87) 747 Standing, firing rifle, long stride	7.50	11.25	15.00
(B88) 747 Standing, firing rifle, cast helmet	6.50	9.75	13.00

	G	VG	M
(B89) 748 Running with rifle, tin helmet	7.50	11.25	15.00
(B90) 748 Running with rifle, cast helmet	8.00	12.00	16.00
(B91) 749 Charging with gas mask, rifle, tin helmet	5.00	7.50	10.00
(B92) Charging with gas mask, rifle, cast helmet	5.50	8.25	11.00
(B93) Army Motorcyclist in cap, also in blue as cop	11.00	16.50	22.00
(B93A) Same as above, larger, motor variation, post-war	20.00	30.00	40.00
(B94A) 715 Cowboy with tin hat brim	5.75	8.63	11.50
(B95) 752 Cowboy with lasso	5.50	8.25	11.00
(B95a) 752 Cowboy with lasso, Post-War version, lasso goes directly through hands	4.00	6.00	8.00
(B96) 753 Cowboy with pistol	4.50	6.75	9.00
(B97) 754 Indian with tomahawk and shield	3.25	4.88	6.50
(B97a) Same as above, flat base	3.25	4.88	6.50
(B98) 755 Indian Kneeling with bow and arrow	4.50	6.75	9.00
(B99) 756? Indian with rifle, long headdress	20.00	30.00	40.00
(B100) 757? Indian standing with bow and arrow	3.00	4.50	6.00
(B101) 758 Cameraman, kneeling, tin helmet	9.00	13.50	18.00
(B102) 759 Stretcher-bearer, open hand	10.00	15.00	20.00
(B102a) 759 Stretcher-bearer, closed hand	6.50	9.75	13.00
(B103) 760 Doctor with stethoscope	7.50	11.25	15.00
(B104) 761 Lying wounded, tin helmet	6.25	9.38	12.50
(B105) 762 Advancing in crouch, tin helmet	8.00	12.00	16.00
(B106) 764 Advancing, raised rifle, tin helmet	9.25	13.88	18.50
(B107) 765 Thrusting with gun muzzle; tin helmet	6.50	9.75	13.00
(B107a) 765, same as above, cast helmet	50.00	75.00	100.00
(B108) 766 Clubbing with rifle, tin helmet	12.50	18.75	25.00
(B109) 766 Clubbing with rifle, cast helmet	30.00	45.00	60.00
(B110) 769 Cook holding roast	9.50	14.25	19.00

	G	VG	M
(B111) 768 (?) Soldier peeling potatoes	6.00	9.00	12.00
(B112) Soldier eating......	16.00	24.00	32.00
(B113) Prone with long binoculars, tin helmet...	13.00	19.50	26.00
(B114) Prone with short binoculars, tin helmet...	20.00	30.00	40.00
(B115) Sitting with rifle, tin helmet...............	10.50	15.75	21.00
(B116) Officer in cap holding orders No.773.........	8.50	12.75	17.00
(B117) 774 Soldier with AA gun, tin helmet........	8.00	12.00	16.00
(B118) 774 Soldier with AA gun, cast helmet........	8.75	13.13	17.50
(B119) 775 Wounded on crutches	9.75	14.62	19.50
(B120) 776 Standing at searchlight, smooth lens, elevation wheel.........	20.00	30.00	40.00
(B120a) 776 Standing at searchlight, smooth lens, no elevation wheel......	No Price Found		
(B121) 776 Standing at searchlight, ridges along base (this and following have ridged lenses)......	7.50	11.25	15.00
(B122) 776 Standing at searchlight, smooth base connected to searchlight, no elevation wheel......	15.00	22.50	30.00
(B123) 776 Standing at searchlight, low seat, not connected to searchlight.	6.50	9.75	13.00
(B124) 776 Standing at searchlight, high seat, two rivets in front of left foot.	12.50	18.75	25.00
(B125) 776 Standing at searchlight, high seat, no rivets in front of left foot.	10.00	15.00	20.00
(B126) 777 Marching with pack, tin helmet........	5.50	8.25	11.00
(B127) 777 Marching with pack, cast helmet.......	6.50	9.75	13.00
(B128) 778 Officer with gas mask, cast helmet........	6.50	9.75	13.00
(B129) 779 Firing from behind wall, cast helmet.	20.50	30.75	41.00
(B130) 780 Falling with rifle, cast helmet...........	10.50	15.75	21.00
(B131) 781 Digging, cast helmet...............	17.50	26.25	35.00
(B132) 782 Leaning out, with field phone, antenna, cast helmet............	21.00	31.50	42.00

B147 B148 B149 B150 B151

B152 B153 B154 B155 B156

Photo by Bill Kaufman

B157 B158 B159 B160 B161 B162 B163 B164

B165 B166 B167 B168 B169 B170 B171 B172

Photo by Bill Kaufman

B173 B174 B175 B176 B178 B182 B183 B184 B185

B186 B187 B188 B189

Photo by Bill Kaufman

	G	VG	M
(B133) 783 Crouching with binoculars, cast helmet...	6.25	9.38	12.50
(B134) 784 Parachutist landing	9.00	13.50	18.00
(B135) 785 Skier in white, cast helmet, 1940, with separate metal skis. (Meant to be Finn)......	10.50	15.75	21.00
(B136) 785 Skier in white, no skis...............	8.00	12.00	16.00

B194   B195   B196   B197

B198

Photo by Don Pielin

B199   B200   B205

B225   B227   B226
Photo by Don Pielin

B201   B202   B203   B204   B206

B207   B208   B209   B210   B211   B212
Photo by Ed Poole

	G	VG	M
(B137) Skier in brown, no skis	10.00	15.00	20.00
(B138) 785 Skier in red, meant to be Russian....	No Price Found		
(B139) Diver with axe.....	200.00	300.00	400.00
(B140) 788 Marching with slung rifle, cast helmet...	8.00	12.00	16.00
(B141) 789 Soldier with AA gun, cast helmet, sitting..	7.00	10.50	14.00
(B142) 790 Two soldiers on raft, cast helmet........	24.00	36.00	48.00
(B143) 791 Two-man rocket team	6.25	9.38	12.50
(B144) 792 Mechanic with airplane engine, prop spins	15.00	22.50	30.00
(B144a) Same as above, variation in engine......	No Price Found		
(B145) Soldier kneeling with anti-tank gun, cast helmet	15.00	22.50	30.00
(B146) Doctor treating soldier	37.50	56.25	75.00
(B147) 951 Radio operator with separate antenna ($\frac{2}{3}$ price without antenna)...	10.50	15.75	21.00
(B148) 952 Walking with dog, tin helmet........	9.00	13.50	18.00
(B149) 953 American Legionaire in overseas cap, tall, made for 1937 Legion convention in New York, 12 known color combinations........	66.00	99.00	132.00
(B150) 954? American Legionaire flag-bearer, tall, cloth flag, made in 1937, as above, four known..............	300.00	450.00	600.00
(B151) 961 Typist with typewriter and wooden table	10.00	15.00	20.00
(B151A) 961 Typist alone..	4.50	6.75	9.00
(B152) Motorcycle with side-car..................	9.00	13.50	18.00
(B153) Two-man machine-gun car, number 45.....	20.00	30.00	40.00
(B154) 714 Pirate........	6.50	9.75	13.00
(B155) Knight with pennant	6.50	9.75	13.00
(B155a) Knight with pennant, flat underbase, may be Jones..............	No Price Found		
(B156) 712 Knight with shield................	5.50	8.25	11.00
(B156a) 712 Knight with shield, early version, flat underbase, rather than			

	G	VG	M
concave, may be Jones...		No Price Found	
(B157) 610? Woman with dog	5.50	8.25	11.00
(B158) 611 Man with over-coat over arm	3.75	5.63	7.50
(B159) 612? Redcap with bags, black	10.00	15.00	20.00
(B160) 613 Railroad Porter, black	5.50	8.25	11.00
(B161) 614? Train conductor	4.50	6.75	9.00
(B162) 615 Train mechanic.	5.75	8.63	11.50
(B163) 616 Little boy in jacket	5.25	7.38	10.50
(B164) 617 Little girl in coat	4.75	7.63	9.50
(B165) 618 Woman with pocketbook	7.50	11.25	15.00
(B166) 619 Old man......	6.00	9.00	12.00
(B167) 620 Minister walking	11.00	16.50	22.00
(B168) 620 Minister holding hat	5.50	8.25	11.00
(B169) 621 Newsboy......	4.00	6.00	8.00
(B170) 622 Shoeshine Boy..	4.50	6.75	9.00
(B171) 623 Detective with pistol	33.00	49.50	66.00
(B172) 624 Burglar........	22.50	33.75	45.00
(B173) 625 Bride..........	7.50	11.25	15.00
(B174) 626 Groom........	7.00	10.50	14.00
(B175) 627? Little girl in rocking chair..........	4.25	6.38	8.50
(B176) **628 Boy Skater.....**	4.75	7.63	9.50
(B177) **629 Girl Skater.....**	4.50	6.75	9.00
(B178) **630 1/2 Man and Woman on Park Bench..**	9.00	13.50	18.00
(B179) Seated man and woman in winter coats...	6.00	9.00	12.00
(B180) **635 Man Speed Skater**	4.50	6.75	9.00
(B181) **636 Girl Figure Skater**...............	4.00	6.00	8.00
(B182) Boy Scout with staff.	5.50	8.25	11.00
(B183) 802 Boy Scout saluting	14.50	21.75	29.00
(B184) 803 Boy Scout signaling	14.50	21.75	29.00
(B185) Scout frying eggs over fire.............	16.50	24.75	33.00
(B186) 850 Policeman, arm raised	5.00	7.50	10.00
(B186a) Same as above, oval base, not shown........	3.00	4.50	6.00
(B187) Fireman with axe...	10.00	15.00	20.00
(B187a) Fireman with axe, flat base (not shown)....		No Price Found	
(B188) 852 Fireman with hose..................	10.00	15.00	20.00
(B189) 853 Mailman.......	6.00	9.00	12.00

B219   B220   B221

B222   B223

Photo by Ed Poole

B213   B214   B215   B216   B217

B224   B232   B233   B234   B235   B236

B237   B218   B238   B239   B240   B241

Photo by Ed Poole

	G	VG	M
(B190) **495 Man on skis....**	6.00	9.00	12.00
(B191) **496 Girl on skis....**	6.00	9.00	12.00
(B192) **497 Man on Sled...**	5.25	7.88	10.50
(B193) **498 Girl on Sled....**	5.00	7.50	10.00
(B194) **499 Santa Claus on Sled**	10.00	15.00	20.00
(B195) **500 Santa Claus on Skis**..................	24.00	36.00	48.00
(B195a) **500 Santa Claus on Skis,** no skis, or poles, and no holes for them...		No Price Found	
(B196) Santa Claus with hol-ly sprig..............	32.00	48.00	64.00
(B197) Santa Claus seated, bag of toys at side, made to ride in sleigh.........	100.00	150.00	200.00

B242 B243 B244 B245 B246 B255 B256 B257

B258 B259 B260 B261 B262

Photo by Ed Poole

B228 B229 B230 B231 B247 B248 B250 B249 B251

B252 B253 B254 B263 B265 B266 B267 B268 B269 B270

Photo by Don Pielin

	G	VG	M
(B198) **510 One Horse Open Sleigh** (Sleigh, horse, seated man and woman).	25.00	37.50	50.00
(B199) **530 Man Pulling Children on Sled**	9.00	13.50	18.00
(B200) **535 Young Man Putting Skates on Girl Sitting on Bench**	13.00	19.50	26.00

Post-World War II

	G	VG	M
(B201) **701** Flagbearer, pot helmet	14.50	21.75	29.00
(B202) **703?** Kneeling, firing rifle	12.00	18.00	24.00
(B203) **705** Port Arms	11.00	16.50	22.00
(B204) **707** Order Arms	11.00	16.50	22.00
(B205) 708 Officer with Sword	11.50	17.25	23.00
(B206) **728** Prone Machine Gunner	10.50	15.75	21.00
(B207) 737 Tommy-Gunner	6.00	9.00	12.00
(B208) **747** Standing Firing Rifle	5.50	8.25	11.00

	G	VG	M
(B209) 774 AA Gunner	6.25	9.38	12.50
(B210) 777 Marching at Slope	10.00	15.00	20.00
(B211) **788** Marching, rifle slung	6.00	9.00	12.00
(B212) **789** AA Gunner	9.50	14.25	19.00
(B212a) Cowboy, two pistols, one in air (not shown)	8.00	12.00	16.00
(B213) Drum Major	14.50	21.75	29.00
(B214) Drummer	17.00	25.50	34.00
(B215) Bugler	17.50	26.25	35.00
(B216) Clarinetist	16.50	24.75	33.00
(B217) Tubist	16.00	24.00	32.00
(B218) Sailor	13.00	19.50	26.00

BARCLAY POD FOOT SERIES, Circa 1950s to 1971

	G	VG	M
(B219) **81 Two Soldier Crew at Radar Equipt**	14.00	21.00	28.00
(B220) **82 Three Soldier Crew at Range Finder**	22.00	33.00	44.00
(B221) **83 Two Soldier Crew at Searchlight**	10.50	15.75	21.00
(B222) **84 Two Soldier Crew at Mobile Cannon**	7.50	11.25	15.00
(B223) **85 Two Soldier Crew at A.A. Gun**	12.50	18.75	25.00
(B224) **187 Officer on Horse** (pot helmet)	25.00	37.50	50.00
(B225) **188 Cowboy on Horse** (lasso)	5.00	7.50	10.00
(B226) **189 Indian on Horse**	10.50	15.75	21.00
(B227) **190 Cowboy with Pistol on Horse**	10.00	15.00	20.00
(B228) **800 Black Knight w/Sword & Shield**	25.00	37.50	50.00
(B229) **801 Knight w/Red & Blue Shield & Sword**	25.00	37.50	50.00
(B230) **802 Knight w/Orange & Black Shield & Sword**	6.25	9.38	12.50
(B231) **803 Knight w/Red & Green Shield & Sword**	4.00	6.00	8.00
(B232) **901 Soldier Flag Bearer**	4.75	7.63	9.50
(B233) **903 Soldier Sniper** (kneeling)	4.50	6.75	9.00
(B233A) 903 same as above, in red	4.50	12.00	16.00
(B234) **906 Soldier Charging**	4.50	6.75	9.00
(B235) **908 Soldier Officer**	3.75	5.63	7.50
(B235A) 908 Soldier Officer in blue	9.25	13.88	18.50
(B236) **909 Soldier Bugler**	3.50	5.25	7.00
(B237) **919 Sailor White Uniform**	4.00	6.00	8.00

B271   B272   B273   B274   All others are 300 series

Photo by Don Pielin

	G	VG	M
(B238) **920 Sailor Blue Uniform**	4.50	6.75	9.00
(B239) **922 Marine**	3.50	5.25	7.00
(B240) **928 Soldier Machine Gunner Lying Flat**	4.50	6.75	9.00
(B241) **929 Soldier w/Pistol, Crawling**	7.00	10.50	14.00
(B242) **937 Soldier, Charging Machine Gunner** (holding tommy gun)	3.75	5.63	7.50
(B243) **938 Soldier Bomb Thrower**	4.50	6.75	9.00
(B244) **941 Aviator**	5.50	8.25	11.00
(B245) **947 Soldier Marksman**	3.50	5.25	7.00
(B246) **948 Soldier Running** .	3.00	4.50	6.00
(B247) **950 Cowboy w/Pistol Shooting**	2.50	3.75	5.00

	G	VG	M
(B248) **951 Cowboy w/Rifle** .	3.50	5.25	7.00
(B249) **952 Cowboy w/Lasso**	4.50	6.75	9.00
(B250) **953 Cowboy w/Pistol** (upraised)	5.50	8.25	11.00
(B251) **954 Indian w/Shield & Tomahawk**	5.00	7.50	10.00
(B252) **955 Indian w/Rifle** . .	2.50	3.75	5.00
(B253) **956 Indian w/Knife & Spear**	5.00	7.50	10.00
(B254) **957 Indian w/Bow & Arrow**	4.00	6.00	8.00
(B255) **960 Soldier, Wounded, w/Crutches**	10.00	15.00	20.00
(B256) **961 Soldier, Wounded Head & Arm**	5.00	7.50	10.00
(B257) **962 Nurse**	11.00	16.50	22.00
(B258) **974 Soldier, Anti-Aircraft Gunner**	5.00	7.50	10.00
(B259) **977 Soldier Under Marching Orders** (Marching)	3.50	5.25	7.00
(B260) **988 Soldier, Marching w/Gun on Back** (Gun slung over shoulder)	3.75	5.63	7.50
(B261) **990 Soldier w/Bazooka**	5.00	7.50	10.00
(B262) **991 Soldier Flame Thrower**	3.75	5.63	7.50
(B262a) 991, same as above, in red	8.00	12.00	16.00

Japanese "Barclays". Most were nearly exact copies, even to the early Barclay "eye", but the sailor flagbearer appears to be a conversion of B49. Other known copies resemble B16, B18, B55.

BARCLAY Box, circa 1939, known to be used for Train Figures and a signal corps set.
Photo by Bill Kaufman

"Midi" Size (Smaller Than Pod Foot)

	G	VG	M
(B263) Flame Thrower	6.00	9.00	12.00
(B264) Bugler	6.00	9.00	12.00
(B265) Officer With Binoculars	6.00	9.00	12.00
(B266) Talking on Field Phone	6.00	9.00	12.00
(B267) Advancing With Rifle	6.00	9.00	12.00
(B268) Marching, slung rifle	6.00	9.00	12.00
(B269) Firing Bazooka	6.00	9.00	12.00
(B270) Firing Tommygun	6.00	9.00	12.00
(B270a) Walking forward, rifle at side, pointing down	10.00	15.00	20.00
(B271) Cowboy with Rifle	3.00	4.50	6.00
(B272) Cowboy with Pistol	3.00	4.50	6.00
(B273) Indian with Hatchet	3.00	4.50	6.00
(B274) Indian with Rifle	3.00	4.50	6.00

More Japanese "Barclays". Value in mint is about $30.00.
Photo courtesy Richard Prindiville

After the War, Barclay introduced a number of small civilians to go with the increasingly popular HO trains. These sell for five dollars apiece in mint condition. They consist of: 350 **Policeman**; 351 **Man**; 352 **Woman**; 353 **Conductor**; 354 **Redcap**; 355 **Oiler**; 356 **Brakeman**; 357 **Engineer**; 358 **Porter**; 359 **Dining Steward**; 360 **Hobo**; 361 **Newsboy**; 362 **Mailman**; 363 **Fireman**; 366 **Peg-Legged Gateman**; 369 **Woman Carrying Baby**; 370 **Little Boy**; 371 **Little Girl**; 372 **Bride**; 373 **Groom**.

	G	VG	M
BARCLAY Box only, circa 1939, 15"x4½"x2", 12 soldiers, coast gun, searchlight pictured, plus pictures of cowboys, Indians and Boy Scouts on sides of box. These boxes are known to have contained train figures and "No.50/30 7-Piece Signal Soldier Set"	80.00	120.00	160.00
BARCLAY Boxed set of winter figures, post-war	100.00	150.00	200.00

MANOIL
(See also Vehicles, Aircraft, Ships, Trains and Miscellaneous)

Manoil began production of toy soldiers in 1935. It was in business as early as 1927 under the name Jack Manoil, turning out metal lamps and novelties at 34 West Houston Street in New York City. The company changed its name to Man-O-Lamp Corporation on July 11, 1928, and was owned by Maurice Manoil (12/4/1893-9/15/74) and Jack Manoil (1/29/02-9/1/55), two brothers who had emigrated from Rumania in the early 1900s. The final name-change to Manoil Manufacturing Co., Inc. took place on July 7, 1934.

The two brothers were essentially partners, with Maurice handling the business end of the operation and Jack, who oversaw the creative area, working closely with Walter Baetz (1894-1978), who sculpted all the company's toys.

Manoil advanced firmly into toy-making in 1934, with seven vehicles, and moved to other addresses as it grew, leaving Manhattan in 1937 for Brooklyn, and then in June, 1940, moving to Waverly, New York (which afforded excellent shipping by rail), employing 225 people at its peak.

With the onset of World War II, Manoil shut down, but then resumed production of soldiers in a fine-grained composition form (employing sulphur) in January, 1944. Brittle, the pieces were ultimately unsuccessful, and their manufacture ended by the end of the year.

After the Second World War, the company introduced several new lines of soldiers, (also containing some of its pre-War soldiers and its appealing Happy Farm series), but they were no longer distributed as widely.

Manoil's soldiers have a distinctive jauntiness to them, at times veering on caricature, the latter trait becoming more pronounced as the years wore on. In 1953 the firm moved to a smaller location in Waverly, changing its name to Jack Manoil Specialty Company, but went out of business shortly after Jack's death. Baetz and Jack Manoil were both keenly interested in the company's soldiers and would work late into the night as they collaborated on ideas for them. One of Baetz's continuing concerns was to design the molds so that there was no structural weakness in the soldiers as a result of air bubbles. For this reason, many of Manoil's soldiers were redesigned a number of times, sometimes with subtle and sometimes with broad variations.

Unlike Barclay, Manoil also produced plastic toys, selling millions of vehicles and airplanes in its later years. Models of Manoil and Barclay soldiers are being reproduced (see Leading Collectors and Dealers), hollow-cast from the original molds. All bold words and numbers are Manoil's own description.

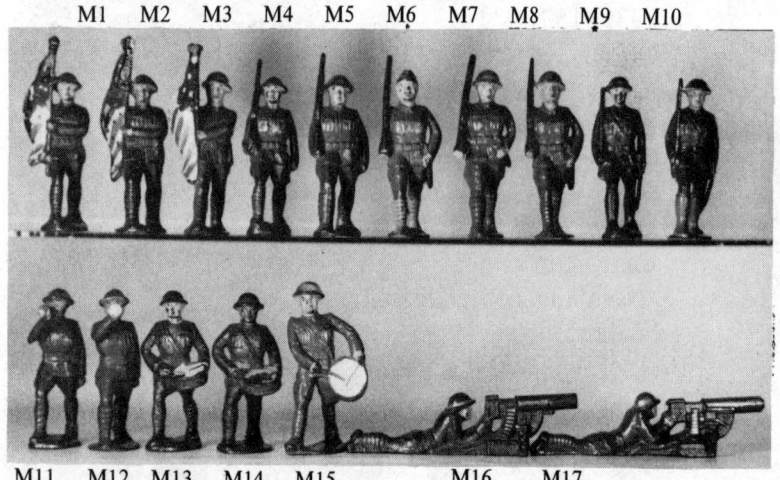

M1 M2 M3 M4 M5 M6 M7 M8 M9 M10

M11 M12 M13 M14 M15   M16 M17
Photo by Bill Kaufman

M38b
Photo by Norbert Schachter
Courtesy Peter & Marjorie Ruben

M58a
Photo by Don Pielin

M23
Photo by Ed Poole

	G	VG	M
(M1) **7 Flag Bearer,** hollow base version	30.00	45.00	60.00
(M2) **7 Flag Bearer,** second version	5.00	7.50	10.00
(M3) **7 Flag Bearer,** third version	5.00	7.50	10.00
(M4) **8 Parade,** hollow base version	15.00	22.50	30.00
(M5) **8 Parade,** stocky version	8.00	12.00	16.00
(M6) **8 Parade,** campaign cap straight on head	12.00	18.00	24.00
(M7) **8 Parade,** number on back	30.00	45.00	60.00
(M8) **8 Parade,** fifth version	4.50	6.75	9.00
(M9) **9 Officer,** hollow base version	26.00	39.00	52.00
(m10) **9 Officer,** second version	7.50	11.25	15.00
(M11) **10 Bugler,** hollow base version	40.00	60.00	80.00
(M12) 10 Bugler, second version	7.50	11.25	15.00
(M13) **11 Drummer,** hollow base version	20.00	30.00	40.00

This rare GREY IRON, Palm Tree, 1¾″ high, sold at an auction in 1983 for $560. It was originally sold as part of GREY IRON's Ethiopians and Italians toy soldier set.

Photo courtesy of John Alliston.

(left to right)
Mix-ette Mixer, Wash-o-Matic Washing Machine, Linda Lee Laundromat, Jig-Saw-Matic Jigsaw, Kitchen-ette Stove and Sink.

Photo by Ron Chojnacki.
Courtesy of Don Hultzman.

(Above)
MARX, "Reversible Coupe, The Marvel Car".

Photo courtesy of Dick and Nancy Dice.

(Above)
MANOIL, 702 Coupe and 703 Wrecker.

Photo by Bill Kaufman.
Courtesy of the Good Old Days Store.

(Below)
Pre-WW II, BARCLAY vehicles.

Photo courtesy of George Buhler

TOOTSIETOY,
0805 Mack "Tootsietoy Dairy"
Semi-Trailer Truck,
1932.

KEYSTONE,
"Moving Van,
Long Distance Hauling".

Photo courtesy of Mapes Auctioneers and Appraisers.

"Champion" Wrecker, 7½″ long.

*Photo by Bill Kaufman.
Courtesy of the Good Old Days Store.*

CRAGSTAN,
"Schoolbus",
(left to right)
CRAGSTAN, Western Locomotive
and New Bell Ringer
Choo-Choo.

Photo by Ron Chojnacki.
Courtesy of Don Hultzman.

(top to bottom)
Tank M-4,
a Combat Tank, Tank X-3,
and Tank M-103.

Photo by Ron Chojnacki.
Courtesy of Don Hultzman.

WOLVERINE,
Diving Submarine, 13″ long.
(see SHIPS)

Photo by Bill Kaufman.
Courtesy of the
Good Old Days Store.

Fire Pumper, cast iron, 11″ long.

Photo by Bill Kaufman.
Courtesy of the Good Old Days Store.

OHIO,
Fire Truck, 10½″ long.

Photo by Bill Kaufman.
Courtesy of the
Good Old Days Store.

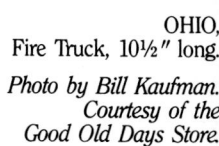

HUBER,
Steam Roller, cast iron,
8″ long.

*Photo courtesy of Dick and
Nancy Dice.*

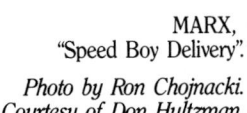

MARX,
"Speed Boy Delivery".

*Photo by Ron Chojnacki.
Courtesy of Don Hultzman.*

NY-LINT,
"Elgin Street Sweeper".

*Photo by Bill Kaufman.
Courtesy of the
Good Old Days Store.*

NIFTY,
Toonerville Trolley.

*Photo courtesy of
Bob Black, Jr.*

MARX,
"Toytown Dairy", tin wind-up.

*Photo by Bill Kaufman.
Courtesy of the Good Old Days Store.*

AUBURN RUBBER,
#231 "Infantry Set",
copyright 1939, sold
for $100.

*Photo by Bill Kaufman.
Courtesy of the
Good Old Days Store.*

AUBURN RUBBER,
Toy Soldiers, boxed set,
sold for $60.

*Photo by Bill Kaufman.
Courtesy of the
Good Old Days Store.*

SOLJERTOYS,
boxed set, circa 1932.

Photo by Ed Poole.

IDEAL, Soldiers.

*Photo by Bill Kaufman.
Courtesy of Hank Anton.*

Toy Soldiers
made by unknown manufacturers
(see "Unknown" in the SOLDIERS section).

Photo courtesy of Hank Anton.

Mint boxed set of "Unknowns"
UC12, UC13, UC15, UC16.
These were probably produced in
New Jersey, by two ex-Barclay workers.

Photo courtesy of Hank Anton.

IDEAL, Train Figures.

*Photo by Bill Kaufman.
Courtesy of Hank Anton.*

JONES,
Farmer and Wife with
BARCLAY Animals.

*Photo courtesy of
Bob Black, Jr.*

(left to right)
Bear-The Cashier, Old
Fashion-Telephone Bear,
Washing Bear, Ice Cream Eating
Bear.

*Photo by Ron Chojnacki.
Courtesy of Don Hultzman.*

(left to right)
Balloon Blowing Bear,
Balloon Blowing Monkey, Bubble
Blowing Monkey.

*Photo by Ron Chojnacki.
Courtesy of Don Hultzman.*

(left to right)
Teddy-The Rhythmical Drummer,
Major Tooty, McGregor,
Cycling Daddy.

*Photo by Ron Chojnacki.
Courtesy of Don Hultzman.*

(left to right)
Warpath Indian, Nutty
Mad Indian, Indian Joe.

*Photo by Ron Chojnacki.
Courtesy of Don Hultzman.*

(left to right)
Drinking Captain, High
Jinks of the Circus, CRAGSTAN Playboy.

Photo by Ron Chojnacki.
Courtesy of Don Hultzman.

(left to right)
Roaring Gorilla, Mighty Kong,
Dancing Merry Chimp.

Photo by Ron Chojnacki.
Courtesy of Don Hultzman.

(above photo, left to right)
Super Astronaut, Attacking
Martian, Smoking Robot.

Photo by Ron Chojnacki.
Courtesy of Don Hultzman.

CHEIN,
"Ferris Wheel",
1930's version.

Photo by Ron Chojnacki.
Courtesy of Don Hultzman.

KEYSTONE, Riding Airplane.

Photo courtesy of Bob Black, Jr.

HUBLEY, Plane.

Photo courtesy of Bob Black, Jr.

STRAUSS, "Mailplane", tin wind-up.

Photo by Bill Kaufman. Courtesy of the Good Old Days Store.

TOOTSIETOY, 719 Crusader.

Photo by Bill Kaufman. Courtesy of the Good Old Days Store.

MARX, Castle Fort.
Photo courtesy of Bob Black, Jr.

BUILT-RITE, #100-A.
Photo courtesy of Ed Poole.

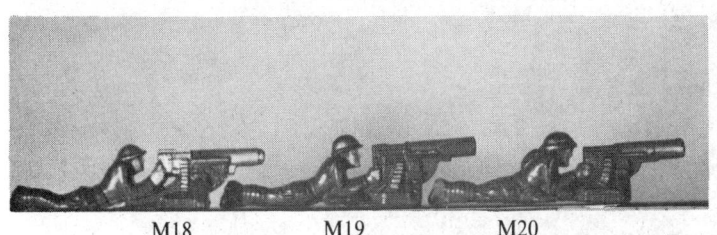

M18　　　M19　　　M20

M21　M22　M23　M24　M25　M26　M27a　M27

Photos by Bill Kaufman

M28　M29　　M30　M31　M32　M35　M36

M37　M38　M38a　M39　　M40　　M41

Photo by Bill Kaufman

	G	VG	M
(M22) **13 Cadet,** second version	6.00	9.00	12.00
(M23) **14 Sailor,** hollow base	20.00	30.00	40.00
(M24) **14 Sailor,** second version	5.00	7.50	10.00
M25) **15 Marine,** hollow base	30.00	45.00	60.00
(M26) **15 Marine,** second version	5.50	8.25	11.00
(M27) **16 Ensign**	10.00	15.00	20.00
(M27a) **16 Ensign,** hollow base	22.50	33.75	45.00
(M28) **17 Signal Man,** hollow base version	19.00	28.50	38.00
(M29) **17 Signal Man,** second version	5.50	8.25	11.00
(M30) **18 Cowboy,** hollow base version	15.00	22.50	30.00
(M31) **18 Cowboy,** second version	7.00	10.50	14.00
(M32) **18A Cowboy With Hands Up**	7.50	11.25	15.00
(M33) **18A Cowboy With Hands Up** (subtle variation)	7.50	11.25	15.00
(M34) **20 Doctor** (same as 20K, but in white)	5.00	7.50	10.00
(M35) **20K Doctor** (Khaki) . .	6.00	9.00	12.00
(M36) **21 Nurse**	4.50	6.75	9.00
(M36a) **21 Nurse,** no hem in skirt, shorter, etc	No Price Found		
(M37) **Indian with hatchet** . .	40.00	60.00	80.00
(M38) **22 Indian,** with knives, straight hair on side	6.00	9.00	12.00
(M38aa) **22 Indian** with knives, same as above, braided hair on side (not shown)	No Price Found		
(M38a) **22 Indian,** with knives, right toes off base	6.00	9.00	12.00

	G	VG	M
(M14) **11 Drummer,** stocky version	9.00	13.50	18.00
(M15) **11 Drummer,** vertical drum	9.00	13.50	18.00
(M16) **12 Machine Gunner (Prone),** grass on base . . .	10.00	15.00	20.00
(M17) **12 Machine Gunner (Prone),** flat base, no grass	7.00	10.50	14.00
(M18) **12 Machine Gunner (Prone),** spaces under body	7.00	10.50	14.00
(M19) **12 Machine Gunner (Prone),** no aperture between hands and gun	8.00	12.00	16.00
M20) **12 Machine Gunner (Prone),** no aperture, pack on back	8.00	12.00	16.00
(M21) **13 Cadet,** hollow base	20.00	30.00	40.00

M42　　M43　　M44　　M45　　M46　　M47

M48　M49　M50　M51　　M52　M53

Photo by Bill Kaufman

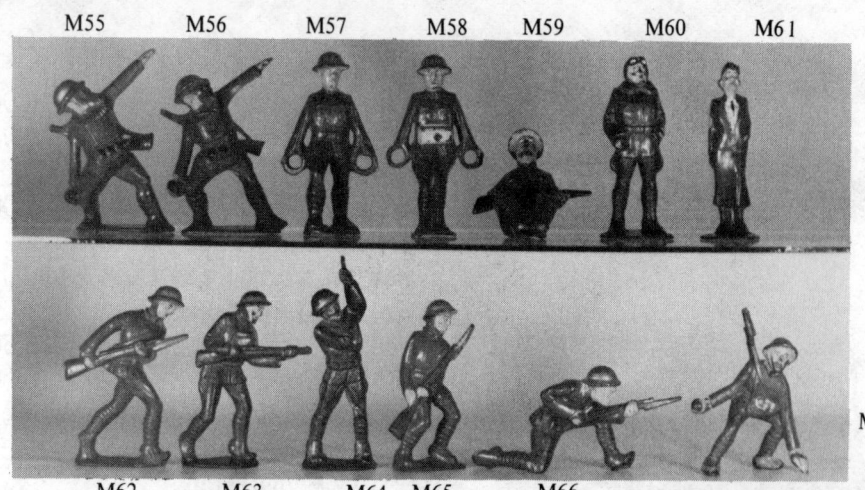

Photo by Bill Kaufman

M36a   M36
Photo by K. Warren Mitchell

	G	VG	M
M38b) 22 Indian, with knives, sarong-like garment, only one known...	No Price Found		
(M39) 23 Machine Gunner Sitting, seated on four pillows, bullets feed from ammo box.............	10.00	15.00	20.00
(M40) 23 Machine Gunner Sitting, markings under base................	No Price Found		
(M41) 23 Machine Gunner Sitting, squarer-looking, markings near right leg..	8.50	12.75	17.00
(M42) 24 Cannon Loader...	8.00	12.00	16.00
(M43) 25 Sniper (Kneeling), hollow base, (may not be Manoil)...............	37.50	56.25	75.00
(M44) 25 Sniper (Kneeling), folding rifle...........	40.00	60.00	80.00
(M45) 25 Sniper (Kneeling), short thin rifle........	8.00	12.00	16.00
(M46) 25 Sniper (Kneeling), longer, thicker rifle.....	7.50	11.25	15.00
(M47) 26 Sniper, folding rifle................	40.00	60.00	80.00
(M48) 26 Sniper.........	7.00	10.50	14.00

	G	VG	M
(M48a) 26 Sniper, shorter rifle, angle different on underside of rifle.......	8.00	12.00	16.00
(M49) 27 Tommy Gunner, bloated version.........	15.00	22.50	30.00
(M50) 27 Tommy Gunner, second version.........	5.50	8.25	11.00
(M51) 28 Observer........	9.00	13.50	18.00
(M52) 29 Wounded Soldier (Walking)	9.00	13.50	18.00
(M53) 30 Wounded Soldier (Lying)	7.00	10.50	14.00
(M54) 30 Wounded Soldier (Lying), number on back, shorter head..........	8.00	12.00	16.00
(M55) 31 Bomb Thrower, three grenades in pouch..	7.00	10.50	14.00
(M56) 31 Bomb Thrower, two grenades in pouch...	8.00	12.00	16.00
(M57) 32 Stretcher Carrier, no medical kit..........	6.00	9.00	12.00
(M58) 32 Stretcher Carrier, medical kit...........	7.00	10.50	14.00
(M58a) 32 Stretcher Carrier, medical kit, number on back, buttons on uniform, different pockets and collar from above........	35.00	52.50	70.00

M79　M80　M81

M82　M83　M84　M85　M86

Photo by Bill Kaufman

M87　M88　M89　M90　M91　M92

M93　M94　M95　M96　M97　M98　M99　M100

Photo by Bill Kaufman

M101　M102　M103　M104　M105　M106

M107　M108　M109　M110　M111

Photo by Bill Kaufman

	G	VG	M
(M59) 33 Sitting Soldier...	9.50	14.25	19.00
(M60) 34 Aviator........	8.00	12.00	16.00
(M61) 35 Hostess, in white or green.............	24.00	36.00	48.00
(M61a) 35 Hostess in Khaki	No Price Found		
(M62) 36 Soldier With Bayonet Charging......	14.00	21.00	28.00
(M63) 37 Soldier With Gun Charging.............	15.00	22.50	30.00
(M64) 38 Soldier With Gun Butting..............	8.50	12.75	17.00

	G	VG	M
(M65) 39 Soldier With Bayonet Jabbing.......	12.00	18.00	24.00
(M66) 40 Soldier (Kneeling With Bayonet)........	18.00	27.00	36.00
(M67) 41 Soldier (Crouching With Hand Grenade)....	30.00	45.00	60.00
(M68) 42 Field Doctor (Crawling)............	15.00	22.50	30.00
(M69) 43 Officer (Lying Down - Shooting Revolver).............	11.00	16.50	22.00
(M70) 44 Crawling Scout With Gun, left leg high (only two known).......	42.00	63.00	84.00
(M71) 44 Crawling Scout With Gun, left leg lower.	20.00	30.00	40.00
(M72) 45 Observer (With Periscope)............	11.00	16.50	22.00
(M73) 46 Anti-Aircraft Gunner, barrel of gun drops below arm.............	6.50	9.75	13.00
(M74) 46 Anti-Aircraft Gunner, barrel of gun ends at arm.................	7.00	10.50	14.00
(M75) 47 Anti-Aircraft Searchlight............	6.50	9.75	13.00
(M75a) 47 like above, with tin lens..............	55.00	82.50	110.00
(M75b) 47 like M75, number on back, helmet looks as if it was adapted to look like WW II helmet...............	7.00	10.50	14.00
(M76) 48 Navy Gunner	8.50	12.75	17.00
(M77) 49 Policeman.......	7.50	11.25	15.00
(M78) 49 Policeman, slightly larger version (not shown)	7.50	11.25	15.00
(M79) 50 Bicycle Dispatch Rider.................	8.00	12.00	16.00
(M80) 51 Motorized Machine Gunner.......	22.00	33.00	44.00
(M81) 52 Motorcycle Rider, number over rear wheel, grass base.............	11.00	16.50	22.00
(M81a) 52 Same as above, motor variation (not shown)	No Price Found		
(M82) 52 Motorcycle Rider.	18.00	27.00	36.00
(M83) 53 Sitting Soldier Without Gun..........	10.00	15.00	20.00
(M84) 54 Sitting Soldier Eating..............	17.00	25.50	34.00
(M85) 55 Sitting Soldier At Table With Phone & Map	9.00	13.50	18.00
(M86) 56 Paymaster.......	70.00	105.00	140.00
(M87) 57 Camouflage Sharpshooter Lying Down....	9.00	13.50	18.00

	G	VG	M
(M88) **58 Parachute Jumper**	8.00	12.00	16.00
(M89) **59 Soldier Writing Letter**	30.00	45.00	60.00
(M89a) Same as above, foot not curled up, pencil is flat		No Price Found	
(M90) **60 Cook's Helper With Ladle,** normal helmet	10.50	15.75	21.00
(M91) **60 Cook's Helper with Ladle,** helmet looks as if it was adapted to look like WW II helmet . .	48.00	72.00	96.00
(M92) **61 Soldier With Camera**	20.00	30.00	40.00
(M92a) **Soldier With Camera,** thinner arm	20.00	30.00	40.00
(M93) **62 Soldier With Gas Mask & Gun**	9.50	14.25	19.00
(M94) **63 Soldier With Gas Mask With Flare Pistol.**	5.50	8.25	11.00
(M95) **64 Soldier Playing Banjo**	16.50	24.75	33.00
(M96) **65 Deep Sea Diver** . .	8.50	12.75	17.00
(M97) **65 Deep Sea Diver with "65" on chest**	8.00	12.00	16.00
(M98) **66 Soldier With Gun on Parade with Overseas Cap**	19.00	28.50	38.00
(M99) **67 Soldier With Gun And Pack Marching**	4.00	6.00	8.00
(M100) **68 Soldier Boxing** . .	30.00	45.00	60.00
(101) **77 Lineman & Telephone Pole,** pole comes with two different-shaped bases, oval or diagonal	20.00	30.00	40.00
(M102) **78 Anti-Tank Gun,** round shield, all 4 variations based on Vickers 2.95 mountain gun	9.50	14.25	19.00
(M103) **78 Anti-Tank Gun,** squared shield	12.00	18.00	24.00
(M103a) **78 Anti-Tank Gun,** angled shield (not shown).		No Price Found	
(M104) **78 Anti-Tank Gun,** wooden wheels (not shown)	37.50	56.25	75.00
(M105) **79 Soldier marching with gun slung at angle** . .	70.00	105.00	140.00
(M106) **80 Anti-Aircraft Machine Gunner**	9.50	14.25	19.00
(M107) **81 Machine Gunner and Helper,** aperture between hand and machine gun	11.00	16.50	22.00

M112a M113 MJ14 M115 M116 M117 M118
Photo by Bill Kaufman

M119 M120 M121 M122 M123 M124
Photo by Bill Kaufman

M125 M126 M127

M128 M129-M131
Photo by Bill Kaufman

M132 M133 M134 M135 M137 M138 M139
Photo by Don Pielin

	G	VG	M
(M108) **81 Machine Gunner and Helper,** no aperture .	7.50	11.25	15.00
(M109) **82 Anti-Aircraft With Range Finder**	8.00	12.00	16.00
(M110) **83 Soldier Trench Mortar**	9.00	13.50	18.00
(M111) **84 Soldier With Shell**	10.50	15.75	21.00
(M112) **85 Aviator Holding Bomb**	7.00	10.50	14.00
(M112a) **85 Aviator Holding Bomb** (hand variation) . . .	10.00	15.00	20.00
(M113) **86 Aviator Mechanic With Propellor,** away from head	75.00	112.50	150.00

M141 M142   M143 M144   M145 M146

M177 M178 M179 M180 M181   M182

M147 M148   M149 M150   M151 M154
Photo by Don Pielin

M183   M184   M185   M186
Photo by Ed Poole

M152 M153   M155 M156 M157 M158 M159 M160 M161

M187 M188   M189 M190   M191 M192 M193

M162   M163 M164 M165 M166 M167 M168 M169
Photo by Don Pielin

M194   M195   M196   M197
Photo by Ed Poole

M173

M170 M171 M72   M174   M175   M176
Photo by Ed Poole

	G	VG	M
(M117) **89 Radio Operator (Lying Down)**	11.00	16.50	22.00
(M118) **90 Soldier Digging Trench**	22.00	33.00	44.00
(M119) **91 Soldier With Barbed Wire**, wide-faced version	12.50	18.75	25.00
(M120) **91 Soldier With Barbed Wire**	9.00	13.50	18.00
(M121) **92 Fire Fighter** in white or grey (add $17.00 to grey in mint)	23.00	34.50	46.00
(M122) **93 Soldier On Guard Duty**	55.00	82.50	110.00
(M123) **94 Soldier Running With Cannon**	7.50	11.25	15.00
(M124) **94 Soldier Running With Cannon**, wood wheels, thin face	13.00	19.50	26.00
(M125) **99 Finn with Skis**	16.50	24.75	33.00

	G	VG	M
(M114) **86 Aviator Mechanic With Propellor**	60.00	90.00	120.00
(M115) 87 Aviator carrying bomb sight	10.50	15.75	21.00
(M115a) 87 Aviator carrying bomb sight, smaller base (not shown)		No Price Found	
(M116) **88 Radio Operator Standing**	15.00	22.50	30.00

M198   M199   M200   M201

M202   M203   M204   M205   M206

Photo by Ed Poole

	G	VG	M
(M126) 100 Finn Machine Gunner	14.00	21.00	28.00
(M127) 101 Soldier Jumping with Chute	30.00	45.00	60.00
(M128) 102 Soldier Jumping With Machine Gun	33.00	49.50	66.00

HAPPY FARM SERIES

	G	VG	M
(129) 41/1 Bench	3.00	4.50	6.00
(M130) 41/2 Girl	2.25	3.38	4.50
(M131) 41/3 Young Man . . .	2.25	3.38	4.50
(132) 41/4 Man Carrying Sack on Back	13.00	19.50	26.00
(M133) 41/5 Farmer Pitching Sheaves	15.00	22.50	30.00
(M134) 41/6 Farmer Sharpening Scythe	11.00	16.50	22.00
(M135) 41/7 Blacksmith Making Horse-Shoes	6.50	9.75	13.00
(M136) 41/8 Farmer Cutting With Scythe	8.00	12.00	16.00
(M137) 41/9 Farmer Cutting Corn	11.00	16.50	22.00
(M138) 41/10 Farmer Sowing Grain	6.00	9.00	12.00
(M139) 41/11 Man Carrying Sheaves Under Arm	11.00	16.50	22.00
(M140) 41/12 Scarecrow With Top Hat	6.00	9.00	12.00
(M141) 41/13 Farmer Carrying Pumpkin	6.50	9.75	13.00
(M142) 41/14 Darky Eating Watermelon	30.00	45.00	60.00
(M143) 41/15 Scarecrow With Straw Hat	6.50	9.75	13.00
(M144) 41/16 Watchman Blowing Out Lantern	5.50	8.25	11.00
(M145) 41/17 Hod Carrier With Bricks	7.00	10.50	14.00

	G	VG	M
(M146) 41/18 Man Chopping Wood	11.00	16.50	22.00
(M147) 41/19 Mason Laying Bricks	14.00	21.00	28.00
(M148) 41/20 Man Dumping Wheel Barrow	12.00	18.00	24.00
(M149) 41/21 Old Man Fixing Shoe	12.00	18.00	24.00
(M150) 41/22 Blacksmith With Wheel	12.00	18.00	24.00
(M151) 41/23 Carpenter Carrying Door	5.50	8.25	11.00
(M152) 41/24 Hound	5.50	8.25	11.00
(M153) 41/25 Carpenter Sawing Lumber	13.00	19.50	26.00
(M154) 41/26 Carpenter With Square	15.00	22.50	30.00
(M155) 41/27 Sheperd With Flute	19.00	28.50	38.00
(M156) 41/28 Lady With Pie	9.50	14.25	19.00
(M157) 41/29 Lady With Child	8.00	12.00	16.00
(M158) 41/30 School Teacher	14.00	21.00	28.00
(M159) 41/31 Girl Watering Flowers	10.00	15.00	20.00
(M160) 41/32 Woman Lifting Hen From Nest	6.50	9.75	13.00
(M161) 41/33 Woman With Butter Churn	11.00	16.50	22.00
(M162) 41/34 Woman Laying Out Wash On Grass .	11.00	16.50	22.00
(M163) 41/35 Woman Sweeping With Broom . .	11.00	16.50	22.00
(M164) 41/36 Man Juggling Barrel (double price in khaki)	15.00	22.50	30.00
(M165) 41/37 Man Planting Tree	12.00	18.00	24.00
(M166) 41/38 Girl Picking Berries	16.00	24.00	32.00
(M167) 41/39 Farmer At Water Pump	9.00	13.50	18.00
(M168) 41/40 Boy Carrying Wood	10.00	15.00	20.00
(M169) 41/41 Stacks of Sheaves	10.00	15.00	20.00
(M169a) Boxed Happy Farm Set (10 pieces), $150.00 mint with box			

End Happy Farm Listing, Beginning Post-WW II

MANOIL Composition

	G	VG	M
(MC1) Prone machine-gunner	26.00	39.00	52.00
(MC2) Seated machine-gunner	25.00	37.50	50.00
(MC3) Motorcyclist	25.00	37.50	50.00
(MC3a) Motorcyclist, mirror variation of above	25.00	37.50	50.00
(MC4) Firing camouflaged AA gun	25.00	37.50	50.00

MC1
Photo by Bill Kaufman

MC2   MC4   MC3   MC5 (Vehicles)

MANOIL "X" LINE

Recently, previously unknown Manoils were found in the collection of Manoil relatives Marjorie and Peter Ruben. Some of these are hollow, and perhaps were actually produced and sold. Other are solid lead, and presumably were prototypes which for one reason or another were never produced. Those marked with an "H" after the code number are hollow, and those with an "S", solid. Those in the 500 series are not the same size as the ones they resemble in that series. The MXH 45/18 Soldier with Bazooka Cannon listed and pictured in the previous edition was included by mistake and has been removed from this volume. An MXS no number, tall cowboy was auctioned in 1983 as one of a lot of soldiers.

MXS16   MXS24   MXH50   MXH57   MXS62   MXS82   MXS 521 through MXS 530

MXS83   MXH88   MXH89   No. Nr.   MXH94
Poto by Norbert Schachter
Courtesy Marjorie and Peter Ruben

MXS 531 through MXS 535
Photo by Norbert Schachter
Courtesy Marjorie and Peter Ruben

MXS1 Military School Cadet?	No Price Found
MXS2 Cadet	No Price Found
MXS3 Sailor	No Price Found
MXS4 Cowboy, gun raised	No Price Found
MXH50 Bicycle Dispatch Rider, WW II helmet	No Price Found
MXH57 Camouflage Sharpshooter Lying Down, WW II helmet	No Price Found
MXS62 Soldier with Gas Mask and Gun, WW II helmet	No Price Found
MXS82 Anti-Aircraft with Range Finder, WW II helmet	No Price Found
MXS83 Soldier Trench Mortar, WW II helmet	No Price Found
MXH88 Radio Operator Standing, one-piece puttees	No Price Found

MXH89 Radio Operator (Lying Down), one-piece puttees	No Price Found
MXS No Number Standing with Periscope, WW II helmet	No Price Found
MXH94 Soldier Running with Cannon, WW II helmet	No Price Found
MXS16 Sailor	No Price Found
MXS24 Cannon Loader, WW II helmet	No Price Found
MXS521 Flag Bearer	No Price Found
MXS522 Parade	No Price Found
MXS523 Soldier in Poncho	No Price Found
MXS526 Observer	No Price Found
MXS527 Aircraft Spotter	No Price Found
MXS530 Machine Gunner (lying)	No Price Found
MXS531 Machine Gunner Sitting	No Price Found

	G	VG	M
MXS532 Sniper (kneeling)..	No Price Found		
MXS533 Soldier with gas mask and flare pistol....	No Price Found		
MXS534 Sniper.........	No Price Found		
MXS536 Anti-Aircraft Gunner..............	No Price Found		
MXS535 Soldier Throwing Hand Grenade........	No Price Found		
MXS No Number Soldier with gas mask, gun, camouflaged helmet.....	No Price Found		
MXS No Number Tommy Gunner, leaning back....	No Price Found		
MXS No Number Tall cowboy, firing two guns.	No Price Found		
M23a Sailor, hollow base, painted black, possibly for export to Cuba.........	No Price Found		

Unnumbered Manoil "X" line soldiers
Photo by Norbert Schachter
Courtesy Marjorie and Peter Ruben

MXS1 MXS2 MXS3 MXS4 M23a
Photo by Norbert Schachter
Courtesy Marjorie & Peter Ruben

	G	VG	M
(M170) Flag Bearer (thin), circa late 1945........	12.50	18.75	25.00
(M171) Parade (thin), circa late 1945.............	6.50	9.75	13.00
(M172) Tommy Gunner (thin, circa late 1945)....	6.50	9.75	13.00
(M173) Machine Gunner Sitting (thin), circa late 1945	30.00	45.00	60.00
(M174) Machine Gunner Lying (thin), circa late 1945.................	45.00	67.50	90.00
(M175) Sniper (thin), circa late 1945.............	No Price Found		
(M176) 45/6 Parade (thin), all 45s circa late 1945...	13.00	19.50	26.00
(M177) 45/7 Flag Bearer...	12.00	18.00	24.00
(M178) 45/8 Parade.......	9.00	13.50	18.00
(M179) 45/9 Combat......	10.00	15.00	20.00
(M180) 45/10 At Attention (present arms).........	9.00	13.50	18.00

	G	VG	M
(M181) 45/11 Sniper......	10.00	15.00	20.00
(M182) 45/12 Tommy Gunner	10.00	15.00	20.00
(M183) 45/13 Soldier With Bazooka Cannon (some marked "45/18"........	10.50	15.75	21.00
(M184) 45/14 Soldier With Shell For Bazooka (some marked "46/14"........	11.50	16.75	23.00
(M185) 45/15 General (some "46/15")	50.00	75.00	100.00

M207   M208   M209   M210
Photo by Don Pielin

M213   M215   M214   M218   M216   M212

M221   M217

M81a
Photo by Don Pielin

	G	VG	M
(M186) 45/16 Mine Detector (some "46/16")	10.00	15.00	20.00
(M187) 521 Flag Bearer, all 500s circa 1950.......	7.50	11.25	15.00
(M188) 522 Parade........	8.50	12.75	17.00
(M189) 523 Soldier in poncho	17.00	25.50	34.00
(M190) 524 Combat.......	7.50	11.25	15.00
(M191) 525 Aviator holding bomb..............	8.00	12.00	16.00
(M192) 526 Observer......	9.00	13.50	18.00
(M193) 527 Aircraft spotter.	7.50	11.25	15.00
(M194) 528 Soldier with bazooka	8.50	12.75	17.00

	G	VG	M			G	VG	M
(M195) **529** Motorcycle rider	8.50	12.75	17.00	(M209) **C-29 Mounted**				
(M196) **530** Machine gunner				**Cowboy**............	11.50	16.50	23.00
(lying)	8.50	12.75	17.00	(M210) **C-30 Mounted**				
(M197) **531** Machine gunner				**Cowboy Shooting**.......	10.50	15.75	21.00
sitting	8.50	12.75	17.00	(M211) C2 Ranch fence,				
(M198) **532** Sniper (kneeling)	8.50	12.75	17.00	gate	50.00	75.00	100.00
(M199) **533** Soldier with gas				(M212) C12 Blanket over				
mask with flare pistol....	8.00	12.00	16.00	Fence Section.........	15.00	22.50	30.00
(M200) **534** Sniper........	8.00	12.00	16.00	(M213) C18 Small Calf....	8.00	12.00	16.00
(M201) **535** Soldier throwing				(M214) C20 Bull, head				
hand grenade..........	8.50	12.75	17.00	turned	6.00	9.00	12.00
(M202) **536** Anti-Aircraft				(M215) C19 Cow feeding...	6.00	9.00	12.00
gunner	6.50	9.75	13.00	(M216) C28 Short Cactus..	4.50	6.75	9.00
(M203) **537** Soldier with				(M217) C14 Brahma Bull...	6.00	9.00	12.00
tommy gun............	20.00	30.00	40.00	(M218) C26 Large Cactus..	15.00	22.50	30.00
(M204) **538** Soldier firing up	7.50	11.25	15.00	(M219) C1 Fence.........	5.00	7.50	10.00
(M205) **539** Stretcher bearer	37.50	56.25	75.00	(M220) C25 Small Horse...		No Price Found	
(M206) **540** Wounded				(M221) Horse for Mounted				
Soldier (lying).........	40.00	60.00	80.00	Cowboy	10.00	15.00	20.00
My Ranch Corral Series				(M222) Horse for Mounted				
(M207) **C-23** Cowboy Rider.	5.00	7.50	10.00	Cowgirl..............	10.00	15.00	20.00
(M208) **C-24** Cowgirl Rider.	7.50	11.25	15.00					

GREY IRON

Grey Iron made the only 3¼" cast iron soldiers. The company began in 1840 as the Brady Machine Shop in Mount Joy, Pennsylvania, where it has remained to this day, and in 1881 was organized as the Grey Iron Casting Company, Limited. As early as 1903 it was manufacturing toy banks and stoves, cap pistols, wheeled toys and trains, as well as a number of non-toy items. On August 14, 1917, the company was granted two patents for their 40 mm solid cast iron Grey Klip Armies, which they then manufactured through 1941, the last of the series emerging in 1938 as "Uncle Sam's Defenders", painted khaki rather than nickel-plated, as the earlier versions had been. The soldiers were not successful at first, but with the advent of a new distributor, the company was swamped with orders, and in January, 1933, introduced a new line of thirty-five different cast iron soldiers, in an approximately 3" size (four Revolutionary War soldiers; an infantryman, a foot officer, a flagbearer and a mounted officer, may have been introduced earlier, as they are numbered lower, but were not part of the 1933 announcement).

The figures tended to be slight, and while apparently successful, were superseded in July 1936 by Grey's "Iron Men" series, a slightly larger, more robust model, which continued to be sold until World War II ended all toy production. Designers for the soldiers were at least two; Edward Musser and Samuel S. Schmidt. The soldiers were hand-poured and then painted on an assembly-line basis, and at least initially were sold for a dime, while their competitors charged a nickel. Grey is still in business today as the John Wright division of Donsco, and has recently been producing, on an erratic basis, some unpainted soldiers from its old molds. Some years ago, the author saw, at a Pennsylvania flea market, some crude, cast iron Continental Soldiers, about 2½" high, which he believes may be early Grey Iron, but none have surfaced since, and there is no evidence that Grey made them. However, they would be valuable to serious collectors, and in mint would probably bring about $30 apiece. All bold words and numbers are Grey's own description.

198

GREY IRON (GA) Set 1 Co.A
Courtesy the late Karl Zipple

GREY IRON (GB) Set 2, Company B
Courtesy the late Karl Zipple

GREY IRON (GC) SEt 3 Company C
Courtesy the late Karl Zipple

GREY IRON (GD) Set 4 Troop D
Courtesy the late Karl Zipple

GREY IRON (GE) Set 5 Battery E
Courtesy Don Pielin

GREY IRON (GF) Set 6 Battery F
Courtesy Don Pielin

GREY IRON (GG) Set 5 Aviation Corps   (Above two photos)
Courtesy the late Karl Zipple

GREY IRON (GH) Uncle Sam's Defenders
Courtesy the late Karl Zipple

Greyklip Armies	G	VG	M
(GA) Set 1/Company A, at attention, consists of bugler, officer, flag-bearer, drummer, rifleman, price per each	1.50	2.25	3.00
(GB) Set 2/Company B, marching, consists of bugler, officer, flag-bearer, drummer, rifleman, price per each	2.00	3.00	4.00
(GC) Set 3/Company C, charging, consists of bugler, officer, flag-bearer, drummer, rifleman, price per each	1.50	2.25	3.00
(GD) Set 4/Troop D, consists of four mounted troopers, one mounted officer, troopers all look alike, price per each	3.00	4.50	6.00
(GE) Set 5/Battery E, two-piece set, led by officer from Troop D, second piece is a gun limber with four horses, several attached soldiers, price for second piece	5.00	7.50	10.00
(GF) Set 6/Battery F, consists of shell stack, loader bending, loader standing, gunner, cannon, price per each	2.50	3.75	5.00
(GG) Set 5/Aviation Corps, consists of pilot (two of the same figure in set) and plane with detachable wing. Pilot sells for $5.00 in mint, price for plane, with wing	6.00	9.00	12.00
(GH) Uncle Sam's Defenders, consists of charging rifleman, machine-gunner, charging officer, rifleman at attention, flagbearer, officer saluting, price per each (double the price on saluting officer and flagbearer)	3.50	5.25	7.00

End Greyklip Armies

	G	VG	M
(G1) 1 Colonial Soldier . . .	6.00	9.00	12.00
(G2) 1A Colonial Foot Officer	6.50	9.75	13.00
(G3) 1B Colonial Color-Bearer	No Price Found		
(G3a) 1B Colonial Color-Bearer, 1950s version, with rifle barrel drilled out for flag	10.00	15.00	20.00
(G4) 1MA Colonial Mounted Officer	20.00	30.00	40.00
(G5) 2 Cadet, early version .	6.00	9.00	12.00
(G6) 2 Cadet	6.00	9.00	12.00
(G7) 2A Cadet Officer, early	6.00	9.00	12.00
(G8) 2A Cadet Officer	5.00	7.50	10.00
(G9) 3 U.S. Infantry, Shoulder Arms, early	5.50	8.25	11.00
(G10) 3 U.S. Infantry, Shoulder Arms	6.00	9.00	12.00
(G11) 3/1 U.S. Infantry, Port Arms (same as 10) . .	6.50	9.75	13.00
(G12) 3A U.S. Infantry Officer, early	6.25	9.38	12.50
(G13) 3A U.S. Infantry Officer	5.50	8.25	11.00
(G14) 3AP Traffic Officer (same as above, in blue) . .	7.50	11.25	15.00
(G15) 3AR Red Cross Officer (same as above, with armband)	9.50	14.25	19.00
(G16) 4 U.S. Infantry, Port Arms, early	4.50	6.75	9.00
(G17) 4A U.S. Doughboy Officer With Field Glasses	9.00	13.50	18.00
(G18) 4/1 U.S. Doughboy Signaling	6.00	9.00	12.00
(G19) 4/2 U.S. Doughboy Combat Trooper	8.50	12.75	17.00
(G20) 4/3 U.S. Doughboy With Range Finder	25.00	37.50	50.00
(G21) 4/4 U.S. Doughboy Ammunition Carrier	25.00	37.50	50.00
(G22) 4/5 U.S. Doughboy Sharpshooter	6.50	9.75	13.00
(G23) 4/6 U.S. Doughboy With Bayonet	7.50	11.25	15.00
(G24) 5 U.S. Infantry, Charging, early	4.50	6.75	9.00
(G25) 6 U.S. Doughboy, Port Arms, early	8.00	12.00	16.00
(G26) 6 U.S. Doughboy, Shoulder Arms	5.50	8.25	11.00
(G27) 6A U.S. Doughboy Officer, early	4.50	6.75	9.00
(G28) 6A U.S. Doughboy Officer	5.00	7.50	10.00
(G29) 6/1 U.S. Doughboy Charging	4.50	6.75	9.00

G1 G2 G3 G3a   G4 G5 G6 G7 G8

G9 G10 G11 G12 G13   G15 G16   G17 G18
Photo by Ed Poole

G19   G20   G21   G22   G23   G24   G25

G26   G27   G28   G29   G30   G31   G32   G33
Photo by Bill Kaufman

G34   G35   G37   G38   G39 G40 G41

G42   G45   G46   G47   G48   G49   G50
Photo by Bill Kaufman

	G	VG	M
(G34) **8M U.S. Cavalryman,** early	10.00	15.00	20.00
(G35) **8M U.S. Cavalryman**	11.50	17.25	23.00
(G36) **8M U.S. Cavalry Color Bearer With Silk Flag** (not shown, same as G34)	No Price Found		
(G37) **8MA U.S. Cavalry Officer,** early	15.00	22.50	30.00
(G38) **8MA U.S. Cavalry Officer**	16.00	24.00	32.00
(G39) **9 U.S. Marine,** early	5.00	7.50	10.00
(G40) **9 U.S. Marine**	4.00	6.00	8.00
(G41) **10 Royal Canadian Police,** early, (same as G16)	7.50	11.25	15.00
(G42) **10 Royal Canadian Police**	7.00	10.50	14.00
(G43) **10M Royal Canadian Mounted Police** (same as G34)	10.00	15.00	20.00
(G44) **10M Royal Canadian Mounted Police** (same as G35)	11.50	17.25	23.00
(G45) **11 Indian,** with hatchet, early	6.00	9.00	12.00
(G46) **11 Indian Chief,** with knife	7.00	10.50	14.00
(G47) **11/1 Indian Brave,** shielding eyes	6.00	9.00	12.00
(G48) **11/2 Chief Attacking,** upraised tomahawk	36.00	54.00	72.00
(G49) **11M Indian Mounted,** early	8.00	12.00	16.00
(G50) **11M Indian Mounted,** lying on horse	30.00	45.00	60.00
(G51) 11/1M **Indian Scout Mounted,** firing pistol reward	100.00	150.00	200.00
(G52) **12 Cowboy,** early	4.50	6.75	9.00
(G53) **12 Cowboy**	4.50	6.75	9.00
(G54) 12/1 **Hold-Up Man**	5.50	8.25	11.00
(G55) **12/2 Cowboy With Lasso,** with lasso price is 15.00 mint	6.00	9.00	12.00
(G56) **12/3 Bandit,** surrendering	40.00	60.00	80.00
(G57) **12M Cowboy Mounted,** early	12.00	18.00	24.00
(G58) **12M Cowboy Mounted**	10.00	15.00	20.00
(G59) **12/1M Masked Cowboy Mounted** (not shown)	125.00	187.50	250.00
(G60) **13 U.S. Machine Gunner,** early	6.00	9.00	12.00

	G	VG	M
(G30) **6/2 U.S. Doughboy Sentry**	5.50	8.25	11.00
(G31) **6/3 U.S. Doughboy Bomber,** crawling	8.00	12.00	16.00
(G32) **6/4 U.S. Doughboy Grenade Thrower**	7.50	11.25	15.00
(G33) **7 U.S. Doughboy Charging,** early	4.50	6.75	9.00

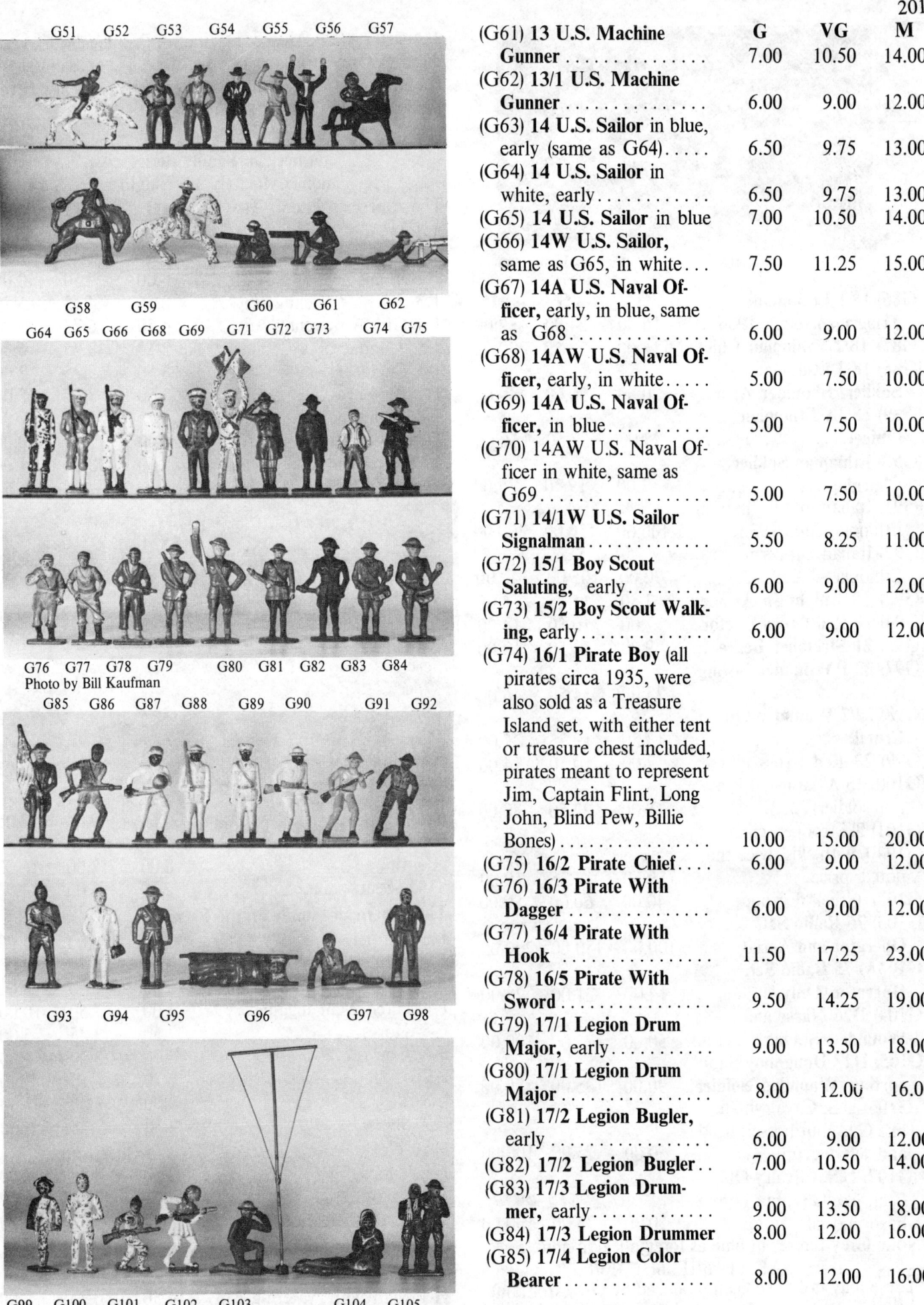

Photo by Bill Kaufman

Photo by Bill Kaufman

	G	**VG**	**M**
(G61) **13 U.S. Machine Gunner**	7.00	10.50	14.00
(G62) **13/1 U.S. Machine Gunner**	6.00	9.00	12.00
(G63) **14 U.S. Sailor** in blue, early (same as G64)	6.50	9.75	13.00
(G64) **14 U.S. Sailor** in white, early	6.50	9.75	13.00
(G65) **14 U.S. Sailor** in blue	7.00	10.50	14.00
(G66) **14W U.S. Sailor,** same as G65, in white ...	7.50	11.25	15.00
(G67) **14A U.S. Naval Officer,** early, in blue, same as G68	6.00	9.00	12.00
(G68) **14AW U.S. Naval Officer,** early, in white	5.00	7.50	10.00
(G69) **14A U.S. Naval Officer,** in blue	5.00	7.50	10.00
(G70) **14AW U.S. Naval Officer** in white, same as G69	5.00	7.50	10.00
(G71) **14/1W U.S. Sailor Signalman**	5.50	8.25	11.00
(G72) **15/1 Boy Scout Saluting,** early	6.00	9.00	12.00
(G73) **15/2 Boy Scout Walking,** early	6.00	9.00	12.00
(G74) **16/1 Pirate Boy** (all pirates circa 1935, were also sold as a Treasure Island set, with either tent or treasure chest included, pirates meant to represent Jim, Captain Flint, Long John, Blind Pew, Billie Bones)	10.00	15.00	20.00
(G75) **16/2 Pirate Chief**	6.00	9.00	12.00
(G76) **16/3 Pirate With Dagger**	6.00	9.00	12.00
(G77) **16/4 Pirate With Hook**	11.50	17.25	23.00
(G78) **16/5 Pirate With Sword**	9.50	14.25	19.00
(G79) **17/1 Legion Drum Major,** early	9.00	13.50	18.00
(G80) **17/1 Legion Drum Major**	8.00	12.00	16.00
(G81) **17/2 Legion Bugler,** early	6.00	9.00	12.00
(G82) **17/2 Legion Bugler** ..	7.00	10.50	14.00
(G83) **17/3 Legion Drummer,** early	9.00	13.50	18.00
(G84) **17/3 Legion Drummer**	8.00	12.00	16.00
(G85) **17/4 Legion Color Bearer**	8.00	12.00	16.00

G106　G107　Courtesy Hank Anton

	G	VG	M
(G86) 18/1 Ethiopian Tribesman, circa 1936...	16.00	24.00	32.00
(G87) 18/2 Ethiopian Chief.	15.00	22.50	30.00
(G88) 18/3 Ethiopian Soldier, Shoulder Arms..	20.00	30.00	40.00
(G89) 18/3A Ethiopian Officer	25.00	37.50	50.00
(G90) Ethiopian Soldier, Charging............	13.00	19.50	26.00
(G91) Italian infantryman in Ethiopia, circa 1936.....	100.00	150.00	200.00
(G92) Italian Officer in Ethiopia	70.00	105.00	140.00
(G93) 19 Knight In Armor.	7.50	11.25	15.00
(G94) 20 Red Cross Doctor.	7.00	10.50	14.00
(G95) 21 Stretcher Bearer..	9.00	13.50	18.00
(G97) 22/1 Wounded Sitting	23.00	34.50	46.00
(G98) 22/2 Wounded On Crutches..............	13.50	19.75	27.00
(G99) 23 Red Cross Nurse.	7.00	10.50	14.00
(G100) 25 Aviator (24 is a non-soldier)...........	15.00	22.50	30.00
(G101) Ski trooper, circa 1940, with skis twice the noted price...........	9.50	14.25	19.00
(G102) Greek Evzone.....	40.00	60.00	80.00
(G103) 75 Radio Set, Operator and Aerial....	100.00	150.00	200.00
(G103A) 75 Radio Set, Operator Only........	14.00	21.00	28.00
(G104) D26 Nurse and Wounded Soldier.......	50.00	75.00	100.00
(G105) D27 Doughboy Supporting Wounded Soldier	90.00	135.00	180.00
*(G106) U.S. Cavalryman, like G34, but horse's head and left leg up........	50.00	75.00	100.00
*(G107) U.S. Cavalry Officer, like G37, but horse's head and left leg up.....	50.00	75.00	100.00

(Note: Grey figures in blue as foreign legion double price; 6AF, 6F, 6/1F, 6/3F, 13/F
*These may not have been produced by Grey Iron, but instead by Distinctive Products Inc., which incorporated

January 2, 1929. Most of Distinctive Products' work was done at Grey Iron and one of its designers, Samuel S. Schmidt, was one of its directors. Distinctive may also have made small Continental soldiers.

American Family Series
(approximately 2¼" high)

The American Family Travels	G	VG	M
T-1 Man in traveling suit...	3.00	4.50	6.00
T-2 Woman in traveling costume	5.00	7.50	10.00
T-3 Boy in traveling suit...	2.75	4.13	5.50
T-4 Girl in traveling suit...	4.50	6.75	9.00
T-5 Conductor...........	2.50	3.75	5.00
T-6 Engineer...........	3.50	5.25	7.00
T-7 Porter.............	2.50	3.75	5.00
T-8 Policeman..........	3.75	5.25	7.50
T-9 Postman...........	5.00	7.50	10.00
T-10 Newsboy..........	5.50	8.25	11.00

T1 T2　T3 T4　　T5 T6 T7　　T8 T9 T10 T11 T12 T13

F1 F2 F3 F4　　　F11 F7 F9 F8 F12 F7 F6　　F5
Photo by Don Pielin

	G	VG	M
T-11 Preacher...........	6.00	9.00	12.00
T-12 Old Colored Man — sitting	8.00	12.00	16.00
T-13 Seat..............	2.00	3.00	4.00

The American Family on the Farm

	G	VG	M
F-1 Farmer.............	2.00	3.00	4.00
F-2 Farmer's wife........	4.50	6.75	9.00
F-3 Girl...............	5.00	7.50	10.00
F-4 Hired Man digging....	5.00	7.50	10.00
F-5 Horse.............	2.50	3.75	5.00
F-6 Cow..............	2.00	3.00	4.00
F-7 Calf..............	1.70	2.55	3.40
F-8 Pig...............	2.00	3.00	4.00
F-9 Sheep.............	2.50	3.75	5.00
F-10 Goat.............	No Price Found		
F-11 Goose............	2.50	3.75	5.00
F-12 Dog..............	2.00	3.00	4.00
F-13 Gate with Post......	3.75	5.63	7.50
F-14 Fence.............	No Price Found		

The American Family At Home

	G	VG	M
H-1 Man with watering can	4.50	6.75	9.00

	G	VG	M
H-2 Woman with basket...	5.00	7.50	10.00
H-3 Boy flying kite........	10.00	15.00	20.00
H-4 Girl skipping rope.....	6.00	9.00	12.00
H-5 Old man sitting.......	2.50	3.75	5.00
H-6 Old woman sitting.....	5.00	7.50	10.00
H-7 Colored cook.........	8.00	12.00	16.00
H-8 Colored man digging...	8.50	12.75	17.00
H-9 Garageman..........	3.00	4.50	6.00
H-10 Delivery boy........	5.00	7.50	10.00
H-11 Milkman...........	5.50	8.25	11.00
H-12 Dog..............	2.00	3.00	4.00
H-13 Lawn Seat.........	2.00	3.00	4.00

The American Family On The Beach

	G	VG	M
B-1 Man in bathing suit....	2.00	3.00	4.00
B-2 Woman in bathing suit.	7.50	11.25	15.00
B-3 Boy in summer suit....	6.00	9.00	12.00
B-4 Girl in slacks........	3.25	5.63	6.50
B-5 Old man sitting.......	2.50	3.75	5.00
B-6 Boy with life preserver.	8.00	12.00	16.00
B-7 Girl with sand pail.....	7.50	11.25	15.00
B-8 Boy with ball........	7.50	11.25	15.00
B-9 Girl catching ball......	3.25	5.88	6.50
B-10 Life Guard.........	10.00	15.00	20.00
B-11 Life Guard's chair....	No Price Found		

	G	VG	M
B-12 Life boat............	12.00	18.00	24.00
B-13 Bench.............	3.50	5.25	7.00
B-14 Cabana............	No Price Found		

The American Family On The Ranch

	G	VG	M
R-1 Cowboy with lasso....	3.75	5.25	7.00
R-2 Cowboy rider.........	3.00	4.50	6.00
R-3 Cowboy squatting.....	1.50	2.25	3.00
R-4 Boy in cowboy suit....	1.50	2.25	3.00
R-5 Girl in riding suit......	3.75	5.25	7.00
R-6 Cowgirl rider.........	1.50	2.25	3.00
R-7 Stallion..............	2.50	3.75	5.00
R-8 Bucking Broncho.....	6.00	9.00	12.00
R-9 Colt..............	4.00	6.00	8.00
R-10 Burro.............	No Price Found		
R-11 Calf.............	4.00	6.00	8.00
R-15 Rooster and Chickens, each	1.50	2.25	3.00
R-16 Ducks.............	No Price Found		

R1 R3 R6/R7 R10 R11   R2/R8 R5 R4 R9
Photo by Don Pielin

B1 B2 B3 B4 B5 B6 B7 B8 B9   B11 B10 B12

L to R: H1 to H11   Photo courtesy Don Pielin

NOTE: Among the Grey Iron figures reported as being reproduced are G1, G2, G45, G46, G47, G48, G54, G93, T5, T6, H8.

AUBURN RUBBER

Although AUBURN (also Aub-Rub'r) was founded in 1913, in Auburn, Indiana, as the Double Fabric Tire Corporation, making auto tubes and tires for Model T Fords, etc., it didn't produce its first toy until 1935, with five soldiers. The prototype was a Palace Guard, which AUBURN President and chief stockholder A. L. Murray had obtained in England. The model was taken to a local pattern-maker who made patterns from it, and then the company made the original molds from lead and molded sample toys for Murray. These samples were next taken to an artist and decorated per Murray's instructions. Presented to buyers, they immediately caught on. The soldiers were molded in 24" rubber presses, each containing forty to sixty soldiers, with cure time approximately 6-12 minutes. The soldiers, once trimmed, were dipped in a base laquer (advertised as "pure vegetable dyes") and then sent down a decorating conveyor, where as many as 24 women, using small camel hair brushes, added finishing touches, painting the faces, shoes, belts, buttons, medals, and finally eyes. After drying, each was wrapped individually in waxed paper and packed three dozen to a chipboard carton and twelve dozen to a corrugated carton for shipment. Design of the soldiers was credited to Edward McCandlish, a free-lance artist. The soldiers sold well from the beginning, with approximately 200 of the 400 AUBURN employees (AUBURN consistently made non-toy products as well) involved in them and other toys on a two-shift basis. Shortly after the first soldiers were introduced, animals and wheeled vehicles, the first a Cord automobile, were marketed, all successfully. AUBURN produced no soldiers during the war, and few after, though it continued to make toys in great quantity (70,000 wheeled items a day in 1962, for example). In 1960 the toys portion of AUBURN was purchased by the town of Deming, New Mexico, where it remained until it went out of business in 1969. AUBURN'S soldiers, all approximately the standard 3¼" length, went through three stages. The first were frail-looking, with long, thin bodies; the second, which emerged as early as September, 1936, were stockier and larger-headed, and the third, introduced in 1941, were more well-proportioned and realistic. Unlike its competitors, AUBURN produced no cowboys, Indians, sailors or civilians, except for baseball and football players and two farm workers. AUBURN'S infantry came in colors other than brown. There were several shades of blue, at least one of which was meant to represent U.S. Marines. It is speculated that the white were meant to represent the U.S. Navy, and the yellow, Italian Army in Ethiopia. At least two blue-grey soldiers have turned up, and these may have represented enemy troops or West Point cadets. It is thought that some Auburn Ethiopians remain to be discovered.

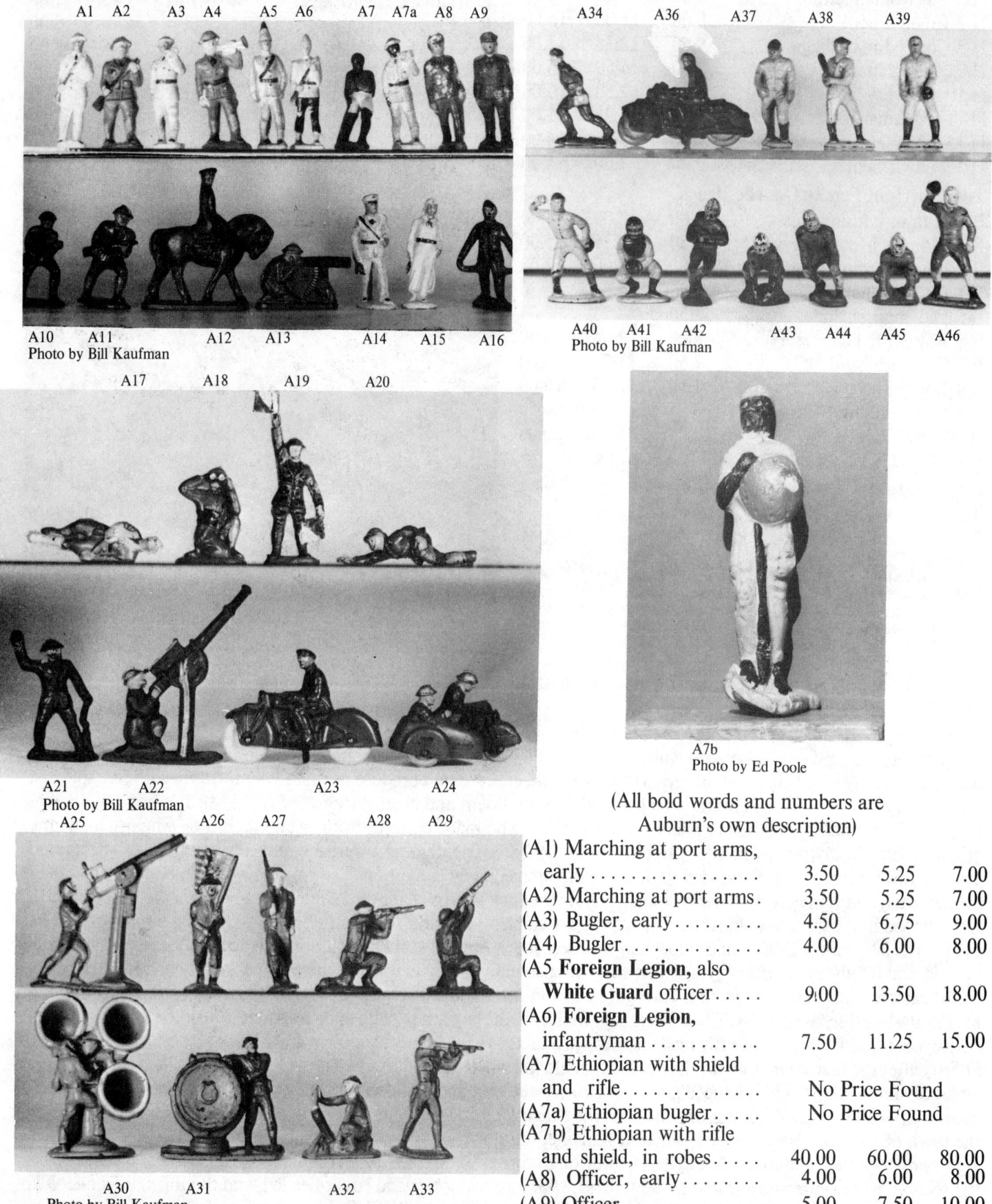

Photo by Bill Kaufman

Photo by Bill Kaufman

Photo by Bill Kaufman

A7b
Photo by Ed Poole

(All bold words and numbers are
Auburn's own description)

(A1) Marching at port arms, early	3.50	5.25	7.00
(A2) Marching at port arms.	3.50	5.25	7.00
(A3) Bugler, early	4.50	6.75	9.00
(A4) Bugler	4.00	6.00	8.00
(A5 **Foreign Legion,** also **White Guard** officer	9.00	13.50	18.00
(A6) **Foreign Legion,** infantryman	7.50	11.25	15.00
(A7) Ethiopian with shield and rifle	No Price Found		
(A7a) Ethiopian bugler	No Price Found		
(A7b) Ethiopian with rifle and shield, in robes	40.00	60.00	80.00
(A8) Officer, early	4.00	6.00	8.00
(A9) Officer	5.00	7.50	10.00

AUBURN, top: Howitzer, 155 mm, 7" long, Tank, model of Marmon-Herrington "Beauty", 4½" long.
Bottom:: Tank, 3¼" long, Fieldpiece, 75 mm, 7" long.
Photo and caption by Ed Poole.

	G	VG	M
(A25) **Aircraft Defender**	7.50	11.25	15.00
(A26) **Color Bearer**	7.50	11.25	15.00
(A27) **Marching Soldier**	6.00	9.00	12.00
(A28) **Firing Soldier**	5.00	7.50	10.00
(A29) **272 Plane Shooter** ..	4.00	6.00	8.00
(A30) **Sound Detector**	15.00	22.50	30.00
(A31) **Searchlight**	17.50	26.25	35.00
(A32) **296 Trench Mortar** ..	12.50	18.75	25.00
(A33) **Tank Defender** (?)	15.00	22.50	30.00
(A34) **Tank Soldier** (?), running with box	10.00	15.00	20.00
(A35) **Tank Soldier** (?), running, looking skyward, in pilot helmet and goggles (not shown)	No Price Found		
(A36) **Motor Scout**	15.00	22.50	30.00
(A37) Baseball Player, runner	10.00	15.00	20.00
(A38) Baseball Player, batter	12.50	18.75	25.00
(A39) Baseball Player, fielder	12.50	18.75	25.00
(A40) Baseball Player, pitcher	15.00	22.50	30.00
(A41) Baseball Player, catcher	12.50	18.75	25.00
(A42) Football Player, running with ball	12.50	18.75	25.00
(A43) Football Player, center	12.50	18.75	25.00
(A44) Football Player, crouching	12.50	18.75	25.00
(A45) Football Player, lineman on all fours	12.50	18.75	25.00
(A46) Football Player, quarterback passing	15.00	22.50	30.00

	G	VG	M
(A10) **Charging Soldier** with tommy gun, early	25.00	37.50	50.00
(A11) **Charging Soldier** with tommy gun	5.50	8.25	11.00
(A12) Cavalry officer, mounted	10.00	15.00	20.00
(A13) Machine Gunner	4.50	6.75	9.00
(A14 Doctor	4.00	6.00	8.00
(A15) Nurse, in white or khaki uniform	6.00	9.00	12.00
(A16) Stretcher-bearer	4.25	6.38	8.50
(A17) Soldier lying wounded	5.00	7.50	10.00
(A18) Kneeling with binoculars	4.00	6.00	8.00
(A19) **Signalman**	5.50	8.25	11.00
(A20) Crawling, rifle slung over shoulder	10.00	15.00	20.00
(A21) Grenade thrower	6.00	9.00	12.00
(A22) **Aircraft Gunner**	4.00	6.00	8.00
(A23) Motorcyclist, in khaki or blue as police	7.50	11.25	15.00
(A24) Motorcycle with sidecar	20.00	30.00	40.00

ALL-NU
(See also Vehicles, Animal-Drawn, Paper)

Frank Krupp (1/24/98-8/30/65), former sculptor and mold-maker for Barclay, was the owner of All-Nu, (his partner in the early stages was David Reader, brother of Barclay's chief salesman, Irving Reader), which was incorporated on February 16, 1938. Originally located at 55-57 Main Street, Yonkers, New York, the company later moved in the summer or fall of 1941 to a second-floor loft at 67 Irving Place in Manhattan. (The "Marching Majorettes" were produced in Yonkers as well as in Manhattan.) Krupp, a trained artist, designed all of All-Nu's toys as well as its novelties and souvenirs, and formed the company immediately upon leaving Barclay. Its first product was a lead souvenir horse, its two halves soldered together, and it is not known when All-Nu produced its first soldiers, which Krupp sculpted in clay over a wire armature without making preliminary sketches. The company was small, with about five or six pourers, six or seven women painters, and few other workers, and was just beginning to get off the ground (its "majorettes", which included all the girl musicians, were sold in 1941 at Woolworth's) when the advent of World War II ended all lead production. Krupp then drew, painted and produced cardboard soldiers and weapons, but they were not successful. Although All-Nu was not dissolved as a corporation until December 15, 1950, it was essentially out a business a year or two after the War began. Around 1946, Krupp resumed toy-making, this time with a new partner. The company, Faben Products, at 47 Walker Street in Manhattan, produced both new toys and novelties and continued All-Nu's prewar horses, mounted hunters, jockeys, and cowboy and cowgirl on bucking broncos. All known All-Nu soldiers are marked "All-Nu" on the underbase.

ALL-NU football players, Cowboy on Bucking Broncho, Cowgirl on Bucking Broncho (far right)
Photo by Bill Kaufman. Courtesy Evelyn Besser.

ALL-NU Dog Musicians. These sell for about $30 apiece in mint condition.
Photo by Bill Kaufman
Courtesy Evelyn Besser

ALL-NU, top row, L to R: Hunter on horse, Woman on horse, Jockey on horse, Mounted cowboy. Bottom row, L to R: ALL-NU "Marching Majorettes"
Photos by Bill Kaufman. Courtesy Evelyn Besser

ALL-NU Advancing with Tommy Gun (gun-tip restored, may not be accurate).
Photo by Ed Poole
Courtesy Gene Coffman

ALL-NU Majorette, with ensign-type cap, cape.
Photo by Don Pielin

	G	VG	M
Marching, slope arms, four known	55.00	82.50	110.00
Advancing, fixed bayonet, two known	No Price Found		
Officer kneeling with binoculars, drawing pistol, only one known	No Price Found		
AA Gunner in campaign cap, only two known	No Price Found		
Prone, firing rifle, none known	No Price Found		
Running in Gas Mask, with Rifle, only one known	No Price Found		
Officer with sword, one known	50.00	75.00	100.00
150? Majorette, baton in air	51.00	76.50	102.00
Majorette, baton held backward, cape-like cloth trailing behind, only one known	No Price Found		
Majorette, ensign-type cap, with cape, only two known	No Price Found		
151? Girl flagbearer	50.00	75.00	100.00
152? Girl fifist	40.00	60.00	80.00
153? Girl bugler	45.00	67.50	90.00
154? Girl saxophonist	40.00	60.00	80.00

ALL-NU Soldiers, photo by Bill Kaufman

	G	VG	M
"Newsreel" Cameraman in helmet, four known	500.00	750.00	1000.00
Seated machine-gunner, one known	86.00	129.00	172.00
Advancing with Tommy Gun, one known	No Price Found		
Grenadier, three known	No Price Found		
Bugler, one known	300.00	450.00	600.00
Signalman, only one known	No Price Found		
Standing, firing rifle, only two known	50.00	75.00	100.00

ALL-NU Continued	G	VG	M
155? Girl drummer........	45.00	67.00	90.00
Mounted Cowboy masked, firing pistol straight ahead	50.00	75.00	100.00
Football player throwing ball (**probably** All-Nu....	No Price Found		
Football player running with ball (**probably** All-Nu)...	No Price Found		
501 (Faben's number) Cowboy on Bucking Broncho	20.00	30.00	40.00
502 (Faben's number) Cowgirl on Bucking Broncho	20.00	30.00	40.00
521 (Faben's number) Jockey on horse........	14.00	21.00	28.00

	G	VG	M
526 (Faben's number) Hunter on horse.......	13.00	20.50	26.00
Woman on horse.........	12.50	18.75	25.00
Polo Player on horse.....	12.50	18.75	25.00

ALL-NU soldiers, as shown in the April, 1941, Toys and Novelties magazine. Courtesy Playthings Magazine.

TOMMY TOY
(See also Vehicles and Aircraft)

Tommy Toy was incorporated October 16, 1935, and recorded its first sale on November 13 of that year. The company was located on the second floor of a parking garage in Union City, New Jersey, on the southwest side of Palisade Avenue near 7th Street. In a 1938 business directory, Tommy Toy's officers are listed as "Pres. Albert D. Greene; V. Pres. Joseph Maulbeck; Sec. Treas. Chas. Weldon; Pur. Agt. Mgr. George Ganzkow", with employees noted as seven men and three women. Also involved was Leon Donze, former co-head of Barclay and presumably the inspiration for the formation of Tommy Toy. Olive Kooken, who did much of the sculpting for Barclay, and Margaret R. Cloninger are the two known to have designed the company's toys. The firm was not a success, and phonebooks of the time indicate it went out of business between August 1938 and May, 1939, with Barclay veterans believing Tommy Toy was bought out by Barclay, which retained the molds, but did not use them. All Tommy Toy soldiers and nursery rhyme figures were marked under their bases with the company name and sometimes with the description of the toy as well. Most of their other toys bore no markings. Unmarked soldiers which appear to be Tommy Toys were actually produced by American Alloy.

TOMMY TOY, Top Row, L to R: "Doctor" in white, "Doctor" in brown, "Officer Gas Mask", "Stretcher Bearer", "Wounded", "Nurse" in brown, "Nurse" in white. Bottom Row, L to R: "Officer", "Ground Arms", "Soldier Marching", "Port Arms", "Soldier Charging", "Hand Grenade", "Soldier Firing", "Machine Gunner". Photo by Bill Kaufman. Courtesy Charles E. Weldon Jr.

TOMMY TOY, Top Row, L to R: "Little Miss Muffet", "Puss In Boots", "Tom, Tom, The Pipers Son", "Jack & Jill", "Humpty-Dumpty". Bottom Row, L to R: "Little Bo Peep", "Old Mother Hubbard", "Old King Cole", "Jack And The Bean Stalk", "Old Mother Witch". Courtesy Don Pielin

	G	VG	M
"Officer"	75.00	112.50	150.00
"Ground Arms"..........	35.00	52.50	70.00
"Soldier Marching"........	35.00	52.50	70.00
"Port Arms"...........	35.00	52.50	70.00
"Soldier Charging"........	75.00	112.50	150.00
"Hand Grenade"........	35.00	52.50	70.00
"Soldier Firing", kneeling firing rifle.............	75.00	112.50	150.00

	G	VG	M
"Machine Gunner", standing firing tommy gun.......	50.00	75.00	100.00
"Officer Gas Mask"........	100.00	150.00	200.00
"Stretcher-Bearer"	100.00	150.00	200.00
"Wounded"	80.00	120.00	160.00
"Doctor", brown uniform..	60.00	90.00	120.00
"Doctor", white uniform...	70.00	105.00	140.00
"Nurse", white uniform....	37.50	56.25	75.00
"Nurse", brown uniform...	37.50	56.25	75.00

	G	VG	M
"Old Mother Hubbard" by Olive Kooken, copyright June 25, 1936.........	27.50	41.25	55.00
"Tom, Tom, The Pipers Son" by Kooken, copyright June 25, 1936.	37.50	56.25	75.00
"Humpty-Dumpty" by Margaret R. Cloninger, copyright June 15, 1936.	35.00	52.50	70.00
"Little Bo Peep" by Cloninger, copyright June 25, 1936	30.00	45.00	60.00
"Jack & Jill" by Kooken, copyright June 25, 1936.	30.00	45.00	60.00

	G	VG	M
"Puss In Boots" by Cloninger, copyright June 25, 1936	20.00	30.00	40.00
"Jack And The Bean Stalk", by Cloninger, copyright August 10, 1936........	30.00	45.00	60.00
"Old King Cole" by Cloninger, copyright August 10, 1936.............	20.00	30.00	40.00
"Little Miss Muffet" by Kooken, copyright August 10, 1936........	20.00	30.00	40.00
"Old Mother Witch" by Kooken, copyright August 10, 1936........	22.50	33.75	45.00

AMERICAN ALLOY

American Alloy produced only toy soldiers, unmarked versions of Tommy Toys, employing new molds. The company was only in business for about a year before the War, ceasing production in 1941 when the government impounded its awaited shipment of lead. It resumed production briefly immediately after the War, still producing soldiers in World War I helmets. American Alloy was located at 1016 Paterson Plank Road in North Bergen, New Jersey. Although the firm had several partners, there were only four employees. Louis Picco, formerly employed with Barclay, was a partner, the company's President, and with J. Bracco, did the casting, selling, and some of the painting. It is not known how many of Tommy Toy's 13 soldiers were produced by American Alloy, though it is presumed all of them were. Those known include the doctor, the grenade-thrower, marcher, officer, charging, tommy-gunner and wounded. There is also a reproduction of the Barclay B132 which has the same paint as American Alloy soldiers, and is possibly a post-War product of the company.

METAL CAST PRODUCTS CO.

The company begin in 1899 as S. Sachs Toy Soldier Manufacturing Company, selling hand-casting molds. These originally were for solid cast toys, but by 1933 Sachs, now known as Metal Cast Products Company, offered, among other casting forms, eight hollow cast molds for soldiers. The company sold their slush cast molds to small businessmen in addition to manufacturing their own soldiers. Thus there appears to be no way of knowing which were made by Metal Cast and which by other individuals or companies, at least one of which is known to have imprinted its own name on molds supplied by Metal Cast. In 1946, Metal Cast was selling its soldiers with WW I helmets; however by the following year, it had updated its line, and its helmeted soldiers now had WW II pot helmets. Some of their soldiers appear to have been copied from Barclay and Manoil figures. On the other hand, Beton Plastic copied several of their pieces from Metal Casts. All bold words and numbers are the company's own description.

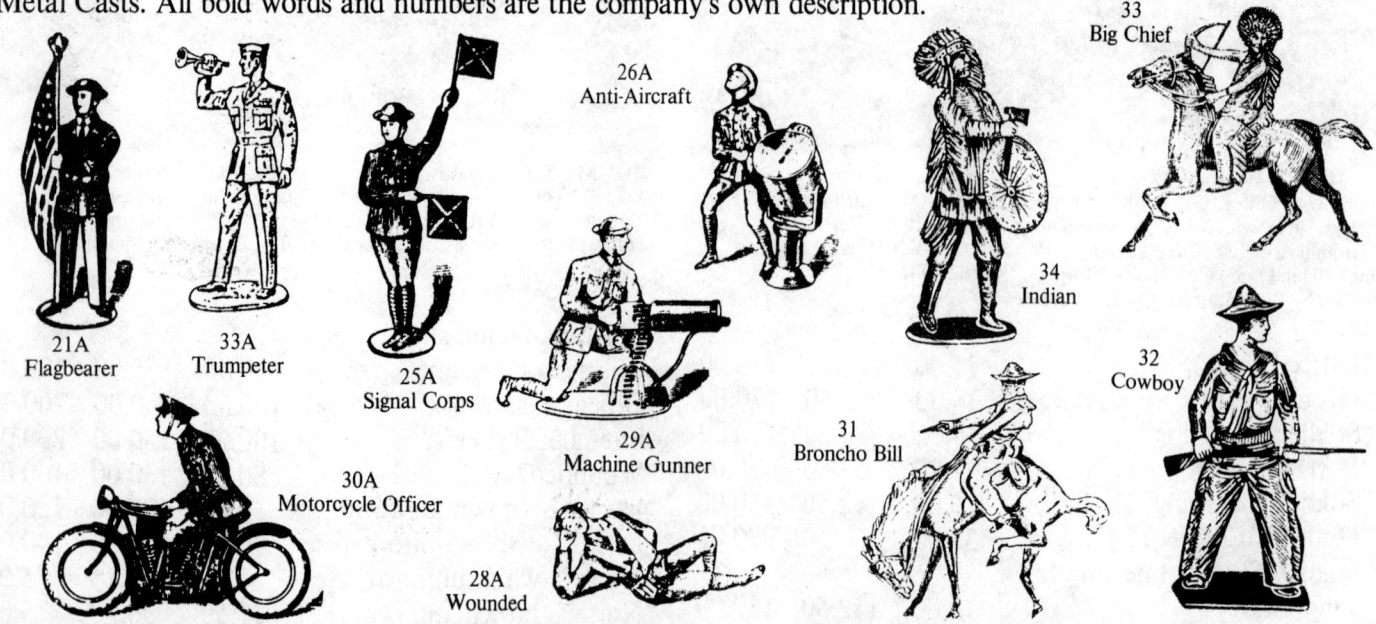

21A Flagbearer
33A Trumpeter
25A Signal Corps
26A Anti-Aircraft
29A Machine Gunner
31 Broncho Bill
33 Big Chief
34 Indian
32 Cowboy
30A Motorcycle Officer
28A Wounded

21
METALCAST Soldiers   24 23 22   Photo by Don Pielin

32A
Photo by Don Pielin

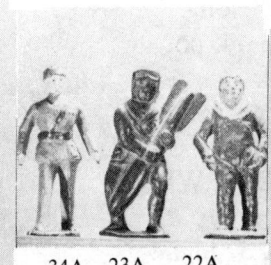

34A 23A 22A
Photo by Don Pielin

23A
Courtesy Hank Anton

38A
Photo by Bill Kaufman

29A   27A   26A   25A   24A

34A   35A   36A   37A
Photo by Ed Poole

Circa 1933

	G	VG	M
21 American Cavalry, mounted, wearing helmet, apprxo. 3" high	8.00	12.00	16.00

22 American Infantry Private, marching in

	G	VG	M
helmet, rifle at slope, approx. 2½" high	2.00	3.00	4.00
23 American Infantry Officer, marching in cap, sword on shoulder approx. 2½" high	2.00	3.00	4.00
24 American Infantry Flag Bearer, wearing helmet	2.00	3.00	4.00
31 Broncho Bill, holding pistol, on bucking broncho		No Price Found	
32 Cowboy holding rifle across waist		No Price Found	
33 Big Chief mounted Indian in war bonnet, holding bow	10.00	15.00	20.00
34 Indian, in war bonnet, holding hatchet and shield	5.00	7.50	10.00

Circa 1946, in WW I Helmets

	G	VG	M
21A Flag Bearer 3⅝" high		No Price Found	
22A Aviator (very similar to Barclay's), 3" high	22.50	33.75	45.00
23A Pilot With Bomb, 3⅛" high, similar to Manoil's	60.00	90.00	120.00
24A Suicide Squad, 3" high, very similar to Barclay's officer with gas mask and pistol	19.00	28.50	38.00
25A Signal Corps, with Semaphore Flags		No Price Found	
26A Anti-Aircraft Soldier, with searchlight		No Price Found	
27A Bomb Thrower, gas mask, slung rifle, throwing grenade		No Price Found	
28A Wounded, lying down, head on hand, arm in sling		No Price Found	
29A Machine Gunner kneeling		No Price Found	

A soldier by an unknown maker (right) next to a Metal Cast (left). It is possible it is a Metal Cast or even a lead Beton, since Beton did cast in lead at first. Price in mint is about $20.
Courtesy Hank Anton   Photo by Ed Poole

	G	VG	M
30A Motorcycle Officer on motorcycle, peaked cap..	90.00	135.00	180.00
31A Cavalry Officer, 3¼" long..................	10.00	15.00	20.00

Circa 1947, WW II Helmets

	G	VG	M
31A Cavalry Officer, in cap, 3¼" high.............	10.00	15.00	20.00
32A Flag Bearer, 3¼" high, in campaign cap.......	No Price Found		
33A Trumpeter, 3" high in campaign cap..........	No Price Found		
34A Marching Private, 3" high, in campaign cap, no weapon, only one known.	20.00	30.00	40.00
35A Infantryman, 3" long, similar to Manoil 44, pot helmet...............	6.00	9.00	12.00
36A Bomb Thrower, 2¾" high, similar to Manoil 31 and Metal Cast 27A, WW II pot helmet.........	6.00	9.00	12.00
37A Suicide Squad, 3" high,, similar to Barclay 778 and Metal Cast 24A........	16.50	24.75	33.00
38A Machine Gunner, 2½" high.................	8.00	12.00	16.00

JONES

Jones' 3¼" hollow lead soldiers probably began in the late 1930s, apparently cutting off in September, 1941. Sculpting was by a Polish immigrant, Henry Kasselowski, who also designed the toy soldiers for Lincoln Log until the 1950s, when England's Crescent took over the Lincoln Log line. Jones was owned by J. Edward Jones, who operated under a number of company names from 1930 into the 1960s, among them Miniature Products, Metal Miniatures, Metal Arts, Military Miniatures, World Miniatures and the Visual History Association. It is now known that the prone German (J3) was made directly over Barclay B61, Kasselowski removing the tin helmet, shaping a German helmet of red wax, then making a plaster cast of the entire figure, from which a bronze mold was made. Many, and perhaps all, of the Jones soldiers were also painted in gray, as "enemy". In 1982, research disclosed that Jones, under the company name of Metal Arts, produced an entirely different set of 3" lead figures from 1929-1931. These are listed at the end of this section. Since they seem to have been a slightly smaller size, it is possible that J1, J2 and J26, which are out of proportion to the later soldiers they were sold with, may have originally been planned as part of the earlier line. None, however, appear in the 1931 photos.

	G	VG	M
(J1) German, kneeling with rifle.................	90.00	135.00	180.00
(J2) German, charging with rifle.................	90.00	135.00	180.00
(J3) German, prone machine-gunner (similar to Barclay No. 728).....	65.00	97.50	130.00
(J4) Observer with binoculars and rifle (similar to Manoil No. 28)	30.00	45.00	60.00
(J5) Wire-cutter, prone.....	100.00	150.00	200.00
(J6) Soldier with rifle, gassed or shot in neck.........	100.00	150.00	200.00
(J7) Stretcher-bearer (similar to Manoil No. 32)......	30.00	45.00	60.00
(J8) Kneeling with AA Gun (similar to Auburn A-22).	35.00	52.50	70.00
(J9) Charging, port arms...	No Price Found		
(J10) Firing machine gun on tree stump............	20.00	30.00	40.00
(J10a) Same as above, No.2 on pocket.............	No Price Found		
(J11) Grenade-thrower, no weapons..............	60.00	90.00	120.00
(J12) Seated, with rifle (similar to Barclay B115).	30.00	45.00	60.00
(J13) Officer in greatcoat, pointing, holding pistol..	100.00	150.00	200.00
(J14) Prone, with rifle, trunk upraised	60.00	90.00	120.00
(J15) Prone, firing double- barreled machine gun....	45.00	67.50	90.00
(J16) Kneeling, firing anti- tank gun (similar to Barclay B145), 3 variations known..........	30.00	45.00	60.00
(J16a) Same as above with barrel brace, "23" on wheel	40.00	60.00	80.00
(J17) Cook with chef's hat, frying pan (similar to Barclay B110)........	30.00	45.00	60.00

J22 J12 J5

J2 J1 J3
Photo by Ed Poole

J4 J7 J8 J10 J13 J14

J16 J19 J20 J23 J30
Photo by Norbert Schachter

J18 J26 J16a J27 J28 J29
Photo by Don Pielin

J25 J17 J31 J39 J33
Photo by Don Pielin

(J18) Ammunition Carrier.. No Price Found
(J19) Motorcyclist with machine gun mounted on motorcycle 40.00 60.00 80.00

	G	VG	M
(J20) Flagbearer (similar to Barclay B7)............	No Price Found		
(J21) Kneeling with searchlight	30.00	45.00	60.00
(J21a) Kneeling with searchlight, "27", "Made in USA" on sides of stanchion	40.00	60.00	80.00
(J22) Seated with phone......	40.00	60.00	80.00
(J23) Kneeling, firing rifle, no stand.............	25.00	37.50	50.00
(J23a) Same as above, shorter rifle...........	65.00	87.50	130.00
(J24) Prone, body arched, firing machine gun......	25.00	37.50	50.00
(J25) Bugler.............	60.00	90.00	120.00
(J26) Soldier with gas mask, plunging rifle down, slightly smaller in size...	62.50	93.75	125.00
(J27) Nurse with bag, like Barclay B82...........	25.00	37.50	120.00
(J28) Doctor with bag, like Barclay B81...........	20.00	30.00	40.00
(J29) Standing firing rifle...	47.50	76.25	95.00
(J30) Wounded supine, like Manoil M53...........	30.00	45.00	60.00
(J31) Cowboy on rearing horse, firing backward (not shown)...........	50.00	75.00	100.00
(J32) Marching with Rifle..	37.50	56.25	75.00
(J33) Cowboy Kneeling....	10.00	15.00	20.00
(J34) Indian on Rearing Horse	40.00	60.00	80.00
(J35) Indian with Bow (may resemble Beton's........	No Price Found		
(J36) Tramp.............	7.50	11.25	15.00
(J37) Farmer.............	7.50	11.25	15.00
(J38) Farmer's Wife.......	7.50	11.25	15.00
(J39) Cowboy on Prancing Horse, similar to Barclay B2.............	No Price Found		
(J40) Knight with shield, flat underbase (may be Barclay).............	No Price Found		
(J41) Knight with pennant, flat underbase (may be Barclay).............	No Price Found		

Jones' Metal Arts 3" Soldiers, 1929-31

	G	VG	M
(MA 1) Father Time with large wings...........	No Price Found		
(MA 2) British Battalion Co. Marine	5.00	7.50	10.00
(MA 3) British Dragoon with movable arm, 1775, mounted	No Price Found		

J24   J15

Photo by Ed Poole

J21   J6   J11   J9

J4 J7 J8   J10 J13 J16 J14 J17

J19   J20   J21a   J23   J30   J32 J33 J34
Photo by Bill Kaufman

Jones Animals

J37   J38   J36   Jones Animals
Photo by Don Pielin

J23a
Photo by Ron Eccles

J40   J41
Photo by Don Pielin

	G	VG	M
(MA 4) British Light Infantryman	5.00	7.50	10.00
(MA 5) American Backwoodsman	No Price Found		
(MA 6) Hessian Grenadier of 1777 Charging	No Price Found		
(MA 7) British Infantry Drummer	No Price Found		
(MA8) British Grenadier . . .	40.00	60.00	80.00
(MA 9) American Marine of 1812	No Price Found		
(MA 10) French Foreign Legion private of 1870 standing on guard	No Price Found		
(MA 11) French Foreign Legion, standing firing, with neckcloth	No Price Found		
(MA 12) Highlander Private Charging	No Price Found		
(MA 13) Highlander Piper Walking	No Price Found		
(MA 14) British 1857 Marine	No Price Found		
(MA15) Cowboy Mounted on Standing Horse 1870 .	No Price Found		
(MA16) Indian lying on galloping horse with rifle aimed	No Price Found		
(MA 17) Cowboy of 1870 . .	No Price Found		
(MA 18) German Officer of 1918, marching	No Price Found		
(MA 19) German Infantryman of 1918, standing, firing	No Price Found		
(MA 20) American Cavalryman of 1918, mounted on standing horse, movable arm	No Price Found		
(MA 21) American 1918 Doughboy Bomber (throwing grenade)	No Price Found		
(MA 22) American 1918 Major, standing in overcoat, holding pistol and pointing, resembles J13, but is not the same	No Price Found		
(MA 23) American Infantry in overcoat, 1918, appears to be at attention	No Price Found		
(MA 24) Seaman 1918	No Price Found		
(MA 25) Boy Scout	No Price Found		
(MA 26) Boy Scout in Shorts	No Price Found		
(MA 27) Boy Scoutmaster standing	No Price Found		

MA10   MA39   MA17   MA9?
Photo by Don Pielin

MA12   MA13   MA?   MA10?
Photo by Don Pielin

MA39 MA17 MA21? MA10

MA13   MA14   MA12   MA8   MA9   MA28
Photo by Don Pielin

(MA 28) American 1929
  Marine . . . .   No Price Found
(MA 29) Midshipman of
  1932 . . . .   No Price Found
(MA 30) West Point Cadet
  of 1929 . . . .   No Price Found
(MA 31) German Infantry
  of 1918 marching with
  movable arm . . . .   No Price Found
(MA 32) Indian Creeping . . .   No Price Found
(MA 33) American Marine
  of 1776 standing . . . .   No Price Found
(MA 34) British Artillery
  Gunner of 1776 . . . .   No Price Found
(MA 35) British Light Co.
  Marines . . . .   No Price Found
(MA 36) British Marine Of-
  ficer with Sword . . . .   No Price Found
(MA 37) Artillery Ensign
  Standing . . . . No Price Found
(MA 38) German Infantry
  Charging (listed, but not
  pictured; possibly J2) . . . .   No Price Found
(MA 39) Indian with
  Tomahawk (not listed or
  pictured, but seems to be
  from this series) . . . .   No Price Found

JONES Pillbox
Photo Courtesy Don Mueller

These large, hollow lead soldiers were probably produced by Jones.
All in photo have their rifle tips off. The standing firing is 4⅜" high,
the marching 4¼" high, and the kneeling firing 2¾" high. In late
1983 these pictured soldiers sold for $125 apiece. The figure on left
is J13.
Photo by Bob Klinedinst

JONES Tank, "22 on side.
Courtesy Gene Parker
(See Vehicles)

JONES Tanks, flame not
touching hull, flame touching
hull.
Photo by Don Pielin
(See Vehicles)

MINIATURE TOY COMPANY - MOULDED MINIATURES
METAL-ART - METAL MINIATURES

Both before and after World War II, at least into the 1950s, J. Edward Jones also made hollowcast 54 mm figures. The following is a list of figures numbered to match the photos shown. Descriptions are provided where possible, with those in bold lettering Jones' own description. Since these photos have been matched against faint Xeroxes of Jones' sale lists, some may be identified incorrectly. Prices are erratic on these, as they have only recently come to be deemed collectible by more than a few.

541 - Sailor, shoulder arms
542 - **West Pointer** parade rest No.2907
543 - Marine with Guidon
544 - Marine at Port Arms
545 - Marine, Shoulder Arms
546 - Crawling with Rifle, in Snow Camouflage
547 - German on Guard
548 - German Charging
549 - Charging in Pith Helmet, British
5410 - Parade Rest with Fixed Bayonet, Chinest Nationalist No.2901
5411 - **1942 U.S. Infantry**
5412 - Highlander, WW I helmet, Shoulder Arms
5413 - U.S. Infantry (?)
5414 - **1948 U.S. Marines,** marching at shoulder arms
5415 - Private at Parade Rest
5416 - **1944 U.S. Cavalry**
5417 - **1190 Herald**
5418 - **1193 English Bowman**
5419 - Robinson Crusoe (prototype, probably never produced)
5420 - **1871 Cowboy**
5421 - Indian Chief, running with rifle
5422 - Indian Standing, Firing
5423 - Right Carry Arms, Italian, WW II, running at trail
5424 - WW I Infantryman, Marching Shoulder Arms
5425 - **Pilot of the 17th Pursuit Squadron, 1937**
5426 - Officer with Binoculars
5427 - Marching Highlander
5428 - **1944 U.S. Aimer**
5429 - Sailor Marching With Drum, British "Blue Jacket"
5430 - **1921 British Guardsman,** shoulder arms
5431 - Greek Evzone

5432 - Civil War (?) at attention
5433 - **1864 Militiaman**
5434 - **1861 Zouave of La.**
5435 - On Guard, circa 18th Century
5436 - U.S. Marine of early 19th century, no pigtail
5437 - U.S. Marine of early 19th century, has pigtail
5438 - 1775 Soldier, modified port arms
5439 - Charging Highlander, circa 1775
5440 - Charging Highlander Officer, circa 1775
5441 - Officer circa 1775
5442 - Naval (?) Officer, circa 1775
5443 - Sailor circa 1775
5444 - French (?) soldier, circa 1775, modified port arms
5445 - French (?) officer, marching
5446 - French (?) soldier, on guard
5447 - Highlander, at ready, 1757 Scotsman, No. 270118
5448 - French (?) soldier circa 1775 at attention
5449 - American (?) Marine, circa 1775
5450 - **Highlander** of 1814, No.1809GB
5451 - **Scotchman,** at ready
5452 - Piper
5453 - Soldier circa 1775, on guard
5454 - 1775 Officer, sword at side
5455 - 1775 Soldier
5456 - 1775 Officer, sword extended
5457 - 1775 Soldier, Rammer Drawn
5458 - **1775 British Ranger,** shoulder arms, 2701LB
5459 - **1775 British Marine,** firing at upward angle, 2705MB
5460 - **1775 Colonial Woman,** deluxe finish is PL1383 **Belle of Baltimore,** ordinary finish is PT2389 **1776 Belle of New Nork**
5461 - **1775 Colonial Man,** deluxe finish is PL1390 **Dandy of Charleston,** ordinary finish is PX2390 **1776 Dandy of Philadelphia**

541   542   543   544   545
Photo courtesy K. Warren Mitchell

546   547   548   549   5410
Photo courtesy K. Warren Mitchell

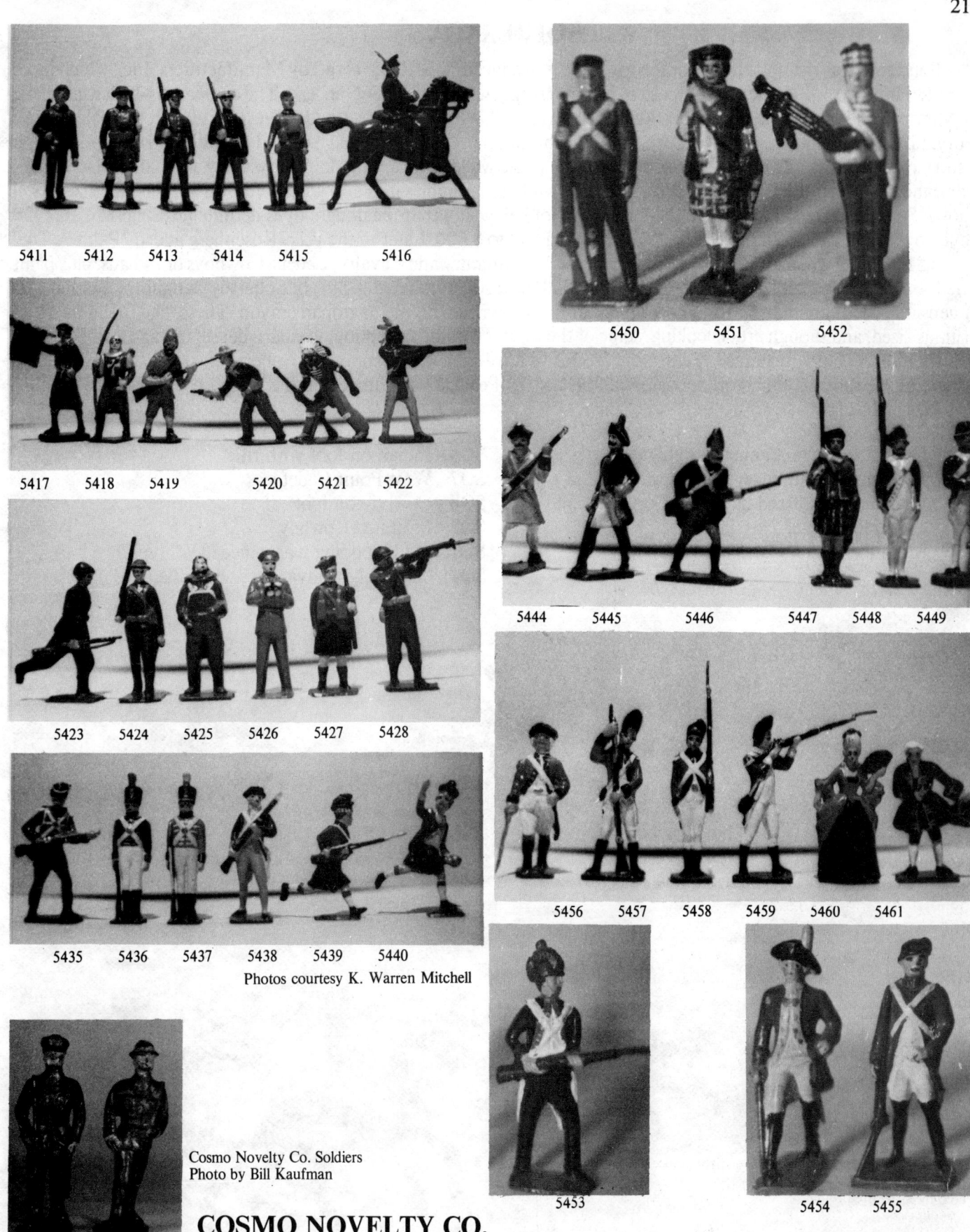

5411   5412   5413   5414   5415   5416

5450   5451   5452

5417   5418   5419   5420   5421   5422

5444   5445   5446   5447   5448   5449

5423   5424   5425   5426   5427   5428

5435   5436   5437   5438   5439   5440

Photos courtesy K. Warren Mitchell

5456   5457   5458   5459   5460   5461

Cosmo Novelty Co. Soldiers
Photo by Bill Kaufman

5453

5454   5455

COSMO NOVELTY CO.

The Cosmo Novelty Co. was reported in the March 1931 Playthings Magazine as selling lead soldiers — including sailors, cadets, Indians and cowboys, boxed in various sets to retail from 25¢ to $5.00. Cosmo had previously been a manufacturer of rhinestone souvenirs. Located at 44 West 36th Street in New York, it appears to have been out of business by 1932, and was listed as a soldier manufacturer as early as 1930. The soldiers illustrated here greatly resemble the two shown in the Playthings article. In the Playthings photo, the rifles are on the right shoulder, but the photo may have been reversed. These pieces are extremely rare, and would probably be worth $20-40 in mint condition.

SOLJERTOYS

Soljertoys was the trade name for the toy soldiers produced by S. Rosenberg Toy Manufacturers, Inc., which incorporated January 14, 1930, for the purpose of manufacturing toys and novelties in lead. The company, which was located at, variously, 37 West 19th Street, 40 West 25th Street, 20 West 17th Street and 7 West 22nd Street, all New York, reorganized in 1934 as the Illfelder Corp. By 1936 the company appears to have ceased operations. In April, 1930, in a story on Soljertoys, Playthings Magazine showed a rifle-wielding charging doughboy along with an Indian doing a war dance, one leg raised. The single doughboy shown here resembles it in every way but is in a three-inch size. As all known Soljertoys are Britains-sized, there is no way of being sure that the doughboy is definitely a Soljertoy. In 1930, Soljertoys sold for ten cents apiece, with sets running 25¢ to $3.00. Later in the year, Rosenberg added "Paint-A-Toy" sets at $1.00 retail which contained 10 lead figures — U.S. Infantry and Cavalry, Cadets, Cowboys or Indians, plus paint. The foot Indians resembled Ideal's I-15. Recently, a boxed set (numbered "750") of Soljertoy doughboys, with a two-dimensional lead cannon, was found with the year "1932" written on the boxtop in crayon. These, like the Indians, are Britains-sized, and though crude-looking, some of the figures contain exceptionally sharp detail. In 1983, the boxed set sold for $80. A company named "Pearlytoys" seems to have some connection with Soljertoys, at least to the extent of producing the same mounted officer, but with the legend "Pearlytoys" stamped on the horse's neck. No known Soljertoys bear markings.

SO1 - Officer with sword, app. 2¼" high
SO2 - Marching left shoulder arms, app. 2⅞" high
SO3 - On guard with fixed bayonet, app. 2¼" high
SO4 - Officer on horse, 2¼" high
SO5 - Mounted Indian Chief
SO6 - Indian on foot with rifle
SO7 - West Point Cadet
SO8 - Cowboy on foot
SO9 - Mounted Cowboy
SO10 - Indian doing war dance (3¼" type?)
SO11 - Doughboy advancing with rifle (3¼" type?)

SO11 Soljertoy doughboy with rifle
Photo by Ed Poole

SO2   SO1   SO3
Photo by Ed Poole

Cannon from Soljertoy set. This cannon was produced by a number of manufacturers, both German and American. Photo by Ed Poole

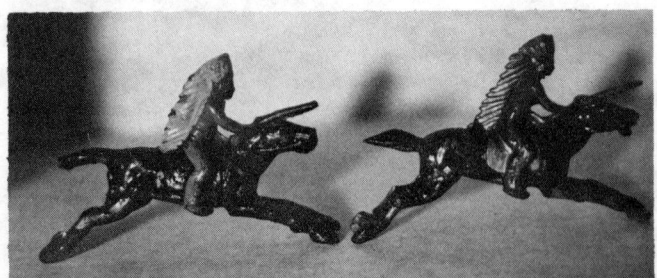

Soljertoy Indian on left, similar Indian on right (notice difference in horses' tails)
Photo by K. Warren Mitchell

Left, Soljertoy SO4, right Pearlytoy mounted officer. The only difference between the two figures is that the Soljertoy is less sharply defined in its details, and most of the "Pearlytoy" trademark found on the Pearlytoy horse's neck has been effaced on the Soljertoy.
Photo by Ed Poole.

UNKNOWN MANUFACTURERS

There are some 3¼" lead soldiers whose manufacturers are unknown. Some or all may have been manufactured by known companies, and where this is suspected, it has been noted. There were also smaller, crudely sculpted lead soldiers which look very much like some of Barclay's toys. Some collectors have believed that these were early Barclay, but none of the ex-Barclay employees queried remember them. These "small Barclays" sell for about $12.00 in mint. All the soldiers listed here are the approximately 3¼" size. Soldiers which appear to be made by the same company are given a common second letter after the U prefix. Some of the soldiers listed in the last edition have been dropped, as they have been identified (see Soljertoy, Cosmo, Jones, Barclay). UC15 and UC16 are known to have been produced by two ex-Barclay employees, probably in North Bergen or West New York, New Jersey, apparently after the Second World War. They look like Barclays, but have inferior lead, paint and detail. UC 6 through UC 18 all appear to be by this company, which lasted only a year or two, and had no more than two or three employees. Recently, UC 12, UC 13, UC 15 and UC 16 turned up in a boxed set.

These recently-discovered figures, all in solid lead and stamped, in white, on the underbase "Made in U.S.A.", appear to have been produced around 1946, and by the same company which made the U 33 Majorette. In addition to those shown, General MacArthur was also produced, and it would seem likely that Winston Churchill was as well. Although no prices have been found, collectors agree that these pieces would be considered valuable. From L to R: General Lafayette?, Nathan Hale?, General DeGaulle, Franklin Delano Roosevelt, Napoleon, Abraham Lincoln, Simon Bolivar?, Stalin, Chiang Kai-shek, Ben Franklin, George Washington.   Photo courtesy Steve Balkin-Burlington Toys.

UD21   UD22   UD23   UD25   UD24

UC28   U26
Photo by Don Pielin

Unpainted solid plastic copies of Barclay soldiers were issued in the late 40s or early 50s. The manufacturer is unknown. No plastic toys were ever made by Barclay. Prices average $3 apiece in mint.
Photo courtesy Don Pielin.

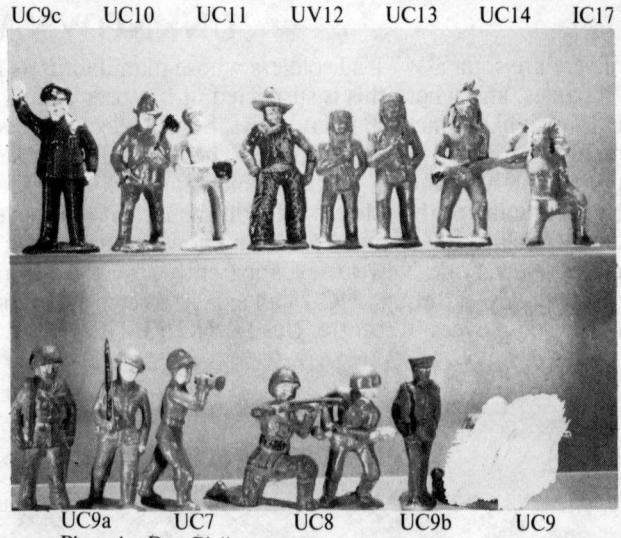

UC9c UC10 UC11 UV12 UC13 UC14 IC17

	G	VG	M
U2 Indian with rifle, hand shielding eyes.........	4.00	6.00	8.00
UC6 Drummer, WW II helmet...............	4.00	6.00	8.00
UC7 Slope arms, WW II helmet...............	4.00	6.00	8.00
UC8 Bugler, WW II helmet.	4.00	6.00	8.00
UC9 Rifle across waist, WW II helmet.............	2.00	3.00	4.00
UC9a Officer with Sword, WW II helmet........	4.00	6.00	8.00
UC9b Kneeling, firing, WW II helmet............	4.00	6.00	8.00
UC9c Traffic Cop........	3.00	4.50	6.00
UC10 Mailman, like Barclay B189..............	3.00	4.50	6.00
UC11 Fireman, like Barclay B187..............	3.00	4.50	6.00
UC12 Cowboy, like Barclay B95................	8.00	12.00	16.00
UC13 Indian with knife, like Barclay B48..........	8.00	12.00	16.00
UC14 Indian, rifle across waist, like Barclay B47...	3.00	4.50	6.00
UC14a Same as above, different size............	3.00	4.50	6.00
UC15 Mounted Indian, like Barclay B1............	10.00	15.00	20.00
UC16 Mounted Cowboy, like Barclay B2.........	9.00	13.50	18.00
UC17 Indian kneeling with tomahawk............	10.00	15.00	20.00
UC18 Indian kneeling with tomahawk, smaller version.	10.00	15.00	20.00
UC18a Cowboy with pistol, like Barclay B96........	4.00	6.00	8.00
UC18b Sailor, 3½" high, like Barclay B51........		No Price Found	
UC18c Marine, like Barclay B59.................		No Price Found	
U19 Indian kneeling with rifle.................	3.00	4.50	6.00
U20 Officer with sword, may be Manoil, looks like Manoil M9 and M10, but larger................		No Price Found	
UD21 Marching at slope, WW II helmet........	20.00	30.00	40.00
UD22 Rifle across waist, WW II helmet........	15.00	22.50	30.00
UD23 With Walkie-Talkie, WW II helmet........	15.00	22.50	30.00

UC9a   UC7   UC8   UC9b   UC9
Photo by Don Pielin

During the World War II era, Breslin Industries produced these Manoil and Barclay copies in Canada. Though cruder than the originals, they are worth at least as much to collectors.
Photo by Don Pielin

U2   UC6   U28

U33   UC9c   U34   U35
U33 U34 and U35 courtesy Bill Adams   Photo by Bill Kaufman

U30   U31a   U32   Photo by Don Pielin   UD25a

	G	VG	M
UD24 Throwing grenade, WW II helmet.........	3.00	4.50	6.00
UD25 Firing bazooka, WW II helmet.............	20.00	30.00	40.00
UD25a Officer in gas mask with pistol, WW II helmet	40.00	60.00	80.00
U26 Prone machine-gunner, recasting of Barclay B63.	4.50	6.75	9.00
U28 Seated machine gunner, WW II helmet, looks like Barclay B79a..........	5.00	7.50	10.00
U29 Football player standing..............	3.00	4.50	6.00
U30 Football player, kneeling..............	3.00	4.50	6.00
U31 Football player, center, kneeling..............	3.00	4.50	6.00
U31a Football Player, kicking..............	3.00	4.50	6.00
U32 Santa on Sled........	No Price Found		
U33 Majorette, solid lead, separate baton, "Made in U.S.A." stamped under base.................	No Price Found		
U34 Soldier crouching with rifle, distorted copy of Manoil M66...........	4.00	6.00	8.00
U35 Crouching Cowboy firing pistol, brace under arm and between legs....	5.00	7.50	10.00

So-called "Small Barclays", oval bases, 60-65 mm. high. TOP: Khaki Troops and West Pointer. BOTTOM: Foreign Troops (red jackets), Mountie, cowboy and sailor. Prices average $12 in mint.
Photo by Ed Poole

More so-called "Small Barclays". TOP: Oval bases, 54 mm high. MIDDLE: Hexagonal bases, 54 mm high. BOTTOM: Left, crudely molded thick hexagonal bases, 54 mm high, center, known Barclay horseman, right, several crude 60 mm types.
Photo by Ed Poole

PLAYWOOD PLASTICS

Playwood Plastics, a subsidiary of Transogram, began production in the spring or summer of 1944, with a factory at 133 Floyd Street, Brooklyn. Its soldiers, sculpted by Max Peinlich, were made of fine-ground sawdust, borax, flour and water. While the war lasted, the company was successful, employing 125 people, but never added to its original line of soldiers, partly because they had all the orders they could handle, and partly because finding metal for molds during war-time was too difficult. The soldiers were numbered in a 400 series, and marked with a P within a triangle.

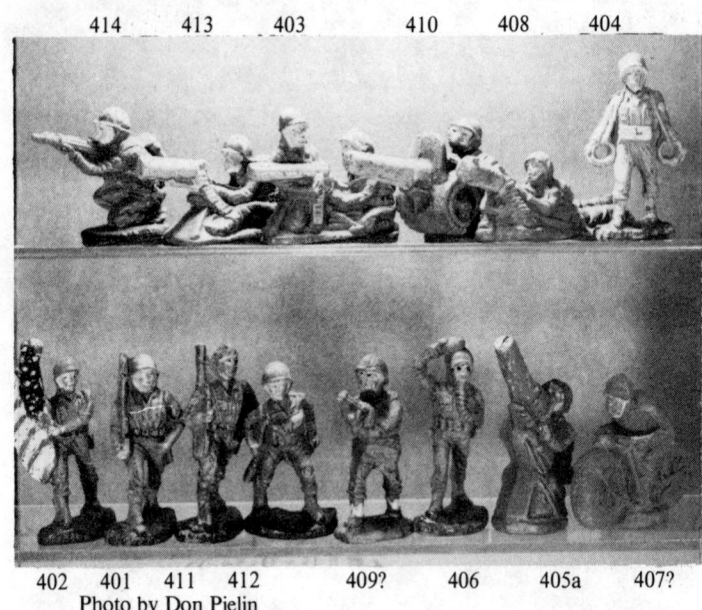

414   413   403   410   408   404

402   401   411   412   409?   406   405a   407?
Photo by Don Pielin

410a   410
Courtesy K. Warren Mitchell

Number unknown, advancing with rifle.
Courtesy K. Warren Mitchell.

407a   407?
Courtesy K. Warren Mitchell

	G	VG	M
401 Marching at Slope in helmet	4.00	6.00	8.00
402 Flagbearer	4.50	6.75	9.00
403 2-Man Machine Gun Team	4.00	6.00	8.00
404 Stretcher-Bearer	7.50	11.25	15.00
405 AA Gunner, triangle base	2.50	3.75	5.00
405a AA Gunner, plow base	No Price Found		
406 In Gas Mask with Flare Gun overhead	4.50	6.75	9.00

	G	VG	M
407? Motorcyclist with pot helmet	4.50	6.75	9.00
407a Looks exactly "438 or 436?"	No Price Found		
408 Prone with Machine Gun, crossed legs	2.50	3.75	5.00
408a Prone with Machine Gun, legs spread	No Price Found		
409? Advancing with Tommy Gun	4.00	6.00	8.00
410 Kneeling with Anti-Tank Gun, square shield, spoked wheels	4.50	6.75	9.00
410a Kneeling with Anti-Tank Gun, rounded shield, wheels not spoked	No Price Found		
411 Marching at Slope in Campaign Cap	6.00	9.00	12.00
412 Paratrooper with Rifle, Parachutes	6.50	9.75	13.00
413 Seated at Machine Gun	4.50	6.75	9.00
414 Kneeling Firing	4.50	6.75	9.00
438 or 436? Motorcyclist, Leather-type Helmet (probably post-War)	No Price Found		
Number unknown, advancing with rifle	No Price Found		

MOLDED PRODUCTS INC.

Molded Products Inc. was incorporated November 29, 1941 by Leslie S. Steinau and his son, Leslie Steinau, Jr. In the advertising display business, with war approaching, they sensed coming shortages would leave them little to advertise, and they purchased the extruding equipment Lionel had employed in making the figures for its Mickey Mouse handcar. Barclay salesman Irving Reader, hearing of the purchase, urged the Steinaus to produce soldiers with the equipment, with Reader utilizing his ties to dimestores as their sales manager. Sculpting was done by Bill Zegel, with the factory employing about thirty people at 203 East 12th Street in Manhattan. The company was highly successful throughout the War, but foundered shortly after it ended, when they no longer had a competitive edge in materials. The figures were made of wood flour, starch, whiting and water, with the distinctive hole in the base and between the legs a result of the soldiers being placed on nails during the drying process.

	G	VG	M
C1 Cowboy	2.00	3.00	4.00
C2 Indian	2.00	3.00	4.00
C3 Parachuting	4.00	6.00	8.00
C3a Parachuting, larger, inside of chute painted white, (not shown)		No Price Found	
C4 Aviator, "X" type front harness	3.00	4.50	6.00
C4a Aviator, square type front harness (not shown)		No Price Found	
C5 Soldier with gas mask, tommy gun and grenade, pot helmet	4.00	6.00	8.00
C6 Soldier with gas mask and pistol, WW I helmet	4.00	6.00	8.00
C7 Soldier with gas mask and pistol, WW II helmet	4.00	6.00	8.00
C8 Prone machine-gunner	4.00	6.00	8.00
C8a Prone machine-gunner, WW I helmet	4.00	6.00	8.00

	G	VG	M
C9 Sitting at AA Gun, WW I helmet	3.50	5.25	7.00
C9a Sitting at AA Gun, WW II helmet	3.50	5.25	7.00
C10 Sailor marching, 3⅝" high	2.00	3.00	4.00
C10a Sailor marching 3¼" high	2.00	3.00	4.00
C11 Marine marching, 3½" high	2.00	3.00	4.00
C11a Marine marching, 3¼" high	2.50	3.75	8.00
C12 Flagbearer	3.50	5.25	7.00
C12a Flagbearer, WW II helmet	3.50	5.25	7.00
C13 Marching, slope arms, WW I helmet	2.75	4.13	5.50
C13a Marching, slope arms, WW II helmet	2.50	3.75	5.00
C14 Officer on horse, WW II helmet	3.50	5.25	7.00
C15 Officer on horse, WW I helmet		No Price Found	

C12a   C13a   C13   C11   C11a   C10   C10a   C10a

C6   C7   C5   C4   C3   C3a
Photo courtesy Don Pielin

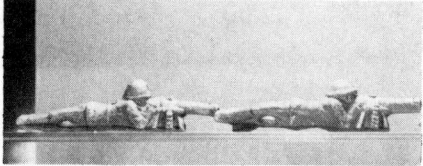

C8   C8a
Photo by Don Pielin

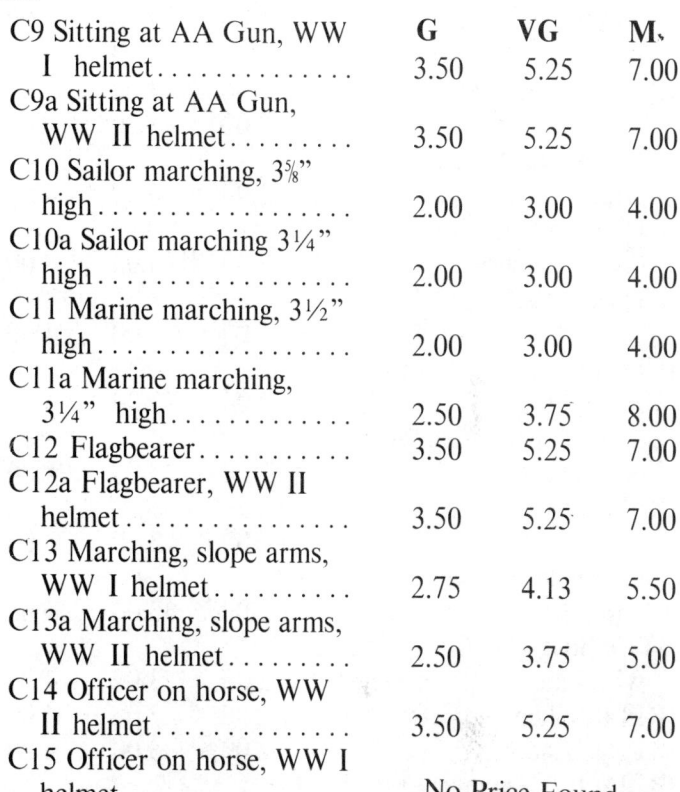

Front and back of C2
Photo by K. Warren Mitchell

C14   C9   C9a
Photo by Don Pielin

222

BETON

Bergen Toy & Novelty Co. (later known simultaneously, and more informally, as Beton), incorporated in 1936, but was in business as early as 1935, producing slush lead soldiers from molds purchased from Metal Cast. In 1938, it became the first company to manufacture acetate plastic figures. The company, owned by Charles Marcak and his wife Elsie, was only marginally successful, though its figurines were ubiquitous in dimestores of the 1940s and 1950s, and about 1958 it was sold to Rel Plastics. It is not known who sculpted toys for the company, which was located variously in Calstadt, Rutherford and Hackettstown (its last location), New Jersey.

	G	VG	M
Pre-1945			
(BT1) Marching Soldier....	2.00	3.00	4.00
BT2) Drummer Soldier.....	2.00	3.00	4.00
(BT3) Bugler Soldier.......	2.00	3.00	4.00
(BT4) Saluting Soldier.....	2.00	3.00	4.00
(BT5) Ammo Carrier Soldier	2.00	3.00	4.00
(BT6) Standing Firing Soldier..............	2.00	3.00	4.00
(BT7) Standing with Tommy Gun Soldier..........	2.00	3.00	4.00
(BT8) Grenade-thrower Soldier..............	2.00	3.00	4.00
(BT9) Officer Kneeling with Binoculars............	2.00	3.00	4.00
(BT10) Soldier Lying with Machine Gun..........	2.00	3.00	4.00
(BT11) Soldier Kneeling with Tommy Gun..........	2.00	3.00	4.00
(BT12) Soldier Charging with Bayonet..........	2.00	3.00	4.00
BT13) Soldier in Gas Mask with rifle.............	2.00	3.00	4.00
(BT14) Soldier Signalman...	2.00	3.00	4.00
(BT15) Cadet............	2.00	3.00	4.00
(BT16) U.S. Cavalry Officer, mounted.............	2.50	3.75	5.00
(BT17) Big Chief (mounted Indian holding bow).....	2.00	3.00	4.00
(BT18) Broncho Bill (mounted cowboy on bucking broncho).......	2.00	3.00	4.00
(BT19) Cowboy with hand on holster............	1.50	2.25	3.00
(BT20) Cowboy with Lasso.	1.50	2.25	3.00
(BT21) Cowboy with Pistol.	1.50	2.25	3.00
(BT22) Indian Leader (club raised high)............	2.00	3.00	4.00
(BT23) Indian Chief (with spear)...............	1.50	2.25	3.00
(BT24) Indian Warrior (hatchet touching head).....	1.50	2.25	3.00
(BT25) Indian with Bow...	1.50	2.25	3.00
(BT26) Indian with Arrow (holding arrow in one hand)...............	2.00	3.00	4.00
(BT27) Indian with Spear (Brave, not chief).......	2.00	3.00	4.00
(BT28) U.S. Cadet, Mounted	2.50	3.75	5.00

BETON Catalog, circa 1953
Courtesy Harold Frutchey

	G	VG	M
(BT29) Officer, Mounted (in peaked cap)............	2.00	3.00	4.00

Post-War Betons, With Copyright Dates
(some pieces were in production long before these dates)

	G	VG	M
(BT30) Baby Goat, September 1, 1949......	1.00	1.50	2.00
(BT31) Bear, January 2, 1952..............	1.00	1.50	2.00
(BT32) Buffalo, June 5, 1952	1.50	2.25	3.00
(BT33) Bugler, WW II Helmet, October 1, 1949.	2.00	3.00	4.00
(BT34) Bull, September 1, 1949................	1.00	1.50	2.00
(BT35) Calf, September 1, 1949................	1.00	1.50	2.00

Beton FOOTMEN

Trade Mark Reg. U.S. Pat. Off.

585 COWBOYS ASSORTED   RETAIL 10¢ ALL NUMBERS

Cowboy w/hand on holster   Cowboy w/lasso   Cowboy w/pistol

586 INDIANS ASSORTED

Indian Leader   Indian Chief   Indian Warrior

Indian w/bow   Indian w/arrow   Indian w/spear

NOT ILLUSTRATED:
582 COWBOYS AND INDIANS ASSORTED
590 POPULAR ASSORTMENT OF ALL FOOTMEN

All Numbers Packed: 2 dozen to handling box
Weight: 4 pounds per gross

BERGEN TOY & NOVELTY CO., INC.
FACTORY and MAIN OFFICE: HACKETTSTOWN, N. J.

BETON Catalog, circa 1953
Courtesy Harold Frutchey

Beton SMALL MOUNTED FIGURES

BETON Catalog, circa 1953
Courtesy Harold Frutchey

	G	VG	M
(BT36) Camel, January 2, 1952	1.00	1.50	2.00
(BT37) Charging Infantryman, WW II Helmet, October 1, 1949	2.00	3.00	4.00
(BT38) Running Infantryman, WW II helmet, October 1, 1949	2.00	3.00	4.00
(BT39) Chicken, September 1, 1949	.50	.75	1.00
(BT40) Clown, February 25, 1952	2.00	2.50	3.00
(BT40A) Colt, March 4, 1950	1.00	1.50	2.00
(BT41) Combat Infantryman, January 15, 1952	2.00	3.00	4.00
(BT42) Cow, July 1, 1949 ..	1.00	1.50	2.00
BT43) Cowboy Rider with hat in hand, May 1, 1950	2.00	2.50	3.00
(BT44) Crocodile, April 15, 1952	1.00	1.50	2.00
(BT45) Dancer, Standing on one foot, May 2, 1955 ...	1.00	1.50	2.00
(BT46) Dancing Girl, January 15, 1952	1.00	1.50	2.00

	G	VG	M
(BT47) Drummer, WW II helmet, October 1, 1949 .	2.00	3.00	4.00
(BT48) Duck, September 1, 1949	1.00	1.50	2.00
(BT49) Elephant, February 1, 1952	1.50	2.25	3.00
(BT50) Farm Boy, July 1, 1949	1.50	2.25	3.00
(BT51) Farmer, July 1, 1949	1.50	2.25	3.00
(BT52) Farmerette, July 1, 1949	1.50	2.25	3.00
(BT53) Female Goat, September 1, 1949	1.00	1.50	2.00
(BT54) Giraffe, January 15, 1952	1.50	2.25	3.00
(BT55) Goat, September 1, 1949	1.00	1.50	2.00
(BT56) Goose, September 1, 1949	.50	.75	1.00
(BT57) Gosling, September 1, 1949	.50	.75	1.00
(BT58) Hand Grenade Thrower, WW II helmet, October 1, 1949	2.00	3.00	4.00

224

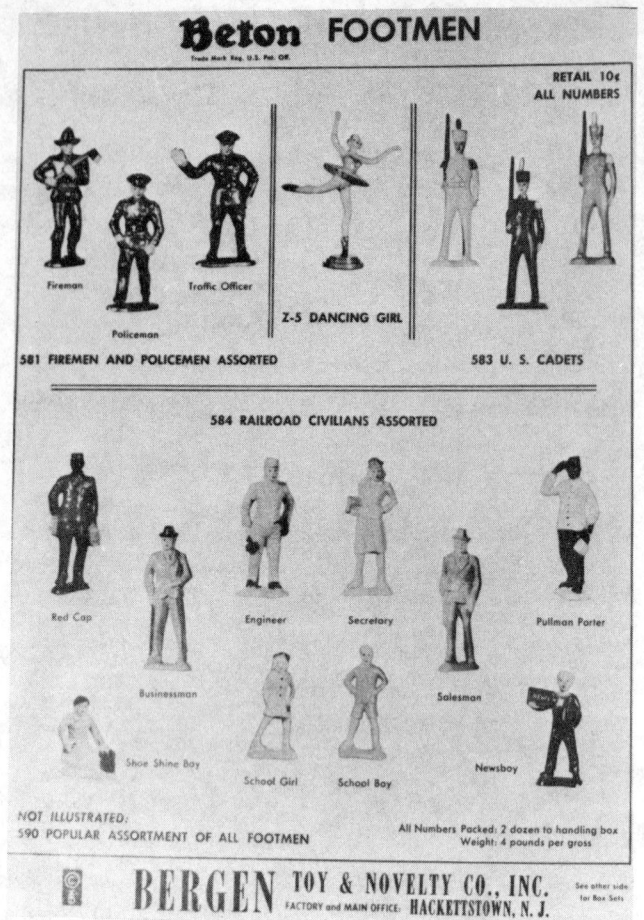

BETON Catalog, circa 1953
Courtesy Harold Frutchey

BETON Catalog, circa 1953
Courtesy Harold Frutchey

	G	VG	M
(BT59) Hippopotamus, February 2, 1953.......	1.00	1.50	2.00
(BT60) Indian Rhinoceros, February 10, 1953......	1.50	2.25	3.00
(BT61) Indian Warrior holding Flag and Shield, 5" high, January 2, 1952.	1.50	2.25	3.00
(BT62) Indian Warrior holding Lasso, 4" high, January 2, 1952........	1.50	2.25	3.00
(BT63) Infantry Flagman, WW II helmet, July 16, 1951	2.00	3.00	4.00
(BT64) Infantry Parachute Jumper, July 16, 1951...	2.00	3.00	4.00
(BT65) Infantry with Walkie-Talkie, July 16, 1951	2.00	3.00	4.00
(BT66) Infantry Flamethrower (Soldier), August 10, 1951........	2.00	3.00	4.00
(BT67) Infantryman Holding Bazooka, September 17, 1951	2.00	3.00	4.00

(BT68) Infantryman Wearing Gas Mask and holding

	G	VG	M
Automatic, August 10, 1951	2.50	3.75	5.00
(BT69) Infantryman with Field Glasses, kneeling, October 1, 1949........	2.00	3.00	4.00
(BT70) Infantryman with Gas Mask, carrying rifle, October 1, 1949........	2.00	3.00	4.00
(BT71) Kangaroo, April 15, 1952	1.00	1.50	2.00
(BT72) Kneeling Machine Gunner, October 1, 1949.	2.00	3.00	4.00

This cadet and Indian may have been produced by Metal Cast, or, more likely, produced by Beton before they turned from lead to plastic. They are worth about $10 in mint.
Photo by Don Pielin

	G	VG	M
(BT73) Lamb, Head Turned, September 1, 1949......	1.00	1.50	2.00
(BT74) Large Running Horse with Saddle, October 2, 1950.........	1.50	2.25	3.00
(BT75) Leopard, January 15, 1952.................	1.00	1.50	2.00
(BT76) Lion, September 24, 1951.................	1.00	1.50	2.00
(BT77) Machine Gunner, holding gun at waist, WW II helmet, October 1, 1949.................	2.00	3.00	4.00
(BT78) Machine Gunner in Prone Shooting Position, WW II helmet, October 1, 1949.................	2.00	3.00	4.00
(BT79) Marching Rifleman, WW II helmet, October 1, 1949.................	2.00	3.00	4.00
(BT80) Moose, February 1, 1952.................	1.50	2.25	3.00
(BT81) Munitions Carrier, WW II helmet, October 1, 1949.................	2.00	3.00	4.00
(BT82) Panther, January 15, 1952.................	1.50	2.25	3.00
(BT83) Pig, September 1, 1949.................	1.00	1.50	2.00
(BT84) Polo Player, August 24, 1951.............	2.00	3.00	4.00
(BT84a) Prancing Horse, January 1, 1950........	1.50	2.25	3.00
(BT85) Ram, September 1, 1949.................	1.00	1.50	2.00
(BT86) Reindeer, February 1, 1953.................	1.00	1.50	2.00
(BT87) Rider, Cadet, February 1, 1951.......	1.50	2.25	3.00
(BT88) Rider, Canadian Mounted Policeman, February 1, 1951.......	2.00	3.00	4.00
(BT89) Rider, Cavalry Officer, February 1, 1951..	1.50	2.25	3.00
(BT90) Rider, Cowgirl, July 16, 1951..............	2.00	3.00	4.00
(BT91) Rider, Cowboy Holding Hat, February 1, 1951.................	1.50	2.25	3.00
(BT92) Rider, Hunter, February 1, 1951.......	1.50	2.25	3.00
(BT93) Rider, Huntress, February 1, 1951.......	1.50	2.25	3.00
(BT94) Rider, Jockey, 3" high, February 1, 1951..	1.50	2.25	3.00

	G	VG	M
(BT95) Rider, Jockey, 2" high, February 1, 1951..	1.50	2.25	3.00
(BT96) Rifleman, WW II helmet, standing firing, October 1, 1949........	2.00	3.00	4.00
(BT97) Rooster, September 1, 1949.............	.50	.75	1.00
(BT98) Running Cow, July 1, 1949.............	1.00	1.50	2.00
(BT99) Saddled Standing Horse, March 4, 1950...	1.50	2.25	3.00
(BT100) Saluting Infantryman, WW II helmet, October 1, 1949........	2.00	3.00	4.00
(BT101) Seal, April 15, 1952	1.00	1.50	2.00
(BT102) Sheep, 3" long, September 1, 1949......	.50	.75	1.00
(BT103) Signaller, WW II helmet, October 1, 1949.	2.00	3.00	4.00
(BT104) Sitting Down Cow, August 21, 1950........	1.00	1.50	2.00
(BT105) Small Cowboy Holding a Rifle, September 20, 1950.....	1.50	2.25	3.00
(BT106) Small Riders, Cowboy holding a Guitar, September 20, 1950.....	1.50	2.25	3.00
(BT107) Small Riders, Cowgirl, 3" high, September 20, 1950.....	1.50	2.25	3.00
(BT108) Small Running Horse, 4" long, September 1, 1950.............	1.00	1.50	2.00
(BT109) Standing Horse, February 21, 1950......	1.00	1.50	2.00
(BT110) Swine, September 1, 1949.................	.50	.75	1.00
(BT111) Tiger, January 15, 1952.................	1.00	1.50	2.00
(BT112) Trainer, Holding a Whip, February 25, 1952	2.00	3.00	4.00
(BT113) Turkey, September 1, 1949.............	.50	.75	1.00
(BT114) Zebra, February 15, 1952.................	1.00	1.50	2.00

BETON Plastic Soldiers — Photo by Ed Poole

PLASTIC TOYS INC.

Until 1982, when ads and articles regarding Plastic Toys Inc. were discovered in back issues of toy trade magazines, it was thought that the unmarked, integrally cast-base soldiers they produced were made by Beton. There was at least one tie to the latter company, aside from the fact that Plastic Toys Inc.'s soldiers were replicas of Beton's, and that was that O.J. Sharpe, the executive vice president of the firm, had previously served as sales manager for Beton. The company, originally located in Cambridge, Ohio, and later in Byesville, was formed in early 1944, and began delivering its soldiers to retailers in July of that year. By 1945, it had produced "several million", according to one of its ads. The company also manufactured three ships, farm animals, barnyard fowl, and later in its history, cowboys and Indians which bore no resemblance to Beton's figures. Prices for their soldiers are the same as for the Betons.

PLASTIC TOYS INC. Soldiers Set
Photo by Bill Kaufman

PLASTIC TOYS INC. Soldiers
Photo by Bill Kaufman

AUSLEY

Ausley Industries, Inc. began in 1943 in Atlanta, Georgia, and later moved to Thomasville, Georgia. Robert C. Ausley, its owner, founded it as a way of earning extra income. Its original soldiers were lead, and produced from home-casting sets. However, in 1948, when lead became too expensive, and soldiers no longer were as popular, Ausley turned to plastic figures, sculpting the company's single cowboy and Indian himself. The cowboys and Indians, which had movable arms, were produced in plastic injection molds, and sold well until the outbreak of the Korean War, when sales slackened drastically due to a renewed demand for soldiers. Ausley's other business precluded his putting any more time into the company, and it ended production in 1950. All told, Ausley produced about 250,000 lead and plastic figures. The cowboys and Indians retailed at a dime apiece. Today, their value is about $2.00 each.

AUS 1 - Cowboy with two moving arms
AUS 2 - Indian with two moving arms

Boxed set of Ausley Cowboys and Indians
Photo by Elizabeth Ausley

MILLER

Although cast in plaster, a fragile material, Miller soldiers were sold in the toy sections of 5&10s in 1950 and 1951 at 19 cents apiece. Five inches high, they were always marked on the top of the base "Miller 1950" or "Miller 1951". All the guns were plastic and separate. Those figures sold while this book was being compiled averaged $13.00 apiece in mint condition. The following list was compiled by K. Warren Mitchell.

(ML 1) Stretcherbearer
(ML 2) Wounded man on separate cloth and wire
  stretcher
(ML 3) Nurse with Plasma
(ML 4) General MacArthur
(ML 5) Officer with Binoculars
(ML 6) Soldier Kneeling with Sentry Dog
(ML 7) Soldier Kneeling with Flame-Thrower
(ML 8) Soldier Kneeling with Walkie-Talkie
(ML 9) Soldier Prone with Bazooka
(ML 10) Soldier Prone with Rifle

(ML 11) Soldier in Foxhole Firing Rifle
(ML 12) Soldier Walking with Flag
(ML 13) Soldier advancing with rifle (possibly also with
  tommy gun)
(ML 14) Soldier throwing Grenade
(ML 15) Soldier charging with Machine Gun
(ML 16) Soldier planting flag
(ML 17) Soldier marching with rifle
(ML 18) Kneeling with Bazooka

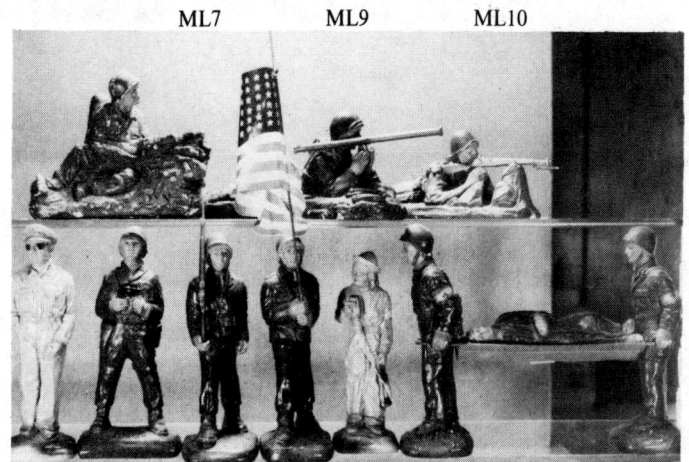

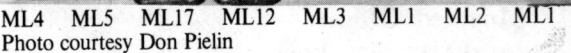

Photo courtesy Don Pielin

Photo courtesy Don Pielin

Two very simple 2½" solid lead figures of a man and woman.

LINCOLN LOG

These figures, about 2" high, were introduced in 1928. Beginning in 1933, some were also produced by Wright under the name Noveltoy Miniatures. The following listing is Lincoln Log's own description, if in bold type.

LL13 LL14 LL1 LL12 LL22 LL23 LL19 LL16 LL17 LL18
Photo by Don Pielin

LL24 LL25 LL28 LL26 LL27 LL29 LL33 LL34 LL35 LL36 LL37 LL38
Photo by Don Pielin

	G	VG	M
LL1 Foot Soldier of 1812	3.00	4.50	6.00
LL2 Indian with Gun	2.00	3.00	4.00
LL3 Indian with Gun (warbonnet)	2.00	3.00	4.00
LL4 Indian with Bow	2.00	3.00	4.00
LL5 Indian with Bow, (warbonnet)	2.00	3.00	4.00
LL6 Indian Crawling	2.00	3.00	4.00
LL7 Cowboy - Foot (with lasso)	2.00	3.00	4.00
LL8 Cowboy - Foot (firing pistol)	2.00	3.00	4.00
LL9 Indian - Mounted (with rifle)	2.50	3.75	5.00
LL10 Indian - Mounted (with bow)	2.50	3.75	5.00
LL11 Cowboy - Mounted (firing pistol)	2.50	3.75	5.00
LL12 Foot Soldier of 1776	3.00	4.50	6.00
LL13 Mounted Officer of 1776	15.00	22.50	30.00
LL14 Mounted Officer of 1776 (larger casting)		No Price Found	
LL15 Pioneer - Foot	2.00	3.00	4.00
LL16 Foot Soldier of 1918 (marching)	3.00	4.50	6.00

	G	VG	M
LL17 Foot Soldier of 1918 (charging)	3.00	4.50	6.00
LL18 Machine Gunner (prone)	3.00	4.50	6.00
LL19 Mounted Officer	4.00	6.00	8.00
LL20 Royal Canadian Police (foot)	4.00	6.00	8.00
LL 21 Mounted Officer (Mountie)		No Price Found	
LL22 Sailor (foot)	3.00	4.50	6.00
LL23 West Point Cadet (foot)	2.50	3.75	5.00
LL24 Og	20.00	30.00	40.00
LL25 Nada	10.00	15.00	20.00
LL 26 Big Tooth	7.50	11.25	15.00
LL 27 Three Horn	10.00	15.00	20.00
LL 28 Ru		No Price Found	
LL 29 Rex		No Price Found	
LL 30 Abe Lincoln		No Price Found	
LL 31 Farmer	2.00	3.00	4.00
LL 32 Farmer's Wife	2.00	3.00	4.00
LL 33 Conductor	2.50	3.75	5.00
LL 34 Engineer	2.50	3.75	5.00
LL 35 Red Cap	3.00	4.50	6.00
LL 36 Telegram Boy	2.50	3.75	5.00
LL 37 Policeman	2.50	3.75	5.00
LL 38 Passenger	2.00	3.00	4.00
LL 39 Oxen Team	4.00	6.00	8.00

TOOTSIETOY

TOOTSIETOY produced a line of four flat 1½" high metal soldiers beginning in 1938. The figures were a Seated Machine-Gunner, Charging Soldier, Marching Rifleman, and Colorbearer. These were sold 10 on a card for a dime. Today, they sell for about $2.00 apiece in mint.

TOOTSIETOY Soldiers & Ambulance.
Photo by Ed Poole

ARCADE

Arcade's solid cast iron soldiers were oddly streamlined, in an art deco style. Five types are known, and appear to have been first produced in 1939. They came in at least two finishes, nickel and light bronze, as a way of forming separate armies. A set of 56 pieces included, in addition to the soldiers, an ambulance, an anti-aircraft gun and three planes, two with two engines, and one with four. In 1939, the set sold for $1.00. Despite being made of iron, and presumably near-indestructible, Arcade's soldiers turn up rarely, and sell for about $5 apiece in mint. The numbers and descriptions that follow are Arcade's own.

7721 Soldier "Sentry", 1⅝" high
7722 Soldier "Skirmisher", 1⅝" high
7723 Soldier "Sniper", 1¼" high

7724 Soldier "Marksman", 1⅝" high
7725 Soldier "Grenadier", 1¾" high

AMERICAN SOLDIER CO.

The American Soldier Co. was perhaps the first commercial mass producer of hollow lead toy soldiers in the United States. The company originally used Britains' soldiers in its sets with pop guns, and later developed its own figures. The soldiers came with a display tray, credited to C. W. Beiser, with patents recorded in Germany on April 11th, 1903, and in England on April 12th, 1904, and in the U.S. on February 21st, 1905. Its address appears to have been Glendale, Brooklyn, New York. In September, 1930, Selchow & Righter of 200 Fifth Avenue, New York, announced the purchase of all rights, patents, trade-marks, machinery and stocks of the "American Hero" cowboy and Indian sets "formerly manufactured by the American Soldier Company". These continued to be sold with trays and pop guns. A 28-piece American Soldier Co. set with soldiers, tents and rifle, with cardboard table and tilting bases in fair-good condition sold for $880 in 1982 at Christie's, New York. In November, 1981, a smaller set in the original box in excellent condition sold for $80.

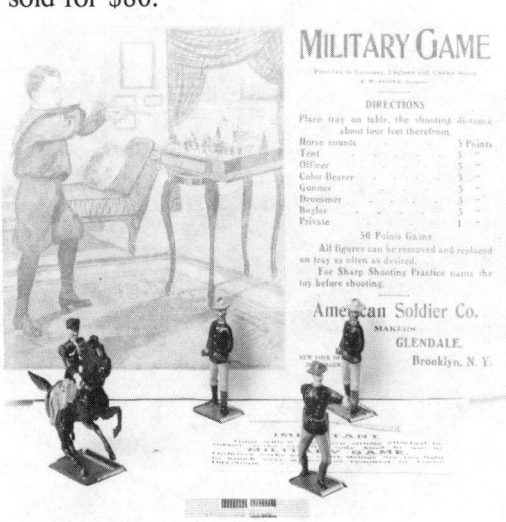

A four-piece American Soldier Co. game sold June 1982 for $352 at Christie's.
Courtesy Christie's New York

AMERICAN SOLDIER COMPANY U.S. Troops, 54 mm high
Photo by Ed Poole

IDEAL

IDEAL Toy Co. of Bridgeport, Connecticut, produced toy soldiers circa 1920-1924, and was owned by Lewis David Christie. The soldiers, hollowcast of lead, were approximately 54 mm. high, and were crude in design. In 1923-24 there was a "Metal Toy & Soldier Co." located at the same address, 252 Middle Street. Whether this was Ideal is not known. It possibly may have been the name of the firm before Christie bought it.

	G	VG	M		G	VG	M
(I-1) Infantryman with campaign hat	4.00	6.00	8.00	(I-8) Sailor at slope arms	5.00	7.50	10.00
(I-2) Bugler, brown uniform	4.00	6.00	8.00	(I-9) Sailor, rifle thrust out at angle	5.00	7.50	10.00
(I-3) Bugler, blue uniform	4.00	6.00	8.00	(I-10) Kneeling rifleman, steel helmet	3.00	4.50	6.00
(I-4) Officer with sword, grey uniform	4.00	6.00	8.00	(I-11) Train figure, conductor?	No Price Found		
(I-5) Officer with sword, blue uniform	4.00	6.00	8.00	(I-12) Train figure, signalman	No Price Found		
(I-6) Infantryman with rifle, cap, blue uniform	4.00	6.00	8.00	(I-13) Train figure, woman	No Price Found		
(I-7) Officer, blue uniform, no weapons	4.00	6.00	8.00	(I-14) Indian, arm raised	3.00	4.50	6.00
				(I-15) Indian, with rifle	3.00	4.50	6.00

I-1 I-2 I-4 I-5 I-6 I-3 I-7 I-8 I-9

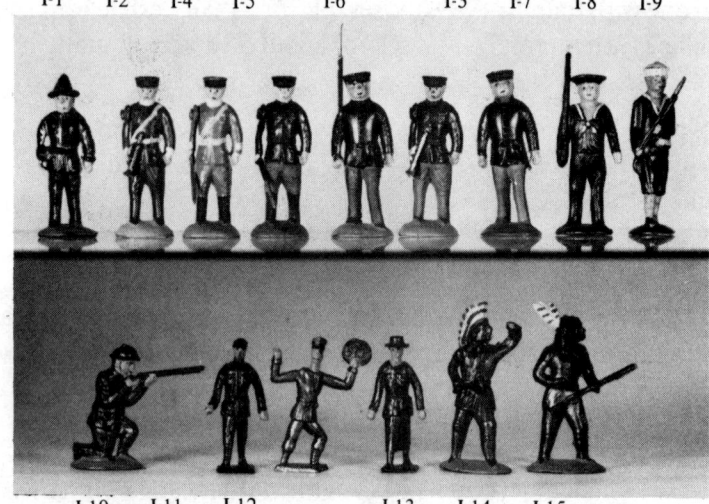

I-10 I-11 I-12 I-13 I-14 I-15
Photo by Bill Kaufman
Courtesy Hank Anton

McLOUGHLIN BROS.

McLoughlin Bros. was probably the earliest mass manufacturer of American soldiers, dating from the turn of the century. The New York-based company's figures were originally solid, and it is believed the company later produced hollow lead soldiers in about a 2¼" size, among them American doughboys, but this has not been established. A set of 18 U.S. Infantry wearing spiked helmets, one of them a drummer, circa 1890, were offered recently for $300.00. A boxed set of "Soldiers On Parade", containing 19 West Point Cadets marching at slope, plus one officer, with a patent date of April 7, 1914, was offered in near mint condition for $125.00.

A twelve-piece "Cavalry Soldiers" turn of the century boxed set by McLoughlin Bros. sold at auction at Christie's for $460 in October, 1981.
Photo courtesy Christie's New York

A 37-piece McLoughlin Bros. turn of the century "Infantry and Cavalry Soldiers" boxed set (see accompanying photo of box cover) sold for $480.00 at auction in October, 1981 at Christie's.
Courtesy Christie's New York

MARX

MARX produced a large number of 3½" flat tin lithographed soldiers in the 1930s and after which are attractive to collectors. The following list was compiled by collector Gene Parker. Individual figures average $3.00 in mint condition, except for the rarer prone figures, which average $6.00 in mint.

1MA 2AM 3MA 5MA 6MA 7MA 8MA 9MA

10MA 11MA 12MA 13MA 15MA 16MA 17MA 17MA
Photo by Ed Poole

18MA 20MA 21MA 22MA 24MA 25MA 26MA 27MA

28MA 29MA 30MA 32MA 33MA 34MA 35MA 36MA
Photo by Ed Poole

37MA 38MA 39MA 40MA 41MA 42MA 43MA

44MA 45MA 46MA 47MA 48MA 49MA 50MA 51MA
Photo by Ed Poole

(1MA) U.S. Cavalry
(2MA) Infantry Private, marching
(3MA) Infantry Private, attention
(4MA) Infantry Private, lying prone fixing bayonet
(5MA) American Infantry "Doughboy"
(6MA) Air Force Mechanic
(7MA) American Cowboy standing
(8MA) American Cowboy on horseback
(9MA) Infantry Private, kneeling firing rifle
(10MA) Infantry Sergeant
(11MA) Gordon Highlander
(12MA) Italian Bersaglieri
(13MA) King Royal Rifle Corps
(14MA) Royal Scots Greys
(15MA) Seaman Equipped for landing force
(16MA) Signalman, Navy
(17MA) Infantry Private, charging, two versions
(18MA) Infantry Private w/automatic rifle, lying prone, brown uniform
(19MA) Infantry Private w/automatic rifle, lying prone, blue uniform
(20MA) Sharpshooter w/rifle, green uniform
(21MA) French Infantry
(22MA) Indian Sikh
(23MA) Uhlan (Prussian Cavalry Soldier)
(24MA) Russian Infantry
(25MA) German Infantry
(26MA) Infantry First Lieutenant
(27MA) American Indian, standing
(28MA) Bandit, on horse
(29MA) Howitzer
(30MA) Ski Trooper on patrol
(31MA) Marine Corps Private
(32MA) Radio Operator
(33MA) Red Cross Nurse
(34MA) Machine Gun Unit, private w/30 cal m/g
(35MA) Tank Commander, standing
(36MA) Infantry Captain
(37MA) Chief Petty Officer
(38MA) Parachute Trooper
(39MA) 3-inch Anti-Aircraft Gun
(40MA) Marine Corps Officer
(41MA) Motorcycle Messenger
(42MA) Wounded Soldier
(43MA) Flame Thrower
(44MA) Pilot, with papers
(45MA) Pilot, adjusting gloves
(46MA) Sniper, camouflaged
(47MA) Infantry Colonel
(48MA) Captain Commands Battleship
(49MA) Officer in full dress uniform

Marx Castle Fort

Marx Castle/Fort box

MARX Set with popgun, "Soldiers of Fortune"
Photo by Ed Poole

MARX Set with cannon, "Soldiers of Fortune"
Photo by Ed Poole

	G	VG	M
(50MA) General			
(51MA) 50 cal. machine gun			
(52MA) Fireman, sold with fire truck			
MARX Soldiers of Fortune, set of eight with pop gun.	15.00	22.50	30.00
MARX Soldiers of Fortune, set of eight with cannon.	10.00	15.00	20.00

	G	VG	M
MARX Soldiers of Fortune, Fort Dix Barracks	15.00	22.50	30.00
MARX Soldiers of Fortune, set of 24 with pop gun	15.00	22.50	30.00
MARX Anti-Tank set, anti-tank gun, exploding tanks, soldiers, circa 1940	40.00	60.00	80.00

MARX PLAYSETS

These sets, with plastic figures and metal buildings, were produced in the 1950s and 1960s, and have become increasingly popular in the past few years. The following list is not complete, but simply a compilation of those sets that appeared for sale recently. 90% of the sculpture was by Joe Ferriot of Ferriot Bros., of Akron, Ohio.

Alamo No.3442	20.00	30.00	40.00
Alamo, Walt Disney Official Davy Crockett at the, No.3520	20.00	30.00	40.00
Babyland Nursery No.3380.	45.00	67.50	90.00
Battle of Little Big Horn	20.00	30.00	40.00
Battleground No.4756	30.00	45.00	60.00
Beachhead Landing Set No.4939	50.00	75.00	100.00
Ben Hur	75.00	112.50	150.00
Cape Canaveral No.4524	45.00	67.50	90.00
Captain Gallant No.4729	62.50	93.75	125.00
Captain Solar Space Academy No.7020	65.00	97.50	130.00
Farm Set No.3942	35.00	52.50	70.00
Fort Mohawk No.3752	20.00	30.00	40.00
Happitime International Airport No.5931	62.50	93.75	125.00
Jungle Playset No.3716	30.00	45.00	60.00
Knight and Viking Set No.4733	70.00	105.00	140.00
Lone Ranger Set No.3969	50.00	75.00	100.00
Lone Ranger Rodeo, no number, figures early, no bases, has Lone Ranger on foot (see MOVIES)			
Medieval Castle Fort No.4709	37.50	56.25	75.00

	G	VG	M
Modern Farm Set No.3938.	16.00	24.00	32.00
Modern Farm Set No.3940.	35.00	52.50	70.00
Presidents of the U.S.......	17.50	26.25	35.00
Prince Valiant No.4706 (see COMIC CHARACTER).			
Rex Mars Planet Patrol No.7040	27.50	41.25	55.00
Rin Tin Tin of Fort Apache No.3658 (see MOVIES)			
Roy Rogers Ranch Set No.3979, early, figures have no bases..........	45.00	67.50	90.00
Roy Rogers Rodeo Ranch, Happitime No.3992, early	45.00	67.50	90.00
Roy Rogers Rodeo Ranch No.3996 (see MOVIES)			
Sears Happitime Complete Dairy Farm No.5944....	50.00	75.00	100.00
Sears Stock Farm No.6005.	35.00	52.50	70.00
Super Circus No.4320.....	150.00	225.00	300.00
U.S. Armed Forces Training Center No.4151........	50.00	75.00	100.00
U.S. Army Training Center No.4122, early.........	50.00	75.00	100.00
U.S. Army Training Center No.4133	10.00	15.00	20.00
U.S. Army Training Center No.4153	45.00	67.50	90.00
Untouchables No.4676....	225.00	337.50	450.00
Zorro, Official Walt Disney Playset No.3754........	27.00	40.50	54.00

MARX Captain Gallant Playset figures
Photo by Paul Stadinger

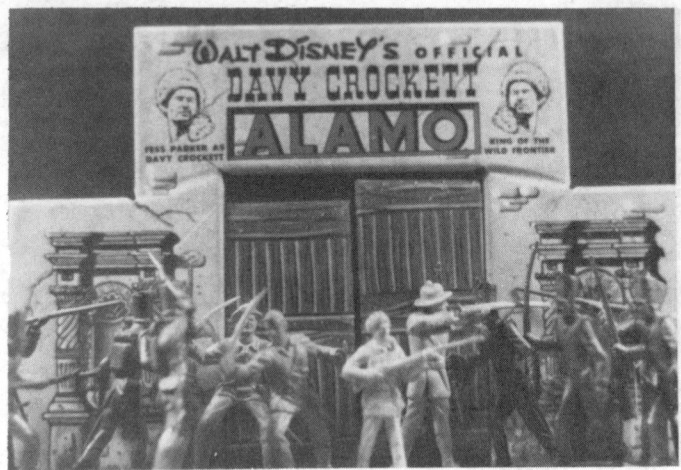

MARX Alamo Playset figures and gate
Photo by Paul Stadinger

MARX Untouchables Playset figures
Photo by Paul Stadinger

MARX Rin Tin Tin Playset figures
Photo by Paul Stadinger

WARREN

Warren's soldiers are particularly prized by those who are attracted to Wm. Britain's soldiers, being roughly the same 54 mm size, and equal in quality. The company, located in New York, New York, was in business from only 1936-1939, and thus its toys are rare. There were about 60 pieces in all, some possibly sculpted by owner John Warren, and the others by former Tommy Toy sculptress Margaret Cloninger, who later married Warren. Warren produced only American soldiers, infantry, cavalry and horse artillery. In 1936, the line was mainly U.S. Cavalry and light Field artillery, with infantry being added in 1937. In 1936 the individual soldiers sold for fifty cents up, and the boxed sets from $2.50 to $20.00. In 1937, one-dollar boxed sets were added. In June, 1982 at Christie's East, a set of 16 U.S. Infantry, in steel helmets, standing at attention, with flagbearer, officer with sword (one head missing, one base broken) sold for $418.00. At the same auction, 4 sets of Warren's No.34 3" guns in original boxes, sold for $242.00. Warren's Scout Car and Staff Car were in very limited production, and are each worth a minimum of $200.00 in mint. Foot figures average $35 apiece and mounted $125 apiece.

WARREN mounted troops
Courtesy Bob Kneale

WARREN Cavalrymen
Courtesy Ed Poole

(Above two photos) WARREN Horse Artillery. This set sold at PB Eighty-Four New York on August 1, 1980 for $550. One of the horses had a broken foreleg.
Photo Courtesy PB Eighty-Four New York

16 Warren U.S. Infantry sold in June, 1982, for $418 at Christie's
Photo courtesy Christie's New York

WARREN foot soldiers   Courtesy Bob Kneale

WARREN Officer's Car No.42 and Three Inch Gun No.34
Courtesy Bob Kneale

COMET

Comet Metal Products was founded in 1919 as a die-casting company by Abraham Slonim. Around 1940 he and his sons Joseph and Samuel began turning out solid-cast lead soldiers in a 54 mm size. Most had moving arms, and some were exact copies of other companies', such as Britains. These pieces are easily identified by the bases, which look like this: ⊂⊃ The company, which was located in Queens, New York, produced ID models of planes, ships and vehicles during the War for the government, and in 1946 formed the Authenticast toy soldier company. The following listing is from what appears to be a summer, 1941 catalog put out by Comet. Prices for boxed sets of mint Comet figures average $40.00.

COMET Boxed Set of FR662 French Foreign Legion charging.
Photo by Bill Kaufman

C1 8 Chinese Infantry Charging
K10 8 Knights in Armor w/Shields
K11 7 Knights in Armor w/Shields (better painting)
K12 6 Knights in Armor w/Shields & Lances
GR50 7 Greek Evzones Marching
GR51 8 Greek Infantry Charging
GR52 8 Greek Evzones Marching (field uniform)
T70 8 Turkish Infantry Charging
T71 Turkish Machine Gun Set
D75 7 Danish Infantry Marching
D76 8 Danish Royal Guards Marching
A100 6 Arabs Running w/Swords
A101 6 Arabs Running w/Rifles
M200 8 Mexican Volunteers Marching
EG450 8 Egyptian Infantry Charging
G500 8 German Infantry Charging
G501 8 German Infantry (SS Troops) Charging
G502 8 German Infantry Marching
G503 German Machine Gun Set
G504 8 German Infantry Running
G505 8 German Infantry (SS Troops) Running
G506 8 German Sailors Marching
G507 8 German Infantry (SS Troops) Marching
G508 German Machine Gun Set (SS Troops)
G509 7 Austro-German Alpine Troops
G511 7 German-Alpine Troops
G514 6 German (SS) Shock Troops
FR650 8 French Infantry Charging
FR652 8 Turcos Charging
FR654 8 Zouaves Charging
FR656 8 Moroccans Charging
FR658 8 Tunisians Charging
FR661 French Machine Gun Set
FR662 8 French Foreign Legion Charging
FR664 8 French Infantry (Maginot Line) Chg.
FR665 8 French Infantry (Maginot Line) Mchg.

FR666 8 French Infantry Marching
SP700 7 Spanish Infantry Charging
E800 7 Black Watch Troops Charging
E803 7 Indian Troops Charging
E804 8 British Navy Marching
E805 8 Australian Anzacs Charging
E806 8 New Zealand Infantry Charging
E807 8 English Infantry Charging
E808 8 British Marines Charging
E809 English Machine Gun Set
E810 8 English Royal Guards Marching
E811 8 English Infantry Running w/Gas Masks
E812 6 English General Staff
E813 7 R.A.F. w/Aeroplane
E814 8 R.A.F. without Aeroplane
E815 8 English Infantry Running
E816 8 English Infantry Marching Route Step
E817 New Zealand Machine Gun Set
E818 8 Canadian Infantry Marching Overseas Co.
E821 8 Sikhs Marching
E822 8 Indian Frontier Troops Marching
E823 6 Indian Malaca Troops Full Dress w/Lance
E824 7 Indian Troops Full Dress Marching
E827 8 Indian Army Marching
E828 Australian Machine Gun Set
I1000 7 Italian Colonial Troops Charging
I1001 8 Italian Infantry Charging
I1002 Italian Machine Gun Set
I1003 8 Italian Infantry Marching
J1050 8 Japanese Infantry Charging
USSR1100 7 Russian Infantry Charging
USSR1101 8 Russian Infantry Marching
USSR1102 7 Siberian Troops Marching
US1250 8 U.S. Infantry Charging Steel Helmets
US1251 8 U.S. Natl. Guard Charging Campaign Hats
US1252 8 West Point Cadets Marching

US1253 8 U.S. Marines Marching
US1254 8 U.S. Sailors Marching (white uniforms)
US1255 8 U.S. Sailors Marching (blue uniforms)
US1256 8 U.S. Infantry Marching Steel Helmet
US1257 8 U.S. Infantry Marching Overseas Caps
US1258 8 U.S. Panama Troops Charging
US1259 8 U.S. Philippine Troops Charging
US1260 8 U.S. Inf. Route Step Marching Steel Helmets
US1261 8 U.S. Inf. Route Step Marching Overseas Cap
US1262 U.S. Machine Gun Set Steel Helmets
US1263 U.S. Natl Guard Machine Gun Set Campaign Hat
US1264 8 U.S. Infantry Crawling w/Gas Masks
US1265 7 U.S. Marine Band
US1266 8 U.S. Infantry Band

US1267 6 American Indians w/Spears
US1268 8 U.S. Infantry Marching Overseas Caps
US1269 6 American Indians w/Tomahawks
US1274 U.S. Machine Gun Set Overseas Caps
US1275 8 U.S. Infantry Crawling Steel Helmets
S1300 7 Swedish Royal Guards Marching
US1776 6 "Spirit of 1776" (Price $8.40 doz.)
US2000 6 Colonial Infantry Marching (Revolution)
US2001 6 Colonial Infantry Charging (Revolution)
E2050 6 British Red Coats Marching (Revolution)
E2051 6 British Red Coats Charging (Revolution)
H2150 6 Hessian Troops Marching (Revolution)
H2151 6 Hessian Troops Charging (Revolution)

BRITAINS
by Joe Wallis

The most-collected of all toy soldiers are those manufactured by Englands' Britains Ltd. The firm was originally owned by William Britain, and in 1893 he introduced a hollow, three-dimensional lead soldier which was to revolutionize the toy soldier industry, and turn Britains into the largest toy soldier manufacturer in the world. Britains stopped producing lead soldiers in 1966, but still makes them in plastic. Prices include the box.

JOE WALLIS is the author of the book *Regiments of All Nations* (see bibliography), a comprehensive 258 page study and identification guide of postwar Britains from 1946-1966. He helped conceive and organize *The Old Toy Soldier Newsletter* when he lived in Chicago. He is one of five owners and the Britains editor of the *OTSN* since its beginning in 1976. (*OTSN* now has over 1,000 subscribers worldwide; its address can be found in the bibliography.) His extensive collection of prewar and postwar Britains has been accumulated over a 20-year period. He was born and raised in West Texas and now works as a grants officer for the Historic Preservation Fund grants program administered by the National Park Service of the U.S. Department of the Interior. He also enjoys Victorian military history and researching the historical background of Britains production.

A WORD ABOUT PRICES AND THIS LISTING
by Joe Wallis

Price alone has not been the predominant factor in selecting items to be included in this guide. Widespread interest by collectors and reasonable availability have been the major criteria. Prices listed are based upon the average prevailing at the time this is written, with unrepresentative aberrations (whether extremely high or very low) being excluded. Truly esoteric items, such as the Civilian Autogiro, which are unlikely to regularly appear on the market have also been excluded.

The rationale for such exclusions is that simply compiling and averaging all the prices of all the items sold over a period of time, without taking into account widely varying defects of condition or completeness inevitably results in an inaccurate median price. A rare item in average condition will generally always command a higher price than a common item in mint condition. Particular care must be exercised with auction prices realized because of "auction fever"; a wealthy but uninformed collector may get carried away and bid far beyond the normal price for an item that has struck his fancy. Such an auction price may not be repeated for many years. By the same token, lack of interest at one particular auction may cause an item to sell for less than it usually brings. No one should expect to receive retail prices for items from a dealer who must pay "wholesale" to provide a profit margin for his business, or when selling an entire collection to one buyer for convenience.

Other factors that cannot be overemphasized with Britains are condition, completeness of sets as issued by the manufacturer, and age of items. As with all old toys, collectors of Britains prize original condition (preferably with original boxes). Repainting, significant paint scratches, broken or structurally repaired pieces, and sets missing pieces will invariably lower not only the price **but may even determine whether an item will sell readily at all.** The accompanying discussion on the

238

importance of condition with toys found throughout this book **must** be kept in mind at all times when dealing with Britains.

The length of time a set was produced and the age of an item (older being harder to obtain in good condition) also affect prices. Some types of soldiers (such as Highlanders) were always produced, but are popular enough to maintain somewhat higher prices than their prevalence would otherwise dictate. Other sets have higher prices than their catalog records would seem to support (e.g. Set No.190, Belgian Chasseurs, which was always in the Britains catalog from 1913 to 1959, but does not seem to have been produced in great quantities.) There are also regional variations in which sets were available in different areas — probably connected with the idiosyncracies of hobby shop and department store orders being repeated without variation year after year.

With this background, the prices in this guide can be used as a general reflection of the market value of Britains sets with original boxes in 1984. Ultimately, however, the price of a Britains item, as with all hard-to-find toys, depends on how badly the seller wants to sell it, and how eagerly the buyer wishes to buy it.

BRITAINS No.2100, Republic of Venezuela.
Courtesy Phillips, New York

Britains No.2112 U.S. Marine Corps Band.
Photo Courtesy Phillips, New York.

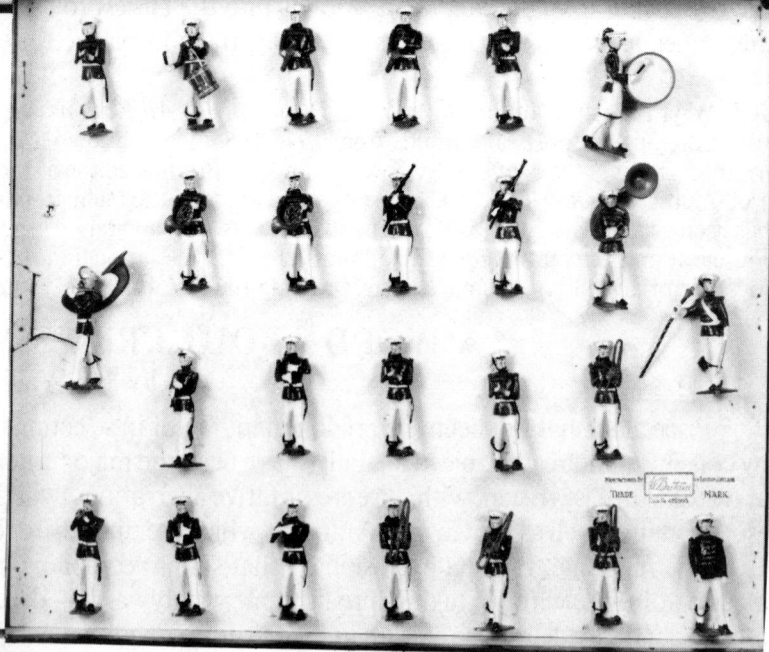

BRITAINS No.2018 Danish Army, Guard Hussar Rgt.
Photo Courtesy Phillips, New York

BRITAINS No.49 South Australian Lancers
Courtesy Christie's East

BRITAINS No.153 Prussian Hussars
Courtesy Christie's East

BRITAINS No.167 Turkish Infantry
Courtesy Christie's East

BRITAINS No.191 Turcos
Courtesy Christie's East

BRITAINS NO.199 Motor Machine Gun Corps (soldier missing
on 3rd motorcycle)
Courtesy Phillips New York

BRITAINS BOXED SETS

Set No.	G	VG	M
1 The Life Guards - walking with tin swords, 1893 version may be first set of British hollow lead soldiers made	150.00	190.00	250.00
Fred Whisstock label (4th version)	80.00	100.00	120.00
2 Horse Guards - mounted with aigulettes, 1953 version	70.00	90.00	115.00
3 Princess Charlotte of Wales' Dragoon Guards . .	125.00	187.50	250.00
8 Queen's Own Fourth Hussars, 1953 version . . .	75.00	100.00	130.00
11 Black Watch - charging with piper, 1950 issue, 6 pcs.	50.00	65.00	80.00
12 Prince Albert's Own Eleventh Hussars - with carbines, 1930 issue	150.00	185.00	230.00
13 Third Hussars - Fred Whisstock label, officer on prancing horse	160.00	200.00	250.00
15 Princess Louise's Argyll & Sutherland Highlanders - running	125.00	150.00	180.00
16 East Kent Regiment (The Buffs)	130.00	160.00	200.00
17 Somerset Light Infantry .	70.00	90.00	110.00
19 West Indian Regiment . .	160.00	210.00	275.00
24 Queen's Royal Ninth Lancers, 1935	100.00	140.00	175.00
27 Infantry Band, 1955 issue	200.00	250.00	300.00
28 Mountain Artillery, 1950 issue	160.00	190.00	225.00
30 Drums and Bugles of the Line - 1908-1912	100.00	150.00	200.00
1930's version	70.00	105.00	140.00
31 King's Dragoons, 1935, black plumes	150.00	200.00	250.00
32 Scots Greys, 1950 issue .	60.00	90.00	120.00
33 Sixteenth Lancers - officer turned to face troops, 1950 issue	80.00	110.00	140.00
34 Grenadier Guards firing .	65.00	90.00	110.00
35 Royal Marines, slope . . .	70.00	95.00	125.00
36 Sussex Regiment, slope, 1950 issue	70.00	90.00	110.00
1910 version	115.00	162.50	230.00
37 Coldstream Guard Band, 1950 issue	175.00	262.50	350.00
39 Royal Horse Artillery, 1950 issue	230.00	290.00	360.00
39B U.S. Cavalry on galloping horse	20.00	30.00	40.00
43 Second Life Guards - full gallop, 1930s painting . . .	180.00	230.00	280.00
44 Second Dragoon Guards, 1935 issue	82.50	123.75	165.00
46 Hodson's Horse; Tenth Bengal Lancers	150.00	190.00	230.00
47 Indian Army cavalry - 1936 issue	100.00	140.00	180.00
48 Egyptian Camel Corps, 1960 issue	60.00	90.00	120.00
49 South Australian Lancers, 1930 issue	175.00	225.00	300.00
52B Royal Canadian Mounted Police - winter dress in picture pack box, 1pc.	15.00	22.50	30.00
66 Thirteenth Duke of Connaught's Own Bombay Lancers, 1950 issue	75.00	100.00	125.00
68 Fourth Bombay Grenadiers, 1935	150.00	180.00	225.00
69 Pipers of the Scots Guard, 1935	80.00	120.00	160.00
71 Turkish Cavalry	165.00	220.00	270.00
74 Royal Welsh Fusiliers - with goat mascot, officer, 1960 issue	60.00	80.00	100.00
76 Middlesex Regiment - at the slope	45.00	67.50	90.00
77 Gordon Highlanders - at slope, with piper, postwar issue	50.00	65.00	85.00
78 Royal Navy Bluejackets, 1930 issue	100.00	130.00	150.00
79 Royal Navy Landing Party, 1960 issue	100.00	150.00	200.00
80 Royal Navy Whitejackets - at trail	80.00	120.00	160.00
82 Scots Guards Pioneers - with axes, flag bearer	50.00	75.00	100.00
83 Middlesex Yeomanry - full gallop	220.00	300.00	400.00
90 Coldstream Guards - firing (24 pcs)	150.00	210.00	260.00
92 Spanish Infantry - at the slope	150.00	200.00	250.00
94 Twenty-first Lancers with steel helmets	200.00	300.00	400.00
97 Royal Marines running at the trail, 1930 issue . . .	150.00	195.00	250.00

	G	VG	M
98 King's Royal Rifle Corps - green uniforms, red facings, 1930 issue........	125.00	187.50	250.00
99 Thirteenth Hussars.....	160.00	220.00	290.00
100 Empress of India's Twenty-first Lancers....	112.50	168.75	225.00
101 Life Guards mounted band in State Dress, 1960 issue................	240.00	310.00	380.00
105 Imperial Yeomanry, 1901 issue...........	240.00	290.00	365.00
107 Irish Guards marching.	85.00	110.00	140.00
108 Sixth Innniskilling Dragoons (khaki).......	220.00	280.00	350.00
109 Dublin Fusiliers - marching at the trail, smooth foreign service helmets, copyright labels, 1901 issue................	240.00	300.00	400.00
111 Grenadier Guards at attention - officer on swayback horse........	105.00	125.00	150.00
112 Seaforth Highlanders - at slope, 1940........	110.00	130.00	160.00
114 Queen's Own Cameron Highlanders - marching, 1930 issue...........	100.00	150.00	200.00
115 Egyptian Lancers, 1950 issue................	80.00	100.00	120.00
117 Egyptian Infantry at attention, 1958.........	110.00	140.00	170.00
118 Gordon Highlanders - officer with binoculars, lying, firing.............	105.00	157.50	210.00
119 Gloucestershire Regiment firing...........	140.00	210.00	280.00
120 Coldstream Guards kneeling firing - officer with binoculars, 1950 issue................	65.00	75.00	90.00
122 The Black Watch - firing.............	140.00	210.00	280.00
123 The Bikanir Camel Corps - with wire tails...	110.00	165.00	220.00
127 Seventh Dragoon Guards - at trot.......	200.00	250.00	300.00
133 Russian Tsarist Infantry - pre war...........	110.00	165.00	220.00
134 Japanese Infantry - charging.............	130.00	195.00	260.00
136 Russian Cossack Cavalry 1935 issue......	100.00	120.00	150.00
137 Royal Army Medical Service, 24 pcs......	225.00	337.50	450.00
138 French Cuirassiers.....	70.00	95.00	120.00
140 French Dragoons.....	225.00	337.50	450.00

	G	VG	M
141 French Infantry of the Line-light blue greatcoats, red trousers............	100.00	125.00	160.00
142 French Zouaves - charging, Post-war..........	40.00	60.00	80.00
144 Royal Field Artillery...	600.00	800.00	1000.00
145 The Royal Army Medical Corps- horse-drawn ambulance.......	240.00	300.00	350.00
145A Royal Army Medical Corps - horse and wagon, khaki................	300.00	380.00	430.00
146 Army Service Corps Wagon - two horse team and crew.............	210.00	250.00	300.00
146A Royal Army Service Corps - active service wagon................	280.00	350.00	400.00
147 Zulu Warriors........	60.00	90.00	120.00
150 North American Indians - on foot.............	50.00	70.00	90.00
152 North American Indians - mounted, with rifles and tomahawks...........	45.00	75.00	90.00
153 Prussian Hussars - Types of the German Army....	170.00	255.00	340.00
154 Prussian Infantry - marching, 1908............	150.00	225.00	300.00
156 Royal Irish Regiment..	125.00	155.00	185.00
157 Highlanders, firing....	70.00	105.00	140.00
160 Territorial Infantry, 1915 issue............	110.00	165.00	220.00
164 Bedouin Arabs of the Desert-mounted with scimitars and jezails.....	50.00	75.00	100.00
165 Italian Cavalry - blue tunics, white kepis, officer with sword............	210.00	270.00	320.00
166 Italian Infantry.......	130.00	160.00	200.00
167 Turkish Infantry......	150.00	190.00	230.00
169 Italian Bersaglieri, 1958 issue................	55.00	82.50	110.00
171 Greek Infantry - running at trail............	200.00	300.00	400.00
178 Austrian-Hungarian Foot Guards..........	110.00	165.00	220.00
179 Cowboys Mounted with Lassos..............	60.00	90.00	120.00
182 Eleventh Hussars - dismounted with horses, 1950 issue............	90.00	115.00	150.00
183 Cowboys on foot - early painting.............	70.00	105.00	140.00
187 Bedouin Arabs - on foot	45.00	67.50	90.00
188 Zulu Kraals - with palm trees	200.00	300.00	400.00

	G	VG	M
189 Belgian Infantry......	120.00	150.00	180.00
190 Belgian Chasseurs.....	130.00	160.00	200.00
191 French Turcos........	150.00	170.00	200.00
192 French Infantry of the Line - with shrapnel proof helmets..............	135.00	175.00	210.00
195 Infantry of the Line - with shrapnel proof helmets, officer with baton................	50.00	75.00	100.00
196 Green Evzones marching, 1950 issue.......	50.00	70.00	90.00
197 Gurkhas at the trail...	60.00	90.00	120.00
199 Motorcycle Machine Gun Corps - with side car and detachable operator..	160.00	200.00	250.00
201 Officers of the General Staff - mounted, Fred Whisstock label........	100.00	150.00	200.00
202 Togoland Warriors - with bows and arrows...	80.00	100.00	125.00
203 Royal Engineers' Pontoon Section..........	480.00	720.00	960.00
205 Coldstream Guards at present.............	105.00	125.00	150.00
206 Warwickshire Regiment	200.00	300.00	400.00
207 Officers and Petty officers.............	125.00	150.00	175.00
212 Royals Scots - with piper at slope, 5 pcs.....	80.00	100.00	120.00
213 Highland Light Infantry - at slope.............	200.00	250.00	300.00
214 Royal Canadian Mounted Police - marching in winter coats....	210.00	250.00	300.00
216 Argentine Infantry - at slope................	120.00	160.00	200.00
219B Yeoman of the Guard Officer with picture pack box, 1 pc.............	12.50	18.75	25.00
220 Uruguyan Cavalry, 4 pcs................	100.00	125.00	150.00
221 Uruguayan Cadets....	160.00	210.00	250.00
224 Bedouin Arabs - mounted and dismounted and on camels, Fred Whisstock label, 11 pcs..	150.00	225.00	300.00
225 Kings African Rifles - at slope................	75.00	105.00	135.00
227 U.S. WWI Doughboys - with campaign hats.....	80.00	100.00	120.00
228 U.S. Marines - winter dress................	55.00	82.50	110.00
229 U.S. Cavalry - 1950s in service dress..........	55.00	82.50	110.00

	G	VG	M
240 Royal Air Force - 1925, light blue uniforms......	75.00	102.50	150.00
241 Chinese Infantry......	137.50	206.25	275.00
258 WW I British Infantry- Fred Whisstock label, with gas masks........	65.00	80.00	100.00
267 U.S. Cavalry and Infantry	160.00	210.00	275.00
276 U.S. Cavalry........	180.00	220.00	260.00
299 West Point Cadets - in summer clothes........	37.50	56.25	75.00
312 Grenadier Guards in greatcoats, 1955 issue...	65.00	80.00	100.00
320 Royal Army Medical Corps	70.00	105.00	140.00
329 Scots Guards Sentry Box and Sentry........	15.00	22.50	30.00
400 The Life Guards - in winter cloaks..........	72.50	108.75	145.00
429 Scots Guards and Life Guards in overcoats and cloaks	125.00	187.50	250.00
432 German Infantry, 1960 issue	50.00	70.00	90.00
1201 Royal Artillery Gun - 5½" long............	10.00	15.00	20.00
1203 Tank of the Royal Tank Corps............	50.00	75.00	100.00
1250 Royal Tank Corps....	125.00	160.00	200.00
1253 U.S. Navy, white jackets...............	65.00	85.00	100.00
1254 Royal Engineers Pontoon Section...........	500.00	700.00	950.00
1257 Yeoman of the Guard (Beefeaters) - with governor	100.00	125.00	150.00
1263 Royal Artillery Gun - thin wheels, 3¾".......	8.00	12.00	16.00
1265 18" Howitzer for Garrison work - 3 shell cases.	40.00	60.00	80.00
1269B Trumpeter of the Life Guard in State Dresss, Picture Pack, 1 pc.......	15.00	22.00	28.00
1283 Grenadier Guards....	40.00	55.00	75.00
1291 Band of Royal Marines	250.00	300.00	360.00
1292 Royal Artillery Gun..	6.00	9.00	12.00
1301 U.S. Military Bank, khaki................	150.00	225.00	300.00
1307 16th Century Knights - in full armor, mounted and on foot............	35.00	50.00	65.00
1318 Machine Gunners....	55.00	82.50	110.00
1321 Green Rolls Royce Armored Car - rubber tires, swivelling gun, black			

	G	VG	M
mudguards and running board	175.00	265.00	350.00
1323 Royal Fusiliers, Seaforth Highlanders, Royal Sussex Regiment with 23 pcs	260.00	325.00	375.00
1325 Gordon HIghlanders, 16 pcs	150.00	200.00	250.00
1325B The Life Guards - trumpeter, regimental dress, Picture Pack box, 1 pc	17.50	26.25	35.00
1330 Royal Engineers General Service Wagon galloping	165.00	210.00	260.00
1333B Life Guard, winter cape, white horse, Picture Pack box, 1 pc	23.00	34.00	46.00
1334 Army Truck, metal wheels	70.00	105.00	140.00
1335 Army Truck - six wheels, 1955 issue	55.00	80.00	100.00
1337B Royal Horse Guard, trumpeter with grey horse in Picture Pack box	22.00	33.00	44.00
1343 Royal Horse Guards - mounted with cloaks	100.00	120.00	140.00
1349 Royal Canadian Mounted Police	70.00	90.00	110.00
1366 French Infantry and machine gunners, 7 pcs	95.00	125.00	150.00
1389 Belgian WW I Infantry	125.00	150.00	195.00
1395 King's Own Scottish Borderers	200.00	300.00	400.00
1413 Police Car with 2 officers, 2 tone brown	235.00	360.00	470.00
1432 Army Tender, with driver	70.00	105.00	130.00
1433 Army Tender split windshield and driver, caterpillar treads	70.00	90.00	110.00
1434 Abyssinian Royal Bodyguard and Tribesmen, 16 pcs	220.00	280.00	350.00
1435 Italian Infantry, khaki green uniforms, 1955 issue	50.00	75.00	100.00
1436 Italian Infantry, foreign service dress, 1936	165.00	247.50	330.00
1437 Italian Carabinieri, 1958 issue	75.00	112.50	150.00
1448 Army Staff Car - twin windshields, 1955 issue	145.00	185.00	250.00
1470 George VI Coronation Coach	185.00	220.00	280.00

	G	VG	M
1475 Display Box, Beefeaters, Outriders, Footmen of the Royal Household	145.00	200.00	250.00
1510 Royal Navy Sailors walking	100.00	130.00	160.00
1512 Army Ambulance, Post War	75.00	100.00	125.00
1515 Coldstream Guards - at slope	60.00	80.00	100.00
1518 British Infantry of the Line, "1815"	100.00	150.00	200.00
1519 Waterloo Highlanders, "1815"	120.00	160.00	200.00
1539 Mammoth Circus, 23 pieces	400.00	600.00	750.00
1542 New Zealand Infantry	60.00	90.00	120.00
1544 Australian Infantry	75.00	112.50	150.00
1554 Royal Canadian Police - on foot, summer dress	60.00	85.00	110.00
1596 South Wales Borderers, famous regiment set, 1937 (box especially important)	150.00	200.00	275.00
1603 Republic of Ireland Infantry - marching, 1939 peak caps	120.00	180.00	240.00
1610 Royal Marines - at "present arms"	100.00	130.00	160.00
1612 Gas Mask Infantry, service dress, bomb throwers	36.00	54.00	72.00
1614 Gas Mask Infantry Digging - assorted positions, 24 pcs	125.00	150.00	175.00
1621 Twelfth Frontier Force Regiment	210.00	315.00	420.00
1631 The Governor General's Horse Guards	60.00	90.00	120.00
1637 Governor-General's Horse and Foot Guards with officers	140.00	190.00	240.00
1638 Sound Locator	15.00	22.50	30.00
1639 Range Finder with operator, post war painting	10.00	15.00	20.00
1641 Underslung Heavy Duty Truck - 18 wheels, driver, white metal wheels	180.00	250.00	300.00
1711 French Foreign Legion - mounted officers and troops at slope	50.00	75.00	100.00
1715 Two-pound Light Anti-Aircraft Gun brass fixings	7.50	11.25	15.00
1717 AA two-pounder on mobile screw jack chassis	20.00	30.00	40.00

	G	VG	M
1720 Band of Royal Scot Greys - mounted......	200.00	300.00	400.00
1722 Drums and Pipes of the Scot Guard........	300.00	370.00	450.00
1723 Royal Army Medical Corps stretcher bearers and nurses...........	80.00	100.00	125.00
1725 4.5" Howitzer......	6.00	10.00	15.00
1726 Regulation Type Limber-rubber tires.....	10.00	15.00	20.00
1728 Predictor and Operator	15.00	20.00	25.00
1729 Height Finder and Operator.............	10.00	15.00	20.00
1730 The Royal Artillery...	60.00	80.00	100.00
1731 Spotter and Chair....	10.00	15.00	20.00
1759 Air Raid Precautions National Service Stretcher Party...............	150.00	200.00	250.00
1791 Royal Corps of Signals - dispatch riders........	70.00	90.00	115.00
1793 Motor Machine Gun - side car with driver and gunner, 2nd version, 1 pc	45.00	67.50	90.00
1828 Infantry of the Battleline - at ease........	190.00	285.00	380.00
1855 Miniature Barrage Truck with winch and balloon...............	60.00	90.00	120.00
1858 British Infantry......	50.00	75.00	100.00
1859 Sentry box with Sentry at ease - steel helmet....	30.00	45.00	60.00
1876 Bren Gun Carrier....	20.00	30.00	40.00
1877 Beetle Truck with Driver...............	42.00	63.00	84.00
1879 00 Scale Gas Cylinder Truck and 4-wheel trailer with cylinders for balloon	110.00	140.00	175.00
1892 Indian Infantry at the trail.................	80.00	120.00	160.00
1893 Indian Army Service Corps - includes mule....	75.00	112.50	150.00
1898 WW I British Infantry - Tommy Gunners......	40.00	55.00	70.00
1901 Cape Town Highlanders...........	85.00	110.00	130.00
1907 Staff - active service order................	75.00	105.00	135.00
1918 The Home Guard - marching with rifles.....	100.00	150.00	200.00
2009 Gelgium Army, le Regiments des Grenadiers	90.00	135.00	180.00
2010 Airborne Regiment - "Red Devils" marching with red berets........	80.00	105.00	125.00
2018 Danish Garde Hussars	225.00	337.50	450.00

	G	VG	M
2019 Danish Livgarde.....	105.00	130.00	165.00
2021 U.S. Military Police, "Snowdrops"...........	45.00	67.50	90.00
2022 Swiss Papal Guards...	90.00	135.00	180.00
2024 Light Goods Van with Driver, 1950s..........	120.00	180.00	240.00
2026 25-Pounder Howitzer.	5.00	8.00	12.00
2027 Red Army Guards in overcoats	70.00	105.00	140.00
2029 The Life Guards - mounted and on foot, 1953	60.00	80.00	100.00
2030 Australian Infantry - 1948, blue ceremonial dress	90.00	110.00	140.00
2033 U.S. Infantry - with steel helmets...........	40.00	60.00	80.00
2035 Swedish Lifeguards - ceremonial dress........	85.00	105.00	130.00
2037 Ski Trooper, 1 pc....	32.50	48.75	65.00
2041 Trailer - universal clockwork unit with keys.	20.00	30.00	40.00
2044 U.S. Air Corps, 1949 blue uniform, marching..	45.00	67.50	90.00
2046 Arab Display, 12 pcs..	150.00	225.00	300.00
2051 Uruguayan Military School Cadets..........	90.00	135.00	180.00
2055 Confederate Cavalry..	50.00	70.00	90.00
2056 Union Cavalry.......	50.00	70.00	90.00
2057 Union Artillery with gunners...............	40.00	50.00	60.00
2058 Confederal Artillery, with gunners..........	40.00	50.00	60.00
2059 Union Infantry......	40.00	60.0	75.00
2060 Confederate Infantry.	40.00	60.00	75.00
2062 Seaforth Highlanders, 1953, with pipers.......	140.00	175.00	225.00
2063 Argyll and Sutherland Highlanders, firing......	60.00	90.00	120.00
2064 155 mm Gun........	35.00	50.00	70.00
2065 Her Majesty the Queen, mounted........	20.00	30.00	40.00
2067 Sovereign's Standard & Escort	110.00	140.00	180.00
2075 Seventh Hussars - 1953	70.00	95.00	120.00
2076 Prince of Wales' 12th Royal Lancers.........	70.00	95.00	125.00
2078 Irish Guards - at "Present Arms"............	70.00	105.00	140.00
2079 The Royal Company of Archers, 14 pcs......	130.00	170.00	200.00
2085 Musical Ride of the Household Cavalry, 2 layer box, 23 pcs........	325.00	487.50	650.00

	G	VG	M
2091 Gloucestershire Regiment at the slope	120.00	160.00	200.00
2092 Parachute Regiment	130.00	170.00	220.00
2093 Band of the Royal Berkshire Regiment	500.00	750.00	950.00
2094 Open State Landau - Duke of Edinburgh	150.00	200.00	250.00
2095 French Foreign Legion in Action	90.00	135.00	180.00
2098 Venezuelan Army Military Cadets	100.00	150.00	200.00
2100 Republic of Venezuela Military Cadets, Infantry and Navy, 23 pcs	250.00	375.00	500.00
2101 U.S. Marine Corps Color Party	75.00	112.50	150.00
2102 Austin Champ jeep-detachable hood	20.00	30.00	40.00
2106 18" Heavy Howitzer for Garrison Work	30.00	45.00	60.00
2107 18" Heavy Howitzer on Tractor Wheels - 2 shell cases	30.00	45.00	60.00
2112 U.S. Marine Corps Band	600.00	800.00	1000.00
2148 The Fort Henry Guard with goat mascot	50.00	75.00	100.00
2150 Centurion Tank - desert warfare variation with aerials	240.00	360.00	480.00
2152 Waterloo Gunners	40.00	60.00	80.00
2175 155 mm Self-propelled gun, on centurion tank body	160.00	220.00	300.00
9145 Royal Scots marching	60.00	90.00	120.00
9149 British Machine Gunners	50.00	75.00	100.00
9158 Ford Henry Guards - with goat	55.00	82.50	110.00
9184 U.S. Sailors marching	40.00	60.00	80.00
9192 Knights of Agincourt	45.00	67.50	90.00
9206 Life Guards	40.00	60.00	80.00
9209 Royal Horse Guards - mounted	60.00	90.00	120.00
9401 Her Majesty's State Coach	150.00	200.00	240.00
9650 The Meet-mounted horsemen	55.00	82.50	110.00

PREMIUMS

The average mint price of premiums was $45.00 in the last edition, falling to $43.63 in this, a decrease of 3%.

TOYS FREE AS THE AIR
By Jim Harmon

Many radio premiums were nearly as free as the wonderful radio shows that advertised them.

We did have to pay the electric bill (or our folks did) to run the radio, and to get the offered toys we did have to send in a box-top from the sponsor's product.

Sometimes it was only that, a proof of purchase (Orphan Annie and Captain Midnight were particularly generous in responding with gifts for inner labels or inner seals from Ovaltine drink mix) and other times, usually only a dime was required "to handle the cost of handling and mailing". (That's really all it did do — the cost of the premium itself came from the advertising budget.)

The lure of the premium to kids then and for grown-up kids who are now collectors is difficult to explain to those who never lived through the era themselves. The ring or badge was more than the toy itself; it was our tangible link to those magical friends on the other side of the speaker cloth.

Those voices were wonderful out there — The rumbling bass of Brace Beemer as the Lone Ranger; the slightly "country" sound of Curley Bradley as Tom Mix; Bret Morrison, whom we recognized even as children was "sophisticated" as Lamont Cranston, alias The Shadow — but they were bodiless and yes, a bit remote.

It was the premium they offered, the same as the one they were using in the story, that put us in touch with them.

There were historic precedents for radio premiums. There were pictures of famous actresses in cigarette packages around the turn of the century, and early radio personalities, such as bandleader Vincent Lopez, offered their autographed pictures. But such footnotes to history aside, radio premiums began with **Little Orphan Annie** in 1931. The plucky little waif from the Sunday comics first gave away sheet music of her theme song ("Who's that little chatterbox with the pretty auburn locks?") and her own photo, but very shortly, she offered a drinking mug that could be used to shake-up Ovaltine powder with milk to make something resembling a soda fountain milk shake. The first significant radio premium, it was the only successful one that encouraged further use of the sponsor's product.

Many different models of the shake-up mug were offered by Annie, and later by Captain Midnight (on both radio and TV). So successful were the offers, shake-up mugs are not rare or high in dollar value. (The most sought after is the orange and blue, embossed — not decaled — Midnight mug.)

It took two more years after Annie came to radio for the fledgling medium to develop its really classic adventure heroes. In 1933, there appeared the Lone Ranger, Tom Mix and Jack Armstrong. Unlike Annie, the two Westerners and the All-American Boy were still around until the 1950s, when television began driving out all radio drama. In those nearly twenty years, these shows offered hundreds of give-away toys, which inspired similar premiums on dozens of other shows.

Any small toy that could be manufactured inexpensively enough might turn up as a premium. Those concerned with the great outdoors were popular. We had compasses, pedometers, telescopes, flashlights, pocketknives, signal mirrors, portable telegraph sets.

The secret society of childhood had its emblems and tokens. So had secret decoders and secret manuals of every size and description. It is these and other **paper** items that have the greatest dollar value. They were the most easily lost or used up in the rush to adulthood. A Captain Midnight Secret Manual is worth more than the metallic decoder it accompanied.

The rarest paper item is the Lone Ranger Frontier Town offered about 1947. To complete this model of a Western village, one had to get four different envelopes by mail, then augment this by buying several packages of Cheerios to cut out the model buildings from the packs. The complete set has been known to sell for hundreds dollars and today might bring $1,000.00, the highest dollar premium.

Perhaps the most popular single type of premium was the ring. Rings let the listener show his loyalty to the fraternity of his favorite hero, but in a less officious and more "grown-up" way than the badge (although they were also highly popular). Besides . . . the rings looked neat, and many of them could **do** things — some of them pretty incredible things.

As with radio premiums in general, the Tom Mix show (and Ralston cereal's premium manufacturer, the Robbins Company) blazed the trail with ingenious ring designs. In 1937, Tom Mix Straight Shooters could get a Signet Ring with their own initial on it. (Years later, Captain Midnight would offer a ring that would ink-stamp your initial.) By 1938, Tom had a ring that let you look in a peep-hole and see a magnified picture of himself and his horse, Tony. (Technology had progressed so much that by the fifties, Straight Arrow offered a similar ring that put your own photo, if supplied, alongside radio's great Indian hero.)

After World War II and the ease in metal rationing, Tom Mix offered a Magnet Ring (good for picking up paperclips — like the one on the stolen plans to the atomic bomb, in Tom's case). His spinning siren whistle ring was neat (but admittedly borrowed in design from Jack Armstrong's 1937 Egyptian Whistle Ring). Tom's Sliding Whistle Ring that played different musical notes (about 1948) was unique, however. His Look-Around Ring concealed an inner mirror that let you see behind you (sort of), a design rustled for a later Tennessee Jed ring.

The final Tom Mix ring looked attractive, sporting a glowing cat's-eye, but the Tiger-Eye Ring was only lightweight plastic in 1949, a far cry from the well-crafted metal rings of a decade earlier. But then, the decade was nearly over, and so was the era, fading in the light of another glowing eye in the living room.

The Shadow's own Glow-in-the-Dark Ring in 1939 had a band composed of two sculpted Shadow figures holding up a jagged blue stone — a proxy lump of his sponsor's product, Blue Coal. One of the very few Shadow premiums and the best-looking, this ring has sold for a record $250.00.

One glowing plastic ring — the identical mold — was used for several different radio shows. The band had two crocodiles holding a setting in their mouths. The oval "stone" was **green** when it was Jack Armstrong's Dragon Eye Ring in 1940. It stayed green for **Terry and the Pirates** in the mid-forties, but it was **black** for Carey Salt's Shadow ring in 1947 (not the rare Blue Coal model). The setting was **red** for Buck Rogers' Ring of Saturn in 1945. It is back to **black** in the slightly lumpy counterfeit being manufactured today, one of the handful of premiums of simple enough design to be faked for profit. The best way to authenticate these rings is by the accompanying paper instruction sheets, naming the famous character whose prize it is.

These rings, as are all radio premiums, are worth whatever you will pay to possess them. A fair average price is $25.00 with $100.00 a top price for very rare, complex and fragile items. No one who is not very familiar with the whole field should pay more. Even though $100.00 or more may be easier to come by today than a dime and a box-top were in those days of yesteryear.

CONDITION OF A PREMIUM AND ITS RELATION TO PRICE

The price of a premium depends not only on its desirability, but on its condition. A premium in mint condition is generally worth twice what that same premium would bring in good condition, with "very good" falling about equally in between good and mint.

"Mint" means just that; the condition in which it was originally issued — perfect, regardless of age, not the slightest blemish. Needless to say this is a fairly rare state of affairs, but enough premiums exist in mint condition to make it a pertinent term. Many people trying to dispose of items are tempted to call an item "mint" when it is really "near mint", "very good", or sometimes just "good". Inevitably this can result in unhappiness all around, and not infrequently, a cancelled sale. "Very Good" indicates a premium that has obviously seen some use, with some signs of wear and aging, but in general having a crispness to its appearance that makes it attractive and collectible to all but the most discriminating.

"Good" signals a premium that has seen considerable wear, shows its age, but is basically sound. A collector will collect it but will often not be wholly satisfied with it as an example of his collection, and thus prices are often drastically below that which the same item in mint can command.

Condition below good results in another drastic drop in price and premiums with missing parts, although otherwise in excellent condition, will usually fall into this lower-priced category.

"Near Mint", "Fine", "Very Fine" and similar terms often found in sellers' descriptions denote conditions between Mint and Very Good, and are priced accordingly.

The key to grading is to avoid wishful thinking. Grading can sometimes be a problem to the uninitiated, but common sense will usually prevail, and when possible, a consultation with an expert in the field can often clear up lingering doubts. A premium in its original mailing envelope or box is worth up to 10 to 20% more, depending on the condition of the container.

Prices on many radio premiums have dropped recently, despite the vehement protestations of some collectors and dealers that this is not so. Perhaps some collectors now have everything they want, or can't afford to invest in these uncertain times. Perhaps many collectors have reached a time in their lives when family and business mean more than collecting.

However, premiums are not likely to become completely worthless. They are fragile antiques of lasting historical value. In the long view, they will become even more valuable than their recent peak prices. The depressed current prices offer an investment opportunity for future gain.

A few **new** authentic premiums have appeared: Boraxo offered a 20 Mule Team model in 1980 (similar to **Death Valley Days** original of the '30s); Cheerios offered a Lone Ranger Deputy Kit in 1981 styled after the movie of that year but similar to earlier offers with mask, badge, etc.; and in 1982 Ralston offered a Tom Mix cereal bowl almost exactly in appearance to a 1940's premium (although there was no such bowl offered then). These are worth perhaps a nominal $5.00 each mint now, but will gain in value, and may be offered by dishonest persons as being older, more valuable premiums than they are.

JIM HARMON is a writer of non-fiction (**The Great Radio Heroes**) and science fiction (including the often-authologized "The Place Where Chicago Was") magazine editor (**Monsters of the Movies**) and writer-producer-co-star with radio's Tom Mix in the 1970s **Curley Bradley, U.S. Marshal** radio and recording series. He has written virtually every imaginable category of fiction or non-fiction, has appeared in movies, radio drama and on many major TV talk shows. Harmon has produced several new radio episodes of **Tom Mix** for Ralston which have been both broadcast and offered on premium record albums. He has also edited a new **Tom Mix** mini-comic book included in specially marked boxes of Hot Ralston, and acted as consultant on a Mix wrist-watch and other premiums. Currently he lives with his wife, Barbara, a microbiologist, and daughter, Dawn, an ice skater, in southern California.

	G	VG	M		G	VG	M
ADMIRAL TELEVISION STUDIO GIVEAWAY — 1953 paper punchout TV studio and characters, features Sky King, Flight to Mars, Walt Disney's Peter Pan and Three Little Pig. 15"x16"	25.00	37.50	50.00	BETTY BOOP pin "Roxy Theatre, New York", large	2.25	3.50	4.50
AMOS & ANDY Pepsodent Give-away-Amos' Wedding	12.50	18.75	25.00	BLONDIE & DAGWOOD GO TO LEISURELAND, 1940, Westinghouse	6.00	9.00	12.00
AMOS & ANDY Puzzle	12.50	18.75	25.00	BOBBY BENSON Code Rule 1935 cardboard decoder, HECKER H-O.	30.00	45.00	60.00
ARCHIE COMICS Club Button	1.00	2.00	3.00	BOBBY BENSON'S GAME CIRCUS, 1934	10.00	15.00	20.00
AUNT JEMIMA BREAKFAST CLUB Badge, metal	5.00	7.50	10.00	BOBBY BENSON JUNIOR BIRDMEN OF AMERICA WINGS, c. 1935, red white and blue metal pinback wings	4.50	6.75	12.00
BARNEY BAXTER Junior Birdmen of America wings, metal, circa late 1930s	5.00	7.50	10.00	BUCK JONES Club Ring	10.00	15.00	20.00
				BUCK JONES Horseshoe Pin	10.00	15.00	20.00
BENDIX RADIO - 5½" WW II military figures circa 1944. Color photos with stands. a. Lt. (jg) Navy; b. Marine 1st Lt. (dress uniform); c. Commander-Coast Guard; d. Army Air Force officer with parachute harness; e. 2nd Lt. with modern Mae West; f. Flier with flying suit; g. Capt. Army Airforce; h. Air officer with furlined jacket and helmet. Price per each	1.00	1.50	2.00	BUCK JONES JR. Sheriff Badge	5.00	7.50	10.00
				BUCK ROGERS Badge, enameled	17.50	26.25	35.00
				BUCK ROGERS Birthstone and initial ring	25.00	37.50	50.00
				BUCK ROGERS Chief Explorer Badge	22.50	33.75	45.00
				BUCK ROGERS lead figures, solid, COCOMALT, Buck, Wilma, Killer Kane, per each	3.50	5.25	7.00
				BUCK ROGERS Flight Commander Whistle Badge	35.00	52.50	70.00
BETTY BOOP face mask - 1931 theatre premium	3.50	5.25	7.00	BUCK ROGERS Girl's charm bracelet	27.50	41.00	55.00
				BUCK ROGERS Helmet	35.00	52.50	70.00

BUCK ROGERS Ring of Saturn
Courtesy Jim Harmon

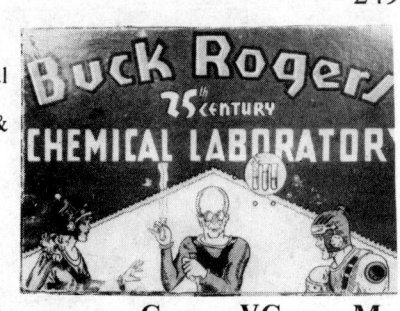

BUCK ROGERS Chemical laboratory.
Courtesy HAKE'S Americana & Collectibles.

	G	VG	M
BUCK ROGERS Knife....	37.50	56.25	75.00
BUCK ROGERS MOR-TON SALT Punch-o-bag, 1930s...............	17.00	25.50	34.00
BUCK ROGERS MOR-TON SALT Spaceship (came in envelope)......	50.00	75.00	100.00
BUCK ROGERS Pendant..	20.00	30.00	40.00
BUCK ROGERS Pinback button, circa 1935, WHITEHEAD AND HOAG, "Buck Rogers in the 25th Century"......	12.50	18.75	25.00
BUCK ROGERS Repeller Ray Ring (seal ring).....	45.00	67.50	90.00
BUCK ROGERS Ring of Saturn, glows in the dark, with red stone.........	50.00	75.00	100.00
BUCK ROGERS Ring of Saturn Instruction Sheet.	15.00	22.50	30.00
BUCK ROGERS Solar Scouts Badge, all brass color...............	12.50	18.75	25.00
BUCK ROGERS Solar Scouts Spaceship Com-mander Badge, 1936 Cream of Wheat premium	12.50	18.75	25.00
BUCK ROGERS Solar Scout Sweater Emblem..	25.00	37.50	50.00
BUCK ROGERS Telescope	37.50	56.25	75.00
BUCK ROGERS items given away for Cream of Wheat green triangle (sold in stores also):			
BUCK ROGERS Films for projector.............	3.50	5.25	7.00
BUCK ROGERS Inter-planetary Game........	45.00	67.50	90.00
BUCK ROGERS lead figures, hollow lead, Buck, Wilma, Huer, Robot, Kane, Ardala, price per each, Britains.........	100.00	150.00	200.00

	G	VG	M
BUCK ROGERS Lite Blaster Flashlight.......	8.00	10.00	25.00
BUCK ROGERS Movie Projector..............	20.00	25.00	30.00
BUCK ROGERS Printing Set (12 rubber stamps)...	17.50	26.25	35.00
BUCK ROGERS Super Dreadnaught, balsa wood	4.00	8.00	12.00
BUCK ROGERS Uniform.	20.00	50.00	75.00
BUFFALO BILL Bamby Bread Horseshoe Badge, late 1930s.............	5.00	7.50	10.00
BUFFALO BILL JR. brass ring, Buffalo in relief on top, TV premium.......	7.50	11.25	15.00
BUSTER BROWN GANG (Smilin' Ed) Ring	7.50	11.25	15.00
BUSTER BROWN GANG tab pins, assorted, price per each.............	2.00	3.00	5.00
Butter-Nut Bread premium, "Sail-Me" glider with 4½" wingspan, c. 1930.......	1.50	2.25	3.00
CAPTAIN FRANKS AIR HAWKS RING........	12.50	18.75	25.00
CAPTAIN FRANKS AIR HAWKS Wings, circa late 1930s, POST'S 40% Bran Flakes Premium........	6.00	9.00	12.00
CAPTAIN GALLANT Medal, c. 1950 dated 1939-1945 with an animal on it.................	5.00	7.50	10.00
CAPTAIN GALLANT Medal, 1950s, this one is a cross with GRI on it...	5.00	7.50	10.00
CAPTAIN HAWK Sky Patrol Propellor Badge, circa late 1930s.........	7.50	11.25	15.00
CAPTAIN MARVEL Club button...............	4.75	7.13	7.50
CAPTAIN MARVEL'S Magic Whistle c. 1943, American Seed Co. Has full color picture of Cap-tain Marvel on both sides and American Seed Co. ad on the inside.......	6.00	9.00	12.00

CAPTAIN MIDNIGHT Code-O-Graph Badge, 1942
Courtesy Jim Harmon

CAPTAIN MIDNIGHT	G	VG	M
Aerial Torpedo Bomber (Airplane), 1941........	25.00	37.50	50.00
CAPTAIN MIDNIGHT American Flag Loyalty Badge, 1940...........	17.50	26.25	35.00
CAPTAIN MIDNIGHT Flight Patrol Wings Badge, 1941...........	17.50	26.25	35.00
CAPTAIN MIDNIGHT Flight Patrol Wings Badge, 1942...........	17.50	26.25	35.00
CAPTAIN MIDNIGHT Code-O-Graph Decoder Pin, 1941, Eagle on top..	22.50	33.75	45.00
CAPTAIN MIDNIGHT Code-O-Graph Badge, 1942, with photo of Captain Midnight..........	28.00	42.00	56.00
CAPTAIN MIDNIGHT Code-O-Graph, 1945, magnifier.............	32.50	48.75	65.00
CAPTAIN MIDNIGHT Code-O-Graph, 1946, Mirromatic............	21.00	31.50	42.00
CAPTAIN MIDNIGHT Code-O-Graph, 1947, works as whistle........	21.00	31.50	42.00
CAPTAIN MIDNIGHT Code-O-Graph, 1948, round, with mirror......	34.00	51.00	68.00
CAPTAIN MIDNIGHT Code-O-Graph, 1949, Key-O-Matic (with key)..	32.50	48.75	65.00

CAPTAIN MIDNIGHT	G	VG	M
Detect-O-Scope, 1941....	30.00	45.00	60.00
CAPTAIN MIDNIGHT Flight Commander Commission, 1956.........	25.00	37.50	50.00
CAPTAIN MIDNIGHT Flight Commander Flying Cross, 1942...........	17.50	26.25	35.00
CAPTAIN MIDNIGHT Flight Commander Ring, 1941.................	25.00	37.50	50.00
CAPTAIN MIDNIGHT Flight Commander Signet Ring, 1957............	30.00	45.00	60.00
CAPTAIN MIDNIGHT Flight Commander Ring, 1959.................	32.50	48.75	65.00
CAPTAIN MIDNIGHT Jumping Bean Target, 1939................	6.00	9.00	12.00
CAPTAIN MIDNIGHT MJC-10 Plane Detector, 1942, distance-finder....	45.00	67.50	90.00
CAPTAIN MIDNIGHT Magic Blackout Lite-Ups, 1942................	15.00	22.50	30.00
CAPTAIN MIDNIGHT 1941 Manual for Decoder	50.00	75.00	100.00
CAPTAIN MIDNIGHT 1942 Manual for Decoder	100.00	150.00	200.00
CAPTAIN MIDNIGHT 1945 Manual for Code-O-Graph................	25.00	37.50	50.00
CAPTAIN MIDNIGHT 1946 Manual for Code-O-Graph................	25.00	37.50	50.00
CAPTAIN MIDNIGHT 1947 Manual for Code-O-Graph................	55.00	82.50	110.00
CAPTAIN MIDNIGHT 1948 Manual for Code-O-Graph................	42.50	63.75	85.00
CAPTAIN MIDNIGHT 1949 Manual for Code-O-Graph................	30.00	45.00	60.00
CAPTAIN MIDNIGHT 1956 Manual for Decoder Badge................	100.00	150.00	200.00
CAPTAIN MIDNIGHT 1957 Manual for Silver Dart decoder..........	100.00	150.00	200.00
CAPTAIN MIDNIGHT Marine Corps Ring, 1942	17.50	26.25	35.00
CAPTAIN MIDNIGHT medal, brass, pictures of			

	G	VG	M
cast, secret word, spinner, 1940	4.75	7.13	9.50
CAPTAIN MIDNIGHT Mystic Eye Detector Ring, 1942	30.00	45.00	60.00
CAPTAIN MIDNIGHT Mystic Sun God Ring, 1946	112.50	168.75	225.00
CAPTAIN MIDNIGHT Printing Ring, 1948	27.50	41.25	55.00
CAPTAIN MIDNIGHT Secret Squadron Decoder Badge, 1955	32.50	48.75	65.00
CAPTAIN MIDNIGHT Secret Squadron Decoder Badge, 1956	32.50	48.75	65.00
CAPTAIN MIDNIGHT Secret Squadron Insignia transfer, 1949	12.50	18.75	25.00
CAPTAIN MIDNIGHT Service Ribbon pin, 1944	14.50	21.75	29.00
CAPTAIN MIDNIGHT Silver Dart Decoder Badge, 1957	30.00	45.00	60.00
CAPTAIN MIDNIGHT Spy Scope, 1947	27.50	41.25	55.00
CAPTAIN MIDNIGHT Surprise Package, 1942	17.50	26.25	35.00
CAPTAIN MIDNIGHT 3-Way Mystic Dog Whistle, 1942	12.50	18.75	25.00
CAPTAIN MIDNIGHT Trick and Riddle Book, 1939 Skelly Oil Premium, 64 pages	12.50	18.75	25.00
CAPTAIN MIDNIGHT Weather Wings, 1940, Predicts weather	17.50	26.25	35.00
CAPTAIN MIDNIGHT Whirlwind Whistling Ring, 1941	22.50	33.75	45.00
CAPTAIN SPARKS Airplane Pilot Training Cockpit, SPARKIES	100.00	150.00	200.00
CAPT. TIM IVORY CLUB Pin — IVORY SOAP, circa 1936	5.50	8.25	11.00
CAPTAIN VIDEO Flying Saucer Ring	12.50	18.75	25.00
CAPTAIN VIDEO Rite-O-Lite	15.00	22.50	30.00
CAPTAIN VIDEO Rocket Launcher and Ships, 1950s	11.00	16.50	22.00
CAPTAIN VIDEO Secret Seal Ring, 1950s	25.00	37.50	50.00

	G	VG	M
CAPTAIN VIDEO Space Fleet Ray Gun, 1952, TV premium — POWERHOUSE	12.50	18.75	25.00
CAPTAIN VIDEO X-9 Rocket Balloon, 1950s	10.00	15.00	20.00
CHANDU THE MAGICIAN Galloping Coin Trick, 1930s	22.50	33.75	45.00
CHANDU THE MAGICIAN Hindu Cones, 1930s	22.50	33.75	45.00
CHARLIE McCARTHY Puppet Doll — 21" high, cardboard, CHASE & SANBORN mailer	12.50	18.75	25.00
CHARLIE McCARTHY RADIO PARTY GAME — Giveaway by Standard Brands, 1938, 21 cardboard figures	17.50	26.25	35.00
CINNAMON BEAR (annual Christmas show, circa 1940s) Silver Star	17.50	26.25	35.00
CISCO KID Badge, western hat on chain, 1950s	6.00	9.00	12.00
CISCO KID cardboard gun, 7" long, Harvest Bread giveaway, clicker sounds when handle squeezed	4.00	6.00	8.00
CISCO KID and PANCHO face masks, 1953, price per each	4.50	6.75	9.00
CISCO KID Triple S Club Kit	17.50	26.25	35.00
CISCO KID Picture Ring, 1950s	22.50	33.75	45.00
COCO WHEATS RADIO CLUB BADGE shape of microphone	12.50	18.75	25.00

CRACKER JACK

Cracker Jack was first introduced in 1893 by the Ruckheim brothers, F.W. and Louis, at the Chicago World's Columbian Exposition. Toys first appeared in the boxes of popcorn and peanuts in 1912 and were bought from various manufacturers. Over 10,000 different have been produced over the years. From 1912 to 1930 they included whistles, tops, yo-yos, brooches and puzzles. From 1930 to 1940 the accent was on miniatures, such as irons, shoes, binoculars, trolley cars, trains, etc. 1940 to 1950 tended towards military items, with plastics being introduced in the late 1940s. Prices can range from $1.00 or less to $50.00. There are about thirty serious Cracker Jack collectors known in this country.

	G	VG	M		G	VG	M
DAVID HARDING COUNTERSPY, Junior Agent Badge	17.50	26.25	35.00	DON WINSLOW Decoder Torpedo	30.00	45.00	60.00
DAVY CROCKETT Gold-plated ring	3.00	4.50	6.00	DON WINSLOW Honor Badge	17.50	26.25	35.00
DICK TRACY Air Detective Ring	27.50	41.25	55.00	DON WINSLOW Magic Slate Secret Code Book	12.50	18.75	25.00
DICK TRACY Badge, "Capt."	32.00	48.00	64.00	DON WINSLOW Ring	17.50	26.25	35.00
DICK TRACY Badge, "Crime Stoppers"	6.00	9.00	12.00	DON WINSLOW USN Secret Code Book, 1935, 16 page OXYDOL giveaway, 7¾"x4"	15.00	22.50	30.00
DICK TRACY Badge, "Detective", picture of Tracy and Junior	9.00	13.50	18.00	DONALD DUCK Punchout figure, circa late 1940s, DONALD DUCK BREAD	5.00	7.50	10.00
DICK TRACY Badge, "Lt."	21.00	31.50	42.00				
DICK TRACY Badge — Republic Pictures	8.00	12.00	16.00	DONALD DUCK Playboard, 1946, 9" high, Comics giveaway	9.00	13.50	18.00
DICK TRACY Badge — "Sgt."	20.00	30.00	40.00	ELSIE THE COW, set of four figural buttons on color illustrated card, BORDEN 1949	4.00	6.00	8.00
DICK TRACY Decoder, green (circa 1938?)	6.00	9.00	12.00				
DICK TRACY Decoder, red (circa 1938?)	6.00	9.00	12.00	FIGHTING DEVIL DOGS Ring, 1938, Republic Pictures serial ring, has bulldog head on top	12.50	18.75	25.00
DICK TRACY Detective Club Badge with secret money pouch in rear	17.00	25.50	34.00				
DICK TRACY Glider Airplane, 1938	12.50	18.75	25.00	FLASH GORDON Ring, 1949 POST TOASTIES CORN FLAKES	5.00	7.50	10.00
DICK TRACY Ring, in shape of Tracy's head	22.50	33.75	45.00	FORT APACHE (Rin Tin Tin) plastic ring 1950s TV premium	4.00	6.00	8.00
DICK TRACY Secret Compartment Ring	27.50	41.25	55.00				
DICK TRACY Secret Service Patrol Member pin, early 1940s	7.50	11.25	15.00	FRANK BUCK Explorer's sun watch, post WW II (offered by Jack Armstrong)	17.50	26.25	35.00
DICK TRACY Secret Service 2nd Year Member pin	15.00	22.50	30.00	FRANK BUCK Leopard Ring	22.50	33.75	45.00
DICK TRACY'S Secret Detective Methods & Magic Tricks. 1939 QUAKER OATS, 68 pages	12.50	18.75	25.00	G. E. Punchout Circus — 65 pieces	22.50	33.75	45.00
				G. E. Rodeo Punchout — 65 pieces	10.00	15.00	20.00
				G-MAN Badge	.50	.75	1.00
DIONNE QUINTS "All Aboard for Shut-Eye Town" paper dolls, PALMOLIVE SOAP	10.00	15.00	20.00	G-MAN Official Signet Ring 1933-35, G-man radio program premium, metal	.75	1.13	1.50

	G	VG	M
GABBY HAYES Antique Cars, 1950s, set for:.....	9.00	13.50	18.00
GABBY HAYES QUAKER Cannon Ring, 1950s....	20.00	30.00	40.00
GABBY HAYES Western Gun Collection, 6 weapons, 3 pistols, 3 rifles, solid non-working, 1950s	7.50	11.25	15.00
GABBY SCOOPS Junior Press Club Card, 1954 CRACKAJACK COMICS	1.25	1.89	2.50
GABBY SCOOPS 1940-41 Press Card, Crackajack Comics	2.50	3.75	5.00
GANGBUSTERS PIN....	14.00	21.00	28.00
GOOFY Playboard, 1946, 9" high, comics giveaway	9.00	13.50	18.00
GREEN HORNET Secret Compartment Ring, hornet seal, glows in dark	75.00	112.50	150.00
Gun, cardboard — Giveaway from Theatorium in Lykens, Pa. Pat'd Dec. 1914 by Spots Spec. Co. Lexington Ky. Swoop downward to produce bang. "The Bang Gun For Young America".............	2.00	3.00	4.00
H.C.B. Club Kit, contains badge, etc., early CREAM OF WHEAT..	12.50	18.75	25.00
HOP HARRIGAN Para-Plane, cardboard plane from GRAPE NUT FLAKES plus two code signal blinkers. Also in tail of plane is a small parachute that drops a cardboard "water" cannister	20.00	30.00	40.00
HOP HARRIGAN (unmarked) Sun Dial Ring..	17.50	26.25	35.00
HOPALONG CASSIDAY Bar 20 compass ring.....	12.50	18.75	25.00
HOPALONG CASSIDY Face Ring............	6.00	9.00	12.00
HOPALONG CASSIDY tin badge, POST RAISIN BRAN Giveaway, Circa 1950s	3.00	4.50	6.00

	G	VG	M
HOWDY DOODY Climber — Cardboard, with string, WELCH'S PREMIUM, 1950s	12.50	18.75	25.00
HOWDY DOODY Face Flashlight Ring, 1950s...	12.50	18.75	25.00
HOWDY DOODY Flicker Key Chain — 3D picture of Howdy Doody flicks to Poll Parrot (POLL PARROW SHOES), 1950s...	4.00	6.00	8.00
HOWDY DOODY Flicker Ring — POLL PARROT Premium, flicks from Howdy to Poll.........	6.00	9.00	12.00
HOWDY DOODY 8" Howdy Doody flexible cardboard figure — WONDER BREAD.....	7.50	11.25	15.00
HOWDY DOODY puppet, MARS CANDY, cardboard, 15" high, 1950s...	5.00	7.50	10.00
HOWDY DOODY Princess dancing puppet, 13" high, joints moveable, 1950s SNICKERS premium...	3.00	4.50	6.00
HOWDY DOODY Princess Spring etc. cardboard figure, 14" high........	4.00	6.00	8.00
I AM A SPY SMASHER button, 1940, Fawcett Comics	6.00	9.00	12.00
INDIAN CHIEF tin badge, POST RAISIN BRAN, circa 1950s............	2.00	3.00	4.00
INDIAN GUM CHIEF'S HEAD RING — GOUDEY GUM card premium, 1930s, silver...	2.50	3.75	5.00
JACK ARMSTRONG Crocodile Ring, glows in dark, green stone.......	57.50	86.25	115.00
JACK ARMSTRONG Big 10 Football Game......	37.50	56.25	75.00
JACK ARMSTRONG Explorer's Telescope.......	12.50	18.75	25.00
JACK ARMSTRONG Flashlight	12.50	18.75	25.00
JACK ARMSTRONG Hike-O-Meter	9.00	13.50	18.00
JACK ARMSTRONG Magic Answer Box.....	20.00	30.00	40.00
JACK ARMSTRONG Ped-O-Meter (Blue or Silver models)	12.50	18.75	25.00

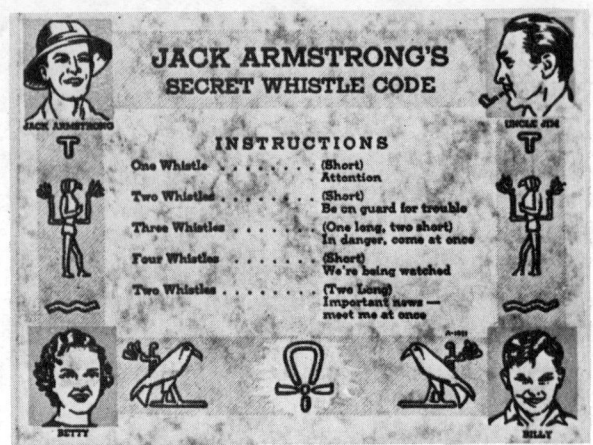

JACK ARMSTRONG Secret Whistle Code Card
Courtesy Jim Harmon

JIMMIE ALLEN Richfield Hi-Octane Flying Cadet wings
Courtesy Jim Harmon

	G	VG	M
JACK ARMSTRONG, Secret Norden Bomb Sight, circa WW II, with three bombs, paper target ships	35.00	52.50	70.00
JACK ARMSTRONG Paper airplane models, many different, price per each	17.50	26.25	35.00
JACK ARMSTRONG Secret Whistle Code Card for Secret Egyptian Coder Siren ring	12.50	18.75	25.00
JACK ARMSTRONG Secret Egyptian Coder Siren Ring, late 1930s, WHEATIES	22.50	37.50	45.00
JACK ARMSTRONG 3-D viewer, filmstrip	17.50	26.25	35.00
JEFF paper mask, 1933 SHELL OIL	6.00	9.00	12.00
JIMMIE ALLEN Colonial Gasoline Flying Cadet wings, late 1930s, bronze	6.00	9.00	12.00
JIMMIE ALLEN High-Speed Gasoline Flying Cadet wings, late 1930s, bronze	6.00	9.00	12.00
JIMMIE ALLEN Richfield Hi-Octane Flying Cadet wings, circa 1930s	6.00	9.00	12.00
JIMMIE ALLEN Richfield Hi-Octane Pilot's Identification Bracelet, late 1930s, all metal	17.50	26.25	35.00
JIMMIE ALLEN Skelly Oil Die-Cut Airplane cadet wings, late 1930s	10.00	15.00	20.00
JIMMIE ALLEN Skelly Oil Flying Cadet Wings, late 1930s, bronze	6.00	9.00	12.00

	G	VG	M
JOE E. BROWN pin	7.00	10.50	14.00
JUNIOR G-MAN Membership kit, circa mid-1930s	12.50	18.75	25.00
JUNIOR G-MEN OF AMERICA, late 1930s, gold-plated tin badge	6.00	9.00	12.00
JUNIOR TEXAS RANGER Badge, 1936 premium	6.00	9.00	12.00
KELLOGG'S Frogmen, 1950s, add baking soda and they swim underwater	6.00	9.00	12.00
KELLOGG'S KRUMBLES — Around-the-World paper dolls. Each cutout from box contains boy and girl, 10: Italy 11: Mexico 13: Franch 17: Czechoslovakia. Price per each	1.00	1.50	2.00
KELLOGG'S Nautilus Nuclear Submarine, 1950s	5.00	7.50	10.00
KELLOGG'S PEP Airplane Carrier, 6½"x10" cut-out sheet with airplane carrier, 5 planes with ¾" wingspan	5.00	7.50	10.00
KELLOGG'S PEP WARPLANES circa 1945, balsa wood models. Price per each	9.00	13.50	18.00
KELLOGG'S PEP WARPLANES circa 1945, balsa, with Superman ad on envelope	4.50	6.75	9.00
KELLOGG'S PEP WARPLANES — Circa 1944, cardboard. Price per each	3.50	5.25	7.00

"THE LIBERTY GUN FOR YOUNG AMERICA-McGrath's

"The Liberty Gun For Young America- McGrath's Big Store", 7" cardboard with photos of Charlie Chaplin. Courtesy HAKE'S Americana & Collectibles.

LONE RANGER Frontier Town, complete Courtesy Hake's Americana & Collectibles

	G	VG	M
Big Store", 7" cardboard with photos of Charlie Chaplin	10.00	15.00	20.00
LITTLE ORPHAN ANNIE Necklace, circa 1936, metal enamel figure of LOA on metal chain	15.00	22.50	30.00
LITTLE ORPHAN ANNIE pinback button, Little Orphan Annie, Member Funy Frosty's Club, mid-1930s	17.50	26.25	35.00
LONE RANGER, A Republic Serial—brass star badge	15.00	22.50	30.00
LONE RANGER Atom Bomb Ring (very common)	12.50	18.75	25.00
LONE RANGER Blackout Kit, 1942, KIX cereal glow in the dark material (two pieces), glow in the dark pledge to flag, glow in the dark Lone Ranger Volunteers armband, plus instruction	25.00	37.50	50.00
LONE RANGER Bond Bread Safety Club Badge, 1938	8.00	12.00	16.00
LONE RANGER Clicker Pistol, black, 1939 movie giveaway, Lone Ranger on one side and ruby on other, Non-moveable silver cylinder	15.00	22.50	30.00
LONE RANGER Deputy Shield — brass with secret compartment	12.50	18.75	25.00
LONE RANGER Flashlight Ring	12.50	18.75	25.00
LONE RANGER Frontier Town — Full set	550.00	825.00	1100.00
LONE RANGER Glow-in-the-dark Belt, 1941	40.00	60.00	80.00
LONE RANGER Hiyo Silver pin, 1938	5.00	7.50	10.00
LONE RANGER Lucky Piece — advertises 17th anniversary — 1933-50 . .	9.00	13.50	18.00

	G	VG	M
LONE RANGER, Mask. About the last radio premium, c.1953 or 1954, back of black mask promotes a personal appearance by "The Lone Ranger and Silver!"	12.50	18.75	25.00
LONE RANGER Movie Film ring, late 1940s CHEERIOS premium . . .	14.00	21.00	28.00
LONE RANGER Pedometer, 1943 CHEERIOS	10.50	15.75	21.00
LONE RANGER Rubber Band Gun and 6 different targets, 1938 MORTON SALT giveaway, cardboard	22.50	33.75	45.00
LONE RANGER Secret Compartment Ring, with picture of Lone Ranger and Silver	20.00	30.00	40.00
LONE RANGER Silver bullet	3.75	4.60	7.50
LONE RANGER Silver bullet, Secret compartment Compass	17.00	25.50	34.00
LONE RANGER Silver Saddle Film Ring, late 1940s, CHEERIOS	27.50	41.25	55.00
LONE RANGER Chief Scout Badge, SILVERCUP BREAD, early 1940s premium, red, blue and gold	37.50	56.25	75.00
LONE RANGER Safety Scout Badge, SILVERCUP BREAD, 1935	9.00	13.50	18.00
LONE RANGER SILVERCUP BREAD Safety Patrol, metal-silver and blue	9.00	13.50	18.00
LONE RANGER Six-Shooter Ring, gun ring with plastic and metal gun attached to top. Turn wheel and flint sparks . . .	18.00	27.00	36.00

	G	VG	M
LONE RANGER Victory Corps Badge, 1942, KIX Cereal	12.50	18.75	25.00
LONE RANGER Weather Ring — color square stone on top with litmus paper. No markings to identify as Lone Ranger . .	17.50	26.25	35.00
MAGIC SHOW Kit, 1946 GENERAL MILLS	12.50	18.75	25.00
MAGICIAN'S BOOK OF CIGARETTE TRICKS, 1933, CAMEL CIGARETTES	4.00	6.00	8.00
MAJOR BOWES — Home Microphone	22.50	33.75	45.00
MALTEX HEALTH CLUB — pinback button	1.50	2.25	3.00
MELVIN PURVIS Junior G-Man Corps Badge, late 1930s	9.00	13.50	18.00
MELVIN PURVIS Junior G-Man Corps Roving Operative Badge, late 1930s	7.50	11.25	15.00
MELVIN PURVIS Law and Order Ring	17.50	26.25	35.00
MELVIN PURVIS Law & Order Patrol Lieutenant's Secret Operator Badge, mid-1930s	6.00	9.00	12.00
MELVIN PURVIS Law & Order Patrol Secret Operator Badge, late 1930s	6.00	9.00	12.00
MELVIN PURVIS Secret Operator, Girl's Division .	6.00	9.00	12.00
MICKEY AND DONALD'S RACE TO TREASURE ISLAND, 1939, 19"x25" STANDARD OIL giveaway . . .	37.50	56.25	75.00
MICKEY AND DONALD'S RACE TO TREASURE ISLAND, 1939, map of U.S. in full color 20"x27", CALCO Gasoline giveaway, with stamps	100.00	150.00	200.00
MICKEY MOUSE CLUB Pinback Button, "Copyright 1928-30 by W.E. Disney", 1¼"	22.50	33.75	45.00
MICKEY MOUSE Globe-Troppers Map, 28"x20", NBC Bread, 1937	68.00	102.00	136.00

	G	VG	M
MICKEY MOUSE Globe-Trotters Map, 28"x22", NBC Bread, with all pictures pasted on	125.00	187.50	250.00
MICKEY MOUSE Globe-Trotters Map, 1930s, PEVELY MILK Premium	75.00	112.50	150.00
MICKEY MOUSE Official Money, 1930s MICKEY MOUSE CONES dollar bills Denomination is "1" (each)	7.50	11.25	15.00
MICKEY MOUSE Playboard, 1946, 9" high, comics giveaway	9.00	13.50	18.00
MORTON SALT "Bat-O-Ball", 1939, features The Shadow (cartoon)	12.00	18.00	24.00
MY-T-FINE Grocery Store folds into an 8"x3" full color grocery store with period products on the shelves, shoppers, workers, etc. Dated 1930 .	17.50	26.25	35.00
NABISCO Finger Puppet Rings, Slim Chants, horse Humbolt, gun, hand, Prairie Mary, Tagalong Boswell, Cold Deck Charlie, Sam Spiel, price per each figure	1.00	1.50	2.00
NABISCO Santa Fe Twin Unit Diesel Train, 1956, includes engine, train, tracks, ground, background	6.00	9.00	12.00
NABISCO Sound-Jet Glider	4.00	6.00	8.00
NABISCO Trailblazers of America cards, six cards make up horse-drawn van and open van, 1956	3.50	5.25	7.00
NABISCO SHREDDED WHEAT Nabisco Flying Circus, 1948, designed by Wallace Rigby, 4"x7" cards, planes, once cut out, can glide. Series of 24. Price per each	.35	.55	.75
THE NEBBS — Detroit Times series No. 27544 (comic strip)	3.75	4.60	7.50
NEW YORK WORLD'S FAIR CHILDREN'S WORLD G-MAN Badge,			

	G	VG	M
giveaway, 3-color brass badge	12.50	18.75	25.00
NEWSBOY BRAND Soups and Vegetables Official Booster Badge, late 1930s	3.00	4.50	6.00
PEP PINS — Little Orphan Annie	5.00	7.50	10.00
PEP PINS — Flash Gordon and Felix the Cat - each .	2.50	3.75	5.00
PEP PINS — The Phantom	2.00	3.00	4.00
PEP PINS — Popeye and Olive Oyl - each	3.00	4.50	6.00
PEP PINS — Superman . . .	3.00	4.50	6.00
PEP PINS — Others, includes Smitty, Inspector, Harold Teen, Skeezix, Corky, Pop Jenks, Goofy, Spud, Andy Gump, Gravel Gertie, Punjab, Hans, Kayo, Smilin' Jack, Dagwood, B.O. Plenty, Mr. Bailey, Shadow, Moon Mullins, Flattop, Rip Winkle, Uncle Willie, Emma, Inspector, Chief Brandon, Vitamin Flintheart, Sandy, Uncle Bim, Sundown, Lillums, Tilda, Uncle Walt, Perry Winkle, Judy, Min Gump, Wilmer, Smoky Stover, Daisy, Ma Winkle, Tess Trueheart, Herbie, Mamie, Breezie, Pat Patton, Maggie, Barney Google, Fat Stuff, Chief Brandon, Toots, Harold Teen, Nina, etc., average .	2.00	3.00	4.00
PEP RINGS — Jack Kramer, Dennis O'Keefe, Burt Lancaster, Sitting Bull, Pocahontas, Pan American Clipper, Douglas F-3D Sky Knight, Republic XF91 Thundercepter, each	1.50	2.25	3.00
PEPSODENT'S Moving Picture Machine shows MICKEY MOUSE, DONALD DUCK, SNOW WHITE AND SEVEN DWARFS in color	70.00	105.00	140.00
PILLSBURY-FARINA Complete Tel-A-Phone Set, 1938, two holders,			

	G	VG	M
mouthpieces, ear phones and 50 feet of line	9.00	13.50	18.00
PINOCCHIO Playboard, 1946 Disney Comics sub. giveaway	9.00	13.50	18.00
POPEYE THE SAILOR MAN Button, ¾" copyright 1935, theatre giveaway	7.50	11.25	15.00
POPSICLE Movie Star coins — Aluminum coins circa early 1930s, includes Irene Dunne, Clark Gable, Marion Davies, Fredric March, Marie Dressler, Gary Cooper . . .	1.50	2.25	3.00
PORCELAIN ENAMEL & MFG Co. 6" West Point Cadet on 3"x6" card with PEMCO ad on back	.50	.75	1.00
POST GRAPE NUTS FLAKES Playing-Filling Station, circa 1950s	2.00	3.00	4.00
POST TOASTIES 1939 Walt Disney cut-out figures, on box, Mickey the Traffic Cop, two types of Pinocchio, etc. Price per each box	7.50	11.25	15.00
POST TOASTIES CORN FLAKES COMIC RINGS 1949, Fritz, Hans, Tillie the Toiler, Toots, Casper, etc.	3.75	4.60	7.50
POST'S CEREAL Junior Detective Club Sergeant Badge, late 1930s	5.00	7.50	10.00
POST'S Explorer Ring, 1947, includes compass, sun watch, sunset predicter and star finder, plastic dome	17.50	26.25	35.00
POST Cereal Rings — 1948, Perry Winkle, Winnie Winkle, Harold Teen, Skeezix, Lillums, Herbie, Smoky Stover, etc.	3.75	5.25	7.50
POST Cereal rings — 1948 — Dick Tracy	7.50	11.25	15.00
POST GRAPE NUTS tin rings, Little King, Phantom, Skeezix, Lillums, Harold Teen	3.00	4.50	6.00
POST RAISIN BRAN Sheriff Badge	1.00	1.50	2.00

L. to R. RADIO ORPHAN ANNIE Decoder Badges, 1938 and 1939
Photo Courtesy Jim Harmon

RADIO ORPHAN ANNIE
Decoder Badge 1936
Courtesy Jim Harmon

RADIO ORPHAN ANNIE	G	VG	M
— Annie and Joe Corntassel button, 1931.....	3.50	5.25	7.00
RADIO ORPHAN ANNIE — Associated Membership Pin, 1934........	4.00	6.00	8.00
RADIO ORPHAN ANNIE Bandana, 1934........	17.50	26.25	35.00
RADIO ORPHAN ANNIE Birthstone Ring, 1935...	11.00	16.50	22.00
RADIO ORPHAN ANNIE Capt. Sparks Aviation Trainer	100.00	150.00	200.00
RADIO ORPHAN ANNIE Circus Cut-outs, 1935...	40.00	60.00	80.00
RADIO ORPHAN ANNIE Code Captain Belt and Buckle, 1940..........	40.00	60.00	80.00
RADIO ORPHAN ANNIE Code Captain Pin, 1939.	17.50	26.25	35.00
RADIO ORPHAN ANNIE Manual, 1934..........	24.00	36.00	48.00
RADIO ORPHAN ANNIE 1935 Decoder Manual...	24.50	36.75	49.00
RADIO ORPHAN ANNIE 1936 Decoder Manual...	21.00	31.50	42.00
RADIO ORPHAN ANNIE 1937 Decoder Manual...	17.50	26.25	35.00

RADIO ORPHAN ANNIE	G	VG	M
1938 Decoder Manual...	17.50	26.25	35.00
RADIO ORPHAN ANNIE 1939 Decoder Manual...	25.00	37.50	50.00
RADIO ORPHAN ANNIE 1940 Decoder Manual...	50.00	75.00	100.00
RADIO ORPHAN ANNIE 1942 Decoder Manual and cardboard decoder...	100.00	150.00	200.00
RADIO ORPHAN ANNIE Decoder Pin, 1935......	12.50	18.75	25.00
RADIO ORPHAN ANNIE Decoder Badge, 1936....	11.00	16.50	22.00
RADIO ORPHAN ANNIE Decoder Badge, 1937....	12.50	18.75	25.00
RADIO ORPHAN ANNIE Decoder Badge, 1938....	7.50	11.25	15.00
RADIO ORPHAN ANNIE Decoder Badge, 1939....	12.50	18.75	25.00
RADIO ORPHAN ANNIE Decoder Badge, 1940....	11.00	16.50	22.00
RADIO ORPHAN ANNIE Foreign Coins, 1937.....	9.00	13.50	18.00
RADIO ORPHAN ANNIE Goofy Circus, 1939.....	10.00	15.00	20.00
RADIO ORPHAN ANNIE Identification Bracelet, 1934	12.50	18.75	25.00
RADIO ORPHAN ANNIE Identification Bracelet, 1935	10.00	15.00	20.00
RADIO ORPHAN ANNIE Identification Tag, 1939.	20.00	30.00	40.00
RADIO ORPHAN ANNIE Magic Transfer Pictures, 1935	10.00	15.00	20.00
RADIO ORPHAN ANNIE Magic Transfer Picture, 1937	7.50	11.25	15.00
RADIO ORPHAN ANNIE Mask, 1933............	12.50	18.75	25.00
RADIO ORPHAN ANNIE Mystic Eye Ring, 1939..	20.00	30.00	40.00
RADIO ORPHAN ANNIE Package, 1942, includes Whirl-O-Matic Decoder, Whistle Badge, booklet, and order blanks........	75.00	112.50	150.00
RADIO ORPHAN ANNIE Pin, 1937.............	5.00	7.50	10.00
RADIO ORPHAN ANNIE Portrait Ring, 1934, ring has head of Annie embossed into top........	12.50	18.75	25.00
RADIO ORPHAN ANNIE Premium Manual, 1937..	12.00	18.00	24.00

	G	VG	M
RADIO ORPHAN ANNIE Premium Manual, 1938..	37.50	46.00	75.00
RADIO ORPHAN ANNIE Punchouts, 1942.......	100.00	150.00	200.00
RADIO ORPHAN ANNIE Ring, 1934............	10.00	15.00	20.00
RADIO ORPHAN ANNIE Ring, 1935...........	12.50	18.75	25.00
RADIO ORPHAN ANNIE Roller Skates, 1938.....	30.00	45.00	60.00
RADIO ORPHAN ANNIE Secret Egyptian Compass and Sundial, 1938......	22.50	33.75	45.00
RADIO ORPHAN ANNIE Secret Society Pin, 1934.	11.00	16.50	22.00
RADIO ORPHAN ANNIE Signet Ring, 1937.......	12.50	18.75	25.00
RADIO ORPHAN ANNIE Silver Star Pin, 1934....	10.00	15.00	20.00
RADIO ORPHAN ANNIE Silver Star Pin, 1935....	10.00	15.00	20.00
RADIO ORPHAN ANNIE Secret Society Silver Star Ring, 1936............	25.00	37.50	50.00
RADIO ORPHAN ANNIE Silver Star Ring, 1937...	20.00	30.00	40.00
RADIO ORPHAN ANNIE Silver Star Ring, 1938...	12.50	18.75	25.00
RADIO ORPHAN ANNIE School Pin, 1939.......	3.00	4.50	6.00
RADIO ORPHAN ANNIE Secret Guard Clicker, 1942	17.50	26.25	35.00
RADIO ORPHAN ANNIE Shake-Up Game, 1931...	6.00	9.00	12.00
RADIO ORPHAN ANNIE Sun Watch, 1938.......	12.50	18.75	25.00
RADIO ORPHAN ANNIE 3-Way Dog Whistle, 1940	17.50	26.25	35.00
RADIO ORPHAN ANNIE Treasure Hunt Game, 1933	15.00	22.50	30.00
RADIO ORPHAN ANNIE Treasure Hunt Game, 1935	7.50	11.25	15.00
RANGE RIDER & Dick West button, PETER PAN Bread, 1950s......	2.50	3.75	5.00
RED RYDER Lucky Coin.	3.00	4.50	6.00
RENFREW OF THE MOUNTED pin-back...	3.25	4.88	6.50
RIN TIN TIN "Ball-in-the-hole" GAMES (sealed coin-size games of Rinty, Rip Masters, Fort Apache, etc.) Each......	5.00	7.50	10.00

	G	VG	M
RIN TIN TIN Ring, plastic, 1950s	2.50	3.75	5.00
RIN TIN TIN set of plastic dinosaurs (Radio-TV 1954)...............	20.00	30.00	40.00
RIN TIN TIN WONDERSCOPE (Telescope-Microscope-Compass) (Radio-TV 1954) w/authentic mailer, (Same item recently, perhaps currently, on sale in stores for under $1.00) .	10.00	15.00	20.00
RIP MASTERS (Rin Tin Tin) plastic rings, 1950s..	4.00	6.00	8.00
ROCKY LANE'S Explorer's Sun Watch, 1951, CARNATION MILK.......	12.50	18.75	25.00
ROY ROGERS Branding Iron Ring............	20.00	30.00	40.00
ROY ROGERS Deputy Badge	1.75	2.63	3.50
ROY ROGERS Microscope Ring, 1947, QUAKER OATS	16.50	24.75	33.00
ROY ROGERS Paint Set, 1950s	7.50	11.25	15.00
ROY ROGERS Signal Badge with mirror, secret compartment and whistle	12.50	18.75	25.00
ROY ROGERS Silver Hat Ring	15.00	22.50	30.00
ROY ROGERS - Trigger's Lucky Horseshoe, full size, black rubber.......	7.50	11.25	15.00
ROY ROGERS Tuck-A-Way Gun.............	5.00	7.50	10.00
SCOOP WARD NEWS OF YOUTH OFFICIAL REPORTER BADGE, late 1930s, Ward's Soft Bun Bread Giveaway....	4.50	6.75	9.00
SECRET THREE Badge, with manual of secret codes................	5.00	7.50	10.00
SGT. PRESTON Distance Finder...............	22.50	33.75	45.00
SGT. PRESTON Fire-Fighting Set..........	22.50	33.75	45.00
SGT. PRESTON Flashlight — Signals, has two filters	15.00	22.50	30.00
SGT. PRESTON Klondike Land Pouch..........	6.25	9.38	12.50
SGT. PRESTON Klondike Movie Film Viewer.....	30.00	45.00	60.00
SGT. PRESTON Pedometer	12.50	18.75	25.00

SGT. PRESTON Police	G	VG	M
Whistle with Nylon Cord, brass, 1950	9.00	13.50	18.00
SGT. PRESTON Skinning Knife	15.00	30.00	45.00
SGT. PRESTON Totem Pole Set	42.50	63.75	85.00
SGT. PRESTON Trail Kit (probably the most complex of all premiums)	30.00	50.00	100.00
SGT. PRESTON Yukon Village	150.00	225.00	300.00
SHADOW Ring, Glow in Dark, "blue coal" jewel on white ring	125.00	187.50	250.00
SHADOW "Carey Salt" Ring (same as J. Armstrong Crocodile ring except for black stone; this ring has been counterfeited; original is smoothly circular with clean-cut design	32.50	48.75	65.00
SHIELD G-Man Club Badge, 1942, Pep Comics premium, lithographed celluloid pinback	7.50	11.25	15.00
SKIPPY S.S.S.S. Captain, pinback button, all celluloid, 1930s	7.50	11.25	15.00
SKIPPY Compass, 1930s? . .	6.00	9.00	12.00
SKY BIRDS Propellor ring, brass and silver, 1930s, GOUDEY GUM premium	2.50	3.75	5.00
SKY KING Azetec Indian Ring	22.50	33.75	45.00
SKY KING Detecto Microscope	17.50	26.25	35.00
SKY KING Detecto Writer	22.50	33.75	45.00
SKY KING Electronic Television Ring	22.50	33.75	45.00
SKY KING Glow in the dark Signal Ring	17.50	26.25	35.00
SKY KING Magni-Glo Ring	12.50	18.75	25.00
SKY KING Mystery Picture Ring	20.00	30.00	40.00
SKY KING Navajo Indian Ring	20.00	30.00	40.00
SKY KING — Small plastic statues of Sky King, Penny, Sky King's horse, Sky King's plane The Songbird, NABISCO			

SKY KING Teleblinker Ring
Courtesy Jim Harmon

	G	VG	M
giveaways in Wheat Honey and Rice Honey, 1950s	7.00	10.50	14.00
SKY KING Signal Scope . . .	30.00	45.00	60.00
SKY KING Stamp Kit	17.50	26.25	35.00
SKY KING Teleblinker Ring	22.50	33.75	45.00
SNOW WHITE Game, TEK TOOTHBRUSH . . .	25.00	37.50	50.00
SPACE PATROL Binoculars, circa 1950s . .	22.50	33.75	45.00
SPACE PATROL Diplomatic Pouch, contains money, stamps, etc . .	25.00	37.50	50.00
SPACE PATROL Goggles .	10.00	15.00	20.00
SPACE PATROL 1951 Jet Glow Code Belt	50.00	75.00	100.00
SPACE PATROL Ring, with secret powder compartment, circa early 1950s	50.00	75.00	100.00
SPACE PATROL Smoke Gun, 1950s	45.00	67.50	90.00
SPACE PATROL Space Helmet, circa 1950s	20.00	30.00	40.00
SPACE PATROL 1952 Space-O-Phone	50.00	75.00	100.00
SPACE PATROL Space Ship, circa 1950s	50.00	75.00	100.00
SPEED GIBSON'S Flying Police Badge, DREIKORN'S BREAD .	11.00	16.50	22.00
STRAIGHT ARROW Indian Head Ring, circa early 1950s	20.00	30.00	40.00
STRAIGHT ARROW Magic Cave Ring, 1949 . .	55.00	82.50	110.00
STRAIGHT ARROW Picture Ring, circa early 1950s	17.50	26.25	35.00

	G	VG	M
STRAIGHT ARROW Puppets and props, 1949, NABISCO radio premium	14.50	21.75	29.00
STRAIGHT ARROW Target Game, lithographed tin target board, 10"x14" NATIONAL BISCUIT COMPANY copyright on the edge...	25.00	37.50	50.00
STRAIGHT ARROW Tom-Tom, circa early 1950s...	12.50	18.75	25.00
STRAIGHT ARROW Wrist Bracelet with secret compartment — circa early 1950s	29.00	43.50	58.00
SUNBRITE "Junior Nurse Corps" brass badge	4.00	6.00	8.00
SUNBRITE "Junior Nurse Corps" pinback button, pictures of Dorothy Hart	3.50	5.25	7.00
SUPERMAN Crusader Ring	37.50	56.25	75.00
SUPERMAN KELLOGG'S Gy Rocket	35.00	52.50	70.00
SUPERMAN KELLOGG'S Silver Jet Airplane Ring, plane flies off	20.00	30.00	40.00
SUPERMAN PIN, 1940s, "Read Superman Action Comics Magazine"	8.00	12.00	16.00
SUPERMAN Planes from PEP cereal, set of 8, 1948	12.50	18.75	25.00
SUPERMAN Premium Club Set — Certificate, Button and Decoder	50.00	75.00	100.00
SUPERMAN Tim Club Ring	35.00	52.50	70.00
SUPERMAN'S Secret Code, circa 1939	20.00	30.00	40.00
SUPERMEN OF AMERICA Button — 1939 version, 1⅜" pinback button	25.00	37.50	50.00
TARZAN Gift Statues, FOULDS, 1930s, Tarzan, Jane, Kala, etc. Price per set	400.00	600.00	800.00
TARZAN Jungle Map and Treasure Hunt WESTON BISCUIT, 1933	50.00	75.00	100.00
TENNESSEE JED Look Around Ring, 1940s	22.50	33.75	45.00
TENNESSEE JED Paper Gun, circa 1940s	17.50	26.25	35.00
TERRY AND THE PIRATES Glow in the Dar ring, crocodiles on sides	17.50	26.25	35.00
TERRY AND THE PIRATES Gold Detector Ring	17.50	26.25	35.00
TEXAS LONGHORN tin badge, POST RAISIN BRAN, circa 1950s	2.00	3.00	4.00
TOM CORBETT SPACE CADET Badge, early 1950s	7.50	11.25	15.00
TOM CORBETT SPACE CADET Belt Buckle Decoder, early 1950s	25.00	37.50	50.00
TOM CORBETT Decoder, cardboard, 1950s	2.50	3.75	5.00
TOM CORBETT Rings, KELLOGGS, 1950-55, 12 different, including: Space Cruiser, Rocket Scout, Space Academy, Space Suit, Space Helmet, Corbett-Space Cadet, Cadet Dress Uniform, Girl's Space Uniform, Parallo-Ray Gun, Strate-Telescope, Sound Ray Gun, per each	5.00	7.50	10.00
TOM MIX Airplane and Parachute	50.00	75.00	100.00
TOM MIX ARM PATCH (TM bar on checkerboard design) 1933 - predominantly blue; 1947 - predominantly red; 1983 - predominantly black (worth probably as much as older versions — only 1000 issued)	20.00	30.00	40.00
TOM MIX Badge — Ranch Boss	27.50	41.25	55.00
TOM MIX Belt Buckle with Secret Compartment, belt glows in dark (offered only on cereal boxes after radio show ended)	50.00	75.00	100.00
TOM MIX Bandana, has TM Brand	37.50	56.25	75.00
TOM MIX Baseball	17.50	26.25	35.00
TIM MIX Baseball bat	17.50	26.25	35.00
TOM MIX Baseball cap	17.50	26.25	35.00
TOM MIX Blowdart Game	35.00	52.50	70.00
TOM MIX Branding Iron, TM Brand	24.00	36.00	48.00
TOM MIX Bullet Flashlight	27.50	41.25	55.00

Get these TARZAN GIFTS FREE

Be the first in your neighborhood to have a *complete* set of these Tarzan gift statues. Your friends will wish they had them, too. It's lots of fun painting these statues. Take them to school and show your teacher what a good artist you are. You can play all kinds of games with them and they make exciting decorations for your room.

Add to your collection *now*. It's much more fun when you have them all.

Moisten colors at beginning for best results. Use clean water and brush at all times. Mix colors in flat dish.

Black and white makes gray. The addition of white to all colors lightens them.

Red and white makes pink. Red, white and yellow makes flesh. Red and yellow makes orange.

Yellow and blue makes green.

Red added to brown makes a rich brown.

To make the coloring of these figures permanent cover with any good furniture wax or still better varnish or shellac.

Gift No. 1
TARZAN
with set of water color paints, brush and color chart.

Gift No. 2
KALA
the Mother Ape

Gift No. 3
NUMA
the Lion

Gift No. 4
JANE PORTER
the Girl

Gift No. 5
SHEETA
the Panther

Follow the directions on this color chart in mixing paints. It's easy to color the statue just like the picture. Never mind if you make a mistake—wash the statue in water and when it is thoroughly dry start over again.

If you need another set of water color paints or a new paint brush, send 2 Directions Panels from any packages of Foulds' Products or 2 tabs from cellophane bags of Foulds' Egg Noodles. Write your name and address plainly. Use the FREE GIFT OFFER Blank.

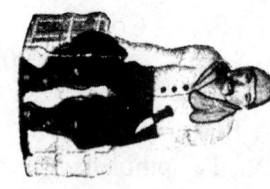

Gift No. 6
WITCH DOCTOR

Gift No. 9
The PIRATE
—a real one

Gift No. 8
D'ARNOT
the French
Lieutenant

Gift No. 10
CANNIBAL
a Tarmangani

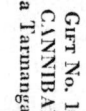

Gift No. 7
THREE MONKEYS
You'll just love these three little fellows

TO THE RADIO STATION WHERE YOU HEARD TARZAN

TARZAN, C/o Radio Station_____

Enclosed are Directions Panels from Foulds Packages for Tarzan gift Statues marked x on this blank. *Three* Foulds panels are necessary for *each* statue wanted. *Two* Directions Panels for set of water colors and paint brush. *Be sure* to *mark X the Gift you want!*

My Name is_____

PRINT PLAINLY

My Address is_____
NO.   STREET   CITY   STATE

Be sure to mark the gift you want!

☐ No. 1 Tarzan, paints, brush and color chart.
☐ No. 2 Kala, the Ape
☐ No. 3 Numa, the Lion
☐ No. 4 Jane Porter
☐ No. 5 Sheeta, the Panther
☐ No. 6 Witch Doctor
☐ No. 7 Three Monkeys
☐ No. 8 Lieut. D'Arnot
☐ No. 9 Pirate
☐ No. 10 Cannibal
☐ Set of Water Colors and Paint Brush

THREE *"Directions"* Panels needed for EACH statue.

	G	VG	M
TOM MIX Bullet Telescope, bird-call device comes with it. approx. 4" long..	17.50	26.25	35.00
TOM MIX Catalog of Straight Shooter Premiums, 8½"x11" b/w sheet with order form on reverse and descriptions and small pictures of premiums on the front. Includes sheepskin vest, rodeo rope, leather cuffs, wood gun, lucky spinner, etc.	12.50	18.75	25.00
TOM MIX Charm Bracelet with charmsteer head, gun, horseman, TM brand	20.00	30.00	40.00
TOM MIX Compass Magnifying Glass, 1937, silver color (Note: Originals have "Japan" written on the back. Imitations have the words "Comet-Japan" on the back)	22.50	33.75	45.00
TOM MIX Compass — Magnifying Glass, 1939, brass	22.50	33.75	45.00
TOM MIX Compass — Magnifying Glass, circa 1948, glows in the dark, plastic	15.00	22.50	30.00
TOM MIX Cowboy Shirt..	27.50	41.25	55.00
TOM MIX Cowboy Vest..	35.00	42.50	70.00
TOM MIX Cowgirl Skirt...	35.00	42.50	70.00
TOM MIX Decoder Badge 1940— moveable 6-shooter points to symbols	14.00	21.00	28.00
TOM MIX Decoder Buttons Instruction Sheet, 1946, Ralston	7.50	11.25	15.00
TOM MIX Decoder Pins — Tom, Tony, Jane, Sheriff, Wash. Price per pin	7.50	11.25	15.00
TOM MIX Deputy Ring, 1934 (Only one specimen known to exist, held by collector "Little" Jimmy Dempsey — possibly a retail store item or prototype never actually offered on the radio as a premium. Value if genuine premium hard to establish; possibly $500 up.)			

	G	VG	M
TOM MIX Glow-in-the-Dark Arrowhead, 1946, has compass and magnifying glass	20.00	30.00	40.00
TOM MIX Gold Ore Badge	12.50	18.75	25.00
TOM MIX Gold Ore Charm, 1940, RALSTON, contains genuine gold ore under plastic dome	12.50	18.75	25.00
TOM MIX "Good Luck" Spinner	12.50	18.75	25.00
TOM MIX Horseshoe nail ring, 1933 (can be verified only by Accompanying papers)	25.00	37.50	50.00
TOM MIX Identification Bracelet	17.50	26.25	35.00
TOM MIX Initial Ring, 1935	25.00	37.50	50.00

TOM MIX Look-Around Ring
Courtesy Jim Harmon

TOM MIX Six-Shooter
Courtesy Jim Harmon

	G	VG	M
TOM MIX Look-Around Ring, circa post 1945....	27.50	41.25	55.00
TOM MIX Lucky Wrist Band, 1936, Ralston Premium, Metal, TM bar brand, with leather strap and buckle	37.50	56.25	75.00

	G	VG	M
TOM MIX Magnet Gun and Signal Arrowhead bracelet, gun and arrowhead glow in the dark	30.00	45.00	60.00
TOM MIX Magnet Ring, 1945	22.50	33.75	45.00
TOM MIX Makeup kit (two grease-paint model, plus five grease-paint model)	125.00	187.50	250.00
TOM MIX 1941 Manual	30.00	45.00	60.00
TOM MIX 1944 Manual	34.00	51.00	68.00
TOM MIX 1946 Manual	27.50	41.25	55.00
MIX Mask, cardboard	32.50	48.75	65.00
TOM MIX Mystery Picture Ring, 1939, with "look-in" picture of Tom Mix and Tony, viewed through one side of the ring	75.00	112.50	150.00
TOM MIX PARACHUTE — 1936 RALSTON premium	37.50	56.25	75.00
TOM MIX Periscope	32.50	48.75	65.00
TOM MIX Periscope (cardboard tube)	27.50	41.25	55.00
TOM MIX Postal Telegraph Set — Blue, metal clicker, 1938	32.50	48.75	65.00
TOM MIX Premium Enclosures and Correspondence: Many picture postcards, letters on Straight Shooter stationery, etc. were sent out to listeners who wrote in to the radio show; these and various coupons, instruction sheets, contest entries are offered by dealers and collectors. Average value:	10.00	15.00	30.00
TOM MIX Telegraph Set — red, uses batteries, 1940	100.00	150.00	200.00
TOM MIX Ralston Straight Shooters Pocket Knife, 1940	22.50	33.75	45.00
TOM MIX Ralston Straight Shooters Walkie-Talkie, 1½" round	17.50	26.25	35.00
TOM MIX RCA TV set - shows photographs or comic strips (brown model, or reddish model)	12.50	18.75	25.00
TOM MIX Secret Code Manual	27.50	41.25	55.00
TOM MIX Sharpshooters Medal, glows in the dark	27.50	41.25	55.00

	G	VG	M
TOM MIX Sheriff of Dobie County Siren Badge, 1946 RALSTON	17.50	26.25	35.00
TOM MIX Signal Arrowhead, 1949 with magnifying glass and "whizzer" flute-type whistle, made of lucite	22.50	33.75	45.00
TOM MIX Signal Flashlight	26.00	39.00	52.00
TOM MIX Signature Ring, pre WW II	27.50	41.25	55.00
TOM MIX Siren Ring, 1945	20.00	30.00	40.00
TOM MIX Six-Shooter — wooden, barrel breaks and cartridge drum spins - 1933	37.50	56.25	75.00
TOM MIX Six Shooter — wooden, barrel spins, 1936	25.00	37.50	50.00
TOM MIX Six-Shooter — wooden, no moving parts, 1939	25.00	37.50	50.00
TOM MIX Spinning Rope, 1936, RALSTON, hemp with wood handle	30.00	45.00	60.00
TOM MIX Spurs — Metal, with plastic glow-in-the-dark rowels. Late	32.50	48.75	65.00
TOM MIX "Square and Fair" Spinner	20.00	30.00	40.00
TOM MIX Straight Shooters Campaign Medal, gold	17.50	26.25	35.00
TOM MIX Straight Shooters Campaign Medal, silver	17.50	26.25	35.00
TOM MIX Sundial Watch	27.50	41.25	55.00
TOM MIX Telephone Set	26.00	39.00	52.00
TOM MIX Telescope, TM brand on side	19.50	29.25	39.00
TOM MIX Tiger Eye Ring, 1949, RALSTON	45.00	67.50	90.00
TOM MIX TM Brand ring, circa 1933	22.50	33.75	45.00
TOM MIX Tri-Color Flashlight	35.00	42.50	55.00
TOM MIX Western Movie Viewer — shows scenes from Tom Mix films, 1935	37.50	56.25	75.00
TOM MIX Whistle Ring, 1945	17.50	26.25	35.00
TOM MIX Wrangler Badge, 1936, RALSTON	30.00	45.00	60.00

TOONERVILLE	G	VG	M
TROLLEY cardboard village put out by COCA COLA	70.00	105.00	140.00
TRIGGER Button, ⅞", POST GRAPE NUT FLAKES	2.00	3.00	4.00
WHEATIES Jogometer	9.00	13.50	18.00
WHEATIES Pedometer, circa late 1940s	5.00	7.50	10.00

WILD BILL HICKOK	G	VG	M
Bunkhouse Set (Cut-out pin-ups of Bill, Jingles, guns, ropes, etc.)	20.00	30.00	40.00
WILK BILL HICKOK Treasure Map & Guide, 1952, KELLOGG'S	17.50	26.25	35.00

COMIC CHARACTER

(See also Premiums, Paper, Mechanical Banks, Vehicles — Arcade; Hubley; Tootsietoy)

Average mint price of these toys in the 3rd edition was $113.16, and this year was $162.99, an increase of 44%. Comic character toys are attractive to collectors as they are often colorful and eye-catching, as well as evocative of happy childhood memories. Popeye continues to be a magnet for collectors, with such as The Yellow Kid, Buck Rogers, Flash Gordon, Tarzan, Superman, Felix the Cat, Barney Google and Happy Hooligan also proving strong lures.

CONDITION OF A COMICS TOY AND ITS RELATION TO PRICE

The price of a toy depends not only on its desirability, but on its condition. A toy in mint condition is generally worth twice what that same toy would bring in good condition, with "very good" falling about equally in between good and mint.

"Mint" means just that; the condition in which it was originally issued — perfect, regardless of age, not the slightest blemish. Needless to say this is a fairly rare state of affairs, but enough toys exist in mint condition to make it an employable term. Many people hoping to dispose of toys are tempted to call an item "mint" when it is really "near mint", "very good", or sometimes even just "good". Inevitably this can result in unhappiness all around, and not infrequently, a cancelled sale.

"Very Good" indicates a toy which has obviously seen use, with signs of wear and aging, but in general having a freshness to its appearance that makes it attractive and collectible to all but the most discriminating.

"Good" signals a toy that has seen considerable wear, shows its age, but is basically sound. A collector will collect it, but will often not be wholly satisfied with it as an example of his collection, and thus prices are often drastically below that which the same item in mint can command.

Condition below good results in another drastic drop in price, and toys with missing parts, although otherwise in excellent condition, will usually fall into this lower-priced category. Rust, even small spots of it can seriously lower the price of a toy. "Near Mint", "Fine", "Very Fine" and similar terms often found in sellers' descriptions denote conditions between Mint and Very Good, and are priced accordingly.

The key to grading is to avoid wishful thinking. Grading can sometimes be a problem to the unitiated, but common sense will usually prevail, and when possible, a consultation with an expert in the field can often clear up lingering doubts. A comic toy in its original box is worth up to 20 to 25% more if the box is in mint condition, with the price dropping as condition lessens.

COMIC CHARACTER

	G	VG	M
ALBERT ALLIGATOR (Pogo) plastic, 1969, approx. 5" high	3.00	4.50	6.00
ALPHONSE, HUBLEY, in a goat-pulled cart, cast iron, 13¾" long, 7½" high, early 1900s, from comic strip team of Alphonse and Gaston, Head-nodder, moveable arms and hands	80.00	120.00	160.00
ALPHONSE, HUBLEY, mule pulling wagon, 6½" long	200.00	300.00	400.00
ALPHONSE, HUBLEY, two goats pulling wagon, cast iron 13¾" long, 7½" high, early 1900s, head-nodder, moveable arms and hands	80.00	120.00	160.00
ANDY GUMP wooden dancing doll 9" tin legs	25.00	37.50	50.00

Alphonse "Nodder"

Alphonse, HUBLEY, two goats pulling wagon
Courtesy Kruse Auctioneers

Silly Goat-pulled Wagon

	G	VG	M
B.O. PLENTY holding SPARKLE PLENTY, circa mid-1940s, tin wind-up, MARX	70.00	105.00	140.00
BABY SNOOKUMS (The Newlyweds) fabric doll, 5½" high	25.00	37.50	50.00
BABY SPARKLE PLENTY paper dolls, SAALFIELD No.1510	7.50	10.75	15.00
BARNEY GOOGLE, cloth and wood, SCHOENHUT	145.00	217.50	290.00

BARNEY GOOGLE Doll, 9" high, wood with composition head, moveable arms and legs	60.00	90.00	120.00
BARNEY GOOGLE glass candy container	112.50	168.75	225.00
BARNEY GOOGLE and SPARKPLUG pulltoy, tin litho, Sparkplug in barn	1150.00	1725.00	2300.00
BARNEY GOOGLE riding SPARKPLUG, wooden	150.00	225.00	300.00
BARNEY GOOGLE tin wind-up, circa 1923	325.00	487.50	650.00
BARNEY GOOGLE and SPARK PLUG, tin wind-up by NIFTY	550.00	825.00	1100.00
BATMAN glasses, 1966	.75	1.13	1.50
BATMAN Handpuppet, cloth body	3.50	5.25	7.00
BATMAN Handpuppet, vinyl, IDEAL	5.00	7.50	10.00
BATMAN Helmet and cape, helmet fits over whole head, 1966, IDEAL	30.00	45.00	60.00
BATMAN Thingmaker set, 1960s	10.00	15.00	20.00
BATMAN Utility Belt, 1941, with belt-radio buckle	50.00	75.00	100.00
BEAUREGARD (Pogo), plastic, 1969	3.20	4.80	6.40
BEETLE BAILEY vinyl figure, 3"	2.00	3.00	4.00
BILLY BATSON (Capt. Marvel) Magic Box	15.00	22.50	30.00
BLONDIE "Blondie's Jalopy", actually has only Dagwood in car, other characters lithoed on chassis	150.00	225.00	300.00
BLONDIE, 1940, WHITMAN 982 paper cut-outs	22.00	33.00	44.00
BLONDIE, 1947, WHITMAN 967 paper cut-outs	16.00	24.00	32.00
BONNIE BRAIDS (Dick Tracy) Doll, 1951	12.50	18.75	25.00
BONNY BRAIDS Paper Dolls - Dick Tracy's Daughter and Wife Tess, SAALFIELD No2724, 1951, cut-outs	19.00	28.50	38.00
BOOB McNUTT tin wind-up, STRAUSS	400.00	600.00	800.00

BOOTS AND HER BUDDIES Paper Dolls, 1943, SAALFIELD 2460	19.00	27.50	38.00
BRINGING UP FATHER, hingee, 1944	7.00	10.50	14.00
BRUTUS (Popeye) cardboard mask, 1940s	4.00	6.00	8.00
BUCK ROGERS Atomic Pistol, 1946, U-235, sparks and pops, DAISY	55.00	82.50	110.00
BUCK ROGERS Battle Cruiser, TOOTSIETOY, 1937, two grooved wheels on top to run on string	52.50	79.25	105.00
BUCK ROGERS binoculars, 1950s	16.00	24.00	32.00
BUCK ROGERS Chemical Laboratory, GROPPER TOYS, 1937	750.00	1125.00	1500.00
BUCK ROGERS Disintegrator pistol, 1936, DAISY	50.00	75.00	100.00
BUCK ROGERS "Flash Blast" Attack Ship, TOOTSIETOY, 1937, two grooved wheels on top to run string, 4½" long	50.00	75.00	100.00
BUCK ROGERS lead figures — these are generally new, from early casting sets. Sell for $2.50 painted.			
BUCK ROGERS Liquid Helium water pistol DAISY, 1936	80.00	120.00	160.00

BUCK ROGERS Rocket Police Patrol.

HENRY Celluloid and tin wind-up.

BUCK ROGERS Battlecruiser,

Flash Attack Ship,

Venus Duo Destroyer.

Courtesy PB Eighty-Four.

BUCK ROGERS Atomic Pistol, Courtesy HAKE'S Americana & Collectibles.

BUCK ROGERS Rocket Pistol, Courtesy HAKE'S Americana & Collectibles

	G	VG	M
BUCK ROGERS "Pop" pistol, 1930s	40.00	60.00	80.00
BUCK ROGERS Rocket Pistol, XZ-31, 1934, DAISY, 9½" long	50.00	75.00	100.00
BUCK ROGERS Rocket Police Patrol, wind-up, MARX 1939	140.00	210.00	280.00
BUCK ROGERS Rocket Ship, Marx Wind-up, 12" long, 1934	175.00	262.50	350.00
"BUCK ROGERS RUBBER BAND GUN", 5"x10" punchouts card, 1940	37.50	56.25	75.00
BUCK ROGERS Sonic Ray Gun, yellow plastic, uses bulb and battery	17.50	26.25	35.00
BUCK ROGERS Strato Kite, 1946	16.00	24.00	32.00
BUCK ROGERS Super-Scope, 1953, NORTON-HONER MFG CO., 8½" long, adjustable plastic telescope	10.00	15.00	20.00
BUCK ROGERS Super Sonic Glasses (binoculars) 1953	15.00	22.50	30.00
BUCK ROGERS U-238 Atomic Pistol & holster set, 1948	42.50	63.75	85.00
BUCK ROGERS U-238 Atomic Pistol & holster set, with box, adventure book, and coupon, 1948, DAISY	62.50	93.75	125.00
BUCK ROGERS "USN Los Angeles" TOOTSIETOY 5" long dirigible	21.00	31.50	42.00

	G	VG	M
BUCK ROGERS Venus Duo Destroyer, TOOTSIETOY, two grooved wheels on top to run on string, 1937	45.00	67.50	90.00
BUCK ROGERS Walkie Talkie	22.50	33.75	45.00
BUSTER BROWN cast iron, painted	75.00	112.50	150.00
BUSTER BROWN in cart pulled by TIGE, cast iron	175.00	262.50	350.00
BUSTER BROWN & TIGE paper dolls, J. OTTMAN LITH. CO., N.Y. Envelope, doll, Tige, 4 suits, 4 hats, plus hat for Tige	35.00	52.50	70.00
BUSTER BROWN & TIGE ring, brass, 1930s	11.00	16.50	22.00
BUSTER BROWN Doll, 23" high	42.50	63.75	85.00
BUSTER BROWN Figure, lead	4.00	6.00	8.00
BUSTER BROWN Secret Agent Periscope, circa 1950	5.75	8.63	11.50
BUTTERCUP (Toots & Casper) stuffed cloth doll, 18" high, jointed head, arms, legs, circa 1924	125.00	187.50	250.00
BUTTERCUP & SPARERIBS, NIFTY, Buttercup beats Spareribs with broom	500.00	750.00	1000.00
CAPTAIN MARVEL Buzz Bomb	2.50	3.75	5.00
CAPTAIN MARVEL Comic Hero Punch-OUts, 1942, SAMUEL LOWE, has Captain Marvel (2), Capt. Marvel Jr., Bulletman, Bulletgirl, Spy Smasher, Ibis, Golden Arrow (2), Minute Man, Freddy Freeman, Mr. Scarlet, Commando Yank, Pinky, Bulletdog	110.00	165.00	220.00
CAPTAIN MARVEL Gun, movie gun with film	125.00	187.50	250.00
CAPTAIN MARVEL Magic Flute, copyright 1946, picture of Captain Marvel on side	10.00	15.00	20.00
CAPTAIN MARVEL Lightning race car, 1948,			

	G	VG	M
FAWCETT, tin wind-up, 4" long..............	42.00	63.00	84.00
CAPTAIN MARVEL Toss Bag...................	5.00	7.50	10.00
CAPTAIN MARVEL JR. Ski Jump, 7"x10", circa 1946, paper, REED & ASSOCIATES, CHICAGO............	3.00	4.50	6.00
CAPTAIN MARVEL'S Magic Picture, circa 1944, REED...............	2.25	3.38	4.50
CAPTAIN MARVEL'S Magic Eyes, circa 1945, REED................	2.50	3.75	5.00
CAPTAIN MARVEL'S Rocket Raider, circa 1944-47, REED........	3.25	4.88	6.50
CHARLIE BROWN Composition bouncing head, 1950s, possibly first Peanuts toy..........	5.00	7.50	10.00
CHESTER GUMP 12" high, oilcloth..........	33.00	49.50	66.00
CHESTER GUMP 13" high oilcloth doll, circa 1920s.	45.00	67.50	90.00
CHESTER GUMP Cart, ARCADE, 1920s, horse, open two-wheel cart, Chester driving.........	200.00	300.00	400.00
COMIC STRIP RINGS, 1953, KING FEATURES, Phantom, Blondie, Barney Google, etc.................	5.00	7.50	10.00
CHURCHY (Pogo) plastic, 1969, 4½" high........	3.50	5.25	7.00
COOKIE (Blondie), SYROC-CO, 1940s.............	7.00	10.50	14.00
DAGWOOD AEROPLANE, 1935, MARX "Dagwood's Solo Flight"...............	200.00	300.00	400.00
DAGWOOD Marionette, 15" wood body, plastic head, hands, feet, "HAZELLE'S", life-like hair, 1940s...........	9.00	13.50	18.00
DAISY MAE AND LI'L ABNER Paper Dolls with Mammy and Pappy Yokum, SAALFIELD No.2360, 1941.........	25.00	37.50	50.00
DAISY MAE WITH LI'L ABNER In Paper Dolls,			

DAISY MAE WITH LI'L ABNER IN PAPER DOLLS. Photo by Jonathan A. Newman Courtesy Barbara and Jonathan Newman

CHESTER GUMP Pony Cart. Courtesy PB Eighty-Four, New York.

	G	VG	M
SAALFIELD No.280, 1942..............	30.00	45.00	60.00
DAN DUNN Det. Corps Secret Operative 28 tin badge, circa 1930s......	15.00	22.50	30.00
DENNY DIMWIT (Winnie Winkle) 11" composition doll..............	100.00	150.00	200.00
DICK TRACY Air Detective Wings, circa late 1930s...............	12.50	18.75	25.00
DICK TRACY AND JUNIOR Knife with Crimestopper whistle and clue detector..........	20.00	30.00	40.00
DICK TRACY Automatic, HUBLEY, with picture of Eagles...............	6.00	9.00	12.00
DICK TRACY click pistol, MARX No.36.........	17.00	25.50	34.00
DICK TRACY Crimestoppers Set, badge, handcuffs, billy club.........	10.00	15.00	20.00
DICK TRACY detective badge with secret compartment, late 1930s, large, metal, leather pouch on back.........	45.00	67.50	90.00
DICK TRACY Detective Fingerprint Set, 1933....	62.50	93.75	125.00
DICK TRACY Electronic Wrist Radio..........	21.00	31.50	42.00
DICK TRACY G-Man wind-up gun..........	20.00	30.00	40.00
DICK TRACY Hingee, paper figures, 1940s, set of six................	7.50	10.75	15.00
DICK TRACY Inspector General badge........	45.00	67.50	90.00

DICK TRACY Click Pistol
Photo Courtesy PB 84
New York

	G	VG	M
DICK TRACY Pen-Lite, 1940s?	17.50	26.25	35.00
DICK TRACY "Police Station" with automatic siren car, 1950s	75.00	112.50	150.00
DICK TRACY Riot Car, circa 1946, MARX, heavy tin or sheetmetal litho, 7½" long, friction motor	29.00	43.50	58.00
DICK TRACY Siren Pistol, red with blue siren, circa late 1930s	22.50	33.75	45.00
DICK TRACY Siren Police Whistle No.64, MARX, tin	20.00	30.00	40.00
DICK TRACY Sparkling Pop Pistol, tin litho, MARX No.96	25.00	37.50	50.00
DICK TRACY Squad Car, convertible, heavy tin or sheetmetal, 20" long, MARX, circa 1948, friction motor with siren and battery-powered flashing light, Dick Tracy and Sam Catchum in plastic	50.00	75.00	100.00
DICK TRACY Sub-Machine Gun, 1946, "Raider"	35.00	52.50	70.00
DICK TRACY Target Game, MARX G25	18.00	27.00	36.00
DICK TRACY Target Game, MARX G34	27.50	41.25	55.00
DICK TRACY tin wind-up police car, 1949	12.00	16.00	24.00
DICK TRACY viewer, 1940s, two films	15.00	22.50	30.00
DICK TRACY JR. Click Pistol No.78, MARX, aluminum	15.50	23.25	31.00
DICK TRACY'S HANDCUFFS FOR JUNIOR, circa 1946, JOHN HENRY PRODUCTS No.700	10.00	15.00	20.00
DICK TRACY Water pistol, plastic, 1955	5.00	7.50	10.00
DON WINSLOW Flashlight Gun	35.00	52.50	70.00

	G	VG	M
ELLA CINDERS 17" high cloth and composition, 1925	100.00	150.00	200.00
ELMER FUDD Handpuppet, 1950s	5.00	7.50	10.00
FAVORITE FUNNIES large size rubber print set, Dick Tracy, Orphan Annie, etc. 14 stamps, pad, booklet	10.50	15.75	21.00
FELIX THE CAT 2" high, cast iron, 1923	25.00	37.50	50.00
FELIX THE CAT 2" high, pot metal nodding head figure, copyright Pat Sullivan on bottom of feet	12.50	18.75	25.00
FELIX THE CAT 2¼" high, lead	32.00	48.00	64.00
FELIX THE CAT 2½" high, cast iron, circa 1930	60.00	90.00	120.00
FELIX THE CAT 4" high, SCHOENHUT, 1925, jointed wood	100.00	150.00	200.00
FELIX THE CAT 6" high, 1924, wooden, GEORGE BORGFELDT CO., standup leather ears, jointed	37.50	56.25	75.00
FELIX THE CAT 6½" rubber squeeze toy	14.00	21.00	28.00
FELIX THE CAT, 7" high, jointed wood figure, circa 1924	60.00	90.00	120.00
FELIX THE CAT, 8" high, tin, with walking feet	30.00	45.00	60.00
FELIX THE CAT 8" wood-jointed doll, 1924	100.00	150.00	200.00
FELIX THE CAT 8" wood-jointed doll, 1930s	50.00	75.00	100.00
FELIX THE CAT 9" wood-jointed, SCHOENHUT, 1923	200.00	300.00	400.00
FELIX THE CAT, 9" high, 1940s, wood, jointed with rubber head	22.50	33.75	45.00
FELIX THE CAT 12" high, wood	10.00	15.00	20.00
FELIX THE CAT 13" high, composition, circa 1930s	70.00	105.00	140.00
FELIX THE CAT Doll, 15" high, stuffed, GUND, hands molded rubber, the rest cloth, circa 1950	42.50	63.75	85.00
FELIX THE CAT, China Set	25.00	37.50	50.00

FELIX THE CAT jointed wood figure, 7"
high
Courtesy PB Eighty-Four, New York

FLASH GORDON Signal Pistol
Photo Courtesy PB 84 New York

FLASH GORDON
Rocket Fighter.
Courtesy PB Eighty-
Four, New York.

	G	VG	M
FELIX THE CAT flasher ring, plastic	6.00	9.00	12.00
FELIX THE CAT on fire truck, gong bell pull toy	30.00	45.00	60.00
FELIX THE CAT on scooter, NIFTY	150.00	225.00	300.00
FELIX THE CAT on tricycle, gong bell pull toy	87.50	131.25	175.00
FELIX THE CAT "pop-up", jointed wood, string-operated, FISHER PRICE	5.00	7.50	10.00

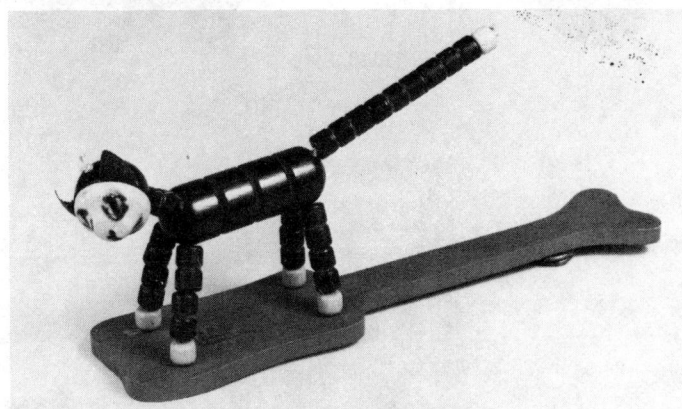

FELIX THE CAT "pop-up"
Courtesy Mapes Auctioneers & Appraisers

	G	VG	M
FELIX THE CAT Pull Car, 12" long, BORGFELDT, 1925	200.00	300.00	400.00
FELIX THE CAT "Speedy Felix" in car	25.00	37.50	50.00
FELIX THE CAT Walker, painted wood and tin	50.00	75.00	100.00
FLASH GORDON aluminum pistol, 10" long, shoots blast of air using rubber diaphragm	15.00	22.50	30.00

	G	VG	M
FLASH GORDON Arresting Ray, MARX, 1936? picture of Flash on handle	50.00	75.00	100.00
FLASH GORDON Atomic Disintegrator, HUBLEY	50.00	75.00	100.00
FLASH GORDON belt, many illos, large plastic buckle showing rocket ship in flight	4.00	6.00	8.00
FLASH GORDON jet-propelled kite	16.00	24.00	32.00
FLASH GORDON Radio Repeater clicker pistol, No.58, MARX	125.00	187.50	250.00
FLASH GORDON Rocket Fighter, MARX wind-up, 12" long, 1939	200.00	300.00	400.00
FLASH GORDON signal pistol, tin litho, MARX, No.74	25.00	37.50	50.00
FLASH GORDON Solar commando; three plastic space men and one ship, 1950s	4.00	6.00	8.00
FLASH GORDON Space Target metal standup, Alex Raymond illustration, 12x14	8.00	12.00	16.00
FLASH GORDON Strat-O-Wagon, 9" long, WYANDOTTE	21.00	31.50	42.00
FLASH GORDON Two way telephone, MARX, circa 1940	15.00	22.50	30.00
FLASH GORDON water gun, plastic	1.10	1.65	2.20
Flying CAPTAIN MARVEL, 1944-47, REED, 7x10", paper	3.00	4.50	6.00

FOXY GRANDPA
A Roly-Poly.
Courtesy Lloyd W.
Ralston Auctions

FOXY GRANDPA
Jack In The Box.
Courtesy Lloyd W.
Ralston Auctions

FOXY GRANDPA	G	VG	M
clockwork figure, tin, German, 8¼" high........	70.00	105.00	140.00
FOXY GRANDPA Jack in the Box, papier mache and paper litho on wood, 1900, 4" square.......	35.00	52.50	70.00
FOXY GRANDPA Nodder, paper mache, 1900, 6" tall...............	41.00	61.50	82.00
FOXY GRANDPA nodder, HUBLEY, circa 1910, cast iron, 6½", Grandpa large-headed in cart pulled by donkey............	210.00	315.00	420.00

FOXY GRANDPA clockwork figure
Courtesy PB 84 New York

FOXY GRANDPA Roly Poly, painted papier mache...............	30.00	45.00	60.00
"GASOLINE ALLEY Garage And Auto Racer", 1924, GIRARD, tin litho garage and "Bearcat Racer" car............	55.00	82.50	110.00

GREMLIN (Gloom) T.E.	G	VG	M
Powers, in leather clothes, 1943	12.00	18.00	24.00
HAPPY HOOLIGAN Donkey Cart, circa 1925, (possibly WILKINS), 10" long.................	115.00	175.50	230.00
HAPPY HOOLIGAN in cart, KENTON, early 1900s, 10¼" long, 7½" high, horse-pulled, head nods, cast iron........	225.00	337.50	450.00
HAPPY HOOLIGAN on a Ladder, SCHOENHUT..	100.00	150.00	200.00
HAPPY HOOLIGAN Police Patrol, KENTON, 18" long, Happy hit by cop as Gloomy Gus drives	1325.00	1987.50	2650.00
HAPPY HOOLIGAN Roly Poly	75.00	112.50	150.00
HAPPY HOOLIGAN walking toy, CHEIN wind-up, 1932, 6" high..........	150.00	225.00	300.00

HAPPY HOLLIGAN
Roly-Poly
Courtesy Lloyd W.
Ralston Auctions

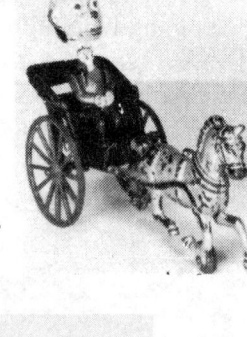

HAPPY HOOLIGAN in cart, horse pulled.

HAPPY HOOLIGAN on a ladder, SCHOENHUT
Courtesy PB 84 New York

	G	VG	M
HECKLE, squeeze toy, 1950s	5.00	7.50	10.00
HENRY, 9½" high rubber squeeze toy, 1950s	6.00	9.00	12.00
HENRY celluloid and tin wind-up, Japanese, Henry sits on elephant's trunk	350.00	525.00	700.00
HENRY "Henry and his Swan", celluloid mechanical	250.00	375.00	500.00
HERBY 10" oilcloth doll	14.00	21.00	28.00
HI-WAY HENRY, wind-up, 1920s, jalopy with man, woman, laundry above roof	1200.00	1800.00	2400.00

HI-WAY HENRY
Courtesy Garth's Auctions Inc.

	G	VG	M
HOPPY THE FLYING MARVEL BUNNY, circa 1944-47, REED, paper	1.50	2.25	3.00
HOWLAND OWL (Pogo), 1969 Plastic, 4½" high	3.00	4.50	6.00
HUMPHREY MOBILE (Joe Palooka) tin wind-up, circa mid-1940s WYANDOTTE	150.00	225.00	300.00

HUMPHREYMOBILE
Courtesy Mapes Auctioneers & Appraisers

	G	VG	M
JANE ARDEN, 1942, SAALFIELD 2408 paper dolls	25.00	37.50	50.00

	G	VG	M
JEEP (Popeye) wood-jointed, 1930s	25.00	37.50	50.00
JEFF 6" composition doll, ball joints, felt clothes	75.00	112.50	150.00
JEFF bendable figure, 1946	62.50	93.75	125.00
JEFF Stick Puppet, 12" high	20.00	30.00	40.00
JIGGS 3" high, hard plastic, 1960s	2.00	3.00	4.00
JIGGS 5" wood-jointed doll	30.00	45.00	60.00
JIGGS 7" high, wood-jointed doll, SCHOENHUT	325.00	487.50	650.00
JIGGS Stick Puppet, 12" high	20.00	30.00	40.00
JOAN PALOOKA doll	37.50	56.25	75.00
JOE PALOOKA, 4" high, wood-jointed	5.00	7.50	10.00
JOE PALOOKA 5½" high wood-jointed doll	22.00	33.00	44.00
JOE PALOOKA Championship belt buckle, circa early 50s. Heavy gold-plated brass buckle shows Palooka with hands raised in victory	6.00	9.00	12.00
JOE PALOOKA Filmatic, 12 different comic strips	7.50	11.25	15.00
JOE PALOOKA Punching Bag, circa 1950	2.50	3.75	5.00
KAYO (Moon Mullins) 9¾" oilcloth doll	12.50	18.75	25.00
KAYO 10" high SUN RUBBER circa 1937, head swivels	100.00	150.00	200.00
KOMIC KAMERA — All metal viewer circa mid-1930s, used to view 35mm film strips. With set of five film strips	32.00	48.00	64.00
KOMIC KAMERA, without film strips	12.50	18.75	25.00
"KRAZY KAT On A Skooter", tin wind-up, NIFTY, 1920s, 7¼" long	130.00	195.00	260.00
LIL ABNER Handpuppet	110.00	165.00	220.00
LIL ABNER AND HIS DOGPATCH BAND, 1945, UNIQUE, wind-up	200.00	300.00	400.00
LITTLE BEAVER Archery Set, 1951	9.00	13.50	18.00
LITTLE KING Walker, plastic, circa 1956	5.00	7.50	10.00
LITTLE KING, wooden pull toy, JAY-MAR, 1938, 4" high	14.00	21.00	28.00

274

LITTLE MARY MIXUP AND HER
FRIEND PEGGY
Photo by Jonathan Newman
Courtesy Barbara and Jonathan Newman

LITTLE ORPHAN
ANNIE, jumping
rope, tin-windup.

	G	VG	M
LITTLE LULU 10" high felt doll	22.50	33.75	45.00
LITTLE LULU 14" high, GEORGENE NOVELTIES, stuffed doll	150.00	225.00	300.00
LITTLE LULU 14" high, doll with mask face, 1944, M.H. BUELL	55.00	82.50	110.00
LITTLE LULU "Shape Book", 1971, WHITMAN No.1970	1.30	1.95	2.60
LITTLE MARY MIXUP AND HER FRIEND PEGGY, 1922, SAALFIELD No.294, paper dolls	30.00	45.00	60.00
LITTLE ORPHAN ANNIE 9½" printed fabric doll, 1930s	26.00	39.00	52.00
LITTLE ORPHAN ANNIE 16¼" oilcloth doll, circa 1920s	80.00	120.00	160.00
LITTLE ORPHAN ANNIE 18" high stuffed doll	60.00	90.00	120.00
LITTLE ORPHANN ANNIE Hingees, 1944, Annie, Sandy, Daddy, Punjab, price per set	14.00	21.00	28.00
LITTLE ORPHAN ANNIE Skipping Rope, tin wind-up, 1930s	200.00	300.00	400.00
LITTLE ORPHAN ANNIE and SANDY, tin wind-up, MARX, 1930s	175.00	262.50	350.00
LITTLE ORPHAN ANNIE stove, 8" high, circa 1930s	18.00	27.00	36.00

	G	VG	M
LITTLE ORPHAN ANNIE Water Pistol	25.00	37.50	50.00
LITTLE ORPHAN ANNIE JUNIOR COMMANDOS, 1943, SAALFIELD No.299	7.50	11.25	15.00
LONESOME POLECAT (Lil Abner), 1950s, rubber squeak toy, REINERT	7.00	10.50	14.00
LUCY 7¾" high squeeze toy	4.25	6.37	8.50
LUCY 8¾" high vinyl squeeze toy	5.00	7.50	10.00
MAGGIE 3" hard plastic, 1960s	2.00	3.00	4.00
MAGGIE 9" high wood jointed doll, SCHOENHUT	325.00	487.50	650.00
MAGGIE & JIGGS, 1920s, NIFTY, seated on 2-wheeled platform, 8" long	675.00	1012.50	1350.00

MAGGIE & JIGGS, 1920s, NIFTY. Courtesy PB Eight-Four, New York

	G	VG	M
MAMA KATZENJAMMER spanking boy as sailor drives mule cart, KENTON, 11½" long	450.00	675.00	900.00
MAMMY YOKUM doll, 21" high, rubber	20.00	30.00	40.00
MANDRAKE THE MAGICIAN Magic Kit, 1949, TRANSOGRAM	24.00	36.00	48.00
MIGHTY MOUSE, rubber, 9" high, no mfr. listed	6.00	9.00	12.00
MOON MAID'S DAUGHTER (Dick Tracy) 16½" doll with space helmet, IDEAL, 1965	27.00	40.50	54.00
MOON MULLINS and KAYO on Hand Car, circa 1940, 6" long, MARX tin wind-up	180.00	270.00	360.00
MOON MULLINS AND MAMIE Face masks, 1933, each	3.00	4.50	6.00
MOVIE KOMICS, reels of film for toy viewers, circa 1940s	5.00	7.50	10.00

	G	VG	M
MRS. BLOSSOM (Gasoline Alley) 17" high oilcloth..	45.00	67.50	90.00
MUTT 8" high composition doll with ball joints, felt clothes...............	75.00	112.50	150.00
MUTT bendable figure, 1946	62.50	93.75	125.00
MUTT Wooden Dancing Doll..................	7.50	11.25	15.00
NANCY 14" high stuffed doll, GEORGENE NOVELTIES	60.00	90.00	120.00
OLIVE OYL 11" GUND marionette	9.00	13.50	18.00
OLIVE OYL Ballerina, LINEMAR tin mechanical	300.00	450.00	600.00
OLIVE OYL Handpuppet, circa 1938, GUND......	6.00	9.00	12.00
OLIVE OYL Hingees No.102, paper punchouts, REED & ASSOCIATES.	1.50	2.25	3.00
OLIVE OYL Mask, card-board, 1940s...........	4.50	6.75	9.00
OLIVE OYL Rubber Squeeze Toy, 1950s.....	7.00	10.50	14.00
OLIVE OYL String and wood puppet, approx. 5" high, JAYMAR circa 1940s	25.00	37.50	50.00

POPEYE "Boom Boom Popeye"
Courtesy Mapes Auctioneers & Appraisers

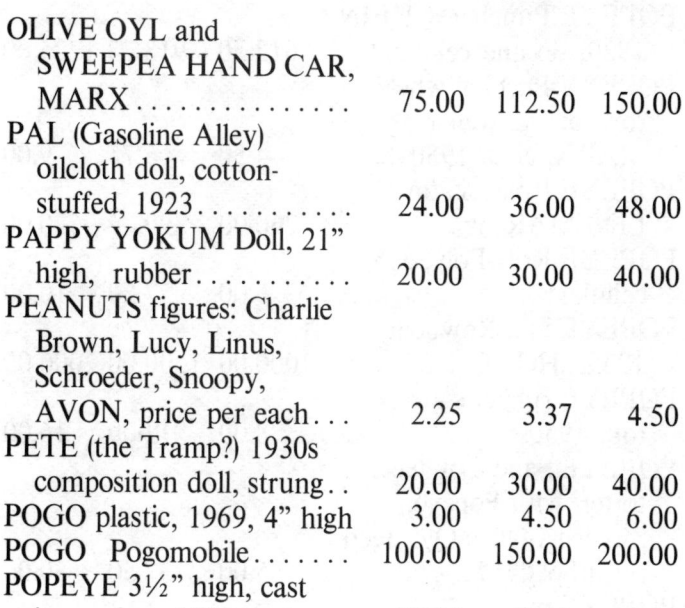

PAL Gasoline Alley, oilcloth, cotton stuffed.

POPEYE Spinach Patrol
Photo by C.B.C. Lee

POPEYE Puncher
Courtesy Sotheby Parke Bernet

	G	VG	M
OLIVE OYL and SWEEPEA HAND CAR, MARX	75.00	112.50	150.00
PAL (Gasoline Alley) oilcloth doll, cotton-stuffed, 1923...........	24.00	36.00	48.00
PAPPY YOKUM Doll, 21" high, rubber.........	20.00	30.00	40.00
PEANUTS figures: Charlie Brown, Lucy, Linus, Schroeder, Snoopy, AVON, price per each...	2.25	3.37	4.50
PETE (the Tramp?) 1930s composition doll, strung..	20.00	30.00	40.00
POGO plastic, 1969, 4" high	3.00	4.50	6.00
POGO Pogomobile.......	100.00	150.00	200.00
POPEYE 3½" high, cast iron, circa 1930........	30.00	45.00	60.00

	G	VG	M
POPEYE 4" high, solid celluloid, 1930s........	25.00	37.50	50.00
POPEYE 7" high, hollow rubber, dated "1935" on back	30.00	45.00	60.00
POPEYE 11" high, CHEIN, circa 1935............	120.00	180.00	240.00
POPEYE 14" high, "Cameo" hard rubber, jointed at neck, hips, shoulders.............	37.50	56.25	75.00
POPEYE 14" high, composition, "Popeye 1935 King Features Syn."........	200.00	300.00	400.00
POPEYE 14" high, wood and composition, jointed arms and legs, "1935"...	90.00	135.00	180.00

"POPEYE EXPRESS"
Photo Courtesy PB Eighty-Four

POPEYE
Rollerskating
Courtesy PB Eighty-
Four, New York

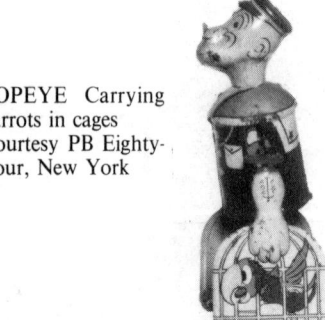

POPEYE Carrying
parrots in cages
Courtesy PB Eighty-
Four, New York

	G	VG	M
POPEYE 15" high, composition, rolling up sleeve....	15.00	22.50	30.00
POPEYE 20" high, rubber arms and head, stuffed body, GUND, circa 1950s	11.00	16.50	22.00
POPEYE Acrobat, MARX tin windup...........	230.00	345.00	460.00
POPEYE Basketball Player, LINEMAR tin windup..	287.50	431.25	575.00
POPEYE "Bifbat" paddle toy, 1929.............	14.00	21.00	28.00
POPEYE "Bo Lo Paddle", 1929................	3.00	4.50	6.00
POPEYE "Boom Boom Popeye", FISHER PRICE, drummer, 491,	See Fisher-Price		

	G	VG	M
POPEYE carrying parrots in cages, MARX wind-up, 1935, 7¾" high........	100.00	150.00	200.00
POPEYE Express — MARX, overhead airplane, 1935, flies over train	314.00	471.00	628.00
POPEYE Express — MARX, Popeye pushing box with parrot, wind-up, 1935	175.00	262.50	350.00
POPEYE Handcar, MARX, 1935, Popeye & Olive Oyl rubber	400.00	600.00	800.00
POPEYE handpuppet.....	2.00	3.00	4.00
POPEYE Hingee paper figures, No.102, REED, 1940s, price per each....	1.50	2.25	3.00
POPEYE in a barrel, CHEIN, 7" high........	115.00	172.50	230.00
POPEYE Jack-in-the-Box, MATTEL Co., tin mechanical, Popeye pops out of spinach can......	14.00	21.00	28.00
POPEYE mask, cardboard, 1940s	4.50	6.75	9.00
POPEYE Moving Van, tin friction, LINEMAR.....	175.00	262.50	350.00
POPEYE One-Man Band, pole with drum and cymbals, rubber Popeye head on top, 69" high........	10.00	15.00	20.00
POPEYE Pirate, click pistol, MARX No.68.........	54.00	81.00	108.00
POPEYE the Pilot, 1930, MARX wind-up........	210.00	315.00	420.00
POPEYE Puncher, CHEIN 1930, tin and celluloid...	612.50	918.75	1225.00
POPEYE Pushing wheelbarrow, plastic walkie, MARX, circa 1950s.....	4.50	6.75	9.00
POPEYE Rollerskating, LINEMAR............	260.00	390.00	520.00
POPEYE Roly-Poly, 3½" celluloid	5.00	7.50	10.00
POPEYE in a Rowboat, 1935, HOGE..........	1000.00	1500.00	2000.00
POPEYE rubber squeeze toy, 1950s.............	8.00	12.00	16.00
POPEYE Sand Toy teeter-totter, with Popeye, Sweepea, Olive Oyl, Jeep, tin litho.............	25.00	37.50	50.00
POPEYE on SPARKPLUG, 1930s,			

FISHER-PRICE, paper litho on wood.........	G	VG	M
	See Fisher-Price		
POPEYE "Spinach Patrol" HUBLEY............	200.00	300.00	400.00
POPEYE Strength Tester, HOLGATE, 14"......	27.00	40.50	54.00
POPEYE String Puppet, approx. 5" high, wood, JAYMAR, circa 1940s..	25.00	37.50	50.00
"POPEYE" The Champ", MARX...............	300.00	450.00	600.00
POPEYE Turnover Tank, LINEMAR tin windup, 1950s, 6" long........	135.00	207.50	270.00
POPEYE Whistle Pipe, NORTHWEST PRODUCTS OF ST. LOUIS, 3½" long, cardboard bowl with illos of Popeye characters, metal stem with whistle at base.....	14.00	21.00	28.00
POPEYE Yazoo Pipe, NORTHWESTERN PRODUCTIONS, ST. LOUIS MO., 1934......	16.00	24.00	32.00
POPEYE & OLIVE OYL Jiggers (Popeye dancing on roof, Olive Oyl playing concertina), MARX.....	330.00	495.00	660.00
PORKY (Pogo) plastic, 1969	2.70	4.05	5.40
PORKY PIG cowboy with lariat, MARX tin windup	100.00	150.00	200.00
PORKY PIG squeeze toy, SUN RUBBER, approx. 6" high, hollow with squeaker, has hands behind back, circa 1940..	20.00	30.00	40.00
PORKY PIG hand puppet, 1950s	.50	.75	1.00
PORKY PIG tin litho windup, 1939, 8½" high, holding umbrella, MARX	125.00	187.50	250.00

PORKY PIG, tin wind-up, holding umbrella, MARX.

PORKY PIG cowboy with lariat
Courtesy Sotheby Parke Bernet

PRINCE VALIANT Castle Fort, MARX, boxed set with knights, etc.......	G	VG	M
	50.00	75.00	100.00
PRINCE VALIANT Shield, tin litho............	11.00	16.50	22.00
PRINCE VALIANT Sword and tin scabbard, 1950s, MATTEL.............	10.00	15.00	20.00
RACHEL (Gasoline Alley) oilcloth doll, cotton-stuffed, 1923..........	40.00	60.00	80.00

RACHEL, Gasoline Alley, oilcloth, cotton stuffed.

RED RYDER BB gun No.111, DAISY........	15.00	25.00	45.00
"RED RYDER Cork Carbine", DAISY, plstic stock	9.00	13.50	18.00
RED RYDER gun and holster set, DAISY......	10.00	15.00	20.00
RED RYDER Pop-Um shooting game, DAISY..	12.50	18.75	25.00
RED RYDER Molding Set, 1948	14.00	21.00	28.00
RED RYDER Target Game, 1939...........	20.00	30.00	40.00
SAD SACK 15½" vinyl doll, 1950...........	30.00	45.00	60.00
SAD SACK 20" high vinyl doll, cloth uniform, STERLING DOLL CO., circa 1952.........	32.50	48.75	65.00
SANDY (Orphan Annie), 5" long, walks, tin wind-up..	46.00	67.00	92.00
SANDY 10½" long oilcloth doll, circa 1920s........	40.00	60.00	80.00
SANDY (Orphan Annie's dog) with suitcase in mouth, tin wind-up.....	125.00	187.50	250.00

SANDY with a suitcase in mouth
Courtesy PB Eighty-Four, New York

	G	VG	M
SCHROEDER (Peanuts) rubber squeeze toy, circa 1960	2.50	3.75	5.00
SECRET AGENT X-9 Gun and Billy Club	2.50	3.75	5.00
SHMOO (Lil Abner) doll, vinyl inflatable, 15" high .	22.50	33.75	45.00
SKEEZIX oilcloth doll, cotton-stuffed, 1924	40.00	60.00	80.00

SKEEZIX, oilcloth, cotton stuffed.

	G	VG	M
SMITTY 9¾" oilcloth doll .	22.00	33.00	44.00
"SMITTY ON A SCOOTER", tin wind-up, MARX, circa 1930, 8" high	250.00	375.00	500.00

"Smitty On A Scooter"
Photo Courtesy PB Eighty-Four

	G	VG	M
SMOKEY STOVER, hard plastic, 3" high, 1960s . . .	2.50	3.75	5.00
SNOOPY rubber squeeze toy, 1958	4.50	6.75	9.00
SNUFFY SMITH Hand-puppet, cloth, with rubber head, GUND, "King Features"	6.00	9.00	12.00

	G	VG	M
SPARKLE PLENTY Paper-doll Set, 1948, SAALFIELD No.5160 . .	7.00	10.50	14.00
SPARKLE PLENTY Washing Machine, KALON RADIO CORP, litho tin, crank action, circa 1947, 13" tall	18.00	27.00	36.00

SPARKLE PLENTY Washing Machine
Courtesy Lloyd W. Ralston Auctions

	G	VG	M
SPARKPLUG, 1920s SCHOENHUT jointed wood figure	132.50	198.75	265.00
"SPARKPLUG" (Barney Google), on wheels, 3¼" high	90.00	135.00	180.00
SPARKPLUG (Barney Google) stuffed cloth	35.00	52.50	70.00
SPARKPLUG Candy Container	100.00	150.00	200.00

SPARKPLUG, 1920s, SCHOENHUT
Courtesy PB Eight-Four, New York

	G	VG	M
STEVE CANYON Jet Helmet	15.00	22.50	30.00
SUPERMAN 13" high, wood and composition, IDEAL, 1940	175.00	262.50	350.00
SUPERMAN Cut-Out Adventure Book	40.00	60.00	80.00
SUPERMAN "Flying Superman", 1950s, plastic	10.00	15.00	20.00
SUPERMAN Holding airplane, MARX tin wind-up, 1940	75.00	112.50	150.00
SUPERMAN Krypto-Ray Gun, DAISY No.94, 1939, with seven film strips	40.00	60.00	80.00
SUPERMAN Krypton Rockets, circa 1939	18.00	27.00	36.00

	G	VG	M
SUPERMAN TANK, tin wind-up, MARX, 1940s.	125.00	187.50	250.00
SUPERMAN TANK, LINEMAR, 1950s, 4" long	100.00	150.00	200.00
SWEEPEA Hingees No.102, 1944, paper punchouts, REED	1.50	2.25	3.00
SWEEPEA Mask, cardboard, 1940s	4.50	6.75	9.00
TARZAN, mask of Akut the Ape, NORTHERN PAPER MILLS, 1933	20.00	30.00	40.00
TARZAN, mask of Numa the Lion, paper, 1933 by NORTHERN PAPER MILLS	20.00	30.00	40.00
TARZAN, mask of Tarzan, 1933, NORTHERN PAPER MILLS, paper	25.00	37.50	50.00
TARZAN In the Jungle dart board game, 1935, large	75.00	112.50	150.00
TARZAN "Tarzan In The Jungle", 1935 battery-operated target game	60.00	90.00	120.00
TERRY AND THE PIRATES Hingees, 1944, set contains Terry, Flip Corkin, Pat Ryan, Burma, Taffy Tucker	12.50	18.75	25.00

THIMBLE THEATRE Mystery Playhouse figures, Olive Oyl, Popeye, Wimpy
Courtesy Mapes Auctioneers and Appraisers

THIMBLE THEATRE Mystery Playhouse "Starring Popeye with Wimpy and Olive Oyl", copyright 1939, HARDING PRODUCTS, Philadelphia, 12x10x3", figures composition, with wooden "Shuffle" feet, individual figures sell for $55.00 in mint ...... No Price Found

	G	VG	M
THREE FLYING MARVELS (Captain, Jr., Mary), paper, circa 1944-47, REED	4.00	6.00	8.00
TOONERVILLE TROLLEY, lead, circa 1923	215.00	322.50	430.00
TOONERVILLE TROLLEY tin wind-up, "copyright 1922 by Fontaine Fox", 7½" high, Skipper driving, NIFTY	300.00	450.00	600.00
TOONERVILLE TROLLEY, 1921, STRAUSS wind-up	310.00	465.00	620.00

"Toonerville Trolley" NIFTY tin wind-up
Courtesy PB Eighty-Four

TOONERVILLE TROLLEY, lead, circa 1923
Courtesy PB Eighty-Four, New York

	G	VG	M
TOONERVILLE TROLLEY, 1⅞" high, sometimes called Crackerjack size	170.00	255.00	340.00
TOONERVILLE TROLLEY — DENT, cast iron	350.00	525.00	700.00
TOONERVILLE Glass Candy Container, 3¼" long	250.00	375.00	500.00
TOONERVILLE TROLLEY, "Powerful			

	G	VG	M
Katrinka", 6½" long, pushing boy in wheelbarrow tin wind-up, LEHMANN, 1923	750.00	1025.00	1500.00
TWEETY BIRD rubber squeeze toy, 1950s	4.00	6.00	8.00
UNCLE WALT (Gasoline Alley), oil-cloth, 26" high	37.50	56.25	75.00
UNCLE WIGGILY, MARX, Crazy Car	125.00	187.50	250.00
WALTER LANTZ ink stamp character set, 12 different rubber stamps	2.50	3.75	5.00
Western Thrills with BILLY THE KID, character from Funny Animals Comics, circa 1944-47, REED, paper toy	1.13	1.70	2.25
WILLIE THE WORM and SAMMY in Car Trouble, paper toy, Fawcett Comics characters, REED, circa 1944-47	1.50	2.25	3.00
WILLIE THE WORM and SAMMY Flying Machine	1.50	2.25	3.00
WILLIE THE WORM and SAMMY Fish-n Fun	1.25	1.88	2.50
WIMPY 3" hard plastic figure, 1960s	2.00	3.00	4.00
WIMPY 3⅛" high, cast iron HUBLEY	40.00	60.00	80.00
WIMPY 4" high, wood-jointed, "by K.F.S."	24.00	36.00	48.00
WIMPY 8" high rubber squeeze toy	30.00	45.00	60.00

	G	VG	M
WIMPY Handpuppet, GUND	9.00	13.50	18.00
WIMPY mask, cardboard, 1940s	4.50	6.75	9.00
WIMPY rubber squeeze toy, 1950s	7.50	11.25	15.00
WIMPY String Puppet, approx. 5" high, wood, JAYMAR, circa 1940s	25.00	37.50	50.00
WOODY WOODPECKER Handpuppet, MATTEL, 1962, "W. LANTZ", rubber head, cloth body	4.00	6.00	8.00
WOODY WOODPECKER, 6½" high, rubber, "Walter Lantz"	2.50	3.75	5.00
YELLOW KID in Cart, KENTON, early 1900s, 10" long 6" high, pulled by mule, cast iron	150.00	225.00	300.00
YELLOW KID in Goat Cart, KENTON, 1890, painted cast iron, 7½" long	110.00	165.00	220.00
YELLOW KID papier mache and wood, SCHOENHUT, 11" high, early 1900s	60.00	90.00	120.00

Yellow Kid in goat cart, KENTON
Courtesy Lloyd W. Ralston Auctions

MOVIES, RADIO, TELEVISION
(see also Paper, Premiums, Banks, Miscellaneous, Comic Character)

The average mint price in this category in the last edition was $58.39, and in this edition averages $103.48, an increase of 77%.

CONDITION OF A TOY AND ITS RELATION TO PRICE

The price of a toy depends not only on its desirability, but on its condition. A toy in mint condition is generally worth twice what that same toy would bring in good condition, with "very good" falling about equally in between good and mint.

"Mint" means just that; the condition in which it was originally issued — perfect, regardless of age, not the slightest blemish. Needless to say this is a fairly rare state of affairs, but enough toys exist in mint condition to make it an employable term. Many people hoping to dispose of toys are tempted to call an item "mint" when it is really "near mint", "very good", or sometimes just "good". Inevitably this can result in unhappiness all around, and not infrequently, a cancelled sale.

"Very Good" indicates a toy which has obviously seen use, with signs of wear and aging, but in general having a freshness to its appearance that makes it attractive and collectible to all but the most discriminating.

"Good" signals a toy that has seen considerable wear, shows its age, but is basically sound. A collector will collect it, but will often not be wholly satisfied with it as an example of his collection, and thus prices are often drastically below that which the same item in mint can command.

Condition below good results in another drastic drop in price, and toys with missing parts, although otherwise in excellent condition, will usually fall into this lower-priced category. Rust, even small spots of it, can seriously lower the price of a toy. "Near-Mint", "Very Fine", "Fine" and similar terms often found in sellers' descriptions denote conditions between Mint and Very Good, and are priced accordingly.

The key to grading is to avoid wishful thinking. Grading can sometimes be a problem for the uninitiated, but common sense will usually prevail, and when possible, a consultation with an expert in the field can often clear up lingering doubts. A toy in its original box is worth up to 10 to 20% more if the box is in mint condition, with the price dropping as its condition lessens.

AMOS & ANDY tin wind-ups, 12" high, eyes move
Courtesy Lloyd W. Ralston Auctions

AMOS & ANDY FRESH-AIR TAXI
Photo Courtesy PB Eighty-Four

	G	VG	M
AMOS tin wind-up, 1930..	215.00	332.50	430.00
AMOS and ANDY in car, glass, 4½" long........	200.00	300.00	400.00
AMOS and ANDY wood jointed dolls, 6" high, price for pair..........	80.00	120.00	160.00
AMOS & ANDY FRESH-AIR TAXI, tin wind-up, MARX, 8" long, 1930s..	265.00	397.50	530.00
ANDY Tin Wind-Up, 12" high.................	205.00	307.50	410.00
BARNEY RUBBLE (Flintstones) 10" high vinyl doll, 1960............	5.25	7.88	10.50

	G	VG	M
BEANY 15" stuffed doll, vinyl head, hands, feet, MATTEL.............	11.00	16.50	22.00
BEANY Doll, 16½" high, talks, MATTEL, 1950s, stuffed cloth body, rubber head.................	16.00	24.00	32.00
BABY HUEY Hand Puppet	2.50	3.75	5.00
BEATLES, Ringo, John, Paul, George, 5" vinyl figures, 1964. Price per each..................	14.00	21.00	28.00
BEN HUR Sword, scabbard and shield, MARX, only produced in 1959, when movie was made........	25.50	38.25	51.00
BETTY BOOP character doll, jointed, 9½" tall, 1930s...............	15.00	22.50	30.00
BETTY BOOP pinback button................	3.50	5.25	7.00
BOB BURNS Bazooka, brass kazoo-like toy, patterned after radio-movie comic Burns' famous musical invention (the Army weapon gets its name from it), metal sliding			

	G	VG	M
tube, M.M. POCHAPIA TOYS, 13" long when not extended, 1930s.........	3.00	4.50	6.00
BOBBA-LOUIE 14" stuffed doll, vinyl head, KNICKERBOCKER, 1959	8.00	12.00	16.00
BOBBA-LOUIE 18" stuffed doll, vinyl face, plush body, KNICKER-BOCKER 1959........	9.00	13.50	18.00
"BOJANGLES DANCES AGAIN", tin litho and wood, 1930s, tap button on base and he dances...	23.00	34.50	46.00
BUCK JONES Rangers chaps.................	30.00	45.00	60.00
BUFFALO BILL JR. belt and buckle (TV), 1950s..	8.00	12.00	16.00
BUGS BUNNY & PORKY PIG talking toy in original box, 1940s, has record that talks........	37.50	56.25	75.00
"BULLET" (Roy Rogers' dog) stuffed doll, circa 1955	9.00	13.50	18.00
CAPTAIN KANGAROO badge, tin shield........	1.00	1.50	2.00
CASPER THE FRIENDLY GHOST 11" stuffed doll, body is beanbag, 1960s..	4.00	6.00	8.00
CASPER THE FRIENDLY GHOST Turnover Tank, LINEMAR tin windup..	100.00	150.00	200.00
CECIL SEA SERPEANT, 8" vinyl...............	11.00	16.50	22.00
CECIL SEA SERPEANT, 18" stuffed doll, MATTEL.............	12.00	18.00	24.00
CECIL SEA SERPEANT, 22" stuffed doll, MATTEL.............	16.00	24.00	32.00
CECIL SEA SERPEANT, stuffed talking doll......	14.00	21.00	28.00
CHARLIE CHAPLIN Tin Wind-Up, 8½" high.....	350.00	525.00	700.00
CHARLIE CHAPLIN Bell Toy, cast iron..........	75.00	112.50	150.00
CHARLIE CHAPLIN, flat tin litho, he tips hat when string is pulled........	7.00	10.50	14.00
CHARLIE CHAPLIN, 1920, MARTIN, clockwork, 7" high, papier mache, lead, wire cane, cloth clothes...........	150.00	225.00	300.00

CHARLIE McCARTHY IN HIS BEN-ZINE BUGGY
Courtesy PB Eighty-Four, New York

CHARLIE McCARTHY, name written on top hat, tin windup.

"CHARLIE MCCARTHY"	G	VG	M
written on top hat, standing erect, tin wind-up, circa 1938.............	90.00	135.00	180.00
CHARLIE MCCARTHY rubber doll, EFFANBEE	20.00	30.00	40.00
CHARLIE MCCARTHY 13" high, composition, mouth moves, 1930s....	32.00	48.00	64.00
CHARLIE McCARTHY in his BENZINE BUGGY, MARX...............	125.00	187.50	250.00
CHARLIE MCCARTHY CAR wind-up, MARX, 1935.................	140.00	210.00	280.00
CHARLIE MCCARTHY Cardboard Puppet, 20" high.................	6.00	9.00	12.00
CHARLIE MCCARTHY Facemask, molded gauze, complete with separate monocle..............	10.00	15.00	20.00
CHARLIE MCCARTHY Handpuppet, composition head, circa 1939........	32.50	48.75	65.00
CHARLIE MCCARTHY paper money...........	4.00	6.00	8.00
CHARLIE MCCARTHY Ventroliquist doll, composition with cloth body, ring pull in back of head to activate lower jaw, 14½" tall.............	225.00	337.50	450.00
CHARLIE MCCARTHY "Charlie McCarthy and Mortimer Snerd Private Car", MARX, two heads sticking out of top of car.	260.00	390.00	520.00
CISCO KID neckerchief with nickel sombrero slide	12.50	18.75	25.00
COWARDLY LION (Wizard of Oz), molded gauze facemask........	12.50	18.75	25.00
DALE EVANS holster outfit	20.00	30.00	40.00

	G	VG	M
DALE EVANS & HORSE, BUTTERMILK, figures by HARTLAND.......	8.00	12.00	16.00
DEPUTY DAWG, 14" high stuffed doll, IDEAL, 1961	9.00	13.50	18.00
DICK VAN DYKE doll from CHITTY CHITTY BANG BANG, 1967, talks, MATTEL........	11.00	16.50	22.00
DRAGNET Crime Lab, 1955, flashlight, signal gun, badge, handcuffs, fingerprint kit, etc......	11.00	16.50	22.00
DRAGNET Jack Webb black police whistle.....	2.20	3.30	4.40
DRAGNET Police Set, gun, handcuffs, badge.......	3.00	4.50	6.00
DRAGNET St. Los Angeles Police No. 714 badge....	3.50	5.25	7.00
DRAGNET talking police car, IDEAL TOYS, circa 1954...............	30.00	45.00	60.00
DRAGNET Water Pistol, circa 1955, 714 badge emblazoned on handle...	7.50	11.25	15.00
ED WYNN FIRE CHIEF, litho on wood, pull toy, SCHOENHUT, 12" long.	90.00	135.00	180.00
FANNY BRICE (Baby Snooks), IDEAL, composition and wire doll...	100.00	150.00	200.00
FARMER ALFALFA (Terrytoons) circa 1950, 17 1/2" high, stuffed body, vinyl head, hands..	21.00	31.50	42.00
FLINTSTONE Choo Choo Train, MARX, "Bedrock Express", tin wind-up, Linemar Co., 13" long, 1950s...............	125.00	187.50	250.00
FLINTSTONE Turnover Tank, LINEMAR tin wind-up, 1950s, 4" long..	125.00	187.50	250.00
FLUB-A-DUB push puppet, plastic, felt, wood, 5" high	21.00	31.50	42.00
FLUB-A-DUB (Howdy Doody) small plastic figure	2.50	3.75	5.00
FRED FLINTSTONE, 5¾" tall, hollow vinyl figure..	1.50	2.25	3.00
FROGGIE THE GREMLIN hollow rubber doll, squeeze toy 5" high, of the Buster Brown radio with TV show, squeeze and tongue sticks out, 1950s	21.00	31.50	42.50
FROGGIE THE GREMLIN, 9¼" squeeze toy..................	25.00	37.50	50.00
FROGGIE THE GREMLIN 10¾" squeeze toy............	25.00	37.50	50.00
GULLIVER'S TRAVELS Boat, wooden (Paramount)	8.00	12.00	16.00
GULLIVER'S TRAVELS Drum, tin, CHEIN, 1939	25.00	37.50	50.00
GULLIVER'S TRAVELS Sandpail, tin, CHEIN...	15.00	22.50	30.00
HAROLD LLOYD Bell Toy, German, 6 1/2" high	100.00	150.00	200.00
HAROLD LLOYD "Funny Face", MARX wind-up walker, 1929...........	145.00	217.50	290.00
HAROLD LLOYD Policeman, 12" high, tin wind-up..............	15.00	22.50	30.00
HENRY FONDA Texas Ranger Sheriff badge, THE DEPUTY, 1951...	4.00	6.00	8.00
HOOT GIBSON lariat.....	15.00	22.50	30.00
HOPALONG CASSIDY Badge, tin with inset photo	10.00	15.00	20.00
HOPALONG CASSIDY Binoculars, circa 1950...	9.00	13.50	18.00
HOPALONG CASSIDY compass	4.00	6.00	8.00
HOPALONG CASSIDY Cowgirl's Outfit........	17.50	26.25	35.00
HOPALONG CASSIDY dart board, 14"x17", stagecoach holdup and target practice, 1950....	5.00	7.50	10.00
HOPALONG CASSIDY Field Glasses, 1940.....	12.50	18.75	25.00
HOPALONG CASSIDY Flashlight Gun, plastic, 8" long, Hoppy's name on side	15.00	22.50	30.00
HOPALONG CASSIDY knife, circa mid-1940s, 3 1/2" long..............	20.00	30.00	40.00
HOPALONG CASSIDY Photo Ring, circa late 1940s	11.50	17.25	23.00
HOPALONG CASSIDY Rocking Horse Cowboy, MARX	79.00	118.50	158.00

	G	VG	M
HOPALONG CASSIDY Shooting Gallery.......	32.50	48.75	65.00
HOPALONG CASSIDY Signet Ring, all metal, late 1940s	5.00	7.50	10.00
HOPALONG CASSIDY Spurs, leather and metal.	6.00	9.00	12.00
HOPALONG CASSIDY Western Frontier set, with figures, stage coach and buildings	55.00	82.50	110.00
HOPALONG CASSIDY woodburning set, 1950, AMERICAN TOY AND FURNITURE CO......	34.00	51.00	68.00
HOPALONG CASSIDY Wrangler Pin..........	3.50	5.25	7.00
HOPALONG CASSIDY Zoomerang Gun, shoots paper, TIGRETT ENTERPRISES, CHICAGO............	8.00	12.00	16.00
HOWDY DOODY 4" high plastic push-puppet, HOHNER, has NBC mike	15.00	22.50	30.00
HOWDY DOODY 6" high, wall walker doll........	6.00	9.00	12.00
HOWDY DOODY 7½" high, 1950s, plastic, cloth clothes, eyes close, mouth opens................	17.50	26.95	35.00
HOWDY DOODY 12" high, moveable jaws, GOLDBERGER DOLLS	12.50	18.75	25.00
HOWDY DOODY 26" ventriloquist dummy.......	20.00	30.00	40.00
HOWDY DOODY Acrobat	12.00	18.00	24.00
HOWDY DOODY and BOB SMITH at the piano, tin wind-up, UNIQUE	200.00	300.00	400.00

HOWDY DOODY
And BOB SMITH At
The Piano
Courtesy PB Eighty-
Four, New York

	G	VG	M
HOWDY DOODY, Clarabell's horn, 1950s...	9.00	13.50	18.00
HOWDY DOODY, Cowboy Gloves, leather, 1950s...	9.00	13.50	18.00
HOWDY DOODY hand puppets, no date no mfr., rubber heads, cloth bodies	3.75	5.63	7.50
HOWDY DOODY Life Preserver, plastic, 1950s, show Howdy, Mr. Bluster, etc.............	10.00	15.00	20.00
HOWDY DOODY marionette, 17" high, wooden arms and legs, composition head.......	25.00	37.50	50.00
HOWDY DOODY Marionette, 16" high, composition head, hands and feet, handpainted features, 1950s.........	25.00	37.50	50.00
HOWDY DOODY Mask, rubber	4.00	6.00	8.00
HOWDY DOODY Piano, Howdy plays it	62.50	93.75	125.00
HOWDY DOODY plastic puppet toys, with levers in back of head to move mouths. Consists of Howdy, Bluster, Clarabell, Princess, Dilly Dally, TEE-VEE Toys No. 549. Price for set	16.50	24.00	32.00
HOWDY DOODY plastic ukulele, EMENEE, 1950s	10.00	15.00	20.00
HOWDY DOODY "Put-In-Head", similar to Mr. Potato Head, but with Howdy characters, Howdy, Bluster, Clarabell, Princess. Price for set	7.50	11.25	15.00
HOWDY DOODY "Pump-Mobile", NYLINT unauthorized Howdy, rides cart, 8½" long, 7" high	60.00	90.00	120.00
HOWDY DOODY Sand Forms, 1952, molds of Howdy, Bluster, Flub-A-Dub, Clarabell, plus shovel	7.00	10.50	14.00
HOWDY DOODY Squeeze toy, 7" high...........	7.50	11.25	15.00
HOWDY DOODY TV Set with paper filmstrips, LEGO, 1950s.........	12.50	18.75	25.00
HOWDY DOODY tin wind-			

	G	VG	M
up, circa 1950, MARX, 5" high, Howdy plays banjo and moves head...	30.00	45.00	60.00
HOWDY DOODY tin wind-up circa 1950, Howdy does jig and Clarabell sits at piano, MARX, 5½" high...	70.00	105.00	140.00
HOWDY DOODY wood-jointed doll, 13" high....	205.00	307.50	410.00
HOWDY DOODY wood-jointed doll, 5½" high, holding NBC mike...	11.00	16.50	22.00
HUCKLEBERRY HOUND 18" stuffed doll, 1959, KNICKERBOCKER....	9.00	13.50	18.00
HUCKLEBERRY HOUND as FIREMAN, rubber, squeeze toy, 1960s...	2.00	3.00	4.00
HUCKLEBERRY HOUND with top hat, rubber squeeze toy, 1960s...	3.75	5.25	7.50
HUCKLEBERRRY HOUND 18" stuffed doll, 1959, KNICKERBOCKER....	9.00	13.50	18.00
HUCKLEBERRY HOUND as FIREMAN, rubber, squeeze toy, 1960s...	3.75	5.25	7.50
HUGH O'BRIAN-WYATT EARP, Dodge City Western Town, MARX, 1950s...	19.00	28.50	38.00
I SPY Ranger Pin...	11.00	16.50	22.00
JACKIE COOGAN glass candy container, 5" high.	800.00	1200.00	1600.00
JACKIE GLEASON "Away We Go" bus, 13"...	7.50	11.25	15.00
JAMES BOND Action Toy Set No. 1 by GILBERT, 1965. Includes figures of 007 as scuba diver, Domino and Largo with Disco Volante's yacht, display box...	17.50	26.25	35.00
JAMES BOND Action Playset No. 2, Bond, Goldfinger, Odd Job and spin-top pool table, display box...	17.50	26.25	35.00
JAMES BOND Action Toy Set No. 3, in display box by GILBERT, 1965, includes figures of 007 on Laser Table, Goldfinger, Odd Job and Dr. No....	17.50	26.25	35.00

	G	VG	M
JAMES BOND Action Playset No. 4, Dr. No, Bond, Domino and fire-spitting Dragon Tank, display box...	17.50	26.25	35.00
JAMES BOND Action Playset No. 5, Bond with baretta, Money Penny, M, and M's secret desk, display box...	17.50	26.25	35.00
JAMES BOND Aston-Martin...	20.00	30.00	40.00
JAMES BOND 007 Attache Case, 11". Code book, rifle, which converts to pistol, bullets, Code-O-Matic, billfold with money and James Bond business cards and instructions, circa 1965...	20.00	30.00	40.00
JAMES BOND Camera, shoots...	15.00	22.50	30.00
JAMES BOND No. 2 with Rifle, 3½" tall, GILBERT, 1965...	1.50	2.25	3.00
JAMES BOND No. 3 in Scuba Suit with Spear Gun, 3½" tall, GILBERT, 1965...	2.00	3.00	4.00
JAMES BOND No. 4 Odd Job, 3½" tall, 1965 GILBERT...	2.25	3.35	4.50
JAMES BOND No. 5 "M", Bond's boss...	2.00	3.00	4.00
JAMES BOND No. 6 Goldfinger...	2.00	3.00	4.00
JAMES BOND No. 7 Miss Moneypenny...	1.50	2.25	3.00
JAMES BOND No. 8 Largo, 3½" tall, 1965, GILBERT...	.75	1.13	1.50
JAMES BOND No. 9 Domino, 3½" tall, 1965, GILBERT...	1.25	1.88	2.50
JAMES BOND No. 10 Dr. No with poison vial...	3.00	4.50	6.00
JERRY MAHONEY ventriloquist dummy...	7.50	11.25	15.00
JETSONS Turnover Tank, LINEMAR tin windup..	150.00	225.00	300.00
JOE PENNER tin wind-up, MARX, circa 1930s, 8" high, tips hat, walks, "Wanna Buy a Duck?"..	125.00	187.50	250.00
KING LITTLE (Gulliver's Travels), IDEAL, 12" jointed composition...	60.00	90.00	120.00

LONE RANGER, "Hiyo Silver, the Lone Ranger Courtesy PB Eighty-Four, New York

MORTIMER SNERD tin wind-up, MARX, Courtesy PB Eighty-Four, New York

	G	VG	M
LAMBCHOP Shari Lewis Handpuppet	3.00	4.50	6.00
LONE RANGER Acme Moviescope Set, 1948, includes 4 films: No.1 Superman, No.2 Lone Ranger, No.3 Lone Ranger, No.4 Lone Ranger. With pop-up box including films and viewer	50.00	75.00	100.00
LONE RANGER and SILVER composition figure, 1938	12.50	18.75	25.00
LONE RANGER Chuck Wagon Lantern	25.00	37.50	50.00
LONE RANGER Deputy Badge, 1950s	15.00	22.50	30.00
LONE RANGER Doll, 20" high, 1938, very realistic, composition head, hands, feet	93.75	140.63	187.50
LONE RANGER flashlight	6.50	9.75	13.00
LONE RANGER film viewer, four films, 1953	12.50	18.75	25.00
LONE RANGER harmonica, MAGNUS, 1950	5.00	7.50	10.00
LONE RANGER Hat, 1930s, official	12.00	18.00	24.00
LONE RANGER Hat, cowboy hat of white felt w/red trim. "Lone Ranger. Hi! Yo! Silver!", inscribed, 1940s	12.50	18.75	25.00
LONE RANGER "Hiyo Silver, the Lone Ranger" tin wind-up, copyright 1938, Lone Ranger on Silver with lasso, MARX	70.00	105.00	140.00
LONE RANGER Official First Aid Kit with contents, 1938, tin litho	11.25	16.88	22.50

LONE RANGER "Official Outfit", 1939, mask, jail

	G	VG	M
keys, badge, silver bullet, glow belt, Lone Ranger buckle, Lee Powell and Chief Thundercloud on belt	75.00	112.50	150.00
LONE RANGER Picture Printing Set, 1939, 8 rubber stamps	16.00	24.00	32.00
LONE RANGER RIDES AGAIN movie viewer, 1939	15.00	22.50	30.00
LONE RANGER Rodeo, MARX set with metal bldgs., plastic figures, etc., 1950s	32.50	48.75	65.00
LONE RANGER Signal Siren, Flashlight, 1950, with silver bullet secret code, UNITED STATES ELECTRIC MFG. CO.	12.50	18.75	25.00
LONE RANGER Silver Bullet Knife, length 3" closed	11.50	17.25	23.00
LONE RANGER "Stringless Marionette" handpuppet, cloth and vinyl	17.50	26.25	35.00
LONE RANGER Strongbox (coinbank)	20.00	30.00	40.00
LONE RANGER Target Game, 1938, MARX	22.50	33.75	45.00
MAN FROM U.N.C.L.E. Ilya Kuryakin	20.00	30.00	40.00
MAN FROM U.N.C.L.E. Napoleon Solo	20.00	30.00	40.00
MATT DILLON, U.S. Marshall badge (Gunsmoke)	3.75	5.25	7.50
MEN INTO SPACE space helmet, retractable visor, space mike, etc. From series starring William Lundigan as Col. McCaulety. Made of fortiflex	7.50	11.25	15.00
MILTON BERLE CAR, two large wheels, two small, MARX, 1950s, "What the Hey," etc. written on car	75.00	112.50	150.00
MORTIMER SNERD, 13" high, IDEAL, composition and wire	60.00	90.00	120.00
MORTIMER SNERD Band, MARX wind-up, 1935, "Hometown Band"	200.00	300.00	400.00

Milton Berle Car
Courtesy Mapes Auctioneers & Appraisers

	G	VG	M
MORTIMER SNERD Jack In The Box, circa 1930s, 8" high.............	32.50	48.75	65.00
"MORTIMER SNERD TEETH", plastic teeth and dental wax, circa 1950................	2.50	3.75	5.00
MORTIMER SNERD Tin Wind-up, MARX, circa 1939, Mortimer's hat tips as he walks...........	71.00	106.50	142.00
"MORTIMER SNERD'S TRICKY AUTO", 1939, MARX..............	120.00	180.00	240.00
MR. MAGOO car, battery, tin litho.............	See Battery Toys		
MR. MAGOO Doll, IDEAL, 15" high.......	18.00	27.00	36.00
OLIVER HARDY Hand-puppet, KNICKERBOCKER....	12.00	18.00	24.00
OLIVER HARDY Roly Poly, 10½" high, plastic...	17.50	26.25	35.00
"OSWALD, Universal Pictures, Irwin Prod". 18½" wind-up, wood and cardboard body with cloth clothes, stuffed arms and head, character created by DISNEY, early........	150.00	225.00	300.00
PINKY LEE vinyl doll. Squeeze and his head pops up, 1950.........	50.00	75.00	100.00
RIFLEMAN (TV) Ranch, MARX..............	19.00	28.50	38.00
RIN TIN TIN and RUSTY Knife, 1950s..........	18.00	27.00	36.00
RIN TIN TIN - MARX Fort Apache Stockade, 1950s	75.00	112.50	150.00

	G	VG	M
ROBIN HOOD Money Pouch, six foreign coins from Richard Greene TV series, 1953-54........	3.75	5.25	7.50
ROBIN HOOD Money Pouch, fifteen foreign coins, from Richard Greene TV series.......	5.00	7.50	10.00
ROBIN HOOD Shield. Badge with embossed Robin Hood and gem stone, circa 1956.......	5.75	8.63	11.50
ROCKY THE FLYING SQUIRREL Bendee figure, 1960s...........	3.50	5.25	7.00
ROOTIE KAZOOTIE Marionette, 14" hard rubber head and hands, wooden shoes and body wearing clothes........	20.00	30.00	40.00
ROY ROGERS, 7½" high, HARTLAND............	37.50	56.25	75.00
ROY ROGERS bandana, large	3.00	4.50	6.00
ROY ROGERS Branding Iron Set..............	11.00	16.50	22.00
ROY ROGERS Double R Bar Ranch, 1950s, tin litho ranch house, MARX	20.00	30.00	40.00
ROY ROGERS "Ranch Lantern", No.90, metal, hurricane type with plastic chimney, 1950s, 7¾" tall.............	20.00	30.00	40.00
ROY ROGERS Mineral City, town with hotel, music hall, cafe, bank, barber shop, trade goods, etc., tin..............	40.00	60.00	80.00
ROY ROGERS Nellie Belle Jeep.................	16.00	24.00	32.00
ROY ROGERS pocket flashlight.............	8.00	12.00	16.00
ROY ROGERS Quickshooter hat.......	7.00	10.50	14.00
ROY ROGERS Riders Lucky Piece...........	4.50	6.75	9.00
ROY ROGERS Rodeo Ranch, MARX........	25.00	37.50	50.00
ROY ROGERS Signal Flashlight	10.00	15.00	20.00
ROY ROGERS Telescope..	20.00	30.00	40.00
ROY ROGERS and TRIGGER pocket knife......	14.00	21.00	28.00
SCARECROW (Wizard of Oz) molded gauze facemask..............	12.50	18.75	25.00

	G	VG	M
SCRAPPY & MARGIE wooden pull toy, 13½" long, he plays xylophone, she revolves, co. Columbia Pictures	150.00	225.00	300.00
SGT. BILKO Holster Set from the CBS TV series "You'll Never Get Rich", starring Phil Silvers. Photo-illustrated box contains leather holster and belt with realistic Army .45 made of silvered die cast metal. Sgt's arm patch and Sgt. Bilko hat with Badge, HALCO BRAND, 1956	7.50	11.25	15.00
SMALL FRY CLUB KIT, 1949, button, etc., Dumont TV show (may be premium)	7.50	11.25	15.00
"SNEAK" Facemask, molded gauze (Gulliver's Travels), 1939	16.00	24.00	32.00
SOUPY SALES dolls, 1965, SUNSHINE DOLL CO.	11.00	16.50	22.00
SPANKY OF OUR GANG 1930s pinback button	6.00	9.00	12.00
STAN LAUREL Handpuppet, KNICKERBOCKER	2.00	3.00	4.00
TALES OF THE TEXAS RANGERS Deputy badge	2.50	3.75	5.00
THREE STOOGES handpuppet, Moe, Curley and Larry, price per each	3.75	5.25	7.50
TIM HOLT Litho Target	4.50	6.75	9.00
TINMAN Facemask (Wizard of Oz) molded gauze	12.50	18.75	25.00
TOM CORBETT SPACE CADET, 14 different figures, MARX, 1950s. Price per set	4.50	6.75	9.00
TOM CORBETT, 7 different figures, same as above, price per set	3.00	4.50	6.00
TOM CORBETT Cosmic Vision Space Helmet, one-way vision, plastic, early 1950s	22.50	33.75	45.00
TOM CORBETT SPACE CADET Molding and Coloring Set, MODEL CRAFT (All Tom Corbett toys 1950-55)	29.00	43.50	58.00

	G	VG	M
TOM CORBETT SPACE CADET Field Glasses, 3 power	12.00	18.00	24.00
TOM CORBETT SPACE CADET Flashlight with built-in signal siren, 7" long, metal, US ALITE Corp	17.00	25.50	34.00
TOM CORBETT Official Outfit, YANKIBOY	20.00	30.00	40.00
TOM CORBETT "Polaris" Rocket Ship, wind-up, MARX, 1952, 12" long, Tom, Astro and Roger looking out of cockpit	125.00	187.50	250.00
TOM CORBETT Space Hat, LEE	5.00	7.50	10.00
TOM CORBETT SPACE CADET official Space Pistol. MARX No.105	15.00	22.50	30.00
TOM CORBETT SPACE CADET Rifle, MARX, No. 0239	32.50	48.75	65.00
TOM CORBETT Space Station	10.00	15.00	20.00
TOM CORBETT SPACE CADET 2-Way Space Phone, ZIMMERMAN	10.00	15.00	20.00
TOM MIX "Circus Wild West", ARCADE circus wagon with driver, two horses, 14½" long, circa 1936. (See Animal Drawn, ARCADE "Big Six")	No	Price	Found
TOM MIX metal and leather spurs, 1934 (not a premium)	50.00	75.00	100.00
TOM MIX Rodeorope, 1928, comes with box and instructions	37.50	56.25	75.00
TONTO (Lone Ranger) 20" high doll, 1938, very realistic, composition head, hands, feet	125.00	187.50	250.00
WILD BILL HICKOCK & JINGLES TV SHOW, 42 piece Western Bunkhouse	20.00	30.00	40.00
WILD BILL HICKOCK Marshal Star Badge with picture of Hickock and Jingles in center	4.50	6.75	9.00
WIZARD OF OZ masks, set of five, EINSON-FREEMAN CO., INC., 1939 "Par-T-Mask"	60.00	90.00	120.00
YOGI BEAR Friction Car, MARX, 1962	15.00	22.50	30.00

DISNEY
(See also Paper, Premiums, Fisher-Price)

The average mint price of Disney toys in the last edition was $107.84, and in this edition it is $131.60, an increase of 22%.

Although Walt Disney was involved in animation as early as 1920, his first really notable character was Oswald the Rabbit, introduced in 1927. However, Disney did not own the rights, which eventually fell into the hands of another animator, Walter Lantz. Mickey Mouse first appeared in the 1928 short "Plane Crazy", but the third Mickey cartoon, "Steamboat Willie", seems to have been the first released, on November 18, 1928, and Mickey was a success from that point on. Minnie Mouse also appeared in the latter film, with Pluto emerging in 1930, though not called that till 1931, Goofy debuting in 1932, and Donald Duck in 1934. Mickey Mouse toys were first produced in 1930, and since then the stream of Disneyana has been unending, and apparently all of it deemed collectible.

CONDITION OF A DISNEY TOY AND ITS RELATION TO PRICE

The price of a Disney toy depends not only on its desirability, but on its condition. A toy in mint condition is generally worth twice what the same toy would bring in good condition, with "very good" falling about equally in between good and mint.

"Mint" means just that; the condition in which it was originally issued — perfect, regardless of age, not the slightest blemish. Needless to say this is a fairly rare state of affairs, particularly with the early Disney toys, but these items do exist, which means that full value must be given the term, or unhappiness all around will result.

"Very Good" indicates a toy that has obviously seen use, with some signs of wear and aging, but in general having a freshness to its appearance that makes it attractive and collectible to all but the most discriminating.

"Good" signals a toy that has seen considerable wear and shows its age, but is otherwise basically sound. A collector will collect it, but will often not be wholly satisfied with it as an example of his collection, and thus prices are often drastically below that which the same item in mint can command.

Condition below good results in another drastic drop in price, and toys with missing parts, although otherwise in excellent condition, will usually fall into this lower-priced category. "Near Mint", "Fine", "Very Fine" and similar terms often found in sellers' descriptions denote conditions between Mint and Very Good, and are priced accordingly.

The key to grading is to avoid wishful thinking. Grading can sometimes be a problem to the uninitiated, but common sense will usually prevail, and when possible, a consultation with an expert in the field can often clear up lingering doubts. A toy on its original card or in its original box is worth up to 10 to 20% more.

	G	VG	M		G	VG	M
BABES IN TOYLAND, tin litho wind-up Indian on rollerskaes, LINEMAR, 1950s, 6½" tall	100.00	150.00	200.00	Co., 1950s, Plastic wind-up, 5" high	30.00	65.00	60.00
BASHFUL 1½" lead figure, BRITAINS	20.00	30.00	40.00	CLEO facemask (Pinocchio) by GILLETTE, 1939	5.00	7.50	10.00
BASHFUL, Approx. 12" high, 1938 IDEAL	50.00	75.00	100.00	CLEO THE GOLDFISH (Pinocchio) SUN RUBBER squeeze toy	5.0	7.50	10.00
BASHFUL Party Mask, 1937	5.40	8.10	10.80	DAVY CROCKETT AUTO-MAGIC PICTURE GUN	6.00	9.00	12.00
BASHFUL stuffed doll	30.00	45.00	60.00	DAVY CROCKETT BADGE, 1950s	2.25	3.38	4.50
BIG BAD WOLF Halloween Costume, 4' high	22.50	33.75	45.00	DAVY CROCKETT Coonskin Hat	9.00	13.50	18.00
BIG BAD WOLF celluloid pinback, 1¼"	12.50	18.75	25.00	DAVY CROCKETT doll, 8" high, FORTUNE TOY, 1950s	5.00	7.50	10.00
BIG BAD WOLF Stuffed toy in tux, with carnation, glass eyes, 20" tall	150.00	225.00	300.00	DAVY CROCKETT Flying Arrows, balsa wood figures to be made into flying arrows. Copyright 1955	3.00	4.50	6.00
CINDERELLA wind-up, 4¾" high, IRWIN, umbrella, spins and dances	17.50	26.25	35.00				
CINDERELLA & PRINCE - Dancing, No.7000, Irwin							

DAVY CROCKETT "Fron-tierland Davy Crockett Outfit", gun, coonskin hat, etc.	G	VG	M
	17.50	26.25	35.00
DAVY CROCKETT hand-gun, pop-action, tin litho, 1950s	15.00	22.50	30.00
DAVY CROCKETT PLAY KNIFE, 1950s	3.13	4.69	6.25
DAVY CROCKETT Powder Horn, DAISY	5.50	8.25	11.00
DAVY CROCKETT Prairie Wagon, 5" long	3.75	5.25	7.50
DISNEYLAND FERRIS WHEEL, circa late 1956, CHEIN, tin wind-up, 17" high	90.00	135.00	180.00

Donald Duck Duet
Courtesy Mapes Auctioneers & Appraisers

DISNEYLAND
Ferris Wheel
Courtesy HAKE'S
Americana &
Collectibles

DISNEYLAND ROLLER
COASTER, CHEIN, 10"
high 140.00 210.00 280.00
DOC 1½" lead figure,
BRITAINS 20.00 30.00 40.00

DONALD DUCK Xylophone
Player
Courtesy Lloyd W. Ralston
Auctions

DONALD DUCK, 6" high,
SIEBERLING,   rubber,
long-billed
Courtesy HAKE'S Americana &
Collectibles

DOC (Snow White), approx. 12" high, 1938 IDEAL	G	VG	M
	50.00	75.00	100.00
DOC, 11½" high, stuffed molded oil-cloth face, IDEAL	40.00	60.00	80.00
DOC party mask, 1937	5.00	7.50	10.00
DONALD DUCK 4" high tin windup, LINEMAR	80.00	120.00	160.00
DONALD DUCK 6" high durmmer, mechanical	75.00	112.50	150.00
DONALD DUCK 6" high, SEIBERLING RUBBER, long-billed	85.00	127.50	170.00
DONALD DUCK 10" high, SUN RUBBER	12.50	18.75	25.00
DONALD DUCK 13" stuff-ed doll, long-billed, KNICKERBOCKER	75.00	112.50	150.00
DONALD DUCK 13½" high, GUND, circa 1949	14.00	21.00	28.00
DONALD DUCK 13½"high, CHARACTER NOVEL-TY, 1940	80.00	120.00	160.00
DONALD DUCK 16" high, long bill, 1930s	20.00	30.00	40.00
DONALD DUCK ACROBAT, LINEMAR, 1950s, 8½" high	70.00	105.00	140.00
DONALD DUCK "CHOO CHOO" No. 450	See Fisher-Price		
DONALD DUCK DELIVERY TRICYCLE, plastic, 5" MARX	14.50	21.75	29.00
DONALD DUCK DOC-TOR KIT	25.00	37.50	50.00
DONALD DUCK DUET, small Donald, large Goofy, circa 1945, MARX tin wind-up	150.00	225.00	300.00

DONALD DUCK Jigger, 11" high, papier mache windup	G	VG	M
	400.00	600.00	800.00
DONALD DUCK MOUSEKETEERS HAT	4.00	6.00	8.00
DONALD DUCK on paddle, string-puller, long-billed, FISHER PRICE..	80.00	120.00	160.00
DONALD DUCK pulltoy, baton-twirler, FISHER PRICE No. 400.......	See Fisher-Price		
DONALD DUCK pulltoy, No. 765, plastic feet, 1950s FISHER PRICE..	See Fisher-Price		
DONALD DUCK pulltoy, FISHER PRICE, 6½" long, long-billed, on platform	See Fisher-Price		
DONALD DUCK pull toy, FISHER PRICE No. 400, 1940, 10" tall, 7½" long, wooden figure with moveable arms and legs, composition head.......	See Fisher-Price		
DONALD DUCK pull toy-wagon, circa 1940, FISHER PRICE No. 544	10.00	15.00	20.00
DONALD DUCK pull toy, with Xylophone, circa 1938, FISHER PRICE No. 185..............	See Fisher-Price		
"DONALD DUCK RAILROAD CAR" with Pluto, Doghouse, 10" long, LIONEL No. 1107.	300.00	450.00	600.00
DONALD DUCK Rubber Boat, SUN RUBBER CO., circa 1940s........	5.00	7.50	10.00
DONALD DUCK Skier, MARX, 1940s, plastic Donald	110.00	165.00	220.00
DONALD DUCK Teapot, OHIO ART...........	6.00	9.00	12.00
DONALD DUCK Walker, celluloid windup, long-billed, 3½" high........	130.00	195.00	260.00
DONALD DUCK and PLUTO in red roadster, SUN RUBBER, 1930s, about 6½" long........	7.50	11.25	15.00
DONKEY (Pinocchio) rubber, SEIBERLING 1940.	25.00	37.50	50.00
DOPEY 1½" lead figure, BRITAINS............	20.00	30.00	40.00

DOPEY DOLL, 9" composition with velvet clothes, KNICKERBOCKER....	G	VG	M
	50.00	75.00	100.00
DOPEY, Approx. 12" high IDEAL 1938..........	60.00	90.00	120.00
DOPEY Doll, MADAME ALEXANDER, 1938...	50.00	75.00	100.00
DOPEY Hand Puppet, composition, 1938, CROWN TOYS, bell, buckling belt	37.50	56.25	75.00
DOPEY Marionette, circa 1952, PETER PUPPET PLAYTHINGS	7.50	11.25	15.00
DOPEY party mask, 1937..	5.40	8.10	10.80
DOPEY 10" rubber squeeze toy, 1950s............	6.00	9.00	12.00
DOPEY tin wind-up, MARX, 1938..........	125.00	187.50	250.00
DUMBO tin windup, MARX, Dumbo flips over	130.00	195.00	260.00

DOPEY Tin Wind-up, MARX
Courtesy PB Eighty-Four, New York

DONKEY (Pinocchio) rubber, 4" high
Photo Courtesy HAKE'S Americana & Collectibles

ELMER ELEPHANT 5" celluloid and string figure, 1930s	30.00	45.00	60.00
ELMER ELEPHANT pull toy, FISHER PRICE, 1936	See Fisher-Price		

ELMER ELEPHANT, rubber SEIBERLING, head moves.
Courtesy Hake's Americana & Collectibles

Bashful, IDEAL, approx. 12" high, 1938
Courtesy HAKES'S Americana & Collectibles

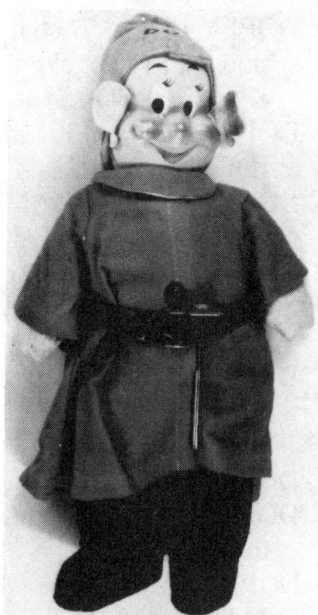

Dopey, IDEAL, approx. 12" high, 1938
Courtesy HAKE'S Americana & Collectibles

Grumpy, IDEAL, approx. 12" high, 1938
Courtesy HAKE'S Americana & Collectibles

Happy, IDEAL, approx. 12" high, 1938
Courtesy HAKE'S Americana & Collectibles

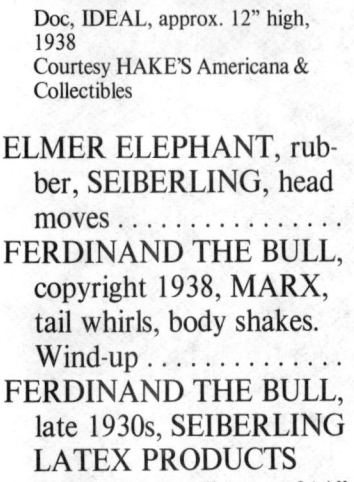

Doc, IDEAL, approx. 12" high, 1938
Courtesy HAKE'S Americana & Collectibles

Sneezy, IDEAL, approx. 12" high, 1938
Courtesy HAKE'S Americana & Collectibles

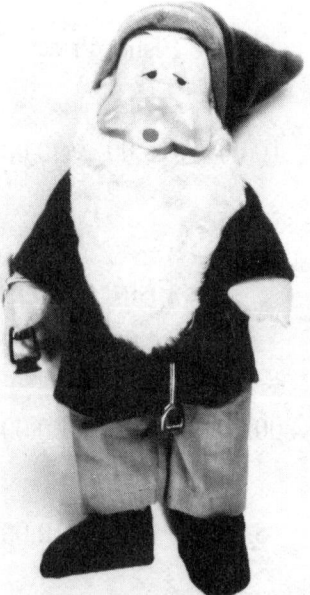

Sleepy, IDEAL, approx. 12" high, 1938
Courtesy HAKE'S Americana & Collectibles

Snow White, IDEAL, 15" high, 1938
Courtesy HAKE'S Americana & Collectibles

	G	VG	M
ELMER ELEPHANT, rubber, SEIBERLING, head moves	42.00	63.00	84.00
FERDINAND THE BULL, copyright 1938, MARX, tail whirls, body shakes. Wind-up	50.00	75.00	100.00
FERDINAND THE BULL, late 1930s, SEIBERLING LATEX PRODUCTS hard rubber, 6" long, 3½" high	31.00	46.50	62.00

	G	VG	M
FERDINAND THE BULL, jointed, wood, 9"	35.00	52.50	70.00
FERDINAND & MATADOR, 1938, MARX tin wind-up	90.00	135.00	180.00
FIGARO (Pinocchio) paper mask, 1939, GILLETTE	5.00	7.50	10.00
FIGARO tin wind-up, MARX, 1940, 4¾" long	80.00	120.00	160.00
GEPETTO facemask (Pinocchio) by GILLETTE 1939	5.50	8.25	11.00

FERDINAND THE BULL,
1938, MARX

	G	VG	M
GEPETTO 5½" wood figure holding his chin, MULTI PRODUCTS 1940	15.00	22.50	30.00
GOOFY 5¼" high tin windup, LINEMAR	107.50	161.25	215.00
GOOFY, "Goofy the Walking Gardener", MARX tin windup	350.00	525.00	700.00
GOOFY 1930 tin figure . . .	100.00	150.00	200.00
GRUMPY lead figure, 1½" high, BRITAINS	20.00	30.00	40.00
GRUMPY DOLL, stuffed, oilcloth face, velvet pants, 11" high, 1938	30.00	45.00	60.00
GRUMPY, 11½" high, stuffed molded oilcloth face, IDEAL	40.00	60.00	80.00
GRUMPY, IDEAL, approx. 12" high, 1938	30.00	45.00	60.00
GRUMPY PARTY MASK, 1937	12.00	18.00	24.00
GRUMPY rubber squeeze toy, 1950s	3.50	5.25	7.00
HAPPY 1½"lead figure, BRITAINS	20.00	30.00	40.00
HAPPY 3¼" high, SEIBERLING RUBBER, 1938	21.00	31.50	42.00
HAPPY marionette, MADAME ALEXANDER, 9½" high, 1938	47.50	67.75	95.00
HAPPY party mask, 1937 . .	12.00	18.00	24.00
HAPPY rubber squeeze toy, 1950s	3.50	5.25	7.00
HAPPY, approx. 12" high, IDEAL, 1938	50.00	75.00	100.00
JIMINY CRICKET 12" approx., rubber head, wooden feet, cloth body, GUND	12.50	18.75	25.00
JIMINY CRICKET 13" high, latex head, hands and feet, cloth body	25.00	37.50	50.00
JIMINY CRICKET 14" high, CROWN TOY, felt and cloth	80.00	120.00	160.00

MICKEY MOUSE, 5" high
wood doll, FUN-E-FLEX,
leather ears
Courtesy HAKE'S Americana &
Collectibles

MICKEY MOUSE 7" high,
wood-jointed, early,
BORGFELDT
Courtesy HAKE'S Americana &
Collectibles

MICKEY MOUSE 11" high,
cloth, "Walt Disney Mickey
Mouse Geo. E. Borgfeldt & Company, New York" on bottom of
one foot
Courtesy HAKE's Americana &
Collectibles

MICKEY MOUSE Felt Doll,
STEIFF, 12" high
Courtesy Lloyd W. Ralston
Auctions

	G	VG	M
JIMINY CRICKET 15½" high, CROWN TOY, felt and cloth	42.50	63.75	85.00
JIMINY CRICKET facemask (Pinocchio) 1939 from GILLETTE . .	5.50	8.25	11.00
JIMINY CRICKET Handpuppet, vinyl and cloth, GUND	4.50	6.75	9.00
JIMINY CRICKET, LINEMAR, tin litho wind-up, 1950s, 5½" tall .	125.00	187.50	250.00

MICKEY MOUSE Drum, OHIO ART, 6"
diameter, tin
Courtesy HAKE'S Americana & Collectibles

MICKEY MOUSE
Acrobat
Photo Courtesy PB
Eighty-Four

MICKEY MOUSE "Mickey-In-The-Box"
Photo Courtesy PB Eighty-Four,
NY

MICKEY MOUSE Circus Train Set
Courtesy PB Eighty-Four, New York

	G	VG	M
JIMINY CRICKET pushing bass fiddle, MARX walkie	6.00	9.0	12.00
JUNGLE BOOK Dancing Bear, MARX, plastic windup	25.00	37.50	50.00
LUDWIG VON DRAKE, 7" rubber squeeze toy, circa 1960	4.50	6.75	9.00
LUDWIG VON DRAKE, litho tin windup, LINEMAR, 1950s, 6" tall	125.00	187.50	250.00
LUDWIG VON DRAKE rubber squeeze toy, 1960s	10.00	15.00	20.00
MAD HATTER puppet (Alice in Wonderland)	11.00	16.50	22.00
MAD HATTER'S Taxi, LINEMAR, 5" long	50.00	75.00	100.00
MICKEY AND DONALD on back of alligator, MARX, 1950s	8.00	12.00	16.00
MICKEY AND DONALD Handcar, windup, plastic, 1948, MARX	75.00	112.50	150.00
MICKEY AND DONALD in fire truck, late 1930s, rubber	9.00	13.50	18.00
MICKEY AND MINNIE MOUSE TEA SET, circa 1935, 13 pieces	75.00	112.50	150.00
MICKEY AND MINNIE MOUSE Swing Toy, celluloid with red and green flag. 11½" tall	200.00	300.00	400.00

	G	VG	M
MICKEY ON PLUTO, rocks, tin windup, LINEMAR, 1950s	800.00	1200.00	1600.00
MICKEY MOUSE, first toy made by BORGFELDT of NY in 1930, wooden Mickey with jointed hands, arms, legs and wire tail, leather ears. "Copyright 1928-1930 by Walter E. Disney"	150.00	225.00	300.00
MICKEY MOUSE larger-size squeeze toy with clothes, 1950, SUN RUBBER	5.00	7.50	10.00
MICKEY MOUSE with red shirt and yellow pants, squeeze toy, SUN RUBBER 1950	4.00	6.00	8.00
MICKEY MOUSE, 3½" high, SEIBERLING RUBBER, 1930s	47.50	71.25	95.00
MICKEY MOUSE 5" high wood doll, FUN-E-FLEX leather ears	55.00	82.50	110.00
MICKEY MOUSE 5½" high, vibrates, LINEMAR tin windup	90.00	135.00	180.00
MICKEY MOUSE 6" high, rubber, circa 1935, SEIBERLING	93.00	146.50	186.00
MICKEY MOUSE 7" high, wood jointed, early BORGFELDT	150.00	225.00	300.00

MICKEY MOUSE 8" high, SUN RUBBER	G	VG	M
SUN RUBBER	32.50	48.75	65.00
MICKEY MOUSE 8" high, wooden, jointed arms and legs, circa 1933	350.00	525.00	700.00
MICKEY MOUSE 9½" high, "DELL", rubber	7.50	11.25	15.00
MICKEY MOUSE 10" high, SUN RUBBER, 1940s	2.00	3.00	4.00

Mickey Mouse Circus
Courtesy PB Eighty-Four

	G	VG	M
MICKEY MOUSE 11" high, cloth "Walt Disney Mickey Mouse Geo. E. Borgfeldt & Company, New York" on bottom of one foot	90.00	135.00	180.00
MICKEY MOUSE 12" high, 1930s, KNICKERBOCKER	150.00	225.00	300.00
MICKEY MOUSE 12" high, felt doll, early 1930s, STEIFF	425.00	637.00	850.00
MICKEY MOUSE 12" high, BORGFELDT	350.00	525.00	700.00
MICKEY MOUSE 12" high, "Cowboy Mickey", KNICKERBOCKER, 1936	400.00	600.00	800.00
MICKEY MOUSE 17", rubber, LAKESIDE MFG. CO.	35.00	52.50	70.00
MICKEY MOUSE 18" high, felt, CHARACTER CO., circa 1939-40	40.00	60.00	80.00
MICKEY MOUSE 21" high, circa 1933	175.00	262.50	350.00
MICKEY MOUSE, 31" high, all felt dressed, opening in back for storing things, black jacket with yellow buttons, red pants, bells on toes of yellow shoes	11.00	16.50	22.00

MICKEY MOUSE
Racing Car
Courtesy PB Eighty-Four, New York

MICKEY MOUSE Acrobat, clockwork trapeze, celluloid Mickey	G	VG	M
MICKEY MOUSE Acrobat, clockwork trapeze, celluloid Mickey	110.00	165.00	220.00
MICKEY MOUSE Airmail, rubber	60.00	90.00	120.00
MICKEY MOUSE Banjo, 1930s, 17" long	60.00	90.00	120.00
MICKEY MOUSE BEVERAGES felt soda jerk hat, show Mickey from shoulders up saying "have one on me", 5"x11", circa 1930	30.00	45.00	60.00
MICKEY MOUSE BUBBLE BUSTER GUN, metal Mickey standing at gun sight. Cast iron	45.00	67.50	90.00
MICKEY MOUSE cardboard mask, circa 1935	7.50	11.25	15.00
MICKEY MOUSE Circus, GEO. BORGFELDT 6/3785, 1931, two wood figures revolving on swinging mechanism, 11" long	75.00	112.50	150.00
MICKEY MOUSE CIRCUS TRAIN SET, LIONEL No. 1536, Engine, tender, containing Mickey, three carriage cars, dining car, Mickey Mouse Circus, Mickey Mouse Band, composition Mickey, and track	900.00	1350.00	1800.00
MICKEY MOUSE CIRCUS TRAIN, Mickey			
"MICKEY'S DELIVERY" Pluto on Tricycle-Cart, tin litho wind-up, celluloid head on Pluto, LINEMAR, 1950s, 5½" long	125.00	187.50	250.00

Mickey Mouse Hand Car. Photo courtesy PB Eighty-Four

	G	VG	M
shoveling tender, three Disney Circus cars, wind-up train, red, circa 1931.	525.00	787.50	1050.00
MICKEY MOUSE Clicker, tin litho, circa 1930, Mickey showing teeth while playing violin.....	10.00	15.00	20.00
MICKEY MOUSE CLUB Auto-Magic Picture Gun, 1946, projects films.....	17.00	26.50	34.00
MICKEY MOUSE CLUB Newsreel.............	15.00	22.50	30.00
MICKEY MOUSE Drum, OHIO ART, 6" diameter, tin.................	35.00	52.50	70.00
MICKEY MOUSE Drum Set, tin and cardboard, circa 1940, Minnie watching while Mickey juggles...............	125.00	187.50	250.00
MICKEY MOUSE EXPRESS tin litho train set, MARX...............	180.00	270.00	360.00
MICKEY MOUSE Ferris Wheel, tin, 16½" high...	175.00	262.50	350.00
MICKEY MOUSE Hand Car, orange base........	350.00	500.00	800.00
MICKEY MOUSE Hand Car, green base........	300.00	400.00	700.00
MICKEY MOUSE Hand Car, red base.........	250.00	300.00	550.00

	G	VG	M
MICKEY MOUSE holding flag, cast iron, 1930s....	60.00	90.00	120.00
MICKEY MOUSE JAZZ DRUMMER, finger-activated tin toy, NIFTY 4¾" high............	40.00	60.00	80.00
MICKEY MOUSE KNICKERBOCKER doll, 1935, 22" high........	275.00	412.50	550.00
MICKEY MOUSE, lead, 2½" high, 1933, ALLIED TOYS...............	10.50	15.75	21.00
MICKEY MOUSE Marionette, circa 1930, 9½" high, felt body stuffed with cotton........	68.75	103.12	137.50
MICKEY MOUSE Marionette, Peter Puppet Playthings Co., 1950s, 14" tall.............	25.00	37.50	50.00
"MICKEY MOUSE Meteor Five-Car Train, Walt Disneys" tin litho, MARX, 43" long.......	75.00	112.50	150.00
MICKEY MOUSE "Mickey-In-The-Box", 7" high jack-in-the-box.....	125.00	187.50	250.00
MICKEY MOUSE Movie-Jecter, 1935..........	37.00	55.50	74.00
MICKEY MOUSE Movie Projector No. E-18,			

L to R: MINNIE MOUSE DOLL 14½" high, MICKEY MOUSE DOLL, 21" high
Courtesy PB Eighty-Four, New York

MINNIE MOUSE 16" high, cloth, early 30s
Courtesy HAKE'S Americana & Collectibles

	G	VG	M
KEYSTONE, 1930s, 10" high	150.00	225.00	300.00
MICKEY MOUSE ORGAN GRINDER, Minnie Mouse dancing on organ pushed by much larger Mickey	400.00	600.00	800.00
MICKEY MOUSE piano, wooden, grand, with decal showing Mickey playing, Minnie listening, circa 1935	60.00	90.00	120.00
MICKEY MOUSE Pocket Knife, 1935	20.00	30.00	40.00
MICKEY MOUSE "Puddle Jumper", No. 310, FISHER-PRICE, circa 1950s	See Fisher-Price		
MICKEY MOUSE Puppet, approx. 10" high, "GUND"	4.00	6.00	8.00
MICKEY MOUSE Puppet, early 40s style, very large composition head, hands and feet, the rest of the body wood, cloth costume, felt ears	50.00	75.00	100.00
MICKEY MOUSE Puppet, PELHAM 24" high, rubber legs and arms, wood body	125.00	187.50	250.00
MICKEY MOUSE Racing Car, red lithographed tin wind-up car with Mickey at the wheel, 4" long	75.00	112.50	150.00
MICKEY MOUSE Roly Poly, celluloid, early, 4" high	1.25	1.88	2.50

	G	VG	M
MICKEY MOUSE "SANTA CAR with MICKEY MOUSE and HIS GIFT PACK" hand car, LIONEL No. 1105, 1935	450.00	675.00	900.00
MICKEY MOUSE "Scooter Jockey", MAVCO CO., 1950s, all plastic, 6" high, wind-up	100.00	150.00	200.00
MICKEY MOUSE Sparkler Toy, 1930s, 5½" tall	150.00	225.00	300.00
MICKEY MOUSE Tambourine, NOBLE & COOLEY CO., 1936, 9" heavy paper head, Mickey juggling while Minnie watches	80.00	120.00	160.00
MICKEY MOUSE Tea Service, 24 piece, tin	50.00	75.00	100.00
MICKEY MOUSE Tin flute	10.00	15.00	20.00
MICKEY MOUSE Tin Washboard set, circa 1935	25.00	37.50	50.00
MICKEY MOUSE Tool Chest, 1935, HAMILTON METAL . .	90.00	135.00	180.00
MICKEY MOUSE on Tricycle, tin litho wind-up, celluloid Mickey, 1940s, 3½" long	95.00	144.50	190.00
MICKEY MOUSE, TUMBLING, 1947, MARKS BROS., 8" high .	17.50	26.25	35.00
MICKEY MOUSE VIEWER, with film of "Brave Little Tailor", 1946	9.00	13.50	18.00

	G	VG	M
MICKEY MOUSE WASHER, 1932, or 33, OHIO ART CO., tin litho washing machine, 7" high, two scenes with Mickey, Minnie, Pluto	12.50	18.75	25.00
MICKEY MOUSE Xylophone, tin wind-up, 1930s	275.00	412.50	550.00
MICKEY MOUSE Xylophone Player, LINEMAR tin windup, 1950s, 6" high	110.00	165.00	220.00
MICKEY MOUSE CLUB Bow and Arrow Set, circa 1955	4.25	6.38	8.50
MICKEY MOUSE CLUB Snap-on ears, plastic, 1950s	3.00	4.50	6.00
MICKEY'S AIRMAIL, 1930s, SUN RUBBER	25.00	37.50	50.00
MICKEY'S TRACTOR, 1930s, SUN RUBBER, Mickey's head turns, 4½" long	32.50	48.75	65.00
MINNIE MOUSE, wooden, JUNE FLEX	80.00	120.00	160.00
MINNIE MOUSE 3" high, wooden, jointed	10.00	15.00	20.00
MINNIE MOUSE, 7" high, FUN-E-FLEX	175.00	262.50	350.00
MINNIE MOUSE 10½" high, SUN RUBBER, 1940s	11.00	16.50	22.00
MINNIE MOUSE 12" high, 1930, wearing dress, high heels, undies	62.50	93.75	125.00
MINNIE MOUSE 14½" high, early cloth figure dressed in a red and white polka dot skirt, wearing composition heeled shoes.	80.00	120.00	160.00
MINNIE MOUSE 16" high, cloth, early 1930s	37.50	56.25	75.00
MINNIE MOUSE cardboard mask, circa 1935	7.50	11.25	15.00
MINNIE MOUSE cowgirl, KNICKERBOCKER, 18" high, 1936	225.00	337.50	450.00
MINNIE MOUSE Hand-puppet, PETER PUPPET PLAYTHINGS, circa 1952	7.50	11.25	15.00
MINNIE MOUSE Knitter, tin litho windup, LINEMAR	135.00	202.50	270.00

	G	VG	M
MINNIE MOUSE Lead, 2½" high, 1933, ALLIED TOYS	10.50	15.75	21.00
MINNIE MOUSE Marionette, circa 1930, 9½" high, felt body stuffed with cotton	68.75	103.13	137.50
MINNIE MOUSE Marionette, 13" wood and composition, 1950s	37.50	52.50	75.00
MINNIE MOUSE Puppet, PELHAM, 24" high, rubber legs and arms, wood body	125.00	187.50	250.00
MINNIE MOUSE Rolypoly, celluloid, 4"	2.00	3.00	4.00
MINNIE MOUSE WASHING MACHINE, 1950, PRECISION SPECIALTIES, INC.	30.00	45.00	60.00
MOUSKETEERS HAT, 50% wool, 50% rayon, by DENAYALUEE, 1950s	6.00	9.00	12.00
MOUSEKETEERS OUTFIT, Western Style	11.00	16.50	22.00
OSWALD THE RABBIT, circa 1927, 6½" long celluloid crib toy	55.00	82.50	110.00
"PARADE ROADSTER" MARX lithographed tin wind-up. Convertible car decorated with Mickey and other characters, with Donald at the wheel, Pluto and Mickey and Minnie Mouse as passengers, 1950s, 11¼" long	100.00	150.00	200.00

Pinocchio, Cloth and Jointed Wood Figure, KREUGER
Courtesy PB Eighty-Four, New York

PINOCCHIO Doll, IDEAL, 8" high
Courtesy Lloyd W. Ralston Auctions

	G	VG	M
PECOS BILL, MARX wind-up	32.50	48.75	65.00
PETER PAN 9¾" high, SUN RUBBER, circa 1952	8.50	12.75	17.00
PETER PAN Marionette, circa 1952, PETER PUP-PET PLAYTHINGS	7.50	11.25	15.00
PETER PAN Tea Set, circa 1953, 23 pieces	17.50	26.25	35.00
PINOCCHIO cloth and jointed wood figure, cloth tag	75..00	112.50	150.00
PINOCCHIO 2½" high, molded wood fiber figure, MULTI PRODUCTS, 1940	5.00	7.50	10.00
PINOCCHIO 5" high, mold-ed wood fiber figure, MULTI-PRODUCTS, 1940	9.00	13.50	18.00
PINOCCHIO 7½" high, jointed, circa 1940, IDEAL	28.00	42.00	56.00
PINOCCHIO 8" high, IDEAL	30.00	45.00	60.0
PINOCCHIO 10½" high, wood and papier mache wind-up, GEORGE BORGFELDT, 1940	170.00	255.00	340.00
PINOCCHIO 11" high, jointed, circa 1940	90.00	135.00	180.00
PINOCCHIO 12" high, IDEAL jointed wood and composition	70.00	105.00	140.00
PINOCCHIO 19¾" high, jointed, circa 1940	50.00	75.00	100.00
PINOCCHIO Handpuppet, GUND, 1950s	2.00	3.00	4.00
PINOCCHIO Paper Mask, GILLETTE, 1939	6.50	9.75	13.00
PINOCCHIO EXPRESS, pull-toy, FISHER-PRICE, 1940, 11" long		See Fisher-Price	
PINOCCHIO ON DONKEY, pull-toy, FISHER-PRICE, 1940, bell-ringer		See Fisher-Price	
PINOCCHIO THE ACROBAT, " Watch Him Go!" tin wind-up, 1939, MARX	100.00	150.00	200.00
PINOCCHIO tin wind-up, MARX, standing erect, eyes skyward, circa 1940 .	125.00	187.50	250.00

PLUTO With Basket, 8" long
Courtesy Lloyd W. Ralston Auctions

PLUTO, plastic wind-up, MARX, metal tail spins.

	G	VG	M
PINOCCHIO, tin litho wind-up, LINEMAR Co., 1950s, 5½" tall	125.00	187.50	250.00
PLUTO hand puppet GUND, 1950s	3.00	4.50	6.00
PLUTO lead cast, 1930s . . .	2.50	3.75	5.00
PLUTO, lead, 2½" high, 1933 ALLIED TOYS . . .	10.50	15.75	21.00
PLUTO, plastic wind-up, MARX, metal tail spins . .	12.50	18.75	25.00
PLUTO 4" long SEIBER-LING RUBBER, circa 1935	22.50	33.75	45.00
PLUTO, 7½" long, SEIBERLINE RUBBER .	35.00	52.50	70.00
PLUTO WITH BASKET paper litho on wood, 8" long		See Fisher-Price	
PLUTO 9" long, wood, jointed	75.00	112.50	150.00
PLUTO, wooden, 3" bend-able legs, circa 1934	17.50	26.25	35.00
PLUTO Drum Major, MARX tin windup	94.00	141.00	188.00
PLUTO "Drum Major" LINEMAR, 1950s' 6½" tall, tin litho wind-up	150.00	225.00	300.00
PLUTO Squeeze toy, SUN RUBBER No. 11520, 1930s	22.50	33.75	45.00
PLUTO, tin litho squeeze-action with cable, LINEMAR, 1950s, 4¼" tall	100.00	150.00	200.00
PLUTO Tin windup, LINEMAR	90.00	135.00	180.00
PLUTO, wooden, hand base, string-operated, many joints, marionette-type, FISHER-PRICE, 1936		See Fisher-Price	
PLUTO ON ROCKERS, wooden, circa 1930s	20.00	30.00	40.00
PLUTO "Watch Me Roll Over", MARX, 1939	75.00	112.50	150.00
PLUTO, sitting position, rubber squeeze toy, 1960s	3.00	4.50	6.00

	G	VG	M
PRACTICAL PIG, tin litho windup, LINEMAR....	75.00	112.50	150.00
SAND PAIL, 1938, OHIO ART tin litho, Mickey, Minnie and Goofy pictured..............	25.00	37.50	50.00
SEVEN DWARFS, all, SEIBERLING RUBBER, 1938, 5½" high........	140.00	210.00	280.00
SI-AM (Lady & Tramp) 16" high, stuffed, vinyl face, GUND, circa 1955......	15.00	22.50	30.00
SLEEPING BEAUTY squeeze toy, sitting with animals, 6½"...........	13.00	19.50	26.00
SLEEPY 1½" lead figure, BRITAINS............	20.00	30.00	40.00
SLEEPY, IDEAL approx. 12" high, 1938.........	50.00	75.00	100.00
SLEEPY party mask, 1937.	5.40	8.10	10.80
SNEEZY 1½" lead figure, BRITAINS............	20.00	30.00	40.00
SNEEZY 3¼" high, SEIBERLING RUBBER, 1938.................	21.00	31.50	42.00
SNEEZY, IDEAL, approx. 12" high, 1938.........	50.00	75.00	100.00
SNEEZY Party Mask, 1937	5.40	8.10	10.80
SNEEZY rubber squeeze toy, 1950s.............	3.25	5.88	6.50
SNOW SHOVEL, 26" long, shows Mickey and Pluto building snowman......	75.00	112.50	150.00
SNOW WHITE 2½" lead figure, BRITAINS......	25.00	37.50	50.00
SNOW WHITE doll, SEIBERLING RUBBER.	165.00	247.50	330.00
SNOW WHITE 13" high, MADAME ALEX- ANDER, 1938.........	85.00	127.50	170.00
SNOW WHITE, IDEAL, 15" high, 1938.........	50.00	75.00	100.00
SNOW WHITE Party Mask	8.00	12.00	16.00
SNOW WHITE Washing Machine, circa 1950, Revell Plastics, 7½" high with wringer...........	25.00	37.50	50.00
SNOW WHITE AND THE SEVEN DWARFS, 4½" dishes, china, with cups, creamer, sugar bowl, 6" plate	80.00	120.00	160.00
SNOW WHITE AND THE SEVEN DWARFS musical top, CHEIN, 6½" across...........	16.00	24.00	32.00

	G	VG	M
SNOW WHITE AND THE SEVEN DWARFS Sew- ing Set HASBRO.......	3.50	5.25	7.00
SNOW WHITE Sink and Stove, WOLVERINE...	40.00	60.00	80.00
THREE LITTLE PIGS clothes washer.........	10.00	15.00	20.00
THREE LITTLE PIGS Mask, 1933 PAR-T- MASK	15.00	22.50	30.00
THREE LITTLE PIGS Sand bucket, 3" tall.....	12.50	18.75	25.00
THREE LITTLE PIGS, wooden pig, circa 1933, BORGFELDT, fiber arms and legs, 3¼" high......	37.50	56.25	75.00
THUMPER 6" friction, MARX, 1950s.........	20.00	30.00	40.00
THUMPER 7" squeeze toy, SUN RUBBER........	19.00	28.50	38.00
THUMPER 14" high, GUND, 1950s.........	12.00	18.00	24.00
THUMPER 17" high, GUND, early 1940s.....	30.00	45.00	60.00
TIMOTHY MOUSE (Dum- bo), stuffed, 17" high, CHARACTER NOVEL- TY, 1942.............	75.00	112.50	150.00
UNCLE SCROOGE Hand- puppet, 1960s? wearing high hat.............	5.00	7.50	10.00
UNCLE SCROOGE Limousine, "$" on back fender	26.00	39.00	52.00
UNCLE SCROOGE Vinyl squeeze toy bank, 7" high, circa 1960.............	20.00	30.00	40.00
WALT DISNEY Television Car, MARX, 1950s, 7½" long..................	100.00	150.00	200.00
WENDY (Peter Pan) handpuppet............	2.50	3.75	5.00
WITCH (Snow White) party mask	6.00	9.00	12.00
ZORRO Hand puppet.....	9.00	13.50	18.00
ZORRO Flintlock Pistol, MARX	3.00	4.50	6.00
ZORRO ring, black top with Z and ZORRO name....	10.00	15.00	20.00

GUNS
(See also Premiums, Comic Character)

Average mint prices of guns in the third edition were $47.26 and in this edition they average $56.28, an increase of 19%.

SOME THOUGHTS ON TOY GUN COLLECTING
by Charles W. Best

Amid all the various toys in the world, the toy gun stands out as the one type most distinctly American and native to the United States, and with good reason. From the earliest days of our history up through the late 19th century, firearms were the primary tool that enabled us to survive, settle, explore, and subdue this land. Firearms gave us our freedom in 1776 and were instrumental in preserving that freedom throughout our first hundred turbulent years. Those years, as we now know, were to become an era of "romantic" wars when boys and young men dreamed of attaining fame and glory on the battlefield or out on the Western Frontier. The War of 1812, the Mexican War, the Civil War, and numerous Indian conflicts were all fought, basically, with small arms, so it is small wonder then that when toys first began to be mass produced after the Civil War, toy guns were among the first to appear on the market. Their success was instantaneous and toy guns remained among our most popular selling toys until as recently as the 1960's.

Although toy guns were patented in the late 1850's they were not manufactured in any quantity until a decade later due to the wartime shortages. These early toy guns were, for the most part, pea shooters and cork poppers and were usually made of wood with metal hardware although iron and lead types may occasionally be found among them. As you might suspect, these early examples are hard to find today and most are known only through their patent drawings. By 1870, inventors, trying to add realism to these toy guns, began using paper caps, a then new invention which had been developed just prior to the Civil War and was known as the Maynard Tape Primer. This tape primer was originally intended to detonate muzzle loading arms and closely resembled a roll of modern day paper caps. Now, for the first time, toy guns could make a loud noise yet still be relatively safe and harmless. Naturally, this spurred the demand for these new toys and designers worked overtime to create new and appealing guns. Their output was prolific and, today, the period from 1870 to 1900 is regarded as the "golden age" of the toy gun and especially the toy cap pistol, in America.

By 1880, the cast iron cap pistol had become the most popular type of toy gun by far and the various toy makers, primarily J. & E. Stevens and Ives, were competing among themselves to see who could produce the most unique and appealing designs. A glance at any collection of these early day toy pistols will show that, in those days, realism was secondary to artistic imagination. Many pistols from this period were literally covered with ornamentation and, in some cases, any resemblance to a real gun was purely coincidental. Leaf and scroll designs were the most popular but pistols can also be found with numerous other designs, including both two and three dimensional figures. Those guns with moving figures are now known as "animated" pistols and even though not as rare as some, are worth much more to a collector than an ordinary-looking pistol from the same period.

Another very desirable pistol from this same era is now known as the "head" pistol and featured a head, either animal or human, which was placed at the breech end of the barrel with the mouth open to receive the cap. Over two dozen varieties of head and animated pistols are known to exist but are so much in demand that they are seldom offered for sale.

The most popular material used to make these early toy pistols was, of course, cast iron, which continued to be used heavily into the 20th century, until the demands of World War II cut off the supply. Many varieties of old toy guns were, however, made of other materials than iron. I have seen examples made from such diverse materials as paper, wood, steel, tin, lead, rubber, zinc, glass, and even wax. During the Second World War, to meet the heavy demand, toy guns were even made of molded sawdust mixed with glue. After the war a few cast iron pistols were produced and assembled, using both new and old parts, but the cost proved to be prohibitive, and makers soon turned to less expensive metals such as steel and die cast zinc. By 1950, most toy pistols were being made of the die cast material and also plastic, both of which continue to be used today.

From almost the very beginning, toy gun makers have felt the need to personalize their products and literally hundreds of different names can be found embossed on these little guns. Some examples that come to mind are: EXCELSIOR, VICTOR, AMERICAN BULLDOG, ACORN, SUN, BOOM, DARB, ACE, DAISY, COWBOY KING, POLO, TRIUMPH, TERROR, etc. Many names were used only once on one particular gun and then dropped while others have reappeared time and again on different guns over the years. This custom of naming toy guns still goes on today and a visit to any toy store will turn up names such as: COWHAND, TOP GUN JR., 007, etc. Many of these names seem to reflect current events or personalities while on others, the meaning has become obscure.

For the toy collector, or would-be collector, the collecting of toy guns and especially pistols, not only offers a large diversity of models and styles but, because of their tremendous popularity in the past, also the opportunity to find and acquire interesting and unusual examples at an affordable price. Guns from as far back as the 1920's and '30's can still be found at flea markets, garage sales, and second hand stores, often at a price that is only a fraction of what other toys from these same years will sell for. At the moment, toy guns are the most overlooked and under-collected of all old toys but, as more books and articles are published, this situation is bound to change. Interest in real antique guns has skyrocketed in recent years and I predict that the toys will not be far behind.

NOTE: Measurements given, in general, are from one end of the gun to the other, rather than on a diagonal from grip to muzzle. Much of the information on manufacturers, measurements, etc., comes from Charles W. Best's excellent book "Cast Iron Toy Pistols" (see bibliography). Dates of manufacture can vary within five years, though most of the later dates are considerably more accurate. Names found on the weapon are in capital letters, as is the manufacturer's name.

CHARLES W. BEST is a leading authority on toy weapons, and has been collecting them in earnest since 1966. His collection is regarded as one of the finest and most comprehensive in existence, and has won many awards at various gun shows. In addition to writing a number of articles on the subject in such magazines as Gun Report and Antique Toy World, he is the author of "Cast Iron Toy Pistols" (see Bibliography).

CONDITION OF A TOY GUN AND ITS RELATION TO PRICE

The price of a toy gun depends not only on its desirability, but also on its condition. Since condition in toy guns varies much less than in most toys, prices in "Good" are much closer to "Mint" than is usually the case.

However, "Mint" means just that; the condition in which it was originally issued — perfect, regardless of age, not the slightest blemish.

"Very Good" indicates a toy which has obviously seen use, with signs of wear and aging, but in general having a freshness to its appearance that makes it attractive and collectible to all but the most discriminating.

"Good" signals a weapon that has seen considerable wear, shows its age, but is basically sound. In cast iron pistols, which are hardy to begin with, and have no paint to wear off, a "good" pistol is worth more comparably to its mint version than a black-painted tin pistol would be to its mint version.

Condition below good results usually in a drastic drop in price, and guns with missing parts, although otherwise in excellent condition, will usually fall into this lower-priced category. Rust, even small spots of it, can seriously lower the price of a gun. "Near Mint", "Very Fine", "Fine" and similar terms often found in sellers' descriptions denote conditions between Mint and Very Good, and are priced accordingly.

The key to grading is to avoid wishful thinking. Grading can sometimes be a problem for the uninitiated, but common sense will usually prevail, and when possible, a consultation with an expert in the field can often clear up lingering doubts. A toy in its original box is worth up to 10 to 20% more if the box is in mint condition, with the price dropping as its condition lessens. A holster in mint condition can be worth as much as 50-100% of its gun's value.

	G	VG	M		G	VG	M
ACE cast iron cap pistol, STEVENS "Made in U.S.A." 5" long, 1930...	12.50	17.50	25.00	ADMIRAL DEWEY cast iron cap bomb.........	50.00	75.00	100.00
ACE cast iron cap pistol, 5" long, 1935............	12.50	17.50	25.00	AEROMATIC GLIDER GUN, steel automatic, circa 1940, shoots balsa airplanes..............	10.00	15.00	25.00
ACME steel cap automatic, repeater, circa 1930.....	5.00	7.50	10.00	AGITATOR, THE, cast iron cap and torpedo			
ACORN cast iron pistol...	47.50	71.25	95.00				

	G	VG	M
shooter, 1908, JOHN FOX, 8¼"............	65.00	97.50	130.00
AIM TO SAVE, circa 1909	100.00	125.00	150.00
AIR RAID WARNING signal pistol............	15.00	20.00	25.00
AMERICA cap pistol, with shield, pat. 1873........	65.00	95.00	125.00
AMERICAN cast iron cap pistol, KILGORE, 1940, 9-5/8"	30.00	45.00	60.00
AMERICAN BULLDOG cast iron .22 cal. blank shooter, 1910, 4½" long, second trigger tips barrel to load, KENTON, handle projects outward.....	25.00	35.00	45.00
AMERICAN BULLDOG cast iron .22 blank shooter, 1920, 4½" long, KENTON, second trigger tips barrel to load, handle curves inward.........	25.00	35.00	45.00
Animated Cap Pistol Cannon..............	140.00	210.00	280.00
ARMY cast iron cap pistol, 1910	17.50	25.00	35.00
ARMY 45 cast iron cap automatic, HUBLEY 1940 "Made in U.S.A." 6-5/8"	15.00	22.50	30.00
ARMY 45 diecast zinc cap automatic, HUBLEY 1940, plastic grips, "Made in U.S.A.", 6½" long....	7.50	12.50	20.00
Army pistol with revolving cylinder, tin litho, MARX No. 625..............	5.00	7.50	10.00
Army sparkling pop gun, MARX No. 197........	5.00	7.50	12.50
ATOMIC DISINTEGRATOR cap pistol, HUBLEY.......	20.00	35.00	50.00
AUTO MAGIC PICTURE GUN, projects film onto wall. 1936. Comes with film and instructions, in box	15.00	22.50	30.00
Automatic Repeater Paper Pop Pistol No. 74, MARX, aluminum......	5.00	7.50	10.00
BANG cast iron cap pistol, KILGORE, "Made in U.S.A.", 6" long........	15.00	22.50	27.50
BANG-O cast iron cap pistol, STEVENS 1938, "Made in U.S.A.", 7" long	10.00	15.00	20.00

Top, L to R: BIG BILL, PLUCK, DICK
Middle, L to R: ATOMIC DISINTEGRATOR, SURE SHOT SAFETY
Bottom, L to R: TIGER, GENE AUTRY 44
Photo Courtesy Garth's Auctions Inc.

	G	VG	M
BANNER, blank-shooting mechanical cast iron pistol	65.00	100.00	150.00
Bell Pistol, WYANDOTTE.	4.00	7.50	10.00
BENJAMIN PUMP early BB gun, before 1910....	40.00	65.00	95.00
BIFF cast iron cap automatic, KENTON, 1935, "Made in U.S.A. Pat. Apld. For", 4½"...	12.50	17.50	25.00
BIFF JR. cast iron cap automatic, KENTON 1935, "Made in U.S.A. Pat. Apld For", 4-1/8" long	12.50	17.50	25.00
BIG BILL cast iron cap pistol, large hammer, "Made in U.S.A." KILGORE 1935, 4-7/8"..	7.50	10.00	15.00
BIG BILL cast iron cap pistol, KILGORE, 1925, 5½" long............	7.00	10.50	14.00
BIG BILL cast iron cap pistol, large hammer, "Made in U.S.A.", KILGORE 1930, 5¾"...	8.25	12.38	17.50
BIG BUSTER cast iron cap automatic, KILGORE 1915, "Patd Jul 2 1907, Made in U.S.A.", 5", two-piece trigger..........	30.00	40.00	60.00

	G	VG	M
BIG CHIEF cast iron cap pistol, KILGORE, 1935, 6" long	12.50	15.00	20.00
BIG CHIEF cast iron cap pistol, KILGORE, 1935, has star and "K", 6"	12.50	15.00	20.00
BIG CHIEF cast iron cap pistol, early-looking, but made in 1930, 3½", DENT "Made in U.S.A."	10.00	12.50	15.00
BIG CLIP cast iron cap pistol, STEVENS 1930, "Made in U.S.A." 6¾"	12.50	15.00	20.00
BIG HORN cast iron cap pistol, revolving cylinder, KILGORE 1939, 8⅜"	25.00	35.00	45.00
BIG INJUN, hammerless	65.00	95.00	150.00
BIGGER BANG large hammer cast iron cap pistol, KILGORE 1930, 6" long	15.00	20.00	25.00
BILLY THE KID cast iron cap pistol, KILGORE, 1930, 6¾"	17.50	25.00	30.00
BLACK JACK cast iron cap pistol, long barrel, KENTON 1930, "Pat. Sept. 11-23", 11"	40.00	50.00	65.00
BLAZE AWAY Dart Pistol, MARX No. G23	5.00	7.50	12.50
BOB cast iron cap pistol, KILGORE, 1930, 5" long	15.00	20.00	25.00
BORDER PATROL cast iron cap automatic, KILGORE, 1930, 4¼" long	7.50	15.00	20.00
BORDER PATROL cast iron cap automatic, KILGORE, 1935, "Pat. Apld. For, Made in U.S.A.", 4½" long	7.50	15.00	20.00
BOSS cast iron mammoth cap pistol, 1925, KENTON, 6¼"	12.50	18.75	25.00
BOY'S DELIGHT Pat. June 1891, cast iron cap pistol.	75.00	100.000	125.00
BOY'S POLICE AUTOMATIC 8" cardboard pop gun, circa 1940s	2.00	3.00	4.00
BRAT cast iron cap pistol, original DENT sample	20.00	30.00	35.00
BRONC cast iron cap pistol, KENTON 1935, "Kenton, Made In U.S.A.", 6"	15.00	20.00	25.00
BUC-A-ROO cast iron cap			

	G	VG	M
pistol, KILGORE 1940, 7¾"	15.00	20.00	25.00
BUCK cast iron pistol, HUBLEY 1930, looks earlier, 3¼"	10.00	12.50	15.00
BUCK JONES SPECIAL DAISY PUMP REPEATER RIFLE, with compass and sun dial in stock, 1937	25.00	40.00	65.00
BUDDY cast iron cap pistol	15.00	20.00	25.00
BUFFALO BILL cast iron cap pistol, KENTON, 1925, "Pat. Setp. 11-23", 11⅜", very long barrel	35.00	50.00	75.00
BUFFALO BILL cast iron cap pistol, KENTON, 1930, "Pat. Sept. 11-23", 13½", perhaps the longest-barreled cap pistol	45.00	75.00	95.00
BUFFALO BILL cast iron cap pistol, STEVENS, 1940, "Made in U.S.A.", 7¾" long	15.00	20.00	25.00
BULL cast iron cap pistol, HUBLEY, 1940, "Pat. Appld. for, Pat. Mch. 25, '24, 6¼"	15.00	17.50	20.00
BULL DOG cast iron cap pistol, HUBLEY, 1935, "Pat. 1,488,046", 6¼"long	10.00	15.00	20.00
BULLDOZER cast iron cap pistol, six-shooter, July 1874	100.00	150.00	175.00
BULL'S EYE cast iron cap pistol, KENTON, 1940, "Gene Autry" signature on grips, 6½"	20.00	25.00	30.00
BULLSEYE SAFETY cast iron pistol, flare barrel, with spring	60.00	85.00	125.00
BUNKER HILL cast iron cap pistol, NATIONAL, 1925, 5¼" long	12.50	18.75	25.00
BUSTER cast iron cap automatic, 1910, KILGORE, 5½"	30.00	45.00	60.00
BUTTING MATCH mechanical pistol, cast iron	200.00	250.00	300.00
Cap Bomb, cast iron, head shape	40.00	65.00	80.00
Cap Bomb, dog's head	40.00	65.00	80.00
Cap Pistol, cast iron, ornate, 1878	50.00	75.00	100.00

Typical Cast Iron Cap Pistols 1900-1910
Top Row, L to R: NEMO, LAS, TIGER 1915
Middle Row, L to R: GO, BUSTER 1910, SCOUT 1890
Bottom Row, L to R: unmarked; NATIONAL, Stevens 1920, unmarked
Courtesy Charles W. Best

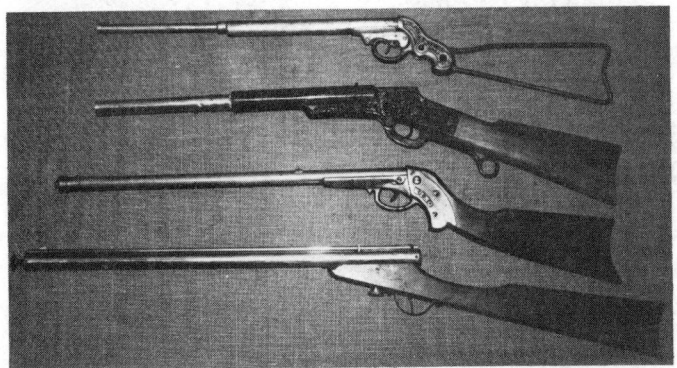

Typical B.B. Guns from the year 1900—Row 1: DAISY 3rd MODEL; Row 2: COLUMBIAN JUNIOR; Row 3: KING; Row 4: BENJAMIN (pump)
Courtesy Charles W. Best

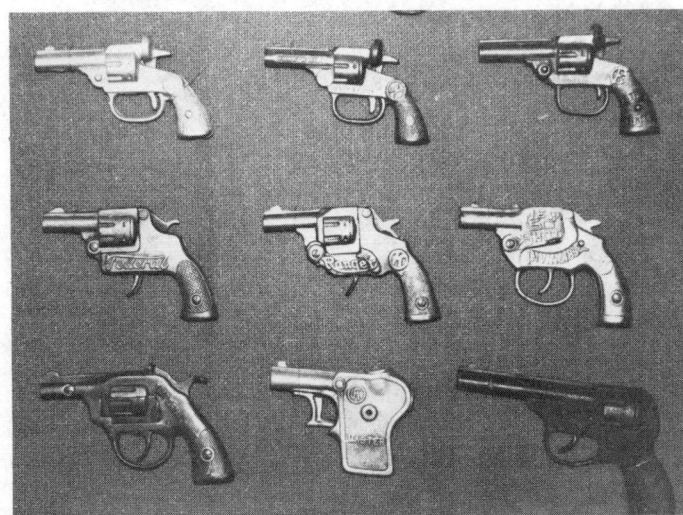

Typical Cast Iron Cap Pistols, 1920-1930 — Top Row, L to R: OH BOY 1922, BUNKER HILL, BIG BILL 1925; Middle Row, L to R: FEDERAL 1920, RANGER 1920, NEW 50 SHOT INVINCIBLE; Bottom Row, L to R: IMPERIAL, MASTER 1922, NATIONAL No. 380.
Courtesy Charles W. Best

	G	VG	M
Cap Pistol, cast iron, revolving cylinder, 1887	65.00	100.00	125.00
Cap Pistol, cast iron, six-shot, dated 1895	85.00	125.00	150.00
Cast iron pistol, ornate, six-shot, 1895	85.00	125.00	150.00
Cast iron pistol, six-shot, pat. Jan. 1895	85.00	125.00	150.00
Cast iron pistol, shoots caps, embossed	20.00	25.00	30.00
Cast iron pistol, shoots caps, plated barrel	15.00	20.00	25.00
Cap pistol, steel, repeating, red, WYANDOTTE, 8" long	7.50	10.00	15.00
CAPTAIN cast iron cap automatic, KILGORE, 1940, 4¼" long	12.50	17.50	22.50
CAVALIER cast iron cap automatic, KILGORE, 1935, "Pat. Appld. For, Made in U.S.A.", 4½"	17.50	22.50	30.00
CHAMP Automatic 5", HUBLEY	4.00	6.00	8.00
CHIEF cast iron .22 cal. blank shooter, KENTON 1915, 6" long, second trigger tips up barrel to load	25.00	35.00	45.00
CHIEF cast iron cap pistol, HUBLEY 1930, "Pat. 1,488,046", 6⅛"	12.50	17.50	25.00
CHIEF cap pistol, aluminum single shot, HUBLEY	5.00	7.50	10.00
CHIEFTAIN cast iron cap pistol, NATIONAL, 1920, 11" long	30.00	35.00	45.00
CHINESE MUST GO mechanical cap pistol	195.00	225.00	395.00
"Click Pistol" MARX No. 32	3.00	5.00	7.50
Click Pistol, MARX, approx. 7¾" long, pressed steel, with box	5.00	7.50	10.00
Click Pistol, tin litho, MARX No. 36	3.00	5.00	7.50
Clicker Pistol, plain black, late 1930s, early 1940s	2.50	5.00	7.50
CLIP JR. cast iron cap pistol, STEVENS, 1935, 5¼"	12.50	17.50	25.00
CLIPPER cast iron cap automatic, KILGORE, 1935 4⅛"	12.50	17.50	25.00
Clown and mule animated pistol	400.00	500.00	600.00

	G	VG	M
COLT cast iron cap pistol, STEVENS 1920, "Patented June 17, 1890, Made in U.S.A.", 5½"...	25.00	35.00	45.00
COLT cast iron cap pistol, STEVENS 1935, 6½"...	20.00	25.00	30.00
COLT .45, die cast HUBLEY.............	10.00	15.00	25.00
COLUMBIA 1885 cast iron cap pistol.............	55.00	75.00	125.00
COLUMBIA 1890 cast iron cap pistol.............	55.00	75.00	125.00
COLUMBIA cast iron cap pistol, pat. June 1891....	55.00	75.00	125.00
COLUMBIAN JUNIOR EARLY BB gun........	100.00	150.00	300.00
COP cast iron cap pistol HUBLEY 1930 "Pat. 1,488,046" or "Pat. Mch. 25 '24", 5"............	15.00	20.00	25.00
Cork-popper pistol, WYAN-DOTTE, spur trigger....	5.00	7.50	10.00
Cork-shooting rifle, MARX No. 206..............	5.00	7.50	10.00
Corn Shooter cap pistol....	35.00	45.00	50.00
COWBOY cast iron cap pistol, IVES, 1890, 7-5/8"	42.50	63.75	85.00
COWBOY cast iron cap pistol, STEVENS, 1935, "Made in U.S.A.', 3½"..	10.00	15.00	20.00
COWBOY cast iron cap pistol, long barrel, STEVENS, 1930, "Made in U.S.A.".............	25.00	30.00	35.00
COWBOY cast iron cap pistol, HUBLEY 1940 "Made in U.S.A.", 8"....	15.00	20.00	25.00
COYOTE die cast HUBLEY.............	7.50	12.50	20.00
DAGGER DERRINGER die cast HUBLEY......	7.50	12.50	20.00
DAISY Buzz Barton Special No. 195, BB gun.......	20.00	35.00	75.00
DAISY cast iron cap pistol, Pat. Apr. 1873.........	50.00	75.00	95.00
DAISY cast iron cap pistol, HUBLEY 1935, 4⅛"....	12.50	17.50	25.00
DAISY "Daisy Mfg. Co. No. 80" water pistol, Pat. 1807839, approx. 7¼" long.................	10.00	15.00	20.00
DAISY Daisy Pump No. 25 BB gun (early).........	15.00	25.00	45.00
DAISY Defender BB gun, No. 140..............	40.00	65.00	100.00

Popular Daisy B.B. Guns from the 1930s (top to bottom)—Daisy BUZZ BARTON SPECIAL, No. 195; Daisy Pump No. 25; Daisy RED RYDER, No. 111; Daisy DEFENDER, No. 140
Courtesy Charles W. Best

	G	VG	M
DAISY early BB gun, 3rd model, with cast iron frame	85.00	125.00	250.00
DAISY Red Ryder BB gun No. 111 (see Comic Character)			
DAISY No. 7 water pistol..	7.50	10.00	12.50
DAISY No. 8 water pistol, all metal, patent 1915...	15.00	20.00	25.00
DAISY Targeteer Air Pistol, circa 1947, 1940s......	7.50	10.00	15.00
DAISY "Daisy No. 118 Targeteer" automatic 10¼" long, target pistol..	10.00	15.00	20.00
DAISY air rifle, cast iron and brass, early, 31" long	75.00	100.00	150.00
DAISY air rifle target, 1935, 4½x5"	.75	1.00	1.25
DAISY CINEMATIC PICTURE PISTOL, circa mid-1940s	25.00	35.00	40.00
DAISY DOUBLE DUTY PISTOL, pops and shoots water from separate barrel, very similar to Buck Rogers pistol (see Comic Character)	15.00	20.00	25.00
DAISY ZOOKA "POP" Pistol, similar to Buck Rogers pistol..........	15.00	20.00	30.00
DANDY cast iron cap pistol, HUBLEY, 1935, can have variety of markings, 5¾"..............	15.00	20.00	25.00
DARB cast iron cap pistol, KENTON 1930, "Pat. Sept.11-23", 5½" long...	15.00	20.00	25.00
Dart Pistol, WYANDOTTE, colorful, fancy lithographing	5.00	7.50	10.00
DERBY cast iron cap pistol, HUBLEY 1930, 7".....	15.00	20.00	25.00

	G	VG	M
DETROIT cast iron cap pistol, 1910, 6-5/8" long	25.00	35.00	45.00
DICK cast iron cap pistol, HUBLEY 1930, 6"	12.50	15.00	20.00
DICK cast iron cap automatic, HUBLEY 1940, "Made in U.S.A.", 4⅛"	10.00	15.00	20.00
DIK cast iron cap pistol, KENTON 1935, "Pat. Sept. 11-23", 4¾"	12.50	15.00	20.00
DIXIE cast iron cap pistol, KENTON 1935, "Made in U.S.A. Pat. Appld. For", 6¼"	15.00	20.00	25.00
DOC cast iron cap pistol, KENTON 1940, "Pat. Sept. 11-23, 4½"	12.50	15.00	20.00
Dolphin animated cap pistol (may actually be Sea Serpent)	275.00	350.00	425.00
Double-barrel cast iron cap pistol, dated 1880	85.00	100.00	125.00
Double-barrel pop gun-rifle, MARX No. 230	5.00	7.50	10.00
Double cap pistol, cast iron	40.00	50.00	75.00
Double cap pistol, cast iron	40.00	50.00	75.00
Double trigger cast iron match-shooting pistol, large, STEPHENS, PA. 1873	75.00	95.00	125.00
DOUGHBOY cast iron cap automatic, KILGORE 1920, "Made in U.S.A.", 5"	15.00	20.00	25.00
DRAGNET Detective Special repeating revolver cap gun, circa 1955	11.00	16.50	22.00

DRAGNET - Detective Special Repeating Revolver Cap Gun, circa 1955
Courtesy HAKE'S Americana & Collectibles

★ KENTON CAP PISTOLS ★

Introducing

NEW NO. 44 DUDE
RIGHT OFF THE RANCH
WITH
PLENTY OF CLASS
MADE TO RETAIL AT 25¢

NO. 44 DUDE

NEW popular priced repeater for 1941—right off the Dude Ranch. This pistol features an entirely new style handle and is designed with class. Note special engraved figure of cowboy on bucking horse on both right and left plastic grips. A repeater type pistol with break action. Furnished in nickel-plated and gun-metal finishes—6½ inches long. Individually packed in Red and Black display carton showing Dude Ranch scene and reproduction of pistol.

GENE AUTRY PISTOLS

GENE AUTRY PISTOLS—still the youngsters first choice—are naturally continued in our line and are offered in two price ranges. With the addition of our new 1941 numbers, we can now offer, as always, a line which will fill your complete requirements.

WRITE FOR NEW 1941 CATALOG SHOWING ENTIRE LINE

★ THE KENTON HARDWARE CO. ★
Kenton, Ohio, U.S.A.

When writing to The Kenton Hardware Co., will you please mention PLAYTHINGS?
JANUARY, 1941—PLAYTHINGS

DUDE
Courtesy Playthings Magazine

	G	VG	M
DUDE cast iron cap pistol, STEVENS 1887, "Pat. Mar. 22 '87", 3½"	40.00	50.00	65.0
DUDE cast iron cap pistol, plastic grips, 1941, KENTON, 6½"	15.00	20.00	25.00
EAGLE cast iron cap pistol, STEVENS, 1895, "Pat. June 17, 1890", 7½"	35.00	50.00	70.00
EAGLE, circa 1940	15.00	20.00	30.00
ECHO cap pistol, six-shooter cast iron, 1881	90.00	110.00	150.00
ECHO cast iron cap pistol, STEVENS 1920, 4¼"	20.00	25.00	35.00
ECHO cast iron cap pistol, STEVENS 1930, "Made In U.S.A.", 4½"	5.00	7.50	10.00
1895 cast iron six shot cap pistol	65.00	100.00	125.00
EXCELSIOR cast iron cap pistol, STEVENS, 1875, "Pat'd Apr. 22, '73", 5¼"	40.00	60.00	75.00
FEDERAL cast iron cap pistol, KILGORE, 1920, 5½"	12.50	18.75	25.00

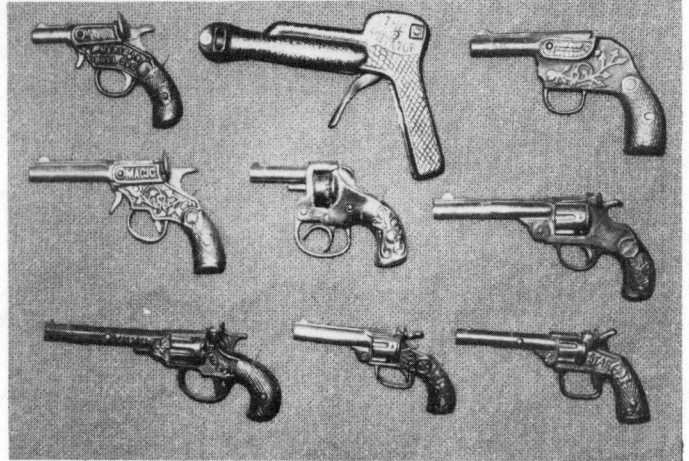

Typical Cast Iron Cap Pistols 1900-1910—Top Row, L to R: AMERICAN BULLDOG 1920, AGITATOR, THE, HANSON-LINDSBORG K.S.; Middle Row, L to R: MAGIC 1900, unmarked .22 blank shooter, unmarked; Bottom, L to R: COWBOY 1890, BOSS 1925, STAR 1910. Courtesy Charles W. Best

	G	VG	M
FEDERAL cast iron cap automatic, KILGORE 1940, 4-7/8", has removeable clip to hold caps	15.00	20.00	25.00
FEDERAL cast iron cap pistol, KILGORE 1920, "Pat. Dec. '14; made in U.S.A."	17.50	25.00	30.00
FEDERAL — KILGORE No. 1 cast iron cap pistol, 1925, 5¼", KILGORE	10.00	15.00	20.00
FEDERAL No. 2 cast iron cap pistol, KILGORE 1925, 6⅜"	25.00	35.00	45.00
Firecracker pistol, filigree handle, cast iron	40.00	65.00	85.00
Five-barrel firecracker pistol, iron and brass, 1877	450.00	600.00	750.00
5-STAR steel dart pistol, WYANDOTTE	5.00	7.50	10.00
FLASH cast iron cap pistol, HUBLEY 1934, "Pat'd" 6¼"	15.00	20.00	25.0
FLINTLOCK die cast, HUBLEY	10.00	15.00	22.50
FLINTLOCK JUNIOR die cast HUBLEY	7.50	12.50	20.00
FLINTLOCK MIDGET, die cast HUBLEY	5.00	7.50	12.50
FOUR WAY cast iron cap pistol, KENTON 1930, "Pat. Appld. For", shoots pea or dart, rubber band and cap, all at same time	30.00	45.00	55.00

	G	VG	M
49-ER cast iron cap pistol, STEVENS 1940, 9"	17.50	25.00	30.00
FOX cast iron cap pistol, HUBLEY 1935, 4½"	12.50	17.50	22.50
FRONTIER cast iron cap pistol, IVES 1890, "Pat. June 21, 1887 and June 17, 1890", Dog's head atop the barrel facing hammer	125.00	175.00	225.00
G-MAN cast iron cap automatic, KILGORE 1935, 6", looks like German Luger, removeable magazine holds caps	25.00	35.00	50.00
G-MAN bakelite-framed cap automatic, KILGORE, 1940, 6"	10.00	15.00	20.00
G-MAN clicker pistol, tin, black	8.00	10.00	12.00
G-MAN wind-up steel spark pistol, painted finish	12.50	20.00	25.00
G-MAN wind-up steel spark pistol, nickel finish with jewels on grip	12.50	20.00	25.00
"G-MAN AUTOMATIC", MARX, sparkles when wound, 1930s	17.50	26.25	35.00
G-MAN automatic sparkling pistol, MARX No. 43 aluminum	5.00	7.50	10.00
G-MAN automatic sparkling pistol, MARX No. 44 aluminum	5.00	7.50	10.00
G-MAN automatic sparkling pistol, MARX No. 85, aluminum	5.00	7.50	10.00
G-MAN gun, MARX No. 707	5.00	7.50	10.00
G-MAN Silent Alarm Pistol, MARX No. 54, tin	8.00	12.00	16.00
G-MAN Tin Wind-up Machine Gun, 1940s, miniature	10.00	15.00	20.00
GANG BUSTERS full size MARX Sub-Machine Gun	30.00	50.00	75.00
GEM cast iron cap pistol, STEVENS, 1900, 3"	20.00	25.00	35.00
GENE AUTRY cast iron die cap pistol, KENTON 1939, 8-3/8"	25.00	30.00	45.00
GENE AUTRY cast iron cap pistol, KENTON 1939, "Made in U.S.A. Pat. Appld. For", 6½"	15.00	22.50	30.00

	G	VG	M
GENE AUTRY cast iron cap pistol, KENTON 1940, "Made in U.S.A.", 6½", red grips	15.00	22.50	30.00
GENE AUTRY cast iron pistol (doesn't fire caps), KENTON, 1940, "Made in U.S.A.", 6½"	15.00	22.50	30.00
GO cast iron cap pistol, 1910, maker unknown, 6¾"	22.50	33.75	45.00
GUARD cast iron cap pistol, KILGORE 1935, "Made In U.S.A.", 6¼"	15.00	20.00	25.00
H-BAR-O cast iron cap pistol, KILGORE 1925, "Made In U.S.A.", 7½"	17.50	25.00	30.00
HAMMERLESS cast iron cap pistol, STEVENS, 1892, "Pat. Appld. For", 7¼", four revolving triggers, hammer concealed	100.00	135.00	175.00
HANSON-LINDSBORG K.S. cast iron firecracker pistol, 1905, HANSON "Pat. Appld. For", 6⅜", fires fire-cracker	35.00	50.00	75.00
HERO cast iron cap pistol, STEVENS, 1937, 5¼"	5.00	7.50	10.00
HERO AUTO cast iron cap automatic, 1920, STEVENS, 4¾"	22.50	33.75	45.00
HI-HO cast iron cap pistol, STEVENS, 1940, "Made In U.S.A.", 7"	12.50	17.50	20.00
HI-HO cast iron pistol, can fire caps, STEVENS 1940, "Made In U.S.A.', 7"	12.50	17.50	20.00
HI-HO cast iron cap pistol, KILGORE, 1940, 6½"	12.50	17.50	20.00
HIO cast iron cap pistol, KENTON 1940, "Pat. Sept. 11-23", 5⅛"	12.50	15.00	20.00
HI-RANGER cast iron cap pistol, STEVENS 1940, 7¾"	15.00	20.00	25.00
HOPALONG CASSIDY 9" revolver, WYANDOTTE, "Hopalong" on both sides of handle, with holster	25.00	30.00	50.00
HOPALONG CASSIDY 10" Revolver with bust of Hopalong, SCHMIDT	25.00	30.00	50.00
HUB cast iron cap pistol, HUBLEY, 1940, 6¼"	12.50	15.00	20.00

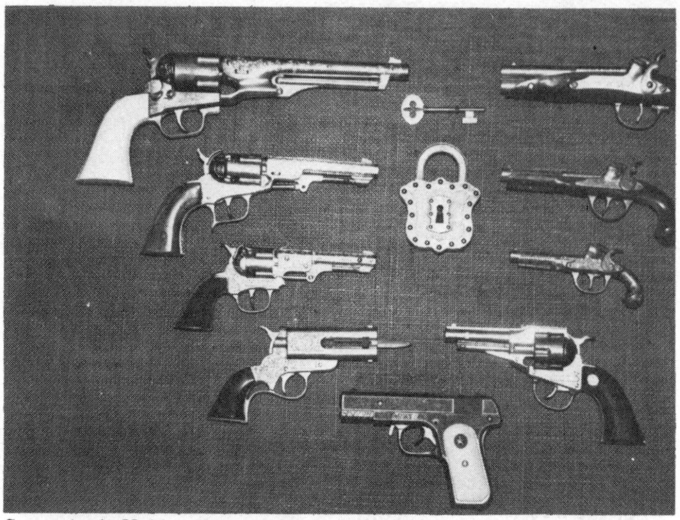

Some classic Hubley die-cast cap pistols from the 1950s:
Row 1: COLT .45; FLINTLOCK
Row 2: PIONEER; Padlock Pistol w/key; FLINTLOCK JR.
Row 3: COYOTE; FLINTLOCK MIDGET
Row 4: DAGGER DERRINGER; REMINGTON .36
Row 5: ARMY .45 (automatic)
Courtesy Charles W. Best

	G	VG	M
HUSTLER cast iron pistol	25.00	30.00	45.00
IDEAL, tin dart-shooter	5.00	7.50	10.00
IMPERIAL cast iron cap pistol, KILGORE, 1935, 5¼"	18.00	27.00	36.00
INDIAN cast iron cap pistol	15.00	20.00	25.00
INVINCIBLE cast iron cap pistol, KILGORE 1935, 5¼", "Pat. Dec. 14"	15.00	22.50	30.00
JACK ARMSTRONG airplane gun, DAISY, 1936	30.00	45.00	55.00
JAX cast iron cap pistol, KENTON, 1930, "Pat. Sept. 11-23", 4"	10.00	15.00	20.00
JUMBO cast iron cap pistol, "Pat. June 17, 1890; Made in U.S.A.", 9½" STEVENS 1895	50.00	75.00	125.00
JR. POLICE CHIEF, cast iron cap automatic, KENTON, 1938, "Made In U.S.A.", 3-7/8"	10.00	15.00	20.00
JUNIOR: POLICE 32 cast iron cap pistol, HUBLEY, 1940, "Hubley; Pat'd. 2088891", 5¼"	15.00	20.00	25.00
JUNIOR SIX-SHOOTER cast iron cap pistol, KILGORE, 1935, 5½"	15.00	20.00	25.00

	G	VG	M
KIDO cast iron cap pistol, KENTON, 1936, "Kenton, Made In U.S.A.", 5⅜"	10.00	15.00	20.00
KILGORE cast iron cap pistol, KILGORE, 1910, 5"	21.00	31.50	42.00
KILGORE cast iron cap pistol, KILGORE, 1912, 5¼"	21.00	31.50	42.00
KING BB gun, early	75.00	110.00	225.00
KING cast iron cap pistol, Pat. Aug. 1879	20.00	30.00	40.00
KING cast iron cap pistol, STEVENS, 1925, "Made In U.S.A.", 4¾"	10.00	15.00	20.00
KIT CARSON cast iron cap pistol, KENTON, 1928, "Pat. Sept. 11-23", 9"	20.00	25.00	30.00
LAS cast iron cap pistol	No Price Found		
LIBERTY, circa 1912 tin, ornate	20.00	30.00	45.00
LASSO 'EM BILL cast iron cap gun, red rubies in handle, cylinder turns, 1930, 9"	25.00	30.00	35.00
LAWMAKER cast iron cap pistol, KENTON, 1941, 8⅜"	20.00	25.00	30.00
LIGHTNING EXPRESS, mechanical cap pistol, train slides forward along barrel to explode cap at end, 5", 1913, Arcade or Kenton	100.00	150.00	195.00
Lion head cast iron cap pistol, Pat. 1890, 5¼", STEVENS	85.00	125.00	150.00
LITTLE BILL cast iron cap pistol, KILGORE 1925, 5"	10.00	15.00	20.00
LITTLE CHIEF FIREFIGHTER, water squirt gun	2.50	5.00	7.00
LONE EAGLE cast iron cap pistol, KILGORE, 1929, 5¼"	20.00	30.00	40.00
LONE RANGER cast iron cap pistol, KILGORE 1938, 8½"	25.00	35.00	50.00
LONE RANGER cast iron cap pistol, KILGORE 1940, 8½"	25.00	35.00	50.00
LONE RANGER click pistol, MARX	15.00	25.00	30.00

	G	VG	M
LONE RANGER 45 Flasher Flashlight Pistol, MARX	15.00	20.00	30.00
LONE RANGER Sparkling Pop Pistol, tin litho, MARX No. 096	17.00	25.50	34.00
LONE RANGER tin pop gun, 1950s, picture of Lone Ranger on handles	15.00	20.00	30.00
LONE RANGER Western Gun collection, circa 1939, six miniature guns mounted on card with history of guns on back	25.00	35.00	50.00
LONG BOY cast iron cap pistol, KILGORE, 1922, 11" long, "Made in U.S.A."	25.00	30.00	35.00
LONG TOM cast iron cap pistol, KILGORE, 1939, 10 3/8"	25.00	30.00	35.00
LOOK OUT dog's head cast iron cap pistol	100.00	150.00	175.00
M&L water pistol, die-cast, rubber ball	2.50	5.00	7.50
MACHINE GUN, cast iron cap automatic, KILGORE, 1938, comes with crank, which when turned, fires the caps rapidly, "Ra-Ta-Ta-Tat", 5"	25.00	30.00	50.00
MAGIC cast iron .22 cal. blank pistol, KENTON 1900, "Pat'd. Oct. 17 '99", 6¼" long, ornate, has second trigger to open barrel for loading	25.00	35.00	45.00
MASCOT cast iron cap automatic, KILGORE 1936, 3⅞"	15.00	20.00	25.00
MASTER cast iron cap automatic, 1922, KILGORE, 4⅝"	16.00	24.00	32.00
MASTER cast iron cap automatic, KILGORE, 1930, 4⅝"	20.00	25.00	30.00
ME AND MY BUDDY, animated pistol with figure, steel, WYANDOTTE	17.50	25.00	35.00
MINUTE MAN cast iron cap rifle, KILGORE 1936, "Pat. Appld. For", "Made in U.S.A.", 20"	80.00	100.00	125.00

Typical Cast Iron Cap Pistols 1910-1920—Top, L to R: HERO AUTO, REX 1914, TERROR 1915, NATIONAL 1915; Middle, L to R: KILGORE 1910, KILGORE 1912, FEDERAL 1920, NEW 50 SHOT INVINCIBLE; Bottom, L to R: NATIONAL 1911, NATIONAL 1909, BIG BUSTER Courtesy Charles W. Best

	G	VG	M
MODEL, Pat. 1890, cast iron, 5⅜"	20.00	25.00	30.00
Monkey and Coconut animated cap pistol, 1878, 4¼", STEVENS	275.00	325.00	395.00
MOONFACE capshooter, STEVENS, circa 1880	500.00	650.00	800.00
NATIONAL cast iron cap automatic, 1915, NATIONAL, 3¾"	16.00	24.00	32.00
NATIONAL cast iron cap pistol, NATIONAL 1909, 4⅞"	25.00	37.50	50.00
NATIONAL cast iron cap pistol, NATIONAL, 1911, 5"	16.00	24.00	32.00
NATIONAL cast iron cap pistol, STEVENS, 1920, 5⅜"	18.00	27.00	36.00
NATIONAL cast iron cap automatic, NATIONAL, 1925, "Made in U.S.A.", 5¼"	15.00	20.00	25.00
NATIONAL No. 380 cast iron cap pistol, 1930s, NATIONAL, 7"	21.00	31.50	42.00
NAVY cast iron cap pistol, KENTON 1930, "Pat. Sept. 11-23", 5½"	15.00	20.00	25.00
NAVY double barrel cap pistol	75.00	100.00	125.00
NEMO cast iron cap pistol, maker unknown, 1910, 6⅝"	21.00	31.50	42.00

	G	VG	M
NEW 50 SHOT INVINCIBLE cast iron cap pistol, 1930, KILGORE, 5½"	10.00	15.00	20.00
NIGGER HEAD cap pistol, cast iron, IVES, 1887, 4½"	100.00	125.00	150.00
"No. 71 Water Pistol" (Daisy?) automatic, approx. 5½" long	10.00	15.00	20.00
NOVELTY cast iron cap pistol, STEVENS, 1885, "Pat. Appld. For", 5"	85.00	125.00	150.00
NU-MATIC PAPER pop gun, 7" long	5.00	10.00	15.00
OFFICER PISTOL, cast iron cap automatic, KILGORE, 1940, 6", modeled after German Luger	30.00	40.00	50.00
Official Detective-Type Submachine Gun, MARX, No. 2146	7.50	10.00	15.00
OH BOY automatic cap, KILGORE, 1933, "Made in U.S.A.; Pat'd. Aug. 8, 1933", works both as automatic and as crank-operated rapid-fire gun, 4-1/8"	15.00	20.00	25.00
OH BOY cast iron cap pistol, NATIONAL, 1922, 5½"	10.00	15.00	20.00
OHIO cast iron cap pistol, KENTON 1930, "Pat. Sept. 11-23", 5⅛"	15.00	20.00	25.00
OK cast iron cap automatic, maker unknown, 1935, 3¾"	10.00	15.00	20.00
OLD IRONSIDES cast iron cap pistol, 10¾"	25.00	30.00	45.00
P-38 steel clicker pistol, circa 1945	7.50	10.00	15.00
Padlock cap pistol, and key, HUBLEY, 4¼"	30.00	40.00	50.00
PAL cast iron cap pistol, KILGORE, 1930, 4"	10.00	15.00	20.00
PAL cast iron cap automatic, KILGORE, 1930, 4"	10.00	15.00	20.00
PAT cast iron cap pistol, KENTON, 1935, "Pat. Sept. 11-23", 6⅛"	10.00	15.00	20.00
PATROL cast iron cap pistol, HUBLEY 1939, "Made In U.S.A.", 6"	10.00	15.00	20.00
PAWNEE BILL, circa 1940	30.00	45.00	60.00

Top, L to R: "Teddy", "Chief"; Middle: "Buffalo Bill"; Bottom, L to R: "25 Jr.", "Pal", "Army 45"
Courtesy Mapes Auctioneers & Appraisers

	G	VG	M
PEA MATIC pea-shooting steel repeater	7.50	10.00	15.00
Pea shooter	10.,00	15.00	20.00
Pea shooter, pewter, highly embossed handle	15.00	25.00	35.00
PEACEMAKER cast iron cap pistol, STEVENS 1940, "Made in U.S.A.", 8½"	15.00	20.00	25.00
PERSUADER cast iron cap pistol, KENTON, 1939, "Made in U.S.A." Pat. Appld. For", 6⅜"	15.00	20.00	25.00
PET, 4¼" HUBLEY	3.00	4.50	6.00
Ping-Pong rifle	5.00	7.50	10.00
PIONEER diecast HUBLEY	7.50	12.50	20.00
PIRATE cap pistol, die cast zinc, with cast iron hammers and trigger, HUBLEY 1941, two-barrel, two hammers that cock, 9⅜"	15.00	20.00	30.00
"Pistol Packin' Mama", wood with cardboard sides, circa 1944, four revolving triggers, 8½" long, shoots wooden pegs	15.00	20.00	25.00
PLUCK cast iron cap pistol, STEVENS 1930, "Made in U.S.A.", 3½", early-looking, at least four versions known, one dating to 1895	15.00	22.50	30.00
POLICE large steel automatic cap pistol, 8"	7.50	10.00	15.00
POLICE bakelite-framed cap automatic, KILGORE, 1940, 5¼"	10.00	15.00	20.00

	G	VG	M
POLICE Chief gun and leather shoulder holster set, circa late 1940s, WYANDOTTE	15.00	20.00	25.00
PONO cast iron cap pistol, KENTON 1936, "Pat. Sept. 11-23", 5⅛"	10.00	15.00	20.00
Powder keg cast iron cap bomb	35.00	50.00	65.00
PRESTO cast iron cap automatic, KILGORE, 1940, 5⅛"	12.50	15.00	20.00
PUNCH & JUDY cast iron animated cap pistol, 1880, 5" "Patented", IVES, Punch explodes cap with nose, on Judy's back	275.00	375.00	450.00
RANGER cast iron cap pistol, KILGORE, 1920, 5⅜"	16.00	24.00	32.00
RANGER cast iron cap pistol, KILGORE, 1939, 8½"	15.00	20.00	25.00
RANGER cast iron cap pistol, KILGORE, 1940, 8½", hammer protrudes more than earlier version	15.00	20.00	25.00
RECORD	2.00	3.50	5.00
"RED RANGER", steel clicker pistol, WYANDOTTE, circa 1939, 8" long, black, red "jewel"	10.00	15.00	20.00
"RED RANGER", steel clicker pistol, WYANDOTTE, 8" long, circa 1941	10.00	15.00	20.00
RED RANGER steel click pistol, WYANDOTTE, 7¾"	10.00	15.00	20.00
RED RANGER steel six shooter repeater with plastic handles, WYANDOTTE, revolving cyclinder	10.00	15.00	20.00
RED RYDER Air Rifle, 1940, DAISY with cast iron lever	35.00	52.50	75.00
RED RYDER Air Rifle, DAISY, circa 1950s	15.00	22.50	30.00
REMINGTON .36 die cast HUBLEY	10.00	15.00	25.00
Repeating Cap Pistol, MARX No. G375, aluminum	5.00	7.50	10.00
REX cast iron cap automatic, 1914, DENT, 4-1/8"	16.00	24.00	32.00

RED RYDER Daisy Air Rifle, circa 1950s
Courtesy HAKE'S Americana & Collectibles

	G	VG	M
REX cast iron cap automatic, KILGORE, 1939, 3⅞"	15.00	20.00	25.00
RIP, circa 1909	55.00	75.00	125.00
ROB ROY, circa 1875	95.00	125.00	150.00
ROCKET SHIP Space Pistol. Late 1940s by IRWIN	10.00	15.00	20.00
ROTOR FIFTY Cast iron cap pistol, KILGORE, 6⅛" long, 1930	25.00	30.00	40.00
ROY ROGERS cast iron cap pistol, 11"	35.00	50.00	75.00
ROY ROGERS Forty Niner pistol and spurs set, 8½" long, 1940s	30.00	40.00	50.00
ROY ROGERS Tuck Away Gun, 2½" derringer, circa early 1950s	5.00	7.50	10.00
ROYAL PISTOL, THE, 1878 cast iron cap mechanical pistol, fires spring-loaded top which is attached to bottom of the barrel, approx. 5", "Pat. Apr. 23 '78"	300.00	350.00	450.00
SAFETY cast iron cap pistol, HUBLEY, 1924, "Pat. Mch 25, '24", 5"	10.00	15.00	20.00
SAFETY FIRST cast iron cap automatic, 1920, "Safe", 3-3/8", maker unknown	20.00	30.00	40.00
SAMBO cast iron cap pistol, hammer hits head, 1887, IVES, "Pat. June 21, 1887, 4-3/8"	75.00	95.00	125.00
SAY I cast iron cap bomb	35.00	45.00	60.00
SCOUT cast iron cap pistol, STEVENS, 1890, "Pat'd. June 17. 1890", 7"	20.00	25.00	35.00
SCOUT cast iron cap pistol, STEVENS, 1935, "Made In U.S.A.", 6¾"	10.00	15.00	20.00
SCOUT cast iron cap pistol, STEVENS, 1940, 6⅛"	10.00	15.00	20.00
SCOUT cap pistol, tin, 1914, automatic	10.00	15.00	20.00
SCOUT JR. cast iron cap pistol, STEVENS, 1935, "Made in U.S.A.", 6"	10.00	15.00	20.00

	G	VG	M
SENATOR cast iron cap pistol, KILGORE 1925, 7" marked with star and "K"	20.00	25.00	30.00
1776-1876 cast iron cap pistol, STEVENS, 1876, 5¼", produced for America's (100th) centennial	85.00	125.00	175.00
SHOO FLY cast iron cap pistol	65.00	80.00	100.00
SHOOT THE HAT cast iron mechanical cap pistol	295.00	395.00	495.00
Shotgun, double-barreled, steel, wood stock 28", both barrels break down, cock and shoot	7.50	10.00	15.00
SIREN SPARKLING AIRPLANE PISTOL, tin litho, MARX No. 182	20.00	28.00	35.00
SIREN SPARKLING PISTOL, tin litho, MARX no. 164	20.00	25.00	35.00
SIX SHOOTER cast iron cap pistol, KILGORE, 1935, 6½"	20.00	25.00	35.00
SIX SHOOTER cast iron cap pistol with plastic-type grips, KILGORE, 1935, 6½"	20.00	35.00	35.00
SIX SHOOTER cast iron cap pistol, KILGORE, 1938, "Made in U.S.A." on hammer, 6½"	20.00	25.00	35.00
SIX SHOOTER cast iron cap pistol, KILGORE, 1938, "Made in U.S.A." on hammer, plastic-type grips, 6½"	20.00	25.00	35.00
SIX SHOOTER cast iron cap pistol, KILGORE, 1930, 7"	20.00	25.00	35.00
SIX SHOOTER AUTOMATIC cast iron cap pistol (not an automatic), KILGORE, 1934, 6½"	20.00	30.00	40.00
6 SHOT cast iron cap pistol, STEVENS, 1895, "Pat'd. U.S.A., Jan. 22, 1895", 6¾"	85.00	125.00	150.00
SLIKO cast iron cap pistol, KENTON, 1930, "Pat. Sept. 11-23", 6¼"	15.00	20.00	25.00

	G	VG	M
SNAPPY JACK, circa 1935, ENGLISH.......	35.00	45.00	60.00
SPARKLING ATOM BUSTER, aluminum, MARX No. 46........	5.00	7.50	10.00
SPARKLING G-MAN Sub-Machine Gun, MARX No. 2308.............	10.00	17.50	25.00
SPARKLING G-MAN Sub-machine Gun, MARX No. 2310.............	10.00	17.50	25.00
SPARKLING Pop Gun, MARX No. 198........	5.00	7.50	10.00
SPARKLING Space Gun, MARX..............	10.00	15.00	20.00
SPARKLING SURE SHOT	5.00	7.50	10.00
SPITFIRE cast iron cap automatic, STEVENS 1940, "Made in U.S.A.", 4⅝".............	15.00	20.00	25.00
SPORT cast iron cap pistol, KILGORE, 1930, "Made in U.S.A.", 7½"........	10.00	15.00	20.00
Spud Gun, tin, automatic, circa 1940.............	10.00	12.50	15.00
Spud Gun No. 504, B.J. Cossman, Hollywood, Calif. die-cast.........	10.00	12.50	15.00
SPY cast iron cap pistol, KILGORE, 1936, "Made in U.S.A.", 4¼"........	10.00	15.00	20.00
STAR pot metal cap pistol, steer on handle........	2.50	4.00	6.00
STAR, circa 1878.........	50.00	65.00	85.00
STAR cast iron cap pistol, 1910, STEVENS, 6¼"..	22.00	33.00	44.00
STEVENS REPEATER cast iron cap pistol, STEVENS, 1930, 6¼", "Mammoth Cap; Made in U.S.A."...............	20.00	25.00	30.00
STEVENS 6-SHOT RAPID LOAD cast iron cap pistol, 1932, STEVENS "Made in U.S.A.", 6½"..	20.00	25.00	30.00
STREAMLINE SIREN SPARKLING PISTOL, tin litho, MARX No. 155	5.00	7.50	10.00
SUN cast iron cap pistol...	65.00	85.00	100.00
S&W cast iron cap gun, 6".	10.00	15.00	20.00
SUPER cast iron cap pistol, KENTON 1930, "Pat. Sept. 11-23", 8¾"......	20.00	25.00	30.00

	G	VG	M
SUPER AUTOMATIC TOM GUN, steel spark automatic............	7.50	10.00	15.00
SUPER NU-MATIC PAPER BUSTER GUN.	5.00	7.50	10.00
SURE SHOT cast iron cap automatic, HUBLEY, 1940, 4¼"............	10.00	15.00	20.00
TARGET cast iron cap pistol, HUBLEY, 1935, "Pat. 1,488,046", 8".....	20.00	25.00	30.00
TEDDY cast iron cap pistol, HUBLEY 1938, 5-5/8"..	10.00	15.00	20.00
TERROR cast iron cap automatic, DENT, 1915, "Pat. Jan. 16 '15", 4¼"..	15.00	20.00	25.00
TERROR, people embossed, cast iron cap pistol......	100.00	125.00	150.00
TEXAN cast iron cap pistol, HUBLEY 1940, "Made in U.S.A.", 9¼" long......	20.00	25.00	30.00
TEXAN JR. cast iron cap pistol, HUBLEY 1941, "Made in U.S.A.", 8⅛" ..	20.00	25.00	30.00
TEXAS cast iron cap pistol, KENTON 1936, "Kenton, Pat'd. No. 1993916", 5¾"................	15.00	20.00	25.00
TEXAS cast iron cap pistol, KENTON, 1930, "Pat. Sept. 11-23", 6⅝"........	15.00	20.00	25.00
THE BIG NOISE, circa 1922.................	25.00	35.00	50.00
THE FORTY FIVE cast iron cap pistol, unusual shape, NATIONAL 1928, "Made in U.S.A.", 11⅛"................	30.00	40.00	50.00
THE SHERIFF cast iron cap pistol, STEVENS, 1940, 8½"............	15.00	20.00	25.00
TIGER cast iron cap pistol, STEVENS, 1915, 6¾"..	20.00	25.00	30.00
TIGER cast iron cap pistol, HUBLEY 1935, 6⅞"....	20.00	25.00	30.00
Tin Tin Gun - 3x5", turn crank and it makes noise, WOODHAVEN METAL STAMPING CO.......	7.50	12.50	17.50
TIP TOP cast iron cap pistol, 1878............	60.00	95.00	125.00
TRAINER..............	5.00	7.50	10.00
TRAPPER cast iron cap automatic, KILGORE, 1935, 4½", fires only single shot, but roll of			

	G	VG	M
caps can be carried in the grip....	25.00	30.00	35.00
TROOPER cast iron cap pistol, HUBLEY 1938, 5⅛"..................	15.00	20.00	25.00
TROOPER SAFETY cast iron cap pistol, KILGORE, 1930, "Pat. Pend; Made in U.S.A.", 10", operates either as straight cap pistol, or can be fired with crank......	35.00	45.00	55.00
TROOPER SAFETY cast iron cap pistol, KILGORE, 1925, 10¼".	20.00	25.00	30.00
25 cast iron cap automatic, STEVENS, 1928, "Pat. Appld. For; made in U.S.A.", 4½".........	15.00	20.00	25.00
25 JR. cast iron cap automatic, STEVENS 1930, 'Made in U.S.A.; Patented", 4⅛"........	10.00	15.00	20.00
25-50 Cast iron cap automatic STEVENS 1935, "Made in U.S.A.; Pat. Appld. For", 4½"..	10.00	15.00	20.00
25-50 Cast iron cap automatic, STEVENS 1935, "Oil Moving Parts; Made in U.S.A. Patented", 4½".......	10.00	15.00	20.00
25-50 Cat iron cap automatic, can be fired rapidly with crank, hole near muzzle holds removeable crank, STEVENS, 1935, "Oil Moving Parts; Made in U.S.A., Patented"......	35.00	50.00	65.00
25-50 TARGET cast iron cap automatic with "silencer" type barrel, STEVENS, 1935, "Oil Moving Parts; Made in U.S.A.; Patented".......	40.00	55.00	75.00
Two Dogs On Bench cap shooter (only two known, the one sold, condition unknown, sold for $3400 in 1981, its last sale.)			
"2 in 1" cast iron cap pistol, 9¼"................	35.00	40.00	50.00
"2 Monkeys", 1882 cast iron animated cap pistol, 4½", maker unknown, monkey			

	G	VG	M
butts head against coconut held by another monkey..............	300.00	375.00	425.00
TWO TIME cast iron cap and rubber band pistol, 1930, KENTON, "Pat. Appld. For", 9¼"......	40.00	50.00	60.00
UNXLD steel cap automatic, 6½", nickel-plated................	7.50	10.00	15.00
U.S.A. LIQUID PISTOL cast iron water pistol, PARKER-STEARNS, 1896, Pat'd. June 30, 1896", 4¾"..........	30.00	40.00	50.00
URICA.................	2.50	5.00	7.50
VICTOR cast iron pistol...	50.00	65.00	85.00
VILLA cast iron cap pistol, DENT, 1934, "Made in U.S.A.", 4¾"..........	20.00	25.00	30.00
VOLUNTEER cast iron cap pistol, STEVENS, 1973, "Pat'd April 22, '73"....	50.00	65.00	85.00
W on one side, S on other, cast iron cap pistol, nickel-plated, normal-size barrel...............	10.00	12.50	15.00
W on one side, S on other, snub nose, single shot, cast iron nickel-plated...	10.00	12.50	15.00
WAR cast iron cap pistol, KENTON, 1930, "Pat. Sept. 11-23", 4¼"......	20.00	25.00	30.00
WARRIOR cast iron cap pistol, maker unknown, 1926, "Pat Appld. For, 1926", 9".............	40.00	45.00	60.00
Water Pistol, WYANDOTTE No. 41........	5.00	7.50	10.00
Water Pistol, WYANDOTTE, unmarked.....	5.00	7.50	10.00
WESTERN cast iron cap pistol, KENTON, 1935, "Pat Sept. 11-23", 7"....	15.00	20.00	25.00
WESTERN cast iron cap pistol, KENTON 1936, "Pat Sept. 11-23", 7", has "jewel" over grips.......	15.00	20.00	25.00
WESTERN cast iron cap pistol, KENTON, 1939, "Made in U.S.A.", 7½"..	15.00	20.00	25.00
WESTO cast iron cap pistol, KENTON, 1936, "Kenton", 7"...............	15.00	20.00	25.00
WESTO cast iron pistol (doesn't fire caps), 1938,			

	G	VG	M		G	VG	M
KENTON, "Kenton", 7".	15.00	20.00	25.00	YANK cast iron cap pistol.	30.00	40.00	50.00
WHOOPIE cast iron cap pistol, KENTON, 1932, 5⅞"	20.00	25.00	30.00	YANKEE cast iron cap pistol, STEVENS, 1895, 5½"	65.00	85.00	110.00
WILD WEST cast iron cap pistol, NATIONAL, 1930, "Made in U.S.A.", 6½"	20.00	25.00	30.00	YORK cast iron cap pistol, KENTON, 1930, "Pat. Sept. 11-23", 7"	20.00	25.00	30.00
WINNER cast iron cap automatic, HUBLEY, 1940, 4⅜"	15.00	20.00	25.00	YOUND SPORTSMAN, circa 1868	75.00	100.00	135.00
WOODSMAN cast iron cap automatic, STEVENS, 1938, "Patented; Made in U.S.A.", 5¼"	25.00	30.00	35.00	ZIP cast iron cap pistol, HUBLEY, 1930, 5"	15.00	20.00	25.00
				ZIP cast iron cap pistol, HUBLEY, 1938, 6"	15.00	20.00	25.00
XTRA cast iron cap pistol, KENTON, 1936, "Made in U.S.A.", 5" long	15.00	20.00	25.00	ZULU cast iron cap pistol, maker unknown, 1890, 6⅝", has decoration of African warrior with spear pursuing bird	75.00	125.00	150.00

Wyandotte Toys
"ARE GOOD AND SAFE"

No. 1427 PISTOL HOLSTER AND BELT

No. 1926 PISTOL HOLSTER AND BELT

No. 3329 MODERNISTIC PISTOL HOLSTER AND BELT

No. 33 REPEATER

No. 34 DOUBLE BARREL POP GUN

No. 14 CLICKER PISTOL

.. AND THE Safest Bet FOR A REALLY PROFITABLE 4th OF July ....

EVERYWHERE the tendency is more and more toward having children celebrate Independence Day in a safe, sane manner, which means that each year at this time, Wyandotte Guns and Pistols are more and more in demand—for they enable youngsters to enjoy the spirit of this holiday to its fullest and yet encounter no danger. These toys produce a loud report and, like all Wyandotte Toys, are absolutely harmless.

The Wyandotte Line of pop and clicker guns and pistols is unusually complete and contains a wide variety of popular numbers in addition to those shown. Send for the new Wyandotte 1935 Catalog and plan now for the biggest 4th of July business you have ever enjoyed.

All Metal Products Co.
WYANDOTTE, MICHIGAN

AIRCRAFT
(See also Tin Wind-Up, Comic Character, Premiums and Paper)

Aircraft in the last edition averaged $88.10 in mint condition, and this year averaged $112.23, an increase of 27%.

CONDITION OF A TOY AND ITS RELATION TO PRICE

The price of a toy depends not only on its desirability, but on its condition. A toy in mint condition is generally worth twice what that same toy would bring in good condition, with "very good" falling about equally in between good and mint.

"Mint"means just that; the condition in which it was originally issued — perfect, regardless of age, not the slightest blemish. Needless to say this is a fairly rare state of affairs, but enough toys exist in mint condition to make it an employable term. Many people hoping to dispose of items are tempted to call a toy "mint" when it is really "near mint", "very good", or sometimes even just "good", Inevitably this can result in unhappiness all around, and not infrequently, a cancelled sale.

"Very Good" indicates a toy which has obviously seen use, with signs of wear and aging, but in general having a freshness to its appearance that makes it attractive and collectible to all but the most discriminating.

"Good" signals a toy that has seen considerable wear, shows its age, but is basically sound. A collector will collect it, but will often not be wholly satisfied with it as an example of his collection, and thus prices are often drastically below that which the same item in mint can command.

Condition below good results in another drastic drop in price, and toys with missing parts, although otherwise in excellent condition, will usually fall into this lower-priced category. Rust, even small spots of it, can seriously lower the price of a toy. "Near Mint", "Fine", "Very Fine" and similar terms often found in sellers' descriptions denote conditions between Mint and Very Good, and are priced accordingly.

The key to grading is to avoid wishful thinking. Grading can sometimes be a problem for the uninitiated, but common sense will usually prevail, and when possible, a consultation with an expert in the field can often clear up lingering doubts. A toy in its original box is worth up to 10 to 20% more if the box is in mint condition, with the price dropping as condition lessens.

	G	VG	M
A.C. GILBERT "Erector" Biplane, with electric motor	40.00	60.00	80.00
ADAM BOMB, circa 1946, wingspan approx. 11", wood and metal	22.00	33.00	44.00
AIRACUDA, 8½" wingspan, circa 1940, blue pressed steel	6.00	9.00	12.00
AIRFORD, small, cast iron, two-passenger, steel wheels, single engine	14.00	21.00	28.00
AIRPLANE, early 1900s, single wing, prop behind tail, pilot, open fuselage	300.00	450.00	600.00
AIRPLANE, wood, ride-on	20.00	30.00	40.00
Airport Set No. 88 by T. COHN CO., circa 1940s. Mechanical tin litho airport with early plastic planes that fly. Control tower controls for stunts, crash truck pumps water, airport bus, gasoline truck, etc.	17.50	26.25	35.00
AMC No. 361 Airplane, twin engine, 5" wingspan, United Boeing embossed on top of wings	75.00	112.50	150.00

A.C. GILBERT "Erector" Biplane, incomplete in photo.
Photo by Bill Kaufman, courtesy Good Old Days Store

	G	VG	M
AMERICAN FLYER Spirit of America, 18" wingspan, 1928	100.00	150.00	200.00
AMERICAN FLYER Spirit of Columbia, "555", pressed tin friction, 18" wingspan	500.00	750.00	1000.
"ANCIENT ART METAL CO., Brooklyn N.Y." Spirit of St. Louis, lead, 5-1/8" wingspan, circa 1927 "Pat. No. 74042"	24.00	36.00	48.00
ARCADE Airplane, cast iron, 6" long	60.00	90.00	120.00
AUBURN RUBBER Clipper plane, 4-engine, apporx. 7" wingspan, USA on port wing, number on starboard wing, circa 1941	3.00	4.50	6.00

Adam Bomb
Courtesy Good Old Days Store, Photo by Bill Kaufman

BARCLAY single-engine "U.S. Army" transport
Photo by Bill Kaufman

"Ancient Art Metal Co." Lindy-type plane
Photo by Bill Kaufman, Courtesy Good Old Days Store

BARCLAY Monoplane, single engine, early
Photo by Bill Kaufman

BARCLAY Lindy-type plane, Dirigible.
Photo by Bill Kaufman, Courtesy Evelyn Besse

	G	VG	M
AUBURN RUBBER ground attack or dive bomber, 4" wingspan, low wing, closed cockpit monoplane, air-cooled engine marked AUB-RUBR under fuselage, circa 1937.....	3.00	4.50	6.00
AUBURN RUBBER pursuit ship, P-40 type, approx. 4" wingspan, US21755 on wings circa 1941.......	3.00	4.50	6.00
AUBURN RUBBER two-engine transport plane, circa 1937............	3.00	4.50	6.00
AUTOGYRO, 6" long, pressed steel, wheels turn blades via gear mechanism............	12.00	18.00	24.00
AUTOMATIC TOY CO. Rocket and Space Ship, No. 305, Friction, tin litho with rubber wheels, sparks, 9" long, 4½" wide, 3" tall, late thirties.	25.00	37.50	50.00

	G	VG	M
AUTOMATIC TOY CO. Silver Eagle aluminum plane, 13" wingspan, wooden wheels, two-engine, 1930s..........	20.00	30.00	40.00
BARCLAY Dirigible, approx. 4-3/8" long, early-mid 30s.............	2.50	3.75	5.00
BARCLAY Lindy-type plane, wingspan approx. 4", early-mid 30s.......	2.50	3.75	5.00
BARCLAY monoplane, single engine, Crackajack size, one-piece, Lindy type, early............	4.00	6.00	8.00

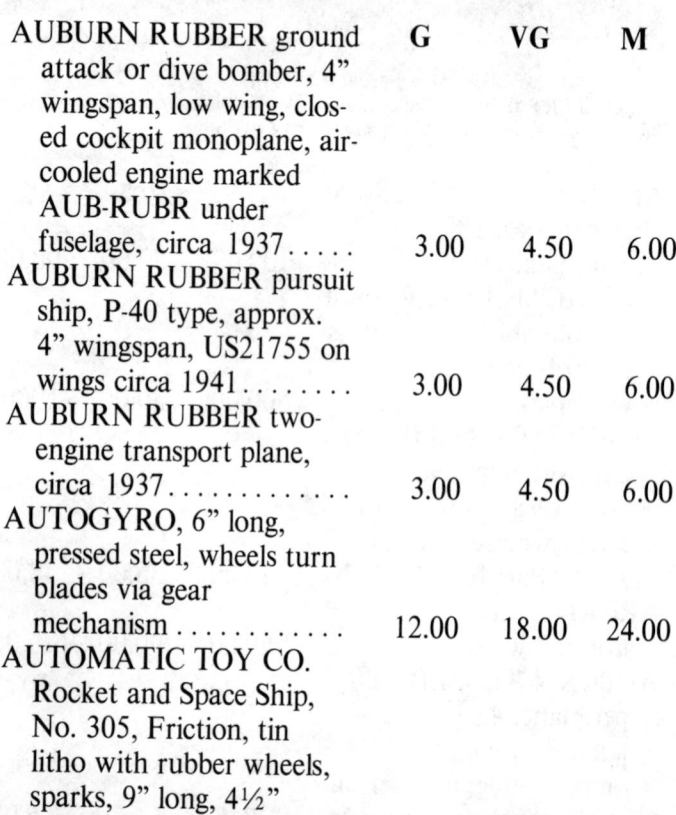

	G	VG	M
BARCLAY monoplane, single engine, slush lead unpainted body, red propellor and red metal wheels	5.00	7.50	10.00
BARCLAY "U.S. Army", small pursuit plane, lead rubber wheels, circa 1941	4.00	6.00	8.00
BARCLAY "U.S. Army" single engine transport, Tootsietoy size, white rubber wheels, circa 1940	2.50	3.75	5.00
BELL AIRACOBRA, pot metal and tin, 4¼"x5¼", "U.S. Army"	11.00	16.50	22.00
BIPLANE, wooden, approx. 7½" wingspan, tin tail, aluminum propellor, pull plane, propellor spins	35.00	52.50	70.00
BOMBER, 4-engine pressed steel, two wooden bombs that drop when button pressed, wooden wheels, wingspan approx. 14"	17.50	26.25	35.00
BUDDY "L" triple hangar and three planes No. 5010, 1931, planes are monocoupes	200.00	300.00	400.00

	G	VG	M
DC-4 type, four-motor passenger, circa 1930s, pressed steel	10.00	15.00	20.00
DENT "Air Express", cast iron, 12" wingspread, sample	380.00	570.00	760.00
DENT "Los Angeles" dirigible, 6¾", circa 1932	120.00	180.00	240.00
DENT "Los Angeles" dirigible, 8½" cast iron, circa 1925	100.00	150.00	200.00
DENT "Lucky Boy", circa 1932	200.00	300.00	400.00
FIGHTER, tin, circa 1940, single engine, four machine guns mounted on wing	15.00	22.50	30.00

DENT "Los Angeles" dirigible

DENT "Lucky Boy" Glider

	G	VG	M
BUDDY "L" Monoplane and Catapult Hangar, 1930-31, No. 2007	75.00	112.50	150.00
BUDDY L single high wing, monoplane, 1929-31 No. 5000	25.00	37.50	50.00
CHEIN Helicopter-Toy Town Airways, litho 13" long, 5½" tall, 1950s	20.00	30.00	40.00
CURTISS TRANSPORT, 9½" wingspan, khaki, pressed steel	4.00	6.00	8.00
DC-3 TRANSPORT, 10" wingspan, pressed steel, circa 1939	3.00	4.50	6.00

	G	VG	M
"FLAGSHIP AMERICA" airplane, metal FORD Tri-Motor, pressed steel, 1930s, 25" wingspan	30.00	45.00	60.00
GIRARD High-Wing Monoplane, 10" wingspan, pressed steel	70.00	105.00	140.00
GIRARD High-Wing Monoplane, 18" wingspan, pressed steel	23.00	34.50	46.00
GIRARD Whiz Skyfighter biplane, early	20.00	30.00	40.00
GLASS AIRPLANE, candy container	5.50	8.25	11.00

GRAF ZEPPELIN, 32" long, pull toy, STEEL CRAFT CO., Murray Ohio	G	VG	M
GRAF ZEPPELIN, 32" long, pull toy, STEEL CRAFT CO., Murray Ohio	150.00	225.00	300.00
HELICOPTER, Army, 13" long, tin litho, friction drive, spinning prop	2.50	3.75	5.00
HUBLEY "America", cast iron, large, trimotor open cockpit, pilot, copilot	800.00	1200.00	1600.00
HUBLEY American Eagle, metal carrier plane. Wings fold, wheels retract and cockpit opens, 9½" long 11" wingspan, 1971	8.00	12.00	16.00
HUBLEY B-17 Bomber, 15" wingspan	40.00	60.00	80.00
HUBLEY Bremen Junkers, single engine monoplane	140.00	210.00	280.00
HUBLEY Corsair-type fighter (wings fold)	9.00	13.50	18.00

HUBLEY DO-X, circa 1935, 5-⅞" wingspan, 6" long, six engines	G	VG	M
HUBLEY DO-X, circa 1935, 5-⅞" wingspan, 6" long, six engines	No Price Found		
HUBLEY Flying Circus, 10" long	5.00	7.50	10.00
HUBLEY "Lindy", 10" wingspan, cast iron	250.00	375.00	500.00
HUBLEY "Lindy", 13¼" wingspan, cast iron	400.00	600.00	800.00
HUBLEY P-38, black rubber tires	8.00	12.00	16.00
HUBLEY piper Cub, pot metal, circa 1940s 5"x8"	11.00	16.50	22.00
HUBLEY Single-Engine fighter, similar to P-40, 3½"	7.50	11.25	15.00
HUBLEY "U.S. Army" plane, folding wheels, 7⅝" wingspan, circa 1941, single engine monoplane	6.50	9.75	13.00

ID MODELS

ID airplane models were manufactured during World War II (and later) at the request of the Navy (initially) and the Army. The craft were manufactured from a variety of materials, including reinforced plaster, papier mache, a hard rubber-like substance, and finally cellulose acetate plastic. Companies manufacturing the planes included V. Roxor Short of Clinton, Ct., L.A. Darling Co., Coldwater, Mich., George Benckenstein, Cincinnati, and Design Center of New York City, with Comet Engraving, H&H Specialty Co. and the Cruver Company, all of Chicago, handling most of the master design and diemaking. By 1961, when production ended, about 425 different planes (or variations of them) had been manufactured. At least one enterprising manufacturer produced more than the military required, and sold them to the public through leading department stores.

ID MODEL "B-17 British Fortress 2", 17" wingspan	17.50	26.25	35.00
ID MODEL "German Junkers 86K" 10" long, copyright 1942	17.50	26.25	35.00
ID MODEL "German Me. 210", 7" long, copyright 1943	17.50	26.25	35.00
ID MODEL P-40, 6" wingspan	6.00	9.00	12.00
ID MODEL PV-2, two engine bomber	4.00	6.00	8.00
JET, USAF, 5" wingspan, friction-powered, tin litho	2.00	3.00	4.00
KD-1 Mak-a-plane—4" long, mechanical, all metal with rubber wheels, 1940s	8.00	12.00	16.00
KEYSTONE Mail Plane, single wing, above fuselage, 24" long	60.00	90.00	120.00

KEYSTONE riding plane, seat over tail, steering bar over cabin, single wing, high, one engine, 23½" long	125.00	187.50	250.00
KEYSTONE riding plane, 28" wingspan, No. 293, "Ride Em" fighter	42.50	63.75	85.00
KILGORE, Seagull, high wing, pusher prop	100.00	150.00	200.00
KINGSBURY Biplane, 15¾" long, circa WWI	200.00	300.00	400.00
KINGSBURY Monoplane, high wing, trimotor, 15" wingspan, clockwork	200.00	300.00	400.00
KINGSBURY Tin Goose, tri-engine, 21" wingspan, 1930s	600.00	900.00	1200.00
KINGSBURY "Trans Atlantic" monoplane, painted pressed steel wind-up, 1930, 11" long	90.00	135.00	180.00

KEYSTONE Riding Airplane, 28" wingspan, No.293 "Ride 'Em"
Fighter.
Courtesy Bob Black Jr.

MARX Pan American 4-motor, 1940, 27"
wingspan
Courtesy Lloyd W. Ralston Auctions

MANOIL Airplanes, L to R: 517, 518, 519, 520
Courtesy Peter and Marjorie Ruben

KINGSBURY "Trans
Atlantic" Monoplane
Courtesy Lloyd W.
Ralston Auctions

	G	VG	M
KINGSBURY "U.S. Air-mail" biplane, 15" long, steel windup	130.00	195.00	260.00
"LINDY" cast iron, nickel prop and wheels, 3½" wingspan	28.00	42.00	56.00
LINDY-TYPE Plane, lead, 2¼" wingspan	2.50	3.75	5.00
LUSCOMBE Airplane, 4" long	30.00	45.00	60.00
MANOIL No. 517, Lockheed F90	3.00	4.50	6.00
MANOIL No. 518 Navion.	5.00	7.50	10.00
MANOIL No. 519 Bonanza B-35	10.00	15.00	20.00
MANOIL No. 520 Ercoupe	10.00	15.00	20.00
MARX "Army Bomber" No. 1025, tri-motor, 26" wingspan, circa 1935	75.00	112.50	150.00
MARX bomber, 18" wingspan, tin litho, sparkling mechanism, camouflaged, four-engine	35.00	52.50	70.00
MARX Friction-powered four-motor transport with whirling propellors, tin litho	9.00	13.50	18.00
MARX Pan American 4-motor, propellor driven,			

	G	VG	M
27" wingspan, 1940 pressed steel	33.00	49.50	66.00
MARX "Pioneer Air Express", 25½" wingspan, tin litho, high wing monoplane	50.00	75.00	100.00
MARX "Sky Cruiser" Two-motored Transport Plane with siren and whirling propellors, Stratoliner 700 18" wingspan, rubber wheels, 1940s	11.00	16.50	22.00
MARX sparkling Rocket Fighter No. 1425, tin litho	9.00	13.50	18.00
MARX Universal Airport with two metal planes	12.50	18.75	25.00
METAL CAST No. 66 Aeroplane, approx. 4½" wingspan, 2-engine, circa 1940s, lead	1.50	2.25	3.00

METAL CAST No. 66 Aeroplane
Photo by Norbert Schachter

METALCRAFT Spirit of St. Louis, 9" long
Courtesy Mapes Auctioneers & Appraisers

	G	VG	M
METALCRAFT Build-A-Zep, builds 21 different 18" zeppelins	64.00	96.00	128.00
METALCRAFT Northrup? Monoplane, wingspan approx. 17", "PURE the Pure Oil Company"	200.00	300.00	400.00
METAL CRAFT Riding Rocket, 24" long	3.00	4.50	6.00
METALCRAFT Spirit of St. Louis, 9" long, came as kit	20.00	30.00	40.00
OHIO ART "Sea Patrol Plane", 9" long, pontoons, moves on water, early 40s wind-up	30.00	45.00	60.00
OHIO ART Seaplane "Hot Job" tin litho, checkerboard wings, spinning propellor, 10" wingspan, 3½" long, 1950s	14.00	21.00	28.00
P-38 glass candy container	15.00	22.50	30.00
Passenger Plane, high-wing, four-engine, approx. 9" wingspan, three wooden wheels	9.00	13.50	18.00
PEDAL CAR, Biplane, 2-motor, 54" long	300.00	450.00	600.00
"PONY BLIMP", 1930,			

	G	VG	M
KILGORE, cast iron, 5¾" long, metal wheels	40.00	60.00	80.00
PULL-TOY, metal airplane	25.00	37.60	50.00
RENWAL B-25, 6¾" wingspan, plastic, circa 1944	5.00	7.50	10.00
"SKY CRUISER" tin litho, 18" wingspan, 2-motor transport, engines turn with friction mechanism	15.00	22.50	30.00
"SPIRIT OF AMERICA" pull toy aeroplane, 14" long, steel and litho	12.00	18.00	24.00
"SPIRIT OF ST. LOUIS", cast iron, 4"x4"	25.00	37.50	50.00
SPIRIT OF ST. LOUIS glass candy container, 4⅜" long	150.00	225.00	300.00
SPIRIT OF ST. LOUIS, 11" wingspread, cast iron	75.00	112.50	150.00
STEELCRAFT "Army Scout Plane", single engine, 22½" wingspan, high-wing, monoplane, 1920s	112.50	168.75	225.00
STEELCRAFT "Army Scout Plane", trimotor, single high wing, 1920s	100.00	150.00	200.00

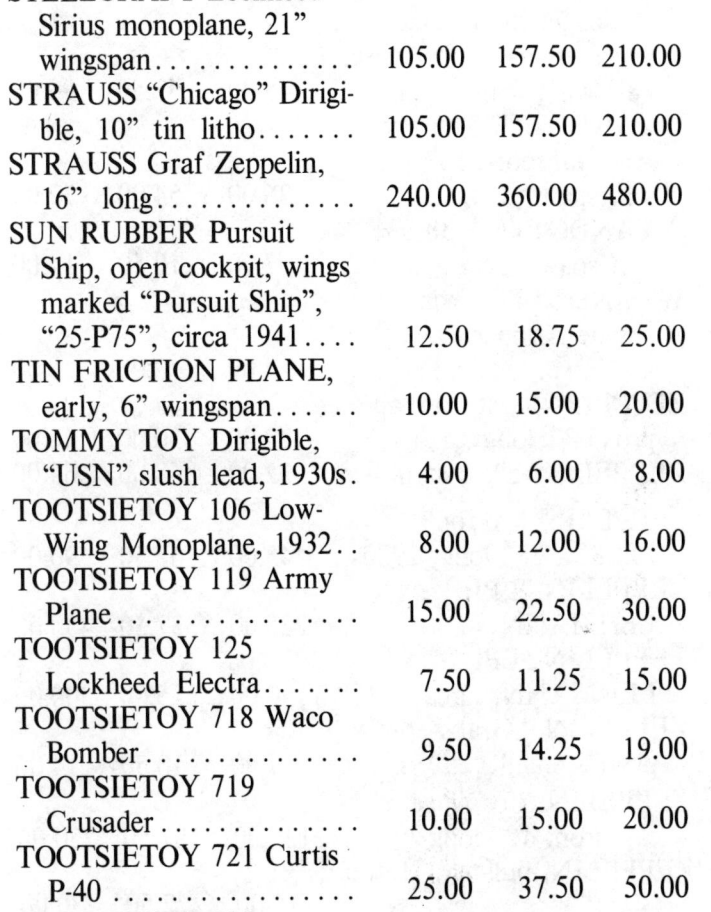

TOOTSIETOY Top Row, L to R: 4649 Tri-Motor Plane, 04460 Aero-Dawn, 4650 Biplane, 4675 Wings, High-Wing Floatplane, Middle Row: 04650 Autogyro, 718 Waco Bomber, 719 Crusader, Bottom Row L to R: 119 Army Plane, 125 Lockheed Electra, 0717 TWA Douglas Airliner, DC4 Super Mainliner.
Photo by Ed Poole

TOMMY TOY "U.S.N." Dirigible
Photo by Bill Kaufman, Courtesy Charles E. Weldon, Jr.

Hubley DO-X

	G	VG	M
STEELCRAFT "Akron" blimp pull toy, 25" long.	55.00	82.50	110.00
STEELCRAFT "Graf Zeppelin" 30½" pressed steel pull toy..............	50.00	75.00	100.00
STEELCRAFT Lockheed Sirius monoplane, 21" wingspan...............	105.00	157.50	210.00
STRAUSS "Chicago" Dirigible, 10" tin litho.......	105.00	157.50	210.00
STRAUSS Graf Zeppelin, 16" long..............	240.00	360.00	480.00
SUN RUBBER Pursuit Ship, open cockpit, wings marked "Pursuit Ship", "25-P75", circa 1941....	12.50	18.75	25.00
TIN FRICTION PLANE, early, 6" wingspan......	10.00	15.00	20.00
TOMMY TOY Dirigible, "USN" slush lead, 1930s.	4.00	6.00	8.00
TOOTSIETOY 106 Low-Wing Monoplane, 1932..	8.00	12.00	16.00
TOOTSIETOY 119 Army Plane...............	15.00	22.50	30.00
TOOTSIETOY 125 Lockheed Electra.......	7.50	11.25	15.00
TOOTSIETOY 718 Waco Bomber..............	9.50	14.25	19.00
TOOTSIETOY 719 Crusader.............	10.00	15.00	20.00
TOOTSIETOY 721 Curtis P-40	25.00	37.50	50.00
TOOTSIETOY 722 Transport Plane, 1941...	8.00	12.00	16.00
TOOTSIETOY 0001 P-38..	11.00	16.50	22.00
TOOTSIETOY 0002 KOP-1 USN	10.00	15.00	20.00
TOOTSIETOY 0003 F9F-2 Panther.............	5.00	7.50	10.00

	G	VG	M
TOOTSIETOY 0007 2-engine airliner, 10 windows each side........	6.00	9.00	12.00
TOOTSIETOY 0008 S-58 Sikorsky Helicopter.....	7.50	11.25	15.00
TOOTSIETOY 0009 Navy Jet Cutlass...........	4.00	6.00	8.00
TOOTSIETOY 0717 Douglas D-C 2 TWA Airliner..............	10.50	15.75	21.00
TOOTSIETOY 0720 Fly-N-Gyro, 1938............	15.00	22.50	30.00
TOOTSIETOY 4482 Bleriot, 1910..........	No Price Found		
TOOTSIETOY 4491 Bleriot, 1910 (smaller)...	No Price Found		
TOOTSIETOY 4649 Tri-Motor Plane..........	25.00	37.50	50.00
TOOTSIETOY 4650 Biplane	20.00	30.00	40.00
TOOTSIETOY 4659 Autogyro	20.00	30.00	40.00
TOOTSIETOY 4675 Wings	12.50	18.75	25.00
TOOTSIETOY 4675 Wings seaplane	12.50	18.75	25.00
TOOTSIETOY 4850 Shooting Star.........	4.00	6.00	8.00
TOOTSIETOY 04650 Autogyro	13.00	19.50	26.00
TOOTSIETOY 04660 Aero-Dawn	12.50	18.75	25.00
TOOTSIETOY 04660 Aero-Dawn seaplane........	12.50	18.75	25.00

324

	G	VG	M
TOOTSIETOY "Atlantic Clipper", approx. 2" long	2.00	3.00	4.00
TOOTSIETOY Beechcraft Bonanza	6.00	9.00	12.00
TOOTSIETOY DC 4 Supermainliner	8.00	12.00	16.00
TOOTSIETOY Navion....	5.50	8.25	11.00
TOOTSIETOY Piper Cub..	6.50	9.75	13.00
TOOTSIETOY "Tootsietoy Airport", hanger and two planes	220.00	330.00	440.00
TOOTSIETOY U.S. Moon Rocket, 3 types, all have 2 wheels to run on string, mid-1960s, replicas of original Buck Rogers spaceships (see Comic Character)............	3.50	5.25	7.00
TOOTSIETOY "U.S.N. Los Angeles" dirigible, two grooved wheels on top to run on string (also was sold as part of Buck Rogers set)...........	21.00	31.50	42.00

TOOTSIETOY "U.S.N. Los Angeles" dirigible, also sold as part of Buck Rogers set, 1937
Photo by Ed Poole

	G	VG	M
Transport Plane, pressed steel, approx. 12" wingspan, four-engine...	12.50	18.75	25.00
TURNER High Wing Monoplane, 18½" wingspan, one engine, 1930s	100.00	150.00	200.00
"UNITED BOEING", two engine cast iron, circa 1941, small...........	16.00	24.00	32.00
"U.S." high-wing monoplane, single engine, 8" wingspan, open iron-work body, spool wheel works prop...........	200.00	300.00	400.00
UX83, cast iron, 3¼" wingspan..............	30.00	45.00	60.00
"UX-99" cast iron, wingspan approx. 4½"..	14.00	21.00	28.00

	G	VG	M
"UX-166", Lindy-type plane, wingspan approx. 5¾", cast iron, nickeled engine and wheels	40.00	60.00	80.00
WATROUS single engine biplane, pressed steel bell toy, 8¼" wingspan, circa 1915	153.00	229.50	306.00
WYANDOTTE Airliner, circa WWII, two engine, wooden wheels........	4.00	6.00	8.00
WYANDOTTE American Airlines Flagship plane, 28" wingspan..........	44.00	66.00	88.00
WYANDOTTE Bomber, Army, pressed steel, two-engine	9.00	13.50	18.00
WYANDOTTE China Clipper, 13" wingspan......	31.00	46.50	62.00
WYANDOTTE City Airport, American Airlines, two hangars, control tower, etc., lights up....	40.00	60.00	80.00
WYANDOTTE High Wing Passenger monoplane, single engine, bullet nose, 18" wingspan..........	45.00	67.50	90.00
WYANDOTTE Military Air Transport, 13" wingspan..............	36.00	54.00	72.00
WYANDOTTE P-38 9¾" wingspan..............	7.00	10.50	14.00
WYANDOTTE Twin engine Airliner, early 4¾"	4.00	6.00	8.00
ZEPPELIN, cast iron, approx. 3" long..........	20.00	30.00	40.00
ZEPPELIN, 5", cast iron..	32.00	48.00	64.00
ZEPPELIN, "Akron", MARX, 28" long, 1930s.	45.00	67.50	90.00
ZEPPELIN "EPL 1", LEHMANN	225.00	337.50	450.00
ZEPPELIN "EPL 2", LEHMANN, circa 1917?	150.00	225.00	300.00
ZEPPELIN, "Graf Zeppelin", small..........	7.00	10.50	14.00
ZEPPELIN, "Los Angeles", cast iron, 12" long......	125.00	187.50	250.00
ZEPPELIN, pull-toy, "Little Giant"................	15.00	22.50	30.00
ZEPPELIN pull-toy, "Macon"...............	15.00	22.50	30.00
ZEPPELIN "Pony DE 107", cast iron, 5½" long	30.00	45.00	60.00
ZEPPELIN, "Sky Ranger", 9" long..............	7.50	11.25	15.00

	G	VG	M
ZEPPELIN "U.S. Akron", potmetal, circa 1932, 6" long	25.00	37.50	50.00
ZEPPELIN, "ZEP", cast iron, 4" long	30.00	45.00	60.00
ZEPPELIN, "ZEP", cast iron, 6¾" long DENT . .	45.00	67.50	90.00
ZEPPELIN, "Goodyear" decals, 25" long, hatch opens	80.00	120.00	160.00
ZEPPELIN, 6" long, silver, pull toy, circa 1920-30s, cast iron	30.00	45.00	60.00
ZEPPELIN, metal, 25" long	20.00	30.00	40.00
ZEPPELIN, metal, 26½" long	20.00	30.00	40.00
ZEPPELIN, metal, 27½" long	30.00	45.00	60.00

WYANDOTTE high wing passenger monoplane, bullet nose.

SHIPS
(see also Tin Wind-Up, Paper)

Mint prices in this category averaged $244.36 in the last edition, and in this edition averaged $287.84, an increase of 18%.

CONDITION OF A TOY AND ITS RELATION TO PRICE

The price of a toy depends not only on its desirability, but on its condition. A toy in mint condition is generally worth twice what that same toy would bring in good condition, with "very good" falling about equally in between good and mint.

"Mint" means just that; the condition in which it was originally issued — perfect, regardless of age, not the slightest blemish. Needless to say this is a fairly rare state of affairs, but enough toys exist in mint condition to make it an employable term. Many people hoping to dispose of toys are tempted to call an item "mint" when it is really "near mint", "very good" or sometimes just "good". Inevitably this can result in unhappiness all around, and not infrequently, a cancelled sale.

"Very Good" indicates a toy which has obviously seen use, with signs of wear and aging, but in general having a freshness to its appearance that makes it attractive and collectible to all but the most discriminating.

"Good" signals a toy that has seen considerable wear, shows its age, but is basically sound. A collector will collect it, but will often not be wholly satisfied with it as an example of his collection, and thus prices are often drastically below that which the same item in mint can command.

Condition below good results in another drastic drop in price, and toys with missing parts, although otherwise in excellent condition, will usually fall into this lower-priced category. Rust, even small spots of it, can seriously lower the price of a toy. "Near Mint", "Fine", "Very Fine" and similar terms often found in sellers' descriptions denote conditions between Mint and Very Good, and are priced accordingly.

The key to grading is to avoid wishful thinking. Grading can sometimes be a problem for the uninitiated, but common sense will usually prevail, and when possible, a consultation with an expert in the field can often clear up lingering doubts. A toy in its original box is worth up to 10 to 20% more if the box is in mint condition, with the price dropping as its condition lessens.

	G	VG	M
"ADIRONDACK" Sidewheeler, cast iron, approx. 13" long	260.00	390.00	520.00
ADMIRAL DEWEY'S FLAGSHIP from the White Fleet, wood and paper, 6" long	14.00	21.00	28.00
ADMIRAL DEWEY FLAGSHIP Paper litho on wood, 30" long, c. 1900	150.00	225.00	300.00
Aircraft Carrier "Libertania", wood and tin litho ship with lead planes, 27¾" long	30.00	45.00	60.00

Aircraft Carrier "Libertania"
Courtesy Mapes Auctioneers & Appraisers

	G	VG	M
AIRCRAFT CARRIER "65", tin litho, large, circa 1950s	10.00	15.00	20.00

	G	VG	M
ARCADE "Showboat", cast iron, approx. 10¾" long, circa 1934	375.00	562.00	750.00
"ATOMIC SUBMARINE", remote-controlled, tin litho	10.00	15.00	20.00
ATWOOD MOTORS, CALIFORNIA "Amazon Side-Wheeler", plastic and metal, circa 1950s	125.00	187.50	250.00
AUBURN RUBBER Battleship, 8¼" long, circa 1941	3.85	5.77	7.70
AUBURN RUBBER Cruiser	3.85	5.77	7.70
AUBURN RUBBER Freighter, 8" long, circa 1941	4.00	6.00	8.00
AUBURN RUBBER Submarine, 6½" long, circa 1941	3.00	4.50	6.00
AUTHENTICAST French warships including Richelieu, Algiers, Fantasque and others, each	20.00	30.00	40.00
AUTHENTICAST German Warships, scale models including Narvik, Galster and others, each	20.00	30.00	40.00

"Baby" cast iron racing boat
Photo by Bill Kaufman
Courtesy Good Old Days Store

Battleship "Admiral", 1890, 20"
long
Courtesy Lloyd W. Ralston
Auctions

BLISS Battleship New York, 36"
long
Courtesy Lloyd W. Ralston
Auctions

	G	VG	M
BATTLESHIP, Tin Friction, 9½" long, circa 1920s	48.00	72.00	96.00
BATTLESHIP "U.S.S. Washington", tin litho, circa 1941, MARX	12.50	18.75	36.00
BATTLESHIP "U.S.S. Washington", MARX, camouflaged tin litho, circa 1941	18.00	27.00	36.00
"BIG BANG BATTLESHIP", 8¼" long . . .	25.00	37.50	50.00
BIG BANG GUNBOAT, 8" long, cast iron, early	15.00	22.50	30.00
BLISS "Battleship New York" paper litho and stained wood, 1890 36"x22'	320.00	480.00	640.00
BLISS "Marguerite" sailing schooner, 22" long	250.00	375.00	500.00
BOAT, Hot Air, tin with driver, 9" long	25.00	37.50	50.00
BOAT, pull motor, metal . . .	25.00	37.50	50.00
BOAT, tin friction, lithographed	20.00	30.00	40.00
BOAT, tin friction, painted, early	15.00	22.50	30.00
BOAT, tin friction, painted, early	60.00	90.00	120.00
BOAT, tin friction, 13" long, two smokestacks, four lifeboats	40.00	60.00	80.00

	G	VG	M
AUTHENTICAST Japanese Warships including Fuso, Kaga, Mogani and others, each	20.00	30.00	40.00
AUTHENTICAST U.S. Scale Model Warships, World War II including: Iowa, Enterprise, Sims and Farragut, and submarine Sarge, each	20.00	30.00	40.00
B-LO submarine, metal, pat. no. 1318048	40.00	60.00	80.00
"BABY" cast iron racing boat, circa 1930, wheeled, 4½" long, HUBLEY? . . .	17.50	26.25	35.00
BATTLESHIP "Admiral" paper litho 1890, 20" long	140.00	210.00	280.00
BATTLESHIP, cast iron, 14½" long	120.00	180.00	240.00
BATTLESHIP "Columbia", paper and wood, 1882, 36" long	235.00	352.50	470.00
BATTLESHIP, glass, approx. 3" long, candy container	4.00	6.00	8.00
BATTLESHIP, HILLCLIMBER, 15" long, pressed steel	80.00	120.00	160.00
BATTLESHIP, lead, may be BARCLAY	4.00	6.00	8.00
BATTLESHIP Oregon, 25" long, paper litho and wood	110.00	165.00	220.00
BATTLESHIP "Rover", paper litho and wood, 20" long	110.00	165.00	220.00

Boat, tin friction, 13" long, two smokestacks, four lifeboats
Courtesy PB 84 New York

	G	VG	M
BOUCHER "Gee Whiz" speedboat, painted sheetmetal, heavy clockwork motor, bronze propellor, 25" long	140.00	210.00	280.00

BUDDY L No. 3000 Tugboat
Photo Courtesy Thomas W. Sefton

"Columbia" riverboat, 1890, 2' long
Courtesy Lloyd W. Ralston Auctions

FALLOWS "Jumbo" riverboat, 14" long
Courtesy Lloyd W. Ralston

	G	VG	M
BRADLEY "Columbia" side paddlewheeler, paper litho on wood, 24" long, c. 1890	80.00	120.00	160.00
BUDDY L No. 3000 Tugboat, 1929-30	750.00	1125.00	1500.00
"C.C. JR." Brass-mounted Wood Boat, wind-up motor concealed within the rudder controlled from the wheel in the circular cockpit with a start-stop lever, 14½" long	40.00	60.00	80.00
CANOE, Wood, 6" long	5.00	7.50	10.00
CHEIN speedboat, 14" long	3.50	5.25	7.00
"Columbia" riverboat, 1890, paper litho, tin litho, wood, working walking beam, 2' long	280.00	420.00	560.00
CRUISER, glass approx. 3" long, candy container	4.00	6.00	8.00
DAYTON Battleship, 16" long, friction, circa 1920	80.00	120.00	160.00
DENT ADIRONDACK, 15" long, cast iron	160.00	240.00	320.00
DENT Battleship New York, circa 1900, 21",			

	G	VG	M
largest cast iron boat made	490.00	735.00	980.00
DESTROYER, on wheels, 12" long, cast iron	700.00	1050.00	1400.00
FALLOWS "Constitution" sidewheeler, 10" long	1500.00	2250.00	3000.00
FALLOWS "Jumbo" river-boat, side-wheel, painted tin, 1880, 14" long, mechanical walking beam	400.00	600.00	800.00
FALLOWS "Volunteer IXL", 16" long	700.00	1050.00	1400.00
"Ferry Go" twin pad-dlewheel ferry boat pull toy, tin litho 14" long	50.00	75.00	100.00
FLEISCHMANN Ocean Liner, 1930, painted tin clockwork, working, 20½" long	200.00	300.00	400.00
GEORGE BROWN "Atlantic" sidewheel riverboat, painted and stenciled tin, 14" long	1100.00	1650.00	2200.00

FLEISCHMANN Ocean Liner, 1930, 20½" long
Courtesy Lloyd W. Ralston Auctions

GEORGE BROWN "Atlantic" sidewheel riverboat, 14" long
Courtesy Lloyd W. Ralston Auction

	G	VG	M
GUNBOAT, tin friction, large wheel rises above deck, circa early 1920s, smokestack	50.00	75.00	100.00
GUNBOAT, tin friction, rocks back and forth on wheels, 10" long	45.00	67.50	90.00
GUNBOAT, 19" long, friction	90.00	135.00	180.00
GUNBOAT, two guns, 2 small stacks, 2 stories above deck, wheeled, friction, 1920s or earlier	60.00	90.00	120.00
HILL CLIMBER pressed steel battleship, 18" long	212.50	318.75	425.00

KEYSTONE Aircraft Carrier, wooden, 12" long
Courtesy Mapes Auctioneers & Appraisers

	G	VG	M
HUBLEY "Penn Yan" motorboat, 15" long, 5 people, very rare, unauthorized by Penn Yan, which stopped Hubley's production.....	1000.00	1500.00	2000.00
IDEAL Varsity Racing Scull, 8 rowers, coxswain, 1890, 14" long, cast iron, oars move...........	900.00	1350.00	1800.00
IVES "Miss Liberty" speedboat, 13½" long, steam-powered	225.00	337.50	450.00
IVES U.S. Merchant Marine Boat, painted pressed tin clockwork...	200.00	300.00	400.00

IVES, U.S. Merchant Marine, painted pressed tin clockwork.

	G	VG	M
IVES "Vim" speedboat, 10½" long...........	100.00	150.00	200.00
IVES "Vixen" speedboat, 12" long.............	90.00	135.00	180.00
"JOHNSON'S SEA HORSE" cast iron speedboat with figure, 10½" long.................	300.00	450.00	600.00
"KEARSAGE" gunboat, 13¾" long, cast iron....	90.00	135.00	180.00

"Kearsage" gunboat
Courtesy PB 84 New York

	G	VG	M
KEYSTONE Aircraft Carrier, wooden, 12" long...	9.00	13.50	18.00
KEYSTONE Battleship, wooden, approx. 2' long with guns, airplanes take off from a spring on deck of ship..........	9.00	13.50	18.00

	G	VG	M
KEYSTONE Battleship, under 2' length, early 1940s	3.00	4.50	6.00
KEYSTONE Ferryboat, wooden, circa 1930s, two wood cars, two wood trucks, 14" long........	30.00	35.00	60.00
KEYSTONE fishing boat, wooden, 12" long, circa 1940s	8.00	12.00	16.00
KINGSBURY Boat, 10" long.................	20.00	30.00	40.00
LIFE BOAT, steel, 11" long by 5¼" wide, simple design, circa late 1930s..	12.00	18.00	24.00
LIONEL CRAFT 18" long, complete with stand and crew	200.00	300.00	400.00
LIONEL CRAFT, without stand or crew..........	110.00	165.00	220.00
MANOIL No. 79 Submarine, lead alloy......	12.50	18.75	25.00
MARX "Carribean" friction Luxury Liner, sparkling, 15" long, 3½" tall......	10.00	15.00	20.00
MARX Mosquito Fleet Putt Putt Boat.........	16.00	24.00	32.00
OHIO Battleship, friction, 16" long, painted pressed steel.................	65.00	97.50	130.00
ORKIN Craft speedboat, clockwork, 29" long.....	125.00	187.50	250.00
"PRISCILLA" Side-Wheeler approx. 10" long, DENT or WILKENS, cast iron.	120.00	180.00	240.00
PULL TOY boat by HUSTILAR TOY CORP, STERLING, ILL, wood with some metal parts, oarsmen row in unison...............	4.00	6.00	8.00
"PURITAN" Sidewheeler, cast iron, approx. 10½" long.................	240.00	350.00	480.00

SIDE WHEELER BOAT, tin, "The Star", height, with stand, 21". Length 14½".

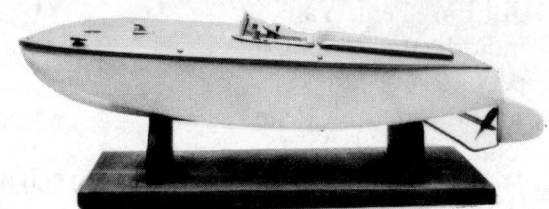

Speedboat on cradle, 1930, 25" long
Courtesy Lloyd W. Ralston Auctions

Steamship, alcohol burner, circa 1885, 19" long
Courtesy Mapes Auctioneers & Appraisers

WOLVERINE "Sandy Andy" Ferry

	G	VG	M
ROW BOAT with four men and oars, cast iron, mechanical, 9" long.....	350.00	525.00	700.00
ROW BOAT, tin rubber band driver, 9" long with man rowing..........	20.00	30.00	40.00
SCHIEBEL Battleship, circa 1927, unpowered......	55.00	82.50	110.00
SCHIEBEL Battleship, wood stacks and large wood guns and turrets, friction motor, circa 1920	75.00	112.50	150.00
SCULL, 9-man crew, U.S. HARDWARE, 14" long, wheeled..............	800.00	1200.00	1600.00
Shore Patrol, battery operated, tin boat, 9" long.................	1.00	1.50	2.00
SHOWBOAT, cast iron, 11" long.................	300.00	450.00	600.00

	G	VG	M
SIDE WHEELER BOAT, "The Star", tin, height, with stand, 21", length 14½"	1600.00	2400.00	3200.00
SIDE-WHEELER, cast iron, approx. 5½" long......	55.00	82.50	110.00
SIDE-WHEELER, cast iron, 8" long..............	45,.00	67.50	90.00
SIDEWHEELER, cast iron, 10½" long............	45.00	67.50	90.00
SIDEWHEELER, tin clockwork, 11" long.....	30.00	45.00	60.00
"SINKING BATTLESHIP", WALBERT MFG., rubber-band torpedo strikes die on ship and sinks it...............	80.00	120.00	160.00
"SPEED BOAT", 5¼" long	34.00	51.00	68.00
"SPEED BOAT", cast iron, with rider, 4¾" long, early	30.00	45.00	60.00
SPEED BOAT, Wood, rubber-band propelled...	10.00	15.00	20.00

SPEED BOAT on cradle, 1930, painted pressed steel, brass hatch cover, floating compass and gear shift in upholstered cockpit, 25" long, clockwork motor.......	G	VG	M
	100.00	150.00	200.00
SS UNITED STATES, tin friction, 6½" long.....	3.00	4.50	6.00
STEAMBOAT, tin, self-propelled, 17" long......	50.00	75.00	100.00
Steamer, lithographed paper on wood, 39" long, 22½" high..................	200.00	300.00	400.00
STEAMSHIP, alcohol burner, ca. 1885, 19" long..................	100.00	150.00	200.00

STERLING 56" scale model, all wood and metal of Battleship Missouri, radio control, with three electric motors	G	VG	M
	150.00	225.00	300.00
SUBMARINE, "575", tin litho, remote-controlled, circa 1960.............	10.00	15.00	20.00
SUBMARINE, Steel, 6" long..................	25.00	37.50	50.00
TILLICUM Convoy Set, MILTON BRADLEY, 1940s, 2 destroyers, 3 freight boats, 3 ocean liners, 2 patrol boats, painted wood, destroyers 5½" long, other about 4½" long.............	20.00	30.00	40.00

TOOTSIETOY
(Compiled by Ed Poole)

	G	VG	M
1034 Battleship, 6" long, 1939 on.............	5.00	7.50	10.00
1035 Cruiser, 5½" long, 1939 on.............	4.00	6.00	8.00
1036 Carrier, 6" long, 1939 on	4.00	6.00	8.00
1037 Transport, 6" long, 1939 on.............	4.00	6.00	8.00
1038 Freighter, 6" long, 1940 on.............	4.00	6.00	8.00

	G	VG	M
1039 Tanker, 6" long, 1940 on.............	4.00	6.00	8.00
127 Destroyer, 4" long, 1939	3.75	5.63	7.50
128 Submarine, 4" long, 1939 on.............	3.75	5.62	7.50
129 Tender, 4" long, 1940 on	3.50	5.25	7.00
130 Yacht, 4" long, 1940 on	4.00	6.00	8.00

TOOTSIETOY, top L to R: 1037 Transport 1039 Tanker.
Bottom L to R: 129 Tender, 130 Yacht
Photo by Ed Poole

TOOTSIETOY, Top L to R: 1034 Battleship, 1036 Carrier.
Middle L to R: 1035 Cruiser, 1037 Liner.
Bottom l to R: 127 Destroyer, 128 Submarine
Photo by Ed Poole

TOOTSIETOY MIDGET SERIES

	G	VG	M
Battleship..............	1.00	1.50	2.00
Destroyer..............	1.00	1.50	2.00
Carrier.................	1.00	1.50	2.00
Cruiser	1.00	1.50	2.00
Tug...................	1.00	1.50	2.00
Submarine.............	1.00	1.50	2.00
TURBO BOAT, pressed, tin, 10½" long........	10.00	15.00	20.00
U.S. NAVAL BASE, SUPERIOR	15.00	22.50	30.00

	G	VG	M
"U.S. SUBMARINE", 13" long, painted wood, fires torpedo for target set....	5.00	7.50	10.00
U.S. WASP, Carrier 27" long, wood storage under deck for planes........	12.50	18.75	25.00

WILKINS Riverboat, 10½" long. Courtesy Mapes Auctioneers & Appraisers

	G	VG	M
WEEDEN "Dewey" Steamboat, 15½" long, circa 1900	400.00	600.00	800.00
WEEDEN Launch, steam-driven, 20" long	350.00	525.00	700.00
WEEDEN Steamboat, live steam, 15" long	225.00	337.50	450.00
WILKINS "City of New York" riverboat, 15" long	440.00	660.00	880.00
WILKINS Riverboat, 5¾" long	70.00	105.00	140.00
WILKINS Riverboat, 7½" long, circa 1910, cast iron	105.00	157.50	210.00
WILKINS Riverboat, 10½" long, cast iron	150.00	225.00	300.00
WILKINS Rowers, circa 1890, 4-man crew and coxswain in 10" long, big-wheeled boat, cast iron . .	320.00	480.00	640.00
WOLVERINE Diving Submarine, 13" long	39.00	58.50	78.00
WOLVERINE " Sandy Andy Ferry", tin litho, 13½" long	20.00	30.00	40.00
WOLVERINE Sandy Andy "Ferrygo", 11" long, tin and wood	90.00	135.00	180.00
WYANDOTTE Pocket Battleship, 7" long, tin litho, wheeled	11.60	17.40	23.20

	G	VG	M
WYANDOTTE, "S.S. America", 7" long, moves on metal wheels, 1930s . .	15.00	22.50	30.00
WYANDOTTE, "Sand-o'Land", 10" long, tin litho sandtoy, wood wheels, 1940s	3.50	5.25	7.00
YACHT-TYPE ship, 28" long with spring-wind motor, either IVES or BING	650.00	925.00	1300.00

WOLVERINE Diving Submarine
Courtesy Mapes Auctioneers & Appraisers

FISHER-PRICE TOYS
by John Murray

On October 1, 1930, in East Aurora, New York, the Fisher-Price Toy Company began operation. Uniquely located on a small side street in a small town atmosphere, it would grow and eventually be considered one of the major manufacturers of toys.

Herman Fisher and Irving Price shared their names in developing a name for their new company. Herman Fisher, a past employee of the FairChild Company, a manufacturer of games, and Irving Price, who had sound experience with the Woolworth Company, would form the guidelines by which they would run their new company.

The first manufacturing facility was located on Church Street in East Aurora, New York. To date it still exists, but was sold by Fisher-Price in the 1970s due to lack of use for the facility.

The Church Street facility would be considered a small area for any type of manufacturing today, but would serve as the main and only facility for Fisher-Price toys for the first twenty years.

The most important factor in constructing this new company was to create a work force that could contribute their efforts towards a smooth, profitable venture. Among the most important employees would be Helen M. Schelle and Margaret Evans Price.

Helen M. Schelle was the first secretary and treasurer of Fisher-Price toys. She developed her skills in the retail management field through a business in which she operated, the Walker Toy Shop, in Binghamton, New York. Given the opportunity to manage the early company's activities, Helen proved to be a great asset to the advancement of Fisher-Price toys.

Margaret Evans Price was the company's first artist and designer for their new line of toys. She developed her early skills as a writer and illustrator for Rand McNally and Harper & Brothers, and by creating children's art for Strecher Lithography Company of Rochester, New York. Many of Margaret Evans Price's art work can still be found on early post cards, valentines, and children's books. These early paper collectibles are most often marked "M.E.P."

Margaret created the early art work for the reproduction of color lithography for the toys. She was also talented in drawing, produced designs for early toys, and contributed in the development of her concepts to Fisher-Price's early line of toys. The Roycroft printers contributed their skills to produce the sales catalogs that prospective retailers would use to choose the toys that they would market.

The most important early development for the company was the forming of the labor force that would generate their efforts towards building the new toy line that would be sold to the public in 1931. The initial work force that first year was approximately 25 employees. As typical of any small town like East Aurora, most employees were neighbors, friends, and relatives, who contributed to a work force that took great pride in the product that they made, since many of the operations were done by hand labor.

Many of the early operations, such as band sawing, drilling, nailing, and painting were shared by these early employees. Quality control would be created by one employee checking the other and making any corrections immediately.

As Fisher-Price began toymaking, numbers were assigned to each toy. This number system started at Number 5 and went up into the thousands. To add to the confusion for collectors today, many of the numbers have been used more than once on various toys.

With the abundance of pine and its ease of workability, this was the main wood used in construction of Fisher-Price toys. During the 30s, another material was used, a heavy cardboard, in which brass eyelets were inserted to prevent wear from spinning axles.

Creating action from child power was of great importance. The use of bellows was common to produce sound, and, as time passed, the introduction of bells was added to create sound and action.

Because of the immense amount of time required to assemble various toys, cottage-type industries were set up by employees, families, and residents of East Aurora. Toys such as the Pop-up Kritter were completely hand assembled in area homes. Because of the large demand, this would prove to be a quick and efficient method of assembly.

As the demand for Fisher-Price toys consistently rose, they began to use the skills of a freelance designer, Edward Savage, a mechanical engineer from the University of Minnesota. He created some of Fisher-Price's most successful toys. In his home in Rochester, New York, Savage created such toys as the Pop-up Kritters, Snoopy Sniffer, and many of the wind-up toys. The most popular of the toys that he created was the Snoopy Sniffer, which was produced from the 30s to the 80s, in four different versions.

After well over a decade of positive growth for Fisher-Price toys in the 30s and 40s, Fisher-Price would meet a major challenge of limited production.

With the United States entering World War II, Fisher-Price, like many companies, served its patriotic duty in a quite different type of manufacturing.

Because of the type of manufacturing that Fisher-Price was set up for, the ability to create and produce wood products set the basis for essential goods needed for war production. Ship fenders, first aid kits, cots, bomb crates, and glider ailerons were among the items produced from 1943 - 1946.

During this time of near non-existent toy manufacturing, very limited toy production continued on a material-availability basis. These toys were made from scraps of wood, with bells and some metal parts painted instead of plated. Toys made during this time sometimes used parts from similar toys, leaving odd and sometimes unusual variations.

As the World War came to an end, normal production began to resume. Well into the 50s, Ponderosa Pine, with a proven durability, was the main source of material in Fisher-Price toys. As wood became more difficult to obtain, the experimentation with plastics as a new material began. The first toy to use this new material successfully was the Busy Bee. Because of the ease of molding, durability, and bright colors, plastic was more prevelant in toys of the 50s.

In 1951, Fisher-Price moved to its new manufacturing facility on Girard Avenue in East Aurora, New York. The Girard Avenue facility handled most operations well into the late 50s. In 1957, Tri Mold of Kenmore, New York, a plastics manufacturer, became a subsidiary of Fisher-Price and their main molding facility.

As the demand for plastics became greater and greater, a new molding facility was built in Holland, New York. This was completed in July 1962. The Holland plant produced many of the plastic parts used in the construction of a more plastic-dominated toy line.

As the 60s advanced, plastic would eventually take over as the main material used to produce toys.

In 1969, The Quaker Oats Company acquired Fisher-Price toys. Three years prior to this acquisition, Herman Fisher resigned as president of the company, and was chairman of the board until the Quaker Oats acquisition. Since Fisher-Price was taken over by Quaker Oats, a plant in Medina, New York, was built, and numerous plants and facilities both nationally and internationally were created.

Considered one of the oldest and largest manufacturers of toys, Fisher-Price has its main offices at the Girard Avenue address in East Aurora, New York.

JOHN J. MURRAY was born and raised in the Buffalo, New York, area. He presently resides in Eden, a suburb of Buffalo,. John began collecting and researching Fisher-Price toys about six years ago. The fact that he is employed with Fisher-Price in their Research and Development Art Department has given him knowledge of early to present toymaking. John admits that the joy of collecting wooden Fisher-Price toys is endless, as this area of collecting is rapidly becoming a field all its own. Their uniqueness, their bright and colorful lithos, and their endless shapes and sizes all combine to make collecting them a hobby of real enjoyment. Any collector who wishes to contact John may do so by sending a SASE to him at Box 29, Eden, New York 14057. John would like to thank Fisher-Price toys and both past and present employees for their assistance. A special thanks to Ross MacKearnin for his volunteered time towards photography.

CONDITION

There are many factors that may contribute to values of Fisher-Price toys. The most important factor to consider is the paper lithography. Most Fisher-Price toys found have what I call "edge wear." Edge wear may be considered as wear only around the outer corners or edge of the toy. Most toys found with edge wear may also be called normal-wear toys. Any toys with this type of wear most often fall in a value class of good/very good. When determining the condition of a toy, other areas of importance to the litho would be the amount of soil on the litho, and the extent to which it has faded and/or lost its color. These areas may be considered as less important, unless there is more than slight soiling or discoloration. When a Fisher-Price toy has advanced conditions of wear, soiling, or missing litho, the toy would be considered as less than good condition, and therefore, a value of less than good (poor) would be placed on it.

The next area that is of importance with regard to condition of the toy in determining value would be paint and originality. Toys with slight paint wear on wheels, bases, and handles would fall into the good/very good condition category, unless however, there is litho damage as stated above. Any parts missing also affect the value of the toy, especially lithography parts, such as arms, legs, and heads. These are especially important, since once the litho is gone, there is no means of replacement. Also lessening the value of a toy would be missing wheels and axles.

A toy which is mint is one that has absolutely no wear or damage on a complete basis. (Litho, paint, wheels, etc. in mint condition). These toys will reflect the highest of values. Boxes for older Fisher-Price toys may add up to 20% more for a mint toy, depending upon the condition of the box. Boxes from toys from the 1930s would be of the most value because of age, and are most often missing. Always consider condition of the box towards a value of a toy.

The last area that seems to have led the way demanding higher prices would be comic characters and the use of other company's names on Fisher-Price toys. Most often toys of this nature have much higher values placed on them than other Fisher-Price toys, due to the fact that there are many Disney, Popeye, and other comic-area collectors.

Because a toy may be a Disney, Popeye, or comic figure does not necessarily mean that it may be a rarer toy. There are many other Fisher-Price toys that are much rarer, since rarity is based on the amount of toys produced over a given period of time, and the amount still in existence.

Also, many toys that had accessories or figures that were often misplaced will bring higher values. Often these accessories and/or figures are difficult to locate separately from the toy itself. If a toy is found mint in the box with accessories, this most certainly will demand higher pricing.

The prices reflected in this guide for Fisher-Price toys were established by taking an average of toys seen at toy shows, flea markets, dealers, and collectors.

777 SQUEAKY THE CLOWN
Photo by Ross MacKearnin, Courtesy John Murray

770 DOC & DOPEY DWARFS
Photo by Ross MacKearnin, Courtesy John Murray

777 TEDDY ZILO
Photo by Ross MacKearnin, Courtesy John Murray

765 TALKING DONALD DUCK
Photo by Ross MacKearnin, Courtesy John Murray

	G	VG	M		G	VG	M
7 Looky Fire Truck	15.00	25.00	45.00	28 Bunny Egg Cart	5.00	10.00	20.00
8 Bouncy Racer	5.00	10.00	25.00	50 Baby Chick Tandem Cart	10.00	15.00	20.00
10 Bunny Cart	5.00	10.00	25.00	100 Musical Sweeper	15.00	20.00	25.00
11 Ducky Cart	10.00	20.00	35.00	120 Cackling Hen (white)	20.00	35.00	50.00
16 Ducky Cart	5.00	10.00	25.00	123 Cackling Hen (red)	15.00	30.00	40.00

491 BOOM BOOM POPEYE
Photo by Ross MacKearnin, Courtesy John Murray

480 LEO THE DRUMMER
Photo by Ross MacKearnin, Courtesy John Murray

494 PLUCKY PINOCCHIO
Photo by Ross MacKearnin, Courtesy John Murray

	G	VG	M
123 Roller Chimes (with push stick)	8.00	14.00	20.00
125 Uncle Timmy Turtle (with glasses) (see picture)	40.00	60.00	75.00
131 Toy Wagon	20.00	35.00	50.00
132 Dr. Doodle	15.00	35.00	45.00
137 Pony Chime	10.00	20.00	35.00
138 Pony Chime	10.00	20.00	35.00
139 Tuggy Turtle	15.00	25.00	45.00
140 Katy Kackler (see picture)	20.00	40.00	55.00
145 Musical Elephant (with original ears) (see picture)	60.00	85.00	135.00
150 Timmy Turtle	30.00	45.00	65.00
151 Happy Hippo	15.00	25.00	40.00
155 Moo-oo Cow	30.00	40.00	65.00
156 F/P Circus Wagon (see picture)	65.00	85.00	125.00
161 Looky Chug-Chug (with tender)	40.00	65.00	85.00
164 Mother Goose	15.00	20.00	30.00
166 Bucky Burro	40.00	60.00	75.00
168 F/P Chug Chug (with 2 cars)	15.00	20.00	30.00
168 Snorky Fire Engine (with all figures)	30.00	40.00	60.00
169 Snorky Fire Engine (with all figures)	30.00	40.00	60.00
170 American Airlines Flagship (with original propellors)	135.00	160.00	225.00
175 Gold Star Stage Coach (with baggage-two) (see picture)	75.00	90.00	125.00
177 Donald Duck Xylophone (see picture)	60.00	80.00	125.00
180 Snoopy Sniffer (see picture)	30.00	50.00	75.00
185 Donald Duck Xylophone	75.00	110.00	145.00
190 Molly Moo-Moo	45.00	65.00	85.00
191 Golden Gulch Express	20.00	30.00	40.00
192 Playland Express	10.00	20.00	30.00
195 Teddy Bear Parade	125.00	155.00	195.00
200 Winky Blinky Fire Truck	30.00	40.00	60.00
210 Pluto the Pup	30.00	45.00	60.00
211 Walt Disney's Elmer the Elephant	35.00	50.00	65.00
215 Streamliner Express	155.00	185.00	235.00
220 Looky Chug-Chug (see picture)	45.00	65.00	85.00
225 Musical Sweeper	10.00	15.00	25.00
230 Musical Sweeper	10.00	15.00	25.00

	G	VG	M
234 Nifty Station Wagon (with roof and four figures) see picture	65.00	95.00	145.00
237 Riding Horse (with original tail)	125.00	185.00	225.00
301 Bunny Basket Cart	10.00	15.00	30.00
302 Chick Basket Cart	5.00	15.00	25.00
303 Bunny Basket Cart	10.00	15.00	30.00
305 Walking Duck Cart	15.00	20.00	35.00
307 Bouncing Bunny Cart	15.00	25.00	35.00
310 Mickey Mouse Puddle Jumper	20.00	30.00	40.00
314 Queen Buzzy Bee (see picture)	10.00	15.00	20.00
325 Buzzy Bee	10.00	15.00	20.00
333 Butch the Pup	10.00	15.00	25.00
350 Go'n Back Mule (with original ears)	125.00	175.00	225.00
400 Donald Duck Drum Major	40.00	60.00	85.00
400 Tailspin Tabby (original pull loops) (see picture)	25.00	35.00	55.00
401 Bunny Cart	20.00	35.00	45.00
406 Bunny & Cart	20.00	30.00	45.00
407 Chick & Cart	10.00	30.00	45.00
410 Stoopy Storky (with original cardboard feet)	60.00	75.00	95.00
415 Lop-Ear Looie (see picture)	75.00	90.00	125.00
415 Super-Jet (see picture)	40.00	50.00	65.00
432 Mickey Mouse Choo-Choo (early version)	75.00	90.00	125.00
433 Dizzy Donkey (see picture)	35.00	40.00	55.00
434 Ferdinand the Bull (see picture)	125.00	145.00	195.00
440 Goofy Gertie	60.00	75.00	95.00
440 Pluto Pop-Up	40.00	50.00	65.00
444 Puffy Engine	15.00	20.00	25.00
444 Fuzzy Fido (see picture)	35.00	45.00	65.00
445 Hot Dog Wagon (see picture)	55.00	75.00	95.00
445 Nosey Pup (see picture)	15.00	25.00	35.00
450 Donald Choo-Choo	45.00	70.00	90.00
450 Jolly Jumper	15.00	20.00	35.00
454 Donald Duck Drummer (see picture)	65.00	75.00	110.00
455 Tailspin Tabby	30.00	40.00	55.00
462 Barky Dog	15.00	20.00	30.00
472 Peter Bunny Cart	65.00	85.00	110.00
472 Jingle Giraffe	45.00	70.00	85.00
473 Merry Mutt	30.00	40.00	60.00
476 Mickey Mouse Drummer	70.00	90.00	125.00
476 Cookie Pig	5.00	10.00	15.00

757 HUMPTY DUMPTY
Photo by Ross MacKearnin, Courtesy John Murray

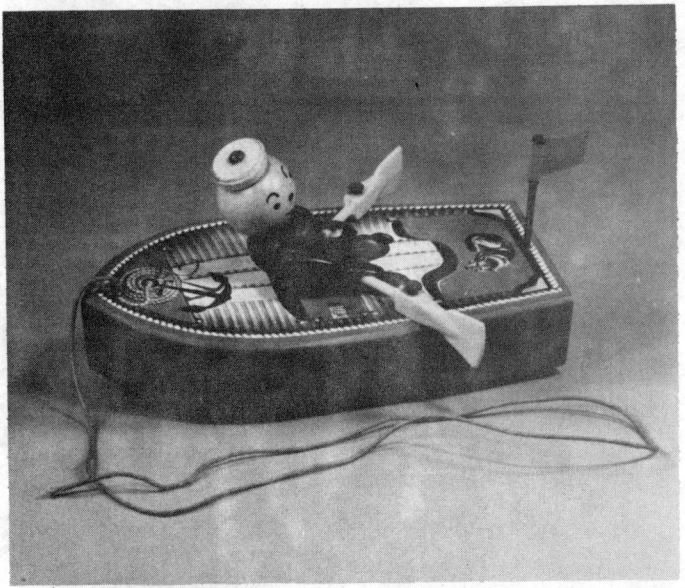

730 RACING ROWBOAT
Photo by Ross MacKearnin, Courtesy John Murray

703 POPEYE THE SAILOR
Photo by Ross MacKearnin, Courtesy John Murray

145 MUSICAL ELEPHANT
Photo by Ross MacKearnin, Courtesy John Murray

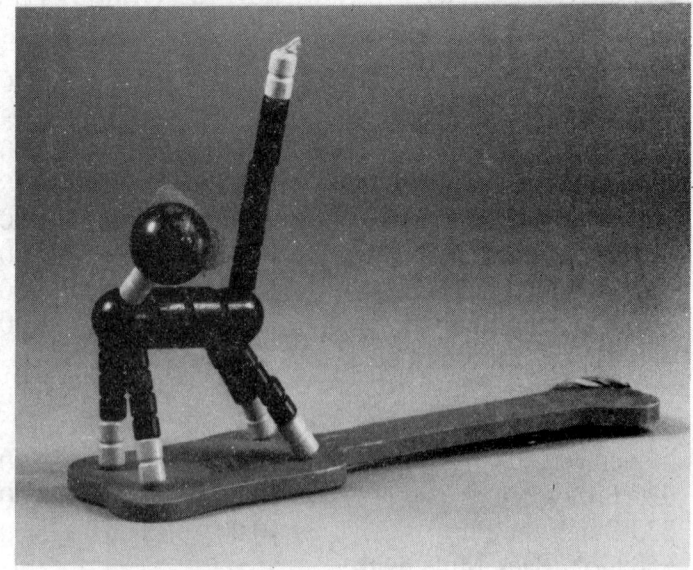

400 TAILSPIN TABBY
Photo by Ross MacKearnin, Courtesy John Murray

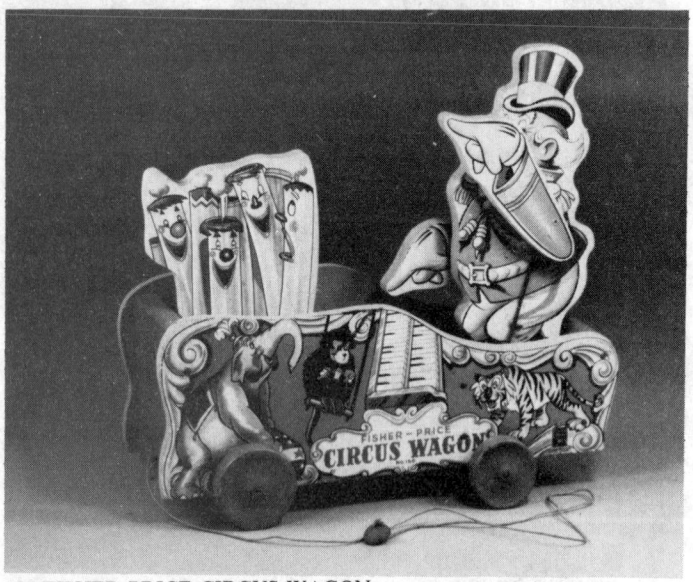

156 FISHER PRICE CIRCUS WAGON
Photo by Ross MacKearnin, Courtesy John Murray

415 LOP-EAR-LOOIE
Photo by Ross MacKearnin, Courtesy John Murray

177 DONALD DUCK XYLOPHONE
Photo by Ross MacKearnin, Courtesy John Murray

415 SUPER JET
Photo by Ross MacKearnin, Courtesy John Murray

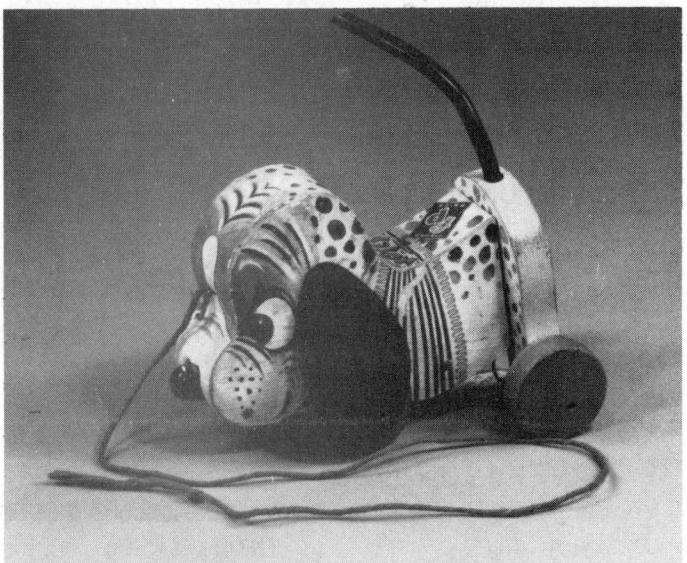

445 NOSEY PUP
Photo by Ross MacKearnin, Courtesy John Murray

454 DONALD DUCK DRUMMER
Photo by Ross MacKearnin, Courtesy John Murray

485 MICKEY MOUSE CHOO CHOO
Photo by Ross MacKearnin, Courtesy John Murray

678 KRISS KRICKET
Photo by Ross MacKearnin, Courtesy John Murray

472 PETER BUNNY CART
Photo by Ross MacKearnin, Courtesy John Murray

698 TALKY PARROT
Photo by Ross MacKearnin, Courtesy John Murray

166 BUCKY BURRO
Photo by Ross MacKearnin, Courtesy John Murray

125 UNCLE TIMMY TURTLE
Photo by Ross MacKearnin, Courtesy John Murray

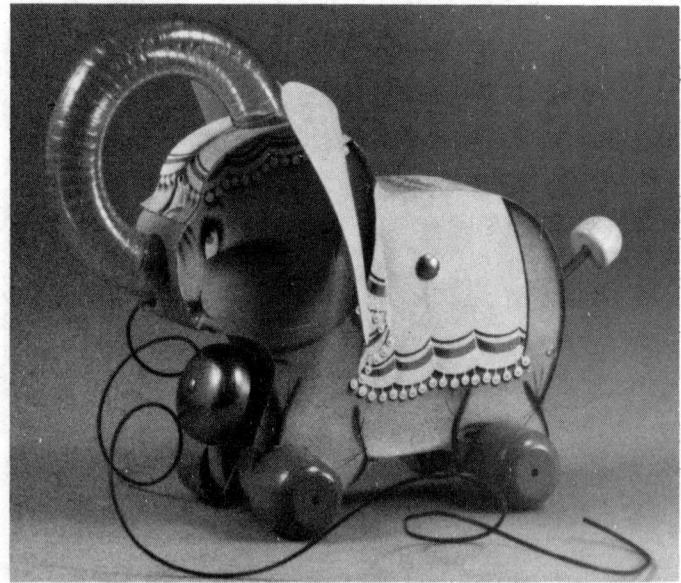

735 JUGGLING JUMBO
Photo by Ross MacKearnin, Courtesy John Murray

	G	VG	M
477 Dr. Doodle	60.00	85.00	110.00
478 Pudgy Pig	5.00	10.00	15.00
479 Donald Duck & Nephews (with 2 nephews)	75.00	90.00	125.00
480 Leo the Drummer (see picture)	50.00	65.00	85.00
485 Mickey Mouse Choo-Choo (see picture)	30.00	40.00	65.00
487 Bunny Cart	40.00	65.00	85.00
488 Popeye Spinach Eater	75.00	115.00	135.00
491 Boom-boom Popeye (see picture)	85.00	120.00	145.00
494 Plucky Pinocchio (see picture)	65.00	125.00	155.00
495 Sleepy Sue	10.00	15.00	25.00
498 Happy Helicopter	35.00	60.00	85.00
508 Bunny Bell Drummer	25.00	45.00	65.00
533 Thumper Bunny	75.00	115.00	135.00
544 Donald Duck Cart	60.00	85.00	125.00
600 Tailspin Tabby Pop-up	40.00	50.00	65.00
610 Tailspin Tabby	40.00	50.00	65.00
616 Chuggy Pop-Up	45.00	60.00	75.00
617 Whistling Engine	30.00	45.00	60.00
621 Suzie Seal (ball)	10.00	15.00	20.00
623 Suzie Seal (umbrella)	10.00	15.00	20.00
625 Playful Puppy	15.00	20.00	30.00
626 Playful Puppy	15.00	20.00	30.00
634 Tiny Teddy	15.00	20.00	35.00
635 Tiny Teddy	15.00	20.00	25.00
636 Tiny Teddy	15.00	25.00	35.00
640 Wiggily Woofer	20.00	40.00	55.00
642 Smokie Engine	10.00	25.00	35.00
653 Allie Gator	30.00	35.00	45.00
654 Tawny Tiger	15.00	30.00	45.00
656 Bossy Bell	10.00	15.00	25.00
658 Lady Bug	10.00	15.00	25.00
662 Merry Mousewife	10.00	15.00	25.00
674 Sports Car	15.00	20.00	35.00
678 Kriss Kricket (see picture)	20.00	30.00	50.00
686 Perky Pot	10.00	15.00	25.00
695 Pinky Pig	15.00	30.00	45.00
698 Talky Parrot	20.00	35.00	55.00
703 Popeye the Sailor (see picture)	125.00	165.00	195.00
707 Fido Zilo	20.00	35.00	50.00
712 Teddy Tooter	40.00	60.00	85.00
720 Pinocchio Express	100.00	140.00	165.00
721 Peter Bunny Engine	45.00	65.00	95.00
728 Buddy Bullfrog	15.00	25.00	40.00
730 Racing Rowboat (see picture)	40.00	50.00	65.00
733 Fisher-Price General Hauling	50.00	70.00	95.00
733 Mickey Mouse Safety Patrol	80.00	120.00	145.00

314 QUEEN BUZZY BEE
Photo by Ross MacKearnin, Courtesy John Murray

434 FERDINAND THE BULL
Photo by Ross MacKearnin, Courtesy John Murray

7 LOOKY FIRE TRUCK
Photo by Ross MacKearnin, Courtesy John Murray

733 FISHER PRICE GENERAL HAULING
Photo by Ross MacKearnin, Courtesy John Murray

450 DONALD DUCK CHOO CHOO
Photo by Ross MacKearnin, Courtesy John Murray

479 DONALD DUCK & NEPHEWS
Photo by Ross MacKearnin, Courtesy John Murray

745 ELSIE'S DAIRY TRUCK
Photo by Ross MacKearnin, Courtesy John Murray

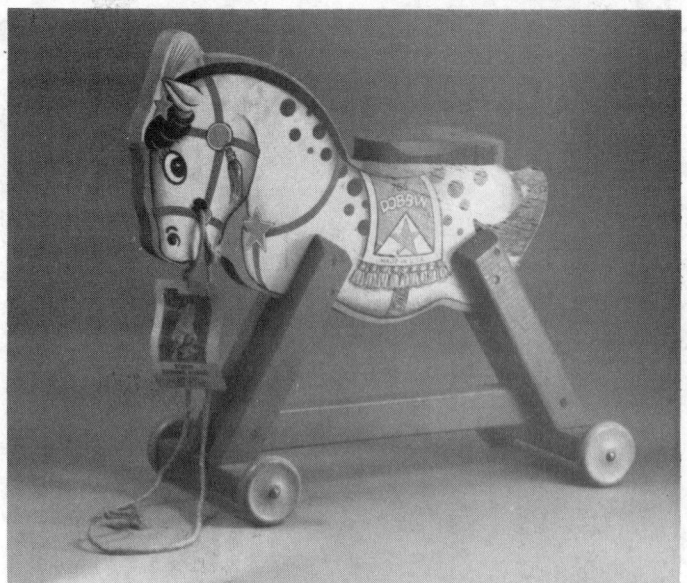

765 DANDY DOBBIN
Photo by Ross MacKearnin, Courtesy John Murray

445 HOT DOG WAGON
Photo by Ross MacKearnin, Courtesy John Murray

444 FUZZY FIDO
Photo by Ross MacKearnin, Courtesy John Murray

	G	VG	M
735 Juggling Jumbo (see picture)	40.00	75.00	95.00
738 Dumbo Circus Racer (original arms)	125.00	185.00	225.00
738 Shaggy Zilo	20.00	30.00	40.00
739 Poodle Zilo	20.00	30.00	40.00
742 Dashing Dobbin	65.00	110.00	145.00
745 Elsie's Dairy Truck (with 2 milk bottles-deduct $15.00 for each missing bottle) (see picture)	70.00	145.00	195.00
750 Hot Dog Wagon	70.00	95.00	135.00
750 Space Blazer	70.00	110.00	155.00
752 Teddy Xylophone	30.00	40.00	85.00
755 Jumbo Rollo	45.00	60.00	85.00
757 Humpty-Dumpty (see picture)	50.00	75.00	125.00
758 Pony Chime	30.00	50.00	65.00
765 Dandy Dobbin (see picture)	60.00	100.00	130.00
770 Doc & Dopey Dwarfs (see picture)	160.00	195.00	245.00

	G	VG	M
775 Gabby Goofies	5.00	10.00	20.00
776 Gabby Goofies	5.00	10.00	20.00
777 Teddy Bear Zilo	25.00	45.00	60.00
777 Squeaky the Clown (see picture)	35.00	45.00	70.00
785 Blackie Drummer	95.00	135.00	165.00
794 Big Bill Pelican (with cardboard fish-add $10.00)	20.00	40.00	65.00
795 Musical Duck	30.00	45.00	60.00
798 Chatter Monk	20.00	30.00	45.00
799 Quacky Family	10.00	15.00	25.00
810 Timber Toter	30.00	40.00	60.00
875 Looky Push Car (with steering wheel push stick)	35.00	45.00	65.00
900 Big Performing Circus)with all accessories)	75.00	125.00	200.00
926 Cement Mixer	45.00	70.00	95.00
983 Safety School Bus (with all figures)	30.00	45.00	65.00
984 Safety School Bus (with all figures)	25.00	40.00	60.00
999 Huffy Puffy Train (with 4 cars)	30.00	40.00	75.00

175 GOLD STAR STAGE COACH
Photo by Ross MacKearnin, Courtesy John Murray

220 LOOKY, CHUG, CHUG
Photo by Ross MacKearnin, Courtesy John Murray

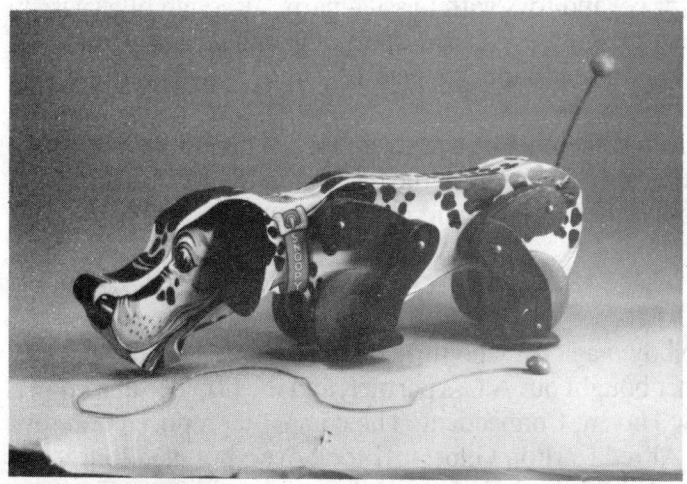

180 SNOOPY SNIFFER
Photo by Ross MacKearnin, Courtesy John Murray

234 NIFTY STATION WAGON
Photo by Ross MacKearnin, Courtesy John Murray

140 KATY KACKLER
Photo by Ross MacKearnin, Courtesy John Murray

433 DIZZY DONKEY
Photo by Ross MacKearnin, Courtesy John Murray

MISCELLANEOUS

Average mint price in this category in the last edition was $165.42, and in this edition it is $187.61, an increase of 13%.

CONDITION OF A TOY AND ITS RELATION TO PRICE

The price of a toy depends not only on its desirability, but on its condition. A toy in mint condition is generally worth twice what that same toy would bring in good condition, with "very good" falling about equally in between good and mint.

"Mint" means just that; the condition in which it was originally issued — perfect, regardless of age, not the slightest blemish. Needless to say this is a fairly rare state of affairs, but enough toys exist in mint condition to make it an employable term. Many people hoping to dispose of toys are tempted to call an item "mint" when it is really "near mint", "very good", or sometimes even just "good". Inevitably this can result in unhappiness all around, and not infrequently, a cancelled sale.

"Very Good" indicates a toy which has obviously seen use, with signs of wear and aging, but in general having a freshness to its appearance that makes it attractive and collectible to all but the most discriminating.

"Good" signals a toy that has seen considerable wear, shows its age, but is basically sound. A collector will collect it, but will often not be wholly satisfied with it as an example of his collection, and thus prices are often drastically below that which the same item in mint can command.

Condition below good results in another drastic drop in price, and toys with missing parts, although otherwise in excellent condition, will usually fall into this lower-priced category. Rust, even small spots of it, can seriously lower the price of a toy. "Near Mint", "Fine", "Very Fine" and similar terms often found in sellers' descriptions denote conditions between Mint and Very Good, and are priced accordingly.

The key to grading is to avoid wishful thinking. Grading can sometimes be a problem for the uninitiated, but common sense will usually prevail, and when possible, a consultation with an expert in the field can often clear up lingering doubts. A toy in its original box is worth up to 10 to 20% more if the box is in mint condition, with the price dropping as condition lessens.

A.C. GILBERT

Alfred Carlton Gilbert, Jr. (1884-1961) began as a schoolboy magician who turned to producing magic kits under the name of Mysto Manufacturing Company. In 1916 his father bought out A.C.'s partner, and the firm became known as A.C. Gilbert Company, located on Erector Square in New Haven, Connecticut. The company produced non-toys as well as its various toy sets. Upon Gilbert's death, his son, Alfred Carlton Gilbert III took over, but died four years later. Since his death, the company has passed through several hands, with many of its items still being manufactured today, including what is probably its most famous product, the Erector Set.

	G	VG	M		G	VG	M
A.C. GILBERT Big Boy tool chest No. 6........	12.00	18.00	24.00	A.C. GILBERT Erector Set No. 2, 1919, "Patented Jan. 16th 1917, Patented May 6th 1918" includes box.................	20.00	30.00	40.00
A.C. GILBERT No. 12052 Chemistry Experiment Lab, in three-piece metal box	10.00	15.00	20.00	A.C. GILBERT Erector Set No. 2½..............	7.50	11.25	15.00
A.C. GILBERT "Electric Eye" early photoelectric toy, 1935, in metal box with original instruction booklet	10.00	15.00	20.00	A.C. GILBERT Erector Set No. 4, 1919, price includes box.............	22.50	33.75	45.00
A.C. GILBERT Erector Motor, early, 2½" x 2" x 3"	20.00	30.00	40.00	A.C. GILBERT Erector Set No. 4, 1930...........	125.00	187.50	250.00
				A.C. GILBERT Erector Set No. 4, 1940...........	160.00	240.00	320.00
A.C. GILBERT Erector Set No. 1	12.50	18.75	25.00	A.C. GILBERT Erector Set No. 4½, copyright 1938.	11.00	16.50	22.00
A.C. GILBERT Erector Set No. 2, Junior, copyright 1949	5.00	7.50	10.00	A.C. GILBERT Erector Set No. 6½, electric engine..	65.00	95.50	130.00

A.C. GILBERT Erector Set	G	VG	M
No. 7, builds steam shovel, price includes wood box...........	150.00	225.00	300.00
A.C. GILBERT Erector Set No. 7½, makes truck...	85.00	127.50	170.00
A.C. GILBERT Erector Set No. 8½.............	30.00	45.00	60.00
A.C. GILBERT Erector Set No. 9, price includes wood box............	25.00	37.50	50.00
A.C. GILBERT Erector Set No. 10, giant deluxe set, includes box approx. 30x30", makes zeppelin (fabric included), Hudson and Tender, White Truck, etc............	900.00	1350.00	1800.00
A.C. GILBERT Erector Set No. 217, makes train engine and tender, price includes wood box......	55.00	82.50	110.00
A.C. GILBERT Erector Set "The New Erector, World's Greatest Toy, Copy. 1928", "A.C. Gilbert Co., New Haven Conn. USA", complete set with box and directions	12.50	18.75	25.00
A.C. GILBERT Erector How To Make 'Em Book, 1938, tells how to make various projects with Erector Set........	5.00	7.50	10.00
A.C. GILBERT Erector Hudson Locomotive....	237.50	356.25	475.00
A.C. GILBERT Erector Set Manual of Instructions for set Number 4, 1928, illustrated	2.50	3.75	5.00
A.C. GILBERT Erector, very large set, comes with big white truck, trains, crane	90.00	135.00	180.00
A.C. GILBERT Helicopter Set No. 10181........	30.00	45.00	60.00
A.C. GILBERT Microscope Set No. 6, circa 1938 with Polaroid Jr. microscope, original manual, vials, test tube and other equipment	25.00	37.50	50.00
A.C. GILBERT Mysto Erector Set No. 1, 1A, 2A, 3A. Price per each..	50.00	75.00	100.00

A.C. GILBERT No. 10053,	G	VG	M
Rocket Launcher.......	45.00	67.50	90.00
A.C. GILBERT Telegraph Outfit	5.00	7.50	10.00
A.C. GILBERT Trumodel Set No. 77, 1929.......	30.00	45.00	60.00
A.C. GILBERT Wood Tool Box and Tools.........	6.00	9.00	12.00
Air Raid Warden Junior Kit, felt hat, arm band, gas mask, whistle, window sign, forms and street-plan sheets, stethoscope, book of instructions, WW II era...	15.00	22.50	30.00
ALL-NU Horse, not made to have rider..........	10.00	15.00	20.00
Alligator, cast iron, 9".....	10.00	15.00	20.00
Alligator, cast iron, two-part, 9" long..........	20.00	30.00	40.00
American Badge ring, circa 1930s or 1940s, heavy metal, may have been premium	4.00	6.00	8.00
AMERICAN LOGS — similar to Lincoln Logs, circa WWII, price includes box............	4.00	6.00	8.00
AMERICAN TOY CO. Dancing Black Women, two	600.00	900.00	1200.00
"Anti-Aircraft Rapid-Fire Machine Gun", cast iron, on wheels............	30.00	45.00	60.00
ARCADE Bathroom Set, 3-piece, cast iron tub, stool sink.............	14.00	21.00	28.00
ARCADE "Don't Park Here" cast iron sign, 4½" high................	4.50	6.75	9.00
ARCADE "Don't Park Here" sign, painted cast iron, 1920, 5" tall......	15.00	22.50	30.00

ARCADE "Don't Park Here" sign, 1920, 5" high
Courtesy Lloyd W. Ralston Auctions

ARCADE Farm Wagon, "Whitehead & Kales Co.", 6½"............	70.00	105.00	140.00
ARCADE Gas Pump, 6"..	35.00	52.50	70.00

	G	VG	M
ARCADE Grand Piano and bench, 3"..........	80.00	120.00	160.00
ARCADE tools, cast iron No. 779N, small, nickel finish, screwdriver, hammer, monkey wrench, pipe wrench, crescent wrench and S wrench, came in set of 6, 1938. Price per each........	2.00	3.00	4.00

ARCADE Tools

ARCADE Weapons

	G	VG	M
ARCADE weapons, cast iron, No. 778N, small nickel finish, cutlass, pistol, automatic, aerial bomb, tommy gun, airplane, came in set of six, 1938. Price per each.	2.50	3.75	5.00
ARCADE Pump and Tub..	25.00	37.50	50.00
ARCADE Windmill, cast iron, 15¼" high.......	100.00	150.00	200.00
ARKITOY Play Lumber by G.B. LEWIS CO., 1926, No. 3................	11.00	16.50	22.00
Artascope, optical toy, circa 1920, pressed steel, spin base with multi-colors, see thru mirrors..........	25.00	37.50	50.00
AUBURN RUBBER Calf, circa 1937............	.75	1.13	1.50
AUBURN RUBBER Chicken, circa 1937.....	.75	1.13	1.50
AUBURN RUBBER Collie, circa 1937............	.75	1.13	1.50
AUBURN RUBBER Colt, circa 1937	.75	1.13	1.50

	G	VG	M
AUBURN RUBBER Cow, circa 1937	.75	1.13	1.50
AUBURN RUBBER Duck, circa 1937	.75	1.13	1.50
AUBURN RUBBER Fence Section, circa 1937......	.75	1.13	1.50
AUBURN RUBBER Horse, circa 1937............	.75	1.13	1.50
AUBURN RUBBER Pig, circa 1937............	.75	1.13	1.50
AUBURN RUBBER Piglet, circa 1937............	.75	1.13	1.50
Baby Buggy, cast iron.....	35.00	52.50	70.00
Baby Buggy, cast iron, 4¼" high.................	14.00	21.00	28.00
Baby Carriage, tin, with folding cloth top, 7¾" long.................	26.00	39.00	52.00
Badge, "Dick Steel News Service"..............	20.00	30.00	40.00
Badge, G-MAN, lead......	2.50	3.75	5.00
Badge, Jet Ranger........	5.00	7.50	10.00
Badge, Junior Counter Spy Agent with picture, No. 161731..............	6.00	9.00	12.00
Badge, "Junior Detective", heavy six-pointed star badge with copper insert, nickel badge..........	2.75	4.13	5.50
Badge, Junior G-Man, circa late 1930s, brass, shield-shaped, eagle on top.....	3.75	5.25	7.50
Badge, Junior Secret Agent, metal.................	4.00	6.00	8.00
Badge, "The Purple Mask" detective badge.........	6.50	9.75	13.00
Badge, "Sheriff", six-pointed star, black oval insert and word "Oklahoma", nickeled metal.............	8.00	12.00	16.00
Badge, Wyatt Earp Marshall, six-pointed........	3.00	4.50	6.00
Baggage Cart, cast iron, 5" high.................	36.00	54.00	72.00
BALDWIN Chicken on nest, marbles for eggs, 5" long.................	20.00	30.00	40.00
Barbed Wire (Army), 8" long, for toy soldiers....	6.00	9.00	12.00
Barbed Wire, mesh, for toy soldiers	4.00	6.00	8.00
BARCLAY Searchlight, swivels on base, 3"......	8.00	12.00	16.00
BARCLAY No. 209 Work horse	5.00	7.50	10.00
BARCLAY No. 210 Horse.	5.00	7.50	10.00

	G	VG	M
BARCLAY No. 211 Grazing Horse	5.00	7.50	10.00
BARCLAY No. 212 Standing Cow	5.00	7.50	10.00
BARCLAY No. 213 Grazing Cow	5.00	7.50	10.00
BARCLAY No. 214 Lying Cow	5.00	7.50	10.00
BARCLAY No. 215 Bull	5.00	7.50	10.00
BARCLAY No. 217 Standing Sheep	5.00	7.50	10.00
BARCLAY No. 218 Resting Sheep	5.00	7.50	10.00
BARCLAY No. 219 Ram	3.50	5.25	7.00
BARCLAY No. 220 Pig	3.50	5.25	7.00
BARCLAY Mess Table, two benches (wooden)	15.00	22.50	30.00
Bear and Black Boy with hammers, mechanical, 13" long	240.00	360.00	480.00
BEAUT MFG. CO. Wagon No. 50	3.00	4.50	6.00

BEAUT MFG. CO. Wagon
Courtesy George Buhler, Photo by Bill Kaufman

	G	VG	M
Bell Toy, Acrobats holding bells, GONG BELL No. 54	850.00	1275.00	1700.00
Bell Toy, Alligator ridden by Black Boy, 5½" long, N.N. HILL, 1910, cast iron	545.00	817.50	1090.00
Bell Toy, Alligator Snapping at teasing boy, cast iron, 9¼" long	1300.00	1950.00	2600.00
Bell Toy, ALTHOF BERGMANN, tin "Chime & Design Patd. May 19th 1874", 3 women or boy soldiers, one with flag, two with rifles	1600.00	2400.00	3200.00
Bell Toy, bear, iron, bounces in air	150.00	225.00	300.00
Bell Toy, bear on tricycle, 4" long	66.00	99.00	132.00
Bell Toy, Billy Goat, GONG BELL No. 51, cast iron, goat mechanically butts bell, 7½" long, 1900	200.00	300.00	400.00

Bell Toy, Horse, FALLOWS, tin
Courtesy Lloyd W. Ralston Auctions

Bell Toy, Clown & Pig, 1900
Courtesy Lloyd W. Ralston Auctions

Bell Toy, Bill Goat, GONG BELL No. 51
Courtesy Lloyd W. Ralston Auctions

Bell Toy, Goat, FALLOWS
Courtesy Lloyd W. Ralston Auctions

Bell Toy, Hunter and Rabbit, N.N. HILL
Courtesy Lloyd W. Ralston Auctions

Bell Toy, "Oriental Clown & Poodle"
Courtesy Lloyd W. Ralston Auctions

	G	VG	M
Bell Toy, bird and bell, tin and iron, 6" long	160.00	240.00	320.00
Bell Toy, Boy and Goat, ALFHOF BERGMANN, tin 9" long	330.00	495.00	660.00
Bell Ringer, Boy Scouts, iron, rest pressed steel, heart-shaped tin wheels, 13½" long	120.00	180.00	240.00

	G	VG	M
Bell Toy, Boys Eating Bananas, cast iron	200.00	300.00	400.00
Bell Toy, Cinderella Chariot, 9¼" long	60.00	90.00	120.00
Bell Toy, Clown and Pig, 1900, painted cast iron, 6¼" long	140.00	210.00	280.00
Bell Toy, Clown bell-ringers riding back to back on a mule	1000.00	1500.00	2000.00
Bell Toy, clown and black man on see-saw, circa 1905, 6½" long, six colors, WATRESS, cast iron	95.00	142.50	190.00
Bell Toy, Comic Characters, two, pressed steel and iron, 3 bells, pierced heart wheels	225.00	337.50	450.00
Bell Toy, Elephant on Platform, FALLOWS, 6¾" long	120.00	180.00	240.00
Bell Toy, Elephant with bell in trunk, N.N. HILL, circa 1905	250.00	375.00	500.00
Bell Toy, "Eskimo & Bear", pressed steel body, iron figures	80.00	120.00	160.00
Bell Toy, Goat, FALLOWS, 1880, painted tin, 14" long x 14" tall	700.00	1050.00	1400.00
Bell Toy, Goat, Lamb and Girl on platform, GEORGE BROWN, tin, 11" long, early	320.00	480.00	640.00
Bell Toy, Goat, tin, circa 1890, small woman at left leg of goat, 7½" high, either Althof Bergmann or Ives	225.00	337.50	450.00
Bell Toy, Horse, FALLOWS	180.00	270.00	360.00
Bell Toy, horse, 9¼" long, tin	230.00	345.00	460.00
Bell Toy, horse, tin, pulling heart-shaped wheels	55.00	82.50	110.00
Bell Toy, IVES, 9½" long white horse pulling heart-shaped wheels, circa 1896	434.00	651.00	868.00
Bell Toy, horse and rider, 9" long, heart-shaped wheels, tin	360.00	540.00	720.00
Bell Toy, Hunter and Rabbit, N.N. HILL, 1900, cast iron, rabbit pops out of hole, 6½" long	325.00	487.00	650.00

Bell Toy, Billy Goat, tin, circa 1890
Photo Courtesy PB Eighty-Four

Pull Toy, Sheep, tin, circa 1890
Photo Courtesy PB Eighty-Four

	G	VG	M
Bell Toy, Jack and Jill on seesaw, 7½" long, cat iron and tin	800.00	1200.00	1600.00
Bell Toy, Jockey on Horse, early, 7½" long	120.00	180.00	240.00
Bell Toy "Landing of Columbus", 7" long	150.00	225.00	300.00
Bell Toy, Monkey and Coconut, N.N. HILL, 6" long	130.00	195.00	260.00
Bell Toy, "Money and Dog", heart wheels, 7" long, cast iron and tin	54.00	81.00	108.00
Bell Toy, Monkey on a Log, cast iron, GONG BELL MFG. CO., circa 1900	250.00	375.00	500.00
Bell Toy, Monkey on Tricycle, J&E STEVENS, 8" high, cast iron	190.00	285.00	380.00
Bell Toy, Monkey Riding Elephant, FALLOWS, 10" long, tin, clockwork	900.00	1350.00	1800.00
Bell Toy, Mule kicks bell, No. 42	350.00	525.00	700.00
Bell Toy, nursery rhymes on drums, one horse	190.00	285.00	380.00
Bell Toy, "Oriental Clown & Poodle" No. 44, painted cast iron, 1900, cloth in hoop, 13" long, poodle jumps through hoop and back	600.00	900.00	1200.00

Bell Toy, Monkey
Riding Elephant,
Fallows

Bell-Ringer, Trick Pony, GONG BELL CO., 1893
Photo Courtesy PB Eighty-Four

	G	VG	M
Bell Toy, STEVENS, "Evening News Baby Quieter", 1890s cast iron, 8" long, man reading paper to baby	800.00	1200.00	1600.00
Bell Toy, "Teddy Roosevelt"	60.00	90.00	120.00
Bell Toy, Trick Pony, GONG BELL CO., 1893, "39", cast iron, 5¼" high	166.00	249.00	332.00
Bell Toy, Victory in a shell-form chariot, cast iron, mounted with bell and eagle	1500.00	2250.00	3000.00
Bell Toy, Watermelon, N.N. HILL BRASS CO., circa 1905, 8½" long	500.00	750.00	1000.00
Bell Toy, Wild Mule Jack, cast iron	300.00	450.00	600.00
Bicycle, early, wood-spoked, 67" long	100.00	150.00	200.00
Bicycle, Wheeler, red-painted	500.00	750.00	1000.00
BLISS Brooklyn Bridge, 1880s, 4' long x 11" tall, paper litho and stained wood, mechanical	300.00	450.00	600.00

BLISS Brooklyn Bridge
Courtesy Lloyd W. Ralston Auctions

	G	VG	M
Blocks, The Brownie, by MCLAUGHLIN BROS., 1891, 20 litho blocks	175.00	262.50	350.00
Blocks, LEECRAFT CIRCUS BLOCKS, 12 wooden blocks, painted with lion, tiger, letters and numbers, contained in wooden pull-toy cage, 1930s	14.00	21.00	28.00
Blocks, set of six puzzle blocks depicting the Three Bears, Old Mother Hubbard, Little Bo-Peep, Puss in Boots, Jack the Giant Killer and Red Riding Hood. Copyright 1892	35.00	52.50	70.00
Blocks, nested, 6, paper litho on cardboard, picturing children and animals, 1920, CRAMER PUBLISHING CO.	9.00	13.50	18.00
Blocks, 16, embossed, wooden, 1¾" square, red and blue, alphabet and pictures, 7½" square box, Dutch scene on cover, THE EMBOSSING COMPANY'S TOY BLOCKS, USA, price includes box	6.25	9.38	12.50
Blocks, 64, wooden, 1¼" square, very colorful, letters and numbers on sides,			

	G	VG	M
box 6" square, price includes box............	11.00	16.50	22.00
Bones Player, SECOR, 1880, cloth-dressed, cast iron, wood and tin figure with hair, painted pot metal-head, clockwork mechanism in body.....	900.00	1350.00	1800.00

Bones Player
Courtesy Lloyd W. Ralston Auctions

	G	VG	M
Boo Berry, rubber squeeze toy..............	3.00	4.00	6.00
Boxers, Black, mechanical wind-up with IVES clockwork mechanism...	650.00	975.00	1300.00
Boy climbing windmill, tin, weight driven, 16" high, 1900s..............	80.00	120.00	160.00
Boy on Sled friction toy, rear wheels have spokes..	65.00	97.50	130.00
Boy on Tricycle, boy celluloid, trike tin, wind-up...............	80.00	120.00	160.00
Boy on Velocipede, papier mache, cloth and cast iron, wind-up, STEVENS & BROWN or ALTHORP & BERGMANN, circa 1870-1880, 10¾" long...	250.00	375.00	500.00
Boy Scout Five-In-One Mystery Hidden Compass	20.00	30.00	40.00
BRADLEY'S INTER-CHANGEABLE COMBINATION CIRCUS in wooden box with label. Patented May 30, 1882. Contains 35 3"x5¼" interchangeable panels which make up a changeable 15¾"x9" circus scene.........	100.00	150.00	200.00
Brochure, framed, illustrating mechanical			

	G	VG	M
banks, cap pistols, cannon, etc., J.E. STEVENS, CONN...........	55.00	82.50	110.00
BUDDY L tool chests, 1927-28, four different, per each, includes tools..	125.00	187.50	250.00
Bulldog, kid-covered wind-up, walks and turns head, 7½" long..........	94.00	141.00	188.00
Cackling Hen, cardboard, drum, 2¼"x3½", with brown plaster chicken standing on top of drum, metal side handle activates cackling, dated 1936.............	7.00	10.50	14.00
Candy Container, tin, shaped like cannon, candy comes out barrel when crank is turned, "WEST BROS. CO. Grapeville, Pa.", 7½" long........	40.00	60.00	80.00
Candy Container shaped like a desk phone, glass base with cast pewter mouthpiece and wooden receiver, paper labels "lines busy", 4¼" high..	7.00	10.50	14.00
Cannon, ARCADE howitzer, 4" long, circa 1941............	14.00	21.00	28.00
Cannon, AUBURN RUBBER (AUBRUBR) Fieldpiece, 75mm, 7" long	9.00	13.50	18.00
Cannon, AUBURN RUBBER Howitzer, 155mm, 7" long..........	7.50	11.25	15.00
Cannon, BALDWIN, No. 890, 16" long, wood and metal...........	15.00	22.50	30.00
Cannon, BARCLAY, barrel elevated, 2½" long.....	8.00	12.00	16.00
Cannon, BARCLAY, circa 1931 (may be first Barclay cannon, from 1924)....	10.00	15.00	20.00
Cannon, BARCLAY Coast Defense Rifle, 4½" long, 5-man..........	15.00	22.50	30.00
Cannon, BARCLAY Howitzer, 4 wheels, loop hitch horizontal, 3" long.	8.00	12.00	16.00
Cannon, BARCLAY Howitzer, 4 wheels, loop hitch vertical, 3" long...	8.00	12.00	16.00

Cannon, BARCLAY, circa 1931 (may be Barclay's earliest, from 1924)
Courtesy Ed Poole

BARCLAY, top row, L to R: Cannon, spring-firing, spoked wheels, 4" long,
Cannon, barrel elevated, Cannon, spoked wheels, 3" long, Cannon, 7¾" long.
Bottom row, L to R: Coast Defense Rifle, Mortar, heavy, Searchlight
Photo by Ed Poole

Cannon, "Big Bang", approx. 23" long
Photo by Bill Kaufman, Courtesy Good Old Days Store

	G	VG	M
Cannon, BARCLAY Mortar, heavy, swivels on base, 3" long	10.00	15.00	20.00
Cannon, BARCLAY, 4" long, Post-WWII, very large wheels	4.50	6.75	9.00
Cannon, BARCLAY, silver, black rubber wheels, 7¾" long	10.00	15.00	20.00
Cannon, BARCLAY, spoked wheels, 3" long	4.00	6.00	8.00
Cannon, BARCLAY, spring-firing, spoked wheels, 4" long	6.00	9.00	12.00
Cannon, BIG BANG, 8½" long	17.00	25.50	34.00
Cannon, BIG BANG, 9" long	15.00	22.50	30.00
Cannon, BIG BANG, 12" long	11.00	16.50	22.00
Cannon, BIG BANG, 13"	9.00	13.50	18.00
Cannon, BIG BANG, 16" long	11.00	16.50	22.00
Cannon, BIG BANG, No. 10, 18" long	12.00	18.00	24.00
Cannon, BIG BANG, 23" long	22.00	33.00	44.00
Cannon, BIG BANG, 24" long	20.00	30.00	40.00
Cannon, BIG PARADE, cast iron	17.00	25.50	34.00

	G	VG	M
Cannon, "Boy Ranger", fires marbles, cast iron	66.00	99.00	132.00
Cannon, "Boy Scout Machine Gun", 19" with 8¼" wheels	20.00	30.00	40.00
Cannon, brass, with wood base, 9" long	20.00	30.00	40.00
Cannon, carbide, 9" long, wheels	20.00	30.00	40.00
Cannon, Carbide, 11" long, side mounted ammo loader	15.00	22.50	30.00
Cannon, carbide, 4-wheel cast iron, 13½"	55.00	82.50	110.00
Cannon, carbide, cast iron, 15"	34.00	51.00	68.00
Cannon, cast iron, 5" long	10.00	15.00	20.00
Cannon, cast iron on wood base, 5½" long	4.00	6.00	8.00
Cannon, cast iron, 6" long	5.00	7.50	10.00
Cannon, cast iron, 6½" long	10.00	15.00	20.00
Cannon, cast iron, 7" long, early	18.00	27.00	36.00
Cannon, cast iron, 7" long, gold paint	3.00	4.50	6.00
Cannon, cast iron, 7" long, pat. 1894	10.00	15.00	20.00
Cannon, cast iron, 8" long, unusual design	14.00	21.00	28.00
Cannon, cast iron, 9" long, Pat. 1888	24.00	36.00	48.00
Cannon, cast iron with turned barrel, "Hotchkiss", 9½" long	10.00	15.00	20.00
Cannon, cast iron, 9¾" long	9.00	13.50	18.00
Cannon, cast iron, 10" long, black	5.00	7.50	10.00
Cannon, Army, cast iron with brass barrel, 10½" long, mechanically elevated barrel	16.00	24.00	32.00
Cannon, cast iron, 11" long	25.00	37.50	50.00
Cannon, cast iron, 12" long, IVES?, works on black powder	19.00	28.50	38.00

	G	VG	M
Cannon, cast iron, 14" long	50.00	75.00	100.00
Cannon, cast iron, 14" long, on 4-wheel platform	30.00	45.00	60.00
Cannon, cast iron, 15½"	22.50	33.75	45.00
Cannon, cast iron, 15½", "Young America", "Rapid Fire Gun"	50.00	75.00	100.00
Cannon, cast iron, fires caps, mounted on wood base	3.00	4.50	6.00
Cannon, Coast Defense Gun, 5" long, camouflaged, litho tin	10.00	15.00	20.00
Cannon, "Dainty" cast iron, on wood base, 10" long	94.00	141.50	188.00
Cannon, DAVID CARLIN mortar, circa WW I, 15" long, cast iron	50.00	75.00	100.00
Cannon, die cast, approx. 5½" long, old type, shoots	3.00	4.50	6.00
Cannon "Disappearing Coast Defense Gun", THOMAS & SKINNER, Indianapolis, 15" wood and steel, fires	20.00	30.00	40.00
Cannon, field, World War I, cast iron, 15¾"	24.00	36.00	48.00
Cannon, firecracker, cast iron, 4" long, "Pat Apr. 23 1895"	14.00	21.00	28.00
Cannon, GREY IRON, 4½" long	6.00	9.00	12.00
Cannon — Howitzer, circa 1930, double-barreled, 9" long, wood-handled firing lever	5.00	7.50	10.00
Cannon, howitzer type, die cast, shoots, approx. 5" long, spring mechanism, pre WWII	3.00	4.50	6.00
Cannon, IDEAL, 1920s	9.00	13.50	18.00
Cannon, IVES, muzzle-loader, 1900, cast iron, 2 wheels	50.00	75.00	100.00
Cannon, IVES, cast iron, brass barrel	14.00	21.00	28.00
Cannon, IVES, red wheels, brass cannon, 7" long	26.00	39.00	52.00
Cannon, KENTON, firecracker type	14.00	21.00	28.00
Cannon, KILGORE, 2" cast iron firecracker mortar, rubber cannon ball	19.00	28.50	38.00
Cannon, KILGORE, 4½" cast iron firecracker cannon, rubber cannon ball	16.00	24.00	32.00

	G	VG	M
Cannon, MANOIL 19 Metal Action Cannon, early version, "USA"	6.00	9.00	12.00
Cannon, MANOIL 69, metal spoked wheels	5.00	7.50	10.00
Cannon, MANOIL 69, solid wood wheels	6.00	9.00	12.00
Cannon, MANOIL 69, solid wood wheels variant	6.00	9.00	12.00
Cannon, MANOIL "Metal Action Cannon No., 200, later version of 19, "Made in USA"	6.00	9.00	12.00
Cannon, MARX Anti-Aircraft Gun, No. 617	12.50	18.75	25.00
Cannon, "Phoenix", 8" long, brass barrel with touch hole	100.00	150.00	200.00
Cannon, PREMIER, large thick barrel, large wheels, cast iron	4.00	6.00	8.00
Cannon, pressed steel base 9½"	11.25	16.62	22.50
Cannon, RALSTOY No. 23	5.00	7.50	10.00
Cannon, RALSTOY No. 34	5.00	7.50	10.00
Cannon, RALSTOY 3¾" long	5.00	7.50	10.00
Cannon, RANGER JR. cast iron, 10" long	40.00	60.00	80.00
Cannon, rapid fire, cast iron, embossed eagle	106.00	159.00	212.00
Cannon, "Remember The Maine", W.S. HAWKES FOUNDRY, Dayton, Ohio, 13" long, circa 1900	100.00	150.00	200.00
Cannon, sheetmetal, shoots small marbles, 14" long, blue with red wheels	8.00	12.00	16.00
Cannon, silver, with red wooden wheels, approx. 3" long	1.75	2.63	3.50
Cannon, tin, pull lever for corks, 14" wood wheels	24.00	36.00	48.00
Cannon, tin, striped spring-loaded barrel with lever	16.00	24.00	32.00
Cannon, tin, two-wheel, 7¼", 4" high, circa 1915	20.00	30.00	40.00
Cannon, tinplate, 7" long, spring action	5.00	7.50	10.00
Cannon, TOOTSIETOY, approx. 3¾" long, pre WW II, shoots	4.00	6.00	8.000
Cannon, TOOTSIETOY, 40MM AA gun, pre WW II	4.00	6.00	8.00
Cannon, TOOTSIETOY, 155 MM gun, pre WW II	4.00	6.00	8.00

	G	VG	M
Cannon, TOOTSIETOY, 155 MM self-propelled howitzer, 1950s.......	3.00	4.50	6.00
Cannon, TOOTSIETOY, 1930s, approx. 5½" long, shoots..............	10.00	15.00	20.00
Cannon, WYANDOTTE, shoots marbles, 14".....	8.00	12.00	16.00
Captain Action, posable plastic figure..........	15.00	22.50	30.00
Captain Action Costumes, Superman, Batman, Aquaman, Captain America, The Phantom, per each..............	7.50	11.25	15.00
Carousel, ALTHOF BERGMAN, 1870, painted tin, wood base, cloth canopy, 20" tall, clockwork, bisque head doll, wood body, tin arms, turns, cranks and gives motion	900.00	1350.00	1800.00

Carousel, ALTHOF BERGMANN, 1870
Courtesy Lloyd W. Ralston Auctions

	G	VG	M
Carousel Horse, hand-carved, American-made, with jeweled eyes and man and eagle saddle, 64" high, 55" long.........	2600.00	3900.00	5200.00
Carpet Sweeper, miniature Bissell	7.00	10.50	14.00
Cat, cardboard, standing on piece of wood, circa 1900	1.50	2.25	3.00
Catalog: AUBURN RUBBER, pre WW II.......	VALUE RARE		
Catalog: Baltimore Price Reducer, 1928, illustrated with toys, games, etc.....	7.00	10.50	14.00
Catalog: BARCLAY, pre-WWII	VALUE RARE		
Catalog: BILT E-Z, 1924...	1.60	2.40	3.20
Catalog: Butler Bros. 1889, tin toys, squeak toys, etc.	10.00	15.00	20.00

	G	VG	M
Catalog: Butler Bros. 1891, illustrated with mechanical banks, toys, dolls, etc..............	10.00	15.00	20.00
Catalog: Butler Bros. 1930, illustrated with toys, banks, etc..............	14.00	21.00	28.00
Catalog: DENT Hardware Co., 1900, 40 pages.....	26.00	39.00	52.00
Catalog: DENT Hardware Co., 1905.............	16.00	24.00	32.00
Catalog: DENT Hardware Col., Fullerton, Pa., undated..............	VALUE RARE		
	7.00	10.50	14.00
Catalog: DENT Hardware Col, Fullerton, Pa., iron toys	7.00	10.50	14.00
Catalog: "Dunham", Buckley & Co., New York, 1895, toys, etc....	20.00	30.00	40.00
Catalog: Ehrich Bros., New York, 1892, illus of banks, toys, dolls, etc....	20.00	30.00	40.00
Catalog: EUREKA TRICK & NOVELTY CO., circa 1875, 32 pages.........	7.00	10.50	14.00
Catalog: A.J. Fisher, N.Y. 1877, illustrating cap pistols, etc.............	14.00	21.00	28.00
Catalog: IVES Yachts, Ships and Shipping, circa 1915, 24 pages..............	30.00	45.00	60.00
Catalog: Illustrated brochure of cap pistols and animated cap pistols by IVES and WILLIAMS..	7.00	10.50	14.00
Catalog: KENTON HARDWARE CO., No. 16, 1920s, 112 pages.......	66.00	99.00	132.00
Catalog: KENTON HARDWARE CO., 1934, illus in color	90.00	135.00	180.00
Catalog: KINGSBURY Toys, Motor Driven, 1936, 16 pages.........	34.00	51.00	68.00
Catalog: KNAPP Electric Toys No. 35...........	1.70	2.55	3.40
Catalog: MANOIL, circa 1939	75.00	112.50	150.00
Catalog: "McCadden & Bros." Philadelphia, illustrated iron and tin toys, banks, mechanical toys, dolls, games, etc....	40.00	60.00	80.00
Catalog: Mickey Mouse Merchandise Catalog,			

	G	VG	M
1935, by Kay Kamen Co., 80 pages, hundreds of illustrations of Mickey Mouse items	200.00	300.00	400.00
Catalog: Nicol & Co., 1895, illustrating banks, etc.	5.00	75.0	10.00
Catalog: Popsicle Pete Radio News and Premium catalog, early	27.50	41.25	55.00
Catalog, Popsicle Pete's 1949 four-page gift list	3.00	4.50	6.00
Catalog: SCHOENHUT 1903	80.00	120.00	160.00
Catalog, SCHOENHUT 1918	45.00	67.50	90.00
Catalog, SCHOENHUT Circus, 1928	50.00	75.00	100.00
Catalog, SCHOENHUT Humpty Dumpty Circus Toys (other toys as well), circa 1915, many illustrations	30.00	45.00	60.00
Catalog: SELCHOW & RIGHTER, 1894-5, games and toys, illustrated trains, boats, bell toys, mechanical banks, etc.	90.00	135.00	180.00
Catalog: SELCHOW & RIGHTER, 1908-1909, 108 pages	66.00	99.00	132.00
Catalog: SMITH-MILLER (Smitty) 1954	10.00	15.00	20.00
Catalog: State, Adams & Dearborn Sts., Chicago, illustrated	3.00	4.50	6.00

Catalog: SMITH-MILLER (Smitty), 1954
Photo by Bill Kaufman
Courtesy Ray Funk

SMITH-MILLER
Famous Trucks in Miniature

	G	VG	M
Catalog: Carl P. Stern, illustrating cap pistols, etc.	14.00	21.00	28.00
Catalog: J.E. STEVENS CO. 1906, illustrations of iron toys and mechanical banks	24.00	36.00	48.00
Catalog: J.E. STEVENS CO. No. 51, Export	25.00	37.50	50.00

	G	VG	M
Catalog: STRUCTO TOYS, 1931, 8 pages	7.00	10.50	14.00
Catalog: SUPPLEE-BIDDLE of Philadelphia, 1936, 180 pages, many toys	50.00	75.00	100.00
Catalog: Thorsen & Cassady, 1894, guns, etc.	16.00	24.00	32.00
Catalog: Tom Mix 1936 Premium Catalog	17.50	26.25	35.00
Catalog: WARD'S 1953 Xmas Catalog, 318 pp	10.00	15.00	20.00
Catalog: WARD'S 1955 Xmas Catalog, 296 pp	10.00	15.00	20.00
Catalog: A.C. WILLIAMS CO., Ohio, illustrating still banks, cast iron toys, airplanes, etc.	74.00	111.00	148.00
Catalog, WALT DISNEY CHARACTER MERCHANDISE 1940-41	175.00	262.50	350.00
Catalog: WOOLWORTH'S Christmas Catalogs, pre-WWII	VALUE RARE		
Catalog: WOOLWORTH'S Christmas 1951	12.50	18.75	25.00
Cathedral Music Box, tin litho, of organ pipes and cherubs, plays loud or soft according to speed of cranking, 5x5x7", no markings	50.00	75.00	100.00
Champion Express Wagon, 8" long, cast iron	5.00	7.50	10.00
Charlie Tuna rubber squeeze toy	4.50	6.75	9.00
CHEIN Drum, 6"x3½"	4.50	6.75	9.00
CHEIN Easter Egg with chicken on top, opens up to hold candy, circa 1938, tin, 5½"	5.00	7.50	10.00
CHEIN Helicopter, "Toy Town Airways", 1950s, 13" long, friction drive	20.00	30.00	40.00
CHEIN Musical Church, tin, circa 1937	27.50	41.25	55.00
CHEIN Sand-Toy, monkey bends and twists, 7" high	17.00	25.50	34.00
CHEIN See-saw Sand Toy, sand poured through funnel activates girl and boy on see-saw, 1930s	28.00	42.00	56.00
CHEIN Teeter-Totter, 11" works by pouring water or sand onto board	15.00	22.50	30.00

	G	VG	M
CHEMCRAFT Beginners Chemistry set No. 602 by PORTER, 1956.......	11.00	16.50	22.00
CHICAGO Printing Press, No. 15..............	16.00	24.00	32.00
Children's Telephone (set of two), 1920.............	9.00	13.50	18.00
Chimes Bell-Ringer with Elephant, 7" long.......	34.00	51.00	68.00
Climbing Monkey brings coconuts down from palm tree, tin, 18" high, "Monkey Shines, Emporium Specialists"......	40.00	60.00	80.00
Clock, tin, transfer scene of coach and four, works with small pendulum, "Lux Clock Mfg. Co., Waterbury, Conn. USA", 7" high..............	30.00	45.00	60.00
Clockwork Dancers, pair, with melting cloth costumes on wood base, 9½" high.............	240.00	360.00	480.00
Clown, balancing, copper, clown holding arched balancing pole weighted at both ends with lead balls, standing on one leg on small round platform on stationary metal ladder 6½" high. Move clown in any direction and he won't fall off platform...	15.00	22.50	30.00
Clown, balancing on pedestal, painted wood, circa 1920, 15" high.....	37.50	56.25	75.00

Clown, balancing on pedestal, painted wood, circa 1920, 15" high
Courtesy Mapes Auctioneers & Appraisers

	G	VG	M
Clown, clockwork, early, cloth suit, 9½" high.....	210.00	315.00	420.00
Clown, wind-up, papier mache and cardboard, 43" high................	90.00	135.00	180.00

	G	VG	M
Coffee Grinder, cast iron, 4" high.................	26.50	39.75	53.00
"Consul", the educated monkey, tin hand toy, monkey automatically adds, subtracts, multiplies, and divides, 5½x6", dated June 27, 1916..........	25.00	27.50	50.00
Conveyor Belt, wood......	14.00	21.00	28.00
Cot, Army, canvas with steel frame, circa early 1940s	4.00	6.00	8.00
Count Chocula, rubber squeeze toy...........	3.00	4.50	6.00
Cow, papier mache, 44" long	46.00	69.00	92.00
Crackle (KELLOGG'S RICE KRISPIES) handpuppet...........	6.00	9.00	12.00
Crackle (KELLOGG'S RICE KRISPIES) squeeze toy, 8½"..............	3.00	4.50	6.00
Cupboard, cast iron, open work has diamond and heart pattern, two doors and one drawer........	26.00	39.00	52.00
Dancing Figure, mechanical, on wood base, in clothing	200.00	300.00	400.00
Dancers, black, AUTOMATIC TOY WORKS, New York City, 1870, on box, clockwork, carved wood and jesso bodies, clothes, 6¼"w x 10¼" t..............	360.00	540.00	720.00

Dancers, black, AUTOMATIC TOY WORKS, 1870
Courtesy Lloyd W. Ralston Auctions

Davy Crockett Indian Target Set by KEYSTONE WOOD COMPANY. Davy Crockett rifle, all wood and hardboard litho set that pre-dates Davy popularity of the 50s, made about 1949. Wood

	G	VG	M
stagecoach and horses, wood covered wagon and horses, Indians, bear, etc.	15.00	22.50	30.00
"Dealer" Marble Board Game, 24" long, "JS"	35.00	52.50	70.00
Doctor's Set, TRANSOGRAM, 1948, Little Country Doctor, full doctor set, chest and bag	18.00	27.00	36.00
DOEPKE No. W-11 Freddie Fireplug, wooden, comes apart		No Price Found	
Dog, mechanical cloth, walks, 4" high	3.00	4.50	6.00
Donkey, cast iron, 4¼"	3.00	4.50	6.00
Drum, metal body, litho, red white and blue design, varnished wooden hoops, leather "ears", sheepskin head and fiber bottom, with wooden drumsticks, circa 1910	8.00	12.00	16.00
Drum, about 1920, circus decor, tin litho	17.50	26.25	35.00
Drum, 13" diameter, metal with drumsticks	5.00	7.50	10.00
Drum, 13" diameter, wooden, with harness	5.00	7.50	10.00
Electric Stove, works, 1930s	16.00	24.00	32.00
Ferris Wheel, made for World Columbian Exposition in Chicago, 1893, 20" high, clockwork motor, lead passengers	600.00	900.00	1200.00
Flagpole, wooden, with flag that raises and lowers, approx. 8" high	20.00	30.00	40.00
Flying Propellor Ring, heavy metal, circa 1930s-40s, could have been a premium	4.00	6.00	8.00
Fort, RICH TOYS, Clinton, Iowa, 9x11x21, wood, pressed wood and metal with moveable drawbridge circa 1940	35.00	52.50	70.00
Frankenberry rubber squeeze toy	3.00	4.50	6.00
Froggie, rubber squeeze toy, REMPEL, 1940s	9.00	13.50	18.00
Fruit Brute, rubber squeeze toy	3.00	4.50	6.00
G-MAN siren pocket signal, metal, oval-shaped,			

	G	VG	M
WALT REACH TOYS, turn metal crank on side and makes siren sound	3.00	4.50	6.00
Giraffe, 97" high, stuffed cloth	166.00	249.00	332.00
Glass Candy Container shaped like dog	30.00	45.00	60.00
Glass Candy Container, Dolly's milk bottle	2.50	3.75	5.00
Glass Candy Container, shaped like rabbit, VICTORY GLASS	12.50	18.75	25.00
Glass candy container shaped like train engine, 3" long	7.50	11.25	15.00
Glass candy container shaped like a train lantern, 3½" high	5.00	7.50	10.00
Glass candy container, Stop and Go, glass, etc., traffic signal	100.00	150.00	200.00
Glass candy container shaped like a train lantern, tin top and base, "Victory Glass Inc.", 3½" high	3.00	4.50	6.00
Grandfather's Clock, tin, has weights that make hands rotate and pendulum swing, but is not a working clock, transfer decorated, 8¾" high	20.00	30.00	40.00
Grandfather Clock, 9½" high	6.00	9.00	12.00
GREY IRON Clever Clowns Trapeze Set	150.00	225.00	300.00
Grocery Store, tin, 14", scales, cash register, wrapping paper, order pad and pencil, "Little Toy Town Grocery Store", shelves with small boxes of products	66.00	99.00	132.00
H.K. Electric Engine, patented 1908, uses D.C. current	40.00	60.00	80.00
Handwashing Machine with wringer	5.00	7.50	10.00
HASBRO, "Mr. Potato Head", 1950s, plastic car and boat trailer, plus all the parts to create different faces	5.00	7.50	10.00
HESS Dynamobil	160.00	240.00	320.00
Hitch, DENT, two-horse, cast iron 14¼"	12.50	18.75	25.00

	G	VG	M
Hitch, front, for goat cart, two goats............	180.00	270.00	360.00
Hitch, two-horse for caisson, 9½" with figure........	15.00	22.50	30.00
Hitch for log wagon, two-oxen, HUBLEY, 10¼"..	54.00	81.00	108.00
Hitch, HUBLEY, three-horse, for large fire engine, 9" horses.......	26.00	39.00	52.00
Hitch, back, cast iron, for log, KENTON.........	16.00	24.00	32.00
Hitch, KENTON, cast iron, two-horse, with driver, 9"	11.00	16.50	22.00
Hitch, three-horse, cast iron, 5¼"................	3.00	4.50	6.00
Hitch, three-horse, cast iron, 7¼"................	3.00	4.50	6.00
Hitch, three-horse, large front-end, 9" horses.....	34.00	51.00	68.00
Hitch, three-horse, cast iron, 11½" long...........	20.00	30.00	40.00
Hitch, three-horse, cast iron, 15"................	36.00	54.00	72.00
Hobby Horse, "Black Beauty", wooden, 34" long...	12.50	18.75	25.00
"Hometown Favorite Store", S.S. KRESGE CO., MARX tin litho........	25.00	37.50	50.00
"Home Town Movie Theatre", early 30s MARX tin litho theatre with paper movie reel...	25.00	37.50	50.00
Horse, American painted tin, 1870, 4½" long.....	69.00	103.50	138.00

Horse, American painted tin, 1870, 4½" long
Courtesy Lloyd W. Ralston

	G	VG	M
Horse, cast iron, 7" high...	50.00	75.00	100.00
Horse, cast iron, 5".......	15.00	22.50	30.00
Horse, cast iron, standing, 10" high.............	11.00	16.50	22.00
Horse and Rider, tin, on tin rockers, with bell, 6" long	45.00	67.50	90.00
Horse in Hoop, GEORGE BROWN, early.........	250.00	375.00	500.00
Horse, sheet metal, with cast iron jointed legs, full form, 10¾" long, 11" high................	100.00	150.00	200.00
Horse Race, circular track within rectangular box, circa 1900, lever-activated	50.00	75.00	100.00

Horses in Hoops, ALTHOF BERGMANN Courtesy Lloyd W. Ralston Auctions

	G	VG	M
Horses in Hoops, ALTHOF BERGMANN, American painted tin, 1880, 4½" diameter	800.00	1250.00	1600.00
HUBLEY Ferris Wheel, early, cast iron, brass and tin, clockwork	300.00	450.00	600.00
HUBLEY Giraffe for circus wagon, large...........	125.00	187.50	250.00
HUBLEY grasshopper pull toy, cast iron..........	350.00	525.00	700.00
HUBLEY Jantzen Beach Patrol, 8" long, circa 1932, man on surfboard riding through waves....	450.00	675.00	900.00
HUBLEY Jantzen Surf Girl, 8" long, 1932, girl surfboard rider, cast iron....	700.00	1050.00	1400.00

HUBLEY Jantzen Surf Girl Photo Courtesy Lloyd W. Ralston

	G	VG	M
HUBLEY Jumbo the Elephant, on wheels.....	10.00	15.00	20.00
HUBLEY Marathon Rider (bicyclist), cast iron......	120.00	180.00	240.00
HUBLEY Old Dutch Cleanser Woman, cast iron	425.00	637.50	850.00
Hurdy-Gurdy, turn crank and play tune, shows animal playing cello.....	14.00	21.00	28.00
"I Hear A Call", dog with knapsack	34.00	51.00	68.00
Ice Box, "Alaska", cast iron, has glass cube of ice in top, 5" high...........	25.00	37.50	50.00
Iron and Trivet, cast iron...	20.00	30.00	40.00
Iron, tin, 5" high.........	5.00	7.50	10.00
Iron, tin, 3½" high.......	9.00	13.50	18.00

IVES Strukt-iron set, 1915
Courtesy Lloyd W. Ralston Auctions

IVES Mechanical Bear
Courtesy PB Eighty-Four, New York

IVES, BLAKESLY & WILLIAMS Mule Dancers
Courtesy Lloyd W. Ralston Auctions

IVES Fire Engine House
Courtesy Lloyd W. Ralston Auctions

IVES Black Dancers, clockwork, circa 1880
Photo Courtesy PB Eighty-Four

	G	VG	M
IVES Barrel Walkers, circa 1890, wood and paper litho balance toy, acrobat, ballerina, monkey	125.00	187.50	250.00
IVES Bear, mechanical wind-up	600.00	900.00	1200.00

	G	VG	M
IVES Black Dancers, clockwork, circa 1880, 11" high	250.00	375.00	500.00
IVES Boy smoking cigar and holding stomach, cast iron	35.00	52.50	70.00
IVES "Elephant Car", circus cage, cast iron, "serpent eggs" magic trick can be burnt in elephant's trunk, "Greatest Show on Earth"	330.00	495.00	660.00
IVES Fire Engine House, circa 1890, cast iron and wood, 16" long	460.00	690.00	920.00
IVES Juggler, clockwork, early	1000.00	1500.00	2000.00
IVES Mechanical Bear, patent 1872	240.00	360.00	480.00
IVES Struktiron set, 1915	100.00	150.00	200.00
IVES Struktiron, 1916, non-motorized, with box	100.00	150.00	200.00
IVES Struktiron, building set, 1916, motorized, with box	75.00	112.50	150.00

IVES Walking Elephant, "Pat. 1873", cast iron, 3½" long, walks down incline, moving legs and trunk	G	VG	M
	100.00	150.00	200.00
IVES Women Churning Butter, "Patented March 31st 1874", 8½" high	850.00	1275.00	1700.00
IVES, BLAKESLEY & WILLIAMS, 1890, Mule Dancers, mechanical revolving, paper litho, painted tin, wooden box, clockwork, 8" tall	1600.00	2400.00	3200.00
Jack-In-The-Box, monkey	60.00	90.00	120.00
Jockey, small, on very large horse, on base, tin, 14½" high, wheeled	250.00	375.00	500.00
"Jolly Jungleers", MILTON BRADLEY, 1932, derringer type pistol shoots over animal targets	22.50	33.75	45.00
JONES Pillbox	60.00	90.00	120.00
Jumping Jack, composition and wood	70.00	105.00	140.00
Junior G-Man Whistle	12.50	18.75	25.00
Kaleidoscope, "C. BUSH, Prov. R.I. 1874", wood, brass & glass, 14" high	220.00	330.00	440.00
Kaleidoscope, STEVENS	21.00	31.50	42.00
Kangaroo, cast iron, 6¼" long, "Jumps"	114.00	171.00	228.00
KENTON Baggage Cart, 6"	30.00	45.00	60.00
KENTON Dray Wagon, lithographed paper on sides, driver, 15½" long	26.00	39.00	52.00
KENTON Driver, small size	1.50	2.25	3.00
KENTON Driver with high hat for pleasure vehicle	5.00	7.50	10.00
KENTON Egyptian Toys — Rhino, Lion, Elephant, offered at $175 each, condition unspecified			
KENTON Elephant — "Land-on Roosevelt 1936"	60.00	90.00	120.00
KENTON Musicians, 8, for Kenton Band Wagon	17.50	26.25	35.00
KENTON Polar Bear, cast iron	3.00	4.50	6.00
KENTON Stove, cast iron, marked "Oak" on door	12.00	18.00	24.00
KENTON Stove, with warming shelves and stove plates, high back for smokestack, "Royal" on door and shelves, 10" high	20.00	30.00	40.00

"Kid Flyer"
Courtesy PB 84 NY

"Kid Flyer" boy on scooter, tin litho, string-wound, 8½" long	G	VG	M
	80.00	120.00	160.00
Kingpin Bowling Game, "BALDWIN MFG. CO. Brooklyn NY No. 300", circa 1940	15.00	22.50	30.00
KINGSBURY Fire Station, No. 8, clockwork bell and door, 9"x10"x13"	125.00	187.50	250.00
"Knockout Target Shooting Gallery", lithographed tin with rifle, many targets	25.00	37.50	50.00
Ladder for fire trucks, cast iron	1.00	1.50	2.00
Ladders, stamped steel, from HUBLEY and ARCADE trucks	8.00	12.00	16.00
Lamb, tin, 2¼" long	18.00	27.00	36.00
Lawnmower, ARCADE, circa 1920, iron and wood	17.50	26.25	35.00
LINCOLN LOGS, Set No. 1A, JOHN WRIGHT, pat 1920	2.66	3.99	5.32
LINCOLN LOGS, 1923	5.00	7.50	10.00
LINCOLN LOGS, in wooden box	10.00	15.00	20.00
LINCOLN LOGS, pre WW II, large set, price includes box	20.00	30.00	40.00
LINCOLN TIMBERS, pre WW II, with box	5.00	7.50	10.00
"Lindstrom's Little Show", cardboard and wood theatre with seven show strips	75.00	112.50	150.00
Lion in Hoop, tin 6¼" high	80.00	120.00	160.00
LIONEL Science Kit, circa 1960	17.50	26.25	35.00
Machine Gun, GREY IRON, rapid fire, 9" long, cast iron, 1930s	40.00	60.00	80.00
Machine Gun, wood and steel, gravity fed, wooden bullets	4.00	6.00	8.00
Magic Lantern	60.00	90.00	120.00

Magic Lantern, KEYSTONE, "Radioptocin"	G	VG	M
	26.00	39.00	52.00
Magic Lantern Projector, tin, embossed deer on door and side, 8" long	8.00	12.00	16.00

Man on Bicycle, animated, tin, high wheel bike, bell on top of bicycle, 10½" high	G	VG	M
	360.00	540.00	720.00
Man, smoking, clockwork mechanism	500.00	750.00	1000.00

MARBLES

Marbles are known to date back as far as ancient Rome, when they were made of clay. Marbles are divided into types, such as "Indian Swirls", "Clambroth", "Lutz Type Swirls", etc. Size numbers range from 000, which equals ½ inch, to 8, which equals one and ⅛ inch. There are estimated to be 8-10,000 current collectors of marbles, about 600 of whom belong to the Marble Collectors' Society of America (see Leading Collectors and Dealers).

	G	VG	M		G	VG	M
Marbles, antique, half gallon	17.50	26.25	35.00	Marbles, ¾" swirl marbles, several	9.00	13.50	18.00
Marbles, clay, 2 for	20.00	30.00	40.00	Marbles, swirl, 2" diameter	3.50	5.25	7.00
Marbles, with sulphide animal centers, price per each marble	15.00	22.50	30.00	Marbles, swirl, 11 marbles	30.00	45.00	60.00
Marbles, glass, with spiral swirls, up to $20 apiece in mint				Marbles, bag of swirls	18.75	29.12	37.50
				Marbles, bag of swirls	16.25	24.12	32.50
				Marbles, lot of assorted marbles	5.00	7.50	10.00

MANOIL Target, lead, either "4-5-6" or "7-8-9". "1-2-3" doesn't appear to exist, except in a version produced by collectors Ed Poole and Ron Eccles. Manoil's order number for the targets, without specifying which, was 76			
	40.00	60.00	80.00

Manoil Targets,
"4 5 6", "7 8 9"
Photo by Don Pielin

Marionette Show, electrically operated, Santa Claus' workshop with 23 moving figures and four moving animals making presents, 46" high, 72" long, 24" deep	630.00	945.00	1260.00
Marky Maypo rubber squeeze toy, 1960s	3.00	4.50	6.00
MARX Air-Sea Power game	7.50	11.25	15.00
MARX Air-Sea Power Bombing Set	7.50	11.25	15.00

MARX Army and Navy Mechanical Target No. G169	G	VG	M
	7.50	11.25	15.00
MARX Army Code Sender, 9½" Morse key and phone, pressed steel	6.00	9.00	12.00
MARX Ballerina, 6" high, operated by sawtooth bar, pulled through	45.00	67.50	90.00
MARX Bear Cyclist, metal, lever action	50.00	75.00	100.00
MARX Bust 'Em Target Game No. G38	7.50	11.25	15.00
MARX Cat with Ball, cable-operated, tin litho	6.50	9.75	13.00

MARX Cat with Ball, cable operated
Courtesy Mapes Auctioneers & Appraisers

MARX "Champion Skater" ballet dancer, pull spinning rod out of motor, place skater in upright position and he spins	50.00	75.00	100.00

MARX "Climbing Fireman", tin and plastic
Courtesy Mapes Auctioneers & Appraisers

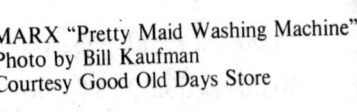

MARX "Pretty Maid Washing Machine"
Photo by Bill Kaufman
Courtesy Good Old Days Store

	G	VG	M
MARX "Climbing Fireman", tin and plastic.	25.00	37.50	50.00
MARX Co. A Barracks, tin litho building, 6x8x12"..	7.00	10.50	14.00
MARX Colonial Doll House No. 4052............	24.00	36.00	48.00
MARX Deluxe Dial Typewriter, 1930s......	12.00	18.00	24.00
MARX Dial Typewriter No. 1000A, 1930s.........	9.00	13.50	18.00
MARX Dishwasher K54, circa 1950s...........	4.00	6.00	8.00
MARX Doll House No. 4021................	5.00	7.50	10.00
MARX Doll House No. 4030................	7.50	11.25	15.00
MARX Headquarters, tin litho, U.S. Army Training Center, 5x8x11"........	12.50	18.75	25.00
MARX Indian Warfare Set, metal bldgs. and plastic figures, 1950s.........	12.50	18.75	25.00
MARX Junior Dial Typewriter No. 2109, circa 1930s.............	20.00	30.00	40.00
MARX Kitchen Sink K47, circa 1950s...........	4.00	6.00	8.00
MARX Little Red Schoolhouse set, 1950s..	15.00	22.50	30.00
MARX Pete the Parrot battery operated talking parrot perched on a lithographed tin branch, eyes light up, tail, wings and beak move........	135.00	212.50	270.00
MARX "Pretty Maid Washing Machine", circa 1930s, 4½" high.......	25.00	37.50	50.00

	G	VG	M
MARX Refrigerator, K42, circa 1950s............	4.00	6.00	8.00
MARX Rex Mars Planet Patrol 45 Cal. machine-gun, tin and plastic, winds up. 22" long............	22.00	33.00	44.00
MARX Searchlight, tin litho, 3½" high........	8.00	12.00	16.00
MARX Stove K39, circa 1950s	4.00	6.00	8.00
MARX Swinging Arm Target Game No. G52...	17.50	26.25	35.00
MARX Swinging Arm Target Game No. G55...	17.50	26.25	35.00
MARX Suburban Colonial Dollhouse, metal......	5.00	7.50	10.00
MARX Tunnel, tin litho, 8"x10"x7" depicts farm scene, rolling hills, houses	5.00	7.50	10.00
MARX Typewriter No. 1110, metal and plastic, circa 1950s-1960s.......	9.00	13.50	18.00
MATTEL Jack in the Music Box, circa 1950s........	2.50	3.75	5.00
Meat Grinder with clamp, die cast..............	2.50	3.75	5.00
MECCANO Set 0........	.62	.93	1.25
MECCANO Set 1........	22.50	33.75	45.00
MECCANO Set 1A.......	11.00	16.50	22.00
MECCANO Set 1X.......	100.00	150.00	200.00
MECCANO Set 2........	50.00	75.00	100.00
MECCANO Set 2A.......	16.00	24.00	32.00
MECCANO Set 3........	20.00	30.00	40.00
MECCANO Set 3A.......	20.00	30.00	40.00
MECCANO Set 4........	200.00	300.00	400.00
MECCANO Set 4A.......	32.00	48.00	64.00
MECCANO Engineering Erector Set...........	5.00	7.50	10.00
MECCANO Microscope Set, 1933.............	5.00	7.50	10.00
Merry-Go-Round, wind-up, lithographed paper and wood, with four bisque			

	G	VG	M
figures riding fur-skinned papier mache horses.....	466.00	699.00	932.00
Merry-Go-Round, wood and lithographed paper Jenny musical wind-up with five horse-form seats........	166.00	249.00	332.00
Microphone, WARD toy...	40.00	60.00	80.00
Monkey, mechanical, in red pants, red-checked shirt, squeeze metal lever attached to 34" spiral wire and monkey jumps alongside you, hitting cymbals, 10" high.......	7.50	11.25	15.00
Monkey on String, 8" high.	11.00	16.50	22.00
Monkey string-climber.....	15.00	22.50	30.00
Monkey, stuffed, red felt cap and jacket, glass eyes, moveable arms and legs, move his tail and head moves from side to side, and up and down, circa 1910, 9½" high........	14.00	21.00	28.00
Mound of Earth, tin litho, 4" long (for toy soldiers).	2.00	3.00	4.00
Mound of Rocks, tin litho (for toy soldiers)........	5.00	7.50	10.00
Movie-Jector, hand crank..	25.00	37.50	50.00
Movie Projector, "Flip Movies", turn crank and flip cards from "Midgette" movies, with film, circa early 1930s...........	56.00	84.00	112.00
"Movie Projector Gun", film only, 1937, Box 1 contains Chaplin, Gasoline Alley, Babe Ruth, Buffalo Bill, Harold Teen; Box 2 contains Dick Tracy, Terry & Pirates, Smitty, Orphan Annie, Winnie Winkle; Box 3 contains Clyde Beatty, Gumps, Little Joe, Tiny Tim, Buffalo Bill; Box 4 contains Gasoline Alley, Chaplin, Tracy, Lone Ranger, Harold Teen. Price per box	3.50	5.25	7.00
Movie Projector, "Uncle Sam", hand cranks, circa 1930s	25.00	37.50	50.00
Music Box, tin, shaped like coffee grinder, 3" high...	22.50	33.75	45.00

	G	VG	M
Musical Spinner Toy, hand-carved bear, spin with hand and hear music box play	64.00	96.00	128.00
MYSTO Erector Set No. 1.	75.00	112.50	150.00
MYSTO Erector Set No. 1A	50.00	75.00	100.00
MYSTO Erector Set No. 2, circa 1915.............	50.00	75.00	100.00
MYSTO Erector Set No. 2A	50.00	75.00	100.00
MYSTO Erector Set No. 3A	50.00	75.00	100.00
Noah's Ark, 6½" long, wooden, 12 animals, Noah.................	50.00	75.00	100.00
Noah's Ark, 11" long, 27 animals	75.00	112.50	150.00
Noah's Ark, BLISS, 13¼" long, 10 animals, wooden	150.00	225.00	300.00
Noah's Ark, cardboard, with animals, 14" long.......	10.00	15.00	20.00
Noah's Ark, CONVERSE, 14" long, carved wooden animals	40.00	60.00	80.00
Noah's Ark with wooden village blocks..........	5.00	7.50	10.00
Noah's Ark, wood litho, 10" long with animals.......	24.00	36.00	48.00
Noise Maker, tin, shaped like old-fashioned phone mouthpiece, 2¼" high...	5.00	7.50	10.00
OHIO ART Barrel organ, musical, 5½" tall.......	5.50	8.25	11.00
OHIO ART Beach Toy Water Pumper, circa 1939, 8½" high, signed "Elaine Ends Hileman"..	5.00	7.50	10.00
OHIO ART Children's Tea Set, tin, 14 pieces.......	1.50	2.25	3.00
OHIO ART Drum, 6"x4"..	4.00	6.00	8.00
OHIO ART Sandpail, 1940s, tin litho..............	4.00	6.00	8.00
OHIO ART Shooting Gallery, key wind.......	35.00	52.50	70.00
OHIO ART Sunnyfield Farms Barn and Silo set with animals, tin litho, 1950s	16.00	24.00	32.00
OHIO ART Toyland Band, drums, bass and snare, cymbals, triangle and sticks, 7½" high........	1.50	2.25	3.00
OHIO ART Washtub, tin litho, wood and metal scrubboard, 1940s......	4.00	6.00	8.00
"Old Kentucky Home" wood litho action toy, six dancers, singer-musicians,			

	G	VG	M
moved by hand crank, 15½" long	366.00	549.00	732.00
Organ Grinder, monkey, 6" wooden, push bottom, squeaks and dances, KOHNER BROS.	4.00	6.00	8.00
Oven, ARCADE, Roper Gas	9.00	13.50	18.00
Paddle Wheel and Tower on base, tin, 14" high	20.00	30.00	40.00
"Paris Coaster", wood-wheeled cart	26.00	39.00	52.00

PARKER BROS. Toy Town Garage Courtesy Lloyd W. Ralston Auctions

	G	VG	M
PARKER BROS., 1910, Toy Town Garage, 3 litho tin penny cars, paper litho garage	550.00	825.00	1100.00
PARKER BROS. "Toy Town Grocery Store" . . .	110.00	165.00	220.00
Phonograph, toy, GENOLA, cranks, with sound horn	110.00	165.00	220.00
Phonograph, toy, NERONA, cranks, sound comes from horn connected to needle, early . . .	90.00	135.00	180.00
Piano, 22½" long	60.00	90.00	120.00
Pig and Piglet in cage, wood, cloth and lithographed paper, spring-loaded squeak toy .	50.00	75.00	100.00
PLAROLA CORPORATION Organ, tin lithographed, with six organ rolls	162.50	243.75	325.00
"Play Store Register", tin and brass, DURABLE TOY AND NOVELTY CO., 4" high	6.00	9.00	12.00
Pop (KELLOGG'S RICE KRISPIES) squeeze toy, 8½" high	3.00	4.50	5.00
Pop (KELLOGG'S RICE KRISPIES) hand puppet .	6.00	9.00	12.00

	G	VG	M
Pram, four-wheel painted wood with leather canopy and wood wheels	66.00	99.00	132.00
"Preacher In The Pulpit" mechanical toy, all wood .	300.00	450.00	600.00
Pull Bell Toy, tin dog standing on platform with bell mechanism on back, 14" long	116.00	174.00	232.00
Pull Toy, Boy on Donkey, 5½"	24.00	36.00	48.00
Pull Toy, Elephant, hide-covered with bisque head, native	70.00	105.00	140.00
Pull Toy, Elephant, tin, 4½" long, 1870, nothing on back	90.00	135.00	180.00
Pull Toy, Elephant, tin, with blanket, iron wheels, 4½" long	25.00	37.50	50.00
Pull Toy, elephant with saddle, tin. Iron wheels, 4½" high	35.00	52.50	70.00
Pull Toy, Elephant, tin, 9" long, early	112.50	168.75	225.00
Pull Toy, Elephant with howdah, cast iron	300.00	450.00	600.00
Pull Toy, Elephants, two, on platform, tin, 12" long . . .	120.00	180.00	240.00
Pull Toy, Goat, 9½" long, tin, early	80.00	120.00	160.00
Pull Toy, four race horses and riders, tin with cast iron wheels, 8¼" long . . .	134.00	201.00	268.00
Pull Toy, horse, galloping, tin, 7" long	40.00	60.00	80.00
Pull Toy, horse, tin, iron wheels, 9" long	75.00	11.250	150.00
Pull Toy, horse, 13¼" high, leather reins, metal stirrups, felt saddle, circa 1880	30.00	45.00	60.00
Pull Toy, horse and animated figure with composition head and tin arms playing drum and cymbal. Horse is tin, wheels, wooden platform, 13½" long	155.00	232.50	310.00
Pull Toy, horse and cart with chicken-shaped sides, iron wheels, tin, 5¼" long	28.00	42.00	56.00
Pull Toy, horse and covered delivery wagon, tin, 5¼" long	25.00	37.50	50.00

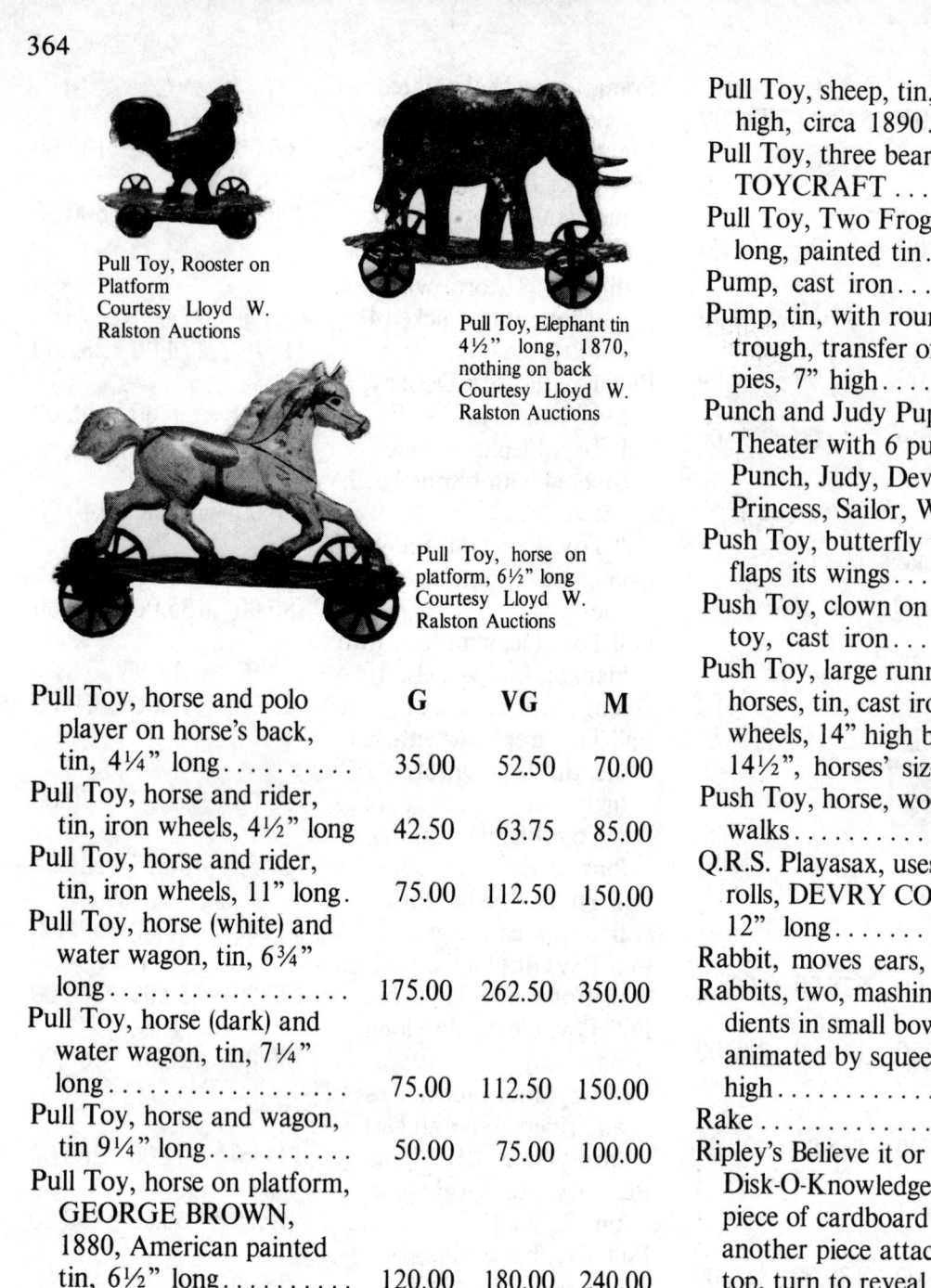

Pull Toy, Rooster on Platform
Courtesy Lloyd W. Ralston Auctions

Pull Toy, Elephant tin 4½" long, 1870, nothing on back
Courtesy Lloyd W. Ralston Auctions

Pull Toy, horse on platform, 6½" long
Courtesy Lloyd W. Ralston Auctions

	G	VG	M
Pull Toy, horse and polo player on horse's back, tin, 4¼" long.........	35.00	52.50	70.00
Pull Toy, horse and rider, tin, iron wheels, 4½" long	42.50	63.75	85.00
Pull Toy, horse and rider, tin, iron wheels, 11" long.	75.00	112.50	150.00
Pull Toy, horse (white) and water wagon, tin, 6¾" long..............	175.00	262.50	350.00
Pull Toy, horse (dark) and water wagon, tin, 7¼" long..............	75.00	112.50	150.00
Pull Toy, horse and wagon, tin 9¼" long...........	50.00	75.00	100.00
Pull Toy, horse on platform, GEORGE BROWN, 1880, American painted tin, 6½" long..........	120.00	180.00	240.00
Pull Toy, horse (race horse) in car, tin "Moxie", 8½" long...............	54.00	81.00	108.00
Pull Toy, horsewoman riding sidesaddle on pony, cast iron.............	66.00	99.00	132.00
Pull Toy, jockey on dog, 10¼" long, tin, early....	370.00	555.00	740.00
Pull Toy, Jockey on Horse, 9" long, tin, hair tail....	600.00	900.00	1200.00
Pull Toy, Jumbo Elephant on wheels, GIBBS, 10" long................	150.00	225.00	300.00
Pull Toy, rooster, tin, 3¼" long................	22.00	33.00	44.00
Pull Toy, rooster on platform, 1890 painted tin, 4¾" long...........	80.00	120.00	160.00

	G	VG	M
Pull Toy, sheep, tin, 6¼" high, circa 1890.......	100.00	150.00	200.00
Pull Toy, three bears by TOYCRAFT..........	7.00	10.50	14.00
Pull Toy, Two Frogs, 7½" long, painted tin.......	150.00	225.00	300.00
Pump, cast iron..........	12.50	18.75	25.00
Pump, tin, with round trough, transfer of puppies, 7" high...........	14.00	21.00	28.00
Punch and Judy Puppet Theater with 6 puppets: Punch, Judy, Devil, Princess, Sailor, Workman	300.00	450.00	600.00
Push Toy, butterfly that flaps its wings..........	30.00	45.00	60.00
Push Toy, clown on log, bell toy, cast iron..........	100.00	150.00	200.00
Push Toy, large running horses, tin, cast iron wheels, 14" high by 14½", horses' size......	234.00	351.00	468.00
Push Toy, horse, wooden, walks................	19.00	28.50	38.00
Q.R.S. Playasax, uses paper rolls, DEVRY CORP., 12" long..............	87.50	131.25	175.00
Rabbit, moves ears, small..	110.00	165.00	220.00
Rabbits, two, mashing ingredients in small bowl, tin, animated by squeezing, 6" high..................	12.00	18.00	24.00
Rake....................	1.50	2.25	3.00
Ripley's Believe it or Not Disk-O-Knowledge, round piece of cardboard with another piece attached on top, turn to reveal questions and answers, 1932, 9½" diameter..........	2.50	3.75	5.00
Road Signs, cast iron, two bases and four signs, read "R.R. Crossing", "Stop", "Hill", "US 30", ARCADE, price per set.....	8.00	10.00	12.00
"Rocket Ring", with futuristic rocket on top of ring, whistles, 1930s.....	3.00	4.50	6.00
Rocking Chair, two-horse, wood and wicker.......	26.00	39.00	52.00
Rocking Horse, cloth and wood.................	40.00	60.00	80.00
Rocking Horse, tin, horse with rider, 6" long....	140.00	210.00	280.00
Rocking Horse, hand carved, all wood..........	26.00	39.00	52.00

Rocking Horse, painted	G	VG	M
wood	66.00	99.00	132.00
Rocking Horse, wood	150.00	225.00	300.00
Rocking Horse, hair mane and tail, saddle, wooden horse, 33" high	200.00	300.00	400.00
Rocking Horse, 36" high on wooden base	90.00	135.00	180.00
Rocking Horse, "Shoo Fly"	15.00	22.50	30.00
Rocking Toy, tin, girl on horse, 3¾" long	34.00	51.00	68.00
Roller Skates, early, metal	7.00	10.50	14.00
Rolmonica, harmonica that plays rolls of tunes, "Blow, crank and play", with three songs, 1930s	70.00	105.00	140.00
Roly Poly, Boy on Horse, circa 1900	50.00	75.00	100.00
Roly Poly Clown, circa 1900, 10" high, papier mache	42.50	63.75	85.00

Sand Toy Set, CHICK ART CO. 19402, includes tin litho frog, sailboat, shovel and round sieve	G	VG	M
	16.00	24.00	32.00
Sandbags, variously marked, for toy soldiers	1.00	1.50	2.00
Sand Pail, tin litho, circa 1940	4.00	6.00	8.00
Sand Toy, Dumping Sandy (WOLVERINE?), 1917, 10" high	36.00	54.00	72.00
Sand Toy, pulley elevator, 8½" high, windmill type	44.00	66.00	88.00
Scales, cast iron, tin tray and four brass weights, 5¾" long	26.00	39.00	52.00
Scales, cast iron, "DAYTON", 3½" high	18.00	27.00	36.00

SCHOENHUT
by Bruce and Blossom Abell

Albert Schoenhut was a German emigrant toy-maker. His company, founded in 1903, made many toys including "The Humpty Dumpty Circus", dolls, toy pianos, other musical instruments, and a myriad of other toy items usually made of wood. The A. Schoenhut Co. closed its doors in 1933 though there were other Schoenhuts who made toys later. The last manufacturer of "Humpty Dumpty Circus" toys was Nelson Delavan of Seneca Falls, N.Y. Mr. Delavan bought the use of the name and manufacturing rights and operated from 1950 to 1953. We have not included pricing information on the Delavans here but they are generally lower priced than the reduced size Schoenhuts which they resemble.

Schoenhut produced many models of his animals and figures over the thirty years of production and we find that invariably model changes had to do with reducing costs to hold established prices. Glass eyes and carved faces gave way to steam pressed heads and painted eyes. Usually the glass-eyed earlier versions demand higher prices than the later models with painted-eyes. In 1923 Schoenhut brought out the "Reduced Size" circus which was about 70% of the size of the comparable full-size counterpart, i.e., full size elephant is about 8¼" long and 5½" high while the reduced size elephant is 6¼" long and 4⅜" high. All of the reduced size were painted-eye and steam pressed heads with very little hand work or shaded paint.

Since there are so many models and variations as well as condition gradations any attempt to price them all would result in unmitigated confusion. We, therefore, have priced each animal, performer, or accessory giving a range of price from a fair condition later model to a mint early piece. All names are taken from the Schoenhut catalogs we own. If a reader would care to identify specific models we would suggest "Schoenhut's Humpty Dumpty Circus from A to Z" by Evelyn Ackerman and Fredrick E. Keller.

Condition as we use it is as follows:

FAIR — As found condition — well worn and soiled — may have some minor parts missing or replaced — considerable paint wear or tiny chips on bisque heads — Original clothing survives but may be damaged, dirty, or moth-eaten. Probably the lowest class that could be displayed.

MINT — Pristine and unplayed with!!! — only concession to age would be loose elastic and slight paint defects caused by age-not wear!

Most items offered for sale will be between these two extremes. Properly restored pieces (not kid repaints or momma's clothes) would be considered better than fair.

BRUCE AND BLOSSOM ABELL have been involved with antique toys for over twenty years and are members of a number of toy collecting groups and clubs. Bruce is associate editor of "The Schoenhut Newsletter" (published by R.W. Zimmerman, 45 Louis Ave., W. Seneca, N.Y. 14244), and both contribute to Antique Toy World and other collector's journals. Their specialty is Schoenhuts, and they enjoy researching the rare pieces and seldom-seen examples, as well as buying, selling, trading, and repairing all kinds of Schoenhut Circus toys.

SCHOENHUT CIRCUS
Listing by Bruce and Blossom Abell

PERFORMERS	FAIR	MINT
Chinaman Acrobat	100.00	350.00
Clown	30.00	150.00
Clown-Reduced	25.00	80.00
Gent Acrobat	140.00	450.00
Hobo	65.00	225.00
Hobo-Reduced	125.00	300.00
Lady Acrobat	80.00	350.00
Lady Rider	65.00	350.00
Lady Rider-Reduced	60.00	150.00
Lion Tamer	65.00	400.00
Negro Dude	80.00	350.00
Negro Dude-Reduced	125.00	300.00
Ringmaster	65.00	400.00
Ringmaster-Reduced	55.00	160.00

SCHOENHUT Clowns
Courtesy PB Eighty-Four

SCHOENHUT Negro Dude, 9" high
Courtesy Mapes Auctioneers & Appraisers

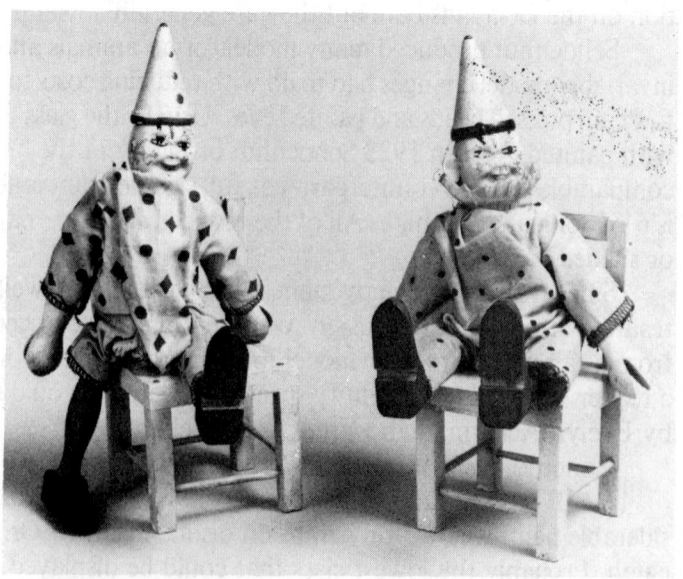

SCHOENHUT Clowns
Courtesy Mapes Auctioneers & Appraisers

SCHOENHUT Circus figures and equipment, circa 1904
Photo Courtesy Garth's Auctions, Inc.

SCHOENHUT Open Mouth - Glass Eyed Early ARABIAN CAMEL
Appears to be Excellent but close examination shows two rear legs substitutes
— because of this, Fair Retail $125.00
Photo and caption courtesy Bruce and Blossom Abell

Barrels and Elephant
Courtesy PB Eighty-Four

ACCESSORIES	FAIR	MINT
Ball	20.00	50.00
Ball-Reduced	30.00	60.00
Barrel	5.00	10.00
Barrel-Reduced	5.00	10.00
Bottle with label	25.00	75.00
Chair	5.00	12.00
Chair-Reduced	5.00	12.00
Flexible Cage	100.00	185.00
Goblet	5.00	10.00
Hoop	15.00	35.00
Hoop-Reduced	15.00	35.00
Horizontal Bar	60.00	175.00
Ladder	8.00	15.00
Ladder-Reduced	10.00	16.00
Pedestal-Tall	12.00	40.00
Pedestal-Short	8.00	25.00
Pedestal-Reduced	8.00	20.00
Table	10.00	40.00
Table-Reduced	12.00	50.00
Tent	350.00	3000.00
Tent-Reduced	300.00	850.00
Tub	8.00	22.00
Tub-Reduced	6.00	18.00
Weight, all 3 sizes		
50 lb., 100 lb., 200 lb.	12.00	60.00
Whip	10.00	25.00
Whip-Reduced	10.00	25.00

ANIMALS	FAIR	MINT
Alligator	65.00	300.00
Brown Bear	55.00	400.00
Brown Bear-Reduced	85.00	300.00
Buffalo	85.00	600.00
Buffalo-Reduced	85.00	250.00
Bulldog	100.00	800.00
Burro	50.00	350.00

	FAIR	MINT
Camel-Arabian 1 hump	60.00	250.00
Camel-Bactrian 2 hump	75.00	600.00
Camel-Bactrian Reduced	75.00	200.00
Cat	150.00	1000.00
Cow	75.00	400.00
Deer	110.00	500.00
Donkey	25.00	140.00
Donkey-Reduced	20.00	50.00
Elephant	35.00	175.00
Elephant-Reduced	35.00	60.00
Gazelle	200.00	1000.00
Giraffe	75.00	300.00
Giraffe-Reduced	75.00	225.00
Goat	45.00	200.00
Goat-Reduced	100.00	250.00
Goose	110.00	300.00
Gorilla	500.00	1500.00
Hippopotamus	85.00	350.00
Hippopotamus-Reduced	85.00	250.00
Horse-Dark	45.00	180.00
Horse-Dark-Reduced	45.00	125.00
Horse-White	45.00	180.00
Horse-White-Reduced	45.00	125.00
Hyena	200.00	1000.00
Kangaroo	180.00	700.00
Leopard	80.00	300.00

SCHOENHUT Donkey and Elephant
Courtesy Mapes Auctioneers & Appraisers

SCHOENHUT GE TIGER AND LEOPARD
About as near mint as we've ever seen — Retail $300.00 either
Photo and caption courtesy Bruce and Blossom Abell

SCHOENHUT GE HORSES, DARK AND WHITE
Dark Horse close to mint but not quite — Retail $150.00
White horse missing platform, otherwise EX — with replacement platform
$135.00
Photo and caption courtesy Bruce and Blossom Abell

	FAIR	MINT
Leopard-Reduced	60.00	175.00
Lion	55.00	650.00
Lion-Reduced	50.00	150.00
Monkey	75.00	350.00
Ostrich	125.00	450.00
Ostrich-Reduced	150.00	400.00
Pig	110.00	450.00
Pig-Reduced	125.00	350.00
Polar Bear	150.00	500.00
Poodle	40.00	500.00
Poodle-Reduced	90.00	250.00
Rabbit	200.00	600.00
Rhinocerous	90.00	450.00

SCHOENHUT GIRAFFE, Open Mouth - Glass eyed early
VG Condition — Retail $175.00
Photo and caption courtesy Bruce and Blossom Abell

Rhinocerous-Reduced	80.00	200.00
Sea Lion	175.00	600.00
Sheep	100.00	350.00
Tiger	60.00	300.00
Tiger-Reduced	50.00	187.50
Wolf	200.00	1000.00
Zebra	55.00	300.00
Zebra-Reduced	55.00	225.00
Zebu	200.00	1200.00

End Schoenhut Circus listing
by Bruce and Blossom Abell

SCHOENHUT Doll Cottage, 14½"x11"	150.00	225.00	300.00
SCHOENHUT Golfer in knickers	130.00	195.00	260.00
SCHOENHUT Golfer in skirt	200.00	300.00	400.00

SCHOENHUT golfer in skirt
Photo Courtesy PB84

SCHOENHUT Hollywood Home buildings, set of six homes, 1928	150.00	225.00	300.00
SCHOENHUT Piano, 6"x6"x5"	42.00	63.00	84.00
SCHOENHUT Piano, 7"x6"x7", five keys	60.00	90.00	120.00

	G	VG	M
SCHOENHUT Piano, 9¾" long, 8" high, 7½" deep, 8 keys..........	50.00	75.00	100.00
SCHOENHUT Piano, 10"x10"x8"............	45.00	67.50	90.00
SCHOENHUT Piano, 10"x11"x8"............	45.00	67.50	90.00
SCHOENHUT Piano, 15½"x9¾"x8", 15 keys..	70.00	105.00	140.00
SCHOENHUT Piano, symphony type, 15½"x10"x7½", 14 keys.	44.00	66.00	88.00
SCHOENHUT Railway Station..............	210.00	315.00	420.00
SCHOENHUT Xylophone.	30.00	45.00	60.00
SEIBERLING LATEX PROD. Panda, rubber squeak toy...........	2.00	3.00	4.00
Sewing Machine, 6" high, circa 1920...........	11.00	16.50	22.00

Sewing Machine, 6" high, circa 1920
Photo by Bill Kaufman
Courtesy Good Old Days Store

	G	VG	M
Shooting Gallery chickens, cast iron, 10¼" long....	11.00	16.50	22.00
Signal Jr. R-70 Twin Wireless Practice Set, two beginner's sending keys, and one advanced key, circa 1920............	17.50	26.25	35.00
Sled, FLEXIBLE FLYER, 37" long.............	4.00	6.00	8.00
Sled, FLEXIBLE FLYER, 60" long.............	25.00	37.50	50.00
Sled, hand-operated mechanical, early, 56" long..............	100.00	150.00	200.00
Sled, push-type, wood and metal, red-painted......	90.00	120.00	180.00

	G	VG	M
Sled, push-type, wood, upholstered...........	54.00	81.00	108.00
Sled, "Star", wood and metal, painted, 71" long..	66.00	99.00	132.00
Sled-Ride, circa 1925, 16½" long, tin, canvas strips and lead riders........	50.00	75.00	100.00
Snap (KELLOGG'S RICE KRISPIES) squeeze toy, 8½" high.............	3.00	4.50	6.00
Snap (KELLOGG'S RICE KRISPIES) hand puppet.	6.00	9.00	12.00
Steam Engine, BIG GIANT Brass Boiler Upright, 11¼"................	55.00	82.50	110.00
Steam Engine, DOLL & CO. upright, cast iron base, 11¼"................	90.00	135.00	180.00
Steam Engine, EMPIRE HORIZONTAL, twin boiler and twin fly......	250.00	375.00	500.00
Steam Engine, EMPIRE, mounted on base board with transmission, concrete mixer, table saw, grinding wheel........	110.00	165.00	220.00
Steam Engine, EMPIRE vertical boiler, stationary, METAL WARE CORP, pat. Jan. 25, 1921......	70.00	105.00	140.00
Steam Engine, HUBER, 8".	150.00	225.00	300.00
Steam Engine, WEEDEN No. 49 with dual flywheels, cast iron base.	200.00	300.00	400.00
Steam Engine, WEEDEN No. 42, 12" high.......	80.00	120.00	160.00
Steam Engine, WEEDEN No. 902, base 7¼"x9"...	70.00	105.00	140.00
Steam Engine, WEEDEN dual flywheel, base 10", 11½" high...........	150.00	225.00	300.00
Steam Engine, WEEDEN, Early cast iron, deluxe model with cast iron boiler front, mounted on wood base inside wooden case, 1880 model.......	125.00	187.50	250.00
Steam Engine, WEEDEN Electric Steam Engine, 3½"x7¼" base........	30.00	45.00	60.00
Steam Engine, WEEDEN, horizontal, 4" cast flywheel, mechanism on top of boiler..........	120.00	180.00	240.00

	G	VG	M
Steam Engine, WEEDEN, horizontal, 6" boiler, stationary	70.00	105.00	140.00
Steam Engine, WEEDEN, upright steam engine, 9½"x7" cast iron base, cast iron mechanism	70.00	105.00	140.00
Steam Engine, WEEDEN Upright Steam Engine on wooden base, 10" tall	45.00	67.50	90.00
Steam Engine, WEEDEN, Upright, early tin, 11" . . .	60.00	90.00	120.00
Steam Engine, WEEDEN, Upright early 11¼"	50.00	75.00	100.00
Steam Engine, WEEDEN, Upright, boiler only. Flywheel assembly mounted on base. Base is 8"x4"	100.00	150.00	200.00
Steam Engine, Wooden Dual Flywheel steam engine, base 10"x7"x11½"	150.00	225.00	300.00
Stichwell Sewing machine, child's floor model, circa 1920s	44.00	66.00	88.00
Stove, cast iron, "American"	60.00	90.00	120.00
Stove, "Daisy', cast white metal, 4¼" high	7.00	10.50	14.00
Stove, "Eagle", cast iron, 4¼" high	28.00	42.00	56.00
Stove, "Eagle", cast iron, 13½" high	75.00	112.50	150.00
Stove, cast iron, 13"x11½" high	40.00	60.00	80.00
Stove, cast iron, ARK, 4"x5"	11.00	16.50	22.00
Stove, electric, one burner, two ovens, chrome-finished steel, porcelain on oven doors, 16" wide, 14" tall	44.00	66.00	88.00
Stove, "Lancaster", "Eagle" on door and shelf, 10¾", cast iron	22.00	33.00	44.00
Stove, wood-burning cast iron, "The Queen"	55.00	82.50	110.00
Stove, wood-burning cast iron, "The Triumph Range"	45.00	67.50	90.00
Stove, tin, with four plate covers, four pans and one skillet, 5" high	34.00	51.00	68.00
Stretcher for 3" toy soldiers, pre-WW II	6.00	9.00	12.00

	G	VG	M
STRUCTO Erector Set, 1910	37.50	55.75	75.00
STRUCTO No. 3	45.00	67.50	90.00
Sulky, cast iron, single casting	24.00	36.00	48.00
Swing, animated, cast iron and pressed steel, for doll, with eagle, wheel	400.00	600.00	800.00
Swinging Clown, tin, base marked "C.D. KENNY CO.", 4¼" high	54.00	81.00	108.00
"The Symmetroscope", wood and tin type of kaleidoscope, 6¼" high, F.P. IRVING, Troy, N.Y.	46.00	69.00	92.00
Tea Kettle, cast iron, 3¼" long	18.00	27.00	36.00
Teeter-Totter, GIBBS TOYS, 14½" high, when inverted, two children work their way down, tin, 1910	60.00	90.00	120.00

Teeter-Totter, GIBBS
Courtesy Garth's Auctions Inc.

	G	VG	M
Tent, Army, two pole, two flags on top, approx. 5" long	5.00	7.50	10.00
Tent, canvas, white, 9" long	5.00	7.50	10.00
Tent, Army, "Field Hangar, U.S. Aviation Corp Squadron 1", two flags atop tent, approx. 9" long	8.00	12.00	16.00
Tent, Army, "U.S. Battery B. Coast Artillery", two poles, two flags on top . . .	6.00	9.00	12.00
Tent, "Guard Tent Co. A" 4¼" high	5.00	7.50	10.00
Tent, "Sail-Me" Co., 6 with box, c. 1931	45.00	67.50	90.00

	G	VG	M
Tent, "U.S. Infantry Co. A", 4½" high, two flags on top	6.00	9.00	12.00
Tent, "U.S. Infantry Co. B".	5.00	7.50	10.00
Tent, paper, 5" high, "State Camp Co. A"	1.50	2.25	3.00
Tent, No. 76, small pup, white with cardboard base, center support	3.00	4.50	6.00
Tin dog with boy rider, 13½" long, on wheeled platform	360.00	540.00	720.00
TINKER TOYS, round box, 12" high	2.50	3.75	5.00
Toledo Scales, 4x4", cast iron	5.00	7.50	10.00
"Tom Thumb" cash register, metal, 6½"x7½"x8¼"by WESTERN STAMPING CO	6.00	9.00	12.00
Tools, GREY IRON, 1933, price per set	5.00	7.50	10.00
Tool Set, GREYCRAFT (Grey Iron) 1940, cast iron, steel and wood	3.00	4.50	6.00
TOOTSIETOY Bathroom set	54.00	81.00	108.00
TOOTSIETOY Bedroom set	30.00	45.00	60.00
TOOTSIETOY Dining Room set	40.00	60.00	80.00
TOOTSIETOY furniture, six chairs, moveable bar, two side tables and a dining table	30.00	45.00	60.00
TOOTSIETOY living room set, two chairs, lamp, gramophone, sofa, secretaire, table	25.00	37.50	50.00
TOOTSIETOY metal kitchen and bathroom furniture, sink, bathtub, toilet, stove, table and cupboard	20.00	30.00	40.00
TOOTSIETOY Music Room, set	70.00	105.00	140.00
Top, Carnival Whistling Top, tin litho circus decor, spring-wound, 4" diameter, LUPOR, 1930s	10.00	15.00	20.00
Top, gyro style, 1918	3.00	4.50	6.00
Top, tin	2.00	3.00	4.00
Top, wooden, circa 1940	1.00	1.50	2.00
TRANSWORLD AIRLINES Jr. Pilot Wings	3.00	4.50	6.00
Tricycle, iron, KILGORE, 2¾"	30.00	45.00	60.00
Tricycle, "Overland", wood and metal	26.00	39.00	52.00
Tricycle, rubber covered wheels, AMERICAN NATIONAL CO	50.00	75.00	100.00
Tricycle, turn of the century, iron, 26" high	50.00	75.00	100.00
Tricycle, turn of the century, iron, 30" high	20.00	30.00	40.00
Tricycle, small metal	14.00	21.00	28.00
Tricycle, wood and metal articulated horseform, 44" long	100.00	150.00	200.00
Tricycle, early, all metal, 41" long, 33" high	100.00	150.00	200.00
Tricycle, wood and metal, 50" long	120.00	180.00	240.00
Tricycle, wood, painted, 38" long	46.00	69.00	92.00
"Trinity Chimes" tone player toy, early	100.00	150.00	200.00
Trix Rabbit, rubber squeeze toy	3.00	4.50	6.00
TURNER Garage, heavy sheet metal, one window on each side, divided into four panes	3.50	5.25	7.00
The Twister, 12" high, in black cloth pants and red stripe shirt with porkpie hat, reminiscent of outfits worn at the Peppermint Lounge where the Twist was born. Stands on a 7" sq. platform, 3½" high, inscribed "Let's Twist!", which is exactly what he does, early 60s	40.00	60.00	80.00
Velocipede, 1890s, 52" wheel diameter	700.00	1050.00	1400.00
Velocipede, 1890s, 58" high	350.00	525.00	700.00
Velocipede, wood, hand-operated, with horse-head motif, painted in blue and yellow, approx. 31" long.	160.00	240.00	320.00
Velocipede, black-painted iron, 37" long	100.00	150.00	200.00
Velocipede, 44" long	66.00	99.00	132.00
Velocipede, L. GOULD & CO., iron, three-wheeled.	74.00	111.00	148.00
Waffle iron, cast iron, WAGNER	2.50	3.75	5.00
Wagon, Champion Express Coaster, 8" with handle..	35.00	52.50	70.00

	G	VG	M
Wagon, "Express", wood spoke wheels..........	250.00	375.00	500.00
Wagon, "Pony Express", 38" long.................	40.00	60.00	80.00
Wagon, wood, for child, 1900	37.50	56.25	75.00
Walking Horse, metal and papier mache wind-up, early 8¼"............	150.00	225.00	300.00
Washing Machine, 1900, salesman's sample......	46.00	69.00	92.00
Washing Machine, tin, works, circa 1940, seashore scene on side...	3.00	4.50	6.00
Water Tank Wagon, 1910, painted pressed steel, 26" long.................	120.00	180.00	240.00

Water Tank Wagon, 1910
Courtesy Lloyd W. Ralston Auctions'

	G	VG	M
"Western Union" telegraph key, battery powered, code printed on front....	10.00	15.00	20.00
Wheelbarrow, cast iron, 4½", 1930...........	12.00	18.00	24.00
Wheelbarrow, cast iron, approx. 5½"............	8.00	12.00	16.00
Wheelbarrow, cast iron, 6½" long............	9.00	13.50	18.00
Wheelbarrow, cast iron, 7" long, with tools, 1915...	7.50	11.25	15.00
Wheelbarrow, 9" long.....	4.50	6.75	9.00
Whirligig of Life, MCLAUGHLIN, 1870s, illusion of motion.......	360.00	540.00	720.00

Whirligig of Life
Courtesy Lloyd W. Ralston Auctions

	G	VG	M
WILKINS Horse and Jockey, 1900, 10", cast iron, wheeled pull toy...	60.00	90.00	120.00

	G	VG	M
Windmill, metal, with pumping apparatus.........	18.00	27.00	36.00
WOLVERINE "Automatic Sand Crane", tin.......	14.00	21.00	28.00
WOLVERINE Bizzy Andy, 11" high sand toy, pat. 1914, steel and tin......	29.00	43.50	58.00
WOLVERINE, Bizzy Andy Trip Hammer, 1917.....	25.00	37.50	50.00
WOLVERINE Organ, tin, turn crank to make organ-like sounds.........	30.00	45.00	60.00
WOLVERINE "Sandy Andy No. 60 Automatic Sand Toy", Patented 1909 and 1911.............	19.00	28.50	38.00
WOLVERINE "Sandy Andy Full Back", 1920s.	100.00	150.00	200.00
WOLVERINE "Sunny Andy" Cable Car Set No. 53, 12" high, circa 1920-30s	42.50	63.75	85.00
WOLVERINE Sunny Andy "Kiddie Kampers" action toy, 5⅝" by 3½", color litho, three boy scouts and two girl scouts in backdrop camp setting, boys chop and saw wood and girls signal with flags, marbles drop down chute, circa 1929............	50.00	75.00	100.00

WOLVERINE "Sunny Andy Kiddie Kampers"
Courtesy Mapes Auctioneers & Appraisers

	G	VG	M
WOLVERINE Sandy Andy sand loader, 1912......	27.50	41.25	55.00
WOLVERINE Sand Loader, tin beach toy, lithographed, circa 1950s....	5.00	7.50	10.00
Woman chasing duck, early tin friction...........	26.00	39.00	52.00
Wood Cage with horse, when gate is open horse pops out and whinnies...	66.00	99.00	132.00

	G	VG	M
Wood Cage, mechanical, rooster flies out when door is open	7.00	10.50	14.00
Wood Mechanical Dancing Figure, clockwork, on box base	60.00	90.00	120.00
Wooden Music Maker, "Auto Phone Co. H.B. Horton's Ithaca, N.Y.", 9½" high, uses player rolls	56.00	84.00	112.00
WYANDOTTE "Carnival", with ferris wheel, carousel and airplane ride, metal . .	35.00	52.50	70.00
WYANDOTTE hen, chubby, tin, lays egg when body pressed down, 8½" long, with eight eggs	14.00	21.00	28.00
WYANDOTTE "Musical" push top, circa 1939	20.00	30.00	40.00
WYANDOTTE "Posse" Shooting Gallery, 14" wide, wind-up gallery	12.00	18.00	24.00
"Zoetrope", wood and cardboard, illusion of motion game, MILTON BRADLEY	200.00	300.00	400.00
"Zulu Blow Gun", copyright 1925, 2' long, 4 arrows, target, instructions, etc. mfd. Battle Creek, Michigan	19.00	28.50	38.00
"Zulu Blow Gun" same as above, different coloring and target, no instruction sheet	17.50	26.25	35.00

WYANDOTTE "Musical" Push Top
Photo by Bill Kaufman
Courtesy Good Old Days Store

WYANDOTTE "Posse" Shooting Gallery
Courtesy Good Old Days Store
Photo by Bill Kaufman

Zoetrope.   Photo Courtesy Milton Bradley

BIBLIOGRAPHY

ANTIQUE TOY WORLD — $20.00 for one year subscription, payable to Dale Kelley, 3941 Belle Plaine, Chicago, Illinois, 60618

A CELEBRATION OF COMIC ART AND MEMORABILIA by Robert Lesser, HAWTHORN

CAST IRON TOY PISTOLS by Charles W. Best, ROCKY MOUNTAIN ARMS & ANTIQUES (Out of Print)

DISNEYANA by Cecil Munsey, HAWTHORN

JIM HARMON'S NOSTALGIA CATALOGUE by Jim Harmon, TARCHER/HAWTHORN

THE AMERICAN DIMESTORE SOLDIER BOOK by Don Pielin, available at $12.50 from Don Pielin, 1009 Kenilworth, Wheeling, Illinois 60090

REGIMENTS OF ALL NATIONS (Postwar Britains) available at $20.00 from Joe Wallis, P.O. Box 2294, Washington, D.C. 20013

OLD TOY SOLDIER NEWSLETTER, $12.00 for one-year subscription, payable to Steve Sommers, 209 North Lombard, Oak Park, Illinois 60302

IT'S ALL IN THE GAME, Biography of Milton Bradley, by James J. Shea, PUTNAM

"The Grey Iron Casting Company of Mount Jay, Pa." by Karl Zipple, published in GUIDON Vol. 30 No. 4, 1972, Vol. 31 No. 2, 1973, and Vol. 32 No. 1, 1974

CAVALCADE OF TOYS by Ruth and Larry Freeman, 1942, CENTURY HOUSE

TOYS IN AMERICA by Inez and Marshall McClintock, 1961, PUBLIC AFFAIRS PRESS, WASHINGTON, D.C.

THE TOY COLLECTOR by Louis H. Hertz, 1969, FUNK & WAGNALLS

ANTIQUE TOYS by Gwen White, 1971, ARCO

THE COMIC BUYER'S GUIDE — Comics, Premiums, Disney items and other toys. 26 issues $10.00. 700 E. State St., Iola, WI 54990

DICTIONARY OF TOYS SOLD IN AMERICA, Volumes I and II, by Earnest & Ida Long, P.O. Box 272, Mokelumne Hills, California 95245, $10 plus postage per volume

MIDWEST PAPER DOLLS AND TOYS QUARTERLY by Janie Varsolona, Box 35 Galesburg, Kansas 66740, $6.50 for one year (four issues).

TOOTSIETOYS, WORLD'S FIRST DIECAST MODELS, by James Wieland and Edward Force, Motorbooks International, Osceola, Wisc.

MARX TOY COLLECTOR NEWSLETTER, Gerritt Beverwyk, 916 Armitage Ave., Chicago, Illinois 60614

"Schoenhut Wooden Toys" by Ann Soules AMERICAN COLLECTOR, April, 1980 P.O. Drawer C-349 Kermit, Texas 79745.

"Black ID Planes", AMERICAN AIRCRAFT MODELER No. 54, September, 1973

"Manoil Variations", 16 page list, $2.87, Peter Ruben, 2 Vera Place, Montclair, NJ 07042

BOX TOP BONANZA, Bimonthly newsletter on Premiums, etc. $18.00 a year, Joel Smilgis, 1115 17th St., Apt. 2, Moline, Illinois 61265

TOY MUSEUMS AND MUSEUMS THAT FEATURE TOYS

Auburn-Cord-Duesenberg Museum
Auburn, Indiana, 46706
(AUBURN toys and Cord and Duesenberg automobiles)

Museum of the City of New York
5th Avenue and 103rd Street
New York, New York

Smithsonian
Washington, D.C.

Daisy Gun Museum
U.S. 71 South
Rogers, Arkansas
(The world's most complete collection of air rifles, dating from the 18th century)

The Toy Museum of Atlanta
2800 Peachtree Road, N.E.
Atlanta, Georgia

Perelman Antique Toy Museum
270 South Second Street
Philadelphia, Pennsylvania

Margaret Woodbury Strong Museum
700 Allen Creek Road
Rochester, New York 14618

Toy Train Museum
Paradise Lane
Strasburg, Pennsylvania

The Sterling Collection
Stone Castle
804 North Third Street
Bardstown, Kentucky

Museum of Childhood
8 Broad Street
Greensport, New York

Islip Town Museum
Montauk Highway
Oakdale, New York

Washington Dolls' House & Toy Museum
5236 44th Street, N.W.
Washington, D.C. 20015

The Toy Museum
42 Bridge St Row
Chester, Cheshire
England

The London Toy & Model Museum
23 Craven Hill
London, England

AUCTIONEERS

These are established firms experienced in disposing of large collections of toys by auction.

PB84 (A Division of Sotheby Parke Bernet Inc. New York)
171 East 84th Street
New York, New York
(212) 472-3584

Philips New York
867 Madison Avenue
New York, New York 10021

Christie's East
219 East 67th Street
New York, New York 10021

Mapes Auctioneers & Appraisers
1600 Vestal Parkway West
Vestal, New York 13850
(607) 754-9193

Hake's Americana & Collectibles — Sample Catalog $2.00
P.O. Box 1444
York, Pennsylvania 17405
(717) 848-1333

Lloyd W. Ralston
447 Stratfield Road
Fairfield, Connecticut 06432
(203) 366-3399

Garth's Auctions Inc.
2690 Stratford Road
Delaware, Ohio 43015
(614) 362-4771

Ted Maurer
1931 N. Charlotte Street
Pottstown, Pennsylvania
(215) 323-1573

Kruse Auctioneers
Kruse Building
Auburn, Indiana 46706

Gene Harris Antique Center
P.O. Box 476-203 So. 18th Avenue
Marshalltown, Iowa 50158
(515) 752-0600

Butterfield & Butterfield
1244 Sutter Street
San Francisco, California 94109
(415) 673-1362

Ken Gooch
Dexter, Iowa 50070
(515) 789-4406

Philip B. Robinson
1010 Gray Street
St. Charles, Illinois 60174

LEADING COLLECTORS AND DEALERS

(It is suggested that, when writing to any of the following, you enclose a stamped, self-addressed envelope.)

JIM HARMON — Radio premiums and tapes, comic books and strips
634 So. Orchard Dr.
Burbank, California 91506

RAY FUNK — Comic books, toys
826 East 8th Street
Upland, California 91786

BARBARA & JONATHAN NEWMAN — Paper toys, old and new
The Paper Soldier
8 McIntosh Lane
Clifton Park, New York 12065

CHARLES W. BEST — Old toy pistols, etc.
6288 South Pontiac
Englewood, Colorado

ALAN LEVINE — Premiums, Big Little Books, Movie Material, Comics, Toys
P.O. Box 1577
Bloomfield, New Jersey 07003

JOHN MURRAY — Fisher-Price
Box 29
Eden, NY 14057

HANK ANTON — Buys, sells, trades, auctions toy soldiers, etc.
92 Swain Avenue
Meriden, Connecticut 06450 (203) 237-5356

JOE WALLIS — Britains Soldiers
P.O. Box 2294
Washington, D.C. 20013

THOMAS W., SEFTON — Standard Gauge Trains, BUDDY L, other toys
San Diego Trust & Savings Bank
Box 1871
San Diego, California

EDWARD K. POOLE — Toy soldiers, 1/36 scale ID vehicles and old wooden military vehicle kits
926 Terrace Mt. Drive
Austin, Texas 78746

DON PIELIN — Toy soldiers
1009 Kenilworth
Wheeling, Illinois 60090

ED & ELAINE LEVIN — Comic and Celebrity toys
Nickelodeon Antiques
13826 Ventura Blvd.
Sherman Oaks, California 91403

OLD FRIENDS — Disney toys, etc.
202 East 31st Street
New York, New York

SECOND CHILDHOOD — Antique toys
283 Bleecker Street
New York, New York

SPEAKEASY ANTIQUES — Antique toys, etc.
799 Broadway
New York, New York

MEMORABLE THINGS — American and foreign toy soldiers, vehicles, etc.
P.O. Box 10505
Towson, Maryland 21204
(Shop Address: 31 W. Allegheny Avenue, Towson, Maryland, 2nd floor)

JOHN GROSS — Soldiers of all types
Fife & Drum, Theatre Arcade
824 W. Lancaster Ave.
Bryn Mawr, Pa. 19010

RICHARD MACNARY — Marx Trains, Coca-Cola vehicles, wood, cardboard, paper toys, soldiers
4727 Alpine Drive
Lilburn, Georgia 30247

ECCLES BROTHERS — Comic Figures, Toy Soldiers and Vehicles from original molds and tin helmets
R.R. No. 1, Box 253-D
Burlington, Iowa 52601

BILL LANGO — Barclay vehicles, animals and soldiers from original and new molds
127-74th Street
North Bergen, New Jersey 07047

K. WARREN MITCHELL — Soldiers of all types
5880 Yorkland Court
Columbus, Ohio 43232

STEVE BALKIN — Toy Soldiers, including Warren
BURLINGTON TOYS
1082 Madison Avenue
New York, New York 10028

GERALD C. WAGNER — Old Toy Trains, especially foreign
4455 Hermosa Way
San Diego, California 92103

MARBLE COLLECTORS' SOCIETY OF AMERICA — Stanley A. Block, Executive Director
P.O. Box 222
Trumbull, Connecticut 06611

HERMAN & FLORENCE LOTSTEIN — Trains, toys and books on toys
Cook's Antique Flea Market
Rt. 29, Lambertville, New Jersey

BRUCE & BLOSSOM ABELL — Schoenhut toys, including repairs
Christmas Past
P.O. Box 247
Algonquin, Illinois 60102

V.J. MEDCALF — Britains and other soldiers
115 South 4th Street No. 1
Reading, Pa. 19602

G. SCOTT MORLAN — Parts for Britains soldiers
P.O. Box 10701
Costa Mesa, California 92627

THE TRAIN COLLECTORS ASSOCIATION
National Business Office
Box 248
Strasburg, Pennsylvania 17579

SHAMUS O.D. WADE — Britains and other soldiers
37 Davis Road
Acton, London W. 3 ENGLAND

G.M. HALEY — Britains and other soldiers
"Hippins" Blackshaw head
Hebden Bridge, W. Yorks ENGLAND

DON HULTZMAN — Tin wind-up and Battery-operated, also repairs, restorations
5026 Sleepy Hollow Road
Medina, Ohio 44256

PETER RUBEN — Manoil Toys
2 Vera Place
Montclair, New Jersey 07042

CONTINENTAL HOBBY HORSE — Toys and Trains
P.O. Box 193
Sheboygan, Wisconsin 53081

FRED THOMPSON — New designs of Smitty vehicles
Smith-Miller Inc.
P.O. Box 139
Canoga Park, Ca. 91305

REX MILLER — Premiums
Supermantiques
Star Route 331-J
East Prairie, Missouri 63845

JOANNE AND RONALD RUDDELL — Britains and other soldiers
LONDON BRIDGE COLLECTOR'S TOYS
1344 Rt. 100S
P.O. Box 426
Trexlertown, PA 18087

GEORGE HALL — Battery-operated toys
Hallmark Antiques
2435 Telegraph Ave.
Oakland, CA 94612

DANNY FUCHS — Superman toys, games, etc.
209-80 18th Ave.
Bayside, NY 11360

Coming
OCTOBER '84

American Premium Guide To
ELECTRIC TRAINS
Identification & Values
by Richard O'Brien

This new 2nd edition again has it all: LIONEL, MARX, AMERICAN FLYER, IVES, BUDDY L, DORFAN, TOOTSIETOY, UNIQUE, plus others; however, each category has been added to with more listings and photos. This guide includes the engines, cars and accessories with descriptions, prices and photos. Richard O'Brien (author of "Collecting Toys") has had the aid of the top train collectors from across the country in making this the best guide on trains; such as: Richard MacNary, Steven and Catherine Hintze, Terry Amadon, Frank Ferrara, Thomas Sefton, Jerry Wagner, Herman Lotstein, Heinz Mueller, Mr. & Mrs. Stacy Feller, J. McAuliffe and Charles Vessell.

$10⁹⁵

Other Identification And Value Guides From Books Americana, Inc.

Depression-Era Glassware	9⁹⁵	Old Fishing Lures & Tackle	14⁹⁵
Collecting Antique Bird Decoys	14⁹⁵	Collector Prints (Old & New)	14⁹⁵
Hummel Figurines & Plates	9⁹⁵	American Premium Record Guide	
300 Years of Kitchen Collectibles	10⁹⁵	3rd Edition - October '84	14⁹⁵
Collecting Toys	14⁹⁵	Collecting Rhinestone Jewelry	10⁹⁵
Answers To Questions About Old Jewelry		American Premium Guide to Olde Cameras	9⁹⁵
2nd Edition - October '84	10⁹⁵	Collecting Art Nouveau	10⁹⁵
Vintage Clothing (1880-1960)	10⁹⁵	Medical-Dental-Pharmaceutical Collectibles	9⁹⁵
Scouting Collectibles	10⁹⁵	Paper Collectibles	9⁹⁵
Country-Store Antiques	10⁹⁵	Collecting Farm Antiques	10⁹⁵
North American Indian Points	7⁹⁵	Jukeboxes/Slot Machines - Nov. '84	10⁹⁵
North American Indian Artifacts	10⁹⁵	Encyclopedia of Golf Collectibles - Oct. '84	14⁹⁵
American Indian Pottery	29⁹⁵		